Marx and
Engels on the
Population Bomb

Marx and Engels on the Population Bomb

selections
from the
writings of Marx and Engels
dealing with the theories
of Thomas Robert Malthus

Edited by Ronald L. Meek

Translations from the German by
Dorothea L. Meek and Ronald L. Meek

Foreword by Steve Weissman

The
Ramparts
Press

NOTE ON REFERENCES

Throughout this volume references are given to the
English editions of the following books, which are also
available in International Publishers editions:

KARL MARX   *Capital*, vol. 1, 1947
            The Poverty of Philosophy, n.d.
            Letters to Kugelmann, 1934
            Theories of Surplus Value, 1952
            Critique of the Gotha Programme, 1938

FREDERICK ENGELS   *Anti-Dühring*, 1939
                   Ludwig Feuerbach, 1941
                   Dialectics of Nature, 1940

KARL MARX AND
FREDERICK ENGELS   *Selected Correspondence*, 1942
V. I. LENIN   *Selected Works*, 12 vols., 1943
JOSEPH STALIN   *Economic Problems of Socialism
                in the USSR*, 1952

COPYRIGHT © BY RONALD L. MEEK
FIRST PUBLISHED AS "MARX AND ENGELS ON MALTHUS"
BY LAWRENCE & WISHART, LONDON, 1953,
AND INTERNATIONAL PUBLISHERS, NEW YORK, 1954.
REPRINTED WITH PERMISSION OF
INTERNATIONAL PUBLISHERS CO., INC.
SECOND EDITION COPYRIGHT © 1971 BY
RAMPARTS PRESS, INC.
BERKELEY, CALIFORNIA
LIBRARY OF CONGRESS CATALOG CARD NUMBER: 71-132220
SBN: 0-87867-002-5   ORDER NO. 20777
ALL RIGHTS RESERVED
TRADE DISTRIBUTION BY SIMON & SCHUSTER, NEW YORK
MANUFACTURED IN THE UNITED STATES OF AMERICA

Contents

Foreword   ix

Part One
MALTHUS—YESTERDAY AND TODAY:
AN INTRODUCTORY ESSAY

1. Malthus Yesterday   3
   The Theory of Population   3
   Economic Theory in General   10

2. Marx and Engels on Malthus   16
   General Criticisms   16
   The Theory of Population   18
   The "Law of Diminishing Returns"   23
   The Theory of Value and Surplus Value   28
   The Theory of Capitalist Crises   31

3. Malthus Today   37
   The Theory of Population   37
   Economic Theory in General   42
   Malthus and Imperialism   46

   Notes on the Translations   50

Part Two
MARX AND ENGELS ON THE
MALTHUSIAN THEORY OF POPULATION

Introductory Notes   53

1. The Myth of Overpopulation   56
   from Engels's *Outlines of a Critique of Political Economy* (1844)

2. The English Poor Law   64
   from Marx's article on *Social Reform* (1844)

3. A Declaration of War on the Proletariat   70
   from Engels's *The Condition of the Working Class
   in England in 1844* (1845)

4. The Reserve Army of Labor   75
   from Engels's *The Condition of the Working Class
   in England in 1844* (1845)

5. Barton, Malthus and Ricardo on "Overpopulation"   82
   from Marx's *Theories of Surplus Value*, vol. 2
   (written 1861–63)

6. The Pressure of Population upon the
   Means of Employment   85
   from Engels's letter to Lange of 29 March, 1865

7. Parson Malthus   88
   from Marx's *Capital*, vol. 1 (1867)

8. Relative Surplus-Population under Capitalism   91
   from Marx's *Capital*, vol. 1 (1867)

9. The "Iron Law of Wages"   117
   from Engels's letter to Bebel of 18–28 March, 1875, and
   from Marx's *Critique of the Gotha Programme* (1875)

10. Population and Communism   119
    from Engels's letter to Kautsky of 1 February, 1881

11. The Malthusian Theory in Reverse   122
    from Engels's letter to Danielson of 9 January, 1895

Part Three
MARX ON MALTHUS AND
ECONOMIC THEORY IN GENERAL

Introductory Notes   125

1. Malthus as an Apologist   127
   from Marx's *Theories of Surplus Value*, vol. 2
   (written 1861–63)

2. Malthus on Value and Surplus Value   139
   from Marx's *Theories of Surplus Value*, vol. 3
   (written 1861–63)

3. Malthus on Overproduction and Overconsumption   171
   from Marx's *Theories of Surplus Value*, vol. 3
   (written 1861–63)

Part Four
MARX AND ENGELS ON
MALTHUS AND DARWINISM

Introductory Notes   193

1. Bourgeois Society and Animal Society   195
   from Marx's letter to Engels of 18 June, 1862

2. Malthusianism and the "Struggle for Existence"   196
   from Marx's letter to Kugelmann of 27 June, 1870

3. Darwinism and Society   197
   Engels's letter to Lavrov of 12 November, 1875

4. Dühring on Malthus and Darwin   201
   from Engels's *Anti-Dühring* (1878)

5. Darwinism—A Summary View   208
   from Engels's *Dialectics of Nature* (written 1872–82)

Index of Authors   213

Foreword

Back in 1798—a year in which the French Revolution was still conjuring up hopes of the perfectibility of man and of society—the Reverend Thomas Robert Malthus issued his famous law of population: mankind's propensity to beget, he warned, would soon outstrip the earth's capacity to provide.

Half a century later another prophet branded the good parson "a shameless sycophant of the ruling classes" and "a bought advocate" of those who opposed a better life for Merrie England's poor. By arguing that poverty was a natural condition and misery a necessary check on growing numbers, the contemptible Malthus was, Karl Marx claimed, simply selling scientific and moral arguments to selfish opponents of reform. The real problem wasn't too many people or too little food, said Marx, but that private capitalists owned the means of meeting men's needs.

Today this war of words roars on. Professional ecologists chastise the political left for "blindly following the outdated Marxist line that the population problem can be ignored until we reform the economic system." And a new generation of unregenerate Marxists yells back that "the population bombers only divert attention from the real issues and pave the way for world-wide race war and genocide."

The debate is classic, and classically dull. Rhetorically, at least, it would be better left to those endless meetings in out-of-the-way auditoriums and to unread forewords to scholarly reprints such as this.

But the issue won't disappear. Because of the debate, many who have worked together against imperial adventure, poverty and racism now find themselves fighting each other across ill-defined barricades. Without the debate, many more—either fearful of the deep dark masses stirring below, or freaked by the whole modern trip and anxious to end it with a quick cultural vasectomy—are making the population control movement into a far-too-holy crusade. The whole scene is scary, and perhaps more immediately dangerous than the life-and-death questions which the neo-Malthusians confusedly pose and the Marxists contemptuously ignore.

More words, especially old words, won't undo the danger: survival is just not the kind of question which encourages sanity. But this collection of Marx's and Engels's scattered critiques, together with the omnipresent editions of the old Malthus, does offer a firsthand view of the old and recurring controversy and, as this preface attempts to show, an opportunity to get beyond "the outdated line" of both Marx's followers and their critics.

The Whole Earth

Properly speaking, the problem posed by the neo-Malthusians isn't really Malthusian at all. In his *Essay on the Principle of Population,* Parson Malthus offered some rather common-sense projections on the geometric growth of populations, and compared them unfavorably to an off-the-top-of-his-head assertion that "subsistence increases only in an arithmetical ratio." In practice, of course, it didn't work out that way. Common sense in nineteenth-century Europe was changing, and in the process undoing Malthus's geometry. Large peasant families had provided extra farmhands and a measure of social security for old age; in the new industrial Europe of the nineteenth century, extra children were simply extra mouths to feed—and, with the breakdown of family solidarity, ungrateful ones at that. Seeing this, and the parallel rise in health care and life expectancy, people quite sensibly started having fewer children. Scientists later termed this cutback in child production the "demographic transition"; our great-great-grandparents simply called it separate beds, unnatural devices, or pulling out. Except for the work of a few pioneers like Francis Place, there was no major family planning campaign and certainly no pill.

Scientific farming and technology were even more unkind to Malthus's agricultural arithmetic, which woefully (and rather geometrically) understated the enormous nineteenth-century rise in food production.

The neo-Malthusians, even as they resurrect the old parson's fame and pessimism, are undermining his science still more, undoing the original terms of the population-food equation. They still hawk the old geometry, and with population now doubling once every thirty-five years, paint some rather ghastly nine-hundred-year projections of earth as a standing-room-only sardine can and spaceship. But that is just a showman's ship. The doubling—and quite possibly the old can herself—won't go on that long, and few of the population controllers are optimistic enough to think that it will.

What they see as the limit, moreover, is not simply the limited potential of food production. "In the long run," writes Stanford biologist Paul Ehrlich, "the progressive deterioration of our environment may cause more death and misery than any conceivable food-population gap." Mankind, even in our present numbers, is wrecking the entire life support system. We are eating up not just hard-grown food but also water, minerals, fuels and even air much faster than nature can regenerate them. We are dumping into the soil, sea and sky, fertilizers, pesticides and chemical wastes faster than nature can absorb and recycle them. We are disrupting complex natural cycles and interactions, mass-producing a simplified and unstable environment that is increasingly vulnerable to massive and quite natural disaster. Everything, the first law of ecology explains, is connected to everything else, and it is this everything, this entire ecology, which we are *progressively* destroying, and which, with the poetic justice of a more classic (and simplified) age, might destroy us.

Alert to this whole world of troubles, and not simply to food production, the neo-Malthusians quickly confound the answer given Reverend Malthus by the nineteenth century, and by most Marxists. This time around, we can't simply wait for science and technology to get us out of the hole. New miracle grains, mechanization, fertilizers, pesticides and irrigation might well do for agricultural growth in the Third World what an earlier green revolution did for food in the old world. But we now know the cost in environmental destruction: modern agriculture will destroy the soil, rob foods of needed nutrients, and spread DDT and other poisons into everything from mothers' milk to the fish ponds which provide essential proteins to the single-celled sea algae which (normally) produce about half the world's oxygen. Worse, since the large expanse of undifferentiated seed strains offers an invitingly simple target for some super-pest or crop disease, the present hastily produced green revolution might not even deliver the agricultural goods.

We can't simply wash our hands of these problems and forswear the modern world. But the next modern-day technocrat—or Marxist—who simply echoes the nineteenth century's paean to progress should get his foolish mouth shut with a good-sized fistful of organic dirt.

The Ecology of the Market

Preservation of the whole earth also requires a little more quiet from the neo-Malthusians themselves, for—by their own testimony—it is now clear that population growth, while a very real problem, is not the prime problem, and population control is not the first solution. Long before the DDT sets in, the "teeming masses" are discovering that there is now *too much food and too few people who can afford to buy it*. The reason is simple: the green revolutionaries are not growing food for people, they are producing commodities for profit. The Rockefeller and Ford foundations produce seeds which require costly applications of fertilizer and pesticide; the petro-chemical companies (like the Rockefellers' Standard Oil) produce the fertilizer and pesticides to sell at a profit; the larger farmers find it easier to afford the new methods if they displace already underemployed farmhands and tenants with new machinery; the "excess farm populations," many of them now in the cities, have no money to buy bread. Let them eat cake?

Even rationally organized and distributed, there might by now still be too little nourishing food for too many people, and even that balance at possibly disastrous cost to the entire eco-system. But, equally important to a holistic, ecological view, it is capitalism which creates this irrationality and hastens the destruction of the environment in most of the world, and without destroying capitalism, neither green revolutions nor population control will put food in the mouths of those who cannot afford to pay for it.

Population is even less the chief culprit in the advanced capitalist countries. In *The Population Bomb*, Ehrlich paints a devastating picture of our dying planet: "too many cars, too many factories, too much detergent, too much pesticide, multiplying contrails, inadequate sewage treatment plants, too little water, too much carbon dioxide"—all traced to a single source, "too many people." Yet pollution is now growing, by rough estimate, some six or seven times faster than population growth. Demands for power are growing about eight times faster, and *Environment* magazine even suggests that in two centuries, not nine, the doubling population of power plants alone—without counting fuel supplies, water for cooling, transformers and transmission lines—could take up all the physical space in the United States. Similarly, the growth of detergents correlates less with population growth than with merchandising budgets and soap operas, while growing automobile populations seem to have a very close relationship to suburban sprawl, planned obsolescence, the organization of our cities, and—again—advertising. Jet contrails and the coming SST, of course, have nothing to do with more people.

The comparisons could go on, but the point is a simple one: the growing number of people—whether as consumers, drivers, clothes-wearers, or clothes-washers—is far less the cause of environmental destruction than our society's dynamic efforts, direct and indirect, to get more people to have more "needs," to buy more products and to accept more waste. Merchandisers, to make their work a little easier, might prefer baby booms and population explosions. But cut back population and they'll simply sell more second cars and recreation vehicles, more expensive "anti-pollutant" gasoline, summer homes, electric toothbrushes, and paper sleeping bags to help enjoy the wilds. Industrial polluters are already arguing that people are the problem behind pollution, and no wonder. They know it's cheaper to create consumers out of a smaller population than to clean up production or possibly cut it back.

It's called capitalism, and it's the very same system which the two nineteenth-century political-economists, Marx and Malthus, described at such length and so differently. The different descriptions, discussed by Ronald Meek in his introductory essay to this collection, still divide socialist and bourgeois economists, and neither approach is adequate. Marx and the socialists, basing their theories on labor as the measure of value, are unsatisfying in their explanations of prices, the workings of the market, and the sphere of consumption; Malthus and the capitalists, taking the self-serving categories of the marketplace for science, ignore power and celebrate the crucifixion of mankind on the iron cross of supply and demand. Yet both sides, with some quibbling over language, would have to agree that it is capitalism which determines the way in which we in the "free world" dominate ourselves and our environment.

Other societies, socialist or communist, can and often do *choose* to follow in our footsteps, trampling on man and nature. But, as long as we retain the private, profit-seeking control of capital, *we have no choice.* Our economy has to keep trying to grow and expand, creating new needs and new wastes, and our social institutions have to fall in behind.

Why don't we simply stop our silly growthsmanship? We can't. If one producer slows down in the mad race, he'll be eaten up by his competitors. If all conspire together to restrain growth permanently, the unemployment and cutbacks will make today's recession look like full employment, and the resulting unrest will make today's dissent look like playtime at Summerhill.

"Accumulate, accumulate," cried Marx. "That's Moses and the prophets."

Stop Population First

Neo-Malthusians, at least the more liberal of them, are coming closer to this critique of capitalism. They sometimes sound so radical that they might well work themselves free of their grants from foundations. "The battle to save our planet is not just a battle for population control and environmental sanity," Ehrlich has said; "it is also a battle against exploitation, against war, and against racism." But this *nouveau radicalisme* notwithstanding, the first priority is still population control. "Whatever your cause," Ehrlich concludes, "it's a lost cause unless we control population." Stop population growth first; then take on "the other causes," or even the system itself.

This liberal, one-step-at-a-time problem-solving seems at first quite practical. But in practice it's the same tunnel vision that brought us to the brink of ecocide in the first place. We could as well urge DDT as a solution to the food shortage, or nuclear power as a replacement for fossil fuels, and then pray that we solve the radiation problem sometime before we all die of poison.

The danger of the population control priority is most clearly marked in the poorer nations. Seventy per cent of the world's present population lives in the "developing" countries of Asia, Africa and Latin America. These people live with hunger, poverty and generally oppressive dictatorships, and also with record-shattering birth rates, averaging three-and-a-half per cent per year. The "untrammeled copulation of these spawning millions," the neo-Malthusians argue, drains off resources that could otherwise be used for education, industrialization, and the exploitation of natural resources. Only when population growth levels off, they contend, will we see growing per capita living standards, political stability, and the long-awaited development of the Third World.

Like most development economics, the emphasis on population growth is a shuck. Per capita numbers tell us nothing about which groups in the population get how much, or about what part of the social surplus goes to build schools and hospitals rather than into Swiss bank accounts and the New York Stock Exchange. Reduce the number of people and, likely as not, those who control the processes of production and distribution will simply reduce the share which they let trickle down to the poor.

Control, just as the Marxists claim, is key, and it is largely the control of development by international financial interests which causes both the relative abundance of people and the laggard growth of industrial and even agricultural employment. Probably the largest single cause for the Third World population explosion, particularly since World War II, is the export from the developed to the underdeveloped world of highly advanced death-control technology. In Latin America, for example, the American army at the turn of the century drained the fever-producing swamps of Puerto Rico, Cuba and the Panama Canal Zone, and then during World War II rid the Brazilian Northeast of malaria. The Rockefeller and Kellogg foundations and the United States government helped eliminate a whole rash of diseases, first in the port cities and then in the interior, while United Fruit and Standard Oil provided modern health care for their workers.

Motives obviously were mixed, from canal-building and military occupation to commercial penetration and the social gospel of wealth. Yet, whether the intent was crass or Christian, the overall effect was the same: the creation of health enclaves as little integrated into the rhythms of indigenous development as the oil fields, banana plantations or tin mines.

The same foreigners of course controlled the other side of the development equation—the job-creation technology—and here they were not so open-handed. Where Europe's industrial revolution provided factories to absorb growing urban populations, the colonial developers were more interested in preserving the flow of raw materials to their own overdeveloping factories, and then selling finished consumer goods and light machinery back to the colonies. This might create more waste in the metropole and even more unemployment among uncompetitive colonial craftsmen or displaced agricultural workers, but such was the way of progress. Even when foreign capital finally did invest in local factories, it brought in overdeveloped technology, perhaps a bit too backward for serious competition with metropolitan production but always too advanced and capital-intensive to give much work to idle hands.

The two processes—death control and disemployment—

continue, to the point that Western capitalism has no prospect at all of ever exploiting, in the Marxist sense, the worldwide surplus of non-value-producing people. They are, to the capitalist, simply a waste, no longer even useful as a reserve army of the unemployed. Worse, they are a threat: idle hands for the devil's work of revolution and, if successful, competitors for their own markets and raw materials.

Controlling the Population

The obvious solution, short of shared industrialization, was birth control. Elsewhere I have tried to show in detail just how completely the rich and well-born have perverted a humanitarian movement to their own ends, or in brief, "why the population bomb is a Rockefeller baby." [1] Here it is enough to remember that the top population planners have consistently integrated their thinking with capitalist strategies to keep the less-developed countries in their place. Through their efforts, the existence of an approved population planning program is now an official string on American aid for "economic development," and a world population policy is part of liberal plans to channel foreign aid through the World Bank and the United Nations Development Program.

Where we once intervened to defend the free world from communism or to promote free enterprise economic development, our interventions will bear the banner of population control. "We must," Ehrlich writes in *The Population Bomb*, "use our political power to push other countries into programs which combine agricultural development and population control."

The likely outcome of all this humanitarianism, in short, is genocide. Population controllers already talk of putting

1. Reprinted from *Ramparts* in *Eco-Catastrophe*, Canfield Press, 1970.

temporary sterilants in food and water, while some of their more adventurous colleagues, no doubt impressed by pin-point bombing in Southeast Asia, would spray whole popula-tions from the air. If we're so willing to napalm peasants to protect them from communists, we could quite easily use a little sterilant spray to protect them from themselves.

Yet, short of genocide, the program has little chance of significantly reducing population growth. For by locking countries into the capitalist scheme, we reduce the possi-bility of providing the economic security, political trust, and new roles for women which motivate people to reduce the size of their families. In the absence of these motivations, traditional villagers, understanding sterilization and other techniques to be a plot, will more than likely fight to protect themselves and their families.

Bringing It All Back Home

Making population control the priority raises similar problems with American blacks, who, with unusual unanimity, regard it as just another approach to their extermination. Ehrlich, aware of their fears and in con-trast to most Malthusians, directs his appeal for smaller fami-lies to the high-consuming, high-waste-producing middle-class whites. "We can't expect members of minorities, or the poor, or any other group which is not given a fair share in our society to cooperate in an effort to save our civilization—unless we make it their civilization, too," he explains.

But again, the very appeal for voluntary middle-class family planning seems destined to produce a coercive middle-class self-righteousness that will support the enforce-ment of yet another middle-class standard on the minority poor. Population controllers Kingsley Davis and Garret Hardin are already branding voluntary family planning hope-lessly futile, while Ehrlich publicly favors a rather coercive and discriminatory elimination of tax exemptions for more than two children. In a class- and race-divided society such as ours, this child tax or other uses of state power in family planning will lead in the direction of outright genocide. But long before that point, coercive family planning campaigns will spark the militant reaction of the minorities and, from their point of view quite rightfully, encourage the traditional nationalist cry for more children, until there is a rational and equitable planning of society.

Even within the already privileged middle class, the priority on population control is counterproductive. Behind the apparent success of family planning campaigns among the college-educated middle class is the overall disillusionment, especially among women, with their life's allotment of a corporation-based social life, a suburban home, and 2.2 children. Women are leading the move to define new social roles and, in the process, are challenging the entire male-oriented domination of man and nature. It is still too early to speak of any generally accepted ecological ethic, or of a new post-scarcity demographic transition to normal single-child and childless families, but these revolutionary social and cultural changes, and the movements for their realization, seem far more productive of ecological sanity and reduced family size than the largely negative neo-Malthusian goal of zero population growth. The effort to reform our civilization is, in fact, the only way to save it.

Coming Together

Caught up in their misdirected and self-defeating priority, the population planners refuse to take their ecological warnings and their holistic ecological perspective seriously. The backsliding is of course well lubricated by Ford and Rockefeller, and encouraged by their own social and intellectual preferences. Few have tried seriously to put their scientific training directly to the cause of revolution from below, or to think through the problems of population and ecology from the perspective of the Black Panthers, Women's Liberation, or the Cuban and Chinese revolutions. Given their education, their access to the powerful, and their friends and neighbors, they always find it more sensible to work for reform from within and from above.

Yet, as their more far-reaching critique is rejected by the elite they want so desperately to reform, the neo-Malthusians, or at least the ecologists among them, will increasingly turn toward the movements for revolution. Ideas without a social force are impotent and, to their proponents, frustrating. Hopefully, the Marxists will at that point be able to tear themselves away from their prejudices and welcome the ecologists as something other than "ideological criminals." For, even apart from their large following, the ecologists do bring a perspective which, integrated with Marx's emphasis on social class and economic process, might once again give the revolutionary movement a claim to ideological hegemony in the advanced industrial countries.

Earlier Marxists viewed capitalism as a closed system, in which advances by the capitalists would increase the misery of the workers. Then, when they saw the fantastic growth of the overall economic pie, if not of the workers' share, they emphasized the relative impoverishment of the working class compared to the capitalists, and located this avoidance of the initial capitalist contradiction in imperial expansion and the impoverishment of the colonial world. Now, with the perspective offered by ecology, it is clear that the West's economic growth involved a massive deficit spending of our natural environment, impoverishing the entire world, and especially future generations.

Capitalism will only carry us beyond any hope of repayment. A democratic and revolutionary socialism at least offers the chance of balancing our accounts with nature and with man—and, as the ecologists are the first to comprehend, it is not simply workers and peasants whose very lives depend upon that chance.

STEVE WEISSMAN

PART ONE

Malthus— Yesterday and Today: An Introductory Essay

1 Malthus Yesterday

The Theory of Population

In the last decade of the eighteenth century, the rulers of Britain were greatly alarmed by the enthusiasm for the French Revolution which was sweeping through the country. The Revolution was breeding dangerous thoughts, not only in the minds of intellectuals like Godwin and poets like Wordsworth, but also in the minds of the working people—the laborers, artisans and small shopkeepers of cities like London and Glasgow. The French Revolution left no one unaffected. "Everything," wrote a contemporary, "not this or that thing, but literally everything, was soaked in this one event."[1]

Those who feared radical social reform fought back against those who hoped and worked for it. A regime of thought-control, terror and physical repression was instituted. The Habeas Corpus Act was suspended; there were many trials for high treason, often with savage sentences; and there was pitiless persecution of those who were suspected of harboring "democratic" thoughts. But physical repression was not enough. Those who feared reform had also to take sides in the great battle of ideas which was raging at the time, in order to overcome the new notions of "the perfectibility of man and of society" which were beginning to grip wide sections of the people.

To their aid, in 1798, came the Reverend Thomas Robert Malthus, with his famous *Essay on the Principle of Population, as it Affects the Future Improvement of Society.*

The *Essay*, at least in its first origins, was quite frankly intended as a political tract, aimed (as Marx noted) "against

1. Henry Thomas Cockburn, *Memorials of His Time* (1856), p. 80.

3

the French Revolution and the contemporary ideas of reform in England (Godwin, etc.)." [2] Malthus himself tells us as much in his Preface. "The following Essay," he writes, "owes its origin to a conversation with a friend, on the subject of Mr. Godwin's Essay, on avarice and profusion, in his Enquirer. The discussion started the general question of the future improvement of society; and the Author at first sat down with an intention of merely stating his thoughts to his friend, upon paper. . . ." [3] The first edition of the *Essay,* then, took the form of an open attack against those who believed in "the perfectibility of man and of society"—that is, against those who believed in what Malthus called "the possible existence of a society, all the members of which, should live in ease, happiness, and comparative leisure; and feel no anxiety about providing the means of subsistence for themselves and families." [4] Malthus maintained that the "principle of population" was "conclusive against the perfectibility of the mass of mankind." [5]

The main argument of the first edition of the *Essay* was as simple as it was sensational. Here is a short summary, in Malthus's own words:

> The power of population is indefinitely greater than the power in the earth to produce subsistence for man.
>
> Population, when unchecked, increases in a geometrical ratio. Subsistence increases only in an arithmetical ratio. A slight acquaintance with numbers will show the immensity of the first power in comparison of the second.

2. Below, p. 188.
3. *Essay,* 1st ed. (London: Macmillan & Co., 1926), p. i. The "friend," as we now know, was actually Malthus's father, Daniel Malthus, who was a strong believer in the possibilities of social improvement.
4. *Ibid.,* pp. 16–17.
5. *Ibid.,* p. 17.

By that law of our nature which makes food necessary to the life of man, the effects of these two unequal powers must be kept equal.

This implies a strong and constantly operating check on population from the difficulty of subsistence. This difficulty must fall somewhere; and must necessarily be severely felt by a large portion of mankind. . . .

This natural inequality of the two powers of population, and of production in the earth, and that great law of our nature which must constantly keep their effects equal, form the great difficulty that to me appears insurmountable in the way to the perfectibility of society.[6]

It will be seen that this argument is chiefly founded upon two propositions—that population when unchecked "increases in a geometrical ratio," whereas "subsistence increases only in an arithmetical ratio." Upon the validity of these "ratios" the argument as a whole stands or falls. It is true that the emphasis on the "ratios" was toned down a little in later editions of the *Essay*, but it is not true—as is often suggested by Malthus's modern admirers—that Malthus eventually came to set little store by them.[7] "Malthus," wrote Engels, "puts forward a calculation upon which his whole system is based. Population increases in geometrical progression—1+2+4+8+16+32, etc. The productive power of the land increases in arithmetical progression—1+2+3+4+5+6. The difference is obvious and horrifying, but is it correct?"[8] Malthus's attempts to demonstrate its correctness are extremely unsatisfactory, to say the least of it. The "geometrical ratio" he takes to be proved by the contemporary growth

6. *Ibid.,* pp. 13–16.
7. Cf. Kenneth Smith, *The Malthusian Controversy* (London: Routledge & Paul, 1951), p. 223.
8. Below, pp. 62–3.

of population in the United States of America, where he asserts (on very doubtful authority) that "the population has been found to double itself in twenty-five years." Therefore, he says, we will take this result as our rule, and assume "that population, when unchecked, goes on doubling itself every twenty-five years, or increases in a geometrical ratio."[9]

If the evidence for the "geometrical ratio" is unsatisfactory, that for the "arithmetical ratio" is even more so. In fact, Malthus adduces no evidence whatsoever for it—all that he does is to assert that it is "the very utmost that we can conceive." Let us allow, he says, "that by great exertion, the whole produce of the Island might be increased every twenty-five years, by a quantity of subsistence equal to what it at present produces. The most enthusiastic speculator cannot suppose a greater increase than this."[10] But this is merely an assertion, and by no means a proof. As Engels pointed out, it ignores (among other things) the fact that "science advances in proportion to the body of knowledge passed down to it by the previous generation, that is, in the most normal conditions it also grows in geometrical progression."[11] The "arithmetical ratio" was in fact purely chimerical.[12] Later on Malthus's followers began to substitute the so-called "law of diminishing returns" for the discredited "arithmetical ratio," and Malthus himself relied increasingly upon this "law" in successive editions of his *Essay*. But this does not save the "principle of population" from collapse. The "law of diminishing returns," as will be shown below,[13] is just as chimerical as the "arithmetical ratio."

Notwithstanding these fairly obvious defects, the success of the *Essay* among the ruling classes was immediate and considerable. Not only did it appear to prove that society was not "perfectible," but it also seemed to reveal that it was

9. *Essay* (1st ed.), pp. 20-21.   10. *Ibid.*, p. 22.
11. Below, p. 63.   12. Cf. below, p. 138.   13. Pp. 23–27.

useless to attempt any major reform even within the present framework of society. In particular, it was impossible "to remove the wants of the lower classes of society." "The truth is," said Malthus, "that the pressure of distress on this part of a community is an evil so deeply seated, that no human ingenuity can reach it."[14] All that can possibly be proposed, he argued, are "palliatives," such as the abolition of the Poor Laws.

It was on this application of the principle of population to the question of reform within the present framework of society, and in particular to the question of the Poor Laws, that Malthus concentrated in the second and subsequent editions of the *Essay*. In his preface to the second edition of 1803, he remarks that in the course of the discussion he "was naturally led into some examination of the effects of this principle on the existing state of society. It appeared to account for much of that poverty and misery observable among the lower classes of people in every nation, and for those reiterated failures in the efforts of the higher classes to relieve them."[15] As the broader perspectives opened up by the French Revolution faded, and the problems of poverty and pauperism were brought into greater prominence by the developing Industrial Revolution and the dislocation caused by the Napoleonic Wars, this application of the principle received more and more emphasis.

When the first edition of Malthus's *Essay* appeared, the English Poor Law legislation was still based on the old principle that an individual could obtain relief only in his own parish. In 1795, in the face of a great increase in pauperism, the so-called "Speenhamland system" had been widely introduced, whereby wages were subsidized from the rates according to a sliding scale varying with the price of bread. This system was beneficial at that time to certain of the

14. *Essay* (1st ed.), p. 95.   15. *Essay* (2d ed.), p. iii.

larger employers of labor—particularly the agricultural employers—since it meant that part of their wage bill would be paid by their smaller competitors, upon whom the burden of the poor rate fell very heavily. The Speenhamland system encouraged employers to cut wages, and resulted in an even greater spread of pauperism among the working people.

Malthus was opposed to the Poor Laws from the beginning. "The poor-laws of England," he said in the first edition of the *Essay*, "tend to depress the general condition of the poor" because their tendency is "to increase population without increasing the food for its support."[16] This theme received much greater stress in the second and subsequent editions. Malthus's work was more influential than that of any other single individual in helping to secure the passing of the new Poor Law of 1834, a measure which was based above all on the interests of the industrial bourgeoisie. The principle of population provided a "scientific" basis for the "reform" of the Poor Law—and also a *moral* basis. In a notorious passage in the second edition, Malthus disposed of the idea that the poor had any "natural right" to support:

> A man who is born into a world already possessed, if he cannot get subsistence from his parents on whom he has a just demand, and if the society do not want his labor, has no claim of *right* to the smallest portion of food, and, in fact, has no business to be where he is. At nature's mighty feast there is no vacant cover for him. She tells him to be gone, and will quickly execute her own orders, if he do not work upon the compassion of some of her guests. If these guests get up and make room for him, other intruders immediately appear demanding the same favor.... The guests learn too late their error, in counteracting those strict orders to all intruders, issued by the great mistress of the feast, who, wishing

16. *Essay* (1st ed.), p. 83.

that all guests should have plenty, and knowing that
she could not provide for unlimited numbers,
humanely refused to admit fresh comers when her
table was already full.[17]

This revealing passage was expunged from subsequent editions, but the basic idea behind it—that the poor are not
entitled to claim relief as a right—was upheld by Malthus to
the end. And not only had the poor no right to relief, but
they must also be punished for their poverty.[18] "Dependent
poverty ought to be held disgraceful,"[19] said Malthus, and it
ought to be made as disagreeable as possible. These ideas
were eventually incorporated in the new Poor Law of 1834,
which abolished all "outdoor relief" for the able-bodied,
compelling the indigent to receive relief inside a workhouse,
and thus forcing the weavers, petty craftsmen and casual
farm laborers into the factories. The "workhouse system" of
industrial England, against which the Chartists—and the
Webbs—struggled, was one of the first fruits of the
Malthusian theory of population.[20]

In his preface to the second edition, Malthus stated that
he had "endeavored to soften some of the harshest conclusions of the first essay."[21] But in actual fact the amount of
"softening" was negligible. It is true that he now suggested
that there might be some hope of improvement if the poor
voluntarily delayed marriage, and therefore procreation, until they were in a position to support a family. But he himself does not seem to have placed much reliance on this
remedy, and all the fundamental doctrines of the original
Essay survived to the last edition with only superficial
changes. The Essay was swollen by the addition of a great
deal of historical and statistical material (much of it of very

17. Essay (2d ed.), pp. 531–32.
18. Cf. below, p. 68.   19. Essay (1st ed.), p. 85
20. Cf. below, part 2, items 2 and 3.   21. Essay (2d ed.), p. vii.

dubious validity), but there were no really radical alterations in the theory itself. Whatever the intentions of its author may have been, the Malthusian theory of population remained to the end what it had been at the beginning—an apology for the condition of the working people, and a warning against all attempts to ameliorate the condition of society. As such it did yeoman service during Malthus's lifetime. And it is still doing yeoman service today, over a century after Malthus's death.

Economic Theory in General

Insofar as it prepared the way for the new Poor Law of 1834, and thus for the removal of the last obstacle which hindered the flow of cheap labor from the country to the towns, Malthus's theory of population was a welcome gift to the industrial bourgeoisie. But it was also by no means unwelcome to the "agricultural interests," who feared radical social reform even more than the industrial bourgeoisie did, and upon whom the burden of the poor rate (at least in certain districts) was beginning to fall with crippling force. Indeed, if the theory of population had been opposed to the general interests of the landed proprietors, Malthus would probably have found excellent reasons for opposing it. For whenever the interests of the landed proprietors and the industrial bourgeoisie came into serious conflict—as they did more and more in the first three decades of the nineteenth century over such issues as the Corn Laws and parliamentary reform—Malthus invariably came down on the side of the landed proprietors. And this is the key to the understanding of his economic theory in general. "Malthus wants bourgeois production," said Marx, "insofar as it is not revolutionary, insofar as it is not a historical force, but merely creates a broader and more convenient material basis for the 'old' society." [22] This attitude colored all his economic writings. "His writings of 1815 on protective tariffs and ground rent," wrote Marx,

> were intended to corroborate his earlier apology for the poverty of the producers; but in particular they were intended to defend reactionary landed property against "enlightened," "liberal" and "progressive" capital, and above all to justify a retrograde piece of legislation put forward in England in the interests of the aristocracy as against the industrial bourgeoisie. Finally his *Principles of Political Economy*, directed against Ricardo, had essentially the aim of confining the absolute demands of industrial capital, and the laws according to which its productivity develops, within limits which would be "advantageous" and "desirable" from the point of view of the landed aristocracy, the State Church to which Malthus belonged, government officials, and tax-consumers. [23]

The English landed proprietors at this time were certainly in sore need of an advocate. The industrial bourgeoisie, who were obsessed—and for their time rightly obsessed—with the great importance of the accumulation of capital, were attacking them in the economic field on two separate fronts. First, they argued, the legislation restricting the import of corn from abroad, while it certainly meant high rents for the landlords, also meant dear bread, and therefore high wages, low profits for the capitalists, and less accumulation of capital. Second, they maintained that the greater part of the rent which the landlords received was generally spent by them on consumer goods and personal services, so that comparatively little of it was saved and accumulated as capital. Other things being equal, then, it was better that the "net revenue" of society should flow into the hands of the industrial bourgeoisie rather than into those of the landlords, since more of it

22. Below, p. 176.   23. Below, pp. 135–36.

would then be accumulated as capital. The industrial bourgeoisie habitually displayed that habit of "parsimony" which
Adam Smith had so highly praised, while the landlords were
notable for that "prodigality" which Adam Smith had correspondingly condemned.

What the landlords needed at this time was an apologist
who would prove on their behalf that there was something
sacrosanct about the rent which they received, that there
were serious dangers inherent in an over-rapid accumulation
of capital, and that even though they spent most of their
income instead of saving it they were still performing a useful social function in the modern capitalist world.

To their aid came the Reverend Thomas Robert Malthus,
with his pamphlet *An Inquiry into the Nature and Progress
of Rent* (1815), and, later, with his book *Principles of Political Economy* (1820).

The first of these two works, in which Malthus put forward the new theory of differential rent (based on the "law
of diminishing returns") which was subsequently to become
associated with Ricardo's name,[24] did not, on the whole,
have the political effect which Malthus intended. Malthus's
aim was twofold. First, he wanted to disprove the assertion,
then frequently being made, that the landlord was no better
than a common monopolist, whose monopoly was injurious
to the consumers. The payment of rent to the landlord,
Malthus argued, was not evidence of the existence of a common monopoly at all: on the contrary, it was "a clear indication of a most inestimable quality in the soil, which God has
bestowed on man—the quality of being able to maintain
more persons than are necessary to work it."[25] Second, he
wanted to provide a theoretical basis for the defense of the
Corn Laws—a defense which he himself put forward, shortly
after the publication of his pamphlet on rent, in a new pam-

24. See below, p. 125.   25. Malthus, *Inquiry*, p. 16.

phlet entitled *The Grounds of an Opinion on the Policy of Restricting the Importation of Foreign Corn* (1815). But Ricardo, Malthus's main opponent in the field of economic theory, had little difficulty in turning the tables completely on him. Ricardo took over Malthus's theory of rent, combined it with a theory of profit which he had already developed independently, and on this theoretical basis demonstrated convincingly that "the interest of the landlord is always opposed to the interest of every other class in the community. His situation is never so prosperous, as when food is scarce and dear: whereas, all other persons are greatly benefited by procuring food cheap."[26] And he appended to this demonstration a set of arguments, erected on the same theoretical basis, designed to show the advantages of a free trade in corn. Ricardo, in short, suggested very persuasively that Malthus's theory of rent, when properly expounded and interpreted, proved virtually the opposite of what Malthus had tried to make it prove.

The argument of Book 2 of Malthus's *Principles of Political Economy*, however, was a harder nut to crack. In this part of the *Principles*, which dealt with "The Progress of Wealth," Malthus maintained that the "present distresses" were in large measure due to the over-rapid accumulation of capital in recent years. If accumulation were too rapid, he argued, the production of commodities might well increase at a greater rate than the distribution of the purchasing power necessary to buy them, so that a "general glut" of commodities would result from this relative deficiency of "effective demand." Since there was an ever-present tendency for this sort of thing to happen under capitalism, the permanent existence of a class of "unproductive consumers"—who would consume without at the same time producing anything—was vitally necessary, in order to keep the

26. David Ricardo, *Works and Correspondence,* Sraffa's ed., vol. 4, p. 21.

economic system functioning at a full employment level. As Marx put it:

> In order to charm out of his bosom the awful con-
> flict between the desire for enjoyment and the chase
> after riches, Malthus, about the year 1820, advo-
> cated a division of labor, which assigns to the capital-
> ist actually engaged in production, the business of
> accumulating, and to the other sharers in surplus
> value, to the landlords, the place-men, the beneficed
> clergy, etc., the business of spending. It is of the
> highest importance, he says, "to keep separate the
> passion for expenditure and the passion for
> accumulation."[27]

In this theory, there were ingeniously combined both a warning against the over-rapid development of capitalism, and an
apology for the continued existence under capitalism of
people like the landlords and their "unproductive" associates
who did nothing except consume.

Ricardo, who saw the cause of the "present distresses"
rather in a deficiency of capital than in an excess of it,
attacked this theory with all the force he could muster. He
recognized clearly enough that Malthus's argument was fundamentally apologetic, and he also recognized the superficiality of the reasoning by which it was supported. In his *Notes
on Malthus*, Ricardo's brief and exasperated comments on
Malthus's defense of "unproductive consumers" reveal his
attitude plainly. For example:

> A body of unproductive laborers are just as neces-
> sary and as useful with a view to future production,
> as a fire, which should consume in the manufacturers
> warehouse the goods which those unproductive
> laborers would otherwise consume. . . . In what way

27. *Capital* (Allen and Unwin ed.), vol. 1, p. 607.

can a man's consuming my produce, without making
me any return whatever, enable me to make a
fortune? ... I cannot express in language so strong
as I feel it my astonishment at the various propositions advanced in this section. ... Mr. Malthus is a
most powerful ally of the Chancellor of the
Exchequer. ...[28]

And although Ricardo went much too far in the opposite
direction, even denying the very possibility of a "general
glut" of commodities under capitalism, his reply to Malthus
convinced most of his contemporaries. Malthus's explanation
of unemployment in terms of "effective demand," unlike his
theory of population, did not become popular in his lifetime.
Oddly enough, it had to await our own times before becoming fashionable. Today, as an important constituent part of
Keynesian economic doctrine, a modified variant of the
Malthusian theory of effective demand has been made to
play a role just as reactionary as that which Malthus intended
the original theory to play.

28. *Works and Correspondence,* vol. 2, pp. 421–33.

2 Marx and Engels on Malthus

General Criticisms

"The hatred of the English working class against Malthus," wrote Marx, ". . . is therefore entirely justified. The people were right here in sensing instinctively that they were confronted not with a *man of science* but with a *bought advocate*, a pleader on behalf of their enemies, a shameless sycophant of the ruling classes."[1] It was for this reason that Marx and Engels spent so much time and energy in attacking Malthus's doctrines.

They recognized, of course, that Malthus had his merits. Marx, for example, praised Malthus for protesting against the extension of the working day.[2] Again, we can infer from the number of times that elementary statements by Malthus are quoted approvingly in *Capital* that Marx admired his facility for expressing familiar classical propositions; and Marx was always prepared to admit that Malthus at least had "a certain interest in theoretical sophistication."[3] Marx also appreciated the superiority of Malthus *when compared with certain other "vulgar" economists*, such as Say and Bastiat.[4] In particular, Malthus was obviously superior to those economists who put forward "the pitiable doctrines of harmony in bourgeois political economy"[5] —i.e., the doctrines which suggested that there was no real conflict of interests between

1. Below, p. 147.
2. Cf. *Capital*, vol. 1, p. 539, fn: "All honor to Malthus that he lays stress on the lengthening of the hours of labor, a fact to which he elsewhere in his pamphlet [*Inquiry into the Nature and Progress of Rent*] draws attention." Cf. also *ibid.*, p. 568.
3. Below, p. 141.
4. Cf. *Critique of Political Economy* (Chicago: C. H. Kerr & Co., *ca.* 1904), p. 34, fn.   5. Below, p. 137.

social classes under capitalism. Malthus at least had the merit of laying emphasis on the disharmonies—in fact, as Marx says, "he clings to them with parsonic satisfaction, amplifies them and blazons them forth."[6] Malthus, he says in another place, "is not interested in disguising the contradictions of bourgeois production; on the contrary, he is interested in emphasizing them."[7] But Marx did not consider this particular merit to be a very outstanding one. For one thing, Malthus had not discovered the contradictions himself, and the reasons why he was interested in emphasizing them were hardly admirable. And for another, the accounts which he gave of these contradictions were superficial and false, and the "remedies" which he proposed were purely apologetic. Such merits as he possessed were greatly outweighed by his deficiencies.

The most important *general* feature of the criticisms of Malthus made by Marx and Engels is their repeated emphasis on his "sin against science." This "sin against science," according to Marx, took two main forms. First, it took the form of his "shameless and mechanical plagiarism."[8] The charge of plagiarism, of course, is notoriously difficult to bring home in cases where the text is not actually *copied*, since the boundaries between the legitimate and illegitimate use of another's work, and between the conscious and unconscious use of it, are often not easy to define. But in the case of Malthus, each of his three major theoretical contributions—the theory of population, the theory of rent, and the theory of effective demand—had been substantially anticipated by earlier writers, and it must be admitted that this series of coincidences is at least highly suspicious. Second, Malthus's "sin against science" took the form of the blatantly *apologetic* character of his conclusions, to which reference has already been made above. As Marx points out on a

6. Below, p. 138.   7. Below, p. 184.   8. Below, pp. 131–32.

number of occasions, Malthus's conclusions were generally either in the interests of the ruling classes as a whole as against the workers, or in the interests of the more reactionary sections of the ruling classes as against the more progressive sections. Malthus "had other things in mind than a scientific treatise on population growth," says a modern commentator on the *Essay*,[9] and this is essentially the burden of Marx's complaint against Malthus's work as a whole. Whether Malthus was as *conscious* of his "sin against science" as the very strong language used by Marx and Engels sometimes seems to imply is, I think, open to doubt. But it is certainly true that Malthus's work forms a pattern which suggests, to say the least of it, that he was often influenced by what he *wanted* to prove to a far greater extent than any competent scientist has a right to be.

The Theory of Population

Marx, in a letter to Schweitzer of 24 January 1865, criticizing the work of Proudhon, made the following comment:

> . . . In a strictly scientific history of political economy the book [Proudhon's *What is Property?*] would hardly be worth mentioning. But sensational works of this kind play their part in the sciences just as much as in the history of the novel. Take, for instance, Malthus's book *On Population*. In its first edition it was nothing but a "sensational pamphlet" and *plagiarism* from beginning to end into the bargain. And yet what a *stimulus* was produced by this *libel on the human race!*[10]

The "stimulus" which the principle of population produced

9. Kenneth Smith, *Malthusian Controversy*, pp. 244–45.
10. Marx and Engels, *Selected Correspondence*, p. 170.

was indeed a strong and far-reaching one. There was probably no other idea which exercised so great an influence on economic theory and practice during the first half of the nineteenth century, and certainly no other which aroused such impassioned attacks and defenses. And it was destined to exercise considerable influence even outside the strictly economic sphere: for example, it was an important factor in the early development of Darwinism.[11] The "stimulus" was strong from the beginning, and its strength is by no means exhausted today.

How did it come about that the Malthusian theory, which had few pretensions to scientific profundity and was shot through and through with fallacies, was able to exercise this enormous influence? One of the main reasons was that the *actual phenomenon* which Malthus described and which he tried to account for—the widespread poverty and pauperism among the working people—was a *real* phenomenon which could not be ignored and which was crying out for an explanation. Malthus was "right, in his way," said Engels, "in asserting that there are always more people on hand than can be maintained from the available means of subsistence"[12]—although the pressure of population was really against the *means of employment* rather than against the means of subsistence. Malthus's critics might attempt to prove his principle of population to be wrong, but they could not "argue away the facts which led Malthus to his principle."[13] Thus even apart from all questions of what Marx called "party interest,"[14] there was a presumption in favor of Malthus's explanation of the facts until a better one had been put forward.

"Party interest," however, played an important role in securing the wide acceptance of the theory in ruling-class circles. An explanation of human misery in terms of an

11. See part 4 below.   12. Below, p. 76.
13. Below, p. 60   14. Below, p. 88

"eternal law of nature," such as Malthus's principle of population, has an obvious appeal for political reactionaries, since it diverts attention from the part played in the creation of this misery by class exploitation in general and by particular systems of class exploitation such as capitalism.[15] One cannot do away with an "eternal law of nature." If it is nature and not human society which is responsible for the misery, all one can do, at the very best, is to mitigate some of the effects of this "eternal law" and suffer the remainder with a good grace.

To Marx and Engels, interested as they were in discovering the basic laws of social change, and in particular the "law of motion" of bourgeois society, any explanation of social phenomena such as overpopulation under capitalism in terms of an "eternal law" was bound to appear superficial and inadequate. This was the basis of their main *general* criticism of Malthus's theory of population. As early as 1847, in his first economic work, Marx attacked the tendency of economists to "represent the bourgeois relations of production as eternal categories," and criticized Ricardo for applying the specifically bourgeois conception of rent to "the landed property of all ages and all countries."[16] The Marxist position was stated by Engels in a letter to Lange of 29 March 1865:

> To us so-called "economic laws" are not eternal laws
> of nature but historic laws which arise and disappear;
> and the code of modern political economy, insofar
> as it has been drawn up with proper objectivity by
> the economists, is to us simply a summary of the
> laws and conditions under which alone modern bour-
> geois society can exist—in short the conditions of its
> production and exchange expressed in an abstract
> and summary way. To us also, therefore, none of

15. Cf. *Capital*, vol. 1, p. 539, fn.
16. *The Poverty of Philosophy*, p. 135.

these laws, insofar as it expresses *purely bourgeois conditions*, is older than modern bourgeois society; those which have hitherto been more or less valid throughout all history only express just those relations which are common to the conditions of all society based on class rule and class exploitation. To the former belongs the so-called law of Ricardo, which is valid neither for feudal serfdom nor ancient slavery; to the latter belongs what is tenable in the so-called Malthusian theory.[17]

And even in the case of those laws and conditions which have had a limited validity throughout the whole history of class society, Marx and Engels maintained that the most interesting and important thing about them was the different ways in which they operated in different types of class society. Thus Marx and Engels denied that "the law of population is the same at all times and at all places." On the contrary, they maintained, "every stage of development has its own law of population."[18]

It was not enough, of course, merely to assert this—it had to be *proved*. Marx and Engels do not seem to have made any direct attempt to formulate the laws of population appropriate to earlier forms of class society; had they done so, they would probably have framed these laws in terms of the particular form of pressure of the direct producers

17. Below, pp. 85–86. Cf. Josef Stalin, *Economic Problems of Socialism in the U.S.S.R.*, p. 8: "One of the distinguishing features of political economy is that its laws, unlike those of natural science, are impermanent, that they, or at least the majority of them, operate for a definite historical period, after which they give place to new laws." It should be noted, however, that Stalin in this work (for reasons which lie outside the scope of the present discussion) lays more emphasis on the economic laws which are common to all forms of society than the founders of Marxism were accustomed to do.

18. *Capital*, vol. 1, p. xxix (author's preface to the 2d ed.).

against the "means of employment" which was generated by each of these types of society. They considered that the most important job they had to do was to formulate the actual law of population peculiar to the present, bourgeois stage of development, and to demonstrate that this new, *specific* law fitted the contemporary facts better than the old, *"eternal"* law which Malthus had put forward. Marx's main formulation of the law is reproduced below,[19] and a brief summary—which necessarily does much less than justice to the original—is all that is required here.

To understand the reason for the emergence of "relative surplus population" under capitalism, says Marx, one must consider the influence of the *growth of capital* upon the lot of the laboring class. And here the most important factor is the composition of capital and the changes it undergoes in the course of the accumulation process. As accumulation proceeds, the value of the means of production (constant capital) tends to rise relatively to the sum total of wages (variable capital). "The accumulation of capital," says Marx, ". . . is effective . . . under a progressive qualitative change in its composition, under a constant increase of its constant, at the expense of its variable constituent." This relative diminution of the variable part of capital proceeds simultaneously with the progress of accumulation and the concentration of capital that accompanies it. Now "the demand for labor is determined not by the amount of capital as a whole, but by its variable constituent alone," so that the demand for labor "falls relatively to the magnitude of the total capital, and at an accelerated rate, as this magnitude increases." Although the demand for labor increases absolutely as the total capital increases, it does so "in a constantly diminishing proportion." Thus "it is capitalistic accumulation itself that constantly produces, and produces in the direct ratio of its own

19. Below, part 2, item 8.

energy and extent, a relatively redundant population of laborers, i.e., a population of greater extent than suffices for the average needs of the self-expansion of capital, and therefore a surplus population." And after discussing briefly the various ways in which these changes may work themselves out, Marx sums the matter up as follows:

> The laboring population therefore produces, along with the accumulation of capital produced by it, the means by which itself is made relatively superfluous, is turned into a relative surplus-population; and it does this to an always increasing extent. This is a law of population peculiar to the capitalist mode of production; and in fact every specific historic mode of production has its own special laws of population, historically valid within its limits alone. An abstract law of population exists for plants and animals only, and only insofar as man has not interfered with them.[20]

It is on the basis of this central thesis that Marx goes on to discuss in greater detail, and with a wealth of historical illustration, the laws of the expansion and contraction of the "industrial reserve army" and the different forms which "relative surplus population" assumes in modern society. It was in this way that Marx and Engels completed their criticism of Malthus's law of population—by formulating a new law capable of replacing it.

The "Law of Diminishing Returns"

As mentioned above, it was not long before the so-called "law of diminishing returns" was brought in as

20. The quotations in this paragraph will be found reproduced below, pp. 91–94.

the main theoretical foundation for the idea that food production cannot increase as fast as population. Since many of the modern "neo-Malthusians" still rely to a greater or lesser extent upon this "law," something should be said here about the Marxist attitude towards it.

In our own times, this "law" is usually formulated in a very general and abstract manner, in terms of the so-called "factors of production"—i.e., land, labor and capital. If we suppose that one "factor" or group of "factors" is held constant, and that to it is applied another "factor" or group of "factors" in successive equal amounts, then, it is said, after a certain point the successive amounts of output added will diminish. But the law was originally formulated with *land* as the "fixed factor" and labor and capital as the "variable factors," and it is this application of it which is important in the present connection. Each additional investment of labor and capital in land, it is argued, must necessarily produce after a point not a corresponding but a diminishing quantity of product. It is this "universal" and "natural" feature of agriculture which is held to be largely responsible for the alleged "overpopulation" which exists in many areas of the world.

In an interesting footnote in *Capital*, referring to the work of the great chemist Liebig, Marx gives a short history of this "law":

> To have developed from the point of view of natural science, the negative, i.e., destructive side of modern agriculture, is one of Liebig's immortal merits. . . . It is, however, to be regretted that he ventures on such haphazard assertions as the following: "By greater pulverizing and more frequent plowing, the circulation of air in the interior of porous soil is aided, and the surface exposed to the action of the atmosphere is increased and renewed; but it is easily seen that the increased yield of the land cannot be propor-

tional to the labor spent on that land, but increases in a much smaller proportion. This law," adds Liebig, "was first enunciated by John Stuart Mill in his *Principles of Political Economy,* vol. 1, p. 17, as follows: 'That the produce of the land increases, *ceteris paribus,* in a diminishing ratio to the increase of the laborers employed . . . is the universal law of agricultural industry.' This is very remarkable, since Mill was ignorant of the reason for this law.". . . Apart from Liebig's wrong interpretation of the word "labor," by which word he understands something quite different from what political economy does, it is, in any case, "very remarkable" that he should make Mr. John Stuart Mill the first propounder of a theory which was first published by James Anderson in A. Smith's days, and was repeated in various works down to the beginning of the nineteenth century; a theory which Malthus, that master in plagiarism (the whole of his population theory is a shameless plagiarism), appropriated to himself in 1815; which West developed at the same time as, and independently of, Anderson; which in the year 1817 was connected by Ricardo with the general theory of value, then made the round of the world as Ricardo's theory, and in 1820 was vulgarized by James Mill, the father of John Stuart Mill; and which, finally, was reproduced by John Stuart Mill and others, as a dogma already quite commonplace and known to every schoolboy.[21]

It was in this "law of diminishing returns," as Marx noted elsewhere, that "Malthus found the real ground for his theory of population and . . . his pupils now seek their final sheet anchor."[22] Marx and Engels always held this "law" in the greatest contempt. "The area of land is limited—that is

21. *Capital,* vol. 1, pp. 514–15, fn.
22. *Selected Correspondence,* p. 27.

perfectly true," said Engels. "But the labor power to be employed on this area increases together with the population; and even if we assume that the increase of output associated with this increase of labor is not always proportionate to the latter, there still remains a third element—which the economists, however, never consider as important—namely, science, the progress of which is just as limitless and at least as rapid as that of population."[23]

Lenin, in his book on *The Agrarian Question and the "Critics of Marx,"* puts forward a detailed criticism of the 'law of diminishing returns." He is attacking a writer called Bulgakov, who "makes the 'law of diminishing returns' the cornerstone of his 'theory of agrarian development,' " and uses it as the basis for an "absurd attempt to revive Malthusianism." Bulgakov implies that technical progress in agriculture should be regarded as a "temporary" tendency, whereas the "law of diminishing returns" should be regarded as possessing "universal significance"—an argument which leads Lenin to remark that "this is the same as saying that the stopping of trains at stations represents the universal law of steam transport, while the motion of trains between stations is a temporary tendency which paralyzes the operation of the universal law of stopping." The "law of diminishing returns," says Lenin,[24]

> does not apply at all to cases in which technique is progressing and methods of production are changing; it has only an extremely relative and restricted application to cases in which technique remains unchanged. That is why neither Marx nor the Marxists refer to this "law," and why so much noise about it is made only by representatives of bourgeois science like Brentano, who are quite unable to rid them-

23. Below, p. 63.
24. The quotations in this paragraph are taken from vol. 12 of the *Selected Works of Lenin,* pp. 51–58.

selves of the prejudices of the old political economy, with its abstract eternal and natural laws.

The "law of diminishing returns," therefore, has to be rejected, and with its rejection the Malthusian principle of population is left without any theoretical basis.

The rejection of this "law" also meant that the "Ricardian" theory of rent, which was originally founded upon it, required substantial amendment. The economists who first developed this theory (with the exception of Anderson) were under what Marx called a "primitive misconception of differential rent . . . to the effect that it necessarily requires a progress toward worse and worse soil, or an ever decreasing productivity of agriculture."[25] In actual fact, Marx argued, this was not so:

> The law of rent, as laid down by Ricardo in its simplest form, apart from its application, does not assume the diminishing fertility of the soil but (*in spite of the fact that the general fertility of the soil increases as society develops*) only presupposes *different* degrees of fertility in different pieces of land, or different results from the successive application of capital to the same land.[26]

It was on this basis that Marx developed his own theory of differential rent. "The main point in all this," he wrote to Engels in an early letter sketching out his theory, "remains to square the law of rent with the progress of the fertility of agriculture in general; this is the only way in which the historical facts can be explained and the only way of superseding Malthus's theory of the deterioration, not merely of the labor force but of the land."[27]

---

25. *Capital*, vol. 3, (Kerr ed.), p. 772.
26. *Selected Correspondence*, pp. 29–30. See also below, pp. 129–31.
27. *Ibid.*, p. 28.

The Theory of Value and Surplus Value

One of the most important general charges which Marx and Engels made against Malthus was that when dealing with economic theory he was almost exclusively concerned with the superficial aspects of market phenomena, and not at all interested in or even aware of the real social relationships lying behind them. This concern with appearances only, which marked Malthus off as a "vulgar" economist *par excellence*, was particularly evident in his theory of value and profit.

There are two alternative ways of looking at economic phenomena. First, you can "hold fast to the appearance," and accept the explanations of these phenomena given by the capitalists themselves as the last word. If you ask a businessman how the value of his commodity is determined, he will probably reply that it is determined by "what the market will bear"—i.e., by what the consumers are prepared to pay. And if you ask him how this value is made up, he will probably answer to the effect that it includes compensation for the labor and raw materials he has purchased, and for the depreciation of his buildings and machinery, *plus* an "addition" of profit at so much per cent on the total capital he has laid out. Profit thus appears as something which is simply "added on" to the price of the finished commodity by the capitalist.

Or, second, you can try to go behind these appearances and penetrate to the real social relationships which ultimately determine them. The value of a commodity then appears, not as the expression of a relation between consumers and finished goods, but rather as the expression of a relationship between men as producers. And profit appears, not as something which is "added on" by the capitalist, but rather as something which is, as it were, secreted in the process of production by virtue of the particular social relationship existing between wage laborers and capitalists.

In the work of Adam Smith, these two ways of looking at economic phenomena, the superficial and the profound, are to be found side by side. In that of Ricardo, the profound predominates, and it was precisely for this reason that the Ricardian system, in spite of its many defects, was able to serve as the foundation for the work of the so-called "Ricardian socialists," and, later, for that of Marx. In Malthus, however, the superficial predominates, and it was only natural that Marx and Engels should have made this aspect of his work a special target for criticism.

The value of a commodity, Malthus argued, ought to be "measured," not by the quantity of labor required to produce it (as Ricardo and Marx maintained), but rather by the quantity of labor which it would "command" on the market—i.e., by the quantity of labor which the amount of money obtainable for the commodity would hire at the current wage rate. Malthus was led to this theory of value by his consideration of an important economic phenomenon peculiar to capitalist society. It is a condition of the production and reproduction of a commodity under capitalism that the amount of labor which it will command should be greater than the amount of labor incorporated in it, for the amount of profit received by the capitalist depends upon the size of this excess. For example, if a capitalist hires ten men for a day to produce a commodity, he will clearly not be prepared to repeat the process unless the price he gets for the commodity is sufficient to enable him to hire *more than* ten days' labor. His aim is not to produce commodities, but to produce profit; and "the excess quantity of living labor for which the commodity is exchanged constitutes the source of profit."[28] The sole merit of Malthus's work on value and

28. Below, p. 142.

profit theory, Marx argues, is the emphasis which he lays on this point. And this merit is canceled out again immediately by reason of the fact that when he proceeds to formulate his theory of value he "confuses the utilization of money or commodities as capital, and consequently their *value* in their specific function as capital, with the *value* of the commodities as such."[29] In other words, having correctly observed that "when commodities or money . . . are exchanged in the form of capital for living labor, they are always exchanged for a greater quantity of labor than is contained in them,"[30] he incorrectly concludes from this that *all* purchasers of *all* commodities, when paying for them "at their value," give in exchange for them a greater quantity of labor than is contained in them (or "a value which contains a greater quantity of labor, which amounts to the same thing").[31] This is the origin of Malthus's theory that the value of a commodity ought to be "measured" by the quantity of labor which it will exchange for or command, and not by the quantity of labor contained in it.

This superficial theory of value leads Malthus to a superficial—and apologetic—theory of profit. What Malthus really does in this analysis, as Marx points out, is to transform all buyers into wage laborers, making them return to the capitalist more labor than is contained in the commodities; whereas in reality—

> his profit is actually derived from the fact that, having *paid* for only a part of the labor contained in the commodities, he *sells all* the labor contained in them. . . . What Malthus does not understand is the difference between the sum total of labor contained in a commodity and the quantity of paid labor contained in it. It is precisely this difference which constitutes the source of profit.[32]

29. Below, p. 143.   30. Below, p. 144.
31. Below, p. 150.   32 Below, pp. 148–49.

Marx, by emphasizing this difference between the paid and unpaid labor contained in a commodity, and by making his important distinction between labor and labor power, was able to show that surplus value was in fact derived from the sale of the commodity *at its value* (that is, for a quantity of labor equal to that contained in it). Malthus, on the other hand, not understanding this—and probably not wishing to understand it—was led directly to "the vulgar idea of profit as originating upon alienation, deriving surplus value from the fact that the seller sells the commodity *above* its value (that is, for more labor time than is contained in it)."[33] What Malthus's theory actually comes down to, said Marx, is this:

> The value of a commodity consists in the value which the buyer pays for it, and this value is equal to the equivalent (value) of the commodity plus an excess over and above this value, surplus value. Thus we arrive at the vulgar concept. Profit arises from the fact that a commodity *is sold dearer than it is bought*. The buyer buys it for a greater quantity of labor, or embodied labor, than it has cost the seller.[34]

To this theory of profit it seems appropriate to apply a comment which Marx later applies to Malthus's concept of value—that it is "the completely commonplace way of looking at the matter which we meet with in everyday life," the concept "held by the Philistine who is steeped in competition and knows nothing except its outward show."[35]

The Theory of Capitalist Crises

Malthus's theory of value, Marx noted, "is curiously in accord with his aim—to act as an apologist for

33. Below, p. 149.   34. Below, p. 150.   35. Below, pp. 166–67.

the state of affairs in contemporary England, with its land-lordism, 'State and Church,' retired officials, tax collectors, tithes, national debt, stock exchange jobbers, law-court officials, parsons and hangers-on."[36] For Malthus's theory of value, as we have just seen, led him to regard profit as "originating upon alienation," and from this it was only a short step to Malthus's famous apology for "unproductive consumers" and his explanation of capitalist crises in terms of a deficiency of effective demand.

If profit arises only in the way described by Malthus, it is extremely difficult to see how this profit is actually going to be realized by the capitalists. The demand of the working class alone is clearly not sufficient to enable the capitalists to realize a profit, since working-class demand is limited to the wages which the capitalists pay to the workers, and the capitalists will obviously expect to get back something over and above these wages. Consequently, as Marx says,

> a demand other than that of the workers, buyers other than the workers themselves, are necessary, or there would be no profit. Where are they going to come from? If they are themselves capitalists, themselves sellers, then we have . . . [a] mutual swindling within the capitalist class—each nominally raises the price of the commodity which he sells to the other, and each gains as seller what he loses as buyer. Thus [according to Malthus] *it is necessary to have buyers who are not sellers*, in order that the capitalist [can] realize his profit and sell the commodities "at their value." Hence the necessity for landowners, retired officials, holders of sinecures, parsons, etc., not forgetting their lackeys and other hangers-on.[37]

This is the theoretical basis for Malthus's plea for the greatest possible increase in the "unproductive classes," and his

36. Below, p. 175.   37. Below, p. 151.

answer to the accusation by the Ricardians (already mentioned above) that these classes (and in particular the landlords) no longer performed any useful function in a capitalist society.

If capitalism is going to expand, said Malthus, then the class of "unproductive consumers" must expand with it if crises are to be avoided, for crises are caused by a deficiency of effective demand which is inherent in the capitalist system. The root cause of crises, according to Malthus, was a contradiction *in the sphere of exchange*, which tended (if accumulation were too rapid) to prevent the amount of purchasing power distributed to consumers being sufficient to buy the commodities produced at prices which would give the capitalists a reasonable profit.

Malthus, as we have seen, was not concerned to disguise the contradictions of bourgeois production, but rather to emphasize them—"on the one hand," as Marx said, "in order to demonstrate that the poverty of the working classes is necessary . . . and on the other hand in order to demonstrate to the capitalists that a well-fed tribe of Church-and-State servants is indispensable for the creation of an adequate demand for their commodities."[38] And Marx was quite prepared to give Malthus credit for emphasizing these contradictions—but only as against those of his contemporaries who denied their existence. Malthus's theory of crises, like that of Sismondi (from whom much of it was probably borrowed),[39] was essentially an "underconsumption" theory—i.e., a theory which puts forward a discrepancy between production and consumption as the basic cause of crises. The Marxist theory of crises, on the other hand, points out—

> that it is precisely in the periods which precede crises that the workers' consumption rises,[40] that

38. Below, p. 184.   39. Cf. below, p. 177 ff.
40. Cf. *Capital*, vol. 2, pp. 475–76.

underconsumption (to which crises are alleged to be due) existed under the most diverse economic systems, whereas crises are the distinguishing feature only of one economic system—the capitalist system.[41] This theory attributes crises to another contradiction, namely, the contradiction between the social character of production (socialized by capitalism) and the private, individual mode of appropriation.[42] ... The two theories of crises of which we are speaking give totally different explanations of them. The first theory attributes crises to the contradiction between production and consumption by the working class; the second attributes them to the contradiction between the social character of production and the private character of appropriation. Consequently, the former sees the root of the phenomenon *outside of* production ... ; the latter sees it precisely in the conditions of production. To put it more briefly, the former attributes crises to underconsumption ... , the latter attributes it to anarchy of production. Thus, while both theories attribute crises to a *contradiction* inherent in the economic system itself, they differ entirely on the point of the nature of this contradiction.[43]

This does not mean, however, that the Marxist theory denies that the contradiction between production and consumption, and the phenomenon of underconsumption, actually exist. It fully recognizes this fact, as Lenin points out,

but puts it in its proper, subordinate, place as a fact that relates only to one of the departments of capitalist production taken as a whole. It teaches that this fact cannot explain crises, which are called forth by another, more profound, the fundamental contra-

41. Cf. Engels, *Anti-Dühring*, p. 314.   42. Cf. *ibid.*, part 3, chap. 2.
43. V. I. Lenin, *A Characterization of Economic Romanticism*, English ed. (Moscow: Foreign Languages Publishing House), pp. 63–64.

diction in the present economic system, namely, the contradiction between the social character of production and the private character of appropriation.[44]

Nor does it mean that the Marxist theory denies that it is the lack of demand for commodities which makes crises *possible*. But the question is:

> Does pointing to this condition which makes crises possible mean explaining the cause of crises? Did not Ephrucy[45] understand the difference between pointing to the possibility of a phenomenon and explaining its inevitability? Sismondi says: crises are possible because the manufacturer does not know the demand; they are inevitable because under the capitalist mode of production there can be no balance between production and consumption (i.e., the product cannot be realized). Engels says: crises are possible, because the manufacturer does not know the demand; they are inevitable, but not by any means because the product cannot be realized in general. This is not so: the product can be realized. Crises are inevitable because the collective character of production comes into conflict with the individual character of appropriation.[46]

What it *does* mean, however, is that crises are in fact inseparable from capitalism, and will continue to break out so long as capitalism exists. "If capitalism could adapt production," writes Stalin,

> not to the obtaining of the utmost profit, but to the

44. *Ibid.*, pp. 64–65.
45. B. Ephrucy, a Russian writer, had written in an article on Sismondi that "on the question of the causes of crises . . . . , we have every right to regard Sismondi as the founder of those views which were subsequently developed more consistently and more clearly" —i.e., of the Marxist theory.
46. *Ibid.*, pp. 68–69.

systematic improvement of the material conditions of the masses of the people, and if it could turn profits not to the satisfaction of the whims of the parasitic classes, not to perfecting the methods of exploitation, not to the export of capital, but to the systematic improvement of the material conditions of the workers and peasants, there would be no crises. But then capitalism would not be capitalism. To abolish crises it is necessary to abolish capitalism.[47]

47. Josef Stalin, *Report to the Sixteenth Congress of the C.P.S.U.(B.)*, English ed. (Moscow: Foreign Languages Publishing House), pp. 18–19. Cf. Stalin's treatment of the "basic economic laws" of capitalism and socialism in his *Economic Problems of Socialism in the U.S.S.R.*, pp. 42–46.

3 Malthus Today

The Theory of Population

In our own times, new doctrines concerning "the perfectibility of man and of society," scientific rather than utopian in character, have come to guide the practical day-to-day activities of large sections of mankind. Inspired by Marxism, tremendous social revolutions have occurred in the Soviet Union, China and the People's Democracies—revolutions in which "everything, not this or that thing, but literally everything," has been soaked. In those countries where capitalism still holds sway, those who fear radical social change are again facing a challenge, but a challenge far stronger than anything of which their predecessors in Malthus's time ever dreamed. Once again it is necessary for them to fight back not only on the physical plane, but also in the realm of ideas. And to their aid, faithful as always, has come the Reverend Thomas Robert Malthus. The main theoretical weapons which Malthus used against the progressive classes of his own time are being taken from the armory of reaction, dusted and polished, and used against the progressive classes of today.

The Malthusian theory of population, for example, in various modernized forms, is very much in vogue today, particularly in the United States. The basic idea of the modern Malthusians is essentially the same as that of Malthus himself—that population tends to increase faster than the means of subsistence. Malthus's prophecy that world population would eventually outstrip world food supplies, they argue, may shortly be fulfilled. "Never before, in history," says William Vogt in his *Road to Survival*, "have so many hundreds of millions teetered at the edge of the precipice." [1]

1. William Vogt, *Road to Survival* (English ed., 1949), p. 265.

"There are too many people in the world," says the same author elsewhere in the book, "for its limited resources to provide a high standard of living."[2] Such ideas as these, it is evident, are useful weapons against those who feel that if the world is in fact teetering at the edge of a precipice today it is for a very different reason, and who are striving to bring about those social and economic conditions in which alone a high standard of living for everyone can eventually be guaranteed.

Some of the modern Malthusians put the principle of population to uses which might have shocked even Malthus himself. In the hands of writers like Vogt, Malthusianism becomes an important weapon in the "cold war." For example, we are told of India that "in all the world there is probably no region of greater misery, and almost certainly none with less hope";[3] of China that she "quite literally *cannot feed more people*";[4] and of the Soviet Union that she is "certainly overpopulated; there is little possibility that she can raise her people to our [i.e., the American] status."[5] It comes as no surprise, therefore, that we should then also be told that "the greatest potential threat to world peace" comes from certain of the "overpopulated" countries—and in particular, of course, from the Soviet Union. "The major threat in Asia," Vogt writes, ". . . is mounting population pressure in the Soviet Union."[6] The Malthusian principle can be used, in addition, to discourage attempts to assist these "overpopulated" countries. Where it finds "overpopulation," says Vogt, the Food and Agriculture Organization of the United Nations should include contraception programs in its conservation and food-production programs, and "should not ship food to keep alive ten million Indians and Chinese

2. *Ibid.*, p. 78. 3. *Ibid.*, p. 227. 4. *Ibid.*, p. 224.
5. *Ibid.*, p. 229. 6. *Ibid.*, p. 238.

this year, so that fifty million may die five years hence."[7] And above all, the principle can be used as a justification for American "leadership" of the Western world. "The British people," says Vogt in a curious passage,

> stimulated by the presence of American GIs, have cast longing eyes toward the American standard of living. The Socialist government, counting on "economic" and "political" prestidigitation that hung in the air without any base on the land, promised to lift the United Kingdom by its own bootstraps, without recognizing that the bootstraps had been worn to the breaking point. Unless we [i.e., America] are willing to place fifty million British feet beneath our dining-room table we may well see famine once more stalking the streets of London. And hand in hand with famine will walk the shade of that clear-sighted English clergyman, Thomas Robert Malthus.[8]

Vogt is a "popular" writer, whose aim is to shock by the brutality of his sentiments. But there are other "neo-Malthusians," more subtle and sophisticated and therefore more dangerous, who use Malthus's doctrine in order to reveal a so-called "dilemma of science." Professor A. V. Hill, for example, in his presidential address to the British Association in 1952, chose to speak on this theme. The application of scientific methods to combat diseases, to improve rural and industrial health, and to increase the supply of medical equipment and services, he said, must necessarily increase the pressure of population upon the world's food resources. Hence science is placed in the following dilemma:

Had it been possible to foresee the enormous success

---

7. *Ibid.*, pp. 281–82. Cf. pp. 224–25: "The greatest tragedy that China could suffer, at the present time, would be a reduction in her death rate."

8. *Ibid.*, pp. 71–72.

of this application, would humane people have agreed that it could better have been held back, to keep in step with other parallel progress, so that development could be planned and orderly? Some might say yes, taking the purely biological view that if men will breed like rabbits they must be allowed to die like rabbits, until gradually improving education and the demand for a higher standard of life teach them better. Most people would still say no. But suppose it were certain now that the pressure of increasing population, uncontrolled by disease, would lead not only to widespread exhaustion of the soil and of other capital resources but also to continuing and increasing international tension and disorder, making it hard for civilization itself to survive: Would the majority of humane and reasonable people then change their minds? If ethical principles deny our right to do evil in order that good may come, are we justified in doing good when the foreseeable consequence is evil? . . .[9]

Professor Hill assumes that Malthus's doctrine is essentially true—that population "naturally" increases faster than the supply of food, and that war and famine and disease (the Malthusian "checks") are therefore the inevitable lot of mankind. He is thus able to transform into a dilemma of science something which is in fact a dilemma of the capitalist system.

The modern Malthusians, however, are hard put to it to make convincing use of some of Malthus's original arguments. In particular, the basic principle can no longer be plausibly presented as if it were *purely* a "natural" law which it is quite impossible for man to circumvent. For example, it has become perfectly obvious in the course of the last century and a half that insofar as certain areas of land have

9. Quoted by J. D. Bernal in *The Modern Quarterly,* vol. 8, no. 1, p. 45.

declined in fertility this has very largely been the fault not of nature but of man himself—or, rather, of systems of land ownership and forms of social organization based on exploitation which encourage the squandering of natural resources. And it is also becoming fairly widely known "first, that of the 50 per cent of the globe's soil which can be cultivated, only 10 per cent is being used; and second, that production per acre in most of the world could be greatly increased by rational agricultural practices."[10] Thus it is becoming increasingly difficult for the "neo-Malthusians" to deny that political and economic factors are at least *relevant* to the question of the relation between population and food supplies. What has to be denied by the modern Malthusians, therefore, is that political and economic factors are *fundamental*, and that insofar as the relation between population and food supplies does at the moment constitute a real problem in certain countries, it cannot be effectively solved except *on the basis* of radical political and economic changes. Some modern Malthusians therefore assert that man has been "tricked" (presumably by socialists) into "seeking political and/or economic solutions for problems that are political, economic, social, geographic, psychological, genetic, physiological, etc."[11] To talk in such terms as these, of course, is to disguise the primary causes of the trouble by giving them equal status with the secondary causes. As Lenin once remarked, "critical flirtation with Malthusianism inevitably results in a descent to the most vulgar bourgeois apologetics."[12]

10. J. de Castro, *Geography of Hunger*, p. 25.
11. Vogt, *Road to Survival*, p. 53.
12. *Selected Works*, vol. 12, p. 59.

Economic Theory in General

There is obviously *some* poverty and distress which cannot possibly be associated, even by the most extreme of the "neo-Malthusians," with any "pressure of population against the means of subsistence." The working people of capitalist countries have not, in general, begun to find themselves conspicuously redundant in relation to the existing means of subsistence. Indeed, it is the bogey of underpopulation, rather than that of overpopulation, which is generally raised up before them nowadays. But they have periodically found themselves redundant in relation to the existing *means of employment*. Malthus himself once wrote that "the difficulty of procuring the means of subsistence" is occasioned "partly by the necessary state of the soil, and partly by a premature check to the demand for produce and labor."[13] In the great majority of cases it is this "premature check" which is the really important phenomenon. Under capitalism, the Malthusian pressure of population against the means of subsistence is largely a myth, whereas the periodical pressure of working people against the means of employment is a grim reality.

Malthus, as we have seen, tried to explain the latter form of redundancy in terms of an overall deficiency of "effective demand," and Ricardo replied by denying the very possibility of a "general glut." Subsequent orthodox economists continued in effect to deny this possibility for almost a century—with much less excuse than Ricardo—until the great depression of the early 1930s made it urgently necessary for them to bring their theory a little more closely into touch with reality.

What they needed was a new economic theory which,

13. *Supplement to the Encyclopaedia Britannica* (1824), vol. 6, p. 316.

while no longer denying the theoretical possibility of periodical and chronic unemployment, would explain it in such
terms as to suggest that it could be done away with *within
the capitalist social structure* if the appropriate measures
were taken by the government. The socialist challenge could
no longer be effectively met by denying the theoretical possibility of slumps or by blaming them on the workers. It could
only be met by demonstrating that the economic advantages
of socialism could in fact be obtained under capitalism,
provided the latter was "regulated" or "controlled" in the
right way. The new "General Theory" put forward by
Keynes in 1936 was eventually found to be eminently suitable for these purposes. This theory, which was essentially
intended as a means for saving monopoly capitalism from
economic ruin, was subsequently presented to the working
class movement as a means for achieving its historic demands. Reformism in the labor movement in the West today
is based almost entirely on the economic theory of Keynes.

Keynes greatly admired Malthus. The *Essay on Population*
is described by Keynes as "profoundly in the English tradition of humane science—. . . a tradition marked by a love of
truth and a most noble lucidity, by a prosaic sanity free from
sentiment or metaphysic, and by an immense disinterested-
ness and public spirit."[14] And the Malthusian doctrine of
effective demand came in for especial praise from Keynes.
"If only Malthus, instead of Ricardo," says Keynes, referring
to this doctrine, "had been the parent stem from which
nineteenth-century economics proceeded, what a much wiser
and richer place the world would be today!"[15] Again, in the
General Theory, Keynes remarks that "in the later phase of
Malthus the notion of the insufficiency of effective
demand takes a definite place as a scientific explanation

14. John Maynard Keynes, *Essays in Biography* (London: Macmillan
& Co., 1933), p. 120.
15. *Ibid.*, p. 144.

of unemployment."[16] And there is a great deal more in this panegyrical strain, contrasting strangely with the contempt which Keynes often expressed for Marx.

There is little doubt that Keynes owed much to Malthus's general approach to the problems of unemployment and crisis. This is how Keynes himself described Malthus's basic approach to economic phenomena, comparing it with that of Ricardo:

> According to Malthus's good common-sense notion prices and profits are primarily determined by something which he described, though none too clearly, as "effective demand." Ricardo favored a much more rigid approach, went behind "effective demand" to the underlying conditions of money on the one hand and real costs and the real division of the product on the other hand, conceived these fundamental factors as automatically working themselves out in a unique and unequivocal way, and looked on Malthus's method as very superficial. . . . Malthus, by taking up the tale much nearer its conclusion, had a firmer hold on what may be expected to happen in the real world.[17]

This statement was intended, of course, as pro-Malthus propaganda, but if the emotive language is ignored it will be found to reveal very clearly the completely superficial character of Malthus's—and by implication Keynes's—approach to economic problems. The main task of political economy, surely, is to seek for the *underlying causes* of the phenomena which we observe on the market. To say nothing more than that prices and profits are determined by "effective demand" is, as Ricardo specifically recognized, to say nothing at all. It is necessary to go behind "effective demand" to the real social relationships which ultimately determine these

16. Keynes, *General Theory of Employment, Interest and Money* (London, Macmillan & Co., 1936), p. 362.
17. Keynes, *Essays in Biography*, pp. 122–23.

market phenomena. If we "take up the tale much nearer its conclusion" we stand a good chance of missing its beginning and thereby losing the whole point of it. If we say nothing at all about these ultimate determining forces, our theory may well turn out to be "good common sense" from the bourgeois point of view. But the "good common sense" of the businessman is not necessarily—or indeed usually—a reliable guide to the understanding of the *basic causes* of economic phenomena. The businessman "holds fast to the appearance, and takes it for the last word"—and calls the result "good common sense." Why, then, as Marx asked, the necessity for any *science* at all?[18]

Keynes always claimed Malthus as "the first of the Cambridge economists,"[19] and it is at any rate true that Keynes himself followed in the Malthusian tradition in economic theory. That tradition, as we have seen, expressed itself in two main ways—first, in a superficial approach to the problem of value and surplus value which abstracted from real social relationships; and second (and dependent upon this), an explanation of capitalist crises in terms of a subordinate contradiction in the sphere of exchange rather than in terms of the basic contradiction in the sphere of capitalist production. In the first of these fields, Keynes seems to have seen nothing seriously wrong with the orthodox theories of value and distribution, which, as he put it, come into their own again if and when the "central controls" secure full employment.[20] And in the second field, Keynes was equally a Malthusian—so much so, indeed, that many of the criticisms which Marx and Lenin made of the theories of crises put forward by Malthus and Sismondi can be applied with little modification to the theories of Keynes. Starting off from this general approach, then, it is not surprising that Keynes,

18. *Letters to Kugelmann*, p. 74.
19. Keynes, *Essays in Biography*, pp. 144–45.
20. Keynes, *General Theory*, pp. 378–79.

like Malthus, should eventually have decided that the main economic evils of capitalism could be done away with (by bolstering up "effective demand," etc.) without doing away with capitalism itself.

Malthus and Imperialism

The theories of Malthus, now as always, are serving as weapons in the hands of people who, whether they are aware of it or not, are hindering the progress of mankind towards a fuller and more abundant life. If the social struggles of the early nineteenth century were essentially summed up in the controversy between Malthus and Ricardo, those of our own times are perhaps not unfairly summed up in that between Malthusians and Marxists. For this reason, it is thought that the present volume, which sets out the main passages in which Marx and Engels criticized Malthus's theories, may serve a useful purpose.

We should not expect, of course, that the detailed criticisms of Malthus made by Marx and Engels can all be automatically and mechanically applied to the doctrines of his present-day admirers and successors. A surprising number of them *can* be so applied: what is remarkable here, as in most other aspects of the work of Marx and Engels, is the startling *modernity* of their approach. But what the selections provide which is really useful to the working-class movement of today is a sustained application of *the Marxist method* to the criticism of certain doctrines which, in different forms and disguises, have been serving the cause of reaction for a century and a half and are still faithfully serving it today.

These doctrines have today become an important part of the ideological stock-in-trade of imperialism in its present state of crisis. The imperialist countries are facing economic stagnation at home and the revolt of millions of people in the colonial territories abroad, while all the time the Soviet Union and the People's Democracies are growing from strength to strength. In this desperate situation imperialism must seek for allies: it must try to persuade wide sections of the people, if not to join actively in its attempts at repression, at least to adopt a passive attitude towards them. And it has found that Malthusian doctrines, in the various forms which they assume today, are an ideal means of persuasion.

Malthus has all the answers the imperialists need. Do you think there is any hope for the future of humanity? Malthus will tell you (through the mouth of Sir Charles Darwin) that "in the very long run of a million years the general course of human history is most of the time likely to be what it has been for most of the past time, a continual pressure of population on its means of subsistence, with a margin of the population unable to survive."[21] Do you think that the colonial territories, if they manage to emancipate themselves from imperialist rule, will be able to improve their standard of living? Malthus will tell you, through the mouths of his modern followers, that there is no possible hope of their doing this—so they might just as well remain dependent. Do you think there is any hope for India, one of the customary text-book examples of an "overpopulated" country? The "neo-Malthusians" will tell you that there is no hope at all— any increase in food production would soon be followed by a corresponding increase in India's "teeming millions." And if you suggest that two centuries of British rule in India may have had something to do with the present situation, and that experience in the West does not seem to bear out the theory that a rise in the standard of living necessarily causes a corresponding rise in the birth rate, the "neo-Malthusians" will reply to the effect that the "law of population" is an

21. Quoted by J. D. Bernal in *The Modern Quarterly*, vol. 8., no. 1, pp. 48–49.

"eternal" law, a "natural" law, and therefore cannot possibly be abrogated. Suppose, finally, that you begin to suspect that the "neo-Malthusians" may be wrong, and look around you at what is going on in the Soviet Union, where the great plans for the increase of food production are making a mockery of the Malthusian theory of population and the "law of diminishing returns." Suppose that you then demand that a socialist system be introduced in Britain, so that we can make similar plans to improve our standard of living. Malthus will then tell you, through the mouths of the Keynesians, that the most serious economic defects in the capitalist system can be cured within the framework of that system, without the necessity of introducing socialism.

And not only this. Malthusian doctrines, in their present-day forms, are encouraging preparations for war, and reducing opposition to the actual waging of war. Many Keynesian economists have proclaimed that the only form of government expenditure which will "bolster up effective demand" sufficiently to prevent a slump in the capitalist world today is expenditure on armaments. And, they add, in order to be effective this expenditure must be continuous, and possibly even cumulative. The current arms drive in the West is quite often justified by economists and statesmen on these grounds, and fears are frequently expressed concerning the effect upon the economies of the Western bloc of the ending or even the diminution of the present program. It is well known that the possession of arms is apt to encourage the use of them. And although there have as yet been few people openly to advocate on Malthusian grounds the use of these arms to reduce the population in "overpopulated" countries like China and the U.S.S.R., there is no doubt that "neo-Malthusian" doctrines are helping to weaken the opposition which any such action would immediately provoke. After all, the advocacy of infanticide or the cessation of medical supplies to "overpopulated" countries is not very far

from the advocacy of more widespread and efficient measures to reduce the population. The struggle against
Malthusianism is an integral part of the struggle for peace in
the world today.

R. L. M.

Glasgow
12 February 1953

Notes on the Translations

The following items have been newly translated into English for this volume: sections one, two, five, ten, and eleven in part two; the entirety of part three; section one of part four. The sources are given in the notes with which each of the sections begins.

Footnotes with no indication as to the author are by Marx or Engels, as the case may be; those marked —K. (in the *Theorien* selections) are by Kautsky; and those marked —Ed. are by the present editor.

Marx's quotations from British authors have in every case been reproduced in the original English. Except in the cases of Smith and Ricardo, the editions used by Marx have generally been referred to. A number of references have been added and corrected, and some attempt at standardization has been made.

Italics in the text represent the emphases of Marx and Engels; italics in the quotations represent the emphases of the authors quoted, unless otherwise indicated. The use of foreign words and phrases in the original text is remarked upon in the footnotes only when they are in English.

Square brackets [] have been used for two purposes: (*a*) in the text of the *Theorien* selections, to indicate words and phrases inserted by Kautsky to make Marx's meaning clearer; and (*b*) in the quotations, to indicate additions or amendments made by Marx or Engels.

These notes apply only to the newly translated items. All the others have been transferred from the indicated sources with only very minor technical alterations.

PART TWO

Marx and Engels on the Malthusian Theory of Population

Introductory Notes

The items included in this part have been selected in order to illustrate the development of the views of Marx and Engels on population theory over the whole period of fifty years from the beginning of their collaboration to the death of Engels.

In the beginning, it was Engels rather than Marx who was the economist. Engels's remarkable article *Outlines of a Critique of Political Economy,* which was published in the *Deutsch-Französische Jahrbücher* in 1844, was in fact the starting-point of Marx's economic studies. In this article, and, a year or so later, in his book *The Condition of the Working Class in England in 1844,* Engels summed up what he had so far learned from his theoretical studies in political economy and from his personal observations of economic conditions in England. In spite of occasional traces of immaturity and overexuberance—in 1844 Engels was only twenty-four years of age—both works are to be ranked among the great classics of socialist thought. The first item appearing below is a general criticism of the Malthusian theory of population from the *Outlines;* the third item is an extract from *The Condition of the Working Class* dealing with Malthusianism and the Poor Laws; and the fourth item is another extract from *The Condition of the Working Class* in which the pressure of the workers against the means of employment is more fully discussed.

In the summer of 1844, when Marx was engaged in his first serious economic studies, an article entitled "The King of Prussia and Social Reform," by "A Prussian" (Arnold Ruge), appeared in *Vorwärts,* a paper issued by the German revolutionary exiles in Paris. Marx objected in particular to Ruge's assumption that the problem of chronic poverty was primarily a political one, and on 7 August 1844, he published in *Vorwärts* his "Critical Comments" on Ruge's contribution. The second item below consists of an extract from Marx's article, in which he discusses the attitude of the English bourgeoisie towards pauperism, illustrating their inability to understand the problem by their uncritical acceptance of Malthus's explanation in terms of an "eternal law of nature."

The fifth item is a short extract from Marx's *Theories of Surplus Value* commenting upon the views of an economist called Barton, one of Ricardo's contemporaries. Barton has some claim to be regarded as one of the pioneers of Marx's own law of population, and the germ of chapter 25 of volume 1 of *Capital,* in which this law was put forward, is to be found in these comments on Barton. The sixth item is a letter from Engels to F. A. Lange, which contains an excellent short survey of the population question; and the seventh is an amusing comment on "Parson Malthus" (and other parsons) from *Capital.*

The later works of Marx and Engels do not contain any *direct* critique of Malthus's "principle of population" comparable in scope to Engels's account of it in the *Outlines.* They obviously felt that the most effective way of refuting Malthus's principle was to provide an alternative theory which would fit the facts of the modern world better than Malthus's did. They were thus more concerned with the positive task of formulating the specific law of population peculiar to capitalism than with the negative task of refuting Malthus's theory in detail. The most important item reproduced in this part, therefore, is the eighth—an extract from chapter 25 of volume 1 of *Capital* in which the new law is formulated.

The Malthusian theory of population had often been used as the basis for the so-called "iron law of wages." Wages, it was argued, must necessarily tend to the subsistence level, since if they rose above this level the population would eventually increase (according to Malthus's principle) until the increased competition for jobs once again reduced wages to the subsistence level. Marx's new law of population was used by him as the basis for a new theory of wages—a theory much less rigid than the old "iron law." The Malthusian basis of the "iron law" is commented upon by Marx and Engels in the ninth item, the occasion being the inclusion of a reference to the "iron law" in the draft program of the German Workers' Party (the famous "Gotha programme") in 1875.

The tenth and eleventh items consist of letters written by Engels to Kautsky and Danielson respectively. The letter to Kautsky contains some interesting comments on the question of the regulation of population in a communist society; and in the letter to Danielson Engels points out that in Europe today it is the means of subsistence which are pressing against the population, rather than the population which is pressing against the means of subsistence.

The sources of the items (which are arranged in chronological order) are as follows:

1. Translated from the *Marx-Engels Gesamtausgabe,* part 1, vol. 2, pp. 396–401.

2. Translated from the *Gesamtausgabe,* part 1, vol. 3, pp. 8–12.

3. From Engels's *The Condition of the Working Class in England in 1844,* English ed. (Allen and Unwin), pp. 284–87.

4. From *ibid.,* pp. 79–85.

5. Translated from Marx's *Theorien über den Mehrwert* (Kautsky ed.), vol. 2, 2, pp. 372–74.

6. From the *Selected Correspondence* of Marx and Engels, English ed. (Lawrence and Wishart), pp. 198–200.

7. From Marx's *Capital,* vol. 1 (Allen and Unwin ed.), pp. 629–30, fn.

8. From *ibid.,* pp. 642–64.

9. From the *Selected Correspondence,* p. 335, and from Marx's *Critique of the Gotha Programme* (Lawrence and Wishart ed.), pp. 21–23.

10. Translated from *Briefe an A. Bebel, W. Liebknecht, K. Kautsky und andere* (Moscow, 1933), part 1, p. 232.

11. Translated from *Die Briefe von Karl Marx und Friedrich Engels an Danielson (Nikolai-on)* (Leipzig, 1929), p. 74.

1 The Myth of Overpopulation

From Engels's *Outlines of a Critique of Political Economy* (1844)

The struggle of capital against capital, labor against labor, and land against land, drives production into a state of feverish activity, in which all natural and reasonable relations are turned upside down. No one capital can stand up against the competition of another if it is not brought to the highest pitch of activity. No one piece of land can be profitably cultivated if its productivity is not constantly being increased. No one worker can hold his own against his competitors if he does not dedicate all his strength to his work. Nobody, in fact, who enters the competitive struggle can endure it without the greatest exertion of his strength, without the abandonment of all truly human purposes. The consequence of this hypertension on the one side is necessarily exhaustion on the other. If the fluctuations of competition are small, if demand and supply, consumption and production, are almost equal to one another, then in the development of production a stage must ensue in which there is so much superfluous productive power in existence that the great mass of the nation has nothing to live on, so that people starve to death from sheer abundance. England has already been in this crazy situation, in this truly absurd condition, for a considerable time: If the fluctuations of competition become stronger, as they necessarily do in such a state of affairs, then we have the alternation of prosperity and crisis, of overproduction and stagnation. The economists have never been able to understand this crazy state of affairs, so in order to explain it they thought up the theory of population, which is just as nonsensical, indeed, even more nonsensical, than this contradiction of the coexistence of wealth and poverty. The economists did not *dare* to see the truth; they did not dare to understand that this contradiction is a simple consequence of competition, because if they had done so their whole system would have collapsed.

For us the explanation of the matter is easy. The productive power at the disposal of mankind is immeasurable. The productivity of the land can be infinitely increased by the application of capital, labor and science. "Overpopulated" Great Britain, according to the calculations of the ablest economists and statisticians (cf. Alison's *Principles of Population*, vol. 1, chaps. 1 and 2),[1] could be so developed in the course of ten years as to produce sufficient corn for six times its present population. Capital increases daily; labor power grows together with population; and science masters natural forces for mankind to a greater extent every day. This immeasurable productivity, administered consciously and in the interests of all, would soon reduce to a minimum the labor falling to the lot of mankind; left to competition, it does the same, but only within the limits imposed by the contradiction. One part of the land is cultivated according to the best methods, while another part—in Great Britain and Ireland thirty million acres of good land—lies waste. One part of the capital circulates with phenomenal speed, while another part lies inert in strong-boxes. One part of the working population works fourteen, sixteen hours a day, while another remains unemployed and idle, and dies of hunger. Or this coexistence of idleness and activity gives way to another pattern: today trade goes well, demand is very considerable and everyone is working, capital is turned over with wonderful speed,

1. Archibald Alison, *The Principles of Population, and their Connection with Human Happiness* (London, 1840).—Ed.

agriculture flourishes, the workers work themselves sick—then, tomorrow, stagnation comes on the scene, agriculture is no longer worthwhile and whole stretches of land remain uncultivated, capital becomes paralyzed in the middle of its course, the workers are unemployed, and the whole country suffers from surplus wealth and surplus population.

The economists cannot regard this account of the matter as the correct one, for if they did, as stated above, they would have to abandon their whole system of competition; they would have to acknowledge the stupidity of its antithesis between production and consumption, between surplus wealth and surplus population. But in order to bring these facts into harmony with theory—since the facts themselves could not be denied—the theory of population was invented.

Malthus, the originator of this doctrine, asserts that population constantly exerts pressure on the means of subsistence; that as production is increased, population increases in the same proportion; and that the inherent tendency of population to multiply beyond the available means of subsistence is the cause of all poverty and all vice. For if there are too many people, then in one way or another they must be eliminated; they must die, either by violence or through starvation. When this has happened, however, a gap appears once more, and this is immediately filled by other propagators of population, so that the old poverty begins anew. Moreover, this is the case under all conditions—not only in the civilized but also in the natural state of man. The savages of New Holland, who live *one* to the square mile, suffer just as much from overpopulation as England. In short, if we want to be logical, we have to recognize *that the earth was already overpopulated when only one man existed.* Now the consequence of this theory is that since it is precisely the poor who constitute this surplus population, nothing ought to be done for them, except to make it as easy as possible for them to starve to death; to convince them that this state of affairs cannot be altered and that there is no salvation for their entire class other than that they should propagate as little as possible; or that if this is not practicable, it is at any rate better that a State institution for the painless killing of the children of the poor should be set up—as suggested by "Marcus,"[2]—each working-class family being allowed two-and-a-half children, and the excess being painlessly destroyed. The giving of alms would be a crime, since it would encourage the growth of surplus population; but it would be very advantageous to make poverty a crime and the workhouse a corrective institution, as has already happened in England under the new "liberal" Poor Law. It is true, of course, that this theory does not accord at all well with the biblical teaching of the perfection of God and of his creation, but "it is a bad refutation which puts forward the Bible against the facts."

Is it necessary for me to give any more details of this vile and infamous doctrine, this repulsive blasphemy against man and nature, or to follow up its consequences any further? Here, brought before us at last, is the immorality of the economists in its highest form. What were all the wars and horrors of the monopoly system when compared with this theory? And it is precisely this theory which is the cornerstone of the liberal system of free trade, whose fall will bring the whole edifice down with it. For once competition has here been proved to be the cause of misery, poverty and crime, who will still dare to say a word in its defense?

Alison, in the work mentioned above, has shattered the Malthusian theory by appealing to the productive power of the soil, and by putting forward in opposition to the Malthusian principle the fact that every grown man can produce more than he himself consumes, a fact without which mankind would not be able to multiply, and would not even

---

2. "Marcus" was the pseudonym of an English author who published in 1838 a pamphlet entitled *On the Possibility of Limiting Populousness*, in which Malthus's theory was carried to an absurdity.—Ed.

be able to maintain itself; otherwise what could the rising generation live on? But Alison does not go to the root of the matter, and therefore finally comes back again to the same conclusion as Malthus. Although it is true that he proves Malthus's principle to be wrong, he cannot argue away the facts which led Malthus to his principle.

If Malthus had not taken such a one-sided view of the matter, he could not have missed seeing that surplus population or labor power is always bound up with surplus wealth, surplus capital and surplus landed property. Population is too great only when productive power in general is too great. The state of affairs in every overpopulated country, in particular England, from the time when Malthus wrote onwards, demonstrates this quite unmistakably. These were the facts which Malthus ought to have examined in their entirety, and whose examination ought to have led to the correct conclusion; instead, he picked out one of these facts, neglecting the others, and thus arrived at his own crazy conclusion. His second mistake was to confuse means of subsistence with means of employment. That population always presses against the means of employment, that the number of people who are propagated corresponds to the number who can be employed, in short, that the propagation of labor power has up to now been regulated by the law of competition and has therefore also been subject to periodical crises and fluctuations—all these are facts, the establishment of which stands to the credit of Malthus. But means of employment are not means of subsistence. The means of employment increase only as the final result of an increase of machine power and capital; whereas the means of subsistence increase as soon as there is any increase at all in productive power. Here a new contradiction in political economy comes to light. The demand of the economists is not a real demand, their consumption is an artifical consumption. For the economists, only those who can offer an equivalent for what they receive are real demanders, real consumers. If, however, it is a fact that every adult produces more than he can himself consume, that children are like trees, returning abundantly the expenditure laid out on them—and surely these are facts?—one would imagine that every worker ought to be able to produce far more than he needs, and that the community ought therefore to be glad to furnish him with everything that he requires; one would imagine that a large family would be a most desirable gift to the community. But the economists, with their crude outlook, know no other equivalent apart from that which is paid over to them in tangible hard cash. They are so firmly entangled in their contradictions that they are just as little concerned with the most striking facts as they are with the most scientific principles.

We shall destroy the contradiction simply by resolving it. With the fusion of those interests which now conflict with one another, there will disappear the antithesis between surplus population in one place and surplus wealth in another, and also the wonderful phenomenon—more wonderful than all the wonders of all the religions put together—that a nation must starve to death from sheer wealth and abundance; and there will disappear too the crazy assertion that the earth does not possess the power to feed mankind. This assertion is the highest wisdom of Christian economics—and that our economics is essentially Christian I could have demonstrated from its every statement, from its every category, and shall in due time so demonstrate. The Malthusian theory is merely the economic expression of the religious dogma of the contradiction between spirit and nature, and of the corruption of both resulting from it. I hope I have shown the futility of this contradiction—which has long been resolved for religion and together with it—in the economic sphere also; moreover, I will not accept any defense of the Malthusian theory as competent which does not begin by explaining to me, on the basis of the theory itself, how a people can die of hunger from sheer abundance, and which does not bring this explanation into harmony with reason and the facts.

The Malthusian theory, however, was an absolutely necessary transitional stage, which has taken us infinitely further forward. Thanks to this theory, as also thanks to economics in general, our attention has been drawn to the productive power of the soil and of humanity, so that now, having triumphed over this economic despair, we are forever secure from the fear of overpopulation. From this theory we derive the most powerful economic arguments in favor of a social reorganization; for even if Malthus were altogether right, it would still be necessary to carry out this reorganization immediately, since only this reorganization, only the enlightenment of the masses which it can bring with it, can make possible that moral restraint upon the instinct for reproduction which Malthus himself puts forward as the easiest and most effective countermeasure against overpopulation. Thanks to this theory we have come to recognize in the dependence of man upon competitive conditions his most complete degradation. It has shown us that in the last analysis private property has turned man into a commodity, whose production and consumption also depend only on demand; that the system of competition has thereby slaughtered, and is still slaughtering today, millions of people—all this we have seen, and all this impels us to do away with this degradation of humanity by doing away with private property, competition and conflicting interests.

However, in order to deprive the general fear of overpopulation of all foundation, let us return once again to the question of the relation of productive power to population. Malthus puts forward a calculation upon which his whole system is based. Population increases in geometrical progression—1+2+4+8+16+32, etc. The productive power of the land increases in arithmetical progression—1+2+3+4+5+6.

The difference is obvious and horrifying—but is it correct? Where has it been proved that the productivity of the land increases in arithmetical progression? The area of land is limited—that is perfectly true. But the labor power to be employed on this area increases together with the population; and even if we assume that the increase of output associated with this increase of labor is not always proportionate to the latter, there still remains a third element—which the economists, however, never consider as important—namely, science, the progress of which is just as limitless and at least as rapid as that of population. For what great advances is the agriculture of this century obliged to chemistry alone—and indeed to two men alone, Sir Humphry Davy and Justus Liebig? But science increases at least as fast as population; the latter increases in proportion to the size of the previous generation, and science advances in proportion to the body of knowledge passed down to it by the previous generation, that is, in the most normal conditions it also grows in geometrical progression—and what is impossible for science? But it is ridiculous to speak of overpopulation while "the valley of the Mississippi alone contains enough waste land to accommodate the whole population of Europe,"[3] while altogether only one-third of the earth can be described as cultivated, and while the productivity of this third could be increased sixfold and more merely by applying improvements which are already known.

3. This appears to be a paraphrase of a passage occurring in Alison's *Principles of Population*, vol. 1, p. 548.—Ed.

He therefore rebels. This is calculated "to *affect* the *prosperity* of [English] manufactures and [English] commerce, to shake the mutual confidence of mercantile men, and to *diminish* the *stability* of ... political and social institutions." [4]

Such is the stupidity of the English bourgeoisie and its press with regard to pauperism, this national epidemic of England.

Let us assume, then, that the reproaches leveled by our "Prussian" at *German* society are well-founded. Does the reason lie in the *unpolitical* condition of Germany? But if the bourgeoisie of *unpolitical* Germany is unable to form a conception of the general significance of *partial* need, the bourgeoisie of *political* England, on the other hand, manages to misunderstand the general significance of universal need—a need whose general significance has been brought to notice partly through its periodical recurrence in time, partly through its extension in space, and partly through the failure of all attempts to remedy it.

"Prussian" further attributes to the *unpolitical* condition of Germany the fact that the *King* of Prussia finds the cause of pauperism in *shortcomings in administration and charity,* and therefore seeks the remedy for pauperism in *administrative and charitable measures.*

Is this way of looking at it peculiar to the King of Prussia? Let us take a brief look at England, the only country where it is possible to speak of large-scale *political* action against pauperism.

The present English Poor Law dates from the Act of the 43rd Elizabeth.[5] What are the methods adopted in this legislation? They consist of the obligation of parishes to support

4. Buret, vol. 1, pp. 400–401; Kay, p. 44.—Ed.
5. For our purposes it is not necessary to go back to the Statute of Laborers of Edward III.

their poor workers, the poor rate, and legal charity. This legislation—charity by administrative act—has lasted for two centuries. After long and painful experience, what is the attitude which Parliament adopts in its Amendment-Bill[6] of 1834?

To begin with, it explains the horrifying increase in pauperism by *"shortcomings in administration."*

The administration of the poor rate, which was in the hands of officials of the respective parishes, is therefore reformed. *Unions* of approximately twenty parishes are formed, and these are united in one single administration. A committee of officials—Board of Guardians[7]—elected by the taxpayers, meets on an appointed day in the headquarters of the Union and decides upon the admissibility of relief. These committees are directed and supervised by government officials, the Central Commission of Somerset House—the *Ministry of Pauperism*, as a Frenchman has aptly called it. The capital supervised by this administration is almost equal to the sum which the French War Office costs. The number of local administrations which it employs reaches five hundred, and each of these local administrations, in its turn, gives work to at least twelve officials.[8]

The English Parliament did not confine itself to the *formal* reform of the administration.

It found the main source of the *acute* state of English pauperism in the *Poor Law* itself. The legal method of combating social distress, charity, promotes social distress. As regards pauperism *in general*, it is looked upon as an *eternal law of nature*, according to the theory of Malthus: "Since population is constantly tending to overtake the means of

6. "Amendment-Bill" is in English in the text.—Ed.
7. In English in the text.—Ed.
8. The information in this paragraph was evidently obtained by Marx from Buret, vol. 1, pp. 156–57 and 233.—Ed.

subsistence, charity is folly, a public encouragement of poverty. The State can therefore do nothing but leave the poor to their fate, at the most making death easy for them."[9] With this humane theory the English Parliament combines the view that pauperism is *poverty which the workers have brought on themselves*, and that it should therefore be regarded not as a calamity to be prevented but rather as a crime to be suppressed and punished.

Thus arose the system of workhouses[10]—i.e., poorhouses, the internal organization of which *deters* the poor from seeking a refuge from death by starvation. In the workhouses, charity is ingeniously combined with the *revenge* of the bourgeoisie upon the poor who appeal to its charity.

England, therefore, began by trying to eliminate pauperism by means of *charity* and *administrative measures*. Then it came to see the progressive growth of pauperism as a necessary consequence not of modern *industry* but rather of the *English poor rate*. It regarded universal need merely as a *peculiarity* of English legislation. What had previously been attributed to a *lack of charity* was now attributed to a *superfluity of charity*. Finally, poverty came to be regarded as the fault of the poor, and they were punished for it as such.

The general significance which pauperism has attained in *political* England is confined to the fact that in the course of development, in spite of the administrative measures, pauperism has grown to be a *national institution*, and has therefore unavoidably become the object of a ramified and widely extended administration—an administration, however, which *no longer* has the task of eliminating it, but of *disciplining* and perpetuating it. This administration has given up trying to stop up the source of pauperism through *positive*

9. For the first sentence of this quotation, see Buret, vol. 1, p. 152.—Ed.
10. "Workhouses" is in English in the text.—Ed.

methods; it is satisfied to dig a grave for it, with policeman-like benevolence, wherever it officially breaks out on the surface of the land. Far from going beyond administrative and charitable measures, the English State has actually re-treated a long way back from them. Now its administration is confined to that pauperism which is sufficiently desperate to allow itself to be caught and imprisoned.

3 A Declaration of War on the Proletariat

From Engels's *The Condition of the Working Class in England in 1844* (1845)

Meanwhile the most open declaration of war of the bourgeoisie upon the proletariat is Malthus's Law of Population and the New Poor Law framed in accordance with it. We have already alluded several times to the theory of Malthus. We may sum up its final result in these few words, that the earth is perennially overpopulated, whence poverty, misery, distress, and immorality must prevail; that it is the lot, the eternal destiny of mankind, to exist in too great numbers, and therefore in diverse classes, of which some are rich, educated, and moral, and others more or less poor, distressed, ignorant, and immoral. Hence it follows in practice, and Malthus himself drew this conclusion, that charities and poor-rates are, properly speaking, nonsense, since they serve only to maintain, and stimulate the increase of, the surplus population whose competition crushes down wages for the employed; that the employment of the poor by the Poor Law Guardians is equally unreasonable, since only a fixed quantity of the products of labor can be consumed, and for every unemployed laborer thus furnished employment, another hitherto employed must be driven into enforced idleness, whence private undertakings suffer at cost of Poor Law industry; that, in other words, the whole problem is not how to support the surplus population, but how to restrain it as far as possible. Malthus declares in plain English that the right to live, a right previously asserted in favor of every man in the world, is nonsense. He quotes the words of a poet, that the poor man comes to the feast of Nature and finds no cover laid for him, and adds that "she bids him begone," for he did not before his birth ask of society whether or not he is welcome. This is now the pet theory of all genuine English bourgeois, and very naturally, since it is the most specious excuse for them, and has, moreover, a good deal of truth in it under existing conditions. If, then, the problem is not to make the "surplus population" useful, to transform it into available population, but merely to let it starve to death in the least objectionable way and to prevent its having too many children, this, of course, is simple enough, provided the surplus population perceives its own superfluousness and takes kindly to starvation. There is, however, in spite of the violent exertions of the humane bourgeoisie, no immediate prospect of its succeeding in bringing about such a disposition among the workers. The workers have taken it into their heads that they, with their busy hands, are the necessary, and the rich capitalists, who do nothing, the surplus population.

Since, however, the rich hold all the power, the proletarians must submit, if they will not good-temperedly perceive it for themselves, to have the law actually declare them superfluous. This has been done by the New Poor Law. The old Poor Law which rested upon the Act of 1601 (the 43rd of Elizabeth), naively started from the notion that it is the duty of the parish to provide for the maintenance of the poor. Whoever had no work received relief, and the poor man regarded the parish as pledged to protect him from starvation. He demanded his weekly relief as his right, not as a favor, and this became, at last, too much for the bourgeoisie. In 1833, when the bourgeoisie had just come into power through the Reform Bill, and pauperism in the country districts had just reached its full development, the bourgeoisie began the reform of the Poor Law according to its own point of view. A commission was appointed, which investigated the administration of the Poor Laws, and revealed a multitude of abuses. It was discovered that the whole working class in the country was pauperized and more or less dependent upon the rates, from which they received relief when wages were low; it was found that this system by which the unemployed were maintained, the ill-paid and the parents of large families relieved, fathers of illegitimate children required to pay alimony, and poverty, in general, recognized as needing protection; it was found that this system was ruining the nation, was

> a check upon industry, a reward for improvident marriage, a stimulus to increased population, and a means of counterbalancing the effect of an increased population upon wages; a national provision for discouraging the honest and industrious, and protecting the lazy, vicious, and improvident; calculated to destroy the bonds of family life, hinder systematically the accumulation of capital, scatter that which is already accumulated, and ruin the taxpayers. Moreover, in the provision of aliment, it sets a premium upon illegitimate children.

(Words of the Report of the Poor Law Commissioners).[1] This description of the action of the Old Poor Law is certainly correct; relief fosters laziness and increase of "surplus population." Under present social conditions it is perfectly clear that the poor man is compelled to be an egotist, and when he can choose, living equally well in either case, he prefers doing nothing to working. But what follows therefrom? That our present social conditions are good for nothing, and not as the Malthusian Commissioners conclude, that poverty is a crime, and, as such, to be visited with heinous penalties which may serve as a warning to others.

1. Extracts from Information received from the Poor Law Commissioners. Published by authority. (London, 1833)

But these wise Malthusians were so thoroughly convinced of the infallibility of their theory that they did not for one moment hesitate to cast the poor into the Procrustean bed of their economic notions and treat them with the most revolting cruelty. Convinced with Malthus and the rest of the adherents of free competition that it is best to let each one take care of himself, they would have preferred to abolish the Poor Laws altogether. Since, however, they had neither the courage nor the authority to do this, they proposed a Poor Law constructed as far as possible in harmony with the doctrine of Malthus, which is yet more barbarous than that of *laissez-faire*, because it interferes actively in cases in which the latter is passive. We have seen how Malthus characterizes poverty, or rather the want of employment, as a crime under the title "superfluity," and recommends for it punishment by starvation. The commissioners were not quite so barbarous; death outright by starvation was something too terrible even for a Poor Law Commissioner. "Good," said they, "we grant you poor a right to exist, but only to exist; the right to multiply you have not, nor the right to exist as befits human beings. You are a pest, and if we cannot get rid of you as we do of other pests, you shall feel, at least, that you are a pest, and you shall at least be held in check, kept from bringing into the world other 'surplus,' either directly or through inducing in others laziness and want of employment. Live you shall, but live as an awful warning to all those who might have inducements to become 'superfluous.' "

They accordingly brought in the New Poor Law, which was passed by Parliament in 1834, and continues in force down to the present day. All relief in money and provisions was abolished; the only relief allowed was admission to the workhouses immediately built. The regulations for these workhouses, or, as the people call them, Poor Law Bastilles, is such as to frighten away everyone who has the slightest prospect of life without this form of public charity. To make sure that relief be applied for only in the most extreme cases and after every other effort had failed, the workhouse has been made the most repulsive residence which the refined ingenuity of a Malthusian can invent.

4 The Reserve Army of Labor

From Engels's *The Condition of the Working Class in England in 1844* (1845)

The worker is, in law and in fact, the slave of the property-holding class, so effectually a slave that he is sold like a piece of goods, rises and falls in value like a commodity. If the demand for workers increases, the price of workers rises; if it falls, their price falls. If it falls so greatly that a number of them become unsalable, if they are left in stock, they are simply left idle; and as they cannot live upon that, they die of starvation. For, to speak in the words of the economists, the expense incurred in maintaining them would not be reproduced, would be money thrown away, and to this end no man advances capital; and, so far, Malthus was perfectly right in his theory of population. The only difference as compared with the old, outspoken slavery is this, that the worker of today seems to be free because he is not sold once for all, but piecemeal by the day, the week, the year, and because no one owner sells him to another, but he is forced to sell himself in this way instead, being the slave of no particular person, but of the whole property-holding class. For him the matter is unchanged at bottom, and if this semblance of liberty necessarily gives him some real freedom on the one hand, it entails on the other the disadvantage that no one guarantees him a subsistence, he is in danger of being repudiated at any moment by his master, the bourgeoisie, and left to die of starvation, if the bourgeoisie ceases to have an interest in his employment, his existence. The bourgeoisie, on the other hand, is far better off under the present arrangement than under the old slave system; it can dismiss its employees at discretion without sacrificing invested capital, and gets its work done much more cheaply than is possible with slave labor, as Adam Smith comfortingly pointed out.[1]

Hence it follows, too, that Adam Smith was perfectly right in making the assertion: "That the demand for men, like that for any other commodity, necessarily regulates the production of men, quickens it when it goes on too slowly, and stops it when it advances too fast." *Just as in the case of any other commodity!* If there are too few laborers at hand, prices, i.e., wages, rise, the workers are more prosperous, marriages multiply, more children are born and more live to grow up, until a sufficient number of laborers has been secured. If there are too many on hand, prices fall, want of work, poverty, and starvation, and consequent diseases arise, and the "surplus population" is put out of the way. And Malthus, who carried the foregoing proposition of Smith farther, was also right, in his way, in asserting that there are always more people on hand than can be maintained from the available means of subsistence. Surplus population is engendered rather by the competition of the workers among themselves, which forces each separate worker to labor as much each day as his strength can possibly admit. If a manufacturer can employ ten hands nine hours daily, he can employ nine if each works ten hours, and the tenth goes hun-

---

1. Adam Smith, *Wealth of Nations* (Edinburgh: A. and C. Black, 1863), McCulloch's ed., sec. 8, p. 36: "The wear and tear of a slave, it has been said, is at the expense of his master, but that of a free servant is at his own expense. The wear and tear of the latter, however, is, in reality, as much at the expense of his master as that of the former. The wages paid to journeymen and servants of every kind, must be such as may enable them, one with another, to continue the race of journeymen and servants, according as the increasing, diminishing, or stationary demand of the society may happen to require. But though the wear and tear of a free servant be equally at the expense of his master, it generally costs him much less than that of a slave. The fund for replacing or repairing, if I may say so, the wear and tear of the slave, is commonly managed by a negligent master or careless overseer."

gry. And if a manufacturer can force the nine hands to work an extra hour daily for the same wages by threatening to discharge them at a time when the demand for hands is not very great, he discharges the tenth and saves so much wages. This is the process on a small scale, which goes on in a nation on a large one. The productiveness of each hand raised to the highest pitch by the competition of the workers among themselves, the division of labor, the introduction of machinery, the subjugation of the forces of nature, deprive a multitude of workers of bread. These starving workers are then removed from the market, they can buy nothing, and the quantity of articles of consumption previously required by them is no longer in demand, need no longer be produced; the workers previously employed in producing them are therefore driven out of work, and are also removed from the market, and so it goes on, always the same old round, or rather, so it would go if other circumstances did not intervene. The introduction of the industrial forces already referred to for increasing production leads, in the course of time, to a reduction of prices of the articles produced and to consequent increased consumption, so that a large part of the displaced workers finally, after long suffering, find work again. If, in addition to this, the conquest of foreign markets constantly and rapidly increases the demand for manufactured goods, as has been the case in England during the past sixty years, the demand for hands increases, and, in proportion to it, the population. Thus, instead of diminishing, the population of the British Empire has increased with extraordinary rapidity, and is still increasing. Yet, in spite of the extension of industry, in spite of the demand for workingmen which, in general, has increased, there is, according to the confession of all the official political parties (Tory, Whig, and Radical), permanent surplus, superfluous population; the competition among the workers is constantly greater than the competition to secure workers.

Whence comes this incongruity? It lies in the nature of industrial competition and the commercial crises which arise from them. In the present unregulated production and distribution of the means of subsistence, which is carried on not directly for the sake of supplying needs, but for profit, in the system under which everyone works for himself to enrich himself, disturbances inevitably arise at every moment. For example, England supplies a number of countries with most diverse goods. Now, although the manufacturer may know how much of each article is consumed in each country annually, he cannot know how much is on hand at every given moment, much less can he know how much his competitors export thither. He can only draw most uncertain inferences from the perpetual fluctuations in prices, as to the quantities on hand and the needs of the moment. He must trust to luck in exporting his goods. Everything is done blindly, as guesswork, more or less at the mercy of accident. Upon the slightest favorable report, each one exports what he can, and before long such a market is glutted, sales stop, capital remains inactive, prices fall, and English manufacture has no further employment for its hands. In the beginning of the development of manufacture, these checks were limited to single branches and single markets; but the centralizing tendency of competition which drives the hands thrown out of one branch into such other branches as are most easily accessible, and transfers the goods which cannot be disposed of in one market to other markets, has gradually brought the single minor crises nearer together and united them into one periodically recurring crisis. Such a crisis usually recurs once in five years after a brief period of activity and general prosperity; the home market, like all foreign ones, is glutted with English goods, which it can only slowly absorb, the industrial movement comes to a standstill in almost every branch, the small manufacturers and merchants who cannot survive a

prolonged inactivity of their invested capital fail, the larger
ones suspend business during the worst season, close their
mills or work short time, perhaps half the day; wages fall by
reason of the competition of the unemployed, the diminution of working-time and the lack of profitable sales; want
becomes universal among the workers, the small savings,
which individuals may have made, are rapidly consumed, the
philanthropic institutions are overburdened, the poor-rates
are doubled, trebled, and still insufficient, the number of the
starving increases, and the whole multitude of "surplus"
population presses in terrific numbers into the foreground.
This continues for a time; the "surplus" exist as best they
may, or perish; philanthropy and the Poor Law help many of
them to a painful prolongation of their existence. Others
find scant means of subsistence here and there in such kinds
of work as have been least open to competition, are most
remote from manufacture. And with how little can a human
being keep body and soul together for a time! Gradually the
state of things improves; the accumulations of goods are consumed, the general depression among the men of commerce
and manufacture prevents a too hasty replenishing of the
markets, and at last rising prices and favorable reports from
all directions restore activity. Most of the markets are distant ones; demand increases and prices rise constantly while
the first exports are arriving; people struggle for the first
goods, the first sales enliven trade still more, the prospective
ones promise still higher prices; expecting a further rise,
merchants begin to buy upon speculation, and so to withdraw from consumption the articles intended for it, just
when they are most needed. Speculation forces prices still
higher, by inspiring others to purchase, and appropriating
new importations at once. All this is reported to England,
manufacturers begin to produce with a will, new mills are
built, every means is employed to make the most of the

favorable moment. Speculation arises here, too, exerting the same influence as upon foreign markets, raising prices, withdrawing goods from consumption, spurring manufacture in both ways to the highest pitch of effort. Then come the daring speculators working with fictitious capital, living upon credit, ruined if they cannot speedily sell; they hurl themselves into this universal, disorderly race for profits, multiply the disorder and haste by their unbridled passion, which drives prices and production to madness. It is a frantic struggle, which carries away even the most experienced and phlegmatic; goods are spun, woven, hammered, as if all mankind were to be newly equipped, as though two thousand million new consumers had been discovered on the moon. All at once the shaky speculators abroad, who must have money, begin to sell, below market price, of course, for their need is urgent; one sale is followed by others, prices fluctuate, speculators throw their goods upon the market in terror, the market is disordered, credit shaken, one house after another stops payments, bankruptcy follows bankruptcy, and the discovery is made that three times more goods are on hand or underway than can be consumed. The news reaches England, where production has been going on at full speed meanwhile, panic seizes all hands, failures abroad cause others in England, the panic crushes a number of firms, all reserves are thrown upon the market here, too, in the moment of anxiety, and the alarm is still further exaggerated. This is the beginning of the crisis, which then takes precisely the same course as its predecessor, and gives place in turn to a season of prosperity. So it goes on perpetually—prosperity, crisis, prosperity, crisis, and this perennial round in which English industry moves is, as has been before observed, usually completed once in five or six years.

From this it is clear that English manufacture must have, at all times save the brief periods of highest prosperity, an unemployed reserve army of workers, in order to be able to produce the masses of goods required by the market in the liveliest months. This reserve army is larger or smaller, according as the state of the market occasions the employment of a larger or smaller proportion of its members. And if at the moment of highest activity of the market the agricultural districts and the branches least affected by the general prosperity temporarily supply to manufacture a number of workers, these are a mere minority, and these too belong to the reserve army, with the single difference that the prosperity of the moment was required to reveal their connection with it. When they enter upon the more active branches of work, their former employers draw in somewhat, in order to feel the loss less, work longer hours, employ women and younger workers, and when the wanderers discharged at the beginning of the crisis return, they find their places filled and themselves superfluous—at least in the majority of cases. This reserve army, which embraces an immense multitude during the crisis and a large number during the period which may be regarded as the average between the highest prosperity and the crisis, is the "surplus population" of England, which keeps body and soul together by begging, stealing, street-sweeping, collecting manure, pushing handcarts, driving donkeys, peddling, or performing occasional small jobs. In every great town a multitude of such people may be found.

5 Barton, Malthus and Ricardo on "Overpopulation"

From Marx's *Theories of Surplus Value,*
vol. 2 (written 1861 - 63)

Barton unquestionably has very great merit. Adam Smith considers that the demand for labor increases in direct proportion to the accumulation of capital. Malthus derives overpopulation from the fact that capital is not accumulated and reproduced on an increasing scale as rapidly as population. Barton was the first to point out that the different organic constituents of capital do not increase at the same rate when capital is accumulated and the productive forces develop, but that on the contrary, in the process of growth that part of capital which resolves itself into wages diminishes in proportion to that part—he calls it fixed capital—which in relation to its size alters the demand for labor only insignificantly. He is therefore the first to establish the following important proposition: "that the number of laborers employed" is not "in proportion to the wealth of the State,"[1] and that it is relatively greater in an industrially undeveloped country than it is in an industrially developed country. In the third edition of his *Principles*, in chapter 31, which deals with machinery, Ricardo—who in his earlier editions had still followed completely in the footsteps of Smith on this point—takes up Barton's correction, but in the same one-sided form in which it is made by Barton himself. The only point in which Ricardo goes further—and this is

1. John Barton, *Observations on the Circumstances which Influence the Condition of the Laboring Classes of Society,* (London, 1817), p. 16.—Ed.

important—is that he not only puts forward, as Barton does, the proposition that the demand for labor does not increase in proportion to the development of machinery, but also affirms that the machine itself causes a "redundancy of people,"[2] thus creating overpopulation. But he incorrectly confines this effect to a case which occurs only in agriculture, but which he also extends to industry, a case in which the net product is increased at the expense of the total product. *In nuce*, however, the whole absurd "theory of population" was overturned by this, and also, in particular, the empty assertion of the vulgar economists to the effect that the workers must strive to keep their rate of reproduction below that of the accumulation of capital. It follows on the contrary from the arguments of Barton and Ricardo that such a restriction on the reproduction of the working population, because of the decrease in the supply of labor and the consequent rise in its price, would only speed up the employment of machinery, the transformation of circulating capital into fixed capital, and would therefore artificially create a surplus population—a surplus which is usually caused not by a lack of means of subsistence but by a lack of means for the employment of the workers, a lack of demand for labor.

Barton's error or shortcoming consists in this—that he conceives of the organic differentiation or composition of capital only in that form in which it appears in the process of circulation—as fixed capital and circulating capital. This distinction, which had already been discovered by the Physiocrats, was further developed by Adam Smith, since whose day it has become a prejudice of the economists—a prejudice, that is, insofar as they see only this difference—which has been handed down to them—in the organic composition of

2. Ricardo, *Principles of Political Economy*, Sraffa's ed., vol. 1, p. 390.—Ed.

capital. This distinction, which has its origin in the process of circulation, has a considerable influence on the reproduction of wealth in general, and therefore also on that part of it which forms the laboring funds.[3] But this is not the decisive factor here. As fixed capital, machinery, buildings, cattle, etc., are distinguished from circulating capital *directly* not through a relationship with wages, but only through their mode of circulation and reproduction.

The direct relation of the different constituents of capital to living labor has no connection with the phenomenon of the process of circulation, being derived not from it but from the immediate process of production; it is the relation between constant and variable capital, the distinction between which is established only on the basis of their relation to living labor.

3. The last two words are in both German and English in the text. —Ed.

6 The Pressure of Population upon the Means of Employment

From Engels's letter to Lange of 29 March, 1865

Meanwhile my involuntary delay in answering you has given me the opportunity of getting your book on the labor question; I have read it with much interest. I too was struck, the very first time I read Darwin, with the remarkable likeness between his account of plant and animal life and the Malthusian theory. Only I came to a different conclusion from yours: namely, that nothing discredits modern bourgeois development so much as the fact that it has not yet succeeded in getting beyond the economic forms of the animal world. To us so-called "economic laws" are not eternal laws of nature but historic laws which arise and disappear; and the code of modern political economy, insofar as it has been drawn up with proper objectivity by the economists, is to us simply a summary of the laws and conditions under which alone modern bourgeois society can exist—in short the conditions of its production and exchange expressed in an abstract and summary way. To us also, therefore, none of these laws, insofar as it expresses *purely bourgeois conditions*, is older than modern bourgeois society; those which have hitherto been more or less valid throughout all history only express just those relations which are common to the conditions of all society based on class rule and class exploitation. To the former belongs the so-called law of Ricardo, which is valid neither for feudal serfdom nor ancient slavery; to the latter belongs what is tenable in the so-called Malthusian theory.

Like all his other ideas, Parson Malthus had stolen this theory direct from his predecessors; all that belongs to him is the purely arbitrary application of the two progressions. In England the theory itself has long ago been reduced to a rational scale by the economists; the pressure of population is not upon the means of subsistence but upon the means of *employment*; mankind is capable of increasing more rapidly than modern bourgeois society can stand. To us a further reason for declaring this bourgeois society a barrier to development which must fall.

You yourself ask how increase of population and increase in the means of subsistence are to be brought into harmony; but except for one sentence in the preface I find no attempt to solve the question. We start from the premise that the same forces which have created modern bourgeois society— the steam engine, modern machinery, mass colonization, railways, steamships, world trade—and which are now already, through the permanent trade crises, working towards its ruin and ultimate destruction—these same means of production and exchange will also suffice to reverse the relation in a short time, and to raise the productive power of each individual so much that he can produce enough for the consumption of two, three, four, five or six individuals. Then town industry as it is today will be able to spare people enough to give agriculture quite other forces than it has had up to now; science also will then at last be applied in agriculture on a large scale and with the same consistency as in industry; the exploitation of the inexhaustible regions fertilized by nature herself in Southeastern Europe and Western America will be carried out on an enormous scale hitherto quite unknown. If all these regions have been plowed up and after that a shortage sets in, then will be the time to say *caveant consules* [to sound the alarm].

Too little is produced, that is the cause of the whole thing. But *why* is too little produced? Not because the limits of production—even today and with present-day means—are exhausted. No, but because the limits of production are determined not by the number of hungry bellies but by the number of *purses* able to buy and to pay. Bourgeois society does not and cannot wish to produce any more. The money-less bellies, the labor which cannot be utilized *for profit* and therefore cannot buy, is left to the death rate. Let a sudden industrial boom, such as is constantly occurring, make it possible for this labor to be employed with profit, then it will get money to spend, and the means of subsistence have never hitherto been lacking. This is the endless vicious circle in which the whole economic system revolves. One presupposes bourgeois conditions as a whole, and then proves that every part of them is a necessary part—and therefore an "eternal law."

7 Parson Malthus

From Marx's *Capital*, vol. 1 (1867)

If the reader reminds me of Malthus,[1] whose "Essay on Population" appeared in 1798, I remind him that this work in its first form is nothing more than a schoolboyish, superficial plagiary of De Foe, Sir James Steuart, Townsend, Franklin, Wallace, etc., and does not contain a single sentence thought out by himself. The great sensation this pamphlet caused, was due solely to party interest. The French Revolution had found passionate defenders in the United Kingdom; the "principle of population," slowly worked out in the eighteenth century, and then, in the midst of a great social crisis, proclaimed with drums and trumpets as the infallible antidote to the teachings of Condorcet, etc., was greeted with jubilance by the English oligarchy as the great destroyer of all hankerings after human development. Malthus, hugely astonished at his success, gave himself to stuffing into his book materials superficially compiled, and adding to it new matter, not discovered but annexed by him. Note further: Although Malthus was a parson of the English State Church, he had taken the monastic vow of celibacy—one of the conditions of holding a Fellowship in Protestant Cambridge University: "Socios collegiorum maritos esse non permittimus, sed statim postquam quis uxorem duxerit, socius collegii desinat esse" (*Reports of Cambridge University Commission*, p. 172). This circumstance favorably distinguishes Malthus

1. This passage is taken from a footnote to a statement in the text to the effect that "Sir F. M. Eden . . . is the only disciple of Adam Smith during the eighteenth century that produced any work of importance."—Ed.

from the other Protestant parsons, who have shuffled off the command enjoining celibacy of the priesthood and have taken, "Be fruitful and multiply," as their special Biblical mission in such a degree that they generally contribute to the increase of population to a really unbecoming extent, whilst they preach at the same time to the laborers the "principle of population." It is characteristic that the economic fall of man, the Adam's apple, the urgent appetite, "the checks which tend to blunt the shafts of Cupid," as Parson Townsend waggishly puts it, that this delicate question was and is monopolized by the Reverends of Protestant Theology, or rather of the Protestant Church. With the exception of the Venetian monk, Ortes, an original and clever writer, most of the population-theory teachers are Protestant parsons. For instance, Bruckner, *Théorie du Système Animal*, Leyden, 1767, in which the whole subject of the modern population theory is exhausted, and to which the passing quarrel between Quesnay and his pupil, the elder Mirabeau, furnished ideas on the same topic; then Parson Wallace, Parson Townsend, Parson Malthus and his pupil, the arch-Parson Thomas Chalmers, to say nothing of lesser reverend scribblers in this line. Originally, political economy was studied by philosophers like Hobbes, Locke, Hume; by businessmen and statesmen like Thomas More, Temple, Sully, De Witt, North, Law, Vanderlint, Cantillon, Franklin; and especially, and with the greatest success, by medical men like Petty, Barbon, Mandeville, Quesnay. Even in the middle of the eighteenth century, the Rev. Mr. Tucker, a notable economist of his time, excused himself for meddling with things of Mammon. Later on, and in truth with this very "principle of population," struck the hour of the Protestant parsons. Petty, who regarded the population as the basis of wealth, and was, like Adam Smith, an outspoken foe to parsons, says, as if he had a presentiment of their bungling interference, "that Religion best flourishes when the Priests are most mortified, as was before said of the Law, which best flourisheth when lawyers have least to do." He advises the Protestant priests, therefore, if they, once for all, will not follow the Apostle Paul and "mortify" themselves by celibacy, "not to breed more Churchmen than the Benefices, as they now stand shared out, will receive, that is to say, if there be places for about twelve thousand in England and Wales, it will not be safe to breed up twenty-four thousand ministers, for then twelve thousand which are unprovided for, will seek ways how to get themselves a livelihood, which they cannot do more easily than by persuading the people that the twelve thousand incumbents do poison or starve their souls, and misguide them in their way to Heaven" (Petty, *A Treatise on Taxes and Contributions*, London, 1667, p. 57).

8 Relative Surplus-Population Under Capitalism

From Marx's *Capital,* vol. 1 (1867)

The accumulation of capital, though originally appearing as its quantitative extension only, is effected, as we have seen, under a progressive qualitative change in its composition, under a constant increase of its constant, at the expense of its variable constituent.[1]

The specifically capitalist mode of production, the development of the productive power of labor corresponding to it, and the change thence resulting in the organic composition of capital, do not merely keep pace with the advance of accumulation, or with the growth of social wealth. They develop at a much quicker rate, because mere accumulation, the absolute increase of the total social capital, is accompanied by the centralization of the individual capitals of which that total is made up; and because the change in the technological composition of the additional capital goes hand in hand with a similar change in the technological composition of the original capital. With the advance of accumulation, therefore, the proportion of constant to variable capital changes. If it was originally say 1:1, it now becomes successively 2:1, 3:1, 4:1, 5:1, 7:1, etc., so that, as the capital increases, instead of $\frac{1}{2}$ of its total value, only $\frac{1}{3}, \frac{1}{4}, \frac{1}{5}, \frac{1}{6}, \frac{1}{8}$, etc., is transformed into labor power, and, on the other

1. Note to the 3d ed. In Marx's copy there is here the marginal note: "Here note for working out later; if the extension is only quantitative, then for a greater and a smaller capital in the same branch of business the profits are as the magnitudes of the capitals advanced. If the quantitative extension induces qualitative change, then the rate of profit on the larger capital rises simultaneously."

hand, $\frac{2}{3}, \frac{3}{4}, \frac{4}{5}, \frac{5}{6}, \frac{7}{8}$ into means of production. Since the demand for labor is determined not by the amount of capital as a whole, but by its variable constituent alone, that demand falls progressively with the increase of the total capital, instead of, as previously assumed, rising in proportion to it. It falls relatively to the magnitude of the total capital, and at an accelerated rate, as this magnitude increases. With the growth of the total capital, its variable constituent or the labor incorporated in it, also does increase, but in a constantly diminishing proportion. The intermediate pauses are shortened, in which accumulation works as simple extension of production, on a given technical basis. It is not merely that an accelerated accumulation of total capital, accelerated in a constantly growing progression, is needed to absorb an additional number of laborers, or even, on account of the constant metamorphosis of old capital, to keep employed those already functioning. In its turn, this increasing accumulation and centralization becomes a source of new changes in the composition of capital, of a more accelerated diminution of its variable, as compared with its constant constituent. This accelerated relative diminution of the variable constituent that goes along with the accelerated increase of the total capital, and moves more rapidly than this increase, takes the inverse form, at the other pole, of an apparently absolute increase of the laboring population, an increase always moving more rapidly than that of the variable capital or the means of employment. But in fact, it is capitalistic accumulation itself that constantly produces, and produces in direct ratio of its own energy and extent, a relatively redundant population of laborers, i.e., a population of greater extent than suffices for the average needs of the self-expansion of capital, and therefore a surplus population.

Considering the social capital in its totality, the movement of its accumulation now causes periodical changes, affecting it more or less as a whole, now distributes its various phases simultaneously over the different spheres of production. In some spheres a change in the composition of capital occurs without increase of its absolute magnitude, as a consequence of simple centralization; in others the absolute growth of capital is connected with absolute diminution of its variable constituent, or of the labor power absorbed by it; in others again, capital continues growing for a time on its given technical basis, and attracts additional labor power in proportion to its increase, while at other times it undergoes organic change, and lessens its variable constituent; in all spheres, the increase of the variable part of capital, and therefore of the number of laborers employed by it, is always connected with violent fluctuations and transitory production of surplus population, whether this takes the more striking form of the repulsion of laborers already employed, or the less evident but not less real form of the more difficult absorption of the additional laboring population through the usual channels.[2]

2. The census of England and Wales shows: all persons employed in agriculture (landlords, farmers, gardeners, shepherds, etc., included): 1851, 2,011,447; 1861, 1,924,110. Fall, 87,337. Worsted manufacture: 1851, 102,714 persons; 1861, 79,242. Silk weaving: 1851, 111,940; 1861, 101,678. Calico-printing: 1851: 12,098; 1861, 12,556. A small rise that, in the face of the enormous extension of this industry, and implying a great fall proportionally in the number of laborers employed. Hat-making: 1851, 15,957; 1861, 13,814. Straw-hat and bonnet-making: 1851, 20,393; 1861, 18,176. Malting: 1851, 10,566; 1861, 10,677. Chandlery: 1851, 4,949; 1861, 4,686. This fall is due, besides other causes, to the increase in lighting by gas. Comb-making: 1851, 2,038; 1861, 1,478. Sawyers: 1851, 30,552; 1861, 31,647—a small rise in consequence of the increase of sawing-machines. Nail-making: 1851, 26,940; 1861, 26,130—fall in consequence of the competition of machinery. Tin and copper-mining: 1851, 31,360; 1861, 32,041. On the other hand: Cotton-spinning and weaving: 1851, 371,777; 1861, 456,646. Coal-mining: 1851, 183,389; 1861, 246,613. "The increase of laborers is generally greatest, since 1851, in such branches of industry in which machinery has not up to the present been employed with success" (Census of England and Wales, 1862, vol. 3. London, 1863, p. 36).

With the magnitude of social capital already functioning, and the degree of its increase, with the extension of the scale of production, and the mass of the laborers set in motion, with the development of the productiveness of their labor, with the greater breadth and fullness of all sources of wealth, there is also an extension of the scale on which greater attraction of laborers by capital is accompanied by their greater repulsion; the rapidity of the change in the organic composition of capital, and in its technical form increases, and an increasing number of spheres of production becomes involved in this change, now simultaneously, now alternately. The laboring population therefore produces, along with the accumulation of capital produced by it, the means by which itself is made relatively superfluous, is turned into a relative surplus population; and it does this to an always increasing extent.[3] This is a law of population peculiar to the capitalist mode of production; and in fact every special historic mode of production has its own special laws of population, historically valid within its limits alone. An abstract law of population exists for plants and animals only, and only insofar as man has not interfered with them.

3. The law of the progressive diminution in the relative magnitude of variable capital, together with its effects upon the condition of the wage-earning class, was suspected rather than understood by some excellent economists of the classical school. In this respect the greatest merit is due to John Barton, although like all the others he mixes up constant with fixed capital and variable with circulating capital. He says: "The demand for labor depends on the increase of circulating, and not of fixed capital. Were it true that the proportion between these two sorts of capital is the same at all times, and in all circumstances, then, indeed, it follows that the number of laborers employed is in proportion to the wealth of the state. But such a proposition has not the semblance of probability. As arts are cultivated, and civilization is extended, fixed capital bears a larger and larger proportion to circulating capital. The amount of fixed capital employed in the production of a piece of British muslin is at least a hundred, probably a thousand times greater than that employed in a similar piece of Indian

But if a surplus laboring population is a necessary product of accumulation or of the development of wealth on a capitalist basis, this surplus population becomes, conversely, the lever of capitalistic accumulation, nay, a condition of existence of the capitalist mode of production. It forms a disposable industrial reserve army, that belongs to capital quite as absolutely as if the latter had bred it at its own cost. Independently of the limits of the actual increase of population, it creates, for the changing needs of the self-expansion of capital, a mass of human material always ready for exploitation. With accumulation, and the development of the productiveness of labor that accompanies it, the power of sudden expansion of capital grows also; it grows, not merely because the elasticity of the capital already functioning increases, not merely because the absolute wealth of society expands, of which capital only forms an elastic part, not merely because credit, under every special stimulus, at once

---

muslin. And the proportion of circulating capital is a hundred or thousand times less. . . . The whole of the annual savings, added to the fixed capital, would have no effect in increasing the demand for labor" (John Barton, *Observations on the Circumstances which Influence the Condition of the Laboring Classes of Society*, London, 1817, pp. 16–17). "The same cause which may increase the net revenue of the country may at the same time render the population redundant, and deteriorate the condition of the laborer" (Ricardo, *Principles of Political Economy*, 3d ed., London, 1821, p. 469). With increase of capital, "the demand [for labor] will be in a diminishing ratio" (*ibid.*, p. 480, n.). "The amount of capital devoted to the maintenance of labor may vary, independently of any changes in the whole amount of capital. . . . Great fluctuations in the amount of employment, and great suffering may become more frequent as capital itself becomes more plentiful" (Richard Jones, *An Introductory Lecture on Pol. Econ.*, London, 1833, p. 13). "Demand [for labor] will rise . . . not in proportion to the accumulation of the general capital. . . . Every augmentation, therefore, in the national stock destined for reproduction, comes, in the progress of society, to have less and less influence upon the condition of the laborer" (Ramsay, *An Essay on the Distribution of Wealth*, Edinburgh, 1836, pp. 90–91).

places an unusual part of this wealth at the disposal of production in the form of additional capital; it grows, also, because the technical conditions of the process of production themselves—machinery, means of transport, etc.—now admit of the rapidest transformation of masses of surplus product into additional means of production. The mass of social wealth, overflowing with the advance of accumulation, and transformable into additional capital, thrusts itself frantically into old branches of production, whose market suddenly expands, or into newly formed branches, such as railways, etc., the need for which grows out of the development of the old ones. In all such cases, there must be the possibility of throwing great masses of men suddenly on the decisive points without injury to the scale of production in other spheres. Overpopulation supplies these masses. The course characteristic of modern industry, viz., a decennial cycle (interrupted by smaller oscillations) of periods of average activity, production at high pressure, crisis and stagnation, depends on the constant formation, the greater or less absorption, and the re-formation of the industrial reserve army or surplus population. In their turn, the varying phases of the industrial cycle recruit the surplus population, and become one of the most energetic agents of its reproduction. This peculiar course of modern industry, which occurs in no earlier period of human history, was also impossible in the childhood of capitalist production. The composition of capital changed but very slowly. With its accumulation, therefore, there kept pace, on the whole, a corresponding growth in the demand for labor. Slow as was the advance of accumulation compared with that of more modern times, it found a check in the natural limits of the exploitable laboring population, limits which could only be got rid of by forcible means to be mentioned later. The expansion by fits and starts of the scale of production is the preliminary to its equally sudden contraction; the latter again evokes the former, but the former is impossible without disposable human material, without an increase in the number of laborers independently of the absolute growth of the population. This increase is effected by the simple process that constantly "sets free" a part of the laborers; by methods which lessen the number of laborers employed in proportion to the increased production. The whole form of the movement of modern industry depends, therefore, upon the constant transformation of a part of the laboring population into unemployed or half-employed hands. The superficiality of Political Economy shows itself in the fact that it looks upon the expansion and contraction of credit, which is a mere symptom of the periodic changes of the industrial cycle, as their cause. As the heavenly bodies, once thrown into a certain definite motion, always repeat this, so is it with social production as soon as it is once thrown into this movement of alternate expansion and contraction. Effects, in their turn, become causes, and the varying accidents of the whole process, which always reproduces its own conditions, take on the form of periodicity. When this periodicity is once consolidated, even Political Economy then sees that the production of a relative surplus population—i.e., surplus with regard to the average needs of the self-expansion of capital—is a necessary condition of modern industry.

"Suppose," says H. Merivale, formerly Professor of Political Economy at Oxford, subsequently employed in the English Colonial Office, "suppose that, on the occasion of some of these crises, the nation were to rouse itself to the effort of getting rid by emigration of some hundreds of thousands of superfluous arms, what would be the consequence? That, at the first returning demand for labor, there would be a deficiency. However rapid reproduction may be, it takes, at all events, the space of a generation to replace the loss of adult labor. Now, the profits of our manufacturers depend mainly on the power of making use of the prosperous moment when demand is brisk, and thus compensating themselves for the interval during which it is slack. This power is secured to them only by the command of machinery and of manual labor. They must have hands ready by them, they must be able to increase the activity of their operations when required, and to slacken it again, according to the state of the market, or they cannot possibly maintain that pre-eminence in the race of competition on which the wealth of the country is founded."[4] Even Malthus recognizes overpopulation as a necessity of modern industry, though, after his narrow fashion, he explains it by the absolute overgrowth of the laboring population, not by their becoming relatively supernumerary. He says: "Prudential habits with regard to marriage, carried to a considerable extent among the laboring class of a country mainly depending upon manufactures and commerce, might injure it. . . . From the nature of a population, an increase of laborers cannot be brought into market in consequence of a particular demand till after the lapse of sixteen or eighteen years, and the conversion of revenue into capital, by saving, may take place much more rapidly; a country is always liable to an increase in the quantity of the funds for the maintenance of labor faster than the increase of population."[5] After Political Economy has thus demonstrated the constant production of a relative surplus population of laborers to be a necessity of capitalistic accumulation, she very aptly, in the guise of an old maid, puts in the mouth of her "beau ideal" of a capitalist the following words addressed to those supernumeraries thrown on the streets by

4. H. Merivale, *Lectures on Colonization and Colonies* (1841), vol. 1, p. 146.

5. Malthus, *Principles of Political Economy*, pp. 254, 319, 320. In this work, Malthus finally discovers, with the help of Sismondi, the beautiful Trinity of capitalistic production: overproduction, overpopulation, overconsumption—three very delicate monsters, indeed. Cf. Frederick Engels, *Umrisse zu einer Kritik der National-Oekonomie, Deutsch-Französische Jahrbücher* (Paris, 1844), p. 107, *et seq.*

their own creation of additional capital: "We manufacturers do what we can for you, while we are increasing that capital on which you must subsist, and you must do the rest by accommodating your numbers to the means of subsistence."[6]

Capitalist production can by no means content itself with the quantity of disposable labor power which the natural increase of population yields. It requires for its free play an industrial reserve army independent of these natural limits.

Up to this point it has been assumed that the increase or diminution of the variable capital corresponds rigidly with the increase or diminution of the number of laborers employed.

The number of laborers commanded by capital may remain the same, or even fall, while the variable capital increases. This is the case if the individual laborer yields more labor, and therefore his wages increase, and this although the price of labor remains the same or even falls, only more slowly than the mass of labor rises. Increase of variable capital, in this case becomes an index of more labor, but not of more laborers employed. It is the absolute interest of every capitalist to press a given quantity of labor out of a smaller, rather than a greater, number of laborers, if the cost is about the same. In the latter case, the outlay of constant capital increases in proportion to the mass of labor set in action; in the former that increase is much smaller. The more extended the scale of production, the stronger this motive. Its force increases with the accumulation of capital.

We have seen that the development of the capitalist mode of production and of the productive power of labor—at once the cause and effect of accumulation—enables the capitalist, with the same outlay of variable capital, to set in action more labor by greater exploitation (extensive or intensive) of each individual labor power. We have further seen that the

6. Harriet Martineau, *The Manchester Strike* (1842), p. 101.

capitalist buys with the same capital a greater mass of labor power, as he progressively replaces skilled laborers by less skilled, mature labor power by immature, male by female, that of adults by that of young persons or children.

On the one hand, therefore, with the progress of accumulation, a larger variable capital sets more labor in action without enlisting more laborers; on the other, a variable capital of the same magnitude sets in action more labor with the same mass of labor power; and, finally, a greater number of inferior labor powers by displacement of higher.

The production of a relative surplus population, or the setting free of laborers, goes on therefore yet more rapidly than the technical revolution of the process of production that accompanies, and is accelerated by, the advance of accumulation; and more rapidly than the corresponding diminution of the variable part of capital as compared with the constant. If the means of production, as they increase in extent and effective power, become to a less extent means of employment of laborers, this state of things is again modified by the fact that in proportion as the productiveness of labor increases, capital increases its supply of labor more quickly than its demand for laborers. The overwork of the employed part of the working class swells the ranks of the reserve, while conversely the greater pressure that the latter by its competition exerts on the former, forces these to submit to overwork and subjugation under the dictates of capital. The condemnation of one part of the working class to enforced idleness by the overwork of the other part, and the converse, becomes a means of enriching the individual capitalists,[7] and

7. Even in the cotton famine of 1863 we find, in a pamphlet of the operative cotton-spinners of Blackburn, fierce denunciations of overwork, which, in consequence of the Factory Acts, of course only affected adult male laborers. "The adult operatives at this mill have been asked to work from 12 to 13 hours per day, while there are hundreds who are compelled to be idle who would willingly work partial time, in order to maintain their families and save their brethren from a pre-

accelerates at the same time the production of the industrial reserve army on a scale corresponding with the advance of social accumulation. How important is this element in the formation of the relative surplus population, is shown by the example of England. Her technical means for saving labor are colossal. Nevertheless, if tomorrow morning labor generally were reduced to a rational amount, and proportioned to the different sections of the working class according to age and sex, the working population to hand would be absolutely insufficient for the carrying on of national production on its present scale. The great majority of the laborers now "unproductive" would have to be turned into "productive" ones.

Taking them as a whole, the general movements of wages are exclusively regulated by the expansion and contraction of the industrial reserve army, and these again correspond to the periodic changes of the industrial cycle. They are, therefore, not determined by the variations of the absolute

---

mature grave through being overworked. . . . We," it goes on to say, "would ask if the practice of working overtime by a number of hands, is likely to create a good feeling between masters and servants. Those who are worked overtime feel the injustice equally with those who are condemned to forced idleness. There is in the district almost sufficient work to give to all partial employment if fairly distributed. We are only asking what is right in requesting the masters generally to pursue a system of short hours, particularly until a better state of things begins to dawn upon us, rather than to work a portion of the hands overtime, while others, for want of work, are compelled to exist upon charity" (*Reports of Insp. of Fact.*, 31 October 1863, p. 8). The author of the *Essay on Trade and Commerce* (London, 1770) grasps the effect of a relative surplus population on the employed laborers with his usual unerring bourgeois instinct. "Another cause of idleness in this kingdom is the want of a sufficient number of laboring hands. . . . Whenever from an extraordinary demand for manufactures, labor grows scarce, the laborers feel their own consequence, and will make their masters feel it likewise—it is amazing; but so depraved are the dispositions of these people, that in such cases a set of workmen have combined to distress the employer, by idling a whole day together" (*Essay, etc.*, pp. 27–28). The fellows in fact were hankering after a rise in wages.

number of the working population, but by the varying proportions in which the working class is divided into active and reserve army, by the increase or diminution in the relative amount of the surplus population, by the extent to which it is now absorbed, now set free. For Modern Industry with its decennial cycles and periodic phases, which, moreover, as accumulation advances, are complicated by irregular oscillations following each other more and more quickly, that would indeed be a beautiful law, which pretends to make the action of capital dependent on the absolute variation of the population, instead of regulating the demand and supply of labor by the alternate expansion and contraction of capital, the labor market now appearing relatively underfull, because capital is expanding, now again overfull, because it is contracting. Yet this is the dogma of the economists. According to them, wages rise in consequence of accumulation of capital. The higher wages stimulate the working population to more rapid multiplication, and this goes on until the labor market becomes too full, and therefore capital, relatively to the supply of labor, becomes insufficient. Wages fall, and now we have the reverse of the medal. The working population is little by little decimated as the result of the fall in wages, so that capital is again in excess relatively to them, or, as others explain it, falling wages and the corresponding increase in the exploitation of the laborer again accelerates accumulation, while, at the same time, the lower wages hold the increase of the working class in check. Then comes again the time, when the supply of labor is less than the demand, wages rise, and so on. A beautiful mode of motion this for developed capitalist production! Before, in consequence of the rise of wages, any positive increase of the population really fit for work could occur, the time would have been passed again and again, during which the industrial campaign must have been carried through, the battle fought and won.

Between 1849 and 1859, a rise of wages practically insignificant, though accompanied by falling prices of corn, took place in the English agricultural districts. In Wiltshire, e.g., the weekly wages rose from seven shillings to eight shillings; in Dorsetshire from seven shillings or eight shillings to nine shillings, etc. This was the result of an unusual exodus of the agricultural surplus population caused by the demands of war, the vast extension of railroads, factories, mines, etc. The lower the wages, the higher is the proportion in which ever so insignificant a rise of them expresses itself. If the weekly wage, e.g., is twenty shillings and it rises to twenty-two shillings, that is a rise of ten per cent; but if it is only seven shillings and it rises to nine shillings, that is a rise of $28\frac{4}{7}$ per cent, which sounds very fine. Everywhere the farmers were howling, and the *London Economist*, with reference to these starvation wages, prattled quite seriously of "a general and substantial advance."[8] What did the farmers do now? Did they wait until, in consequence of this brilliant remuneration, the agricultural laborers had so increased and multiplied that their wages must fall again, as prescribed by the dogmatic economic brain? They introduced more machinery, and in a moment the laborers were redundant again in a proportion satisfactory even to the farmers. There was now "more capital" laid out in agriculture than before, and in a more productive form. With this the demand for labor fell, not only relatively, but absolutely.

The above economic fiction confuses the laws that regulate the general movement of wages, or the ratio between the working class—i.e., the total labor power—and the total social capital, with the laws that distribute the working population over the different spheres of production. If, e.g., in consequence of favorable circumstances, accumulation in a particular sphere of production becomes especially active, and profits in it, being greater than the average profits, attract

8. *London Economist,* 21 January 1860.

additional capital, of course the demand for labor rises and wages also rise. The higher wages draw a larger part of the working population into the more favored sphere, until it is glutted with labor power, and wages at length fall again to their average level or below it, if the pressure is too great. Then, not only does the immigration of laborers into the branch of industry in question cease; it gives place to their emigration. Here the political economist thinks he sees the why and wherefore of an absolute increase of workers accompanying an increase of wages, and of a diminution of wages accompanying an absolute increase of laborers. But he sees really only the local oscillation of the labor market in a particular sphere of production—he sees only the phenomena accompanying the distribution of the working population into the different spheres of outlay of capital, according to its varying needs.

The industrial reserve army, during the periods of stagnation and average prosperity, weighs down the active labor army; during the periods of overproduction and paroxysm, it holds its pretensions in check. Relative surplus population is therefore the pivot upon which the law of demand and supply of labor works. It confines the field of action of this law within the limits absolutely convenient to the activity of exploitation and to the domination of capital.

This is the place to return to one of the grand exploits of economic apologetics. It will be remembered that if through the introduction of new, or the extension of old, machinery, a portion of variable capital is transformed into constant, the economic apologist interprets this operation which "fixes" capital and by that very act sets laborers "free," in exactly the opposite way, pretending that it sets free capital for the laborers. Only now can one fully understand the effrontery of these apologists. What are set free are not only the laborers immediately turned out by machines, but also their future substitutes in the rising generation, and the additional contingent, that with the usual extension of trade on the old basis would be regularly absorbed. They are now all "set free," and every new bit of capital looking out for employment can dispose of them. Whether it attracts them or others, the effect on the general labor demand will be nil, if this capital is just sufficient to take out of the market as many laborers as the machines threw upon it. If it employs a smaller number, that of the supernumeraries increases; if it employs a greater, the general demand for labor only increases to the extent of the excess of the employed over those "set free." The impulse that additional capital, seeking an outlet, would otherwise have given to the general demand for labor, is therefore in every case neutralized to the extent of the laborers thrown out of employment by the machine. That is to say, the mechanism of capitalistic production so manages matters that the absolute increase of capital is accompanied by no corresponding rise in the general demand for labor. And this the apologist calls a compensation for the misery, the sufferings, the possible death of the displaced laborers during the transition period that banishes them into the industrial reserve army! The demand for labor is not identical with increase of capital, nor supply of labor with increase of the working class. It is not a case of two independent forces working on one another. *Les dés sont pipés.* Capital works on both sides at the same time. If its accumulation, on the one hand, increases the demand for labor, it increases on the other the supply of laborers by the "setting free" of them, while at the same time the pressure of the unemployed compels those that are employed to furnish more labor, and therefore makes the supply of labor, to a certain extent, independent of the supply of laborers. The action of the law of supply and demand of labor on this basis completes the despotism of capital. As soon, therefore, as the laborers learn the secret, how it comes to pass that in the same measure as they work more, as they produce more wealth for others, and as the productive power of their labor increases, so in the same measure even their function as a means of the self-expansion of capital becomes more and more precarious for them; as soon as they discover that the degree of intensity of the competition among themselves depends wholly on the pressure of the relative surplus population; as soon as, by trades unions, etc., they try to organize a regular cooperation between employed and unemployed in order to destroy or to weaken the ruinous effects of this natural law of capitalistic production on their class, so soon capital and its sycophant, political economy, cry out at the infringement of the "eternal" and so to say "sacred" law of supply and demand. Every combination of employed and unemployed disturbs the "harmonious" action of this law. But as soon as (in the colonies, e.g.) adverse circumstances prevent the creation of an industrial reserve army and, with it, the absolute dependence of the working class upon the capitalist class, capital, along with its commonplace Sancho Panza, rebels against the "sacred" law of supply and demand, and tries to check its inconvenient action by forcible means and state interference.

The relative surplus population exists in every possible form. Every laborer belongs to it during the time when he is only partially employed or wholly unemployed. Not taking into account the great periodically recurring forms that the changing phases of the industrial cycle impress on it, now an acute form during the crisis, then again a chronic form during dull times—it has always three forms, the floating, the latent, the stagnant.

In the centers of modern industry—factories, manufactures, ironworks, mines, etc.—the laborers are sometimes repelled, sometimes attracted again in greater masses, the number of those employed increasing on the whole, although in a constantly decreasing proportion to the scale of production. Here the surplus population exists in the floating form.

In the automatic factories, as in all the great workshops, where machinery enters as a factor, or where only the modern division of labor is carried out, large numbers of boys are employed up to the age of maturity. When this term is once reached, only a very small number continue to find employment in the same branches of industry, while the majority are regularly discharged. This majority forms an element of the floating surplus population, growing with the extension of those branches of industry. Part of them emigrates, following in fact capital that has emigrated. One consequence is that the female population grows more rapidly than the male, *teste* England. That the natural increase of the number of laborers does not satisfy the requirements of the accumulation of capital, and yet all the time is in excess of them, is a contradiction inherent to the movement of capital itself. It wants larger numbers of youthful laborers, a smaller number of adults. The contradiction is not more glaring than that other one that there is a complaint of the want of hands, while at the same time many thousands are out of work, because the division of labor chains them to a particular branch of industry.[9]

The consumption of labor power by capital is, besides, so rapid that the laborer, half-way through his life, has already more or less completely lived himself out. He falls into the ranks of the supernumeraries, or is thrust down from a higher to a lower step in the scale. It is precisely among the work-people of modern industry that we meet with the shortest duration of life. Dr. Lee, Medical Officer of Health for Manchester, stated "that the average age at death of the

9. While during the last six months of 1866, 80–90,000 working people in London were thrown out of work, the Factory Report for that same half-year says: "It does not appear absolutely true to say that demand will always produce supply just at the moment when it is needed. It has not done so with labor, for much machinery has been idle last year for want of hands" (*Rep. of Insp. of Fact.*, 31 October 1866, p. 81).

Manchester ... upper middle class was thirty-eight years, while the average age at death of the laboring class was seventeen; while at Liverpool those figures were represented as thirty-five against fifteen. It thus appeared that the well-to-do classes had a lease of life which was more than double the value of that which fell to the lot of the less favored citizens."[10] In order to conform to these circumstances, the absolute increase of this section of the proletariat must take place under conditions that shall swell their numbers, although the individual elements are used up rapidly. Hence, rapid renewal of the generations of laborers (this law does not hold for the other classes of the population). This social need is met by early marriages, a necessary consequence of the conditions in which the laborers of modern industry live, and by the premium that the exploitation of children sets on their production.

As soon as capitalist production takes possession of agriculture, and in proportion to the extent to which it does so, the demand for an agricultural laboring population falls absolutely, while the accumulation of the capital employed in agriculture advances, without this repulsion being, as in non-agricultural industries, compensated by a greater attraction. Part of the agricultural population is therefore constantly on the point of passing over into an urban or manufacturing proletariat, and on the lookout for circumstances favorable to this transformation. (Manufacture is used here in the sense of all non-agricultural industries.)[11] This source of relative

10. Opening address to the Sanitary Conference, Birmingham, 15 January 1875, by J. Chamberlain, Mayor of the town, now (1883) President of the Board of Trade.

11. Seven hundred and eighty-one towns given in the census for 1861 for England and Wales "contained 10,960,998 inhabitants, while the villages and country parishes contained 9,105,226. In 1851, 580 towns were distinguished, and the population in them and in the surrounding country was nearly equal. But while in the subsequent ten years the population in the villages and the country increased half a million, the

surplus population is thus constantly flowing. But the constant flow towards the towns presupposes, in the country itself, a constant latent surplus population, the extent of which becomes evident only when its channels of outlet open to exceptional width. The agricultural laborer is therefore reduced to the minimum of wages, and always stands with one foot already in the swamp of pauperism.

The third category of the relative surplus population, the stagnant, forms a part of the active labor army, but with extremely irregular employment. Hence it furnishes to capital an inexhaustible reservoir of disposable labor power. Its conditions of life sink below the average normal level of the working class; this makes it at once the broad basis of special branches of capitalist exploitation. It is characterized by maximum of working time, and minimum of wages. We have learned to know its chief form under the rubric of "domestic industry." It recruits itself constantly from the supernumerary forces of modern industry and agriculture, and specially from those decaying branches of industry where handicraft is yielding to manufacture, manufacture to machinery. Its extent grows as, with the extent and energy of accumulation, the creation of a surplus population advances. But it forms at the same time a self-reproducing and self-perpetuating element of the working class, taking a proportionally greater part in the general increase of that class than the other elements. In fact, not only the number of births and deaths, but the absolute size of the families stand in inverse proportion to the height of wages, and therefore to the amount of means of subsistence of which the different categories of laborers dispose. This law of capitalistic society would sound

---

population in the 580 towns increased by a million and a half (1,554,067). The increase of the population of the country parishes is 6.5 per cent, and of the towns 17.3 per cent. The difference in the rates of increase is due to the migration from country to town. Three-fourths of the total increase of population has taken place in the towns (*Census, etc.*, pp. 11–12).

absurd to savages, or even civilized colonists. It calls to mind the boundless reproduction of animals individually weak and constantly hunted down.[12]

The lowest sediment of the relative surplus population finally dwells in the sphere of pauperism. Exclusive of vagabonds, criminals, prostitutes, in a word, the "dangerous" classes, this layer of society consists of three categories. First, those able to work. One need only glance superficially at the statistics of English pauperism to find that the quantity of paupers increases with every crisis, and diminishes with every revival of trade. Second, orphans and pauper children. These are candidates for the industrial reserve army, and are, in times of great prosperity, as 1860, e.g., speedily and in large numbers enrolled in the active army of laborers. Third, the demoralized and ragged, and those unable to work, chiefly people who succumb to their incapacity for adaptation, due to the division of labor; people who have passed the normal age of the laborer; the victims of industry, whose number increases with the increase of dangerous machinery, of mines, chemical works, etc., the mutilated, the sickly, the widows, etc. Pauperism is the hospital of the active labor army and the dead weight of the industrial reserve army. Its production is included in that of the relative surplus population, its necessity in theirs; along with the surplus population, pauperism forms a condition of capitalist production, and of the capitalist development of wealth. It enters into the *faux frais* of capitalist production; but capital

12. "Poverty seems favorable to generation" (A. Smith). This is even a specially wise arrangement of God, according to the gallant and witty Abbé Galiani. "Iddio fa che gli uomini che esercitano mestieri di prima utilità nascono abbondantemente" (Galiani, *Della Moneta*, in Custodi, *Parte Moderna*, vol. 3, p. 78). "Misery up to the extreme point of famine and pestilence, instead of checking, tends to increase population" (S. Laing, *National Distress*, 1844, p. 69). After Laing has illustrated this by statistics, he continues: "If the people were all in easy circumstances, the world would soon be depopulated."

knows how to throw these, for the most part, from its own shoulders on to those of the working class and lower middle class.

The greater the social wealth, the functioning capital, the extent and energy of its growth, and, therefore, also the absolute mass of the proletariat and the productiveness of its labor, the greater is the industrial reserve army. The same causes which develop the expansive power of capital, develop also the labor power at its disposal. The relative mass of the industrial reserve army increases therefore with the potential energy of wealth. But the greater this reserve army in proportion to the active labor army, the greater is the mass of a consolidated surplus population, whose misery is in inverse ratio to its torment of labor. The more extensive, finally, the lazarus layers of the working class, and the industrial reserve army, the greater is official pauperism. *This is the absolute general law of capitalist accumulation.* Like all other laws it is modified in its working by many circumstances, the analysis of which does not concern us here.

The folly is now patent of the economic wisdom that preaches to the laborers the accommodation of their number to the requirements of capital. The mechanism of capitalist production and accumulation constantly effects this adjustment. The first word of this adaptation is the creation of a relative surplus population, or industrial reserve army. Its last word is the misery of constantly extending strata of the active army of labor, and the dead weight of pauperism.

The law by which a constantly increasing quantity of means of production, thanks to the advance in the productiveness of social labor, may be set in movement by a progressively diminishing expenditure of human power, this law, in a capitalist society—where the laborer does not employ the means of production, but the means of production employ the laborer—undergoes a complete inversion and is expressed thus; the higher the productiveness of labor, the

greater is the pressure of the laborers on the means of employment, the more precarious, therefore, becomes their
condition of existence, viz., the sale of their own labor
power for the increasing of another's wealth, or for the self-
expansion of capital. The fact that the means of production,
and the productiveness of labor, increase more rapidly than
the productive population, expresses itself, therefore, capital-
istically in the inverse form that the laboring population
always increases more rapidly than the conditions under
which capital can employ this increase for its own self-
expansion.

We saw in Part 4, when analyzing the production of
relative surplus value: within the capitalist system all methods for raising the social productiveness of labor are brought
about at the cost of the individual laborer; all means for the
development of production transform themselves into means
of domination over, and exploitation of, the producers; they
mutilate the laborer into a fragment of a man, degrade him
to the level of an appendage of a machine, destroy every
remnant of charm in his work, and turn it into a hated toil;
they estrange from him the intellectual potentialities of the
labor process in the same proportion as science is incorporated in it as an independent power; they distort the conditions under which he works, subject him during the labor
process to a despotism the more hateful for its meanness;
they transform his life-time into working-time, and drag his
wife and child beneath the wheels of the Juggernaut of capital. But all methods for the production of surplus value are
at the same time methods of accumulation; and every extension of accumulation becomes again a means for the development of those methods. It follows therefore that in proportion as capital accumulates, the lot of the laborer, be his
payment high or low, must grow worse. The law, finally, that
always equilibrates the relative surplus population, or industrial reserve army, to the extent and energy of accumulation,

this law rivets the laborer to capital more firmly than the wedges of Vulcan did Prometheus to the rock. It establishes an accumulation of misery, corresponding with accumulation of capital. Accumulation of wealth at one pole is, therefore, at the same time accumulation of misery, agony of toil, slavery, ignorance, brutality, mental degradation, at the opposite pole, i.e., on the side of the class that produces its own product in the form of capital.

This antagonistic character of capitalistic accumulation[13] is enunciated in various forms by political economists, although by them it is confounded with phenomena, certainly to some extent analogous, but nevertheless essentially distinct, and belonging to precapitalistic modes of production.

The Venetian monk Ortes, one of the great economic writers of the eighteenth century, regards the antagonism of capitalist production as a general natural law of social wealth. "In the economy of a nation, advantages and evils always balance one another (il bene ed il male economico in una nazione sempre all' istessa misura): the abundance of wealth with some people, is always equal to the want of it with others (la copia dei beni in alcuni sempre eguale alla mancanza di essi in altri): the great riches of a small number are always accompanied by the absolute privation of the first necessaries of life for many others. The wealth of a nation corresponds with its population, and its misery corresponds with its wealth. Diligence in some compels idleness in others.

13. "From day to day it thus becomes clearer that the production relations in which the bourgeoisie moves have not a simple, uniform character, but a dual character; that in the self-same relations in which wealth is produced, poverty is produced also; that in the self-same relations in which there is a development of the productive forces, there is also a driving force of repression; that these relations produce *bourgeois wealth*, i.e., the wealth of the bourgeois class, only by continually annihilating the wealth of the individual members of this class and by producing an ever-growing proletariat" (*The Poverty of Philosophy*, p. 104).

The poor and idle are a necessary consequence of the rich and active," etc.[14] In a thoroughly brutal way about ten years after Ortes, the Church of England parson, Townsend, glorified misery as a necessary condition of wealth. "Legal constraint (to labor) is attended with too much trouble, violence, and noise ... whereas hunger is not only a peaceable, silent, unremitted pressure, but as the most natural motive to industry and labor, it calls forth the most powerful exertions." Everything therefore depends upon making hunger permanent among the working class, and for this, according to Townsend, the principle of population, especially active among the poor, provides. "It seems to be a law of nature that the poor should be to a certain degree improvident" [i.e., so improvident as to be born *without* a silver spoon in the mouth] "that there may always be some to fulfill the most servile, the most sordid, and the most ignoble offices in the community. The stock of human happiness is thereby much increased, while the more delicate are not only relieved from drudgery ... but are left at liberty without interruption to pursue those callings which are suited to their various dispositions ... it [the Poor Law] tends to destroy the harmony and beauty, the symmetry and order of that system which God and Nature have established in the world."[15] If

14. G. Ortes, *Della Economia Nazionale*, vol. 7 (1777), in Custodi, *Parte Moderna*, t. 21, pp. 6, 9, 22, 25, etc. Ortes says, *l.c.*, p. 32: "In luoco di progettar sistemi inutili per la felicità de'popoli, mi limiterò a investigare la ragione della loro infelicità."

15. *A Dissertation on the Poor Laws.* By a Well-wisher of Mankind (the Rev. J. Townsend), 1786, republished London, 1817, pp. 15, 39, 41. This "delicate" parson, from whose work just quoted, as well as from his *Journey through Spain*, Malthus often copies whole pages, himself borrowed the greater part of his doctrine from Sir James Steuart, whom he however alters in the borrowing. E.g., when Steuart says: "Here, in slavery, was a forcible method of making mankind diligent," [for the non-workers] ... "Men were then forced to work" [i.e., to work gratis for others], "because they were slaves of others; men are now forced to work" [i.e., to work gratis for non-workers]

the Venetian monk found in the fatal destiny that makes misery eternal, the *raison d'être* of Christian charity, celibacy, monasteries and holy houses, the Protestant prebendary finds in it a pretext for condemning the laws in virtue of which the poor possessed a right to a miserable public relief.

"The progress of social wealth," says Storch, "begets this useful class of society ... which performs the most wearisome, the vilest, the most disgusting functions, which takes, in a word, on its shoulders all that is disagreeable and servile in life, and procures thus for other classes leisure, serenity of mind and conventional [c'est bon!] dignity of character."[16] Storch asks himself in what then really consists the progress of this capitalistic civilization with its misery and its degradation of the masses, as compared with barbarism. He finds but one answer: security!

"Thanks to the advance of industry and science," says Sismondi, "every laborer can produce every day much more than his consumption requires. But at the same time, while his labor produces wealth, that wealth would, were he called on to consume it himself, make him less fit for labor." According to him, "men" [i.e., non-workers] "would probably prefer to do without all artistic perfection, and all the enjoyments that manufactures procure for us, if it were necessary that all should buy them by constant toil like that of the laborer. . . . Exertion today is separated from its recompense; it is not the same man that first works, and then reposes; but it is because the one works that the other rests. . . . The indefinite multiplication of the productive powers of labor

---

"because they are the slaves of their necessities," he does not thence conclude, like the fat holder of benefices, that the wage-laborer must always go fasting. He wishes, on the contrary, to increase their wants and to make the increasing number of their wants a stimulus to their labor for the "more delicate."

16. Storch, *Cours d'Economie Politique* (Paris, 1823), t. 3, p. 223.

can then only have for result the increase of luxury and enjoyment of the idle rich."[17]

Finally Destutt de Tracy, the fish-blooded bourgeois doctrinaire, blurts out brutally: "In poor nations the people are comfortable, in rich nations they are generally poor."[18]

17. Sismondi, *De la Richesse Commerciale ou Principes d'Economie Politique,* vol. 1 (Geneva, 1803), pp. 79, 80, 85.
18. Destutt de Tracy, *Traité de la Volunté et de Ses Effets* (Paris, 1826), p. 231: "Les nations pauvres, c'est là où le peuple est à son aise; et les nations riches, c'est là où il est ordinairement pauvre."

9 The "Iron Law of Wages"

From Engels's letter to Bebel
of 18 - 28 March, 1875

... Thirdly, our people have allowed the Lassallean "iron law of wages" to be foisted upon them, and this is based on a quite antiquated economic view, namely, that the worker only receives on the average the *minimum* of the labor wage, because, according to Malthus's theory of population, there are always too many workers (this was Lassalle's argument). Now Marx has proved in detail in *Capital* that the laws regulating wages are very complicated, that sometimes one predominates and sometimes another, according to circumstances, that therefore they are in no sense iron but on the contrary very elastic, and that the thing can by no means be dismissed in a few words, as Lassalle imagines. The Malthusian basis for the law which Lassalle copied from Malthus and Ricardo (with a falsification of the latter), as it is to be found for instance in the *Arbeiterlesebuch* [*Workers' Reader*], p. 5, quoted from another pamphlet of Lassalle, has been refuted in detail by Marx in the section on the *Process of Capital Accumulation*. Thus by adopting Lassalle's "iron law" we commit ourselves to a false statement with a false basis.

From Marx's *Critique of the Gotha Programme* (1875)

Starting from these basic principles, the German Workers' Party strives by all legal means for the *free* *state—and—*socialist society; the abolition of the wage system *together with* the *iron law of wages—*and—exploitation in every form; the removal of all social and political inequality.

I shall return to the "free" state later.

Thus, in future, the German Workers' Party has got to believe in Lassalle's "iron law of wages"! That this shall not be lost, the nonsense is perpetrated of speaking of the "abolition of the wage system" (it should read: system of wage labor) *together with* the "iron law of wages." If I abolish wage labor, then naturally I abolish its laws also, whether they are of "iron" or sponge. But Lassalle's attack on wage labor turns almost solely on this so-called law. In order, therefore, to prove that Lassalle's sect has conquered, the "wage system" must be abolished *"together* with the iron law of wages" and not without it.

It is well known that nothing of the "iron law of wages" belongs to Lassalle except the word "iron" borrowed from Goethe's "great, eternal, iron laws." The word *iron* is a label by which the true believers recognize one another. But if I take the law with Lassalle's stamp on it and consequently in his sense then I must also take it with his basis for it. And what is that? As Lange already showed, shortly after Lassalle's death, it is the Malthusian theory of population (preached by Lange himself). But if this theory is correct, then again I can *not* abolish the law even if I abolish wage labor a hundred times over, because the law then governs not only the system of wage labor but *every* social system. Basing themselves directly on this, the economists have proved for fifty years and more that socialism cannot abolish poverty, *which has its basis in nature,* but can only *generalize* it, distribute it simultaneously over the whole surface of society!

10 Population and Communism

From Engels's letter to Kautsky
of 1 February, 1881

Even if the professorial socialists are persistently demanding that we, the proletarian socialists, should solve for them the problem of how to avoid the possible setting in of overpopulation and the imminent danger of a collapse of the new social order which it would bring with it, this is far from being a sufficient reason why I should do them this favor. I should consider it as a sheer waste of time to remove for these people all the scruples and doubts which they have acquired thanks to their own confused hyper-wisdom, or even, for example, to refute all the awful rubbish which Schäffle alone has put together in his many bulky tomes. It would take a large-sized volume merely to correct the *misquotations* from *Capital* which these gentlemen put in inverted commas. Let them first learn to read and copy before they demand answers to their questions.

Moreover, I do not consider the question to be at all a burning one at a time when American mass-production and *real* large-scale agriculture, which are only now coming into existence, are literally threatening to suffocate us under the weight of the means of subsistence they have produced; on the eve of a revolution which must have this consequence among others, that *the earth will now be populated*—what you say about this on pp. 169–70[1] touches far too superficially on this point—and which in Europe will also be *certain to require* a large increase of population.

1. The reference is to Kautsky's book *Der Einfluss der Volksvermehrung auf den Fortschritt der Gesellschaft* [The Influence of the Increase of Population on the Progress of Society] (Vienna, 1880).—Ed.

Euler's calculation is of exactly the same value as that concerning the kreutzer [2] which is put out at compound interest in the first year of our era, which doubles itself every thirteen years, and which therefore now amounts to about $\frac{1 \times 2^{144}}{60}$ gulden, a lump of silver bigger than the earth. When you say on p. 169 that there is not much difference between the social conditions of America and those of Europe, surely this is only true as regards the large coastal towns, or the outward legal forms in which these conditions are clothed. The great mass of the American population certainly lives under conditions which are extremely favorable to an increase of population. This is proved by the flow of immigration. And yet it will take more than thirty years for the population to double itself. That doesn't scare me!

There is, of course, the abstract possibility that the number of people will become so great that limits will have to be set to their increase. But if at some stage communist society finds itself obliged to regulate the production of human beings, just as it has already come to regulate the production of things, it will be precisely this society, and this society alone, which can carry this out without difficulty. It does not seem to me that it would be at all difficult in such a society to achieve by planning a result which has already been produced spontaneously, without planning, in France and Lower Austria. At any rate, it is for the people in the communist society themselves to decide whether, when, and how this is to be done, and what means they wish to employ for the purpose. I do not feel called upon to make proposals or give them advice about it. These people, in any case, will surely not be any less intelligent than we are.

Incidentally, as early as 1844 I wrote (*Deutsch-Französische Jahrb.*, p. 109): "Even if Malthus were altogether right, it would still be necessary to carry out this

---

2. A small coin, formerly current in Germany and Austria.—Ed.

(socialist) reorganization immediately, since only this re-organization, only the enlightenment of the masses which it can bring with it, can make possible that moral restraint upon the instinct for reproduction which Malthus himself puts forward as the easiest and most effective counter-measure against overpopulation."

11 The Malthusian Theory in Reverse

From Engels's letter to Danielson of 9 January, 1895

I have received your letter of 1 December. I do not understand what Mr. von Struve means when he asserts that Marx *completes* Malthus's theory of population, but does not *repudiate* it.[1] I should have thought that the note on Malthus in volume 1, footnote 75 to chapter 23, 1,[2] would be plain enough for anybody. Moreover, I do not understand how anyone can today speak of a completion of the Malthusian theory that *the population presses against the means of subsistence*, at a time when corn in London costs twenty shillings a quarter, or half the average price of 1848–70, and when it is generally recognized that *the means of subsistence are pressing against the population*, which is not large enough to consume them! And if in Russia the farmer is forced to sell corn which he really should consume, he is forced to do this not by the pressure of population, but by the pressure of the tax collector, the landlord, the kulak, etc., etc. As far as I know, it is the low price of Argentine wheat more than anything else which is to blame for the agrarian distress in the whole of Europe, Russia included.

1. P. von Struve, *Critical Notes on the Development of Capitalism in Russia* (St. Petersburg, 1894).—Ed.
2. Engels refers to the footnote which is partly reproduced above, pp. 83–84.—Ed.

PART THREE

Marx on
Malthus and
Economic
Theory
in General

Introductory Notes

Marx originally intended to conclude *Capital* with a final volume in which "the history of the theory" was to be discussed. Between 1861 and 1863 he prepared a great deal of material with this end in view. After Marx's death, Engels took over this material with the intention of putting it into a publishable form, but he himself died before he had time to do so. The task was therefore entrusted to Kautsky, who edited Marx's manuscript (by no means satisfactorily) and published the work under the title *Theorien· über den Mehrwert* ("Theories of Surplus Value") between 1905 and 1910. An excellent English translation of selections from the work was published in 1951, but up to now there has been no English translation of the important sections dealing with Malthus.

Three extracts from the *Theorien* are translated below. The first of these occurs in the course of Marx's extended discussion of Ricardo, at the beginning of a section dealing with the history of the discovery of the so-called "Ricardian" theory of rent. The "Ricardian" theory of rent, although it has come to be associated with Ricardo's name, was in fact put forward almost at the same time—early in 1815—by four economists (Malthus, West, Torrens and Ricardo), and priorities are very difficult to establish. Almost forty years before this, however, a Scottish farmer called James Anderson had substantially anticipated the theory in a pamphlet on the Corn Laws. Marx, in the first extract from the *Theorien* translated below, begins by discussing the unprincipled manner in which Malthus used Anderson's theory. But the discussion soon leaves this rather specialist field and develops into a general attack upon what Marx calls the "meanness" of Malthus's approach to political economy. The brilliant comparison between the "considerate" character of Malthus's outlook and the "inconsiderate" character of Ricardo's is especially noteworthy.

The second and third of the extracts translated below are both taken from the special section of the *Theorien* which Marx devoted to Malthus. This section follows upon Marx's lengthy study of Ricardo, and immediately precedes a section dealing with "The Dissolution of the Ricardian School." It consists of five parts: (1) Value and Surplus Value; (2) Variable Capital and Accumulation; (3) Overproduction and

Overconsumption; (4) The Author of the *Inquiry*; (5) The Author of the *Outlines*. "Value and Surplus Value" appears below in its entirety as the second extract, and "Overproduction and Overconsumption" in a shortened form as the third. The other parts, which are short and of secondary importance, have not been included.

The second extract contains an exhaustive analysis of Malthus's theories of value and profit. Marx shows in particular how Malthus's superficial theory of value leads him directly to the "vulgar" idea that profit is something which the capitalist simply "adds on" when he sells his commodity. In the third extract, he shows how these theories of value and profit in turn lead Malthus to the apologetic doctrine of "the necessity for an ever-increasing unproductive consumption." The third extract concludes with a remarkable survey of the differences and resemblances between Malthus, Ricardo and Sismondi, and an incisive summary indictment of Malthus's economic work as a whole. A review of Marx's main arguments in these sections will be found in the Introductory Essay in the present volume.

The first extract is translated from volume 2, 1, of the Kautsky edition of the *Theorien*, pp. 304–15, and the second and third from volume 3, pp. 1–29 and 35–61.

1   Malthus as an Apologist

From Marx's *Theories of Surplus Value,*
vol. 2 (written 1861 - 63)

Anderson was a practical farmer. His first
work, in which he *incidentally* discusses the nature of rent,
appeared in 1777,[1] at a time when in the eyes of a large part
of the public Sir James Steuart was still the leading economist, but when general attention was also being directed to
the *Wealth of Nations*, which had appeared in the previous
year. In this situation, the work of the Scottish farmer,
which was concerned with a controversial question of immediate practical interest, and which did not deal with rent
"ex professo" but merely explained its nature in passing,
could not attract any attention. Just as incidentally, this
theory of his turns up again in one or two of his essays in a
three-volume collection, edited by himself, which appeared
under the title *Essays Relating to Agriculture and Rural Affairs,* 3 vols., Edinburgh, 1777–1796.[2] The same goes for
*Recreations in Agriculture, Natural-History, Arts and Miscel-
laneous Literature*, London, which was published in
1799–1802. Both these works were directly intended for
farmers and agriculturists. If Anderson had had a presentiment of the importance of his find, and had put it before
the public on its own in the form of an examination of the
nature of ground rent, or if he had possessed even a part of

1. *An Enquiry into the Nature of the Corn-Laws, etc.* (Edinburgh,
1777). Marx is mistaken in saying that this was Anderson's first work.
—Ed.
2. Marx's reference is to the second edition. The first edition, in one
volume, was published in 1775.—Ed.

the talent for trading in his own ideas which his compatriot McCulloch displayed so successfully with those of other people,[3] matters [would have turned out] differently. When his theory was reproduced in 1815, it appeared straight away in the form of an independent *theoretical* examination of the nature of rent, as is shown by the very titles of the respective works of West and Malthus—*Essay on the Application of Capital to Land*, and *Inquiry into the Nature and Progress of Rent*.

Malthus used this theory of rent of Anderson's in order to endow his law of population for the first time with an economic and real, natural-historical foundation, for his nonsense [borrowed] from earlier writers about the geometrical and arithmetical progressions was a purely chimerical hypothesis. Malthus availed himself of the opportunity at once. And Ricardo, as he himself says in the preface,[4] even made this doctrine of rent into one of the most important elements of the whole system of political economy, and gave to it—not to mention an exact formulation—an entirely new theoretical importance.

Ricardo was evidently unaware of Anderson's work, since in the preface to his *Principles of Political Economy* he speaks only of West and Malthus as the discoverers of the law of rent. Judging from the original manner in which West presents the law, it is possible that he too was unacquainted with Anderson, as Tooke was with Steuart.[5] This is not the case with Malthus. A careful comparison of their work shows that he knows Anderson and uses him. Malthus was altogether a *plagiarist* by profession. One has only to compare

3. Marx is probably referring to McCulloch's habit of publishing the same (often unoriginal) material in several different places.—Ed.
4. To his *Principles of Political Economy*. See Sraffa's ed. of Ricardo's *Works and Correspondence*, vol. 1, pp. 5-6.—Ed.
5. For an explanation of this reference to Tooke and Steuart, see Marx's *Critique of Political Economy* (Kerr ed.), p. 260.—Ed.

the first edition of his work on population with the work by the Rev. Townsend[6] to become convinced that he does not use the latter as raw material, as an independent producer would, but that he copies and paraphrases him, like a slavish plagiarist, although he *nowhere mentions* him, keeping his existence a *secret*. The manner in which Malthus used Anderson is characteristic. Anderson had defended bounties on the export and duties on the import of corn, not in any way out of concern for the landlords, but because he considered that legislation of this kind would lower the price of production of corn and ensure the even development of the productive powers of agriculture. Malthus took over this practical conclusion from Anderson because, like a true member of the English State Church, he was a professional sycophant of the landed aristocracy, whose rents, sinecures, extravagance, heartlessness, etc., he justified from the economic point of view. Malthus defends the interests of the industrial bourgeoisie only insofar as they are identical with the interests of landed property, of the aristocracy, that is, insofar as they are *opposed to* the interests of the mass of the people, of the proletariat; but where the interests of the bourgeoisie and the aristocracy diverge and come into conflict with one another, he stands on the side of the aristocracy in opposition to the bourgeoisie. Hence his defense of *"unproductive laborers,"* overconsumption, etc.

Anderson, on the other hand, had explained the difference between land which pays rent and [land which] does not pay rent, or between pieces of land which pay unequal rents, in terms of the relative infertility of the soil which yields no rent, or which yields a smaller rent, compared with that of the soil which does yield rent, or which yields a larger rent. But he had expressly stated that these degrees of relative fertility of different grades of soil, and thus also the

6. Joseph Townsend, *A Dissertation on the Poor Laws* (1786).—Ed.

relative infertility of the worse grades of soil compared with the better grades, have no connection whatsoever with the absolute fertility of agriculture. On the contrary, he had not only emphasized that the absolute fertility of all grades of soil could be constantly increased, and with the growth of population must be constantly increased, but had also gone further, asserting that the inequalities in the fertility of the different grades of soil could be progressively evened out. He said that the present degree of development of agriculture in England gave no indication of its possibilities of further development. He [also] said that the price of corn could be high and rent low in one country, while in another country the price of corn was low and rent high. This followed from his principle, since in both countries the existence and level of rent are determined by the difference between the fertile and infertile soils, and in neither of them by the absolute fertility; in each of the countries the existence and level of rent are determined only by the differences of degree in the fertility of the grades of soil to be found there, and in neither of them by the average fertility of these grades of soil. He concludes from this that the absolute fertility of agriculture has nothing whatsoever to do with rent. That is why he revealed himself subsequently, as we shall see below, as a confirmed enemy of the Malthusian theory of population, never suspecting that his own theory of rent was destined to serve as the foundation for this monstrous invention. Anderson explained the rise in the price of corn in England between 1750 and 1801, as compared with the period from 1700 to 1750, not at all by the cultivation of progressively more infertile grades of soil, but by the influence of legislation upon agriculture during these two periods.

Now what does Malthus do?

In place of his chimera (also plagiarized) of the geometrical and arithmetical progressions, which he retained as a form of words, Malthus used Anderson's theory to confirm his theory of population. He retained the practical conclusions drawn by Anderson from the theory insofar as they coincided with the interests of the landlords—a fact which alone is sufficient to prove that he understood the connection of this theory with the system of political economy as little as did Anderson himself. Without going into the evidence to the contrary put forward by the discoverer of the theory, he turned it against the proletariat. He left it to Ricardo to make the theoretical and practical progress which was possible with the help of this theory—theoretical progress, in the determination of the *value* of commodities, etc., and in gaining an insight into the nature of landed property; practical progress, in opposing the necessity for private property in land on the basis of bourgeois production, and also in opposing all State measures, such as duties on corn, which augmented this landed property. The only practical conclusions which Malthus drew from the theory were a defense of the protective tariff which the landlords of 1815 were demanding—a sycophantic service to the aristocracy—and a new justification of the poverty of the producers of wealth, a new apology for the exploiters of labor. [Viewed from this angle, his practical conclusion from the theory is also a] sycophantic service to the industrial capitalists.

What characterizes Malthus is the *fundamental meanness* of his outlook; a meanness which only a parson could permit himself to display, a parson who looks upon human misery as the punishment for the Fall of man and stands in general need of "an earthly vale of tears," but who at the same time, out of consideration for the benefices accruing to him, finds it most advantageous, with the help of the dogma of predestination, to "sweeten" the sojourn of the ruling classes in the vale of tears.

This meanness of outlook also reveals itself in his standards of scholarship. *First*, in his shameless and mechanical *plagiarism. Second,* in the *considerate,* not *inconsiderate,*[7] conclusions which he draws from scientific premises. Ricardo was right, for his time, in regarding the capitalist mode of production as the most advantageous for production in general, as the most advantageous for the production of wealth. He wants *production for the sake of production,* and in this [he is] *right.* Those who assert, as Ricardo's sentimental opponents have done, that production as such is not the end, forget that production for the sake of production merely means the development of human productive power, that is, *the development of the wealth of the human race as an end in itself.* If, as Sismondi does, one sets up the welfare of the individual in opposition to this end, this is tantamount to asserting that the development of the species must be *checked* in order to ensure the welfare of the individual—for example, that wars should never be waged, since individuals are necessarily destroyed in them. Sismondi is right only as against those economists who *gloss over* this antithesis or deny it. What is not understood is that the development of the capabilities of the species *man,* although it [proceeds] at first at the expense of the majority of human individuals and of certain human classes, will eventually break through this antagonism and coincide with the development of the individual person, and that therefore the higher development of individuality can only be purchased through a historical process in which individuals are sacrificed. And this is to say nothing of the sterility of such views, since the gains of the species in the human kingdom, as in the animal and plant

7. In the original German the two words are *rücksichtsvoll,* "full of (kind) consideration," and *rücksichtslos,* "without consideration (for other people)." Marx is using the words ironically in order to contrast the "considerate" manner in which Malthus tended to falsify his scientific conclusions in the interests of the landlords and capitalists, with Ricardo's "inconsiderate" lack of concern for the effect of his conclusions upon the interests of any particular class.—Ed.

kingdoms, are always made at the expense of individual advantage. Ricardo's inconsiderateness was thus not only *scientifically honest*, but also, given his point of view, *scientifically necessary*. This means, however, that he was also entirely indifferent as to whether the development of productive power destroyed landed property or whether it destroyed the workers. If this progress reduces the value of the capital of the industrial bourgeoisie, it is just as welcome to him. If the development of the productive power of labor reduces the value of the existing fixed capital by a half, what does that matter, asks Ricardo. The productivity of human labor has doubled. Here, then, is *scientific honesty*. If Ricardo's theories taken together are in the interests of the *industrial bourgeoisie*, this is the case only *because* and insofar as the interests of this class coincide with those of production or of the productive development of human labor. Where they do not coincide but are in conflict with one another, Ricardo comes out just as *inconsiderately* against the bourgeoisie as in other cases he comes out against the proletariat and the aristocracy.

In connection with the characterization of Ricardo, the two following passages are of decisive importance:

> I shall greatly regret that considerations for any particular class, are allowed to check the progress of the wealth and population of the country (Ricardo, *An Essay on the Influence of a Low Price of Corn on the Profits of Stock, etc.,* 1815, Sraffa's ed., vol. 4, p. 41).

When the import of corn is free, "land is abandoned" (*ibid.,* p. 39). [But industrial production is advanced.] Thus landed property is sacrificed to the development of production.

But, in the same case of free import of corn:

> That some capital would be lost cannot be disputed,

but is the possession or preservation of capital the end, or the means? The means, undoubtedly. What we want is an abundance of commodities,[8] and if it could be proved that by the sacrifice of a part of our capital we should augment the annual produce of those objects which contribute to our enjoyment and happiness, we ought not, I should think, to repine at the loss of a part of our capital (*On Protection to Agriculture*, 1822, Sraffa's ed., vol. 4, pp. 248–49).

By *"our capital"* Ricardo means capital which belongs neither to *us* nor to *him*, but which is laid out by *the capitalists* on landed property. But *we* (!) represent the nation as a whole. The increase of *"our"* wealth is the increase of *social* wealth, which is an end in itself, irrespective of those who participate in this wealth!

To an individual with a capital of £20,000, whose profits were £2,000 per annum, it would be a matter quite indifferent whether his capital would employ a hundred or a thousand men, whether the commodity produced sold for £10,000, or for £2,000, provided, in all cases, his profits were not diminished below £2,000. Is not the real interest of the nation similar? Provided its net real income, its rent and profits be the same, it is of no importance whether the nation consists of ten or of twelve millions of inhabitants (*Principles of Political Economy*, Sraffa's ed., vol. 1, p. 348).

Here the "proletariat" is sacrificed to wealth. Insofar as the proletariat is of no importance for the existence of wealth, wealth places no importance on the existence of the proletariat. It is a mere mass—a human mass—and is of no value.

8. Wealth in general.

In these three examples, then, we see Ricardo's scientific impartiality.

But the contemptible Malthus draws from the scientifically established premises—which he always *steals*—only those conclusions which are *acceptable* and useful to the aristocracy as against the bourgeoisie and to both *as against* the proletariat. He therefore wants *production*, not *for the sake of production*, but only insofar as it maintains or consolidates [9] the existing order of things and serves to further the advantage of the ruling classes. His very first book—one of the most remarkable examples in literature of a plagiarism which was successful at the expense of the original work—had the practical aim of proving, in the interests of the then English government and landed aristocracy, that the doctrines of perfectibility of the French Revolution and of its supporters in England were "economically" utopian. In other words, it was a panegyrical tract in favor of the existing state of affairs as against historical development, and in addition a justification of the war against revolutionary France. His writings of 1815 on protective tariffs and ground rent were intended to corroborate his earlier apology for the poverty of the producers; but in particular they were intended to defend reactionary landed property against "enlightened," "liberal" and "progressive" capital, and above all to justify a retrograde piece of legislation put forward in England in the interests of the aristocracy as against the industrial bourgeoisie. Finally his *Principles of Political Economy*, directed against Ricardo, had essentially the aim of confining the absolute demands of industrial capital, and the laws according to which its productivity develops, within limits which would be "advantageous" and "desirable" from the point of view of the landed aristocracy, the State

9. In the manuscript: *ausbaucht.*—K. (Kautsky takes *ausbaucht*, "swells," as a slip for *ausbaut*, "consolidates."—Ed.)

Church to which Malthus belonged, government officials (*Regierungspersonen*), and tax-consumers (*Steuerverzehrer*). But a man who tries to *accommodate* science to a point of view which is not derived from science itself, however erroneous it may be, but which is borrowed from outside, from *extrinsic interests* which are *foreign* to it, I call "*mean.*" Ricardo is not mean when he places the proletarians on the same level as machinery, beasts of burden or commodities, because from his point of view "production" demands that they should be merely machinery or beasts of burden and because in actual fact they are only commodities in capitalist production. This is stoical, objective, and scientific. Insofar as it is possible without sinning against his science, Ricardo is always a philanthropist, as he was in practice. Parson Malthus [it is true, also] reduces the workers to beasts of burden for the sake of production, and even condemns them to live in celibacy and to die of hunger. [But] where the same demands of production reduce the landlord's "rent," or encroach too much on the "tithes" of the State Church or the interests of the tax-consumers, or where they sacrifice that section of the industrial bourgeoisie whose interests hinder progress to that section of the bourgeoisie which advocates the progress of production—that is, where it is a question of any interest of the aristocracy as against the bourgeoisie, or of the conservative and stagnating bourgeoisie as against the progressive bourgeoisie—in all these cases "Parson" Malthus does not sacrifice the exclusive interests to production, but does his best to sacrifice the demands of production to the exclusive interests of the existing ruling classes or sections of them, and to this end he falsifies his scientific conclusions. That is his scientific meanness, his sin against science, quite apart from his shameless and mechanical plagiarism. Malthus's scientific conclusions are *considerate* where the ruling classes in general and the reactionary elements among these ruling classes in particular are concerned; that is, he *falsifies* science on behalf of these interests. His conclusions are, however, *inconsiderate* where the oppressed classes are concerned. And it is not only that he is inconsiderate. He *affects* inconsiderateness, takes a cynical pleasure in this role, and *exaggerates* the conclusions—insofar as they are directed against those living in poverty—to an even *greater* extent than could be scientifically justified from his own point of view.

The hatred of the English working class against Malthus— the "mountebank-parson,"[10] as Cobbett rudely calls him—is therefore entirely justified. The people were right here in sensing instinctively that they were confronted not with a *man of science* but with a *bought advocate*, a pleader on behalf of their enemies, a shameless sycophant of the ruling classes.

The author of an idea can exaggerate it and remain honest; but the plagiarist who exaggerates it always trades on this exaggeration.

[In its] first edition, Malthus's work *On Population*, since it does not contain a [single] new word of science, [is] to be regarded merely as an importunate Capuchin's sermon,[11] an Abraham à Sancta Clara[12] version of the treatment of the subject by Townsend, Steuart, Wallace, Herbert, etc. Since in actual fact it sets out to impress only by means of its *popular* form, it is right that *popular* hatred should be directed against it.

Malthus's only merit, as against the pitiable doctrines of harmony in bourgeois political economy, is precisely his pointed emphasis on the disharmonies. Although in no instance did he discover these, yet in every instance he clings

10. In both German and English in the text.—Ed.
11. I.e., a trivial, canting sermon.—Ed.
12. A Roman Catholic preacher (1642–1709), remarkable for his eccentric writings.—Ed.

to them with parsonic satisfaction, amplifies them and blazons them forth.

Charles Darwin says in the introduction to his work, *On the Origin of Species by Means of Natural Selection, or the Preservation of Favoured Races in the Struggle for Life:*

> In the next chapter the *Struggle for Existence* [13] amongst all organic beings throughout the world, which inevitably follows from the high geometrical ratio of their increase, will be treated of. This is the doctrine of Malthus, applied to the whole animal and vegetable kingdoms (1860 ed., London, pp.4–5).

In his excellent work, Darwin did not see that his discovery of the "geometrical" progression in the animal and vegetable kingdoms overturns Malthus's theory. Malthus's theory is based precisely on the fact that he opposes Wallace's geometrical progression of human beings to the chimerical "arithmetical" progression of animals and plants. In Darwin's work, for example in his discussion of the extinction of species, we find a natural-historical refutation of the Malthusian theory, not only of its fundamental principle but also of its details. Insofar as Malthus's theory was based on Anderson's theory of rent, it was refuted by *Anderson himself.* Ricardo, for example, when his theory leads him to the view that the rise of wages above their minimum does not increase the value of commodities, says so straight out. Malthus wants to keep wages low so that the bourgeoisie should profit.

13. Marx's emphasis.—Ed.

2 Malthus on Value and Surplus Value

From Marx's *Theories of Surplus Value,* vol. 3 (written 1861 - 63)

The works by Malthus which will be considered here are:

1. *The Measure of Value Stated and Illustrated, with an application of it to the alterations in the value of the English currency since 1790,* London, 1823.

2. *Definitions in Political Economy, etc.,* London, 1827. See also the edition of the same work edited by John Cazenove, London, 1853, with "notes and supplementary remarks."

3. *Principles of Political Economy, etc.,* 2nd ed., London, 1836 (1st ed., 1820).

4. The following work by a Malthusian (that is, Malthusian in contrast to the Ricardians) will also be considered: *Outlines of Political Economy, etc.,* London, 1832.

In his work *Observations on the Effects of the Corn Laws, etc.* (1814), Malthus was still saying about Smith:

> Dr. Smith was evidently led into this train of argument, from his habit of considering labor[1] as the standard *measure of value,*[2] and corn as the measure of labor. . . . That neither labor nor any other commodity can be an accurate measure of real value in exchange, is now considered as one of the most

1. That is, the value of labor.
2. Marx's emphasis.—Ed.

incontrovertible doctrines of political economy: and indeed follows, as a necessary consequence, from the very definition of value in exchange (*Observations*, 1st ed., pp. 11–12).

But in his work of 1820, *Principles of Political Economy*, Malthus took up and used against Ricardo this very "measure of value," which Smith himself had never used in the real (*wirklich*) parts of his theory.[3] In the work on rent mentioned above,[4] Malthus himself had held to Smith's other definition, the determination of the value of an article by the quantity of capital (accumulated labor) and labor (immediate) which is required for the production of this article.

It is quite obvious that both Malthus's *Principles*, and the two other works mentioned above which were intended to follow up individual points in the *Principles*, largely owed their origin to the fact that Malthus, jealous of the success of Ricardo's book, was making an attempt to force his way back to that position of predominance into which he had wormed himself, by means of his clever plagiarism, prior to the appearance of Ricardo's book. In addition to this, the exposition of the determination of value in Ricardo's work, although still abstract, was directed against the interests of

3. Earlier in the *Theories of Surplus Value*, Marx refers to the manner in which Adam Smith "moves with great *naïveté* in a continuous contradiction." On the one hand, "he traces the inner connection between the economic categories—or the hidden structure of the bourgeois economic system." On the other hand, "alongside this inner connection he sets up also the connection as it is manifested in the phenomena of competition, and therefore as it presents itself to the unscientific observer" (see *Theories of Surplus Value*, Selections, translated by G. A. Bonner and Emile Burns, pp. 202 ff.). Marx sometimes (as here) refers to the first of these two modes of approach as the "real" part of Smith's theory; at other times (as occasionally below) he refers to it as Smith's "strong side," as opposed to his "weak side"—i.e., to the second mode of approach. Cf. p. 29, above.—Ed.

4. Malthus's *Inquiry into the Nature and Progress of Rent* (1815). —Ed.

the landowners and their hangers-on—interests which Malthus represented even more directly than those of the industrial bourgeoisie. It cannot be denied, however, that Malthus had a certain interest in theoretical sophistication. Nevertheless his opposition to Ricardo—and his method of attack—were possible only because Ricardo had become entangled in all kinds of inconsistencies. Malthus's attack seizes in the first place upon the genesis of surplus value; upon the way in which Ricardo conceives the leveling out of prices of production in the different spheres of employment of capital as a modification of the law of value itself; and upon his general confusion of profit and surplus value (a direct identification of the two). Malthus does not disentangle these contradictions and *quid pro quos,*[5] but takes them over from Ricardo in order to overturn, with the support of this confusion, the basic Ricardian law of value, etc., and to draw conclusions which will be acceptable to his patrons.

Malthus's real merit in these three works consists in the fact that he lays the main emphasis upon the *unequal* exchange between capital and wage labor, whereas Ricardo does not in fact show how the unequal exchange between capital and living labor, between a quantity of accumulated labor and a given quantity of immediate labor, proceeds from the exchange of commodities according to the law of value—i.e., according to the labor time contained in them. Thus Ricardo in fact leaves the origin of surplus value obscure, since with him capital is exchanged directly against labor and not against labor power. Cazenove, one of the few subsequent disciples of Malthus, has a presentiment of this in his preface to the work mentioned above (*Definitions, etc.*), saying:

The *Interchange* of commodities and *Distribution*

---

5. Marx uses this expression in a sense which is now rare, meaning mistakes made by using one thing for another.—Ed.

(*Wages, Rent,* and *Profits*) must be kept distinct from each other. ... *The Laws of Distribution* are not dependent upon those relating to Interchange (*Definitions*, Cazenove's ed., pp. v–vii).[6]

This can only mean that the relation of wages and profit, the exchange of capital and wage labor, of accumulated labor and living labor, does not *directly* conform to the law of exchange of commodities.

If we consider the *utilization* (*Verwertung*) of money or commodities as capital—that is, not their value (*Wert*) but the capitalist *utilization of their value* (*Verwertung*)[7]—it becomes clear that *surplus value* is nothing else but the excess quantity of labor (unpaid labor) which the capital, in the form of money or commodities, commands over and above the quantity of labor which the capital itself contains. The commodity used as capital purchases, over and above the quantity of labor contained in it, an excess quantity of labor which was not incorporated in it. This excess quantity forms the surplus value; and the extent of the gain upon realization (*die Proportion der Verwertung*) depends upon the size of this excess. The excess quantity of living labor for which the commodity is exchanged constitutes the source of profit. Profit (or rather surplus value) does not arise from the equivalent of embodied labor which is given in exchange for an equal quantity of living labor, but from the portion of living labor which is appropriated in this exchange without an equivalent being paid for it, the unpaid labor which capital appropriates for itself in this semblance of an exchange. If we leave out of account the intermediate links in this process—and Malthus is the more justified in doing this since

6. A paraphrase of extracts from three separate passages, not a direct quotation.—Ed.

7. *Verwertung* normally means "utilization" or "turning to account," but commercially it means "realization" or "conversion into money." —Ed.

they are absent in Ricardo—if we consider only the real content and result of the process, then gain upon realization (*Verwertung*), profit, the transformation of money or commodities into capital, are seen to arise not from the fact that the commodities are exchanged in conformity with the law of value, i.e., in proportion to the relative quantities of labor time which they have cost, but rather, on the contrary, from the fact that the commodities or money (embodied labor) are exchanged for a *greater* quantity of living labor than is contained or worked up in them. The sole merit of Malthus in the above works is the emphasis which he lays on this point—a point which stands out less clearly in Ricardo since the latter always presupposes a finished product which is divided between capitalist and worker, without taking into account the exchanges, the intermediate links in the process, which lead up to this division of the product. And this merit is canceled out again by reason of the fact that Malthus confuses the utilization (*Verwertung*) of money or commodities as capital, and consequently their *value* (*Wert*) in their specific function as capital, with the *value* of the commodities as such. Thus in his argument, as we shall see, he falls back on the empty idea of the monetary system that profit arises from alienation (Profit upon expropriation),[8] and entangles himself completely in the most unedifying confusion. Thus instead of going beyond Ricardo, Malthus tries in his work to force political economy back to what it was before Ricardo, and even before Smith and the Physiocrats.

> In the same country, and at the same time, the exchangeable value of those commodities which can be resolved into labor and profits alone, would be accurately measured by the quantity of labor which would result from adding to the accumulated and immediate labor actually worked up in them the varying amount of the profits on all the advances

8. The phrase in brackets is in English in the text.—Ed.

estimated in labor. But this must necessarily be the same as the quantity of labor which they will command (*The Measure of Value*, pp. 15–16).

The labor which a commodity can command is a measure of its value (*ibid.*, p. 61).[9]

I had nowhere seen it stated,[10] that the ordinary quantity of labor which a commodity will command must represent and measure the quantity of labor worked up in it, with the addition of profits (*Definitions*, 1827 ed., p. 196).

Malthus wants to incorporate "profit" in the very definition of *value*, in order that it should be directly derived from this definition, which is not the case with Ricardo. This shows that he has a presentiment of where the difficulty lies.

Moreover it is perfectly ridiculous for him to identify the *value of a commodity* with its *utilization as capital*. When commodities or money (embodied labor, in short) are exchanged in the form of capital for living labor, they are always exchanged for a greater quantity of labor than is contained in them; and if one compares on the one hand the commodities before the exchange and on the other hand the product which results from their exchange with the living labor, then one finds that the commodities have been exchanged for their own value (equivalent) plus an excess over and above their own value, the surplus value. But it is absurd to conclude from this that the value of a commodity is equal to its value plus an excess over and above this value. Thus when a commodity is exchanged as a commodity for another commodity, and not as capital for living labor, it is exchanged—insofar as it is exchanged for an equivalent—for the same quantity of embodied labor as is contained in it.

Thus all that is worthy of note is that according to Malthus profit is already directly included in the value of a

9. A paraphrase, not a direct quotation.—Ed.
10. That is, before his own work *The Measure of Value, etc.*

commodity, and that one thing is clear to him—that a commodity always commands more labor than is contained in it.

It is precisely because the labor which a commodity will ordinarily command measures the labor actually worked up in it with the addition of profits, that it is justifiable to consider it as a measure of value. If then the ordinary value of a commodity be considered as determined by the natural and necessary conditions of its supply,[11] it is certain that the labor which it will ordinarily command is alone the measure of these conditions (*Definitions*, 1827 ed., p. 214).

Elementary Costs of Production: An expression exactly equivalent to the conditions of the supply (*ibid.*, Cazenove's ed., p. 14).

Measure of the Conditions of the Supply . . . : The quantity of labor for which the commodity will exchange, when it is in its natural and ordinary state (*ibid.*, p. 14).

The quantity of labor which a commodity commands represents exactly the quantity of labor worked up in it, with the profits upon the advances, and does therefore really represent and measure those natural and necessary conditions of the supply, those elementary costs of production which determine value (*ibid.*, p. 125).

But the demand for a commodity, though not proportioned to the *quantity* of any other commodity which the purchaser is willing and able to give for it, is really proportioned to *the quantity of labor* which he will give for it; and for this reason: the quantity of labor which a commodity will *ordinarily* command, represents exactly the effectual demand

11. According to Malthus (*Definitions*, p. 213), these conditions are "the accumulated and immediate labor worked up in commodities with the ordinary profits upon the whole advances for the time that they were advanced."—K.

for it; because it represents exactly that quantity of labor and profits united necessary to effect its supply; while the *actual* quantity of labor which a commodity will command when it differs from the *ordinary* quantity, represents the excess or defect of demand arising from temporary causes (*ibid.*, p. 135).

Here too Malthus is right. The condition of the manufacture, that is of the production or rather reproduction, of a commodity on the basis of capitalist production, is that the commodity or its value (the money into which it is converted) should be exchanged in the process of its production or reproduction for a greater quantity of labor than is contained in it; for it is only produced in order to realize a profit.

For example, a calico manufacturer has sold his calico. The condition of the manufacture of further calico is that he should exchange the money—the exchange value of the calico—in the process of reproduction of the calico for a greater quantity of labor than was contained in it or is represented by the money. For the calico manufacturer produces the calico as a capitalist. What he wants to produce is not calico but profit. The production of calico is only a means for the production of profit. But what are the consequences of this? More labor time, more labor, is contained in the newly manufactured calico than in the advanced calico. This surplus labor time, surplus value, also takes the form of surplus product, a *surplus* of calico over that which was exchanged for the labor. Thus a portion of the product does not compensate for the calico which was exchanged for labor, but forms a surplus product belonging to the manufacturer. Or if we consider the whole product, every yard of calico contains an aliquot part, or its value contains an aliquot part, for which no equivalent has been paid and which represents *unpaid* labor. If, then, the manufacturer sells a yard of calico at its value, that is if he exchanges it for money or commodities containing an equal quantity of labor time, he will realize a sum of money or receive a quantity of commodities which do not cost him anything. For he sells the calico, not according to the labor time which he has paid for, but according to the labor time which is contained in it—and he has not paid for a part of this labor time.

The calico contains, let us suppose, labor time equal to twelve shillings. The manufacturer has paid only eight shillings of this. Assuming that he sells the commodity at its value, he will sell it for twelve shillings, thus gaining four shillings. So far as the buyer is concerned, he always pays, on this assumption, *only* the value of the calico. That is, he gives a sum of money which contains as much labor time as is contained in the calico. Three cases are possible here. First, the buyer is a capitalist. The money (that is, the value of the commodity) with which he makes payment likewise contains a portion of unpaid labor. Thus while one of the parties sells unpaid labor, the other buys with unpaid labor. Both realize unpaid labor, the one as seller and the other as buyer. Or, second, the buyer is an independent producer. In this case he receives equivalent for equivalent. Whether the labor which the seller sells to him in the commodity is paid for or not does not concern him. He receives as much embodied labor as he gives. Or, finally, the buyer is a wage laborer. In this case, too, he receives, just like any other buyer—assuming that the commodity is sold at its value—an equivalent in commodities for his money. He receives as much embodied labor in the form of commodities as he gives in the form of money. But for the money which constitutes his wages he has given more labor than is contained in the money. Having thus paid for the money above its value, he therefore also pays for the equivalent of the money, the calico, above its value. The cost is accordingly greater for him as buyer than it is for the seller of any commodity, even though he receives in the commodity an equivalent for his money. He did not receive in the money an equivalent for his labor; rather did he give more than an equivalent in labor. Thus the worker is the only one who pays for all commodities above their value even when he buys them at their value, since he has bought the money, the general equivalent for labor, above its value. This does not mean that the man who sells a commodity to a worker gains any [special] advantage. The worker pays him the value of the labor, which is no more than any other buyer pays him. The capitalist, who sells back to the worker the commodity produced by the worker, certainly realizes a profit on this sale, but only the same profit which he realizes on a sale to any other buyer. In relation to the worker, the capitalist's profit does not originate from the fact that he sells him the commodity *above* its value, but from the fact that earlier, in the process of production, he really bought it from the worker *below* its value.

Just as Malthus transforms the utilization (*Verwertung*) of a commodity as capital into its value (*Wert*), so he consistently transforms all buyers into wage laborers—that is, he makes them give in exchange to the capitalist immediate labor instead of commodities. And according to Malthus they all return to the capitalist more labor than is *contained* in the commodities, whereas on the contrary his profit is actually derived from the fact that, having *paid* for only a part of the labor contained in the commodities, he *sells all* the labor contained in them. Thus, whereas with Ricardo the difficulty [lies in the fact] that the law of exchange of commodities does not directly explain the exchange between capital and wage labor but rather seems to contradict it, Malthus resolves the difficulty by transforming the purchase (exchange) of commodities into an exchange between capital and wage labor. What Malthus does not understand is the difference between the sum total of labor contained in a commodity and the quantity of paid labor contained in it. It is precisely this difference which constitutes the source of profit. Further, he is led to the inevitable conclusion that profit is derived from the fact that the seller sells his commodity not only *above* [the price] which represents its cost *to him* (which the capitalist in fact does), but also above the price which represents *its cost*. He thus reverts to the vulgar idea of profit as originating upon alienation, deriving surplus value from the fact that the seller sells the commodity *above* its value (that is, for more labor time than is contained in it). But what he gains in this way as the seller of one commodity he loses as the buyer of another commodity, and it is absolutely impossible to understand how real "profit" can arise through a general nominal running-up of prices of this type. In particular, it is impossible to understand how the community *en masse* can enrich itself by this procedure, and how any real surplus value or surplus product can come into being. It is an absurd and empty idea.

Adam Smith, as we have seen, naively gives expression to the most contradictory elements, and thus becomes the source, the point of departure, for diametrically opposed ideas. Malthus, relying on these observations of Smith's, makes a confused attempt—which is nevertheless founded on a correct perception and consciousness of an unresolved difficulty —to bring forward a new theory in opposition to Ricardo, and thus to gain pride of place. The transition from this attempt to the meaningless vulgar view is effected as follows:

If we look at the utilization of a commodity as capital—that is, in its exchange with living productive labor—we find that the commodity commands, in the equivalent reproduced by the worker, a surplus of labor time over and above the labor time contained in it, a surplus which constitutes the source of profit. If we now transfer to the *value* of the commodity the concepts appropriate to this *utilization of it as capital*, then each buyer of the commodity must stand in the same relationship to it as a worker does, that is, when buying the commodity, he must give in exchange for it an additional quantity of labor over and above the quantity which it contains. Since *apart from the workers* the other buyers do *not* stand in the same relationship to the commodity as a worker does (even when the worker appears simply as a buyer of commodities, as we have seen, the original basic distinction is maintained indirectly), it must be supposed that when they give in exchange for it a greater quantity of labor than it contains, they do not do this directly, but by giving a value which contains a greater quantity of labor, which amounts to the same thing. The transition is effected by means of this "greater quantity of labor, or, what amounts to the same thing, the value of a greater quantity of labor." What it actually comes down to, then, is this: the value of a commodity consists in the value which the buyer pays for it, and this value is equal to the equivalent (value) of the commodity plus an excess over and above this value, surplus value. Thus we arrive at the vulgar concept. Profit arises from the fact that a commodity *is sold dearer than it is bought.* The buyer buys it for a greater quantity of labor, or embodied labor, than it has cost the seller.

But if the buyer [is] himself a capitalist, a seller of commodities, and if his money—his capital—only represents sold commodities, then it merely follows from this that both [buyer and seller] must sell each other their commodities too dear, thus mutually swindling one another—and swindling one another to the same extent, too, if they both realize only the general rate of profit. From where, then, are the buyers to come who will pay the capitalist a quantity of labor which is equal to the labor contained in his commodity plus his profit? Take an example. A commodity costs the seller ten shillings. He sells it for twelve shillings. By this means he commands not just ten shillings worth of labor, but an additional two shillings worth. But the buyer likewise sells his commodity, which costs ten shillings, for twelve shillings.

Thus each loses as buyer what he has gained as seller. The working class constitutes the only exception. For, since the price of the product is raised above its cost price, they can only buy back a portion of the product, so that another portion of the product, or the price of this other portion, constitutes the capitalist's profit. But since this profit arises from the very fact that the workers are unable to buy back more than a portion of the product, the capitalist class can never realize its profit through the demand of the workers alone. It can never realize it by exchanging the whole product for the wage; on the contrary, it can only do so by exchanging the *whole* wage for no more than a portion of the product. Consequently, a demand other than that of the workers, buyers other than the workers themselves, are necessary, or there would be no profit. Where are they going to come from? If they are themselves capitalists, themselves sellers, then we have the above-mentioned mutual swindling within the capitalist class—each nominally raises the price of the commodity which he sells to the other, and each gains as seller what he loses as buyer. Thus [according to Malthus] *it is necessary to have buyers who are not sellers*, in order that the capitalist [can] realize his profit and sell the commodities "at their value." Hence the necessity for landowners, retired officials (*Pensionäre*), holders of sinecures, parsons, etc., not forgetting their lackeys and other hangers-on. How these "buyers" come to acquire the means of buying—how they must first take away from the capitalists a portion of their product without furnishing an equivalent in order to buy back less than an equivalent with what they have thus taken away—Malthus does not explain. Anyway, this is the basis of his plea for the greatest possible increase in the unproductive classes, so that the seller should find a market, a demand for his supply. And it is for this reason too that the author of the tract on population preaches constant over-consumption, and the appropriation by idlers of as large as possible a proportion of the annual product, as a condition of production. By way of further justification—in addition to that which necessarily follows from the theory—Malthus maintains that capital represents the *impulse towards abstract wealth, the impulse towards profit (Verwertungstrieb)*, which however can only be realized by means of a class of buyers who represent the impulse towards *spending, consumption and prodigality*—that is, the unproductive classes, who are buyers without being sellers. On this basis a pretty squabble [developed] in the '20s between Malthusians and Ricardians (from 1820 to 1830, on the whole, is the great metaphysical period in English political economy). The Ricardians, just like the Malthusians, consider it necessary that the laborer should not himself appropriate his [whole] product, but that a portion of it should go to the capitalist, in order that the worker should have an *incentive to produce*, thus ensuring the growth of wealth. But they are very angry about the Malthusians' view that the landlords, holders of Church and State sinecures, and a whole flock of idle retainers[12] must first appropriate a portion of the capitalists' product without giving any equivalent for it—exactly as the capitalist does in relation to the worker—in order that they may then buy from [the capitalists], at a price which gives a profit to the latter, their own commodities. The Ricardians, however, put up the same argument as against the worker. In order that accumulation should increase, and with it the demand for labor, the worker must gratuitously surrender to the capitalist as much of his own product as possible, so that the capitalist can change back into capital the net revenue which has thus come into existence. The Malthusians [argue] in just the same way. As much as possible [ought] to be taken away for nothing from the industrial capitalists, in the form of rent, taxes, etc., in order that they

12. "Retainers" is in both German and English in the text.—Ed.

should be able to sell back to their involuntary "partners," at a profit, the remaining portion which they retain. According to both the Ricardians and the Malthusians, the worker must not appropriate his own product, lest he lose the incentive to work. The industrial capitalist must give up a portion of his product to the classes which do nothing but consume—*fruges consumere nati*—in order that the latter may again exchange with him, on unfavorable terms, what he has given up. Otherwise the capitalist would lose the incentive to produce, which consists precisely in the fact that he makes a large profit, selling his commodity far above its value. We shall come back again later to this comical struggle. First, [a few more quotations] to show that Malthus comes round to the thoroughly commonplace concept:

> Whatever may be the number of intermediate acts of barter which may take place in regard to commodities—whether the producers send them to China, or sell them in the place where they are produced: the question as to an adequate market for them, depends exclusively upon whether the producers can replace their capitals with ordinary profits, so as to enable them successfully to go on with their business. But what are their capitals? They are, as Adam Smith states, the tools to work with, the materials to work upon, and the means of commanding the necessary quantity of labor (*Definitions*, Cazenove's ed., p. 70).

And this, he imagines, is all the labor bestowed upon a commodity.

Profit is an *excess* over and above the labor thus expended upon the production of the commodity. Thus in reality it is only a nominal addition to the cost price of the commodity. And in order that no doubt concerning his opinion should remain, he quotes approvingly from Colonel Torrens (*On the Production of Wealth*, 1821, ch. 6, sec. 6) in confirmation of his own view: "Effectual demand consists in the power and inclination, on the part of consumers,[13] to give for commodities, either by immediate or circuitous barter, some greater proportion of all the ingredients of capital than their production costs" (*Definitions,* Cazenove's ed., pp. 70–71).[14]

And Cazenove himself, the editor, apologist and annotator of Malthus's *Definitions,* says:

> Profit does not depend upon the proportion in which commodities are exchanged with each other [15] (seeing that the same proportion may be maintained under every variety of profit), but upon the proportion which goes to wages, or is required to cover the prime costs, and which is in all cases determined by the degree in which the sacrifice made by the purchaser (or the labor's worth which he gives) in order to acquire a commodity, exceeds *that* made by the producer, in order to bring it to market (*ibid.,* p. 46).

In order to arrive at these wonderful results, Malthus had to indulge in a considerable amount of theoretical spadework. First and foremost, [having taken up] that side of Adam Smith's doctrine according to which the value of a commodity is equal to the quantity of labor which it commands or by means of which it is commanded or against which it is exchanged, it was necessary to dispose of the

13. The antithesis between buyer and seller becomes one between consumer and producer.
14. This is a paraphrase by Malthus of certain passages appearing on pp. 342 ff. of Torrens's book, and not a direct quotation.—Ed.
15. For if we took account only of the exchange of commodities between capitalists, then, since there is no exchange with workers who have at their disposal *no* commodity other than labor to exchange with the capitalist, Malthus's theory would appear absurd, because there would be merely a mutual raising of prices, a nominal rise in the prices of their commodities. Therefore the exchange of commodities must be abstracted from, and people who do *not* produce commodities must exchange money.

objections which had been brought forward against this view that value could be a measure of value by Adam Smith himself, by his successors—and also even by Malthus.

Malthus's work *The Measure of Value, etc.* (London, 1823) is a very model of intellectual imbecility, winding its way casuistically through its own inner confusion. Its difficult and clumsy style leaves the [open-minded] and insufficiently instructed reader with the impression that the difficulty of making clarity out of the confusion does not lie in the contradiction between confusion and clarity, but in a lack of understanding on the part of the reader himself.

What Malthus had to do first of all was to obliterate again the distinction which Ricardo had made between "value of labor" and "quantity of labor," and to reduce the two conceptions which had stood side by side in Smith's work to one—the incorrect one.

> Any given quantity of labor must be of the same value as the wages which command it, or for which it actually exchanges (*The Measure of Value*, p. 5).

What this statement aims to do is to reduce the expressions *quantity of labor* and *value of labor* to an identity. In itself the statement expresses a mere tautology, an absurd commonplace. Since the wages, or that "for which it (the quantity of labor) actually exchanges," constitute the *value* of this quantity of labor, it is a tautology to say that the *value* of a given quantity of labor is equal to the *wages*, or to the quantity of money or commodities for which this labor is exchanged. In other words, this means nothing else but that the exchange value of a given quantity of labor is equal to its exchange value, *alias* wages. But, even if we leave aside the fact that it is not labor but labor power which is directly exchanged for wages—it is through mixing up these concepts that the nonsense is made possible—even if we leave this aside, it does not in any way follow from what was stated above that a given quantity of labor is equal to the quantity of labor worked up in the wages, or in the money or the commodities in which the wages are expressed. If a worker works for twelve hours and receives as wages the product of six hours, then this product of six hours (since it constitutes the wages, the commodity which is exchanged for the labor) constitutes the value of twelve hours' labor. It does not follow from this that six hours' labor is equal to twelve hours', or that the commodity in which six hours' labor is expressed is equal to the commodity in which twelve hours' is expressed. It does not follow that the value of the wages is equal to the value of the product in which the labor is expressed. It only follows that the value of a given quantity of labor (since the value of labor is measured by the value of labor power, and not by the labor carried out by this labor power) contains less labor than it purchases; and that therefore the *value of the commodity* in which the labor purchased is expressed is very different from the value of the commodities with which this given quantity of labor was purchased or commanded. Malthus draws the opposite conclusion. Since the *value* of a given quantity of labor is equal to its value, it follows, according to him, that the value in which this quantity of labor is expressed is equal to the value of the wages. Hence it follows further that the immediate labor (that is, the labor after the means of production have been deducted) which is absorbed or contained in a commodity does not create a value greater than that which is paid for it—that it only reproduces the value of the wages. From this alone it is self-evident that profit cannot be explained if the value of commodities is determined by the labor contained in them, and that another explanation must be found—that is, if we assume that the value of a commodity must include the profit which it realizes. For the labor worked up in it consists, first, of the labor which is contained in the worn-out machinery, etc., and which therefore reappears in the value of the product; and, second, of the labor contained in the raw materials which are used up. Obviously the labor contained in these two elements before the production of the new commodity does not increase by virtue of the fact that they become elements in the production of a new commodity. Thus there remains, third, the labor contained in the wages which were exchanged for the living labor. But according to Malthus the latter is no greater than the embodied labor for which it was exchanged. Hence it follows that if the value of a commodity were determined by the labor contained in it, it would not yield any profit. Consequently, if it does yield a profit, the latter is an *excess* of its price over and above the labor contained in it. In order to be sold at its value (which includes profit), the commodity must therefore command a quantity of labor equal to the quantity of labor used to produce it, plus an excess quantity of labor representing the profit yielded in the sale of the commodity.

Further, in order that *labor*—not the quantity of labor required for production, but labor as a commodity—should serve as a measure of value, Malthus asserts (*The Measure of Value*, p. 29, fn.) that "*the value of labor is constant.*"[16] There is nothing original in this—it is simply a paraphrase and further elaboration of the thesis put forward by Adam Smith in Book 1, chapter 5, of the *Wealth of Nations*:

> Equal quantities of labor, at all times and places, may be said to be of equal value to the laborer. In his ordinary state of health, strength and spirits . . . he must always lay down the same portion of his ease, his liberty, and his happiness. The price which he pays must always be the same, whatever may be the quantity of goods which he receives in return for it. Of these, indeed, it may sometimes purchase a

16. A paraphrase, not a direct quotation.—Ed.

greater and sometimes a smaller quantity; but it is their value which varies, not that of the labor which purchases them. At all times and places that is dear which it is difficult to come at, or which it costs much labor to acquire; and that cheap which is to be had easily, or with very little labor. Labor alone, therefore, never varying in its own value, is alone the ultimate and real standard by which the value of all commodities can at all times and places be estimated and compared (*Wealth of Nations,* Cannan's ed., vol. 1, p. 35).

Also [related to this is] Malthus's discovery—of which he is so proud and which he says he was the first to make—namely, that value is equal to the quantity of labor contained in a commodity, plus a quantity of labor which represents the profit. But this discovery, too, appears [to be] quite simply an amalgamation of the two theses put forward by Smith (Malthus can never get away from being a plagiarist):

The real value of all the different component parts of price, it must be observed, is measured by the quantity of labor which they can, each of them, purchase or command. Labor measures the value not only of that part of price which resolves itself into labor, but of that which resolves itself into rent, and of that which resolves itself into profit (*ibid.,* p. 52).

Malthus says in this connection:

If the demand for labor rises, the greater earnings of the laborer are occasioned, not by a rise in the value of labor, but by a fall in the value of the produce for which the labor is exchanged. And in the case of an abundance of labor, the small earnings of the laborer are occasioned by a rise in the value of the produce, and not by a fall in the value of the labor (*The Measure of Value*, p. 35; cf. pp. 33–34).[17]

17. In part a paraphrase, not a direct quotation.—Ed.

In the following passage, Bailey very effectively ridicules Malthus's *reasoning* to the effect that the value of labor is invariable—[in connection with which it should be noted that] Malthus's additional line of argument is not that of Smith:

> In the same way any article might be proved to be of invariable value; for instance, ten yards of cloth. For whether we gave £5 or £10 for the ten yards, the sum given would always be equal in value to the cloth for which it was paid, or, in other words, of invariable value in relation to cloth. But that which is given for a thing of invariable value, must itself be invariable, whence the ten yards of cloth must be of invariable value. ... It is just the same kind of futility to call wages invariable in value, because though variable in quantity they command the same portion of labor, as to call the sum given for a hat, of invariable value, because, although sometimes more and sometimes less, it always purchases the hat (Samuel Bailey, *A Critical Dissertation on the Nature, Measures, and Causes of Value, etc.,* London, 1825, pp. 145–47).

In the same work, Bailey ridicules very caustically the absurd arithmetical tables, with their pretensions to profundity, with which Malthus "illustrates" his measure of value. In his *Definitions in Political Economy*, Malthus gives vent to his anger over Bailey's sarcasm, and among other things tries as follows to prove that the value of labor is invariable: "While there is one large class of commodities, such as raw products, which in the progress of society tends to rise as compared with labor, there is another large class of commodities, such as manufactured articles, which at the same time tends to fall; [therefore] it may not be far from the truth to say, that the portion of the average mass of commodities which a given quantity of labor will command in the same country, during the course of some centuries, may not very essentially vary" (*Definitions*, 1827 ed., p. 206).

According to Malthus, the value of labor never changes, but only the value of the commodity which I receive for it. Let us assume that at one time wages equal two shillings for one working day, while at another time they equal one shilling. In the first case the capitalist gives twice as many shillings for the same labor time as he does in the second. But in the second case the worker gives double the quantity of labor for the same product as he does in the first, for in the second case he gives a whole working day for one shilling and in the first only half a working day. Malthus believes, then, that the capitalist gives now more, now fewer shillings for the same labor. What he does not see is that the worker, in exactly the same way, gives more or less labor for a given product.

> Giving more produce for a given quantity of labor, or getting more labor for a given quantity of produce, are one and the same thing in his "view" [Malthus's]; instead of being, as one would have supposed, just the contrary! (*Observations on Certain Verbal Disputes in Political Economy, etc.*, London, 1821, p. 52)

Earlier in the latter work we read the following:

> [Mr. Malthus says:] "In the *same* place, and at the *same* time, the different quantities of day labor, which different commodities can command, will be exactly in proportion to their relative values in exchange," and vice versa. *If* this is true of labor, it is just as true of anything else (*ibid.,* p. 49).
>
> *Money* does very well as a measure at the same time and place. ... But it [Malthus's statement] seems *not* to be true of labor. Labor is not a measure even at the same time and place. Take a portion of corn, such as is at the same time and place said to be

of equal value with a given diamond; will the corn and the diamond, paid in specie, command equal portions of labor? It may be said ... No; but the diamond will buy *money*, which will command an equal portion of labor. ... The test is of no use, for it cannot be applied without being *rectified* by the application of the other test, which it professed to supersede. We can only infer, that the corn and the diamond will command equal quantities of labor, *because* they are of equal value, in money. But we were told to infer, that two things were of equal value, because they would command equal quantities of labor (*ibid.,* pp. 49–50).

It is noted quite correctly in these *Observations* that labor as a measure of value in the sense in which Malthus uses it here, in accordance with one of Smith's concepts, would serve as a measure of value in just the same way as any other commodity, and that in practice it would not be as good as money. Here our whole concern would be only with a measure of value in the sense in which money is a measure of value.

It is never at all the *measure of values* (in the sense of money) which makes commodities commensurable. See my book [*The Critique of Political Economy*], Book 1, p. 45: "It is rather the commensurability of commodities as embodied labor time, that turns gold into money."[18] As values commodities constitute a *unity*, mere expressions of one and the same unity, social labor. The *measure of value* (money) presupposes them as values, and relates only to the expression and the magnitude of these values. The *measure of value* of commodities always relates to the transformation of values into prices, and already presupposes value.

18. In the Kerr ed. of the *Critique* this sentence (in a slightly different translation) will be found on pp. 78–79. In the German original "gold into money" appears as *"Geld zu Geld."*—Ed.

Just as prettily as in the case of the "invariable value of labor," Malthus proves that a rise in the money price of wages must cause a general rise in the money prices of commodities. "If the money wages of labor universally rise, the value of money proportionably falls; and when the value of money falls . . . the prices of goods always rise (*Definitions*, 1827 ed., p. 34).

If the value of money has fallen relatively to labor, then what has to be proved is that the value of all commodities has risen relatively to money, or that the value of money, measured not in labor but in other commodities, has [fallen]. And Malthus proves this by presupposing it.

Malthus's polemic against Ricardo's analysis of value is taken entirely from the propositions, first put forward by Ricardo himself, concerning the modifications which are brought about in the exchange values of commodities, independently of the labor contained in them, by differences in the composition of capital arising out of the process of circulation of capital—different proportions of circulating and fixed capital, different degrees of durability of the fixed capital employed, and different times of turnover of the circulating capital. In short, it rests on Ricardo's confusion between price of production and value—on the fact that he regards the leveling out of the prices of production, which are independent of the quantity of labor applied in the separate spheres of production, as a modification of the values themselves, thus abandoning the whole principle. Malthus takes up these contradictions, which were first discovered by Ricardo himself and brought forward by him against the determination of value by labor time, not in order to resolve them, but in order to revert to absolutely empty concepts, putting forward the *expression* of the contradictory phenomena, their translation into words, as if this were their resolution. In the section below dealing with the dissolution of the Ricardian school, we shall see the same

method used by Mill and McCulloch, who try to talk the
contradictory phenomena into direct accord with the general
law by means of absurdly scholastic definitions and dis-
tinctions, in order to argue the contradictions away—but in
the process the foundation itself goes west. Here are some
of the passages in which Malthus directs against Ricardo
the arguments which Ricardo himself had provided against
the law of value:

> It is observed by Adam Smith that corn is an annual
> crop, butchers' meat a crop which requires four or
> five years to grow; and consequently, if we compare
> two quantities of corn and beef which are of equal
> exchangeable value, it is certain that a difference of
> three or four additional years profit at fifteen per
> cent upon the capital employed in the production of
> the beef would, exclusively of any other consider-
> ations, make up in value for a much smaller quantity
> of labor, and thus we might have two commodities
> of the same exchangeable value, while the accumu-
> lated and immediate labor of the one was forty or
> fifty per cent less than that of the other. This is an
> event of daily occurrence in reference to a vast mass
> of the most important commodities in the country;
> and if profits were to fall from fifteen per cent to
> eight per cent the value of beef compared with corn
> would fall above twenty per cent (*The Measure of
> Value*, pp. 10–11).

Now capital consists of commodities, and a large part of
the commodities of which it is constituted or which enter
into it possesses a price (that is, exchange value in the ordinary sense) which consists neither of accumulated nor of
living labor, but—insofar as we consider only this particular
commodity—of a purely nominal increase [in] value, caused
through the addition of the average profit. Therefore
Malthus says:

Labor is not the only element worked up in capital (*Definitions*, Cazenove's ed., p. 29). What are the costs of production? ... The quantity of labor in kind required to be worked up in the commodity, and in the tools and materials consumed in its production with such an additional quantity as is equivalent to the ordinary profits upon the advances for the time that they have been advanced (*ibid.*, pp. 74–75).

On the same grounds Mr. Mill is quite incorrect, in calling capital hoarded labor. It may, perhaps, be called hoarded labor and profits; but certainly not hoarded labor alone, unless we determine to call profits labor (*ibid.*, pp. 60–61).

To say that the values of commodities are regulated or determined by the quantity of *Labor and Capital* necessary to produce them, is essentially false. To say that they are regulated by the quantity of *Labor and Profits* necessary to produce them, is essentially true (*ibid.*, p. 129).

With reference to this point, Cazenove remarks:

The expression *Labor and Profits* is liable to this objection, that the two are not correlative terms—labor being an *agent* and profits a *result*; the one a *cause*, the other a *consequence*. On this account Mr. Senior has substituted for it the expression *Labor and Abstinence*. ... It must be acknowledged, indeed, that it is not the abstinence, but the *use* of the capital productively, which is the cause of profits (*ibid.*, p. 130, fn.).

For, according to Senior—

He who converts his revenue into capital, *abstains* from the enjoyment which its expenditure would afford him (*ibid.*).[19]

19. This is Cazenove's summary of Senior's views, and not a direct quotation from Senior.—Ed.

A fine explanation! The value of a commodity consists of the labor contained in it plus the profit—of labor which is contained in it, and of labor which is not contained in it but which must be paid for.

Here is another of Malthus's polemics against Ricardo:

> [Ricardo's] proposition that as the value of wages rises profits proportionably fall, cannot be true, except on the assumption that commodities, which have the same quantity of labor worked up in them, are always of the same value, an assumption which probably will not be found to be true in one case out of five hundred; and this, not from accidental or temporary causes, but from that natural and necessary state of things, which, in the progress of civilization and improvement, tends continually to increase the quantity of fixed capital employed, and to render more various and unequal the times of the returns of the circulating capital (*Definitions*, 1827 ed., pp. 31–32).

The same idea is to be found on pp. 53–54 of Cazenove's edition, where Malthus says literally: Ricardo's measure of value is contrary to the natural state of things, since this state of things "in the progress of civilization and improvement, tends continually to increase the quantity of fixed capital employed, and to render more various and unequal the times of the returns of the circulating capital" (*Definitions*, Cazenove's ed., pp. 53–54).

> Mr. Ricardo, indeed, himself admits of considerable exceptions to his rule; but if we examine the classes which come under his exceptions, that is, where the quantities of fixed capital employed are different and of different degrees of duration, and where the periods of the returns of the circulating capital employed are not the same, we shall find that they are so numerous, that the rule may be considered as the exception, and the exceptions the rule (*ibid.*, p. 50).

Malthus, in conformity with the above, defines value as follows:

> The estimation in which a commodity is held, founded upon its *cost to the purchaser* or the *sacrifice* which *he* must make in order to acquire it, which sacrifice is measured by the quantity of labor that he gives in exchange for it, *or* [20] what comes to the same thing, by the labor which it will command (*ibid.*, pp. 8–9).

Cazenove also points out the following as a difference between Malthus and Ricardo:

> Mr. Ricardo has, with Adam Smith, adopted labor as the true standard of cost; but he has applied it to the *producing cost* only. . . . It is equally applicable as a measure of *cost to the purchaser (ibid.,* pp. 56–57).

In other words, the value of a commodity is equal to the sum of money which the buyer must pay, and this sum of money is best estimated in terms of the quantity of simple labor which can be bought with it. [21] But how the sum of money is determined is of course not stated. This is the completely commonplace way of looking at the matter which we meet with in everyday life. It is mere banality, expressed in high-sounding phrases. All that it means, to put it another way, is that *price of production* and *value* are identical—a confusion which in the case of Adam Smith and even more of Ricardo stands in contradiction to their real concepts, but which in the case of Malthus is now raised to the status of a law. This is the concept of value held by the Philistine who is steeped in competition and knows nothing

---

20. Marx's emphasis.—Ed.
21. Malthus *presupposes* the *existence of profit,* in order subsequently to measure the magnitude of its value with an extrinsic measuring-rod. He does not touch on the question of the origin and intrinsic possibility of profit.

except its outward show. How is the price of production determined? By the magnitude of the advanced capital plus profit. And how is the profit determined? What is the origin of the fund out of which it is paid? Where does the surplus product come from in which this surplus value is expressed? If it is only a matter of a nominal rise in the money price, then there is nothing simpler than to raise the value of commodities. And how is the value of the advanced capital determined? By the *value* of the labor contained in it, says Malthus. And how is the latter determined? By the *value* of the commodities in which the wages are laid out. And the value of these commodities? By the value of the labor plus profit. And so we go on, in a vicious circle. If we suppose that the worker is actually paid the value of his labor—i.e., that the commodities (or the sum of money) which form his wages are equal to the value (sum of money) of the commodities in which his labor is realized, so that if he receives wages of 100 shillings he contributes only 100 shillings in value to the raw material, etc., in short to the advanced capital—then profit can only consist of an addition which the seller makes in the sale to the *real* value of the commodity. And this is done by every seller. Thus insofar as capitalists exchange commodities with one another, no one can realize anything by means of this addition, and least of all can a surplus fund be formed in this way from which they can draw their revenue. Only those capitalists whose commodities enter into the consumption of the working class will make a real and not an imaginary profit, since they will sell back the commodities to the workers dearer than they have bought them from them. They will sell back to the workers for 110 shillings a commodity which they have bought from them for 100. This means that they will sell back to them only $\frac{10}{11}$ of the product, keeping $\frac{1}{11}$ for themselves. But what does this mean other than that of the eleven hours, say, which the worker has worked, he is only paid ten; that he is only given the product of ten hours, while one hour or the product of one hour falls to the capitalist without payment of any equivalent? And what in turn does this mean other than that—with reference to the working class—profit is made by their giving a portion of their labor *gratuitously* to the capitalist, and that consequently the "*quantity* of labor [expended]" does not mean the same as the "*value* of labor [expended]"? The other capitalists, however, since they cannot resort to this expedient, will only make an imaginary profit.

How little Malthus has understood of Ricardo's elementary propositions, and how completely he fails to grasp the fact that profit can arise otherwise than through an addition to the price, is strikingly shown, among other things, by the following statement:

> Allowing that the first commodities, if completed and brought into use immediately, might be the result of pure labor, and that their value would therefore be determined by the quantity of that labor; yet it is quite impossible that such commodities should be employed as capital to assist in the production of other commodities, without the capitalist being deprived of the use of his advances for a certain period, and requiring a remuneration in the shape of profits. In the early periods of society, on account of the comparative scarcity of these advances of labor, this remuneration would be high, and would affect the value of such commodities to a considerable degree, owing to the high rate of profits. In the more advanced stages of society, the value of capital and commodities is largely affected by profits, on account of the greatly increased quantity of fixed capital employed, and the greater length of time for which much of the circulating capital is advanced before the capitalist is repaid by the returns. In both cases, the rate at which commodities exchange with each other, is essentially affected by

the varying amount of profits (*Definitions*, Caze-nove's ed., p. 60).

The concept of *relative* wages is one of the greatest merits of Ricardo. The essence of it is that the *value of wages* (and therefore also of *profit*) is absolutely dependent upon the relation which the portion of the working day in which the *worker works for himself* (for the production or repro-duction of his wages) bears to the portion of his time which belongs to the capitalist. This is important from the point of view of economics: in fact, it is only another way of stating the correct theory of surplus value. It is also important from the point of view of the social relations between the two classes. Malthus gets wind of something amiss here, and is therefore obliged to state his objections:

> No writer that I have met with, anterior to Mr. Ricardo, ever used the term wages, or real wages, as implying proportions.[22] Profits, indeed, imply pro-portions; and the rate of profits had always justly been estimated by a percentage upon the value of the advances.[23] But wages had uniformly been con-sidered as rising or falling, not according to any *pro-portion* which they might bear to the whole produce obtained by a certain quantity of labor, but by the greater or smaller quantity of any particular produce received by the laborer, or by the greater or smaller

22. Ricardo speaks of the *value* of wages, which is certainly also ex-pressed as the portion of the product which falls to the worker.
23. Even Malthus himself finds it impossible to say what he means by "the value of the advances," and it is indeed difficult to do so. Accord-ing to him, the value of a commodity is equal to the advanced capital contained in it plus profit. Now since the advanced capital, leaving aside the immediate labor, also consists of commodities, the value of the advanced capital is equal to the advanced capital contained in it plus profit. Thus profit is equal to profit on the advanced capital plus profit. And so ad infinitum.

power which such produce would convey, of commanding the necessaries and conveniences of life (*Definitions*, 1827 ed., pp. 29–30).

Since in capitalist production it is *exchange value*—the increase of exchange value—which is the immediate aim, it is important to know how to measure it. Since the value of the advanced capital is expressed in money (real money or money of account), the extent of this increase is measured by the monetary magnitude of the capital itself, and a capital (sum of money) of a given magnitude—100—is taken as a measuring-rod. Malthus says:

Profits consist of the difference between the value of the capital advanced, and the value of the commodity when sold or used (*ibid.*, p. 241).

3 Malthus on Overproduction and Overconsumption

From Marx's *Theories of Surplus Value,*
vol. 3 (written 1861-63)

From Malthus's theory of value there springs the whole doctrine of the necessity for an ever-increasing unproductive consumption, a doctrine which this theoretician of overpopulation (arising from a lack of means of subsistence) has preached so emphatically. The value of a commodity is equal to the value of the advanced materials, machinery, etc., plus the quantity of immediate labor contained in it, which with Malthus is made equal to the *value* of the wages contained in it, plus an addition of profit on these advances according to the level of the general rate of profit. This nominal addition to the price forms the profit, and is a condition of the supply, that is, of the reproduction of the commodity. These elements make up the price for the buyer, as distinct from the price for the producer; and the price for the buyer is the real value of the commodity. The question now arises, how is this price to be realized? Who is to pay it? And out of which fund is it to be paid?

When considering Malthus's theory, we must make the following distinction (which Malthus himself neglected to make). One section of the capitalists produces commodities which enter *directly* into the consumption of the workers. Another section produces either commodities which enter into this consumption *only* indirectly, that is, by entering as raw materials, machinery, etc., into the capital necessary for the production of means of subsistence; or commodities which *do not enter at all into the consumption* of the workers, since they enter only into the revenue of the non-workers.

[*A passage of about 4,500 words is omitted here.* In this passage—which consists largely of rather sketchy notes obviously intended for later elaboration—Marx assumes for the moment that Malthus's account of value and surplus value is true, and asks whether it would in fact be possible, on this assumption, for the capitalists to realize a profit on the sale of their commodities. Marx argues that the first section of the capitalists—those who produce "commodities which enter *directly* into the consumption of the workers"—could in fact create a real "surplus fund" for themselves merely by making a "nominal addition" to the price of their commodities. By making such an addition, these capitalists could render their workers incapable of buying back their whole product with the wages paid to them, so that the capitalists would thus be able to appropriate a portion of it for themselves. But no other section of the capitalists (on Malthus's assumptions) would be able to create a "surplus fund" artificially in this way. The only way in which these other capitalists could realize a profit would be by making an advantageous exchange with the first section of the capitalists, thus indirectly participating to some extent in the surplus product appropriated from the workers by that section. The main point which Marx is concerned to emphasize in all this is that no profit at all can be "created" or "realized" *merely* through exchanges between capitalists in which the parties simply make a "nominal addition" to the prices of the commodities they sell. It is clear that if this were the case everyone would lose as buyer just as much as he gained as seller, and no profit would result. Profit can only arise if a *real* "surplus fund" is created—and this in fact can only happen through the exploitation of the workers.—*Ed.*]

It is difficult to understand how any profit at all can

originate from these exchanges, in which the parties sell one another their commodities at prices which are uniformly increased, thus defrauding one another in the same proportion.

This defect would be remedied if, in addition to the exchanges of one class of capitalists with their workers and the exchanges of the different classes of capitalists among themselves, there were also exchanges with a *third class of buyers* —a *deus ex machina,* a class which would pay for the commodities at their nominal value without in its turn reselling them, without in its turn carrying on the farce; a class, that is, which passes through the stage M—C, but not through M—C—M; a class which buys without selling. In this case the capitalists would not realize their profit by exchanging their commodities among themselves. They would realize it, in the first place, by means of an exchange with the workers, to whom they would sell back a portion of the whole product for the same money which they have spent in buying the whole product from them (constant capital having been deducted). And they would realize it, in the second place, by means of a sale of a portion both of means of subsistence and luxury goods to the third group of buyers. Since the latter pay 110 for 100, without in their turn selling 100 for 110, a profit of ten per cent—a profit which would not be merely nominal—would thus in fact be realized. This profit would have a two-fold origin, in that as little as possible of the whole product would be sold back to the workers, and as much as possible would be sold to the third class which pays in ready cash without itself selling, which buys in order to consume. But buyers who are not at the same time sellers must be consumers who are not at the same time producers— i.e., *unproductive consumers*; and it is by means of this class of unproductive consumers that Malthus resolves the conflict. But these unproductive consumers must at the same time be solvent consumers; they must engender a real demand, and the sums of money which they possess and which they spend every year must be sufficient to pay not only the production value of the commodities which they buy and consume, but also the nominal addition of profit, the surplus value, the difference between the sale value and the production value. In society, this class will represent consumption for the sake of consumption, just as the capitalist class represents production for the sake of production; the one the "passion for expenditure" and the other the "passion for accumulation" (*Principles*, 2nd ed., p. 326). The impulse towards accumulation is kept alive in the capitalist class through the fact that their receipts constantly [run] at a higher level than their outlays—and it is profit, of course, which supplies the incentive to accumulate. In spite of this zeal of theirs for accumulation, they are not driven into overproduction, or at least only with great difficulty, since the *unproductive consumers* not only form a huge channel for the products which are thrown onto the market, but also refrain from throwing any products onto the market themselves. Thus, however many of them there may be, they do not represent any competition for the capitalists; rather, they all simply constitute a demand without a supply, and they therefore compensate the preponderance of supply over demand on the capitalist side.

But where do the annual means of payment of this class come from? To begin with, the class includes the *landowners*, who appropriate a large part of the annual product under the name of rent, and who spend the money which they have thus taken from the capitalists in the consumption of the commodities produced by the capitalists—a transaction in which they are defrauded. These landowners must not themselves be producers, and, in general, they are not producers. It is important that, insofar as they spend money in purchasing labor, they should not maintain any productive workers, but only co-consumers of their wealth—*menial servants*, who keep the price of means of subsistence high by buying them without themselves helping to increase their supply or that of any other commodity. But these rent-receivers are not enough to create "a sufficient demand." Recourse must be had to artificial methods. These consist in heavy *taxes*, a host of holders of State and Church sinecures, great armies, retired officials, tithes for the parsons, a considerable national debt, and from time to time costly wars. Such are Malthus's "remedies" (*Principles*, 2nd ed., pp. 408 ff.).

Thus the third class, which Malthus brings in as a "remedy," a class which buys without selling and consumes without producing, receives in the first instance a considerable portion of the value of the annual product without *paying* for it, and enriches the producers by virtue of the fact that the latter, having first had to cede to it gratuitously the money required for the purchase of their commodities, subsequently appropriate this money once more by selling their commodities above their value to this class, thus receiving back from it more value in the form of money than they supply to it in the form of commodities. And this transaction goes on repeating itself every year.

Malthus's conclusions follow quite logically from his basic theory of value; but this theory of value itself is curiously in accord with his aim—to act as an apologist for the state of affairs in contemporary England, with its landlordism, "State and Church," retired officials, tax collectors, tithes, national debt, stock exchange jobbers, law-court officials (*Büttel*), parsons and hangers-on ("national expenditure"),[1] against which the Ricardians fought as so many useless, outlived, detrimental and malignant phenomena of bourgeois production. Ricardo disinterestedly defends bourgeois production insofar as it [stands for] as unbridled a development as possible of the social forces of production. He is unconcerned with the fate of the agents of production, whether

1. The words in brackets are in English in the text.—Ed.

they be capitalists or workers. He maintained the *historical* validity and necessity of this stage of development. If his historical sense of the past was very weak, his perception of the mainspring of historical development in his own times was correspondingly strong. Malthus, too, wants as free a development as possible of capitalist production, insofar as only the poverty of its main agents, the working class, is a condition of this development; but according to him this production should at the same time adapt itself to the "needs of consumption" of the aristocracy and its representatives in State and Church, and serve as a material basis for the obsolete demands of those who represent interests inherited from feudalism and absolute monarchy. Malthus wants bourgeois production insofar as it is not revolutionary, insofar as it is not a historical force, but merely creates a broader and more convenient material basis for the "old" society.

First, then, we have the working class, which because of the principle of population is always too numerous relatively to the means of subsistence allotted to it—i.e., over-population due to underproduction. Second, we have the capitalist class, which as a consequence of the same principle of population is always able to sell back their own product to the workers at such a price that they get back only just as much of it as is necessary to keep body and soul together. And third, we have an immense section of society which consists of parasites and self-indulgent drones, in part masters and in part servants, who appropriate gratuitously a considerable quantity of wealth—partly under the name of rent and partly under political titles—from the capitalist class, paying for the commodities produced by the latter above their value with the money they have taken from the capitalists themselves. The capitalist class is spurred on in production by the impulse towards accumulation; the unproductive classes, from the economic point of view, represent merely the impulse towards consumption and prodigality. And this is the only means of escape from overproduction, which exists alongside overpopulation relatively to production. Overconsumption by the classes standing outside production is [recommended] as the best remedy for both overproduction and overpopulation. The disproportion between the working population and production is neutralized by means of the consumption of a portion of the product by those who do not produce, by idlers. The disproportion represented by the overproduction of the capitalists [is canceled out] by the overconsumption of the extravagant rich.

We have seen how childishly weak, trivial and meaningless Malthus is when, basing himself on the weak side of Adam Smith, he tries to put forward a counter-theory in opposition to that formulated by Ricardo on the basis of the strong side of Adam Smith. One could hardly imagine a more comical exhibition of impotence than Malthus's work on value. But as soon as he comes on to the practical conclusions, thus once again entering the field which he occupied as a sort of economic Abraham à Sancta Clara,[2] he is entirely in his element. Nevertheless even here this born plagiarist remains true to himself. Who would think at first sight that Malthus's *Principles of Political Economy* was merely a Malthusianized version of Sismondi's *Nouveaux Principes de l'Economie Politique?* And yet this is in fact the case. Sismondi's book appeared in 1819. One year later Malthus's English caricature of it saw the light of day. Just as previously with Townsend and Anderson, so here too with Sismondi he found a theoretical foothold for one of his bulky economic tracts—in which, incidentally, the new theories which he had learned from Ricardo's *Principles* also came in handy.

Just as Malthus, when opposing Ricardo, fought against those tendencies of capitalist production which were

2. See fn. 12, p. 137, above.

revolutionary in relation to the old society, so with the unerring instinct of a parson he took from Sismondi only what
was reactionary in relation to capitalist production, in relation to modern bourgeois society.

I am excluding Sismondi from my historical survey, since
the criticism of his views pertains to a subject with which I
shall only be able to deal after the present work—the real
movement of capital (competition and credit).

To see that Malthus adopted Sismondi's views, one has
only to look at the heading of one of the chapters of
Malthus's *Principles of Political Economy*: "Of the Necessity
of a Union of the Powers of Production with the Means of
Distribution, in order to ensure a continued Increase of
Wealth" (*Principles*, 2nd ed., p. 361). We read in this
chapter:

> The powers of production, to whatever extent they
> may exist, are not alone sufficient to secure the
> creation of a proportionate degree of wealth. Some-
> thing else seems to be necessary in order to call these
> powers fully into action. This is an effectual and
> unchecked demand for all that is produced. And
> what appears to contribute most to the attainment
> of this object, is, such a *distribution of produce*,[3]
> and such an adaptation of this produce to the wants
> of those who are to consume it, as constantly to
> increase the exchangeable value of the whole mass
> (*Principles*, 2nd ed., p. 361).

Here is a further quotation, equally Sismondian and also
directed against Ricardo:

> The wealth of a country depends partly upon the
> quantity of produce obtained by its labor, and partly
> upon such an adaptation of this quantity to the
> wants and powers of the existing population as is

3. Marx's emphasis.—Ed.

calculated to give it value. Nothing can be more certain than that it is not determined by either of them alone. But where wealth and value are perhaps the most nearly connected, is in the *necessity of the latter to the production of the former*[4] (*ibid.*, p. 301).

This is specially directed against Ricardo—*Principles of Political Economy*, chapter 20, "Value and Riches, their Distinctive Properties."

Ricardo says here, among other things:

> Value, then, essentially differs from riches, for value depends not on abundance, but on the difficulty or facility of production (*Principles*, Sraffa's ed., vol. 1, p. 273).[5]
>
> Riches do not depend on value. A man is rich or poor, according to the abundance of necessaries and luxuries which he can command. ... It is through confounding the ideas of value and wealth, or riches that it has been asserted, that by diminishing the quantity of commodities, that is to say of the necessaries, conveniences, and enjoyments of human life, riches may be increased. If value were the measure of riches, this could not be denied, because by scarcity the value of commodities is raised; but if Adam Smith be correct, if riches consist in necessaries and enjoyments, then they cannot be increased by a diminution of quantity (*ibid.*, pp. 275–76).

4. Marx's emphasis.—Ed.
5. Incidentally, value can also rise together with the "facility of production." Suppose that in a particular country the population increases from one million to six million people, and that the one million had worked a twelve-hour day. Suppose also that the six million develop the forces of production to such an extent that each one, working a six-hour day, produces twice as much as was previously produced in that time. Then wealth would be increased sixfold, and value would increase to three times its former level, according to Ricardo's own view.

In other words, what Ricardo is saying here is this: Wealth consists only of *use values*. He transforms bourgeois production into simple production for use value, which is a fine way of looking at a mode of production dominated by *exchange value*. He regards the specific form of bourgeois wealth as something merely formal, not affecting its content. Hence he also denies the contradictions of bourgeois production, which break out in crises. Hence his completely false conception of money. Hence too, in the process of production of capital, he is not at all concerned with the process of circulation, insofar as it embraces the metamorphosis of commodities, the necessity for the transformation of capital into money. But no one has demonstrated better and more distinctly than Ricardo himself that bourgeois production is not the production of wealth for the *producers* (as he repeatedly calls the workers)—that is, that the production of bourgeois wealth is something entirely different from the production of "abundance," of "necessaries and enjoyments" for the people who produce them. And yet this ought to be the case if production were merely a means of satisfying the requirements of the producers, if production were dominated by use value alone. But the same Ricardo also says:

> If we lived in one of Mr. Owen's parallelograms, and enjoyed all our productions in common, then no one could suffer in consequence of abundance, but as long as society is constituted as it now is, abundance will often be injurious to producers and scarcity beneficial to them (*On Protection to Agriculture*, 1822, Sraffa's ed., vol. 4, p. 222)

Ricardo conceives of bourgeois production, or more exactly capitalist production, as the *absolute form* of production; thus its particular forms of production relations must never get involved in contradictions or fetter the aim of production, which is simply abundance. And this word includes both the mass of use values and their variety, which in their turn condition a rich development of man as producer and an all-round development of his productive abilities. Here Ricardo gets involved in a comical contradiction. When we are speaking about value and wealth, we should have in view only society as a whole. But in speaking of capital and labor, it goes without saying that "gross revenue" exists only in order to create "net revenue." In fact what Ricardo admires in bourgeois production is the fact that its particular forms, when compared with earlier forms, clear the way for an unrestrained development of the forces of production. When they cease to do this, or when the contradictions within which they do it come into prominence, he denies the contradictions, or, rather, expresses the contradictions themselves in a different form, by presenting *wealth as such*—the sum of use values—as something existing on its own, without any regard for the producers, as the *ultima Thule*.

Sismondi has a deeply-rooted presentiment that capitalist production is in contradiction with itself; that on the one hand its forms, its relations of production, stimulated an unbridled development of the productive forces and of wealth; that on the other hand these relations of production are subject to certain conditions; that their contradictions—between use value and exchange value, commodity and money, purchase and sale, production and consumption, capital and wage labor, etc.—are increasingly accentuated with the development of the productive forces. In particular, he senses the basic contradiction: on the one hand, the unfettered development of the productive forces and the growth of wealth, which at the same time consists of commodities requiring to be turned into money; on the other hand, as the foundation of the system, the limitation of the mass of producers to the necessary means of subsistence. For this reason crises for him are not accidents, as they are for Ricardo, but essential outbreaks of the inherent contradictions, occurring on a large scale and at definite periods. He is constantly vacillating: should the *productive forces* be held in check by the State in order to bring them into correspondence with the relations of production, or should the *relations of production* be held in check in order to bring them into correspondence with the productive forces? Here he often escapes into the past; he becomes a *laudator temporis acti,* and wants to mitigate the contradictions by means of the establishment of a different relationship between revenue and capital, or between distribution and production. He does not understand that the relations of distribution are merely the relations of production *sub alia specie*. He forcefully *pronounces judgment upon* the contradictions of bourgeois production, but he does not *understand* them, and therefore he does not understand the process of their resolution either. What lies at the heart of his approach, however, is in fact his presentiment that to the productive forces developed in the womb of capitalist society, to the material and social conditions of the creation of wealth, there must correspond *new* forms of the appropriation of this wealth; that the bourgeois forms are merely transitory and full of contradictions, that they are forms in which wealth always maintains only a contradictory existence, appearing everywhere at the same time as its opposite. Wealth always presupposes poverty, and develops only by developing the latter.

We have now seen the wonderful manner in which Malthus appropriates Sismondi's views. Malthus's theory, in an exaggerated and even more nauseating form, is to be found in a work by Thomas Chalmers (Professor of Divinity): [6] *On Political Economy, in connexion with the Moral State and Moral Prospects of Society,* 2d ed., Glasgow, 1832. Here there come into greater prominence not only the parsonical

6. In English in the text.—Ed.

element in the theory, but also, from the point of view of practice, the member of the State Church who defends "economically" its "bread and fishes" and the whole conglomeration of institutions by which this Church stands or falls.

Malthus's statements concerning the workers, to which reference was made above, are the following:

> The consumption and demand occasioned by the workmen employed in productive labor can never *alone* furnish a motive to the accumulation and employment of capital (*Principles,* 2d ed., p. 315).
>
> No farmer will take the trouble of superintending the labor of ten additional men merely because his whole produce will then sell in the market at an advanced price just equal to what he had paid his additional laborers. There must be something in the previous state of the demand and supply of the commodity in question, or in its price, antecedent to and independent of the demand occasioned by the new laborers, in order to warrant the employment of an additional number of people in its production (*ibid.,* p. 312).
>
> As a great increase of consumption among the working classes must greatly increase the cost of production, it must lower profits, and diminish or destroy the motive to accumulate, before agriculture, manufactures, and commerce have reached any considerable degree of prosperity (*ibid.,* p. 405).
>
> It is the *want of necessaries* [7] which mainly stimulates the laboring classes to produce luxuries; and were this stimulus removed or greatly weakened, so that the necessaries of life could be obtained with very little labor, instead of more time being devoted to the production of conveniences, there is every reason to think that less time would be so devoted (*ibid.,* p. 334).

7. In Malthus's original, only the word "necessaries" is emphasized. —Ed.

Malthus is not interested in disguising the contradictions of bourgeois production; on the contrary, he is interested in emphasizing them, on the one hand in order to demonstrate that the poverty of the working classes is necessary (it is necessary for this mode of production), and on the other hand in order to demonstrate to the capitalists that a well-fed tribe of Church-and-State servants is indispensable for the creation of an adequate demand for their commodities. Thus he also shows that neither increase of population, nor accumulation of capital (*ibid.*, pp. 319–20), nor fertility of the soil (*ibid.*, p. 399), nor "inventions to save labor," nor extension of the "foreign markets" (*ibid.*, pp. 352 and 359), are sufficient to ensure the "continued increase of wealth."[8]

> Both laborers and capital may be redundant, compared with the means of employing them profitably (*ibid.*, p. 414, footnote 7).

Thus Malthus, in opposition to the Ricardians, stresses the possibility of general overproduction. The main statements which he makes in this connection are the following:

> Demand is always determined by *value*, and supply by *quantity* (*ibid.*, p. 316, footnote).

On the same page, Malthus shows that commodities are exchanged not only for commodities but also for productive labor and personal services, and that in relation to these, as in relation to money, there can be a general glut of commodities (*loc. cit.*).[9]

8. Marx's page references here are a little arbitrary. Malthus actually devotes a separate section to the consideration of each of the factors which Marx mentions.—Ed.

9. The passage to which Marx is referring reads as follows: "It is by no means true, as a matter of fact, that commodities are always exchanged for commodities. An immense mass of commodities is exchanged directly, either for productive labor, or personal services: and it is quite

Supply must always be proportioned to *quantity,* and demand to *value* (*Definitions,* Cazenove's ed., p. 65, footnote).

[James Mill] observes, "It is evident that whatever a man has produced, and does not wish to keep for his own consumption, is a stock which he may give in exchange for other commodities. His will, therefore, to purchase, and his means of purchasing, in other words, his demand, is exactly equal to the amount of what he has produced, and does not mean to consume." . . . It is quite obvious that his means of purchasing other commodities are not proportioned to the *quantity* of his own commodity which he has produced, and wishes to part with; but to its *value in exchange;* and unless the value of a commodity in exchange be proportioned to its quantity, it cannot be true that the demand and supply of every individual are always equal to one another (*ibid.,* pp. 64–65; cf. *Definitions,* 1827 ed., pp. 47–49).

If the demand of every individual were equal to his supply, in the correct sense of the expression, it would be a proof that he could always sell his commodity for the costs of production, including fair profits; and then even a *partial* glut would be impossible. The argument proves too much. . . . Supply must always be proportioned to *quantity,* and demand to *value* (*Definitions,* 1827 ed., p. 48, footnote).

[Torrens is wrong in saying that] "increased supply is the one and only cause of increased effectual demand." . . . If it were [true], how difficult would it be for a society to recover itself, under a temporary diminution of food and clothing! But . . . food and clothing thus diminished in quantity, will rise in value, and . . . the money price of the remaining

---

obvious, that this mass of commodities, compared with the labor with which it is to be exchanged, may fall in value from a glut just as any one commodity falls in value from an excess of supply, compared either with labor or money."—Ed.

food and clothing will for a time rise in a greater
degree than in proportion to the diminution of its
quantity, while the money price of labor may remain
the same. The necessary consequence will be, the
power of setting in motion a greater quantity of productive industry than before (*ibid.,* pp. 59–60).

All the commodities of a nation can fall at the
same time, as compared with money or labor. . . .
Thus a general glut is possible. . . . Their prices can
all fall below their costs of production (*ibid.,*
pp. 64–67).[10]

Apart from this, there are only [a few ideas] of Malthus's
concerning the process of circulation to be noted:

If we reckon the value of the fixed capital employed
as a part of the advances, we must reckon the remaining value of such capital at the end of the year
as a part of the annual returns. . . . In reality [the]
annual advances [of the capitalist] consist only of
his circulating capital, the wear and tear of his fixed
capital with the interest upon it, and the interest of
that part of his circulating capital which consists of
the money employed in making his annual payments
as they are called for (*Principles,* 2nd ed., p. 269).

The amortization fund, that is, the fund for the replacement of the wear and tear of the fixed capital, is at the same
time a fund for accumulation.

In his *Essay on Population*, Malthus, with his usual "profound philosophy," makes the following remark in opposition to a plan to provide cows for English cottagers:

It has been observed that those cottagers who keep
cows are more industrious and more regular in their
conduct than those who do not. . . . Most of those
who keep cows at present have purchased them with

10. These statements are paraphrases, rather than direct quotations.—Ed.

the fruits of their own industry. It is therefore more just to say that their industry has given them a cow, than that a cow has given them their industry (*Essay on the Principle of Population*, 7th ed., 1872, p. 471).

And it is also just to say, then, that diligence in labor (together with the exploitation of the labor of others) has given cows to the parvenus among the bourgeoisie, while these cows give an inclination towards laziness to the sons of these parvenus. If one deprived the cows, not of the ability to give milk, but of the ability to command the unpaid labor of others, this would have a very healthy effect upon the diligence of the sons.

The same "profound philosopher" remarks in this chapter:

> It is evident that all cannot be in the middle [classes]. Superior and inferior parts are in the nature of things absolutely necessary, and not only necessary but strikingly beneficial. If no man could hope to rise or fear to fall in society, if industry did not bring with it its reward and indolence its punishment, we could not expect to see that animated activity in bettering our condition which now forms the master-spring of public prosperity (*ibid.*, pp. 473–74).

The inferior classes must exist so that the superior ones should fear to fall, and the superior classes must exist so that the inferior ones can hope to rise. So that indolence should bring with it its punishment, the worker must be poor, and the rentier and the landed proprietor so dear to Malthus's heart must be rich. But what does Malthus understand by "reward for labor"? That the worker must perform a portion of his labor without receiving any equivalent. A fine incentive—if this "reward" were really the incentive rather than hunger. The most that can be said about it is that a worker can hope that he too will one day exploit workers. "The greater the expansion of monopoly," says Rousseau, "the heavier do the chains become for the exploited." This is not the opinion of the "profound thinker" Malthus. His highest hope—which even he himself regards as more or less utopian —is that the middle class should grow in size and that the (working) proletariat should form a smaller and smaller proportion of the total population (even though it grows in absolute numbers). This is in fact the course which bourgeois society follows. Malthus says in the same place:

> We might even venture to indulge a hope that at some future period the processes for abridging human labor, the progress of which has of late years been so rapid, might ultimately supply all the wants of the most wealthy society with less personal effort than at present; and if they did not diminish the severity of individual exertion[11] might at least diminish the number of those employed in severe toil (*ibid.*, p. 474).

Malthus's book *On Population* was a tract against the French Revolution and the contemporary ideas of reform in England (Godwin, etc.). It was an apology for the poverty of the working classes. The *theory* was a plagiarism of Townsend, etc.

His *Essay on Rent* was a tract on behalf of the landlords against industrial capital. The *theory* was a plagiarism of Anderson.

His *Principles of Political Economy* was a tract in the interests of the capitalists against the workers and in the interests of the aristocracy, the Church, and the "tax-devourers" (*Steuerfresser*), etc., against the capitalists. The *theory* was a plagiarism of Adam Smith. Where it was

---

11. The worker must continue to work just as hard as before, and proportionately more and more for others and less and less for himself. (Note by Marx, inserted in the quotation.)

Malthus's own invention, it was pitiably poor. The foundation for the further development of the theory was supplied by Sismondi.

PART FOUR

Marx and Engels on Malthus and Darwinism

Introductory Notes

When Marx first read Darwin's *Origin of Species* at the end of 1860, he remarked in a letter to Engels that "although it is developed in the crude English style, this is the book which contains the basis in natural history for our view" (*Selected Correspondence,* English ed., p. 126). Both Marx and Engels always stressed the fundamental importance of Darwin's discovery that "the stock of organic products of nature surrounding us today, including mankind, is the result of a long process of evolution from a few original unicellular germs" (Engels, *Ludwig Feuerbach,* Lawrence and Wishart ed., p. 56).

One aspect of Darwin's work, however, came in for early criticism from Marx. Darwin believed that the "struggle for existence" which he had demonstrated among organic beings was, in effect, "the doctrine of Malthus, applied to the whole animal and vegetable kingdoms" (see above, p. 124). "It is remarkable," wrote Marx to Engels, "that Darwin recognizes among brutes and plants his English society with its division of labor, competition, opening up of new markets, 'inventions' and Malthusian 'struggle for existence' " (item 1 below).

This question of the "Malthusian" element in Darwinism soon began to assume considerable importance. A number of bourgeois writers, notably F. A. Lange, attempted to subsume the whole of history under "a single great natural law"—the Darwinian "struggle for existence," which they interpreted largely in terms of the Malthusian theory of population. What had happened, in essence, as Engels pointed out in a letter to Lavrov (3) and later almost in the same words in his *Dialectics of Nature* (5), was, first, that certain bourgeois theories such as the theory of competition and the Malthusian theory of population had been transferred from society to animate nature to form the Darwinian theory of the struggle for existence; and, second, that Lange and others had then transferred the same theories back again from organic nature to history and claimed that their validity as "eternal laws of human society" was thereby proved.

Marx and Engels objected strenuously to this "childish" procedure. With reference to the second stage of the process, Marx pointed out that what was actually required was a concrete analysis of the struggle for existence "as represented historically in varying and definite forms of society" (2); and Engels laid stress upon an essential difference between humans and animals which made it impossible "simply to transfer the laws of animal societies to human societies" (3, 5). In addition, Engels cast doubt upon the "unqualified justification" of the first stage of the process. Even in the sphere of nature, he argued, "the one-sided and meager phrase, 'struggle for existence,' . . . can only be taken with a grain of salt" (3); there may indeed be important cases in which the evolution of species may develop *"without any Malthusianism"* at all (5). Nevertheless, it was quite wrong to suggest that the analogy drawn between bourgeois society and animate nature was completely fanciful. It was absurd to imply, as Dühring did, that the *origin* of Darwin's idea of the struggle for existence was to be found in Malthus rather than in the facts. "No Malthusian spectacles," said Engels, "are required in order to perceive the struggle for existence in Nature" (4).

The sources of the items are as follows:

1. Translated from the *Marx-Engels Gesamtausgabe,* part 3, vol. 3, pp. 77–78.

2. From Marx's *Letters to Kugelmann* (Lawrence and Wishart ed.), p. 111.

3. From the *Labour Monthly*, July 1936, vol. 18, no. 7. The translation and notes are by Dona Torr.

4. From Engels's *Anti-Dühring* (Lawrence and Wishart ed.), part 1, ch. 7, pp. 77–82.

5. From Engels's *Dialectics of Nature* (Lawrence and Wishart ed., 1940), pp. 18–20, 208–10, and 235–36.

1 Bourgeois Society and Animal Society

From Marx's letter to Engels of 18 June, 1862

... As regards Darwin, whom I have looked at again, it amuses me that he says he applies the "Malthusian" theory *also* to plants and animals, as if Malthus's whole point did not consist in the fact that his theory is applied *not* to plants and animals, but only to human beings—in geometrical progression—as opposed to plants and animals. It is remarkable that Darwin recognizes among brutes and plants his English society with its division of labor, competition, opening up of new markets, "inventions" and Malthusian "struggle for existence." It is Hobbes's *bellum omnium contra omnes*, and it is reminiscent of Hegel in the *Phenomenology*, where bourgeois society figures as "spiritual animal kingdom," while with Darwin the animal kingdom figures as bourgeois society.

2   Malthusianism and the "Struggle for Existence"

From Marx's letter to Kugelmann of 27 June, 1870

. . . Herr Lange (*Ueber die Arbeiterfrage, etc.*, 2nd. ed.) sings my praises loudly, but with the object of making himself important. Herr Lange, you see, has made a great discovery. The whole of history can be brought under a single great natural law. This natural law is the *phrase* (in this application Darwin's expression becomes nothing but a phrase) "the struggle for existence," and the content of this phrase is the Malthusian law of population or, rather, over-population. So, instead of analyzing the struggle for existence as represented historically in varying and definite forms of society, all that has to be done is to translate every concrete struggle into the phrase, "struggle for existence," and this phrase itself into the Malthusian population fantasy. One must admit that this is a very impressive method—for swaggering, sham-scientific, bombastic ignorance and intellectual laziness.

3 Darwinism and Society

Engels's letter to Lavrov
of 12 November, 1875

My dear Monsieur Lavrov,—Now that I have returned from a visit to Germany I have at last got to your article, which I have just read with much interest. Here are my observations upon it, written in German, as this enables me to be more concise.[1]

(1) Of the Darwinian theory I accept the *theory of evolution* but only take Darwin's method of proof (struggle for life, natural selection)[2] as the first, provisional, and incomplete expression of a newly-discovered fact. Before Darwin, the very people (Vogt, Buchner, Moleschott, etc.) who now see nothing but the *struggle* for existence everywhere were stressing precisely the *cooperation* in organic nature—how the vegetable kingdom supplies the animal kingdom with oxygen and foodstuffs while the animal kingdom in turn supplies the vegetable kingdom with carbonic acid and manures, as Liebig, in particular, had emphasized. Both conceptions have a certain justification within certain limits, but each is as one-sided and narrow as the other. The interaction of natural bodies—whether animate or inanimate—includes alike harmony and collision, struggle and cooperation. If, therefore, a so-called natural scientist permits himself to subsume the whole manifold wealth of historical development under the one-sided and meager phrase, "struggle for existence," a phrase which even in the sphere of nature can only

1. The first and last paragraphs of the letter are written in French; the rest is in German, excepting the two quotations from Lavrov's article, and a few phrases, which are in Russian.
2. This parenthesis is written in English.

be taken with a grain of salt, such a proceeding is its own condemnation.

(2) Of the three convinced Darwinists cited, Hellwald alone seems to be worth mentioning. Seidlitz is only a lesser light at best, and Robert Byr is a novelist, whose novel *Three Times* is appearing at the moment in *By Land and Sea*—just the right place for his whole rodomontade too.

(3) Without disputing the merits of your method of attack, which I might call a psychological one, I should myself have chosen a different method. Each of us is more or less influenced by the intellectual medium in which he chiefly moves. For Russia, where you know your public better than I do, and for a propagandist journal appealing to the bond of sentiment, to moral feeling, your method is probably the better one. For Germany, where false sentimentality has done and is still doing such enormous harm, it would be unsuitable, and would be misunderstood and distorted sentimentally. What we need is hate rather than love—to begin with, at any rate—and, above all, to get rid of the last remnants of German idealism and install material facts in their historic rights. I should, therefore, attack these bourgeois Darwinists something after this fashion (and shall perhaps do so in time):

The whole Darwinian theory of the struggle for existence is simply the transference from society to animate nature of Hobbes's theory of the war of every man against every man and the bourgeois economic theory of competition, along with the Malthusian theory of population. This feat having been accomplished—(as indicated under (1) I dispute its unqualified justification, especially where the Malthusian theory is concerned)—the same theories are next transferred back again from organic nature to history and their validity as eternal laws of human society declared to have been proved. The childishness of this procedure is obvious, it is not worth wasting words over. But if I wanted to go into it further I should do it in such a way that I exposed them in the first place as bad *economists* and only in the second place as bad natural scientists and philosophers.

(4) The essential difference between human and animal society is that animals are at most *gatherers* whilst men are *producers*. This single but cardinal distinction alone makes it impossible simply to transfer the laws of animal societies to human societies. It makes it possible that, as you justly remark, "Man waged a struggle not only for existence but for enjoyment and for the increase of his enjoyments . . . he was ready to renounce the lower enjoyments for the sake of the higher." Without contesting your further deductions from this, the further conclusions I should draw from my premises would be the following: At a certain stage, therefore, human production reaches a level where not only essential necessities but also luxuries are produced, even if, for the time being, they are only produced for a minority. Hence the struggle for existence—if we allow this category as valid here for a moment—transforms itself into a struggle for enjoyments, a struggle no longer for the mere means of *existence* but for the means of *development, socially produced* means of development, and at this stage the categories of the animal kingdom are no longer applicable. But if, as has now come about, production in its capitalist form produces a far greater abundance of the means of existence and development than capitalist society can consume, because capitalist society keeps the great mass of the real producers artificially removed from the means of existence and development; if this society is forced, by the law of its own existence, continually to increase production already too great for it, and, therefore, periodically every ten years, reaches a point where it itself destroys a mass not only of products but of productive forces, what sense is there still left in the talk about the "struggle for existence"? The struggle for existence can then only consist in the producing class taking away the control

of production and distribution from the class hitherto entrusted with it but now no longer capable of it; that, however, is the Socialist revolution.

Incidentally it is to be noted that the mere consideration of past history as a series of class struggles is enough to reveal all the superficiality of the conception of that same history as a slightly varied version of the "struggle for existence." I should therefore never make that concession to these spurious natural scientists.

(5) For the same reason I should have given a different formulation to your statement, which is substantially quite correct, "that the idea of solidarity, as a means of lightening the struggle, could ultimately expand to a point at which it embraces all humanity, counterposing it as a solidarized society of brothers to the rest of the world of minerals, vegetables and animals."

(6) On the other hand I cannot agree with you that the war of every man against every man was the first phase of human development. In my opinion the social instinct was one of the most essential levers in the development of man from the ape. The first men must have lived gregariously and so far back as we can see we find that this was the case.

17 November. I have been interrupted afresh and take up these lines again today in order to send them to you. You will see that my remarks apply rather to the form, the method, of your attack than to its basis. I hope you will find them clear enough; I have written them hurriedly and on re-reading them should like to change many words, but I am afraid of making the manuscript too illegible.

With cordial greetings,
F. Engels.

4 Dühring on Malthus and Darwin

From Engels's *Anti-Dühring* (1878)

"A single and uniform ladder of intermediate steps leads from the mechanics of pressure and impact to the linking together of sensations and ideas." With this assurance Herr Dühring saves himself the trouble of saying anything further about the origin of life, although it might reasonably have been expected that a thinker who had traced the evolution of the world back to its identical state, and is so much at home on other celestial bodies, would have had exact information also on this point. For the rest, however, the assurance he gives us is only half true, unless it is completed by the Hegelian nodal line of measure-relations which has already been mentioned. In spite of all intermediate steps, the transition from one form of motion to another always remains a leap, a decisive change. This is true of the transition from the mechanics of celestial bodies to that of smaller masses on a particular celestial body; it is equally true of the transition from the mechanics of masses to the mechanics of molecules—including the forms of motion investigated in physics proper: heat, light, electricity, magnetism. In the same way, the transition from the physics of molecules to the physics of atoms—chemistry—in turn involves a definite leap; and this is even more clearly the case in the transition from ordinary chemical action to the chemistry of albumen which we call life. Then within the sphere of life the leaps become ever more frequent and imperceptible.—Once again, therefore, it is Hegel who has to correct Herr Dühring.

The idea of purpose provides Herr Dühring with his conceptual transition to the organic world. Once again, this is borrowed from Hegel, who in his *Logic—the Science of the Idea*—makes the transition from chemistry to life by means of teleology or the science of purpose. Wherever we look in Herr Dühring we stumble up against a Hegelian "crudity" which he quite unblushingly hands out to us as his own deep-rooted science. It would take us too far to examine here to what extent it is legitimate and appropriate to apply the ideas of end and means to the organic world. In any case the utilization of the Hegelian "inner purpose"—i.e., a purpose which is not imported into Nature by some third party acting purposively, such as the wisdom of providence, but lies in the necessity of the thing itself—constantly leads, with people who are not well versed in philosophy, to the unthinking interpolation of conscious and purposive activity. That same Herr Dühring who is filled with boundless moral indignation at the slightest "spiritistic" tendency in other people assures us "with certainty that the instincts were primarily created for the sake of the sense of pleasure which is associated with their activity." He tells us that poor Nature "is obliged incessantly to maintain order in the objective world," and moreover in doing so she has to solve more than one problem "which requires on the part of Nature more subtlety than is usually credited to her." But Nature not only *knows* why she does one thing and another; she has not only to perform the duties of a housemaid, she not only possesses subtlety, in itself a very pretty accomplishment in subjective conscious thought; she has also a will. For what the instincts do in addition, fulfilling real natural functions such as nutrition, propagation, etc., "we should not regard as directly, but only indirectly, *willed*." So we have arrived at a consciously thinking and acting Nature, and are thus already standing on the "bridge"—not indeed from the static to the dynamic, but from pantheism to deism. Or is Herr Dühring perhaps just for once indulging in a little "natural-philosophical semi-poetry"?

It is impossible. All that our philosopher of reality can tell us of organic Nature is restricted to the fight against this natural-philosophical semi-poetry, against "charlatanism with its frivolous superficialities and pseudo-scientific mystifications," against the "poetizing features" of *Darwinism*.

The main reproach leveled against Darwin is that he transferred the Malthusian population theory from economics into natural science, that he never got beyond the ideas of an animal breeder, and that in his theory of the struggle for existence he pursued unscientific semi-poetry, and that the whole of Darwinism, after deducting what had been borrowed from Lamarck, is a piece of brutality directed against humanity.

Darwin brought back from his scientific travels the view that plant and animal species are not constant but subject to variation. In order to follow up these ideas after his return home there was no better field available than that of the breeding of animals and plants. It is precisely in this field that England is the classical country; the achievements of other countries, for example Germany, fall far short of what England has achieved in this connection. Moreover, most of these successes have been won during the last hundred years, so that there is very little difficulty in establishing the facts. Darwin found that this breeding has produced artificially, among animals and plants of the same species, differences greater than those found in what are generally recognized as different species. Thus was established on the one hand the variability of species up to a certain point, and on the other, the possibility of a common ancestry for organisms with different specific characteristics. Darwin then investigated whether there were not possibly causes to be found in Nature which—without conscious purpose on the part of the breeder—would nevertheless in the long run produce in living organisms changes similar to those produced by artificial breeding. He discovered these causes in the disproportion between the immense number of germs created by Nature and the insignificant number of organisms which actually attain maturity. But as each germ strives to develop, there necessarily arises a struggle for existence which manifests itself not merely as direct bodily combat or devouring, but also as a struggle for space and light, even in the case of plants. And it is evident that in this struggle those individual organisms which have some particular characteristic, however insignificant, which gives them an advantage in the struggle for existence will have the best prospect of reaching maturity and propagating themselves. These individual characteristics have furthermore the tendency to be inherited, and when they occur among many individuals of the same species, to increase through accumulated heredity in the direction once taken; while those individual organisms which do not possess these characteristics succumb more easily in the struggle for existence and gradually disappear. In this way a species is altered through natural selection, through the survival of the fittest.

Against this Darwinian theory, however, Herr Dühring says that the origin of the idea of the struggle for existence, as, he claims, Darwin himself admitted, has to be sought in a generalization of the views of the economic theorist of population, Malthus, and the idea is therefore marked by all the defects peculiar to the parsonical views of Malthus on the pressure of population.—Now Darwin would not dream of saying that the *origin* of the idea of the struggle for existence is to be found in Malthus. He only says that his theory of the struggle for existence is the theory of Malthus applied to the animal and plant world as a whole. However great the blunder made by Darwin in accepting so naively and without reflection the Malthusian theory, nevertheless anyone can see at the first glance that no Malthusian spectacles are required in order to perceive the struggle for existence in Nature—the contradiction between the countless host of germs which Nature so lavishly produces and the small number of those which ever reach maturity; a contradiction which in fact for the most part finds its solution in a struggle for existence which is often of extreme cruelty. And just as the law of wages has maintained its validity even after the Malthusian arguments on which Ricardo based it have long been exploded, so likewise the struggle for existence can take place in Nature, even without any Malthusian interpretation. For that matter, the organisms of Nature also have their laws of population, which have been left almost entirely uninvestigated, although their formulation would be of decisive importance for the theory of the evolution of species. But who was it that gave the most definite impulse to work in this direction? No other than Darwin.

Herr Dühring carefully avoids an examination of this positive side of the question. Instead, he does nothing but make repeated attacks on the struggle for existence. It is obvious, according to him, that there can be no talk of a struggle for existence among unconscious plants and good-natured plant eaters: "In the precise and definite sense the struggle for existence is found only in the realm of brutality, insofar as animals get their nourishment by seizing prey by force and devouring it." And after he has reduced the idea of the struggle for existence to these narrow limits he can give full play to his indignation at the brutality of this idea, which he himself has restricted to brutality. But this moral indignation applies only to Herr Dühring himself, who is indeed the only author of the struggle for existence in this limited conception and is therefore also solely responsible for it. It is consequently not Darwin who "sought the laws and understanding of all Nature's actions in the kingdom of the brutes"— Darwin had in fact expressly included the whole of organic nature in the struggle—but an imaginary bugbear dressed up by Herr Dühring himself. The *name*: the struggle for existence, can for the matter be willingly handed over to Herr Dühring's exceedingly moral indignation. That the *fact* exists also among plants can be demonstrated to him by every meadow, every cornfield, every wood; and the question at issue is not what it is to be called, whether "struggle for existence" or "lack of conditions for existence and mechanical effects," but how this fact influences the fixity or variation of species. On this point Herr Dühring maintains an obstinate and "identical" silence. Therefore for the time being in regard to natural selection it will certainly continue to be applied.

But Darwinism "produces its transformations and differences out of nothing." It is true that Darwin, when considering natural selection, leaves out of account the *causes* which have produced the variations in separate individuals, and deals in the first place with the way in which such individual variations gradually become the characteristics of a race, variety or species. To Darwin it was of less immediate importance to discover these causes—which up to the present are in part absolutely unknown, and in part can only be stated in quite general terms—than to establish a rational form according to which their effects are preserved and acquire permanent significance. It is true that in doing this Darwin attributed to his discovery too wide a field of action, made it the sole agent in the alteration of species and neglected the causes of the repeated individual variations, concentrating rather on the form in which these variations become general; but this is a mistake which he shares in common with most other people who make any real advance. Moreover, if Darwin produces his individual variations out of nothing, and in so doing applies exclusively "the wisdom of the breeder," the breeder also must produce *out of nothing* his changes in animal and plant forms which are not merely imaginary but occur in reality. But once again, the man who gave the impetus to science to investigate how exactly these variations and differences arise is no other than Darwin.

5 Darwinism—A Summary View

From Engels's *Dialectics of Nature*
(written 1872-82)

With men we enter *history*. Animals also have a history, that of their derivation and gradual evolution to their present position. This history, however, is made for them, and insofar as they themselves take part in it, this occurs without their knowledge or desire. On the other hand, the more that human beings become removed from animals in the narrower sense of the word, the more they make their own history consciously, the less becomes the influence of unforeseen effects and uncontrolled forces on this history, and the more accurately does the historical result correspond to the aim laid down in advance. If, however, we apply this measure to human history, to that of even the most developed peoples of the present day, we find that there still exists here a colossal disproportion between the proposed aims and the results arrived at, that unforeseen effects predominate, and that the uncontrolled forces are far more powerful than those set into motion according to plan. And this cannot be otherwise as long as the most essential historical activity of men, the one which has raised them from bestiality to humanity and which forms the material foundation of all their other activities, namely the production of their requirements of life, that is today social production, is above all subject to the interplay of unintended effects from uncontrolled forces and achieves its desired end only by way of exception and, much more frequently, the exact opposite. In the most advanced industrial countries we have subdued the forces of nature and pressed them into the service of mankind; we have thereby infinitely multiplied production, so that a child now produces more than a hundred adults previously did. And what is the result? Increasing overwork and increasing misery of the masses, and every ten years a great collapse. Darwin did not know what a bitter satire he wrote on mankind, and especially on his countrymen, when he showed that free competition, the struggle for existence, which the economists celebrate as the highest historical achievement, is the normal state of the *animal kingdom*. Only conscious organization of social production, in which production and distribution are carried on in a planned way, can lift mankind above the rest of the animal world as regards the social aspect, in the same way that production in general has done this for men in their aspect as species. Historical evolution makes such an organization daily more indispensable, but also with every day more possible. From it will date a new epoch of history, in which mankind itself, and with mankind all branches of its activity, and especially natural science, will experience an advance that will put everything preceding it in the deepest shade.

The Struggle for Existence.—Until Darwin, what was stressed by his present adherents was precisely the harmonious cooperative working of organic nature, how the plant kingdom supplies animals with nourishment and oxygen, and animals supply plants with manure, ammonia, and carbonic acid. Hardly was Darwin recognized before these same people saw everywhere nothing but *struggle*. Both views are justified within narrow limits, but both are equally one-sided and prejudiced. The interaction of dead natural bodies includes both harmony and collisions, that of living bodies conscious and unconscious cooperation equally with conscious and unconscious struggle. Hence, even in regard to nature, it is not permissible one-sidedly to inscribe only "struggle" on one's banners. But it is absolutely childish to desire to sum up the whole manifold wealth of historical evolution and complexity in the meager and one-sided phrase "struggle for existence." That says less than nothing.

The whole Darwinian theory of the struggle for existence is simply the transference from society to organic nature of Hobbes's theory of *bellum omnium contra omnes*, and of the bourgeois economic theory of competition, as well as the Malthusian theory of population. When once this feat has been accomplished (the unconditional justification for which, especially as regards the Malthusian theory, is still very questionable), it is very easy to transfer these theories back again from natural history to the history of society, and altogether too naive to maintain that thereby these assertions have been proved as eternal natural laws of society.

Let us accept for a moment the phrase "struggle for existence" for argument's sake. The most that the animal can achieve is to *collect*; man *produces*, he prepares the means of life in the widest sense of the words, which, without him, nature would not have produced. This makes impossible any immediate transference of the laws of life in animal societies to human ones. Production soon brings it about that the so-called struggle for existence no longer turns on pure means of existence, but on means for enjoyment and development. Here—where the means of development are socially produced—the categories taken from the animal kingdom are already totally inapplicable. Finally, under the capitalist mode of production, production reaches such a height that society can no longer consume the means of life, enjoyment, and development that have been produced, because for the great mass of producers access to these means is artificially and forcibly barred; and therefore every ten years a crisis restores the equilibrium by destroying not only the means of life, enjoyment, and development that have been produced, but also a great part of the productive forces themselves. Hence the so-called struggle for existence assumes the form: to *protect* the products and productive forces produced by bourgeois capitalist society against the destructive, ravaging effect of this capitalist social order, by taking control of social production and distribution out of the hands of the ruling capitalist class, which has become incapable of this function, and transferring it to the producing masses—and that is the socialist revolution.

Even by itself the conception of history as a series of class struggles is much richer in content and deeper than merely reducing it to weakly distinguished phases of the struggle for existence.

Darwin. The Struggle for Existence.—Above all this must be strictly limited to the struggles resulting from plant and animal *overpopulation*, which do in fact occur at definite stages of plant and lower animal life. But one must keep sharply distinct from it the conditions in which species alter, old ones die out and newly evolved ones take their place, *without* this overpopulation: e.g., on the migration of animals and plants into new regions where new conditons of climate, soil, etc., are responsible for the alteration. If *there* the individuals which become adapted survive and develop into a new species by continually increasing adaptation, while the other more stable individuals die away and finally die out, and with them the imperfect intermediate stages, then this can and does proceed *without any Malthusianism*, and if the latter should occur at all it makes no change to the process, at most it can accelerate it.

Similarly, with the gradual alteration of the geographical, climatic, etc., conditions in a given region (desiccation of central Asia for instance) whether the members of the animal or plant population there exert pressure on one another is a matter of indifference; the process of evolution of the organisms that is determined by it proceeds all the same. It is the same for sexual selection, in which case too Malthusianism is quite unconcerned.

Hence Haeckel's "adaptation and heredity" also can determine the whole process of evolution, without need for selection and Malthusianism.

Darwin's mistake lies precisely in lumping together in "natural selection" or the "survival of the fittest" two absolutely separate things:

(1) Selection by the pressure of overpopulation, where perhaps the strongest survive in the first place, but where the weakest in many respects can also do so.

(2) Selection by greater capacity of adaptation to altered circumstances, where the survivors are better suited to these *circumstances*, but where this adaptation as a whole can mean regress just as well as progress (for instance adaptation to parasitic life is *always* regress).

The main thing: that each advance in organic evolution is at the same time a regression, fixing *one-sided* evolution and excluding evolution along many other directions.

This, however, *a basic law.*

Index of Authors

Abraham à Sancta Clara, 137, 177

Alison, Archibald, 57, 59-60, 63n

Anderson, James, 25, 27, 125, 127-31, 138, 177, 188

Bacon, Francis, 64-65
Bailey, Samuel, 159-60
Barbon, Nicholas, 89
Barton, John, 53-54, 82-84, 94-95n
Bastiat, Frédéric, 16
Bebel, August, 55, 117
Bernal, J. D., 40n, 47n
Bonner, G. A., 140n
Brentano, L., 26
Bruckner, J., 89
Buchner, F. K. C. L., 197
Bulgakov, S., 26
Buret, Eugène, 65n, 66n, 67n, 68n
Burns, Emile, 140n
Byr, Robert, 198

Cantillon, Richard, 89
Castro, J. de, 41n
Cazenove, John, 139, 141-42, 143, 153-54, 164-66, 169, 185
Chalmers, Thomas, 89, 182
Chamberlain, J., 108n
Cobbett, William, 137
Cockburn, Lord, 3n
Condorcet, Marquis de, 88

Danielson, N. F. (Nikolai-on), 54, 55, 122

Darwin, Charles, 19, 85, 138, 193-98, 201-12
Darwin, Sir Charles, 47
Davis, Kingsley, xix
De Foe, Daniel, 88
Dühring, Eugen, 194, 201-2, 204-6

Eden, F. M., 88n
Ehrlich, Paul, xi, xiii, xv, xviii, xix-xx
Ephrucy, B., 35
Euler, Leonard, 120

Feuerbach, Ludwig, 193
Franklin, Benjamin, 88-89

Galiani, Ferdinando, 110n
Godwin, William, 3, 4, 188
Goethe, Johann Wolfgang, 118

Haeckel, Ernst, 212
Hardin, Garret, xix
Hegel, G. W. F., 195, 201-2
Hellwald, F. von, 198
Herbert, Claude-Jacques, 137
Hill, A. V., 39-40
Hobbes, Thomas, 89, 195, 198, 210
Hume, David, 89

Jones, Richard, 95n

Kautsky, Karl, 50, 54-55, 119, 125-26, 135n
Kay, Dr. (J. P. Kay-Shuttleworth), 65-66

Keynes, John Maynard, 15, 43–46, 48
Kugelmann, Ludwig, 194, 196

Laing, S., 110n
Lange, F. A., 20, 54, 85, 118, 193, 196
Lassalle, Ferdinand, 117–18
Lavrov, Peter, 193, 197
Law, John, 89
Lee, Dr., 107
Lenin, V. I., 26–27, 34, 41, 45
Liebig, Justus, 24–25, 63, 197
Liebknecht, Wilhelm, 55
Locke, John, 89

McCulloch, John Ramsay, 64–65, 76n, 128, 163
Malthus, Daniel, 4n
Mandeville, Bernard de, 89
"Marcus," 59
Martineau, Harriet, 99n
Merivale, Herman, 97–98
Mill, James, 25, 163–64, 185
Mill, John Stuart, 25
Mirabeau, Marquis de, 89
Moleschott, Jacob, 197
More, Thomas, 89

North, Dudley, 89

Ortes, Giammaria, 89, 113–15
Owen, Robert, 180

Petty, William, 89–90
Place, Francis, xi
Prévost, Guillaume, 65n
Proudhon, Pierre Joseph, 18

Quesnay, Francois, 89

Ramsay, George, 95n

Ricardo, David, 11, 12–15, 20, 25, 27, 29, 33, 42–44, 46, 50, 54, 64, 82–84, 85, 95n, 117, 125–26, 128, 132–36, 138–44, 148–49, 152–53, 155, 162–63, 165–68, 175–81, 184, 205
Rousseau, Jean Jacques, 188
Ruge, Arnold, 53

Say, Jean Baptist, 16
Schäffle, A. E. F., 119
Schweitzer, Johann Baptist von, 18
Senior, William Nassau, 164
Sismondi, J. D. L. S. de, 33, 35, 45, 98n, 115–16, 126, 132, 177–78, 181–82, 188
Smith, Adam, 12, 25, 29, 50, 76, 82–84, 88n, 89, 110n, 127, 139–40, 143, 149, 153–55, 157–59, 161, 163, 166, 177, 179, 188
Smith, Kenneth, 15n, 18n
Stalin, J. V., 21n, 35–36
Steuart, James, 88, 114–15n, 127–28, 137
Storch, H. Fr., 115
Struve, P. von, 122
Sully, M. de B., 89

Temple, William, 89
Tooke, Thomas, 128
Torr, Dona, 194
Torrens, Robert, 125, 153–54, 185
Townsend, Joseph, 88–89, 114, 129, 137, 177, 188
Tracy, Destutt de, 116
Tucker, Josiah, 89

Vanderlint, Jacob, 89
Vogt, Karl, 197

Vogt, William, 37–39

Wallace, Robert, 88–89, 137–38
Webb, Sydney and Beatrice, 9

West, Edward, 25, 125, 128
Witt, Johan de, 89
Wordsworth, William, 3

INFORMATION PROCESSES:

Educational,

Occupational, and

Personal-Social

The Macmillan Company

Collier-Macmillan Limited LONDON

Preface

The content of this book is focused on how the counselor works with an individual in personalizing the information processes in educational, occupational, and personal-social areas, and with professional persons who also work with that individual. A person is surrounded by information, much of which is abstract. He needs to develop methods of identifying information that has potential personal meaning, as well as methods of analyzing, assimilating, and integrating the information so that it may be of personal value.

In this book, obtaining and utilizing information has been considered an ongoing process rather than a single act. The developmental approach has been used, with the recognition that throughout life informational needs are present but changing. Information has been considered as being more meaningful to the individual when he himself is involved in the processes rather than when information is merely presented to him. As he becomes involved in the information processes, he needs a means of integrating the new information into his self-concept and a means of exploring his perceptions. For information processes to be complete, the individual needs general and specific information plus a feedback for cognitive and affective assimilation.

To formulate a philosophical base and develop guidelines for using information with an individual, the authors applied the principles of communications to the discipline of counseling and guidance. A conceptual model was developed in which the *person* with whom the information is to be used becomes one dimension; the *area* or topic in which the information is needed becomes the second dimension; and the different levels of *depth* that are needed as the information becomes personalized is the third dimension. The depth is dependent upon the need for general, specific, and feedback information.

The book is subdivided into four parts. Part I encompasses the philosophical and historical foundations; Parts II, III, and IV concern the three areas in the information processes—educational, occupational, and personal-social. Although the information processes are interwoven throughout an individual's life, at times he may focus his attention primarily upon one area. The following aspects are presented within each area: basic information; illustrative sources; techniques; suggestions for coding, filing, storage, and retrieval; and means for utilization. For those who wish to read more extensively on a topic, references are included both within and at the end of each chapter.

Acceptance of the principle that man and his world are continually and uniquely changing has created the need for information to be personalized. In each part of the book the information presented illustrates how personalized information may assist an individual to become flexible, adaptable, ready for change, and able to change on the basis of his own evaluation. At the same time, the information is of sufficient breadth and depth to enable the individual to know when his concepts are attuned to reality and can be acted upon. The aim is to help the individual become flexible where flexibility is desired but stable where stability is needed. Information is important in helping individuals to make, prepare for, and facilitate change. The more information processes can be personalized the better the individual can understand and integrate information through both his cognitive and affective processes.

The book is designed as a text for counselor education courses such as "Occupational and Educational Information" and "Career Development." It was written also to assist professional counselors in their work in various settings—schools, higher education institutions, and community agencies. Illustrative materials are provided for children, youth, and adults.

The authors are indebted to the many graduate students who used, criticized, modified, and helped develop ideas for the content of this book. We also express appreciation to Joyce Qualkinbush, Betty Brown, Dorothy Johnson, Tom Springer, Billie Lee, Jan Kuldau, John Quigley, and Lt. Col. Harold Rasmussen.

J. W. H.
L. U. H.

Contents

List of Figures   xv

List of Tables   xvii

PART I FOUNDATIONS   1

Chapter 1 Philosophical Foundations for
            Personalizing Information   3

            Why Personalized Information?
            Why Individuals Want Information
            Philosophical Basis for Personalized Information
            Terminology and Definitions
            Purposes of Personalized Information Processes
            Role of Personalized Information in Education
            Summary
            Selected References

Chapter 2 Historical Events, Trends, and
            Implications   20

            Parsons' Concept of Information for the
                Individual
            Influence of World War I
            Depression and Role of the Federal Government
            World War II and the Changes
            Automation and Cybernation
            Federal Legislation
            Other Major Changes Affecting Information
                Processes
            Trends and Implications
            Summary
            Selected References

Chapter 3 Concepts—Coordination and
            Interrelationships   34

            Contribution of Information to Developmental
                Concept
            Approaches to Collecting Information

The 3-D Concept of Personalized Information
Structure
Levels in Occupational Maturity
Systems Development for Information Utilization
Types of Libraries Needed
Priority Determinants
Selection of Personalized Information
Coordination
Summary
Selected References

**PART II PERSONALIZING EDUCATIONAL
INFORMATION**   **59**

Chapter 4 Determinants of Educational
Opportunities: Characteristics of the
Individual   **61**

Psychology of Individual Difference
Role of the Counselor in Determining Individual
Differences
Measurement Techniques for Assessing Individual
Potential
Characteristics of Individuals Affecting Their
Educational Potential
Changing Educational Objectives
Implications for Personalizing Educational
Information
Types of Educational Information Needed
Educational Potential—A Determinant of Job
Potential
Summary
Selected References

Chapter 5 Implications of Educational Structure
for the Individual   **79**

Taxonomy of Educational Structure
Availability of Educational Opportunities for
Individual
Conditions Within Educational Structure Affecting
Choice by Individuals
Changing Role of Education in Today's World
Implications for Counselors

Summary
Selected References

Chapter   6   Sources and Types of Educational
                Information   99

Educational Information for the Developmental
    Approach—Early Childhood Throughout Life
Educational Information for 3-D Concept
Sources of Educational Information
Types of Educational Information
Evaluative Criteria for Educational Information
Counselor's Techniques for Obtaining Educational
    Information
Techniques for Individuals and Groups for Obtaining
    Educational Information
Mobilizing and Organizing Resources
Summary
Selected References

Chapter   7   Making Educational Information
                Available to Users   127

Accessibility as a Determinant of Extent of Use
Criteria for Housing Educational Material
Physical Facilities for Housing Educational
    Materials
Filing Plans—Values and Limitations
Developing Files to Facilitate the 3-D Concept
Filing Code Based on 3-D Concept
Sample Materials
Criteria of Educational Maturation
Relationship of Ease of Checkout of Information
    to P and D Dimensions
Improving Extensiveness of Use
Methods of Keeping Educational Materials
    Up-to-Date
Summary
Selected References

Chapter   8   Utilizing Educational Information with
                Individuals and Groups   156

"Utilizing Information With" as Compared to
    "Supplying Information To"

Objectives in Using Information with Groups and
Individuals
Needs as a Determinant of Methods
Method Variation as Depth Dimension Changes
Information in Counseling
Selection of Method
Methods of Utilizing Educational Information
Summary
Selected References

PART III PERSONALIZING OCCUPATIONAL
INFORMATION   171

Chapter   9 Implications of Recent Research and
Occupational Theories for the Counselor   173

Research and Theories as Recent Developments
Practitioner's Role in Understanding Research and
Theories
Theories and Research in Vocational Development
and Their Implications
Summary
Selected References

Chapter 10 Effects of the Occupational World on the
Individual   198

Changing Nature of World of Work
Changing Role of Work in Life of Individual
Technological Advances Necessitate Change in Job
and Man
Geographical Considerations in Occupations
Terminology and Definitions
Classification Structures for Occupations
Sociological Implications of Occupation
Demographic Factors
Impediments to Occupational Mobility
Influence of Labor Unions and Collective
Bargaining
Governmental Influence in World of Work
Summary
Selected References

Chapter 11 Sources and Types of Occupational
Information 227

Occupational Information for a Developmental
Approach
Occupational Information for the 3-D Concept
Sources of Occupational Information
Types of Occupational Information
Evaluative Criteria for Occupational Information
Counselor's Techniques for Obtaining Occupational
Information
Techniques for Individuals and Groups for Obtaining
Occupational Information
Summary
Selected References

Chapter 12 Making Occupational Information
Available to Users 256

Needs Determine Use
Considerations for Filing Educational and
Occupational Information Separately
Criteria for Location of Occupational Material
Physical Facilities for Housing Occupational
Material
Codification and Filing Plans—Values and
Limitations
Development of Files to Facilitate 3-D Concept
Sample Materials
Criteria of Occupational Maturity
Improving Extensiveness of Use
Methods of Keeping Occupational Information
Up-to-Date
Summary
Selected References

Chapter 13 Utilizing Occupational Information with
Individuals and Groups 281

A Point of View
Interrelationship of Roles
Using Occupational Information in a Counseling
Relationship
Contribution of Group Work to Individual
Selection of Method

Methods of Utilizing Occupational Information
Summary
Selected References

PART IV PERSONAL-SOCIAL INFORMATION
FOR THE INDIVIDUAL   303

Chapter 14 Integrating Physical and Psychological
Information   305

Variables Involved in Working with Individuals
The Emerging Self
Perception—The Perceived World
Tomorrow Is Sculptured Today
Counselor's Role in Personal Information
Developing a Philosophy of Life
Leisure Time *or* Self-Expressive Time
Team Work
Tests as a Source of Physical and Psychological
   Information
Coding and Filing Physical and Psychological
   Information
Sample Materials and Sources
Utilizing Physical and Psychological Information
Summary
Selected References

Chapter 15 Personalizing Social Information   332

Purposes of Personalized Social Information and
   Counselor's Role
Subgroups and Cultures
The Disadvantaged
Understanding Others to the Extent of
   Participation
The Individual in Relation to the Modern World
Social Mobility—Vertical and Horizontal
Social Problems of Life
Social Activities Contribute to Development
Social Agencies for Referrals and Consultation
Coding, Filing, Storing, and Retrieving Social
   Information
Sample Materials and Sources
Utilizing Social Information

. Summary
Selected References

Chapter 16 Relationship of Economic Conditions to
the Individual   359

Purposes of Personalized Economic Information
Economic Self-Aspiration
Financial Income
Financial Planning
Financial Assistance for Obtaining an Education
    or Training
Financial Assistance in Starting a Private
    Enterprise
Community Agencies Offering Financial
    Assistance
Relationship Between Economic Conditions and
    Leisure Time
Coding, Filing, Storing, and Retrieving Economic
    Information
Subscriptions and Services for Economic
    Information
Reference Books for Economic Information
Sample Material and Sources
Utilization
Summary
Selected References

Chapter 17 Information Pertinent to Peer and Family
Relations   385

Purposes of Family and Peer Information
Role of Counselor
Parental Expectations
Family Relationships
Peer Relationships
Dating Practices
Sex Information
Marriage Responsibilities
Working with Parents
Coding, Filing, Storing, and Retrieval
Material and Sources
Utilization of Peer and Family Information
Summary
Selected References

Chapter 18   Personalized Military Information
             Processes   **405**

             Purposes of Military Information in Counseling and
                Guidance
             Counselor's Role
             Women in the Armed Forces
             Educational Opportunities While in Armed
                Forces
             Occupational Development During Military
                Service
             Military Service and Implications for the Family
             Transition from Military to Civilian Life
             Veterans' Benefits
             Benefits for Veterans' Children
             Keeping Abreast of Changes in Military
                Information
             Coding, Filing, Storage, and Retrieval
             Sample Materials and Sources
             Utilization of Military Information
             Summary
             Selected References

Appendix
   List of Abbreviations   **432**
   Address Index   **433**
Name Index   **447**
Subject Index   **453**

List of Figures

3–1. Three-Dimensional Concept for Use of Information in the Developmental Phase of Guidance. 37

3–2. Schematic Representation of an Individual Obtaining Information over a Period of Time. 40

5–1. Location of Study for Adults in Continuing Education. 84

5–2. Educational Attainment of Young Persons in American Population for Three Selected Years. 86

5–3. High School Graduates, by Percentage by Sex, for Selected Years. 87

5–4. College Graduates Twenty-five Years of Age and Over, by Percentage by Sex, for Selected Years. 88

5–5. Percentage of Population as of April 1, 1966, Not Having Adult Experience with Selected Major Events. 90

5–6. College Enrollment, Public and Private, in Millions of Persons and as Percentage of Total Population. 92

5–7. College Enrollment, 1964 and 1975, per 1,000 Population, by State of Enrollment. 94–95

7–1. Schematic of the 3-D Concept for the Educational Information Area. 137

7–2. Illustrative Captions for Filing Educational Information in File Drawer: Code Based on 3-D Concept. 144

10–1. Percentage of Labor Force in Each Occupational Group for Selected Years. 201

10–2. Next Steps for High School Graduates in the Mid-1960's: Numbers Are Approximates for the Nation. 202

10–3. Female Labor Force Compared to Female Population Shown in Percentage for Total and by Marital Status (Fourteen Years of Age and Over). 206

10–4. Schematic Comparison of Two Different Approaches to Considering Prestige of Occupations—Interoccupational Rankings and Intra-Inter-occupational Rankings. 214

10–5. Employed Persons Fourteen Years of Age and Over by Major Occupational Groups and Sex, March 1967. 216

11–1. Diagrammatic Representation of How Occupational Information plus Experiences Contribute to an Upward (Vertical) and Outward, Broadening (Horizontal) Development, Thus Advancing the Individual's Occupational Maturation. 228

12–1. D.O.T. Codes for Two Occupations, with Code Explanation. 266

16–1. Median Money Income of Families, by Years of School Completed and by White and Nonwhite Families in 1965. 363

16–2. Median Income of Recipients by Age and Sex, 1964. 366

16–3. Families and Unrelated Individuals Grouped in Fifths by Income Rank and Indicated Percentage of Aggregate Income. 1965. 367

18–1. Selective Service Draftees Found Acceptable or Disqualified, and Reasons for Disqualification Expressed in Percentage of Total Examined in 1966. 408

List of Tables

2–1. Educational Attainment of Workers, Eighteen Years Old and Over, by Major Occupational Groups, March 1967.   **25**

2–2. Trends That Will Affect the Personalized Information Processes.   **29**

3–1. Developmental Trends from Early Childhood to Adulthood.   **43**

3–2. Occupational Development Subdivided by "Levels Concept" According to Occupational Understandings Developed, Sources and Kinds of Material Used, Meanings Acquired, and Attitudes Formulated at Each Level.   **46–47**

4–1. Intergenerational Differences in Educational Attainment of Persons in the Labor Force, March 1967.   **75**

4–2. Median Years of School Completed by the Employed Civilian Labor Force in the United States, Eighteen Years Old and Over, by Occupational Group and by Sex.   **75**

7–1. Schematic Coding System for Filing Information Based upon 3-D Concept.   **140–41**

8–1. Schematic Classification of Media and Specific Methods for Utilizing Educational Information with Persons on an Individual and Group Basis.   **164–65**

10–1. Percentage Change in Labor Force by Age (Fourteen and Over) by Decades. Actual 1950 and 1960 and Projected 1970 and 1980 Labor Force Data Used for Determining Percentages.   **215**

10–2. Percentage Distribution of Employed and Unemployed Persons by Occupational Group for 1965; Percentage Shown by Color and Sex for Employed Persons and by Color for Unemployed Persons. 217

10–3. Percentage of Unemployment for 1950 and 1962 and Percentage Change in Unemployment According to Years of Schooling Completed. 219

12–1. The *California File Plan* Developed by Kirk and Michels. 262–63

13–1. Schematic Classification of Media and Specific Methods for Utilizing Occupational Information with Persons on an Individual and Group Basis. 292–93

14–1. Average Weekly Hours of Employment for Selected Years. 319

14–2. Percentage of Office Workers and Plant Workers Who Received Paid Holidays and Paid Vacations Annually in 1966. 320

16–1. Money Income of Persons Fourteen Years Old and Over— Percentage Distribution of Recipients: by Income Level, by Sex, by Total and Nonwhite Population, and by Median Income, 1965. 365

PART I

FOUNDATIONS

If information is to be personalized, then a philosophical foundation is necessary. Making information personal requires a different philosophy from that used when information is treated in the same manner for all persons. Making a lifetime process of the obtaining and utilizing of information necessitates a philosophy different from that used when each piece of information is assumed to be isolated and independent from all other materials.

Occupational and educational knowledge is expanding at such a rapid pace that it can no longer be comprehended by one person. No one person needs to learn all this information, because much of it does not apply to him. Each person, however, needs to find a means for obtaining the information that does have potential personal value for him. A counselor should facilitate the information processes so that they will be personalized.

The use of information in counseling and guidance involves communication and the communication processes. Combining the principles for communication and counseling as they apply to information processes makes possible the formation of guidelines. First, information is essential for communication and for the effective development of an individual. Second, information is generally more meaningful when it is obtained over an extended period of time. Third, information is gained throughout life and is often perceived by one individual differently than it is by another. Thus, the use of information in counseling and guidance is concerned with the processes (obtaining, perceiving, synthesizing, internalizing, and utilizing over an extended period of time) rather than the act alone. Fourth, in any communication or counseling, the individual and his uniqueness become the determining dimension. The

1

person, his needs, his variables, and his stage of development must be considered. Information to be meaningful must be personalized. Fifth, the information area or topic is another dimension, which when understood enables the counselor or the individual or both to focus on the information received. The sixth guideline is that individuals neither want nor need information all on one depth. At times general, broad information is needed. At other times specific, resource information is most helpful. At still other times, the individual is attempting to assimilate the information and needs a feedback so as to have a means of evaluating understandings, ideas, expectations, progress, and his own self-concept.

From the guidelines formulated from communications and counseling, a three-dimensional conceptual model was developed for utilizing information with individuals. The three dimensions determining the information to be used are PEOPLE, AREA, and DEPTH.

Chapter 1

Philosophical Foundations for

Personalizing Information

Life expectancy has increased sufficiently to predict that more than one-half of the present population will be living in the twenty-first century. Change is a certainty, but creating readiness, flexibility, and adaptability to change are challenges. The counselor, helping the individual with his personalized information processes, facilitates the individual's development.

Man as a dynamic living organism is confronted constantly with decisions. In order that he may make the best decisions possible, he must consider all of the pertinent information he can obtain. Often he has the necessary information or can obtain it easily; however, in many instances he needs additional information applicable to his particular situation. From the voluminous information available today, he must select the information he needs and integrate it into his decision-making processes.

Why Personalized Information?

Information is defined as knowledge and also often carries the concept of the communication of knowledge derived from reading, observation, or instruction. Information is defined in a collegiate dictionary as "unorganized or unrelated facts or data." The amount of information in the world is expanding rapidly, and in this century the rate has caused an information explosion. The amount of information is doubling every seven to ten years. A young person entering kindergarten has much to learn, but by the time he graduates from high school the amount of information available will be three to four times as great. If the informa-

3

tion explosion continues at the same rate, then by the time he is ready to retire, the amount of information in the world will be at least sixty-five times that available when he started to school.

Man is surrounded by a vast amount of information and he obtains information from many sources. He starts obtaining information soon after birth and continues to do so throughout life. Much of this information is unorganized and unrelated, but he continues to come in contact with it as he coexists with people, things, and ideas. Schools are established so that information can be communicated effectively. Information is organized in school so that the teacher may assist the individual in learning information. The more the individual perceives the information as having value to him, the more he learns.

Information is available from various sources and the total volume of information is beyond any one person's comprehension even if he wanted to comprehend it all. Information that has meaning to one person may not have meaning to another. Today the challenge is not to get information but rather to select pertinent information. With the information explosion another challenge arises: making sure that one has not omitted from his considerations information that may be important to him.

Man at all ages, birth to death, is in need of some information. At times the need for additional information is intensified; frequently the person can best obtain that information from a teacher, a parent, a specialist in the area in which he seeks information, association with a thing or object, and various other means. At times, however, the counselor may be the best person to assist the individual in his information processes. Information is data, material, or knowledge, and it must be communicated to and perceived in some manner by the individual. The communication, perception, and internalization of information involves many processes, each of which can be most meaningful when personalized. *Information, information processes,* and *personalized information processes* are not synonymous terms. Information processes necessitate the use of information and include communication; thus, they require media and techniques. Personalized information processes assure that the information and processes will be attuned to a particular person.

In counseling and guidance the prevailing philosophy is that information is needed by an individual so that he can make decisions. Certainly a similar statement could encompass one of the objectives in teaching. What then is the difference between the roles of a counselor and a teacher? The two often work conjointly for the individual's benefit. The teacher is employed to impart knowledge, to communicate the knowledge and skills that have been accumulated over ages, and also to expect the individual to discover new ideas for himsellf.

The counselor, in regard to information, tries to help the individual personalize the information that he obtains. The information is used in terms of that individual's present and expected needs, as well as they can be determined. The information is personalized, meaning that a selection is made from all the information available and the individual then interprets and evaluates the information on the basis of its implications for him. A counselor may assist an individual in perception, attitude formation, and internalization of information within his present value system or in the modification of his value structure. In some cases one of the counselor's responsibilities may be to help individuals set new goals, to create new needs. The counselor's goals include broadening the horizons, increasing the expectations, and assisting in obtaining the kind of information that an individual can use personally as he begins to make decisions about himself, about the group of which he is or might become a part, and about his environment or potential environments.

Counselors are not the only people who work with an individual; however, counselors are integral supplemental partners to other professional personnel. In the educational program, counselors must assist teachers, not attempt to replace them, and they must supplement and complement the teachers' work, not work in opposition to them. For counselors who work outside the school system—for example in rehabilitation, state employment, and other community services—their role also may be to assist the people who work with the individual. When counselors in all settings are working directly with the individual, they are helping him utilize information, understand where and how to obtain additional information, recognize the alternatives possible, and learn how to obtain the additional knowledge and skills desired. Persons of all ages—children, youth, and adults, including senior citizens—need at times to have personalized information and an opportunity to work with a counselor.

Why Individuals Want Information

Information is essential for one's growth and development. As one acquires information, he has a greater potential for growth and development if he can integrate the pertinent information into his value systems. The individual can build a reservoir of personalized information fundamental for his decision-making processes. As long as we are living human beings, within a democratic society, decisions (choices) must be made.

> Decision-making at each stage may be regarded as a strategy for acquiring and processing information. If a decision is truly *to be made,* if it is not a foregone conclusion, it must involve some novel elements. The person confronted with the problem of decision-making either does not know what information he needs, does not have what information he wants, or cannot use what information he has. Thus, the

> pressure for making a decision creates a discrepancy between the individual's present state of knowledge (or wisdom) and the state that is being demanded of him. (Katz, 1963, p. 25.)

As long as choices are possible, the need eixsts for personalized information to facilitate the development of the individual; the counselor can contribute to this development. If no choices exist, only a predetermined direction, personalized information is not necessary because the individual can make no decision. In this case, counseling and guidance cannot function for that person because the work of the counselor is to facilitate change. Decision-making is essential to a person's growth and development. In counseling and guidance the developmental concept must prevail. A person is not static but dynamic. The counselor contributes to that dynamic condition by facilitating changes in pace, maturation processes, development, and breadth of perception.

Why do individuals want information? Some, at times, do not realize that they want or need information; therefore, part of the counselor's responsibility may be to create a conscious need for information. Generally speaking, the individual wants information in order to make a choice, plan, or decision; therefore, he is asking for *personalized* information. He is asking for information that applies to him, and he is not concerned whether it applies to anyone else or not.

He wants information so that he may acquire a broader perspective. He wants to take the goggles off; he wants total vision; he wants to broaden his horizon. As he develops, man must constantly come in contact with more and more information, but *not more of the same information*. His information should increase progressively in depth as long as he is considering the same topic. The individual, however, may proceed back and forth from general information depth to specific information depth to relation of the information to himself. If the counselor assists the individual in obtaining and utilizing enough information in depth, the individual may discover that the topic under consideration is no longer of interest or is meaningless for him. When the individual changes topics, he starts the process over again, starts with the broadening concept, then obtains more specific or resource information, and relates the information to himself and his value systems.

When an individual searches for answers to his questions and as he begins the decision-making process, he will become more involved personally in the information processes. He has need for information that can provide him with a feedback so that he can decide whether or not he is making the right kind of choices, whether his decisions are realistic for him. People want to make and are capable of making decisions. They want to have the kind of personalized information that will enable them to evaluate the potential outcome of each alternative.

Once a decision is made, they want a means for continuous personalized information feedback so that they can evaluate progress, benefits achieved, and projected outcomes against new alternatives. Feedback is essential for the individual but frequently is overlooked by those who work with him.

If one listens to taped interviews of counseling sessions, very frequently the counselee has said to the counselor: "What do you think? Am I making the right choice?" He is asking for feedback. The counselor does not have to make the evaluation; the counselee is asking "How can *I* get the kind of information that will give me the feedback I need?" The counselor can and should assist the individual in learning how to obtain the information—the feedback—so essential for continued progressive development.

Information in isolated form may be knowledge, and many pieces of information are available. From the various sources the individual must seek, select, and interpret the information that has value to him. He must more than know and understand many pieces of information. He must personalize and internalize so as to integrate and modify his own perceptions and value systems. He must have continuous information processes for the growth and development so necessary to his own self-fulfillment.

Throughout the book the developmental approach will be stressed—away from the concept of the problem-centered approach. Information may be necessary at times to solve problems, but the overall, long-term viewpoint is that personalized information is a vital part of a person's development. Personalized information processes assure communication of knowledge and go beyond communication to aid the individual in obtaining, learning, internalizing, and utilizing information not in its isolated form but in its interrelationships with other information and particularly with the individual's own value structures. Personalized information processes contribute to the individual's growth and development.

Philosophical Basis for Personalized Information

In psychology in recent years a major philosophical position has developed on the belief that man's freedom lies in his capacity to choose from among the options available and thus to create for himself his "world." The two terms frequently associated with this philosophy are *Dasein-analyse* and *existentialism*. Psychologists who hold to the existentialist philosophy believe man is able to understand himself according to his subjectively observable responses, of which his thoughts are one, although not the most important one. Man is responsible for himself, considers his fellow man as an object of value, exists in a world of reality, and makes his choices in a direction that enhances his development toward his innate potentialities (Ford and Urban, 1963, pp. 451–452).

Not all psychologists hold to the existential philosophy, although much research supports many of the postulates. For counselors the existential philosophy gives importance to information not only as a cognitive process but also as an affective process. Information cannot be considered only from the absolute and statistical viewpoint but must be considered from the subjective viewpoint of each individual. Information may be collected and data analyzed on an impersonal basis, but to have meaning to the individual, information must be personalized and perceived as an integral part of the sequential lifetime processes.

Many philosophies and theories exist. The significant implications from philosophies, theories, research, and bodies of knowledge in the various disciplines cannot be ignored by counselors. Each counselor should study, keep abreast with developments, integrate those viewpoints that will contribute to his professional growth, and then use his own development for the benefit of each individual with whom he works.

The philosophy held by one counselor may differ somewhat from that held by another. However, most counselors' philosophies include the belief that each counselee can change and will change, although the direction, kind, and pace of change may not be known. Probably another belief is that the counselor's role is to broaden the counselee's concepts, to help him understand that regardless of his past, regardless of who he is, opportunities (alternatives) are available even though at times the individual may have to help create them. Alternatives are not static; they, too, are changing. The very living and dynamics of the person makes his alternatives viable.

The question may be asked, "Who determines the growth or change to be made?" One philosophy in guidance and counseling is that the counselor has had more experience than the individual, therefore the counselor should determine the change. The point of view taken in this book is not in agreement with that philosophy. Society may set standards for the individual, but the counselor's role is different. A basic postulate is that *the individual is the one who decides his course of action.* The philosophical concept held is that an individual has the potential for change and he is responsible for his decisions, even though some of his decisions may be based on compromise because of external pressures. The society of which he is a member may be setting the standard for him and may at the same time be the creator of his problem. Thus, the individual may work to join a different group or to bring about a change in the society, the social group, or the situation.

In terms of who determines change, another philosophical postulate that will be basic in this book is that *every person, regardless of who he is, desires to improve himself.* What the individual does, he does because he perceives or feels that the results will be an improvement for him. Man seeks information that will help him to improve himself and to achieve the goals that he has established for himself.

Another philosophical postulate is that *the role of occupational and educational information today is considerably different from its role forty or fifty years ago.* Technological changes have ushered in a new need for personalized information. If one thinks about the information obtained by his grandparents, particularly occupational information, he realizes that they in one way or another obtained information that assisted them to discover what job each might do and where and how to be trained for that job. Generally the job was the same as that of their parents. Today, the most progressive companies are not so much employing a person to do a job as they are searching for talent to buy. Frequently they do not ask, "What do you want to do?" or state, "I think we have a position open in the kind of work you do. Let me first check with the personnel office." Instead the officials of progressive companies are making statements such as "Show me a bright young man or woman, and I'll employ him or her. If we don't have a job for the person in our company, we'll make one." Technical and skilled workers are needed, and progressive companies would like to employ persons with the technical and skilled background needed, but realistically these companies recognize that they must educate and train their own workers. These companies are seeking people who have the potential for continuing education and training, for gaining new skills and knowledge, and for being willing to change. In a society in which employers are searching more than ever before for capable persons who are flexible and who want an opportunity to continue their development, the information used with an individual must have greater breadth and depth than when it was used only to inform a person about an occupation and its requirements. The counselor must move from the idea of having a box of answers to being a person who facilitates the changes desired by the individual.

Each person is constantly becoming, progressing, changing; and personalized information can facilitate change, can affect the direction and pace. What happened yesterday or is happening now to the individual, he cannot do much about, but he can have an influence on what happens tomorrow. Man can affect his own life. Man wants to be responsible for his own decisions, to be the captain of his fate. Many times, however, he lacks the appropriate personal information to make the best possible decision. Each day brings new changes and so-called "truths" of yesterday become progressively out-of-date as today unfolds. Unless the individual adds and integrates the new and different information into his reservoir and dismisses the out-of-date, he will become lost in the social milieu. Adding knowledge is not enough. Personalizing and integrating information, and modifying attitudes are important for formulating a broad and firm foundation on which decision-making can become effective.

An individual gains information from many sources and has many experiences with people, things, and ideas. Working with the counselor is only one of those experiences. Hopefully, the experiences resulting from working with the counselor will be significant ones and over an extended period of time will contribute to the sequential experiences contributing to the counselee's growth and development. The individual needs many kinds of experiences, and the counselor can assist the individual in identifying and obtaining a wide variety of meaningful experiences. Personalized information processes are essential for the selection of these experiences and the means of gaining maximum benefits from them. The developmental approach is based on the long-term meaningful sequential interaction with people, things, and ideas. The obtaining of information on a given topic is generally not done all at one time. The information is pyramidal over an extended period of time and includes not only general and specific information but also the individual's perception of the information in relation to himself.

Youth of today must be prepared for the unknown because of the rapidity of the creation of new occupations. Much educational and occupational information necessary for future decision-making has not yet been identified or recorded. Another postulate is that an individual *must be able to evaluate, discard, and integrate information continually in order to facilitate his decision-making processes as new and varied opportunities arise.* The high school student who will not be entering the labor market for another three to six years probably will have another one to two thousand new occupations to consider that do not exist currently.

Technological advances have been causal factors for the change in the role of information. Technological advancements together with many other changes have made possible another postulate—*almost every individual will change occupations one or more times during his lifetime.* This postulate is a complete reversal from that of the past—not the training of an individual for a job, but the continued education of a person, the creation of a job for his stage of development, and the willingness to assist him in occupational mobility. The one thing known about the world of work is that tomorrow it will be different. In what way different no one is sure. This philosophy contrasts to that of the past, when an occupation was chosen for life. A person who enters the labor market today is, on the average, going to change occupations at least three times in his life, and the number of different positions or specific jobs that he may hold will be more. The individual can anticipate occupational mobility. The changing philosophy necessitates a change in information use, media, and purposes for counseling and guidance. Today a broader scope with more personalized information is needed to assist the individual in understanding and relating himself to an ever-changing world.

The way the counselor uses materials and the purposes he hopes to achieve are important. One should be more concerned about learning than one is about teaching, more concerned about change than about counseling, more concerned about the psychological approach than about the materialistic. Some counselors use the materialistic approach in that they use materials as absolutes or facts and have a tendency to give undue importance to material. They tend to explain each occurrence by the presence or lack of existence or nature of matter. In the information processes the materials, media, and facts are not to become the main theme. The postulate to encompass this point of view might be stated thus: *materials should be used as a means rather than an end*. The counselor should avoid working with materials; instead he should work with individuals and use information to facilitate their development. The developmental approach requires a new concept on the part of counselors rather than a conventional mass approach. Counselors are professional people, not technicians who hand out material according to some prescribed procedure. Counselors can be expected to understand the philosophical, psychological, anthropological, and sociological implications of what the individual is experiencing as he makes decisions regarding his life. A counselor is not effective because he has a piece of information to give an individual; rather he is effective when he assists the individual in obtaining, interpreting, and integrating information essential for making decisions. The decision-making process and decision theory (Gelatt and Clarke, 1967; Thoresen and Mehrens, 1967) have implications for personalizing information processes. The obtaining and internalizing of information extends over a period of time greater than the time during which a decision is made. Decision-making behavior may be unique to each individual; however, the long-term information processes have an integral part in the decision-making.

Another philosophical base for personalized information has its origin in the changing role of education in America today. The vehicle for social mobility in America once was education. Today education is not *the* vehicle for social mobility; it has become even more important—it has become the deciding factor in the kinds of occupations that will be open to an individual when he changes from one occupation to another. The individual's potential for education must be considered, not necessarily how much education he has obtained. The postulate might be stated that *men and women in America today are given the opportunity to change occupations provided that they have the potential for obtaining and are willing to obtain the education or training necessary.* Adult education is assuming a new role, with training for occupational mobility being only one part. Adults of all ages, including senior citizens, are continuing their education with life fulfillment being one of the major goals. Education has entered a new era, and information used by counselors is also entering a new era.

The user becomes the major determinant of what information and media are used. Information appropriate for one person may be inappropriate for another. The needs and maturity level of the user and the depth of information desired are important determinants. Information should be considered from the viewpoint of the potential user and of those who work with him, rather than placing primary emphasis upon external criteria; i.e., kind of paper, format, number of pictures, and so on. The basic philosophy in counseling and guidance is that the individual is fundamental and he, as the user, is the major determinant. The counselor is more concerned about understanding, meanings, and attitudes formed from the information processes than he is with a specific piece of material. Data in the raw form often have little value until interpretation is made by the individual and meaning is added through relationship. The same information used with two different people often has two different meanings; therefore the information processes, rather than the information, become important. The user and his world must be the first consideration in information communications.

Another basic postulate is that *the total information processes in all educational, occupational, and personal-social areas must be considered together rather than separately.* All three areas must be considered and each has a dependency upon the others. The individual may at times highlight one area over another. The informational processes should assist him in bringing all three into focus with one another. His personal-social development has implications for his educational and occupational development and vice versa. The areas are separated in this book for purposes of study, but one of the goals in filing materials is to accentuate the interrelatedness of the information. In many information programs the personal-social area is the smallest in amount of materials and resources available. An examination of current counseling theories would reveal that the emphases are now more upon the personal-social area than upon either the educational or the occupational area. Assuming that counselors do counsel according to the prevailing theories and assuming that change is based upon new information and insights, personal-social information processes should be given even more emphasis.

If information must be communicated to or perceived in some manner by the individual, then *personalized information processes must involve the principles of both—communications and counseling.* The basic considerations must be the person with whom communication is to take place, the areas or topics in which he wants and needs information, and the depth, including general, specific, and psychological involvement, at which information is needed. The depth of information is very important; however, the counselee may not always finish with one depth before moving to the next. He may fluctuate from one depth to another, back and forth, in his needs, as they pertain to a given area or topic. Also he may be at one depth on one topic and at another depth on another topic. The development concept does operate, but not on all topics at the same rate. In addition new topics are introduced from time to time, thus making the depth of information needed on a given topic an important consideration in the information processes.

Information processes are ongoing and extend over a lifetime. Today counselors are being employed not only in schools and higher educational institutions but also in businesses and industries, community agencies, and private practices. A counselor-throughout-life is coming within the realm of reality for more and more people. With counselors available to assist people throughout their lives, new and different ways of personalizing information processes must become a reality also. The counselor needs a concept or model by which he can organize his materials and plan to assist people effectively and efficiently. Materials must be coded, filed, stored, and readily retrieved. The volume of information has expanded tremendously and changes are occurring so rapidly that information becomes outdated in a relatively short time. A composite of the many facets in information seems to give support to the readiness for automation and computer-based information systems to assist in storage and retrieval of pertinent data. The counselor and others who work with the individual will still be needed. Their roles may change, and the counselor may be able to become more concerned with the individual and his information processes rather than with the information.

As previously noted, information becomes most meaningful when it serves a need. *Information contributes most to an individual's growth and development when the information has personal meaning and he can become involved with it.* When he can relate the information to himself, incorporate the new information into his reservoir of knowledge, alter his viewpoints where necessary, crystallize others, and use the information in his ongoing processes, including decision-making, then information has been expanded into the personalized information processes. The information processes must be inclusive enough to help the individual to perceive not only knowledge about people, things, and ideas but also about himself in relation to modifications as they are made or as they may be made.

Terminology and Definitions

If information as it is used in counseling and guidance is to be meaningful to the individual, then that information must include a wide spectrum of information that has potential for personal application. Included must be information about how the individual may be affected and how the information relates to him. Information in counseling and guidance is not the presentation of data in abstraction, but rather a personalizing of information so that the individual can integrate it into his reservoir of knowledge and thus broaden his perspective; so that he can obtain information to answer some of his questions, although probably creating others; or so that he can provide a feedback to being a validation of his concepts, including those about himself and his relation to the area being investigated.

Educational information, as usually defined, includes valid and usable data pertaining to educational or training opportunities, requirements, and so on. In such a definition the emphasis is upon the external factors and not upon how the individual relates to the educational or training possibilities. In this book the definition of educational information is expanded and emphasis is placed upon the implications of the educational information for and to the individual.

The educational information area includes all information essential for and to the individual, i.e., information that will facilitate his understanding of available educational (including training) opportunities, the successive levels of attainment necessary for continued progress, and the means by which additional alternatives may be made available. Also included are information and opportunities for the individual to have continuous feedback on his development; a means of evaluating his educational self-concept, ideas, and goals; understanding of the educational structure and some of its possible implications for him; and an approach to projecting himself into different educational situations prior to an actual tryout. Because education is a lifelong process, the information must assist each child, youth, and adult to obtain maximum benefits from each present and future educational situation in which he is or will be involved. The information should assist the individual in becoming aware of his increased societal expectations commensurate with each additional educational attainment. Trends in American and international education that may affect the individual are an important part of the educational information area. The information should enable each person to obtain, understand, integrate into his value system, and utilize educational information to the extent that it becomes an ongoing process. Also, the individual should became aware of avenues by which the educational structure may be changed. Educational information may be obtained through various media: materials and persons.

Occupational information as usually defined includes valid and usable data pertaining to the world of work, requirements, and so on. The emphasis in such a definition is upon an examination of what does or may exist in occupations, jobs, or positions including working conditions, rewards, and so on. The focus is upon the work performed and conditions prevailing rather than upon an attempt to help the individual to understand the implications of the world of work for him and how he may relate to it. For occupational information to become meaningful it must become personalized—one role of the counselor is to assist the individual in personalizing the occupational information processes.

The occupational information area includes all information that will facilitate the individual's understanding of and ability to utilize information about career fields in general, specific job requirements, work attitudes in an industrial society, and the occupational world's potential contribution to his self-fulfillment. Occupational information is provided to assist the individual in understanding career development and some of the processes through which he may proceed during his working life. The information must be applicable to the individual on his level and the information, to be comprehensive, must provide a means for the individual to understand whether or not he is perceiving and utilizing the information in a meaningful way. Because occupations and the world of work are rapidly changing, occupational information processes are lifelong; the uniqueness and constant fluctuation of individual needs necessitate a personalized process. The information may be obtained through the various media that assist an individual in his occupational development and in an understanding of the people employed in various occupations.

Personal-social information is not as often defined in literature as are educational and occupational information; however, the importance of personal-social information is reflected throughout the literature. Psychological and sociological studies in recent years have contributed much to man's understanding of himself, how he relates to his present environment, and even the assessment of his probable behavior in another potential environment. Today, the counselor has an important role in helping the individual to know himself, understand his present and potential environments, and examine the interrelationships among them. To do this, the individual needs information about himself, social and cultural groups, and some of the forces that do or may affect him in his present and future life.

The *personal-social information area* includes all information that will facilitate the individual's understanding about his present physical and social environments, potential environments of which he may become an integral part, values and limitations of each for his development, military obligations and opportunities, physical and psychological self, and economic conditions that exist or may develop that have implications for him. Personal-social information should assist the individual in becoming more effective in relations with members of his family, peers, and others, and in gaining maximum benefits from his experiences. Personal-social information extends over a lifetime and should be applicable to the individual and his needs. Effective personal-social information will assist the individual in developing realistic expectations and aspirations, leisure time activities for self-fulfillment, and an understanding of his contributions and potential roles in his society. The individual may obtain personal-social information through various media so as to perceive himself as he has been, is, and chooses to become within the limits of his potential.

Purposes of Personalized Information Processes

The preceding definitions of educational, occupational, and personal-social information included statements from which can be developed a list of purposes of personalized information processes in the counseling and guidance program. Personalized information processes are broader than just information. They encompass activities of the individual, the counselor, and others who are assisting the individual which enable him to obtain and interpret, select, internalize, integrate, modify, or crystallize viewpoints, and utilize information. The following list of purposes is a summary and should be supplemented by specific purposes for each of the three areas—educational, occupational, and personal-social.

> To supply information to individuals in order to increase their knowledge in occupational, educational, social, and personal areas, as well as to assist each person in the identification of specific choices that might be realistic for him.
>
> To make available to the individual information on present and potential alternatives.
>
> To facilitate the individual's understanding of his present circumstances and of how their modification may change the possibilities open to him, and thus to instill in him the desire to reevaluate his choices periodically on the basis of new circumstances and potential developments.
>
> To supply comprehensive information to enable an individual to make immediate choices, while also providing him with information for considering long-range alternatives.
>
> To provide, interpret, and relate information at the individual's maturity and educational level.

To assist the individual in obtaining the information necessary for increasing awareness of himself and his present and potential environments. (Hollis and Hollis, 1965, p. 274.)

To the preceding list of purposes should be added the purposes of recognizing the different maturity and educational levels of the individual, the sequential activities necessary for the development approach to become effective, the continuous change in the individual that may make any or all past information out-of-date at any time, and the cognitive and affective processes through which the individual must integrate the personalized information.

Role of Personalized Information in Education

Through personalized information processes in counseling and guidance, resource people and various kinds of information and media are made available and utilized with individuals to help them develop their occupational, educational, and personal-social attitudes and plans. Information is personalized and utilized with the individual so that he may integrate the information into his present knowledge and value systems as a basis for making immediate decisions, if needed, as well as for preparation for future decision-making.

The educational program of America contributes a vast amount of information to individuals and to groups. Teachers are trying constantly not only to help persons comprehend this information but also to interpret it in relation to themselves. Individuals generally are able to understand the implications of knowledge and skills for themselves; however, some individuals, at times, need additional assistance in personalizing this information. The counselor, teacher, and others can work conjointly so that the individual will receive maximum benefits in using this information.

As counselors collect data about an individual and as they study the growth and development of a group, the research should indicate the kinds of information and the media that may be most helpful to the group and to individuals within the group. The counselor may use the information directly with the group or individual, or, as is frequently the case, the counselor may assist the teacher or some other person to obtain and to use the information with the groups or individuals.

Assisting the growth and development of individuals is a general objective of education. The belief that growth and development are continuous processes is a basic premise of education and, in addition, educators hold the belief that an individual's growth and development are influenced by the kind of information available, the types of past and continuing experiences, and the people with whom he comes in contact. With these basic beliefs, the counseling and guidance program, and specifically the personalized information processes, have a very important role in the educational program of the individual, whether he be a child, youth, or adult, including senior citizens.

Summary

Change is inevitable and the direction and rate of change can be affected by man. As the amount of information has increased so has the rate of change increased. So much information is available from so many different sources today that selectivity becomes necessary. Man needs some information in order to make decisions, but he does not want or need all information; instead he wants information of personal meaning to him at a particular time.

Information in counseling and guidance has changed from including only information about occupations, job analysis, and entry requirements to including more information about the individual and his characteristics, the opportunities available to him, and the means for relating himself to the world of work, education, and social groups. Personalized information not only helps to answer questions, but also helps to broaden horizons for the individual. The processes by which an individual obtains, selects, and utilizes information over an extended period of time are of importance to counselors.

SELECTED REFERENCES

Baer, Max F., and Edward C. Roeber. *Occupational Information: The Dynamics of Its Nature and Use.* Chicago: Science Research Associates, Inc., 1964. Pp. 1–14, 359–365.

Borow, Henry, ed. *Man in a World at Work.* Boston: Houghton Mifflin Company, 1964. Pp. xiii–xvii, 411–433.

Ford, Donald H., and Hugh B. Urban. *Systems of Psychotherapy: A Comparative Study.* New York: John Wiley and Sons, Inc., 1963. Pp. 445–480.

Gelatt, H. B., and R. B. Clarke. "Role of Subjective Probabilities in the Decision Process," *Journal of Counseling Psychology,* **14** (July 1967), 332–341.

Hollis, Joseph W., and Lucile U. Hollis. *Organizing for Effective Guidance.* Chicago: Science Research Associates, Inc., 1965. Pp. 273–299.

Hoppock, Robert. *Occupational Information: Where to Get It and How to Use It in Counseling and in Teaching,* 3rd ed. New York: McGraw-Hill, Inc., 1967. Pp. 1–15, 131–133.

Isaacson, Lee E. *Career Information in Counseling and Teaching.* Boston: Allyn and Bacon, Inc., 1966. Pp. 3–18, 390–418.

Katz, Martin. *Decisions and Values, A Rationale for Secondary School Guidance.* New York: College Entrance Examination Board, 1963. 67 pages.

Norris, Willa. *Occupational Information in the Elementary School.* Chicago: Science Research Associates, Inc., 1963. Pp. 4–18, 36–40.

Norris, Willa, Franklin R. Zeran, and Raymond N. Hatch. *The Information Service in Guidance,* 2nd ed. Chicago: Rand McNally & Company, 1966. Pp. 3–27, 485–500.

Peters, Herman J., and James C. Hansen. *Vocational Guidance and Career Development: Selected Readings.* New York: The Macmillan Company, 1966. Pp. 30–40, 188–195, 239–275.

Proceedings, National Seminar on Vocational Guidance (Marquette, Michigan: Northern Michigan University). Jointly sponsored by the American Vocational Association and the American Personnel and Guidance Association, August 24–26, 1966. 151 pages.

Shartle, Carroll L. *Occupational Information: Its Development and Application,* 3rd ed. Englewood Cliffs, N.J.: Prentice-Hall, Inc., 1959. Pp. 1–25.

Thoresen, Carl E., and William A. Mehrens. "Decision Theory and Vocational Counseling: Important Concepts and Questions," *The Personnel and Guidance Journal,* 14 (October 1967), 165–172.

Williamson, E. G. *Vocational Counseling: Some Historical, Philosophical, and Theoretical Perspectives.* New York: McGraw-Hill, Inc., 1965. Pp. 3–14, 199–214.

Chapter 2

Historical Events,

Trends, and Implications

[There is an] urgent necessity for the constant renewal, reexamination, and reevaluation of our knowledge. There are no absolutes in knowledge which can be captured, delineated, and preserved forever unless our interest is in fossils rather than fresh and creative ideas.—ALBEE, 1966, p. 27.

Counseling and guidance started more than half a century ago. Many of today's practices are an outgrowth of the foundations developed over the years. Although comparatively new, counseling and guidance shows tremendous growth and changes are occurring frequently. To better understand its development and to recognize the need for and possible directions of future changes in counseling and guidance, one needs a knowledge of the results of research and of experiences in practice as well as of theories. Many persons and programs have contributed to the advancement of counseling and guidance.

Parsons' Concept of Information for the Individual

Frank Parsons, who was educated as a lawyer and engineer and worked as a professor and teacher, is generally credited with being the founder of the guidance movement in 1908. He was a teacher of career-choosing classes and did individual counseling at the Breadwinners' College and the Vocational Bureau in Boston. Frank Parsons is noted for having started vocational guidance, and, even more important, he helped to initiate the move to individualization.

Parsons placed emphasis upon the person and upon the individual's understanding himself, having a knowledge of the things about himself, and being able to interrelate this knowledge and understanding. He wrote in his book *Choosing A Vocation,* published in 1909, the following:

> In the wise choice of a vocation there are three broad factors: (1) a clear understanding of yourself, your aptitudes, abilities, interests, ambitions, resources, limitations, and their causes; (2) a knowledge of the requirements and conditions of success, advantages and disadvantages, compensation, opportunities, and prospects in different lines of work; (3) true reasoning on the relations of these two groups of facts. Every young person needs help on all three of these points. He needs all the information and assistance he can get. He needs counsel. He needs a vocational counselor. He needs careful and systematic help by experienced minds in making this greatest decision of his life. (p. 5.)

Parsons emphasized a system of counseling in which the individual was the focus of attention and in which the counselor assisted the individual using all the information obtainable.

E. G. Williamson, in his book *Vocational Counseling,* made the following statement:

> Essentially, Parsons' three-part formulation has continued, with some modification, to undergird modern practice until the close of the past decade, a span of almost half a century. By that time, modern techniques of psycho-therapy and the concepts of personality dynamics had made major inroads on certain emphases in counseling. (1965, p. 80.)

Williamson credits three persons as the originators of systems of counseling. In addition to Parsons he listed William Rainey Harper, founder and first president of the University of Chicago, and Lightner Witmer, a clinical psychologist at the University of Pennsylvania. Harper placed emphasis upon individualization of instruction and in one of his speeches stressed the importance of treating every student as if he were the only student in the institution. Williamson, in contrasting Parsons' and Harper's concepts, pointed out that Harper ". . . translated his concept of counseling into personal, social, and academic programs, in contrast with Parsons, who translated his similar concept into a system of personalized relationship centered on the choice of a vocation" (p. 85). Witmer made use of clinical psychology to diagnose learning difficulties and encouraged his assistant, Morris Viteles, 1921, to use clinical techniques in vocational guidance.

From the time of its conception, guidance has placed emphasis upon the individual's understanding of the world of work about him, upon making this occupational information available, and upon helping the individual to relate it to himself.

Influence of World War I

World War I had an influence upon the guidance program particularly in the emphasis placed upon psychological measurements and their application to the individual and his work. Two of the leading persons whose names are frequently mentioned in relation to vocational guidance are Franklin J. Keller, principal of a vocational high school in New York City and at one time Director of the National Occupational Conference, and Morris S. Viteles, Associate Professor of Psychology, University of Pennsylvania. In their book *Vocational Guidance Throughout the World* (1937) they wrote about the effect of World War I.

> In general, the World War [I] emphasized the importance of vocational psychology and accelerated its development in all of the major countries involved. . . . Psychologists were called upon to render service in the classification of Army and Navy personnel and in the selection of men for specialized branches of these services. . . . The success of these methods contributed to their increased use in industry and in vocational guidance after the war. The war also furthered such developments by throwing on the labor market a large number of disabled men for whom some occupation had to be found. The difficulty of finding occupations suitable for disabled men encouraged the psychological analysis of occupations. . . . Thus all elements of the population were drawn behind both the movement for organized vocational guidance and the search for systematic, scientific techniques for use in this program. (p. 294.)

In the 1932 report on the White House Conference on Child Health and Protection by the Committee on Education and Training, F. J. Kelly, Chairman, reported that during World War I occupational research was conducted and job analysis and specifications were made as a means of assisting in employment activities. The Federal Government was a major contributor to occupational research during this time by promoting the study of single occupations by the War Department, the Bureau of Labor Statistics, and the Federal Bureau of Rehabilitation (p. 90).

During this period of national emergency the need was recognized for additional information about jobs, about education, and about individuals. The testing movement made great strides. Terman revised the Binet Individual Test (1916) and during World War I group tests of intelligence, such as the Army Alpha and Beta, were introduced (Stewart and Warnath, 1965, p. 6).

During World War I, in 1917, important Federal legislation, known as the Smith-Hughes Act, was passed. The intent of this act was to provide support for vocational education. At various times, legislative modifications that enlarged and expanded this act have accounted for some of the most influential steps in the history of counseling and guidance, especially in the development of information for individuals and later in providing funds for employing counselors to work with individuals.

Depression and the Role of the Federal Government

During the depression years, the Federal Government helped to change the role of information processes. Millions of people both young and old were out of work. In 1933 the Civilian Conservation Corps was formed. In the same year the Wagner-Beyser Act made possible the creation of the United States Employment Service, which was charged with promoting and developing "a national system of employment offices for men, women, and juniors" (Reed, 1946, p. 68). In the following year, 1934, an occupation research program was established as part of the United States Employment Service "to furnish public employment offices and other cooperating agencies with operating tools which will facilitate the proper counseling, classification, and placement of workers" (Borow, 1964, p. 54). In 1935 the National Youth Administration was established with the objective of encouraging job training, counseling, and placement.

In 1937 Keller and Viteles wrote "No reference to vocational guidance is yet to be found in federal legislation, and very little in the laws of the states" (p. 35). From the very first legislation until the depression the Federal Government had not taken an active role in providing vocational guidance and counseling. During the depression Federal acts were passed that affected the collection and supplying of information and the providing of professional persons to work with individuals in regard to educational and occupational matters.

In 1938 the Federal Government, through the United States Office of Education under the Division of Vocational Education, did organize the Occupational Information and Guidance Service (Borow, 1964, pp. 55–56). The new service was formed following the proposal made for such an organization by the National Vocational Guidance Association at its national convention in 1937 (Borow, 1964, p. 10).

Another significant outgrowth of the depression and the role of the Federal Government was the publication of the first edition of the *Dictionary of Occupational Titles* in 1939. This publication became one of the first major tools in occupational counseling: the dictionary contained specific and accurate information on more than 18,000 American occupations (Borow, 1964, p. 56). In 1940 the United States Congress established the Occupational Outlook Service within the Bureau of Labor Statistics of the United States Department of Labor (Borow, 1964, p. 56).

World War II and the Changes

World War II brought even more changes. America found itself engaged in a war for which it was not prepared. People were needed to fill new jobs as the nation began to turn its attention to production of new items to help in the war. The armed services needed quick information about individuals in order to place them in the best positions, thus creating a greater emphasis on testing.

America by this time had begun to make a shift in the kind of work to be done. The nation, which had been primarily agricultural, was shifting to industrialization, and to the engagement of a tremendous number of workers in service occupations. The shift necessitated a change in the amount of education required by workers to perform jobs. Such a shift had been partially forced by technology and automation. An urgency developed for information about education, about occupations, and particularly about the personal and social areas.

In World War II and immediately following, America took on a look of urbanization and suburbanization. This shift brought about a new way of life in America, a way of life quite different from that in America's early days and quite different from that in the days when Frank Parsons helped to start the guidance movement. Along with this new look, World War II contributed to changing the role of women in America. Women began to be active in different types of occupations, to work as equals with men, and to increase in number and percentage in the labor force. In the world of work, equal rights for individuals regardless of race, sex, or creed began to be practiced, making the need for a new kind of understanding even more important.

Automation and Cybernation

Both *automation* and *cybernation* are terms that have come into use since World War II. The effect of automation and cybernation is changing American society, education, and the working man. The emphasis today has been shifted to technology and automation, resulting in more educational prerequisites for employment. The major occupational group that has increased the most in number of persons employed is the professional and technical group, the one requiring the most education and training (Wolfbein, 1964, p. 204). Not only are the occupations that require the most education expanding the fastest, but the national educational average for the labor force has increased, requiring additional education for workers to remain competitive in the labor market. The workers in clerical and sales groups each have an average education of more than twelfth grade, whereas the people in professional and technical occupations, other than athletics and acting, average almost the equivalent of one-third year of graduate school education. (Table 2-1)

Table 2-1

EDUCATIONAL ATTAINMENT OF WORKERS, EIGHTEEN YEARS OLD AND OVER, BY MAJOR OCCUPATIONAL GROUP, MARCH 1967.

Occupational Group	Median Years of Education
Professional, technical, and kindred workers	16.3
Managers, officials, and proprietors, except farm	12.7
Clerical and kindred workers	12.5
Sales workers	12.5
Craftsmen, foremen, and kindred workers	12.0
Service workers, except private household	11.5
Operatives and kindred workers	10.8
Laborers, except farm and mine	9.5
Farmers and farm managers	9.1
Private household workers	8.9
Farm laborers and foremen	8.6

Source: Based on data from Hamel, Harvey R., "Educational Attainment of Workers, March 1967," *Special Labor Force Report* No. 92, Reprint No. 2559, Bureau of Labor Statistics, United States Department of Labor, p. A-14.

Automation and cybernation have brought about changes in attitudes toward work and have been influential in modifying women's role in and away from home. Today one in every three workers is a woman, with almost one in every two women aged forty-five to fifty-four in the United States in the labor force.

Automation and cybernation have helped to make possible changes in the type of work performed. As the type of work has changed, opportunities have come for workers to upgrade themselves. In recent years workers have been able to upgrade themselves faster than they once were able to do. Because of various factors, such as seniority rights, the older worker has had an opportunity to upgrade himself faster than the younger worker, but the educational attainment of the older worker on the average is less than that of the younger worker. To take advantage of the opportunities for upgrading, many workers have had to obtain additional training or education. This may be one of the major factors in the rapid expansion of continuing education in America.

The changes in the working world require the worker to be flexible and adaptable. His life will be filled with the certainty of uncertainty. He will hold an occupation that is sure to change, but he will not know how or to what his occupation, job, or position will be changed. While working in one position he must be preparing himself for modifications in that position or possibly a vertical or horizontal move to another position, possibly even with a different employer.

Rapid changes in America today have not been isolated. Changes in the technological world have brought about changes in the sociological world as well. These rapid changes are requiring more information for the individual and particularly information not just about the changes, but information that is personalized so that the individual can see the projected implications and usefulness for himself.

Federal Legislation

Federal legislation since Sputnik in 1957 has had a tremendous impact upon guidance. In 1958 the National Defense Education Act (NDEA) became a reality. Title V-A and -B of this act probably did as much as any one thing to expand the counseling and guidance field and to assist in the preparation of counselors, particularly for elementary and secondary schools. In 1964 the act was amended to broaden and extend its scope to include junior colleges, colleges, universities, and technical institutes.

In 1961 the Area Redevelopment Act (ARA) was passed to assist in the vocational training of unemployed and underemployed persons in specific redevelopment areas. This act was the forerunner of the Federal legislation, passed in 1962, known as the Manpower Development and Training Act (MDTA). The MDTA recognized training needs on a nationwide basis rather than restricting training to certain depressed areas. The ARA and MDTA "included provisions for affording personnel and guidance services to persons who have been displaced from the labor market due to industrial, economic or sociological changes and to those who are under-employed for similar reasons" (APGA, 1966, p. 3).

The following year Congress enacted the Vocational Education Act (VEA) of 1963, which according to Grant Venn has already had tremendous implications in education. In time VEA and modifications of it "promises a new philosophy in the relationship between education and work in the United States" (Venn, 1964, p. 62). One of the major shifts in some new Federal legislation has caused educational programs for vocational education to operate in conjunction or cooperation with public employment services. The VEA among other things made funds available for construction of vocational-technical schools. The implications of vocational-technical schools may not be fully understood at this time, but certainly they have affected the educational and vocational information processes for many young persons. The VEA funds have been used to hold many conferences and seminars, which have been instrumental in generating and implementing new concepts applicable to vocations.

The Economic Opportunity Act of 1964 included two major programs: the College-Work-Study Program for needy college students and the Adult Basic Education Program for adults who have less than a grade school education, to help them obtain employment.

In 1965 Congress passed two major acts—the Elementary and Secondary Education Act (ESEA) and the Higher Education Act—which placed a new emphasis upon information and the dispersion of such information to those who can utilize it.

Other Major Changes Affecting Information Processes

In addition to changes already mentioned, many others are taking place in America that are affecting the role of information processes in counseling and guidance programs. For instance, the sociological changes in America today make it important for the individual to obtain personalized information about the society in which he will participate. The sociological changes applicable directly to an individual are sometimes difficult to identify, but the changes are taking place and the counselor's role in helping the individual to obtain the information is becoming of more concern to more counselors today than ever before.

Another change is the role of women in today's society, and specifically women's role in the world of work, which has changed the kind of counseling and guidance needed by girls and women. Some information required by them may not be the same as that needed by boys or men.

An additional change is the rather highly developed labor union organization. The effect of the labor union upon the individual is of tremendous importance, but frequently pertinent information is difficult for him to obtain.

With the Federal Government entering into programs for minority groups, additional emphases have been placed upon information for members of the minority groups. Where and how to obtain this kind of information becomes another item of consideration for the counselor.

The change in concept about the amount of education necessary for an individual has influenced the information processes. At one time elementary school education was considered the desirable amount. Then a high school education became the principal terminating point. Today continuing education for each individual has become a necessity.

Trends and Implications

In addition to the changes already mentioned, the counselor should be concerned with trends, as far as he can determine them, and the implications of the trends upon his work. In the following paragraphs are presented some changes that are occurring or have occurred and that may be trends. Along with each of the possible trends, possible implications are presented. Table 2-2 is a summary of trends that will affect the personalized information processes. Each counselor must keep abreast of changes, trends, and implications. Unless the counselor stays informed, he may find that his skills, techniques, and competencies are soon outdated. The counseling profession is young and changing rapidly.

One of the major trends that will affect the counselor's work is the shift from the concept that a person's education should be confined to the years of his youth to the concept that education is a lifelong, continuous process. Education has for years been considered continuous, but the return to school at various times in life has only in recent years begun to be accepted by the lay person. Education for the upgrading and retraining of people will become a major and continuous part of education. The trend is away from a terminal education and is toward continuing education for increasing one's opportunities and one's self-fulfillment. Adult and community education for career, leisure time, greater knowledge, and self-fulfillment is growing at a rapid pace with education for and during retirement becoming another important segment of continuing education.

In the early years of vocational guidance a counselor's responsibility was to help the individual decide on an occupation for life. Today the task is not selecting one occupation, but preparing the individual to accept an expectation of three or four more occupations during his working life. Therefore, counselors, in the educational systems particularly, can no longer afford merely to help an individual prepare for an occupation, but they must help the individual develop an attitude of flexibility and adaptability. No longer can one think in terms of preparing for a lifetime occupation, but rather preparing for entry into a first occupation.

The preceding trend means then that an education such as the individual receives in a formal school setting and as structured under the single occupation concept is a thing of the past. Rather than the goal of completing elementary school, or graduating from eighth grade or high school, each person must develop an attitude of flexibility and a reliance on continuous education. The expectation of three, four, or more occupations during a working life will force him, in terms of his occupation, to obtain more education to increase his opportunities. These

Table 2-2

TRENDS THAT WILL AFFECT THE PERSONALIZED INFORMATION PROCESSES.

From	$\longrightarrow$	Toward
An occupation for life		Expectation of three or more occupations during working life
Eighth grade education as standard		High school education for all
Socio-economic mobility primarily by educational means		Socio-economic mobility dependent upon characteristics and activities of individual
Employ individual to do a specific job		Create a job for the individual (talent search)
Educate for an occupation		Educate for occupational flexibility (entry with expectation of change)
Long working hours on given job		Increased leisure time or job moonlighting
Problem-oriented counseling and guidance program		Developmental approach with personalized information an integral component
Education confined to childhood and youth years		Continuing education throughout life
Large percentage of high ability persons terminating education early		Large percentage of high and average ability persons continuing education at post-high-school level
Secondary school as almost exclusively college preparatory		Public education assuming greater responsibility for preparing young people to enter into changed and changing world of work

three or four occupations will not necessarily be at the same level, because there will be opportunities for upward mobility within occupations and not just horizontal mobility from job to job.

A few years ago the average schooling was an eighth grade education. Today a high school education is almost a reality for all. The drop-out rate has been reduced and for the drop-outs and potential drop-outs specialized programs are being established. In the late 1940's and in the 1950's a higher percentage of high ability individuals terminated their education earlier than now. Today the trend is toward a proportionate increase of high ability individuals attending college, and this percentage is increasing faster than the percentage of the total group of high school graduates who attend college (Berdie and Hood, 1965, p. 37). Although an increasing percentage of the population is graduating from high school, the percentage of graduates attending college is increasing even more rapidly.

Economic and educational assistance of the culturally disadvantaged by the Federal Government probably will involve more students from these populations in education and training programs and they will remain in these programs for a greater length of time than in the past. Creating a learning atmosphere that will hold these students in school will be a challenge; in addition they must be oriented for flexibility to change.

One of the reasons that culturally disadvantaged individuals lose interest in education is that education usually has a delayed effect— in other words, from the time the student learns to the time he can apply the knowledge a time lag occurs. The culturally disadvantaged want immediate results, want to be taught for immediate use. Once such an individual accepts his ability to learn and begins to progress educationally, he needs help in understanding the opportunities that become available to him through education and in understanding the possible necessity of more education before he can reach his potential level of attainment.

In the past, not so much in America as in some other countries, the individual remained throughout life at the socio-economic level into which he was born. The trend today, which influences the work of the counselor, is toward a social and economic mobility dependent upon the characteristics and activities of the individual. Education is not necessarily the vehicle for climbing the socio-economic ladder that it once was. Personalized information becomes increasingly important in assisting the individual to understand himself and how he may move from one group to another or from one socio-economic level to another. A person who has a high social or high economic level may have mobility downward if he does not assume the responsibility that is essential at that level. The counselor is responsible for trying to help the individual understand the kinds of responsibilities that go with the level at which he is living.

In the past the counselor helped the individual to choose the job or occupation and then outlined an educational program that would qualify him. Many counselors may still use this plan of operation. Actually today the potential educational level of an individual, not the level he has attained, will determine the occupational level into which he may move. Therefore, a reverse of the past is true—*the individual may choose an educational level and strive for it and then the job opportunities may follow.*

In the past a job **was** identified and then a person was employed to fill the job. The **trend** today is to employ a talented person and create a job for him. Today a person does not necessarily have to adjust himself to the scheme of present occupations. Industry is creating jobs for people who have the personality and talent to make major contributions. Those who possess skills, such as technicians, are also being employed by industry even when the company does not have a specific position open. Such people can be retrained for positions that will be open in the company by the time the training is complete. With the rapid change in occupations an individual cannot plan with certainty to enter a particular sequence of occupations because by the time the individual is ready to enter the labor market major occupational changes may have occurred. New occupations are being created at a rapid rate. In the *Dictionary of Occupational Titles, 1965* (D. O. T.), published 16 years after preceding D.O.T., 6,432 jobs new to the Dictionary were listed. On that basis, *an average of 402 new job definitions have developed each year; thus more than one was developed for every day in the year.* The implications for counselors might be more forcefully understood if one recognizes that if this rate of new definitions continues, then during the 13 years that a child spends in elementary and secondary schools, more than 5,000 new job definitions will have been created. Thus *approximately one out of every seven job definitions existing at high school graduation time will not have existed at the time the child started in kindergarten.*

Another trend affecting the need for personalized information is the number of working hours per week on a given job. With shorter working hours, an individual must decide how to spend the additional hours. He may decide to use it for lesiure-time activities or for job moonlighting. Additional information is provided on this topic in Chapter 10. Preparation for his decisions about lesiure time should be based on self-understanding and information about the world into which he wants to project himself.

The approach to guidance and counseling is shifting from problem-oriented counseling to the inclusion of developmental counseling. In the past the counselor spent most of his time with people with problems. Today the change in emphasis and the number of counselors available has made possible a trend in which an individual may come to the guidance office to solve a problem or he may come to promote his growth and development. Personalizing the information processes can contribute to assisting an individual who has a problem, who is attempting to avoid or adjust to situations, or who is making progress and wants to further his growth and development.

Summary

The role of information processes has changed since the days when Frank Parsons first did vocational counseling. Various historical events have affected the role of counseling and guidance and the counselor's role in information processes. Testing was introduced during World War I and expanded in World War II. The Federal Government has affected the guidance movement through such legislation as the Smith-Hughes Act, the George Borden Act, the NDEA, the ARA, the MDTA, the Vocational Education Act, the Economic Opportunity Act, the ESEA, the Higher Education Act, and modifications to some of these acts. The Federal Government has affected the information available by such steps as publication of the *Dictionary of Occupational Titles*, establishment of the Occupational Research Program, and the development of the Occupational Information and Guidance Service within the United States Office of Education and the Occupational Outlook Service within the United States Department of Labor. These changes by the Federal Government are reflections of changes in the society and in the role of counselors.

Recent changes and trends resulting from automation and cybernation, Federal legislation, and sociological factors influence the role of the counselor and the need to personalize information for the individual. Some changes are sufficient in magnitude and innovation to cause trends that have implications for counselors. Trends, such as the expectation of three or more occupations during a working life, the creation of jobs by industry for individuals, education for occupational flexibility, and adult and community education are producing modifications in the information processes and the techniques used by counselors.

SELECTED REFERENCES

Albee, George W. "Psychology and the Body of Knowledge Unique to the Profession of Education," in *The Body of Knowledge Unique to the Profession of Education*. Washington, D.C.: Pi Lambda Theta, 1966. Pp. 27–44.

American Personnel and Guidance Association, Committee on Professional Preparation and Standards, "A Proposal to Improve and Expand Accreditation of Programs of Graduate Preparation in Personnel and Guidance." Washington, D.C.: American Personnel and Guidance Association, Third Draft, Oct. 13, 1966. 15 pages.

Baer, Max F., and Edward Roeber. *Occupational Information: The Dynamics of Its Nature and Use*. Chicago: Science Research Associates, Inc., 1964. Pp. 453–460.

Berdie, Ralph F., and Albert B. Hood. *Decisions for Tomorrow: Plans of*

High School Seniors for After Graduation. Minneapolis: University of Minnesota Press, 1965. Pp. 27–40.

Borow, Henry, ed. *Man in a World at Work.* Boston: Houghton Mifflin Company, 1964. Pp. 3–23, 45–64, 155–173, 215–256, 434–459, 487–533, 557–585.

Brewer, John M. *History of Vocational Guidance: Origins and Early Development.* New York: Harper & Row, Publishers, 1942. 344 pages.

Brewer, John M. *The Vocational Guidance Movement: Its Problems and Possibilities.* New York: The Macmillan Company, 1919; 333 pages.

Keller, Franklin J., and Morris S. Viteles. *Vocational Guidance Throughout the World, A Comparative Survey.* New York: W. W. Norton & Company, Inc., 1937. 575 pages.

Kelley, F. J., Chairman, Section III—Education and Training, Committee on Vocational Guidance and Child Labor, White House Conference on Child Health and Protection, *Vocational Guidance.* New York: The Century Co., 1932. 396 pages.

Parsons, Frank. *Choosing a Vocation.* Boston: Houghton Mifflin Company, 1909. 165 pages.

Peters, Herman J., and James C. Hansen. *Vocational Guidance and Career Development: Selected Readings.* New York: The Macmillan Company, 1966. Pp. 1–19, 227–238.

Reed, Anna Y. *Occupational Placement, Its History, Philosophies, Procedures, and Educational Implications.* Ithaca, N.Y.: Cornell University Press, 1946. 350 pages.

Stewart, Lawrence H., and Charles F. Warnath. *The Counselor and Society, A Cultural Approach.* Boston: Houghton Mifflin Company, 1965. Pp. 3–23.

Tanner, Daniel. *Schools for Youth: Change and Challenge in Secondary Education.* New York: The Macmillan Company, 1965. Pp. 3–114.

Venn, Grant, assisted by Theodore J. Marchese, Jr. *Man, Education, and Work: Postsecondary Vocational and Technical Education.* Washington, D.C.: American Council on Education, 1964. Pp. 38–72, 112–128, 138–156.

Williamson, E. G. *Vocational Counseling: Some Historical, Philosophical, and Theoretical Perspectives.* New York: McGraw-Hill, Inc., 1965. Pp. 72–149.

Wolfbein, Seymour. *Employment and Unemployment in the United States: A Study of the American Labor Force.* Chicago: Science Research Associates, Inc., 1964. Pp. 181–208.

Wrenn, C. Gilbert. *The Counselor in a Changing World.* Wassington, D.C.: American Personnel and Guidance Association, 1962. 195 pages.

Chapter 3

Concepts—Coordination

and Interrelationships

Important, long-term effects of conditioning do not depend primarily on numerous repetitions but on the critical factor of the state of the organism at the time of the conditioning experience and on subsequent developments.

—MCCURDY, 1961, p. 164.

Personalizing information necessitates making the information available when the individual is ready rather than at the convenience of the information provider. Information as an integral part of counseling and guidance is more than information on an occupation and related information on the amount of education necessary to obtain the job. The information processes extend over a lifetime as the individual utilizes information pertinent to areas of his concern and at a depth that has meaning to him. The individual wants the information to be related to himself and himself to the information; thus, a feedback is essential not only at the time of decision but also over an extended period of time.

Contribution of Information to Developmental Concept

The individual lives in an environment of not only biological changes, but also changes in the opportunities and alternatives open to him. The individual is dynamic, an ever-changing person himself. Information can keep him informed of changes and keep him abreast of changes. But even more important, personalized information can help him to be prepared for changes and to contribute to changes; and he himself may be able in part to establish the course and extent of change.

34

Changes do not just happen; they are caused. The rate of change today is greater than at any time in history. Reasons must exist. One of the reasons is increased education and an opportunity for the individual to obtain more information about himself and his world. The counselor has an important role in working with the individual. The counselor is an agent of change—he helps the individual to obtain educational, occupational, and personal-social information that is as personalized as possible and is obtained at the most appropriate time.

If the individual is in a constant state of change, then certainly the developmental concept is fundamental. What is happening probably is based upon what has happened, and what will happen probably will be determined by what is happening. With this developmental concept, information used by the counselor as he works with an individual should be personalized and should be developmental also. The information used in the beginning should be information that helps the individual *broaden his outlook* on a particular topic. As he broadens his outlook, he may want more *specific information,* and then he may begin to want a *feedback* of how he personally relates to the information. The development of the individual occurs in all areas—the educational, the occupational, the personal, and the social. The individual himself needs and wants information in all the areas and at times the persons who work with him also will need to have information in order to facilitate his development. Thus, the counselor has a role not only in helping the individual obtain information, but also in giving information to other people who work with him. Accepting the developmental concept, then, means collecting and utilizing information sequentially over an extended period of time with individuals, based upon their state of readiness and upon the desired purposes to be achieved. The information cannot be accidental, but must be collected according to the area in which the individual does or may need assistance. The approach indicated here of recognizing who is to use the information, the area in which he is to be assisted, and the purposes for which the information is being used, begins to make the information program take on not only a developmental concept but a recognition of the dimensions within that development.

Approaches to Collecting Information

Job analyses have been made by the Federal Government (Chapter 2) and the D.O.T. has been published periodically. The purpose for these studies and the publishing of the D.O.T. was to assist in understanding occupational requirements and to facilitate the job placement of people. The D.O.T. includes a coding system that provides a means for counselors to file information according to specific occupations. The coding system causes evaluation of information in terms of the occupation instead of projected uses with individuals. The coding system tends to produce the selection of specific information about a given occupation. Information that is general and tends to cover several occupations or fields of work is difficult to code and thus is infrequently selected by the counselor for inclusion in his files.

Educational information has not been extensively coded and elaborate filing systems have not been commercially produced. The counselor is often left to his own ingenuity and therefore frequently files information alphabetically, primarily by names of schools or areas of study. Such a file system forces the evaluation of information in terms of the school or area of study rather than the projected use to be made of the information with an individual.

Personal-social information has been, by many counselors, an informal, somewhat accidental collection of information. The filing has for the most part been done alphabetically by topic classification. Counselors often find a need for information with individuals but frequently lack the kind of information needed.

In all three areas the usual approach to collecting, coding, filing, collating, and utilizing have to some extent caused counselors to seek and use information containing specific information about a given topic. The choice of the material used has been primarily evaluated from the external or subject (topic, occupation, school, and so on) viewpoint. This approach is good but frequently is too narrow for the scope of activities performed by counselors. As counselors increase their scope and the kinds of people with whom they work, additional depths of information are needed. The production of information may be dependent upon the development of an approach that will identify more clearly than has previously been done the areas and purposes of the information needed. Just as in chemistry, more elements were discovered and better identification and relationships were understood after the production of the periodic chart. Counselors need an approach or concept that will help them collect and utilize the information useful to the people with whom they do or may work.

The 3-D Concept of Personalizing Information

The information processes in counseling and guidance makes use primarily of the principles underlying communications. When trying to personalize information, the main concern is to communicate that information to the person or persons. In counseling and guidance, information is not an abstraction but rather is of meaning only when it applies to an individual. Counselors are concerned about individuals; counselors want to use information to assist the individual in his development. Personalizing the educational and occupational information processes forces the consideration of three dimensions—*people, areas,* and *depth.* (See Figure 3-1.)

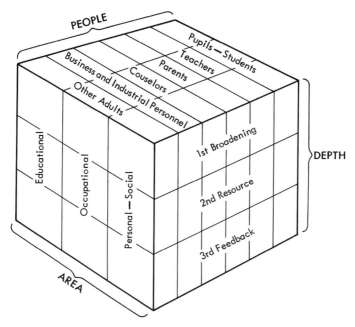

Figure 3-1. THREE-DIMENSIONAL CONCEPT FOR USE OF INFORMATION IN THE DEVELOPMENTAL PHASE OF GUIDANCE.

In the information processes, a counselor at first is not concerned with what the information is, but rather with *whom* it is to be used. The first dimension to be considered by the counselor is the people who will be using the information, so that the information selected can be as personal and as meaningful as possible. Is the information going to be used by a young child, a teen-ager, or an adult? Is the information meant for the teacher or another professional person, such as a fellow member of the counseling staff who works with the individual? Is the information to be used by an employer within the business and industrial community or perhaps by other adults in the community? To whom is the information to be made available? In other words, the first dimension that must be considered is the counselee himself and the other people who are working or may work with him. The first dimension may be entitled *people.* If the people for whom the information is meant are not clearly identified then the other dimensions in the communication process—personalizing information—probably will be unsuccessful.

The second dimension that must be considered is the dimension of *areas* in which the individual is to receive assistance. Simply stated, in what area or body of knowledge is he asking for or needing information? In some cases the initiative for obtaining the information may not be taken by the individual but rather by the counselor, who may use the information to create a readiness. The information areas usually considered in counseling and guidance are educational, occupational, and personal-social.

The third dimension that must be considered is the *depth* of information for which the individual is ready. The purpose for which the information will be used is probably the determinant of the third dimension. One way to subdivide the third dimension into different depths is to examine the purposes for which a counselor helps the individual acquire information. Generally speaking, when the individual knows nothing about a topic and is trying to obtain information, he wants a broadening concept; he is looking for something to broaden horizons for him, information that will make it possible for him to have a broader overview and a better understanding. The broadening concept is a fundamental one at the elementary school level in educational information, in occupational information, and in personal-social information, but it is just as essential to teen-agers and adults. For example, when an individual has been working in an occupation that is being replaced by automation, not only in the company where he has been working but throughout the nation, then to remain employed he is forced to change occupations. He may have been in that occupation for thirty or forty years, but now he must change occupations. If he has been very narrow in his vision of the occupational world, one of the first purposes of information, regardless of his age, is to help broaden his concept about occupations, about opportunities, and about himself. Broadening, then, is the first depth of the three dimensions and may be applicable to a person of any age as he develops and wants to explore new topics.

After a topic has been explored somewhat by an individual, he may want to know more and he may seek specific information—second depth information—on the topic. Examples would be his need for particulars about a certain job, about a school, about society, or about himself; his need to know how well he is doing in a given school subject; or his need to know how well he is achieving in comparison to others. This specific information constitutes the second depth; within this depth is resource information.

The third depth of information—feedback—is one that has been considered by counselors since the very beginning of counseling and guidance, but has been somewhat separated from rather than included in the continuum of information processes. In personalizing information some means must be provided for helping the individual to obtain information for validating his self-concept, for getting a verification of his decisions before total implementation. Some feedback should be almost immediate whereas other feedback may extend over years, or in some instances may be postponed for a given time. For example, if an individual decides that he wants to be a medical doctor, how will he know two years from now whether or not he is making the progress he should be making? What kind of feedback should he expect? Where would he go to get the information?

The three-dimensional concept (3-D) has been formulated from principles established in various areas including counseling and guidance. By using the three dimensions, that is, by starting with considerations about *people* (P), *area* (A), and *depth* (D), the counselor might be on the launching PAD for work with an individual. Not only will these three dimensions provide personalizing information for the counselor, but the concept can serve to identify the kind of information needed by the counselor. The 3-D concept can become a framework for collecting and collating information.

The first depth information is to increase awareness, a removing of blinders, a broadening of horizons. It is the branching out for the individual; it often stirs curiosity.

The second depth information begins to help the individual to know the specifics. He may be able more nearly to complete his spectrum of information on a given topic. The second depth information puts color and detail into the spectrum. It is filling in the unknown—making information a continuum from beginning to end.

The third depth information begins to help the individual to recognize the lines of the spectrum with which he can identify. The individual begins to identify in the breadth of information specifics that apply to him. With adequate third depth information the individual is able to discard information that is not applicable to him at this time under these circumstances and that does not facilitate his development.

The three depths are a continuum extending from the unknown, to awareness, to comprehension, to applicability or selectivity. Personalized information is always in a state of fluctuation for the individual; it is dynamic and ongoing. Additional information at one depth may move the individual into the need for information at another depth. Once he gets specifics, he may say "That topic is not for me"; and then he returns to a need for the broadening depth. Graphically, the accumulation of information on a given topic could be shown as in Figure 3-2. An individual of any age may need and get information at a given depth. When he has obtained the information at one depth, he may continue to seek information at that depth or he may go directly to another depth. He may go back and forth between depths instead of showing progressive or chronological advancement. Personalized information is obtained in

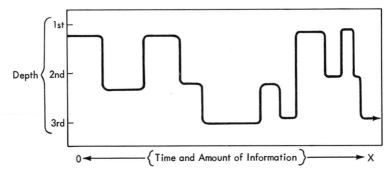

Figure 3-2. SCHEMATIC REPRESENTATION OF AN INDIVIDUAL OBTAINING IN-FORMATION OVER A PERIOD OF TIME.

a sequence, and the information obtained at a given time is dependent upon the person and the area.

Structure

Information in counseling and guidance is more than information on occupations and related information on the amount of education necessary to obtain the job. Counselors are recognizing the importance of information in the development of the individual. Information becomes a particularly vital part of the individual's development if the information can be personalized and made meaningful to him—and he has an opportunity to relate himself to the information. The feedback (third level of the depth dimension) is essential not only at the time of decision but over an extended period, so that the individual is prepared for the decision-making process and following it for an evaluation of the decision made. Information in counseling and guidance should help motivate children, youth, and adults to explore their own opportunities and to see themselves and the world about them as an intriguing, exciting, enjoyable challenge. Personalized information begins to fill a role of helping the individual to open his future even wider, to make his horizons broader, so that he begins to see alternatives that, without the information, he never would have considered.

In this book, personalized educational and occupational information processes are presented from the standpoint of the psychological and sociological approach rather than from a materialistic approach; i.e., the information processes are considered in relation to the personal and social implications for the individual rather than to the universality of facts without consideration of the person and the situation. Materials are used, but materials become a means rather than an end. The stress is placed on the users rather than on the information. The important considerations include with whom the work is to be done; what kind of a person he is; and under his present conditions, what information will help him make the greatest growth. The developmental approach is advocated rather than a chronological or definite time approach. The emphasis is on the individual and his needs for growth and development, rather than on assumptions based on data from other persons. In the past the assumption often has been made that each individual needs certain kinds of information at given grade levels or in given situations. Using the psychological and sociological approach, the emphasis is on the individual and his needs rather than asking, "What age is he now?" or "What should we give him now because he is in this school grade or this company?"

Counselors work with individuals, although at times they may do so in group settings. Always the counselor, as a professional person, is interested in the total individual within the total sociological, psychological setting. The counselor, then, begins to use information with the individual from a personal or perceptual or phenomenological approach, rather than from an external or objective approach (Combs and Snygg, 1959, pp. 10–11). The phenomenological approach seeks to make the information take on meaning from the individual's own point of view rather than from the viewpoint of another person or from an impersonal objective approach. The perceptual view of the individual and how information may help to extend his perceptions are the basis of information selection. With the kind of structure outlined, counselors in different settings have an important responsibility for helping the individuals with whom they work obtain the kind of information that has personal meaning to them as they go through processes of change. Personalized occupational and educational information becomes meaningful for counselors working in community agencies, business and industry, and educational institutions at all levels.

Counseling and guidance activities, including personalizing educational and occupational processes, start early. As Frank Miller stated: "It is in the elementary school that pupils acquire values and form attitudes that will have a lasting effect upon their future behavior" (1961, p. 11). If values and attitudes are formed in the elementary school, then here is where counselors must start to work. Here is the place where information of the first depth must be presented and utilized about the world of work. The second and third depths also must be utilized. As shown in studies on school drop-outs, those who form negative attitudes toward school in the first few grades are more likely to drop out of school before completion of high school than are those who form positive attitudes toward school. Successful experiences in school and sufficient feedback to help the individual develop an understanding of his relationship to education are important. In the early years of school, educational, occupational, and personal-social information becomes an important part of that individual's growth and development. The utilization of information cannot be stopped at the end of elementary school; it must be continued in the junior and senior high school, in the post-high-school, trade, and industrial settings; in the colleges and universities; in the employment services; and in the various community agencies. The individual is constantly undergoing change, growth, and development. To assist him in that growth, in that development, information is needed; and the more pertinent it is to his needs at that time and under those conditions, the more potential the information has for helping his positive growth.

No one kind of information can be given at the expense of another; however, in this book educational information has been placed before the other areas. The reasons are as follows: first, because it is in the educational setting that the counselor probably will begin his work with the individual; and second, because the extent of education that one obtains or is willing to obtain may be the major factor in determining the opportunities that will be available to him, including occupations and certain positions. Personal-social information and occupational information also must be integrated with the educational information. A positive attitude toward learning must become an integral part of the individual's intrinsic values; otherwise, he may find constantly that many doors that would have been open to him are closed. In today's world some of the attitudes that need to be developed are the willingness to obtain additional knowledge, to exchange old concepts for new ones, and to take the viewpoint that learning is a continuous process throughout life.

Levels in Occupational Maturity

From early childhood to adulthood and throughout his life, each person is constantly undergoing developmental changes. Many psychologists have examined the developmental trends from early childhood to adulthood. In Table 3-1 are listed some of the trends, such as the passivity of the individual in early childhood developing toward more activity; early childhood dependence developing toward independence; and the lack of self-awareness in early childhood developing toward awareness of and control over self in adulthood. These developmental changes do not occur in definite degrees, but do occur in each individual. Furthermore, the maturity of an individual is often determined by the extent to which he has reached some of the items that are listed in Table 3-1 under "Adulthood." Likewise, if an individual's development over a period of years has moved him toward self-fulfillment

Table 3-1

DEVELOPMENTAL TRENDS FROM EARLY CHILDHOOD TO ADULTHOOD.

From EARLY CHILDHOOD	*To* ADULTHOOD
Passivity ⟶	Activity
Dependence ⟶	Independence
Minimal behavioral patterns ⟶	Organized behavioral patterns
Erratic, casual, short-lived interests ⟶	Continued, deep, long-lived Interests
Short-time (largely present determined) perspective ⟶	Long-time (past, present, and future) perspective
Subordinate position in family and society ⟶	Equal or superordinate position with adult peers
Lack of self-awareness ⟶	Awareness of and control over self

Source: Based on Chris Argyris, *Personality and Organization, The Conflict Between System and the Individual* (New York: Harper & Brothers, 1957), pp. 49–51.

within an occupation, then probably he has passed through different levels toward occupational maturity.

If the individual shows occupational development rather than merely making an occupational choice, then occupational development occurs over a period of time. Ginzburg (1951), Super (1953, 1957), and others who followed have all indicated that years of time are required for the developmental process. Super, Crites, Gribbons and Lohnes, and others have done research on vocational maturity and readiness. (See Chapter 9 for occupational theories and research.) If the counselor is to accept the concept that the individual needs and takes a period of time for development, then at some point he should reach (or theoretically be able to reach) a state of maturity. The occupational maturity may not be maintained if he does not keep himself abreast of the changes. If the development occurs over an extended period of time, then possibly a continuum with subdivisions could be devised to identify levels of progression toward maturity. These subdivisions, if formulated, would assist the counselor in determining the level of occupational maturity of an individual at a specific time so that the counselor might personalize the information needed by the individual.

Research work by John O. Crites in formulating a Vocational Development Inventory (VDI) and Warren D. Gribbons and Paul R. Lohnes in developing criteria for eight Readiness for Vocational Planning (RVP) scales would lend support to the concept that occupational maturity grows on a continuum over a period of time.

The subdivisions of a continuum extending toward occupational maturity would not be sharply and clearly delineated because regardless of how one might draw the lines, degrees of uncertainty and overlapping will occur. One approach to subdivisions might be to examine and designate levels according to the kinds of occupational understanding that generally have been presented in occupational literature in the past. On such a basis, five levels of occupational maturity may be discerned; however, these levels have not been subjected to extensive research. The five levels should attempt to provide subdivisions that coincide with the individual's understanding from his first concept of the world of work to his understanding of a specific job. The five levels might, therefore, according to the occupational understanding that he possesses be listed as follows (see Table 3-2):

Level 1. General world of work.
Level 2. Occupational fields.
Level 3. Occupational family.
Level 4. Specific occupation.
Level 5. Specific job or position.

The counselor must recognize that all persons holding a job may not have reached the fifth level of occupational maturity. The levels are listed on the basis of occupational understandings and not on the basis of whether the individual is or is not employed. In addition to helping the counselor to recognize the amount of the individual's understanding and thus indicating his occupational development, the chart contains a summary of the *sources and kinds of materials* to be used with that individual, the *meanings to be acquired,* and the *attitudes to be formulated.*

Materials should be selected for use with each individual on the level of his maturity of understanding. Kinds and sources should be determined according to the need of each individual. Materials that may be appropriate for one individual may not be appropriate at that same level for another individual, but the counselor needs a general concept by which he can begin to organize and personalize the material for use with different individuals.

In addition to the *kinds of understanding* that the individual has about occupations and the kinds of materials that might be used with the individual, the counselor is concerned also about what *kinds of meanings* contribute to the development of the individual in his understanding about the total world of work. The counselor is concerned also about *attitudes formed* by the individual. By recognizing the kinds of meanings and attitudes that might be expected, the counselor should be better able to work with the individual and also better able to help others who work with the individual.

In the *first level*, where the individual is acquiring an understanding of the world of work, he can acquire this general understanding through stories about workers, exhibits of products made, pictures of people at different jobs, lists of different kinds of things done by other people, illustrations of how the world of work helps another person, working in different jobs as community helpers, and visits to general places of work so that he can begin to understand people making different contributions in society. These sources and kinds of materials are frequently used in the lower grades in the elementary school because these experiences may be the child's first introduction to the general understanding of the world of work. In addition to these experiences in elementary school, however, the individual constantly needs to broaden his understanding of the general world of work as new jobs and occupations become an intergral part of our society. If an individual becomes so narrow in his concept about an occupation that he fails to keep abreast of the changes in the world of work, then at the age of forty he may have dropped back as far as the first level. The levels of occupational maturity are not directly associated with chronological or physiological development. The levels are sequential and must be considered from a sequential standpoint even though the individual may have limited understanding about things in the other levels; he needs a comprehensive understanding for total occupational development.

On the first level of occupational maturity, the individual is at that stage where he needs to form an attitude about and for work. He must have an understanding of different kinds of needs such as how people share, how they do different tasks, and how they contribute to one another. Without these understandings and meanings, it is questionable whether the individual can have occupational maturity even though he may be working at a job. Such an individual will see the job in a very narrow perspective and he will not be what is considered an occupationally mature person.

In the *second level* the occupational understanding should include different occupational fields. When the counselor obtains materials for use with individuals at this level, he often finds that they are hard to code and file for quick retrieval. The material is broad in that it covers several occupations. The 3-D concept does help to organize such information in a usable way as will be illustrated in the chapter on coding occupational information (Chapter 12). The kinds of materials that can be used besides the broad coverage in books and pamphlets include the individual's talking with persons who are employed in various fields, observing different workers in action, and using different kinds of interest inventories. The individual should begin to have a different

Table 3-2

OCCUPATIONAL DEVELOPMENT SUBDIVIDED BY "LEVELS CONCEPT" ACCORDING TO OCCUPATIONAL UNDERSTANDINGS DEVELOPED, SOURCES AND KINDS OF MATERIAL USED, MEANINGS ACQUIRED, AND ATTITUDES FORMULATED AT EACH LEVEL.

Level	Occ. Understandings Developed	Sources and Kinds of Materials Used	Meanings Acquired	Attitudes Formulated
1	General world of work	Stories about workers Exhibits of products made Pictures of people doing different things Lists of what fathers do (for children) Lists of what mothers do (for children) Illustrative relationships of how the world of work helps another person Books on different occupations, like those held by people in community: grocer, fireman, policeman, secretary, minister, and so on Visits to police, fire stations, and so on (for children) Visits to different plants and companies (for adults) Film strips and recordings	People share People do different tasks Respect for fellow man's contribution Beginning of value concepts Assistance in attitude formation Association among occupations and jobs	Attitudes for work
2	Occupational fields, i.e, social, scientific, managerial, clerical, and so on	Broad coverage books or booklets on fields, fiction and nonfiction Talks by persons in fields Interest inventory (useful if recognition is made of use at second level and not for occupational selection) Trips to observe workers in action	Occupational structure and classification Abilities and personalities associated with occupations Means of meeting individual needs	Attitudes of relationship of individual with field of occupation

3	Occupational family, i.e., health careers, research, farming and so on	Fiction: career stories *D.O.T.*, Vol. II Booklets of explanation of given occupational family, i.e., health career Simple, accurate, highlight information on examples of occupations within field Career days—opportunity to talk with workers	Interrelationship of a group of occupations with the individual's own abilities, desires, potentials, and needs	Attitude toward self and relationship of needs and abilities
4	Specific occupation	Readable, interesting, communicative material on various occupations Three Digit *D.O.T.*, provides 600 occupations for clarification Occupational briefs Class projects such as "Your Future Occupation" Occupational Monographs	Occupation reflects attitudes of individual Choice should be based on assets of individual	Attitude of inter-weaving of self and particulars Past attitudes and values give rise to selection of particular occupation
5	Specific job or position (entry or one into which the individual may change)	Specific job descriptions Specific job abstracts ("Communicative Abstracts") List of people doing similar job who might be willing to give information		Value system gives rise to self-selection of a job

concept of the meanings of occupations, including a recognition that different kinds of occupations require different abilities, and different personalities, and thus provide different kinds of opportunities for meeting the occupational needs of people.

As the individual progresses in his occupational maturity to the *third level* he should begin to know more about the families of occupations that exist, such as health careers, research, farming, and so on. Materials, such as career stories; *Dictionary of Occupational Titles,* Volume 2; talks with workers; and such activities as career days, can be used by or with the individual for an understanding of the relationship of a group of occupations to his own abilities, desires, potentials, and needs. This understanding could help in the attitudes formed about himself and the relationship between his needs and abilities.

The *fourth level* of occupational maturity involves an understanding of specific occupations. The *Dictionary of Occupational Titles,* Volume 1, describes specific occupations, but the counselee would probably prefer more readable, interesting, and communicative material on various occupations. Occupational briefs and occupational monographs are valuable materials for use at the fourth level. The individual should by this time understand himself enough to begin to select occupations that reflect his own idiosyncratic values; he should be selecting occupations that will permit him to use his assets to advantage. At the fourth level his attitude toward the world of work should include an interweaving of self with occupations. He should thus be discovering his role in the world of work, his contribution to society, and a job that might give him self-fulfillment.

At the *fifth level* the individual begins to choose a specific job. For a young person this may be an entry job, whereas for a person who has been previously employed it may mean the selection of a different job or position. Here, the individual needs specific job descriptions, job abstracts, and more specific information about the job or the position. He should begin to use his own value system in selecting or rejecting the various alternatives that are open to him.

The 3-D concept presented in this chapter divides information into three dimensions—people, areas, and depth. If the occupational levels of maturity are superimposed upon the depth dimension in the 3-D concept, then one can readily see that the first level of occupational maturity is primarily the first depth, in which the individual needs information for broadening his knowledge and understanding. Probably the second level would also be included in the first depth. The third, fourth, and fifth levels of occupational maturity require specific information and resource materials as at the second depth in the 3-D concept. At all levels of occupational maturity, feedback must be available so that the individual can test his own development to see if he is making the proper choices. Thus, the third depth—feedback—should be interwoven at all levels.

Systems Development for Information Utilization

Today automation, particularly through data processing, has moved into business and industry and is being used more and more in education. At the present time research studies are being conducted to determine the feasibility of using various automation systems in helping individuals obtain and utilize information. (Research information is supplied in Chapter 9.) Various communication media already are being used in the field of counseling and guidance. Besides the printed page, audio tapes, films, filmstrips, slides, television, radio, and various other communication media are being used. In addition, various gaming techniques, such as those developed by James Coleman and Sarene Boocock at Johns Hopkins University, may help the individual to develop career potentials in simulated decision-making situations.

Computer-assisted information systems for counseling and guidance are also being studied. The computer-assisted information system (CAIS) will make it possible to store information in small amounts of space and to retrieve the information easily at the appropriate time. In addition CAIS will allow handling of a greater amount of information about the individual himself, bringing together the most pertinent information about the individual and the most pertinent information about the educational and occupational opportunities available to him. The CAIS should make possible decisions based upon comprehensive and accurate information rather than on guesswork or sketchy information. CAIS may change extensively the counselor's role in the information processes.

In August, 1966, a conference was held at Ohio State University for the purpose of exchanging research information on the systems under development for vocational guidance. The published report suggests the possible advantages of using some of the systems now being studied. Much research is needed to determine how systems can be used and under what conditions. The production of materials to feed into the systems will also take considerable study. A coding system will be needed to include personal-social and educational as well as occupational information.

The advantages of CAIS in counseling and guidance may be similar to or quite different from those found by business and industry at the time computers were made a part of their operations. Different authorities list different potential advantages. The following is a partial list of potential advantages:

1. Help the individual learn how to decide and how he has decided (Campbell, et al., 1966, p. 2).
2. Make routine tasks a machine function (Campbell, et al., p. 3), enabling the counselor to spend more of his time in professional activities at greater depth.
3. Provide a wider spectrum of educational and occupational information more easily (Campbell, et al., p. 5).
4. Make available ". . . comprehensive, accurate, and relevant data at appropriate choice points in the educational and vocational sequences . . ." (Campbell, et al., p. 19).
5. Help individuals to learn how they use information in the decision-making process (Campbell, et al., pp. 19–20).
6. Require the individual to think about himself and become aware of some of his own qualities.
7. Assist the individual in recognizing that he can become a determining agent in the course of his career and his life (Campbell, et al., p. 20).
8. Begin to make the individual feel responsible for the consequences of his choices (Campbell, et al., p. 20).
9. Provide within a capsule exploration the experiences resulting from certain decisions; these explorations can be done faster and without some of the real life risks.
10. Give the individual a time-extended set of choices to consider prior to the real life decision-making process.
11. Provide periodic information at the depth needed by the individual.

CAIS has not been perfected for general use by counselors. When the use of the CAIS becomes a reality, then hopefully either CAIS equipment or a terminal that is connected to a master CAIS will be available for individuals to use independently or with a counselor. The CAIS can become another means for helping to broaden an individual's outlook. Every device, including the CAIS, used by the counselor in information communication should assist the individual's growth and development. The CAIS, in helping an individual to obtain the most pertinent and comprehensive information available, should enable him to perceive more than he now can through the available systems. In Arthur Combs' words (Speech at Ball State University, Summer, 1966), "Enlarging perception leads to more intelligent behavior."

CAIS research is being conducted at various places. At the University of Pittsburgh computers are used with terminals located several miles away. Individuals can use the terminal to obtain the desired information. At Pennsylvania State University Joseph T. Impellitteri is working with a computerized system in presenting occupational information through slide projections, tape recordings, and computer terminal print-outs. At Harvard University David V. Tiedeman and others are doing research on an information system for vocational decisions (ISVD). The study is often referred to as the Harvard-Needs-Newton Information System for Vocational Decisions.

At the system Development Corporation, Santa Monica, California, John F. Cogswell and others are doing research on the use of computers in counseling and in helping students to choose courses throughout their high school careers. In terms of CAIS, the potentials are great enough and the results sufficient to suggest that a new horizon is before the counselor where not only he but also those with whom he works may broaden their frontiers of thinking.

Types of Libraries Needed

When the emphasis is placed upon the individual user rather than upon materials, the potential user should determine the types of libraries needed. Basically, the libraries can be thought of in terms of two kinds of users: (1) the individual himself, and (2) the people who work with that individual, such as counselors, parents, teachers, and other adults. In considering types of libraries and their location, the counselor should think of the person, why the information is needed, and where and when the information might be needed.

One type of library is needed for *the counselees served,* with information for the counselees to use on their own or in conjunction with other persons. A second type of library needed is a *reference library,* where reference materials are available to the counselee, counselor, or others who work with him. These materials should be similar to those normally found in reference rooms of large libraries. A third type needed is the *professional library,* where professional materials are available to the counselor and other professional personnel with whom the counselor works conjointly. The information available should assist in the professional growth and development of the counselor and other professional personnel. A fourth type is needed for *other persons,* such as parents or business and industrial personnel, who work with the counselee.

The organization of counseling and guidance information may be different than that normally used in city or school libraries; counseling and guidance information materials need not be located separately, with books in one place, pamphlets in another place, and audio tapes somewhere else. In the three-dimensional concept all materials are classified according to people (users), areas (topics), and depth (purposes), and related materials are filed together.

The information is collected for the projected use with a person rather than on some abstract criterion. The main evaluation guidelines for the material become: Who will use it? Under what conditions? For what purpose? and, Will the information complement and supplement the other kinds of information already available to the person? These guidelines do not belittle other evaluation criteria, but the emphases are shifted. The counselor selects material on its potential usefulness to a given individual rather than on the qualities of the material itself, such as format, cost, accuracy, comprehensiveness, and number of pictures.

A counselor may select a given pamphlet, audiotape, filmstrip, or some other form of information for its potential use with an individual even though it is not comprehensive or its style is not like that normally selected for the information library. Thus materials frequently will be selected because all or part of the contents will add to the materials already possessed, rather than because the additional materials are comprehensive in and of themselves. The information utilized often will extend to media beyond the printed page to include audiovisual, resource people, and new media, such as computer-assisted information systems.

One of the most difficult jobs in building an adequate counseling and guidance information library is finding the same information at different reading and comprehension levels. The information needed by an individual is not always directly related to his chronological age. The third dimension—depth—takes the fact into account that a person may have comprehension and sophistication beyond that normally found in the personalized information he desires. For example, he may be thirty years old, a college graduate, and seeking information on the first depth dimension—the broadening dimension. The personalized information made available to him should be compatible with his comprehension and sophistication. For the same topic, however, a ten-year-old fourth grader's reading comprehension and sophistication are different.

Information may be located in the counselor's office, his waiting room, or in some other room that is more convenient for users. For example, in a school it may be realistic to house most of the counseling and guidance information in the school library, instructional materials center, or career resources center. At times the information may have to be moved by movable book carts or some other means into another area more convenient for users. Within their courses teachers frequently use educational, occupational, or personal-social information. If the material can be brought into the classroom and, in some cases, if the counselor can work in the classroom with the teacher and the students, this information may be made more meaningful to the students. For counselors in community agencies, information may be housed in the waiting room or in an adjacent room where the individual can use the information conveniently. The counselor may at times assist the individual in selecting material that will be meaningful to him. If CAIS is available to the counselor, then computer stations should be available also.

Information may have to be divided among various locations. For example, information used primarily by counselors who work with the individual should be housed in the counseling offices or in the counseling and guidance secretarial area. Information used primarily by teachers may be located in the teachers' study-preparation room or the teachers' library. The specific location is not important, but its convenience to those who need information is; in addition, potential users should be surrounded by information to help create a readiness in them for information and for change.

Priority Determinants

Because usually the counselor cannot possibly purchase or produce all the information he desires or needs at a given time, he must establish priorities, which he often does informally and frequently in response to an immediate pressure.

In counseling and guidance the number one priority is always the person who is to receive assistance in the guidance services; e.g., if a school counselor is to work primarily with teachers at this time, then information for teachers should have priority over information for any other individuals.

The second priority should probably be the purposes for which the information is to be used with the individual. The extent and timeliness of the information already available at the needed depth in the specific area determines whether or not additional information should be obtained. The counselor does not always know all the people who will use the information; therefore, his decision on information will have to be made on the basis of the people he knows will use it and those he anticipates will use it. In some cases the anticipated users themselves cannot be identified at the time of decision, but the counselor can surmise the kinds of people who may use the information in the near future; and he will have to select information for the probable needs of these kinds of people.

The third priority probably should be the extent of projected use, including the number of users at a given time and the frequency with which the material is used. The anticipated length of time that the material will be kept and the frequency of its use determine the quantity of information needed and in some cases the amount of duplication of the same material.

Selection of Personalized Information

Information utilization is more than a one-step approach; it is an integral part of a total guidance program. The information program necessitates knowing well each individual so that meaningful information can be obtained either for or with the individual. The selection, obtaining, transmission, utilization, and evaluation of this information are all part of the processes. In addition to this, personalizing information with an individual is frequently more than a one-time contact or a contact for a short duration.

Procedures should be established to ensure the collection, collation, classification, and transmission of information. In the future each counselor may not have to spend as much of his time doing these tasks because part of the information may be made available through a network of computer-assisted information systems (CAIS). Even after CAIS some information will need to be collected locally. Until CAIS is perfected and becomes commonplace, counselors or their assistants will have to collect, collate, classify, and transmit information. In the chapters to follow, specific suggestions and examples are provided for this purpose.

The concept held in the past, that counselors were responsible for obtaining and storing for later use all the information that their counselees might want, is no longer realistic. The counselor cannot know all the present and projected needs of his counselees. Information is in a state of flux; therefore the information obtained today may be out-of-date by the time it is used with a given individual. Another point that should be considered is that *if the counselor obtains all the information that is needed by a given individual, the counselor may be depriving the individual of becoming involved in his own growth and development.* If the depth dimension is sequential, perhaps the counselor needs more comprehensive information at the first depth, only part of the information at the second depth, and lists of techniques and persons for the third depth. The counselor need not collect all the information; instead he facilitates the individual's obtaining and utilizing the information that will be meaningful to him. The counselor then moves from being a person who has a box of answers to being a person who facilitates the changes desired by the individual, thereby personalizing the information so that the individual is able to perceive its pertinency to him. If he perceives that it is pertinent, then he may integrate the information into his own value structure.

Coordination

The developmental approach in utilizing information with an individual necessitates use over an extended period of time. This approach requires capable counselors and a new concept in place of the conventional mass approach (Goodlad, et al., 1966, p. 19). No one person can offer total guidance; therefore, a team or conjoint concept should be utilized. In business and industry, in addition to the counselor who works with the individual, other personnel people, administrators, and the employee's immediate supervisor should become part of the team. In community agencies the counselor and other professional service personnel, administrators, and community agency personnel who work with that individual should all coordinate their efforts. In the school the counselor who works with an individual should coordinate his efforts with those of others, such as the school social worker, psychometrist, teachers, nurse, administrators, and the individual's parents. Professional personnel working conjointly in their areas of specialization and competency to assist the individual can reduce duplication and increase the benefits to the individual. In the counseling and guidance office efforts should be coordinated among the counselors and any other counseling and guidance staff members, including clerical and secretarial personnel.

Referrals are an integral part of the counseling program, assisting the individual in obtaining the information that will be most pertinent to his present situation. The counselor can assist the individual in seeing the person or persons who can provide first-hand information. This person may be in the same building as the counselor or in an entirely different setting. For example, an individual who wants to know about a particular occupation might well be referred to a person who is working in that occupation and who is willing to take the time to work with the individual. The counselor may also provide the names and addresses of people or companies the individual may telephone or write for additional information. Personalizing information includes obtaining information that is more meaningful to an individual than the mass material, which frequently is not appropriate for his use at the second and third depths of the third dimension.

Information in the educational, occupational, and personal-social processes can be personalized by accidental, unprofessional, and uncoordinated means, but the developmental approach is more meaningful if the direction is planned, the sequences of activities are outlined, and progress is evaluated. To accomplish such tasks coordination for integration and continuity is necessary.

[Without coordination] . . . insights developed during elementary school may be inadequately transmitted to the secondary school;

junior high school counselors often do not establish effective communication with senior high school counselors; information transmitted from high school to college is often little more than that included on the formal transcript of grades. (Thompson, 1964, p. 504.)

In a guidance program the counselor should therefore consider the kinds of coordination that will contribute to comprehensive information processes.

Summary

Man is constantly undergoing change, in a state of becoming. His need for personalized information is never fulfilled, but is developmental. The counselor should facilitate the use of information by a *person* in an *area* for which he can use the information and at a *depth* that is meaningful to him. The developmental approach uses information in sequence over an extended period of time.

The developmental approach makes possible a three-dimensional (3-D) concept for the use of information in counseling and guidance. The emphases are upon the person rather than the materials; upon his needs rather than the content and format of materials; upon the area in which he can use information rather than his chronological age or school placement; and upon the purposes to be achieved. The counselor strives to personalize information rather than to factualize information.

As new concepts are developed, the need for a wider variety of information at different depths over an extended period of time makes coding, filing, collating, and retrieval increasingly complex. The computer-assisted information system (CAIS) becomes more meaningful. As CAIS is developed, the counselor can spend more of his time in assisting the individual in obtaining and utilizing personalized information.

SELECTED REFERENCES

Argyris, Chris, *Personality and Organization, The Conflict Between System and the Individual.* New York: Harper & Row, 1957. 290 pages.

Baer, Max F., and Edward Roeber. *Occupational Information: The Dynamics of Its Nature and Use.* Chicago: Science Research Associates, Inc., 1964. Pp. 375–378.

Campbell, Robert E., David V. Tiedeman, and Ann M. Martin, eds. *Systems Under Development for Vocational Guidance.* Columbus, O.: The Center for Vocational and Technical Education, 1966. A report of a Research Exchange Conference, August 18 and 19, 1966, held at Ohio State University; 60 pages. Not copyrighted.

Combs, Arthur W., and Donald Snygg. *Individual Behavior: A Perceptual Approach to Behavior,* revised ed. New York: Harper & Row, 1959. Pp. 3–15.

Crites, John O., "Part II: Proposals for a New Criterion Measure and Improved Research Design," in *Man in a World at Work,* Henry Borow, ed. Boston: Houghton Mifflin Company, 1964. Chap. 14, pp. 324–340.

Ginzburg, E., et al. *Occupational Choice.* New York: Columbia University Press, 1951. 271 pages.

Goodlad, John I., John F. O'Toole, Jr., and Louise L. Tyler. *Computers and Information Systems in Education.* New York: Harcourt, Brace & World, Inc., 1966. Pp. 3–25.

Gribbons, Warren D., and Paul R. Lohnes. "Seven-Year Follow-up Validities of Readiness for Vocational Planning Scales," *The Personnel and Guidance Journal,* 46 (September 1967), 22–26.

Hollis, Joseph W., and Lucile U. Hollis. *Organizing for Effective Guidance.* Chicago: Science Research Associates, Inc., 1965. Pp. 273–299.

Hoppock, Robert, *Occupational Information: Where to Get It and How to Use It in Counseling and in Teaching,* 3rd ed. New York: McGraw-Hill, Inc., 1967. Pp. 16–26; 348–365.

Impellitteri, Joseph T., "A Computerized Occupational Information System," *The Vocational Guidance Quarterly,* 15 (June 1967), 262–264.

Loughary, John W., Deloss Friesen, and Robert Hurst. "Autocoun: A Computer-Based Automated Counseling Simulation System," *The Personnel and Guidance Journal,* 45 (September 1966), 6–15.

McCurdy, Harold Grier. *The Personal World: An Introduction to the Study of Personality,* Claude E. Buxton, ed. New York: Harcourt, Brace & World, Inc. 1961. Pp. 137–176.

Miller, Frank W. *Guidance Principles and Services.* Columbus, Ohio: Charles E. Merrill Books, Inc., 1961. Pp. 8–16.

Norris, Willa. *Occupational Information in the Elementary School.* Chicago: Science Research Associates, Inc., 1963. Pp. 40–41.

Norris, Willa, Franklin R. Zeran, and Raymond N. Hatch. *The Information Service in Guidance,* 2nd ed. Chicago: Rand McNally & Company, 1966. Pp. 373–403; 503–519.

Shertzer, Bruce, and Shelley C. Stone. *Fundamentals of Guidance.* Boston: Houghton Mifflin Company, 1966. Pp. 268–290.

Super, Donald E. "A Theory of Vocational Development," *American Psychologist,* 8 (1953), 185–190.

Super, Donald E. *The Psychology of Careers: An Introduction to Vocational Development.* New York: Harper & Row, 1957. Pp. 69–161.

Thompson, Albert S. "School Settings for Vocational Guidance," *Man in a World at Work,* Henry Borow, ed. Boston: Houghton Mifflin Company, 1964. Pp. 487–509.

Walz, Garry R., and Juliet V. Rich. "The Impact of Information Systems on Counselor Preparation and Practice," *Counselor Education and Supervision,* 6 (Spring 1967), 275–284.

PART II

PERSONALIZING EDUCATIONAL INFORMATION

Recent occupational changes in America require new skills, techniques, and knowledge. Certain occupations are being replaced with new ones, and workers are being retrained or their education broadened for new roles. Education, including training, is becoming a major factor in determining job opportunities. The rate of change in new jobs and new machines is governed to some extent by the rate that workers can be educated or retrained. An industry cannot afford to install new machines nor create new jobs at a faster pace than individuals can be educated. The educational potential (including training) of individuals available is a major determinant of the rapidity of change for each business or industry. Therefore, education is becoming more of a determinant of occupations than occupations are of education.

The education possessed by an individual, his potential, and his willingness to obtain more education may be a key to his occupational maturity or lack of it throughout his life. His relationship to the world of work may depend upon his perception of his educational alternatives. Education, including training, is considered in this book to be lifelong, never terminal, although it may be interrupted at times. Educational information is essential to all: children, youth, and adults.

Educational information has been placed before occupational information in this book in full recognition that the two are most effective when integrated and utilized together. Neither of them is effective without an understanding of and integration with personal-social information. The three areas are separated in this book for the purpose of study, although they must be interwoven as the counselor works with each person.

Chapter 4

Determinants of Educational Opportunities: Characteristics of the Individual

The direction in which education starts a man will determine his future life—PLATO

The doors of opportunities open to an individual are dependent upon many things, but one of the major determinants throughout his life will be the amount of education and training that he possesses or is willing to obtain. Education has always been, and in the years ahead it may be even more so, an opener to doors of opportunity. The days are past when one could think about school as the first eight, ten, twelve, or even fourteen or sixteen years of his life. Education is no longer something to be achieved and completed prior to employment. Education has become a lifelong process and the purposes of education for the individual have broadened to include advancement in occupational work, mobility from one occupation to another, self-fulfillment, preparation for hobbies and recreation, community service, and laying the foundation for major changes in a person's life, such as marriage, parenthood, and retirement.

Abilities, attitudes, interests, and personality of an individual are determinants of the educational alternatives available to him. The extent of educational alternatives today is almost unlimited; however, for a given individual many of the educational doors are not open. In the counseling processes generalities may be the starting point, but the specific alternatives open to the individual must become clearly identifiable. To achieve this goal the individual, with the assistance of the counselor, must examine his own characteristics realistically and evaluate these in terms of educational criteria, purposes, and alternatives. As each educational choice is made by the individual, he probably is aware of some of the advantages to himself, but equally important is whether he also is aware of the doors he closes as he makes the choice. Doors probably are opened by his choice in the educational decision-making processes, but equally or in some cases perhaps even more so, some are closed to him; e.g., the individual who chooses not to take algebra has closed the door for the present toward pursuing careers in many occupations.

Education in the future will become even more concerned with the necessity for additional education for individuals who have left school— some prior to completion even of the eighth grade. Almost one half of the young workers, ages sixteen to twenty-one, who are out of school do not have a high school diploma and over one fourth do not have even an eighth grade education. The ratio is even higher among non-white youth (*Highlights from the 1966 Manpower Report,* pp. 26–27). On the opposite end of the continuum are the senior citizens, past sixty-five years of age, who will number approximately thirty million by the year 2000 and who may want additional education to assist them in a new adventure—retirement. Yes, the characteristics of the individuals differ and those characteristics are determinants of the educational alternatives.

Psychology of Individual Difference

For each individual an optimum combination of situations probably could exist, a combination permitting and stimulating the fullest expression of the individual's potential (McCurdy, 1961, p. 39). The individual is striving to establish himself within "an optimum combination of situations." He, too, however, may not be aware of the "right" combination or even of the possibilities of situational combinations. The role of the counselor, then, becomes one of furnishing additional information that helps to broaden the individual's horizons, broaden in terms of alternatives that may be realistic for him and, equally important, broaden in terms of situations that may be unrealistic for him with his given set of conditions.

Learning has an important hereditary base that has been accepted for years. Psychologists have been attempting to measure with various instruments, such as the Stanford-Binet Intelligence Tests, the differences in individuals for learning. In recent years, educators have been accepting the belief that intelligence of an individual can and does change. Changing conditions within the environment of the individual may in time bring about a change in measured intelligence. Specifically the environment has its influence in the way the individual perceives the environment, including *people, ideas,* and *things,* and the way he integrates the experiences he has into his value system.

With learning being dependent upon many factors and conditions, including heredity and the individual's reactions to people, ideas, and things, the counselor is in no position to predetermine the extent of educational alternatives for a person. The counselor in working with an individual may, however, be in an ideal position to increase the individual's awareness of not only the educational alternatives available, but also the conditions and factors in the individual's own self that may be contributing to or hindering his extent of educational development. The individual may now or in the future be able to alter or reverse the deterring factors or conditions to the extent that they may become contributing factors or conditions, thus utilizing them for his development.

A postulate with which each counselor begins is individual differences—the belief that each person is unique and in many, many ways different from any other person; however, he may have enough commonalities so that some generalizations can be made. The counselor and the individual, if the individual recognizes the commonalities, can start with consideration of the generalizations, but constantly must try to find those unique characteristics that give the individual identity. Once having done so, an attempt should be made to integrate the commonalities and uniquenesses into the foundation of any plan of action. The differences between and within man produce the differences in rate and manner of learning and of living.

The psychology of individual differences forms one of the bases for counseling and guidance. Each individual is different from each other person not only because he started with a unique combination of genes and chromosomes, but also because of his "Gestalt" total of perceived experiences, unique to him, as he relates with people, things, and ideas in a lifetime.

Role of the Counselor in Determining Individual Differences

Several professional persons—teachers, counselors, school social workers, nurses, school psychologists, and so on—are available for working with individuals. Because of the scope, depth, and variety of assistance needed by individuals, a team of professional persons working conjointly with one another potentially can contribute more for the benefit of the individual and of society than could be achieved by the sum total of all of them working independently. The counselor through the use of various tools and techniques, including counseling, available to him can be a valuable member of the team. The number of team members working conjointly for and with an individual will vary from time to time and from situation to situation according to the professional competencies needed and the personnel available.

The counselor's role involves assisting the person in identifying and understanding his own individual differences rather than the counselor determining what the individual differences of the person are or will be. The counselor has a unique position of assisting the person in determining what his commonalities and uniquenesses are and, equally important for the person, what are some implications of these under various projected possible circumstances (alternatives). Increasing the awareness on the part of the person of his own individualities is one facet of the role of the counselor. For the counselor to achieve this role he must seek means for the individual to determine his differences and the counselor must recognize the necessity at times of involving other members of the professional team in order that goals can be achieved.

The counselor in fulfilling his role of identifying individual differences makes use of instruments yielding results that are statistically normed and that yield as objective information as man knows how to obtain. Also he may use other measurement techniques that are as objective as professional and clinical experiences can develop, but that at best can only be said to have professional objectivity rather than statistical objectivity. However, in still other cases because of the uniqueness of the individual or the situation the counselor may need to rely upon subjective judgments—information as reliable as can be obtained, but without the statistical norm or the professional and clinical experience for objectivity.

The counseling and guidance records maintained as a result of working with the individual become an important means for the counselor to cumulate information helpful in reflecting longitudinal consistencies and may provide information enabling identification of changes in the early stages. The measurement techniques used by the counselor in assisting an individual in understanding his potentialities will vary from person to person and with prevailing conditions.

Measurement Techniques for Assessing Individual Potential

The measurement techniques for assessing an individual's potential for continuing his education number in the thousands. Space will not permit a review of these and no attempt is made in this book to identify all measurement techniques. Various reference sources should be studied and the counselor should become professionally competent in using the results obtained from measurement techniques. A brief summary is provided for *objective statistically normed instruments, professional objectivity,* and *subjective judgment,* any one or combination of which a counselor may use to assist an individual in determining his educational potential.

The objective statistically normed instruments are classified generally into (1) *scholastic aptitudes,* used to obtain a measurement of probable success in schools, (2) *achievement*, used to determine how well the individual has learned, (3) *specific aptitudes*, used to determine the probable success of the person in specific areas, (4) *interest inventories*, used to measure the extent of interest the person has in an area (the degree of agreement for bases of measuring interest differ considerably as illustrated by three common bases used: familiarity with vocabulary of the area, preferring to do the kinds of activities most closely related to an area, or possessing interest in common with those who are within an occupation), and (5) *personality measurements*, which attempt to identify personality characteristics. All five classifications of objective instruments have value in assessing an individual's potential for continuing his education in different areas and under different conditions. Buro's Mental Measurement Yearbook is an excellent source for obtaining information on the various instruments.

In addition to objective statistically normed instruments are other measurement techniques, which include professional objectivity and subjective judgment, which may contribute to determining an individual's educational potential. The sources from which data may be obtained and to which professional objectivity and subjective judgment can be applied are classified under four major sources: records, the person himself, professional colleagues, and peers and associates of the individual (Hollis and Hollis, 1965, pp. 194–196). Existing *records* pertaining to the individual may be reviewed to assist in understanding how well the individual has done in various situations. Some of the more frequently used records for this purpose are academic record, activity record, anecdotal records, and counseling and guidance records. The *person himself* may take an active role in supplying and evaluating the information through such means as autobiography, personal-data questionnaire, and role-playing. *Professional colleagues* who know the individual may supply pertinent information of value in assessing the individual's potentials for continuing education within different settings. *Peers and associates of the individual* may offer information that probably will be more subjective than the other three but, to the individual and to the professional counselor working with him, may be of significant value and often is unobtainable from any other means. In this fourth classification the means of obtaining the information may include such techniques as conferences with peers or associates, sociograms, or social acceptance scales.

No one counselor would use all the available objective statistically normed instruments and other measurement techniques in assessing the potentials of any one individual; however, because of individual differences, a counselor needs to know and understand various instruments and techniques so that he may help in selection of appropriate ones for each individual. The choice of techniques used will depend upon various factors, such as age and maturity of the individual, but equally important are the reasons for needing to assess the individual's potential. The need for assessment in the first grade in school is often motivated by the parents or the social agency—the school—rather than by the individual himself. Regardless of the reasons for assessment the point of view taken in this book is that the individual should be helped to understand his potentials and to know the extent of educational success he is achieving. One of the most important attitudes, which might be established by the time the individual is through the first or second grade, is a positive attitude toward education and one in which he is developing a view toward education as an essential ongoing contributing part of his personal development.

The professional counselor recognizes that today's measured assessments of the individual may be different tomorrow because of additional education, other information, changed environment, and so on. Even though the counselor recognizes these possibilities for changes, the individual himself may not. The person may take a test score as a final score or the alternatives identified through the counseling processes as being the only ones now and forever. One goal of the counselor might be to assist the individual in realizing that through time and/or education measured assessment may be altered.

Characteristics of Individuals Affecting Their Educational Potential

In addition to information about certain characteristics of the individual himself, the counselor needs findings from research studies and surveys to assist him in interpretation and prediction. Research findings are available in various sources including entire books on some studies; therefore, space permits including only a few examples of meaningful findings in this section. Studies pertinent to educational planning include those completed by Beezer and Hjelm (1961), Astin (1965), Pemberton (1963), and Berdie and Hood (1965).

In the Cooperative Research Monograph, *Factors Related to College Attendance*, Robert Beezer and Howard Hjelm (1961, pp. 34–37) reported selected findings of three statewide surveys conducted in Arkansas, Indiana, and Wisconsin. The student characteristics found by them to be significant factors related to college attendance may be summarized as follows:

1. More boys than girls attend college.
2. The better a student does academically while in high school the better are the chances of his attending college.
3. More students of high class rank attend college than those of average or below average class rank.

4. The probability of a student's enrolling in college is increased in relation to his mental ability. This statement is especially true for boys.

5. Motives of the individual seem to be extremely important in determining whether or not the individual will go to college. Generally speaking the individual who goes to college places emphasis upon academic and vocational reasons whereas those who placed emphasis upon the immediate, practical, and economic considerations were more likely to plan not to go to college.

6. Financial capability of the individual to pay for college education does affect the decision of the individual in regard to attending a college. The Wisconsin study found that boys were more willing to take advantage of student loans than were girls.

7. Marriage plans of students became an important factor in the probability of the student's enrolling in a college. Being married reduced the probability of enrollment in a college. This was more so associated with females than with males and more with low than with high ability students.

8. Students whose fathers were white-collar workers were much more likely to plan to attend a college than were those students whose fathers were blue-collar workers.

9. The chances that a high school graduate would go to college increased with the amount of schooling completed by his parents. The chances increased with each increment in the educational attainment of the parents. The educational level of the parents appeared to be more important than the occupational level of the parents.

10. Attitudes of parents toward whether their children should or should not attend college or were passive in their encouragement did affect the plans of students for attending college.

11. The size of the high school was associated with the number of students who planned to attend college with the percentage increasing as the size of the graduating class increased.

12. If a college was within commuting distance of the home of the high school graduate, the chances of his attending college were increased.

13. If the high school graduate had attended a high school that was accredited by the regional accrediting agency then the probability of his attending college was increased.

Alexander W. Astin in his study of *Who Goes Where to College?* (1965) started with the results of previous studies by John Holland and R. C. Nichols, in which the basic assumption was that high school graduates have an educational level of aspiration related to a variety of personality characteristics. Astin obtained a set of twenty-five student attributes on each of 127,212 entering freshmen at 248 colleges and universities (Astin, 1965, p. 3). In addition he presented data about the freshmen students and the environmental assessments of nearly all four-year colleges and universities in the United States (Astin, pp. 54–97).

Six factors accounted for a large proportion of the differences among the entering student body—intellectualism, estheticism, status, leadership, pragmatism, and masculinity. "These six factors appear to represent a meaningful scheme for describing the major distinguishing characteristics of entering freshman classes" (Astin, p. 20).

According to Astin, each college and university has eight environmental conditions that can be determined. By plotting an institutional profile, the individual may use the profile to assist him in selecting the institution that best meets his expectations. The eight environment assessments listed by Astin and the significance of a high score in the assessments are as follows:

1. A college that admits "high able students" has an environment that encourages ". . . academic competitiveness, individualism, and scholarship" (p. 55).
2. "The large institution tends to be characterized by an impersonal atmosphere, with personal contacts between faculty and students at a minimum" (p. 55).
3. "Realistic Orientation is characterized by a preference for the practical, the concrete rather than the abstract, and an aversion to intensive emotional experiences" (p. 56).
4. Scientific Orientation tends to emphasize the "acquisition of intellectual, as opposed to social, skills" (p. 56).
5. "Social Orientation is likely to emphasize social interaction and service to others" (p. 56).
6. "Conventional Orientation is characterized by a relatively high degree of conformity among the students and a relatively authoritarian attitude on the part of the faculty and administration" (p. 56).
7. ". . . high Enterprising Orientation tends to encourage the development of verbal and persuasive skills and to foster an interest in power and status" (p. 56).
8. ". . . relatively high Artistic Orientation is likely to emphasize esthetic and humanistic pursuits and to deemphasize sports and similar activities that require the use of gross physical skills" (p. 56).

With information available about colleges and universities, the counselor cannot afford to ignore the studies and should assist individuals to examine their own characteristics and those of the institutions into which they may enter.

Some of the old concepts held about girls and their opportunities for education and employment are rapidly disappearing. In 1965 Mary Dublin Keyserling, Director, Women's Bureau, U.S. Department of Labor, stated:

> Improvement in educational opportunities has equipped women for new and larger roles. Last year about a million girls graduated from high school—a number equivalent to 73 percent of our 17-year-old girls. The percentage of those who enjoy this educational advantage is more than 10 times larger than it was at the turn of the century. The number of women enrolled in college has risen at nearly the same rate—from 3 per 100 girls aged 18 to 21 years in 1900 to 30 per 100 girls in 1963. (*New Approaches to Counseling Girls in the 1960's,* p. 4.)

The persons in special education are definitely concerned with characteristics of individuals that affect educational potential. Approximately one out of every thousand babies born or approximately four thousand each year are profoundly retarded (have IQ's below 20) or severely retarded (have IQ's from about 20 to 35). Children and adults within these classifications need constant care throughout their lives. The moderately retarded (IQ's from about 35 to 50) are trainable, and include about three out of every thousand babies born. Individuals in this group progress to the mental age of approximately six to nine years but generally not beyond a mental age of approximately seven years. Approximately twenty-six out of every thousand births are in the classification of mildly retarded (IQ's from approximately 50 to 70). These individuals can progress to approximately nine to twelve age level of learning. Of school age children one in every five is enrolled in a public school special education program (McQueen, 1964, pp. 2–3).

W. A. Pemberton in *Abilities, Values, and College Achievement* (1963) indicated that the appropriate question is not what is the innate ability of an individual, but rather what is his developed ability. "Developed ability is not a purely intellectual attribute, but is determined in large measure by motivation" (pp. 64–65). He pointed out that motivation assumes an important role in determining the achievements of individuals and that the degree of motivation becomes even more important as the individual increases his educational level.

Ralph Berdie and Albert Hood in *Decisions for Tomorrow* (1965) wrote the results of a survey conducted on almost the entire population of high school seniors in the State of Minnesota in 1961. The discussion of the influences affecting the decisions of high school graduates to attend college included the following (pp. 8–9):

The student's satisfaction with his past school experiences and his emotional reaction to his current and immediately past experiences.

Student's peers, including . . . number and types of friends and associates, their attitudes, habits, plans, families, school experiences, and out-of-school attitudes.

Student's ability.

Student's needs and interests.

His personal adjustment . . . to his peers and friends, to his family, and to his community.

Alternatives available to him.

Berdie and Hood in writing about determinants of post-high-school plans identified needs as concepts rather than attributes of the individual. Needs as a concept are used to help describe the person as he is and as a potential doer of deeds. The six needs they considered as being most relevant to the planning of high school graduates were the need to do something; the need for independence; the need for security; the need for status, recognition, and acceptance; the need for learning and for mastering skills; and the need for role fulfillment (pp. 10–12).

Berdie and Hood found some of the same factors as those reported by Beezer and Hjelm. Berdie and Hood also reported that they found a marked relationship between those who planned to attend college and the family cultural status. The higher the cultural status, the higher the percentage of students who planned to attend college (p. 17). They also found "students planning to attend college indicated a greater social need and more social competencies than students planning to seek jobs" (p. 38). In this regard the students who planned to attend college seemed to express more ease in social situations than those who did not plan to attend college; those who planned to attend college also seemed to have less difficulty with authority figures and had favorable relationships with their own families (p. 105). (Social and family information is presented in Chapters 15 and 17.) Though it may be difficult to determine, the attitudes and personal values of individuals seem to be differentiating factors between students who were planning to go to college and those who were not (p. 105).

Expectancy and experience tables have in the past few years become regular tools for counselors. Research has produced some expectancy and experience tables that can be used in the local situation. The counselor through local research studies can develop tables that will be meaningful to his counselees and may provide information not obtainable otherwise.

These studies and others contribute information for the counselor to use for interpretation and predictions. Findings from other studies and surveys may be obtained through the local library and its loan service, and from reports in periodicals and books.

Changing Educational Objectives

The educational system is continually undergoing change, educational and occupational opportunities are constantly being modified, and the individual himself is a changing organism. The counselor must be aware of these three factors and perhaps even be a contributor to the curricular and educational objectives and changes of the person. Ben Ervin in studying over a thousand 1965 college graduates found that more than one half of them had changed their curricular objectives—major and/or minor—during their college career (p. 46). The graduates indicated that the number one factor causing them to change their curricular objectives was that the "college provided opportunity through general requirements or electives to discover more interesting areas of study" (p. 143). Based on this study, a conclusion may be reached that additional schooling enables an individual to discover additional areas, which may broaden his outlook and may enable him to re-evaluate, thus change, his original goal. Another viewpoint that could be taken is that individuals very frequently do not know and understand themselves well enough when they enter college and thus lose time and/or money by taking courses that may or may not lead directly toward their educational goals. Ervin found that over two thirds of the graduates who did change their objectives were able to do so without adding more than four hours of course work to those required for graduation.

Tying for second position were two factors that had caused graduates to change curricular objectives: "additional knowledge regarding employment opportunities" and "original objective failed to keep my interest" (p. 144). These two factors may be reason enough to indicate that counselors should do more to help individuals know about occupations and employment opportunities and to assist the individual in understanding himself, his interests, and the relationships of these to educational offerings.

According to Ervin's study, the greatest number of changes made in majors and minors during college life of the student did not occur during his first year in college but rather occurred during the second and third year in college. For men, nearly twice as many changed majors during the second year as during the third year. Women students made fewer changes in majors than the men students, but the women made nearly three times as many during the second year as in the third year (p. 146).

While some counselors work to reduce the number of changes in educational objectives in high school, college, and continuing education, consideration might be given as to whether the opposite should not be considered; that is, counselors might work toward making it easier for a student to change educational objectives if he so desires. As individuals grow and mature, their aspirations often change also, thus necessitating a change in their educational objectives. If the counselor is effective in being an agent of change, then not only might he bring about changes within the individual himself, but the counselor might also facilitate the individual's bringing about changes in his environmental alternatives.

Implications for Personalizing Educational Information

The preceding studies cited were primarily on high school seniors, graduates, and college students. The information, however, might be extrapolated to include implications for individuals at other grade levels. If the Berdie and Hood (1965) information about past school experiences does carry significance about the amount of schooling the individual might attain, then all school employees have a role in trying to help each person have a successful, beneficial school experience so that he can see the value of that schooling for him. The more educational information can be personalized when that individual is in school, the better the opportunity of helping him recognize the value of that schooling. The educational information that a person receives in the elementary school as well as in high school or college needs to be personalized. The individual, before he ever attends school the first time, needs educational information to help prepare him for that first school experience. Each individual at every level of education needs personalized educational information in order to be ready for and looking forward to the secondary school, trade or business school, college, or continuing education.

Because education has become one of the major factors in a human life—a factor affecting him from preschool on through elementary, secondary, post-high-school, and continuing education—the counselor working with that individual in a school setting, industrial setting, or community agency has a responsibility for assisting that individual in obtaining educational information that is pertinent to him and his situation. At no time in the history of mankind has the need been greater over a longer span of man's life for educational information to be personalized rather than presented on an impersonal and mass basis.

Types of Educational Information Needed

The types of educational information needed are related to the educational maturity of the individual. The educational maturity is used to express the degree of development of the individual in the understandings and implications of education to society and particularly to himself. Generally speaking, the educational maturity of an individual is congruent with the educational level of attainment but not necessarily so. Some general statements of kinds of educational information needed regardless of educational maturity would include degree of success the person has had in past educational endeavors and the conditions under which he was successful and/or unsuccessful, the educational opportunities available to him (for the second grader compared to the sophomore in college these would be quite different), and some of the implications of educational opportunities if he takes advantage of them and succeeds and also the alternatives remaining should he fail.

At the first depth in the 3-D concept (Chapter 3) of educational information, the kind of information that will broaden the outlook on education will, of necessity, need to be on different reading levels and on different interest levels to meet the needs of each individual. The child who is just beginning to learn to read could have a need for a broadening kind of information about education just as well as, though different from, a potential school drop-out or an employee who has twenty years of seniority in a company that is about ready to expand facilities, increase number of employees, and make promotional opportunities available to qualified employees.

Information on the second depth in the 3-D concept needs to be more specific and often contains more abstract, quantitative information than does either of the other two depths. The second depth generally includes the frequently listed kinds of information, such as number of schools, classes, or sections available; entrance requirements whether for college, trade school, or specific subjects in the local school; accreditation or rating of the educational program; qualifications of the faculty or instructors; number of students in each class or faculty-student ratio; approach used, i.e., laboratory, work-study, lecture, apprenticeship, and so on; facilities and equipment available; length of program; reward received, i.e., pay while attending, certificate or degree upon completion, advancement in salary or standing, and so on; opportunities for engaging in other activities while taking part in the educational program, i.e., extracurricular activities, cultural opportunities, free time, and so on; and generally some kind of information about the alumni and their achievements. The second depth does not include how the individual relates to the information but the information to be personalized must be selected and utilized according to the individual's psychological readiness and according to his opportunity for personal involvement.

The third depth of educational information requires the kind of information that will enable the individual to understand how he is progressing toward his goals or, if lacking, the implications for the directions in which he seems to be developing. The third depth is at the feedback stage, where the individual begins to have information so pertinent to himself and his situation that he is able to have indicators for reality testing. Kinds of information that have meaning here include grades in specific areas, achievement test results, rewards and placing in contests that are allied to the areas considered, recognitions and evaluations by authorities within the area, and so on.

Educational information needs to be personalized to relate to the individual, first to broaden his concepts, second to give him more specifics, and third, to help him integrate information and obtain feedback to test reality for himself. The third depth, feedback, is often omitted from the information processes or it is merely assumed to have occurred. Counselors have a responsibility to try personalizing information to the extent that the individual can begin to relate himself with the educational opportunities available. In the third dimension, the depth dimension, the personalized information broadens his concepts, provides resources and specific information pertinent to topics of concern to him, enables him to integrate himself into the specific part of the educational area being considered, and assists the individual in obtaining feedback information sufficient in quality and quantity to have tentative reality testing for himself. Without the third level the development of realistic expectations may not occur and the modifications of these as the individual develops may not be done at the most beneficial times.

Educational Potential—A Determinant of Job Potential

R. M. Walker (1962, p. 18) reported that almost nine out of ten young men in a survey in 1960 had completed as much as or more schooling than their fathers and almost one out of two had completed more. Each generation is completing more schooling than the previous generation. (See Table 4-1)

The educational level of workers in each occupational group has increased over the past fifteen years. (See Table 4-2). A high school diploma has become a minimum requisite for many business and industrial firms for even production workers or floor cleaners (Venn, 1964, pp. 15–29). The amount of education possessed has in the past determined, to a large extent, the occupational level of the individual. With the increase in educational level of more people today, the relationship may be changing. Without the education the person probably will not be considered, but with the education the person will not have the assurance he once had of being considered. The greatest exceptions will probably continue to occur at the highest occupational levels, e.g., the professional levels. Education is not a passport, but is a prerequisite.

The minimum educational attainment has become a requisite for entry into many firms, but another trend may also be developing. Some companies and certain Federal Government programs are now trying to identify individuals with the potential for completing an educational program outlined for the job(s), then the company or Federal Govern-

Table 4-1

INTERGENERATIONAL DIFFERENCES IN EDUCATIONAL ATTAINMENT OF PERSONS IN THE LABOR FORCE, MARCH, 1967.

Age	Median School Years Completed
20–24	12.6
25–34	12.5
35–44	12.3
45–54	12.1
55–64	10.8
65 and over	9.0

Source: Based on data from Hamel, Harvey R., "Educational Attainment of Workers, March 1967," *Special Labor Force Report* No. 92, Reprint No. 2559, Bureau of Labor Statistics, U.S. Department of Labor, page A-9.

Table 4-2

MEDIAN YEARS OF SCHOOL COMPLETED BY THE EMPLOYED CIVILIAN LABOR FORCE IN THE UNITED STATES, EIGHTEEN YEARS OLD AND OVER, BY OCCUPATIONAL GROUP AND BY SEX.

Occupational group	Women		Men	
	1950[a]	1965[b]	1950[c]	1965[b]
All occupational groups	11.3	12.3	9.5	12.2
Professional and technical	15.8	16.2	16+	16.4
Managers, officials, and proprietors	12.1	12.4	12.2	12.6
Clerical	12.4	12.5	12.2	12.5
Sales	11.6	12.2	12.3	12.7
Craftsmen and foremen	9.9	11.8	9.3	11.7
Operatives	8.7	10.1	8.7	10.8
Laborers, excluding farm and mine	8.6	9.6	8.0	9.5
Private household workers	7.9	8.9	8.1	*
Other service workers	9.1	11.4	8.7	11.2
Farmers and farm managers	8.1	9.0	8.3	8.8
Farm laborers and foremen	6.5	9.0	7.1	8.0

Source: a—Thomas, 1956, p. 49. b—Simon and Grant, 1966, p. 9. c—Thomas, 1956, p. 39.
* Median not shown—base was less than 100,000.

ment will provide the schooling and assure the individual of the job upon satisfactory completion of the program. One of the dangers in preparation of a person for a given occupation is that he may become too narrow and not be able to change with the speed desired if the occupation changes. Fragmented occupational education—education for one specific occupation at the almost exclusion of other occupational and personal-social learning—may be one thing for counselors to help individuals guard against.

As new jobs and occupations are developed, the emphasis upon educational potential may become even more important than the courses one has had. The total person is being considered rather than merely the courses in his credentials. His potential future development is beginning to be one of the major factors in consideration.

Summary

Research and studies of the characteristics of individuals have contributed data and information for understanding of an individual. The information may not only be beneficial to professional persons who work with him but may also assist the individual in understanding himself. The characteristics of an individual determine his potential educational development as well as his ability to take advantage of educational opportunities and alternatives.

The role of the counselor in assisting the individual to identify his characteristics is enhanced through information and data yielded by using as refined measurement techniques as are available. These measurement techniques may involve objective statistically normed instruments—scholastic aptitudes, achievement, specific aptitudes, interest inventories, and personality measurements; professional objectivity; and subjective judgment. Sources that yield information to which professional objectivity and subjective judgment may be applied are academic, activity, and anecdotal records; the person himself; other professional persons who work with the individual; and his peers, parents, and other associates.

Personalizing educational information is influenced by the characteristics of the individual, and his educational maturity determines the types and depth of educational information needed by him to contribute to his development.

SELECTED REFERENCES

Adams, James F. *Counseling and Guidance, A Summary View.* New York: The Macmillan Co., 1965. Pp. 325–331.

Astin, Alexander W. *Who Goes Where to College*. Chicago: Science Research Associates, Inc., 1965. 125 pages.

Baer, Max F., and Edward C. Roeber. *Occupational Information: The Dynamics of Its Nature and Use*. Chicago: Science Research Associates, Inc., 1964. Pp. 217–227, 257–267.

Beck, Carlton E. *Guidelines for Guidance: Readings in the Philosophy of Guidance*. Dubuque, Ia.: Wm. C. Brown Company Publishers, 1966. Pp. 47–61.

Beezer, Robert H., and Howard F. Hjelm. *Factors Related to College Attendance* Cooperative Research, Monograph No. 8, OE-54023, Washington, D.C.: U.S. Government Printing Office, 1961. 42 pages.

Berdie, Ralph F., and Albert B. Hood. *Decisions for Tomorrow: Plans of High School Seniors for After Graduation*. Minneapolis: University of Minnesota Press, 1965. Pp. 3–26, 27–40, 97–105.

Borow, Henry, ed. *Man in a World at Work*. Boston: Houghton Mifflin Company, 1964. Pp. 534–556.

Davis, James A. *Great Aspirations: The Graduate School Plans of America's College Seniors*. Chicago: Aldine Publishing Company, 1964. 319 pages.

Ervin, Ben. *Curricular Objective Changes in Ball State Univeristy Graduates*, Unpublished doctoral dissertation, Indiana University and Ball State University, June 1966. 170 pages.

Highlights from the 1966 Manpower Report, A Summary of the Report Transmitted to the Congress, U.S. Department of Labor, O-221-349. Washington, D.C.: U.S. Government Printing Office, 1966. Pp. 25–32.

Hollis, Joseph W., and Lucile U. Hollis. *Organizing for Effective Guidance*. Chicago: Science Research Associates, Inc. 1965. Pp. 194–196.

Isaacson, Lee E. *Career Information in Counseling and Teaching*. Boston: Allyn and Bacon, Inc., 1966. Pp. 260–278.

McCurdy, Harold Grier. *The Personal World: An Introduction to the Study of Personality*, Claude E. Buxton, ed. New York: Harcourt, Brace & World, Inc., 1961. Pp. 21–52.

McQueen, Mildred, Research Editor. "Present Knowledge and New Development," in *Research Report, Mental Retardation*, Part I. Chicago: Science Research Associates, Inc., 1964. 4 pages.

New Approaches to Counseling Girls in the 1960's, A Report of the Midwest Regional Pilot Conference, Cosponsored by Women's Bureau, U.S. Department of Labor; and Office of Education, U.S. Department of Health, Education and Welfare. Held at the University of Chicago, Center for Continuing Education, February 26–27, 1965. Pp. 2–33, 36–50.

Pemberton, W. A. *Ability, Values, and College Achievement*. Newark, Del.: University of Delaware, 1963. 77 pages.

Simon, Kenneth A., and W. Vance Grant. *Digest of Educational Statistics*. Washington, D.C.: National Center for Educational Statistics, Office of Education, 1966. 124 pages.

Thomas, Lawrence G. *The Occupational Structure and Education*. Englewood Cliffs, N.J.: Prentice-Hall, Inc., 1956. Pp. 27–55.

Venn, Grant, assisted by Theodore J. Marchese, Jr., *Man, Education, and*

Work: Post-Secondary Vocational and Technical Education. Washington, D.C.: American Council on Education, 1964. Pp. 1–37.

Walker, R. M. "Educational Level of Young Men Today Compared with That of Their Fathers," *School Life,* **44** (1962), 18.

Williamson, E. G. *Vocational Counseling: Some Historical, Philosophical, and Theoretical Perspectives.* New York: McGraw-Hill, Inc., 1965. Pp. 47–71.

Wolfbein, Seymour L. *Employment and Unemployment in the United States: A Study of the American Labor Force.* Chicago: Science Research Associates, Inc., 1964. Pp. 201–205.

Chapter 5

Implications of Educational
Structure for the Individual

Education not only for the world of work but also an education for the world in which we live.

The prevailing educational structure influences extent and kind of learning experiences of an individual. The controls on educational institutions and the idiosyncratic value system of the person may encourage him or even prevent him from having an opportunity to develop educationally. The educational aspirations of an individual may be influenced also by the availability of educational opportunities. How a person progresses in his educational maturation may be affected not only by the cognitive processes but also by the affective processes; thus, acquiring and utilizing educational information is a lifelong process. The implications of this concept create a new horizon for counselors.

The comprehensive purposes of an educational program include not only to communicate what has been and what is but also to develop a structure that will prepare persons for today and tomorrow. The educational structure is being expanded to provide continuing education to assist in updating skills and techniques, provide new knowledges for increased or different capabilities, rekindle and create intellectual interests, broaden aspirational outlooks, and supply opportunities for self-fulfillment. The boy or girl entering school this fall will be in or a potential member of the labor force through the first quarter of the twenty-first century. Couple that concept with the need of education to prepare the individual to be an active participating member of a social group(s) for three quarters of a century, based on life expectancy tables, then the counselor has a major role in understanding the implications of the educational structure for the individual.

Taxonomy of Educational Structure

Education in America today includes a large number of people, buildings, and pieces of equipment. The approximate number of schools includes 93,000 elementary, 31,000 secondary, 2,200 colleges and universities, and 35,000 specialty schools. The number of board members alone would be nearly 656,000 and the number of administrators and supervisors would be approximately 166,000. The number of students would be over 36 million in elementary schools, over 13.3 million in secondary schools, 6 million in higher education, and 5 million in specialty schools, or approximately three out of every ten people in the United States. The number of teachers in elementary and secondary public and private schools approximates 2 million (1 per cent of the population) and in the colleges and universities the number of the faculty is over 450,000.

The educational system taxonomy or classification used by the counselor affects the way he organizes informational materials and the way he transmits information to others. If the taxonomy used is for the purpose of personalizing information, then the taxonomy has to be developed from the user's standpoint and what will have meaning to him. The taxonomy, then, should assist the counselor in organizing the information for use *with* the individual. For example, information on the number of schools, programs, and so on may have meaning to a counselor, but may have very little meaning to an individual. Knowing that more than two thousand colleges and universities exist may not be of much assistance to an individual who is trying to select a college or university. What he wants to know, probably, are the colleges and universities that offer the program he wants and under what conditions he can enter that program.

A taxonomy for education can be formulated in several different ways. One of the most frequent ways is to consider *elementary and secondary* schools, including public, private, church-related, military academy, special, home studies, and so on; *occupationally oriented programs*, including on-the-job training, apprenticeships, vocational and trade schools, business schools, and trade or industrial training, such as the programs supported by the Federal Government; and *higher education*, including junior and community colleges and degree-granting colleges and universities.

Another taxonomy of education frequently used within books on education is based on two classifications: *control* of the educational offerings and *kind of program(s)* provided. These two classifications are primarily applicable at the second depth of the 3-D concept and may have tremendous meaning for the individual user seeking specific information about different educational institutions. Frequently when the individual wants educational information, he wants to know the kind of program available or the places where he can get a specific program. In addition he may be concerned about knowing what kinds of controls and restrictions might be placed upon him and/or the kind of students that might be attracted to the institution. The control classification may be a helpful index.

Control

The subdivisions within the control classification include *tax supported* institutions, sometimes listed as local or public. However, state colleges and universities are included within this subdivision; therefore, the words local control are not definitive.

Another type of control is the *military*. Often complete listings of the educational opportunities in the armed services are omitted from the educational information in most reference books. The amount of training and education available today within the military services and controlled by military personnel is becoming a major factor in the educational programs offered in our society. The counselor working with individuals who are in or may be eligible for military service should assist them in considering educational opportunities sponsored by the armed services.

A third type of control is educational institutions that are *church-related*, in which the control is partially, if not totally, by a church. Educational institutions under church control include elementary and secondary schools, colleges and universities, and trade and business schools.

A fourth type of control is the *independent* schools, which are of two types—the nonprofit and the operated-for-profit. Not all, but some of the training institutions operated for profit remain in operation for a short period of time only. Examples are training places for auto body repair and heavy road-machine equipment operation. Because of the short term of operation, counselors may have difficulty in obtaining the kind of information desired about the program.

A fifth control of education is *business and industry*. Today, business and industry are offering educational and training opportunities that have a definite implication for the amount and kind of education many of their employees will receive. One company will offer one kind of education or training and another company in the same kind of business may offer a different education or training program. The trend has been and probably will continue for business and industry to increase their involvement in educational opportunities.

A sixth control group is the *labor unions*. By means of some of the apprenticeship programs, the labor unions control who can start the training and when. Some predictions have been made that the labor unions may in the future control more of the training activities than they have in the past.

Kind of Program(s)

In the second classification—kind of program(s)—the first two subdivisions are the *elementary education* programs and the *secondary education* program. Note the emphasis on program rather than age of child. Basic education programs for educationally deprived adults who have not completed the eighth grade would be listed in the first subdivision.

A third subdivision—*specialty schools*—which in recent years has received attention because of work done by Kenneth B. Hoyt at the University of Iowa, is the program designed for the specialty oriented students (SOS). These programs are designed for preparation in trades, technical occupations, and businesses, primarily on the post–high-school level. Clark and Sloan (1966) in their study, *Classrooms on Main Street, An Account of Specialty Schools in the United States That Train for Work and Leisure,* indicated that the number of specialty schools (thirty-five thousand) exceeds the total number of public and private secondary schools plus the institutions of higher education (p. 4).

A fourth subdivision based on the kind of program offered includes programs for which authorities have not totally agreed on terminology. *Continuing education* seems to be the more accepted term but is frequently referred to as the adult program or extended education. In this subdivision are placed such programs as apprenticeship, Manpower Development and Training Act programs, on-the-job training, and some work experience programs that are offered outside the secondary school or degree-granting institution. Another program that may be included in the continuing education subdivision or may be a separate one, depending upon one's point of view, is the *junior or community college.* The junior college was designed primarily to offer the first two years of college. The community college, in its original concept, was started to serve a geographic area in which the enrollees would be taking more terminal programs. Today the lines of distinction seem to be vague.

A fifth subdivision is the *degree-granting* programs, such as those offered by colleges and universities at both the undergraduate and graduate levels. The professional schools—teaching, medical, theological, and technological—would be included within this subdivision.

Availability of Educational Opportunities for Individuals

Educational opportunities for individuals have been increasing regularly since the beginning of America. Early in American history reading and writing were made available in communities of given sizes. Then schools were expanded, and the three R's became available for all with elementary education being required. At about the turn of the century high schools became a possibility for those living in urban areas; then the high schools were expanded so that today a high school education becomes a possibility for every boy and girl. Even though the possibility may be present, only seven out of every ten will complete high school, with four out of the ten going to college and two completing four-year college programs.

Today the Federal Government has entered into education to the point that many educational opportunities are available for individuals that were not available to them a few years ago. Adults with less than eighth grade education now have specialized programs developed for them (Economic Opportunity Act, Title II-B, Adult Basic Education Program). Education also is being planned for the culturally deprived adult. The Manpower Development and Training Act makes training available for adults who need new or different skills in order to obtain employment in the local labor market. Youth programs are available as exemplified by Youth Corps and other programs for specific groups. Federal legislation as passed by Congress in the 1960's has greatly expanded educational opportunities to the point where almost anyone who wants and needs an education has an opportunity for one.

Business and industry, recognizing the rapid changes being made within their own organizations, have established training programs within their own plants to facilitate the constant upgrading of their employees. In addition, many companies have made arrangements for their employees to enroll in local schools or colleges and take educational programs, either totally or partially at the expense of the company. The educational programs offered by business and industry have been on the increase and probably will continue to increase as both a fringe benefit and a means of upgrading employees.

Adults have had educational classes available to them in recent years both in public and in private schools. In addition, community agencies such as YMCA and YWCA offer courses to assist the adult as well as youth. In the average to larger size communities the educational opportunities for youth and adults include most of the traditional educational courses plus special courses in recreation and leisure time activities. According to Johnstone and Rivera's study (1965, p. 5), adults obtain their education chiefly in institutions that are engaged primarily in functions other than education. NEA, Division of Adult Education Service (1963), listed where adults study in continuing education (Figure 5–1).

For some youth the best opportunities for obtaining an education have been the military services. Education has been provided both within the military service and in post-military-services, where special Federal legislation, such as the GI bill and its modifications, have made educational programs available with the veteran receiving an allowance to assist in paying expenses.

If one examines a United States map with dots on it representing the

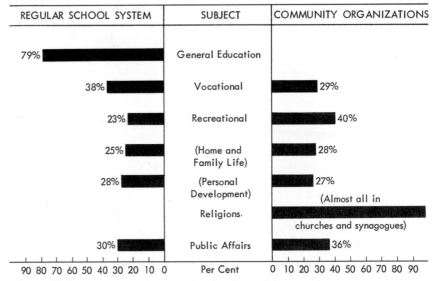

REGULAR SCHOOL SYSTEM	SUBJECT	COMMUNITY ORGANIZATIONS
79%	General Education	
38%	Vocational	29%
23%	Recreational	40%
25%	(Home and Family Life)	28%
28%	(Personal Development)	27%
	Religions.	(Almost all in churches and synagogues)
30%	Public Affairs	36%

90 80 70 60 50 40 30 20 10 0   Per Cent   0 10 20 30 40 50 60 70 80 90

Figure 5–1. LOCATION OF STUDY FOR ADULTS IN CONTINUING EDUCATION.
Source: Based upon Facts and Figures on Adult Education, *NEA, Division of Adult Education Service, Vol. 1, No. 1, pp. 4–5, Apr. 1963.*

colleges and universities existing at twenty-five-year intervals, not only can the increase in number of institutions be noted, but also the geographic distribution that has occurred throughout the country. Thus, the chances are that one or more of the colleges and universities are located within a seventy-five to a hundred-mile radius of the individual's place of residence. In many locations of average or above density in population, a college or university is located within commuting distance of an individual's home. Colleges and universities have been increasing not only in number and in distribution, but also in the kinds of offerings that are provided for individuals. Within the colleges and universities also have been developed institutes, centers, and special programs to serve special needs.

The availability of eduction within the local community does make a difference in the amount of education individuals will obtain. In the Association for Higher Education, *College and University Bulletin,* October 15, 1966, a report was made on the results of tests taken for the Army. The following information was contained in the Bulletin (pp. 1–2):

> More than two-thirds of all Negroes who took the Armed Forces Mental Qualification Test over an eighteen-month period, failed it, according to a survey published in the October *American Education.*

The failure rate for Negroes on the mental tests were 67.5 percent, in contrast to a failure rate of 18.8 percent among non-Negroes. There is a close correlation between the inferior education available to most Negroes and the performance gap, the survey reports.

Of the 767,935 young men who took the Selective Service College Qualification Test last May and June, 81 percent received passing scores of 70 or more.

Students from New England scored the highest, with 93 percent of those who took the test passing it. Southern students scored the lowest, with only 53 percent passing. Physical sciences, mathematics, and humanities students were the top scorers.

The availability of education has been increased through using facilities and equipment other than the usual classroom concept. Educational television and courses taught by radio have greatly expanded the opportunities. Tapes and records also have broadened the availability of courses to those who never would have had the opportunities otherwise. Correspondence and various home-study courses have come of age with over a hundred colleges and universities offering correspondence courses and nearly as many private accredited correspondence schools with a long list of different subjects at various levels. The counselor needs to be aware of the availability of education through various media from a wide variety of public and private institutions.

Many of our forefathers had to discontinue their education because a school or college was not available for them to attend. Such is not the case today; not only is one available but generally several alternatives exist from which the individual may make a choice. The availability of educational opportunity has spread to such an extent that today education may be America's largest enterprise. The counselor's role in working with an individual may be quite different than was the role fifty years ago when counseling and guidance was in its infancy.

With the increased availability of education, more persons are enrolled in education at all levels than ever before, with a higher percentage of them completing a program. The high school enrollment at the turn of the century was 11 per cent of the 14- to 17-year-old youths, but in the mid-1960's the percentage had increased to 94 (Figure 5–2). In 1966–1967 the enrollment in public elementary and secondary schools had reached 44.6 million, an increase of 2.3 per cent over the 1965–1966 school year and 38 per cent greater than ten years before. The adult education, community colleges, summer activities, community centers, and recreational programs are the fastest growing ones, with a 23 per cent increase in 1966–1967 expenditures over the preceding year.

An interesting fact is that so far in the twentieth century more girls

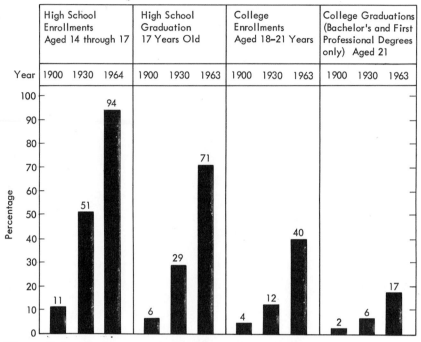

	High School Enrollments Aged 14 through 17			High School Graduation 17 Years Old			College Enrollments Aged 18–21 Years			College Graduations (Bachelor's and First Professional Degrees only) Aged 21		
Year	1900	1930	1964	1900	1930	1963	1900	1930	1963	1900	1930	1963

Figure 5–2. EDUCATIONAL ATTAINMENT OF YOUNG PERSONS IN THE AMERICAN POPULATION FOR THREE SELECTED YEARS.

Source: Based on Trends in Educational Attainment of Women, *U.S. Department of Labor, Women's Bureau, Jan. 1965, p. 3.*

have graduated from high school than boys (Figure 5–3), whereas the number of college graduates has always been the reverse, with more men than women graduating (Figure 5–4).

Conditions Within Educational Structure Affecting Choice by Individuals

Even though the educational opportunities are present for the individual today, many conditions prevail that prevent him from choosing one alternative over another. The admissions standards for the different institutions become an important factor not only in selection of a college or university but also in the selection of private kindergartens or in the selection of a summer-school program. The kinds of tests administered as screening devices frequently become barriers for individuals not only in terms of the scores, but because some people fear taking tests.

The individual differences of people make some programs become attractive for one individual but the same program would not be attrac-

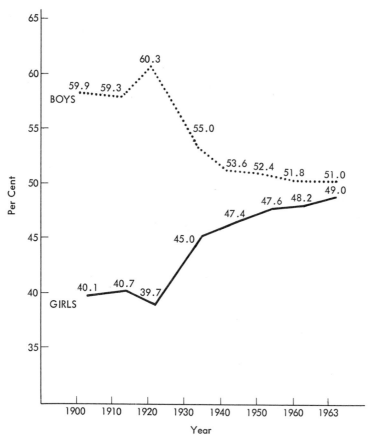

Figure 5–3. HIGH SCHOOL GRADUATES, BY PERCENTAGE BY SEX, FOR SELECTED YEARS.

Source: Based on Trends in Educational Attainment of Women, *U.S. Department of Labor, Women's Bureau, Jan. 1965, pp. 5 and 13.*

tive for another person, even though the program in terms of the course content or desired outcomes may be similar. Flexibility of the program, for example, becomes a determining factor as to whether some people could or could not profitably gain from the experience provided. The quantity and quality of the educational experiences become another condition that frequently affects the choice by an individual. The status that is associated with one program and not with another becomes an important condition that is and must be considered by the individual according to his own idiosyncratic value system. The very fact that one program ends in a certificate and another does not or that one ends in a degree may make the difference in the choice that the individual will make. The reputation that the institution has among the individual's

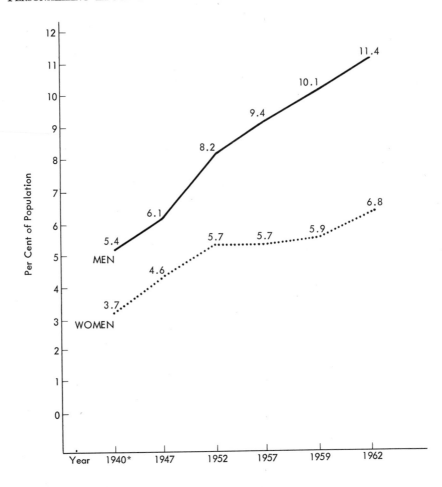

*Excludes Alaska and Hawaii.

Figure 5–4. COLLEGE GRADUATES TWENTY-FIVE YEARS OF AGE AND OVER, BY PERCENTAGE BY SEX, FOR SELECTED YEARS.

Source: Based on Trends in Educational Attainment of Women, *U.S. Department of Labor, Women's Bureau, Jan. 1965, p. 12.*

* Excludes Alaska and Hawaii.

peers or his family may become the important factor determining choice.

Much work has been done to eliminate the financial obstacle that prevented many persons from obtaining an education at the elementary, secondary, or collegiate level. Private loan funds, governmental programs, and private programs of scholarships and fellowships today have made it possible for almost all persons to obtain an education. Even with the financial assistance that is presently available, the cost of one educational program over another is frequently a condition that causes the individual to decide not to enter his first choice educational program.

Rules and regulations within the educational institution have a tremendous effect upon the amount and kind of education of an individual or even available to him. Many schools have been operating on a selecting-out process, whereas schools of the future will need imagination to develop new or modified programs, rules, and regulations that will provide greater variety of opportunities designed to include-in persons. Some educational institutions have designed programs to provide individuals with experiences by integrating education and work. Also industry is providing employees opportunities to attend classes. The prevailing conditions within the educational structure and each institution that the individual may consider affects, or may affect, his educational maturation.

Changing Role of Education in Today's World

Goldstein (1965, p. 2) phrased the changing occupational structure as a shift "from lunchbox to attaché case." The picture may be even more clearly underscored for education by reflecting attitudinal changes also—*the worker of yesterday with his lunchbox has changed to the employee of today with his attaché case.* The role of education has changed and is changing to help set the pace of the changing world and bring about new aspirations. Once the purpose of school was primarily the teaching of the three R's; today education may be taking on an additional role—the development of the ability to think. "If work, in the technological sense, is becoming cognitive, then every worker is going to have to keep going back to school" (Venn, 1965, p. 3). One way to recognize the continuing need for education and for a means of helping young and old to have some of the same understandings (cognitive processes) and feelings (affective processes) is to recognize that a large percentage of the population has never had an adult experience with many of the "recent" social events in history that affect today's world (Figure 5–5).

A factor that affects the role of education is the upward trend in the educational level attained by the population (Figure 5–6). Contributing to this increase in educational level is the large number of persons who take an entry job, then continue education in order to make job or occupational advancement. Also, upward mobility of educational level has occurred within the same occupational group, thus an individual has had to obtain additional education in order to remain in or to enter a given occupational group. In addition, the entry of the Federal Government into mass programs has changed the educational level of minority

No adult experience with:

(1) World War I — not born or under 21 years old on November 11, 1918 (Armistice signed) — 182.6 million persons.
(2) Stock Market Crash — not born or under 21 years old on December 29, 1929 (Black Friday) — 165.4 million persons.
(3) Prohibition — not born or under 21 years old on December 5, 1933 (Adoption of 21st (Repeal) Amendment) — 157.8 million persons.
(4) Pre-Social Security — not born or under 21 years old on January 1, 1937 (Old-Age Insurance in effect) — 150.4 million persons.
(5) Mass Unemployment (over 5.5 million unemployed) — not born or under 21 years old on August 15, 1941 — 139.2 million persons.
(6) World War II — not born or under 21 years old on August 14, 1945 (VJ Day) — 129.6 million perosns.
(7) Korean War — not born or under 21 years old on July 27, 1953 (Armistice signed) — 111.1 million persons.
(8) Pre-Space Age — not born or under 21 years old on October 4, 1957 (Sputnik I) — 102.4 million persons.
(9) Republican President — not born or under 21 years old on January 20, 1961 (Last Day of Eisenhower Administration) — 94.2 million persons.

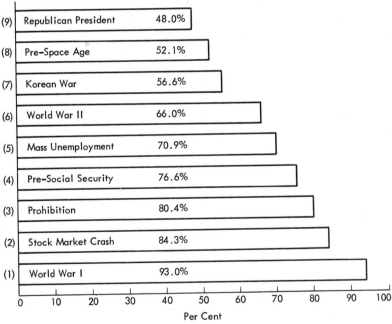

Figure 5–5. PERCENTAGE OF POPULATION AS OF APRIL 1, 1966, NOT HAVING ADULT EXPERIENCE WITH SELECTED MAJOR EVENTS.
Source: Road Maps of Industry, *No. 1549, July 1, 1966, National Industrial Conference Board, Inc.*

groups. As reported by Clark and Sloan (1966, p. 6) and Johnstone and Rivera (1965, p. 144) an increase has occurred in the number and percentages of adults who are enrolled in education for self-improvement and self-fulfillment. Where schools offer the opportunity, many adults and youth are taking schooling in order to learn for leisure-time activities. Education has changed its image and is taking on a different role of helping the individual not only to fulfill his immediate needs but to broaden his concepts for tomorrow.

America is entering the age when nearly one in every five adults, twenty-five years of age and older, has completed a four-year college program (18.2 per cent in 1962, see Figure 5-4). The projected college enrollments will increase in every state in the next few years (Figure 5-7). The day when only children went to school has gradually disappeared in concept to where today not only the children and their parents but in some cases three generations of a family are in school at once.

A few years ago those who did not have the economic backing were unable to obtain the schooling that they needed for their aspirations. Today the economically disadvantaged are not seriously limited in obtaining additional education or training unless they do not have the opportunity to work with a counselor or someone else who can help them recognize opportunities and resources available for assisting them regardless of their economic circumstances.

The day may be disappearing when one can speak of the educated man, because education is becoming a never-ending process, with the additional education not filling but stretching the mind; not closing in, but increasing the individual's ambition to expand himself and his world: ". . . education becomes the link . . . between an individual and his place in society" (Venn, 1965, p. 1).

Material things have been in the past a measure of success in an industrial society such as America's. With the younger generation having less respect for material things, America may be entering into a new era, in which education to the young people may be taking on a new role, with material things decreasing in meaning in their value system (Venn, 1965, p. 2).

Over the next few years the number of unskilled workers probably will remain about the same but the number of persons in the labor force will increase. The new jobs and occupations will require more educational background. Probably by 1970 only 5 per cent of the jobs in the labor force can be filled by the unskilled. In the probable, not too distant, future for each person on the assembly line, ten back-up workers will be required. The educational program has to change to keep pace. The 3-M Company, like many other companies, has introduced in the last five years one out of every four products it markets today. The complexity of equipment and rapidity of advancements have made many workers become ineligible for continued useful employment. The individual had the education for the job at the time he was employed, but the changes

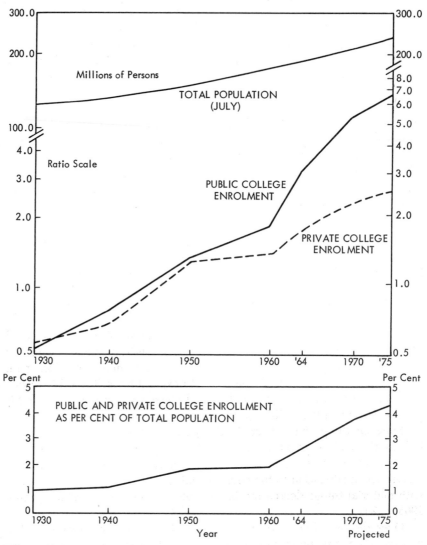

Figure 5–6. COLLEGE ENROLLMENT, PUBLIC AND PRIVATE, IN MILLIONS OF PERSONS AND AS PERCENTAGE OF TOTAL POPULATION.

Degree-credit enrollment in institutions of higher learning is expected to reach about 9.5 million by 1975. This is almost triple the number enrolled in the fall of 1960. Public colleges and universities are slated to absorb the bulk of the increase. Total enrollment was 1.8 per cent of the resident population in 1960. By 1975, this percentage is expected to exceed 4 per cent. The impact of increasing enrollment will be felt most emphatically in the eighteen to twenty-one age bracket. Over 50 per cent of that age group are projected as being college students in 1975, while about 40 per cent were in college in 1960.

Source: Road Map of Industry, *No. 1539, Feb. 1, 1966, National Industrial Conference Board.*

in job requirements make him no longer qualified. However, in many cases additional education has helped the worker to keep pace with the modified requirements, whereas in other cases companies have not been able to offer the training and education fast enough or the worker has not been able to gain or willing to gain the additional skill, knowledge, and attitudes necessary.

Implications for Counselors

With the changing role of education in the lives of individuals and in the world in which they live, important implications may be present for the counselors who will be working with the people of today and tomorrow. One implication may be that counselors will need to assist individuals to view education differently than education has been seen in the past. Education should become an integral part of life's fulfillment rather than an end in itself. "Many people who study outside the formal system do so for reasons having to do with their own fulfillment, and care little for academic credit" (Gardner, 1960, p. 94).

A second implication for counselors may be a recognition that the choice of an entry occupation is often delayed because of the additional schooling being acquired by the individual. The entry into the full-time world of work is often delayed beyond high school, therefore, delaying this particular task of decision-making until the individual is in some kind of post-high-school education and, in some cases, may acutally be engaged in a type of part-time employment. Thus, the choice of an entry occupation is delayed until after the person has been an integral part of a continuing education program (Venn, 1964, p. 149).

A third implication for counselors may be a recognition that the increased number of educational courses, programs, and schools is now so large that the counselor can no longer rely upon himself only to supply individuals with all the possible information that they might need. The sheer number of schools and their requirements, to say nothing of the specifics about their offerings, has become enough to make the counselor realize that educational information now must be rather comprehensive in order for him to fulfill an adequate role in helping the individual to obtain the information needed. The counselor probably needs to recognize that he is taking on a facilitating role rather than a source-of-all-knowledge role. Not only must the counselor be able to help the individual obtain comprehensive, accurate information but also the counselor must facilitate understanding and feeling for the implications of the information so that the individual can achieve a systematic integration into his own value system, rather than depending on incomplete, inaccurate, and sometimes accidental information for his decision-making.

PERSONALIZING EDUCATIONAL INFORMATION

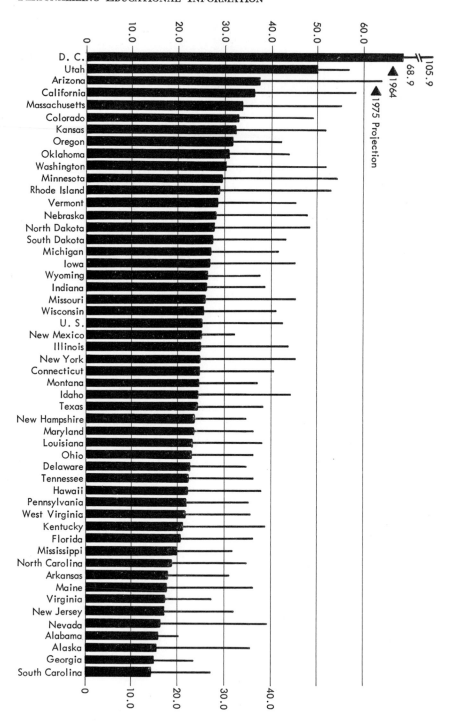

A fourth implication for the counselor may be the recognition of the increase in available resources today to help individuals, not only those of the high social economic class or high ability, but also those in the minority and disadvantaged groups. Resources have become available to help individuals obtain a basic education and a continuing education. The counselor not only should think in terms of the educational setting in which he or the individual is, but also should consider the possible multiple resources available at the next educational step for the person. Also the counselor should assist the individual to recognize implications of resources in each program on a long-term basis as well as immediate ones. The counselor should have available updated resources with which he may help an individual to know about or obtain in order to start, proceed, and complete a given part of his educational objectives.

The fifth implication might be that the individual no longer selects *the* school just as he no longer makes one occupational choice for life. The counselor may assist the individual in selection of the next entry school, college, or training facility, but the individual will make additional selections later as he recognizes and fulfills his continuing educational needs.

With the concept that education is an ongoing, never-ending process, a sixth implication may be one in which the counselor could help the individual recognize that he may be an active participating member in the world of education longer than he will be an active member in the world of work. Education has broadened its objectives and accepted new challenges in which the individual is assisted not only in learning basic information, but also in broadening his scope and assisting him in the development of the ability to think.

Also, a seventh implication may result from the expanding concept

---

Figure 5–7. COLLEGE ENROLLMENT, 1964 AND 1975, PER 1,000 POPULATION, BY STATE OF ENROLLMENT.

Population size and net migration (students going to out-of-state colleges) were the key factors in determining the ratios of college enrollment to population shown in the chart. The projections for 1975 were based on estimates of total population and college age population, as well as existing net migration.

Of the twenty-one states whose 1964 ratio exceeded the national average, only six were east of the Mississippi River. Thus, in the states east of the Mississippi River, where population was high, the ratio was generally smaller than in low population states. Two notable exceptions were California and Massachusetts, both high-ratio states with sizable populations, but with a multitude of large and attractive institutions of higher learning.

The District of Columbia, with its many colleges and universities and its high proportion of nonresident students, had the highest ratio by far. This position is expected to be maintained through 1975.

Source: Road Map of Industry, *No. 1539, Feb. 1, 1966, National Industrial Conference Board.*

of continuing education. With the viewpoint that education is extended over one's lifetime, then the role of the counselor in an individual's life may be recognized by the person and by society as being different from that of the past. Exactly what the implication is for the counselor may not be clearly understood at this time. In the past, a counselor often served as an individual's counselor from three to six years in the schools. This concept may expand and the role of the counselor for an individual may become comparable to the role of a physician or a lawyer in one's life, in which the services are extended over a longer period of time.

Probably an eighth implication is also one that results from the role of education changing in one's life. Counseling, in private practice and in community agencies, outside of the formal school setting, may increase at a faster rate in the future than counseling in schools.

The counselor's hours in a day probably cannot be increased beyond those that are presently being used by counselors, because most counselors probably are working the maximum number of hours they can spend. However, the hours in which a counselor is available may need to change. With the viewpoint that education becomes an integral part throughout one's life rather than centered primarily around serving those who are currently in school or those who are out of work, a counselor may need to be available when the individual has time available. To meet the new challenge the hours that counseling offices are open may need to be extended. Some counselors may work from 8 A.M. to 4 or 5 P.M., whereas others may come on duty at noon and work until 8 or 9 P.M. Other counselors may come on duty at 4 P.M. and go off at midnight. Where only one counselor must serve the demand, his office hours may need to vary each day of the week.

Another implication is that with the changing role of education the educational information of the future must be different in nature than it has been in the past. Not only will this be necessitated because of the change in serving people over a longer period of time, but also in serving more people from a greater variety of backgrounds, with different needs for education, and with varying values for education. With the purposes of education broadening, the counselor of today should recognize educational information as having a more comprehensive base than has been considered in the past.

Summary

The rapidity of expanding choices of education and training opportunities for individuals creates a situation in which accurate, comprehensive, and current information necessary for decision-making must be obtained from many sources. A systematic assimilation of information is necessary so that the individual may integrate the information into his own perceived world, examine alternatives, explore the potential consequences, and approach education or training from a base of reliable information personalized for his purposes and needs.

A taxonomy developed from the user's viewpoint is essential for effectively organizing and utilizing educational information. A taxonomy was suggested based upon control and kinds of educational program(s) provided. A taxonomy is needed more today than ever before with the increase in number of available educational opportunities for children, youth, and adults.

The changing role of education affects the area of counseling and guidance. Such trends as the increased number of people entering educational programs outside the formal school setting and often for the reason of self-fulfillment without regard for academic credit, delayed decision on an entry occupation beyond secondary school level, increased available resources for pursuing education, and the concept of a lifetime of education, have implications for the counselor.

SELECTED REFERENCES

Association for Higher Education, "81% of College Students Pass Selective Service Test," *The College and University Bulletin*. Washington, D.C.: Association for Higher Education, **19** (October 15, 1966). 6 pages.

Baer, Max F., and Edward D. Roeber. *Occupational Information: The Dynamics of Its Nature and Use*. Chicago: Science Research Associates, Inc., 1964. Pp. 91–98, 102–120, 127–135.

Clark, Harold F., and Harold S. Sloan. *Classrooms on Main Street, An Account of Specialty Schools in the United States That Train for Work and Leisure*. New York: Institute for Instructional Improvement, Inc., Teachers College Press, Teachers College, Columbia University, 1966. Pp. 1–10.

Gardner, John W. "National Goals in Education," *Programs for Action in the Sixties, Goals for Americans*. New York: The American Assembly, Columbia University, A Spectrum Book, Prentice-Hall, Inc., 1960. Pp. 81–100.

Gaston, J. Frank, ed. "The Growth of College Enrollment," *Road Maps of Industry*, No. 1539. New York: National Industrial Conference Board, February 1, 1966. 4 pages.

Gaston, J. Frank, ed., and Paul Biederman. "Per Cent of Population (as of April 1, 1966) Not Having Adult Experience With," *Road Maps of Industry*, No. 1549. New York: National Industrial Conference Board, Inc., July 1, 1966. 4 pages.

Goldstein, Harold. "Education and Work Life in a Changing Economy," *Occupational Outlook Quarterly*, **9** (September 1965). 4 pages.

Johnstone, John W. C., and Ramon J. Rivera. *Volunteers for Learning, A Study of the Educational Pursuits of American Adults*. Chicago: Aldine Publishing Company, 1965. Pp. 1–22, 142–162.

National Education Association, "Facts and Figures on Adult Education," Washington, D.C.: Division of Adult Education Service, 1 (April 1963). 6 pages.

Norris, Willa, Franklin R. Zeran, and Raymond N. Hatch. *The Information Service in Guidance*, 2nd ed. Chicago: Rand McNally & Company, 1966. Pp. 161–189.

Venn, Grant. "Needed: A New Education-Work Relationship," *SRA Guidance Newsletter*, September–October 1965. Chicago: Science Research Associates, Inc. 4 pages. Summary of a Speech, Kent State University.

Venn, Grant, assisted by Theodore J. Marchese, Jr. *Man, Education, and Work: Postsecondary Vocational and Technical Education*. Washington, D.C.: American Council on Education, 1964. 184 pages.

Women's Bureau, *Trends in Educational Attainment of Women*. Washington, D.C.: U.S. Department of Labor, January 1965. 17 pages.

Chapter 6

Sources and Types of

Educational Information

The sources of educational information are all about us. The types and media for transmittal are so plentiful that an individual need not rely upon one source, one type, or one medium. He is surrounded with educational information throughout his life but needs assistance in selection of sources and types having personal meaning for him and contributing regularly to his educational maturation.

To have information comprehensive enough to accomplish the scope included in the definition for educational information, various sources should be utilized and all types of literature and other information should be considered. Recognizing that educational information is obtained throughout life and is a vital part of the individual's educational maturation, the counselor should assist in making educational information as meaningful and purposeful as it can be made for the person. Sources will be needed for each person to be served by the guidance program and also will be needed at each of the three depths as the individual progresses throughout life.

Sources of educational information include not only publishers, but also educational and training institutions and literally hundreds of people. The identification of sources appropriate for individual users becomes a major task, and the counselor needs techniques for obtaining comprehensive information. He also needs to assist individuals in identifying the sources and techniques whereby they may obtain the information they need, not only now, but in the future.

Educational Information for the Developmental Approach—Early Childhood Throughout Life

At one time man learned primarily as a result of living and working with his parents. Then in America came, in general, the requirement of an elementary school education. Today the number and the percentage of young people completing high school has increased greatly from pre-World War II days. The rise in college enrollments has shown the desire of man to know even more. A startling figure is the adult education enrollment of 28 million in 1966; the increase rate being one of the fastest for any educational program. "Industry, the armed forces, and business have developed both educational programs and training programs that match in size the entire college and university systems (there are 32,000 programs other than those in colleges and universities that enroll high school graduates)" (Arbolino, 1966, p. 1).

Without a doubt education has become one of man's continued concerns from early childhood throughout life. His motives for obtaining additional training or education vary from time to time; but regardless of the reasons, education is a major contributor to his development. Education may be and often is the basis for horizontal and vertical mobility not only in occupations, but also in social groups. With the necessity of continued education, the need for educational information throughout life becomes a reality. Educational opportunities have increased and means of assessing educational opportunities and individuals have improved to the extent today that the individual can benefit from educational information being personalized rather than mass distributed. Personalized educational information can be utilized with him at various times throughout life rather than the traditionally planned once or twice at specific chronological ages. Educational information may at times assist in *remedying* a problem; at other times, educational information may help *prevent* certain situations; but the role of education in one's life today has become so extensive that educational information becomes an integral part of one's continued *development.*

Educational Information for the 3-D Concept

For a counselor to be most effective in obtaining and utilizing information he needs a philosophical frame of reference with an adaptability concept. The 3-D concept is one that may have application for obtaining and using information with individuals. Applying the 3-D concept to personalize educational information, the counselor should have access to various types of educational information because different classifications of people within each of the people dimensions needs educational information at the different depths, and needs materials at different reading levels. As the counselor attempts to obtain information for a given individual, he not only may need specific information for that person, but also may need information for others who work with that individual. Thus, the counselor, as means for personalizing information are considered, must be concerned about who the person is, what his needs are, and for what reason he is at this time going to utilize educational information. Because other people are working with that individual, a need may exist to supply others with information they can use in working with him, thus bringing about a coordinated team effort for the person's benefit.

To fulfill the 3-D concept, the counselor will have to obtain information from various sources and also will need to know various places where the individual can obtain information himself. The counselor cannot be expected to have compiled previously all information that might be needed by all individuals at the various times during their development. Rather, the counselor will need to know and understand sources of information that will help to fill in the grid of the three-dimensional concept—sources of places, people, material, and ideas, where the counselor and/or the individual might obtain information to meet the individual's needs and assist in his development.

Educational information to be comprehensive enough to cover the 3-D concept must in the first dimension—people—include educational information, not just educational literature, for each potential person to be served in the guidance program. The information must be complete enough so that information can be personalized at a comprehension level whereby the individual can internalize the information into his own value systems. The second dimension—area—is identified by specifying educational information. The third dimension—depth—begins to sharpen the difference between educational information to serve a presently existing need as contrasted to educational information for a developmental approach. Educational information for the depth dimension necessitates three levels of information integrated into the educational maturation processes: (1) to broaden the individual's concepts, horizons, understandings, and curiosities about education and training and the learning processes; (2) to provide resourceful specific information with data and interpretations that will enable the individual to gain a comprehensive, as well as general understanding pertaining to definite educational institutions, programs, or parts thereof; and (3) to enable the individual to obtain a feedback at each stage of his development with an integration of information and self, plus an evaluation of each upon the other. The educational information processes may be highlighted—increased in intensity—at certain times but those times cannot be specified as occurring at the same time for all persons.

The counselor's educational information sources need to be broad and flexible enough to make the 3-D concept become a reality.

Some people take the viewpoint that in kindergarten and the first, second, and third grades the only educational information role is to broaden the knowledge of the individual—the first level in the depth dimension. If the teacher and counselor in the lower elementary school only do the first level, many of the children may become potential dropouts. The individual wants and needs information at all three levels whether he is in kindergarten or graduate school or in an adult training program. The first level information should help broaden his perspectives, lift him to a point where he can see forward, and take the blinders off of him. As soon as a person obtains greater vision, his questions become more specific. As soon as he has a broader perspective, he wants to know more. When he begins to ask specific questions—as a kindergartner, junior high school student, or graduate school person does—more resources of specific educational information at the second level are needed. For the kindergarten child practically none of the educational information can be printed. Educational information for the 3-D concept must be more than unisensory (sight) input. Educational information includes multisensory input, thus necessitating a multimedia approach utilizing all types of educational information.

In the third level—feedback—the educational information should provide ways for the individual to test reality. If educational information is provided comprehensively enough to achieve the 3-D concept, then the individual will have an increased exposure to alternatives available (through the first and second levels) and an opportunity to have an exploration of consequences, often prior to having the full circumstantial experience (third level). The 3-D concept makes possible the interweaving of information at all three levels according to the individual, his purposes at the time, and his educational maturation.

In the first and second level the educational information is more objective and abstract, whereas in the third level the information is more subjective and personally oriented. Often in the third level the information is not in the counselor's files; instead the counselor helps the individual identify kinds of information that will enable him to have checks at various points in his progress toward a goal. Some educational information processes frequently used at the third level include grades, teachers' comments, tests, a counselor for exploration of viewpoints and possibly for gaining new insights, and other people. One of the major tasks might be to assist the individual in determining what kinds of feedback are meaningful for the topic under consideration.

In the 3-D concept the counselor is not in the position of getting all the information and giving it to the individual at any one of the three depths. The counselor works with and for individuals and assists them in identifying and obtaining educational information throughout their development—life. The counselor helps the individual learn how to obtain the most appropriate information at a time when it will be of maximum benefit rather than the counselor's always giving information or making it available, even though sometimes these are also necessary.

Sources of Educational Information

Sources for individuals and counselors to obtain educational information are varied and many in number. When the individual is young he depends primarily upon his parents and other close friends of the family to supply him with the information that establishes his attitudes towards attending school. Some information comes from radio and television programs and other canned media, such as movies, cartoons, and lectures. After he becomes a little older he begins to read, and as he does he begins to obtain information about education, about schooling and training programs, from various kinds of publications from different publishers. He also obtains information about education from interaction with school officials and individuals associated with schools, including students and alumni. Part of his educational information also comes from the educational institution itself. In addition he obtains information from various publicity items, including publications released by the school and other sources, the activities associated with the school, and the image existing about that school. Thus, sources of educational information may be primarily classified under three major headings—*people* (interaction with), *publications* (literature and other "canned" media), and *educational and training institutions*.

A depository of educational information that may well become a major contributor in the future to the availability of information is the Educational Resources Information Center (ERIC) Clearinghouse on Counseling and Personnel Services, The University of Michigan, Ann Arbor. The center is operated as part of the Federal Government's program within the U.S. Office of Education. Value of ERIC as a clearinghouse and information center, the first comprehensive information system designed to serve counselors and others, will be to make available information on the most important developments regardless of the places where the new developments occurred. ERIC acquires, abstracts, indexes, stores, retrieves, and disseminates nationally the most significant and timely educational research and research-related documents. Monthly publications with detailed indexes of all new acquisitions are produced. In addition to the abstracts contained in the monthly publications, any document cited can be obtained at nominal cost either on microfiche or hard copy. Orders are generally filled within one week.

People—Interaction with

Throughout an individual's life he obtains information about educational institutions and education in general from people whom he knows or with whom he comes into contact. Some of these people will be conscious of their role in furnishing educational information that assists the individual in his cognitive and affective processes pertaining to education and training. Frequently, however, individuals are unaware of the role assumed in communicating education information to another person. Thus, the counselor's role is to help a specific individual identify and assess the kinds of information that might be obtained from different people as well as what information has already been obtained from interacting with others.

Just as the individual needs information about specific educational and training programs so does the counselor. He may communicate by writing, telephoning, or interviewing individuals associated with different institutions, such as admissions officers, administrators, or faculty members.

For a classification and listing of people who may be considered as sources for both the professional guidance worker and the individual the following list is suggested. The classification implies difference in possible understandings and kinds of information that can be supplied by each.

PROFESSIONAL PEOPLE ASSOCIATED WITH THE EDUCATIONAL OR TRAINING INSTITUTION
admissions officer
administrator
curricular adviser
teacher, trainer, or instructor

PRESENT OR FORMER ENROLLEES OF THE INSTITUTION
students
alumni

EDUCATIONAL INFORMATION SPECIALISTS
counselor in private practice or public agency
guidance specialists from state department of public instruction
consultant from U.S. Office of Education
educational director, respective business or industry

FRIENDS AND ASSOCIATES
parents
peers
friends
associates

Information obtained by interaction with people who have firsthand information is a fundamental source for comprehensive educational information. People may be a major source of the third depth information—feedback—for the individual. The identification of the appropriate source people for the educational information desired by the individual may necessitate the counselor's contacting the people to ensure that the information they will be able to furnish will be applicable.

Publications—Literature and Other Canned Media

A second source, publications, includes printed materials of various kinds, films, filmstrips, audio and video tapes, phonograph records, cartoons, and other media where the information is recorded—canned—for review by the person when he chooses. The publications source may be divided into four classifications—commercial publishers, associations and organizations, government publishers, and business and industries.

COMMERCIAL PUBLISHERS. The commercial publishers from whom counselors regularly would obtain educational publications would depend upon the setting in which the counselor works. Frequent review of newly published materials is necessary to assure awareness of and possibility of obtaining additional materials that have value to potential users of educational information. The following list contains examples of commercial publishers of educational information. (See Address Index.)

Addison-Wesley Publishing Company, Inc.
Allyn and Bacon, Inc.
American Guidance Service, Inc.
Association Press
Barron's Educational Series, Inc.
Bellman Publishing Company
B'nai B'rith Vocational Service
The Bobbs-Merrill Company, Inc.
Burgess Publishing Company
The Center for Applied Research in Education, Inc.
Chronicle Guidance Publications, Inc.
Columbia University Press
Croner Publications
Educational Directories, Inc.
Education Research Corporation
Educators Progress Service
Golden Press, Inc.
Grosset & Dunlap, Inc., Publishers
Guidance Associates
Guidance Exchange

Harcourt, Brace & World, Inc.
Harper & Row, Publishers
Houghton Mifflin Company
Jossey-Bass, Inc., Publishers
Little, Brown and Company
The Macmillan Company
McGraw-Hill, Inc.
David McKay Co., Inc.
McKnight & McKnight Publishing Co.
Meridith Press, Division of Meridith Publishing Company
Charles E. Merrill Books, Inc.
Julian Messner, Inc.
Methods and Materials Press
National Industrial Conference Board
The New American Library, Inc.
Oceana Publications
Pocket Books, Inc.
Porter Sargent Publishers
Prakken Publications, Inc.
Prentice-Hall, Inc.
G. P. Putnam's Sons
The Ronald Press Company
Science Research Associates, Inc.
Simon and Schuster, Inc.
Sound Seminars
Student Admissions Center
Charles C. Thomas, Publisher
The Viking Press, Inc.
John Wiley & Sons, Inc.

TESTS AND TEST INFORMATION. Commercial publishers of tests and test information for use in the area of educational information are important to counselors, teachers, and others who work with individuals. Test results serve as a source of the third depth—feedback. A list of publishers supplying tests used in educational information would include (see Address Index):

American Guidance Service, Inc.
California Test Bureau
Educational Testing Service
Harcourt, Brace & World, Inc.
Houghton Mifflin Company
Personnel Press, Inc.
The Psychological Corporation
Science Research Associates, Inc.

Associations and Organizations. Associations and organizations, both professional and trade, are actively engaged in publishing material pertaining to education and training that affect their members and that serve recruitment purposes. This information can be pertinent to an individual in his decisions concerning education and training.

A comprehensive list can be obtained from the Superintendent of Documents, U.S. Government Printing Office, Washington, D.C. 20402, in *The Education Directory, Part 4: Education Associations,* which contains names, addresses, administrative heads, and secretaries of over eight hundred special-interest education groups, as well as the name(s) of the official publication(s) and frequency of issue.

The following list contains the names of the associations and organizations more frequently used. (see Address Index.)

Accrediting Commission for Cosmetology Education, Inc.
Adult Education Association
American Association for Higher Education
American Association of Dental Schools
American Association of Junior Colleges
American College Admissions Center
American Council on Education
American Personnel and Guidance Association
American Sociological Association
American Trucking Association, Education Section
Association of College Admissions Counselors
College Entrance Examination Board, Publications Order Office
Council on Hotel, Restaurant, and Institutional Education
Goodwill Industries, Inc. (local)
National Association for Practical Nurses Education Service, Inc.
National Association of Trade and Technical Schools
National Education Association
National Home Study Council
Vocational Rehabilitation Office (local or state)
United Business Schools Association
YWCA and YMCA (local)

Governments. Much educational information can be obtained through publications from government units at the national, state, and local levels. Certain publications are issued regularly, and in addition other publications are released from time to time on research studies, projects, and committee reports. If the title of a publication issued by any U.S. Government Office is known, it can be ordered directly from the Superintendent of Documents, U.S. Government Printing Office. The material is often free or inexpensive.

Names of governmental agencies that are involved in educational activities and are sources of educational information are listed; some with annotations. (Addresses are provided in the Address Index.) The United States Government departments, offices, and bureaus are listed according to the governmental administrative organizations:

DEPARTMENT OF AGRICULTURE
Publishes information pertaining to education for agriculture, agri-business, and extension work.

> Science and Education Director
> Federal Extension Service

DEPARTMENT OF COMMERCE
Publishers demographic information of value in understanding educational levels in different parts of the country.

> Bureau of Census

DEPARTMENT OF DEFENSE
Department of the Air Force
Department of the Army
Department of the Navy
Marine Corps (Department of Navy)

OFFICE OF ECONOMIC OPPORTUNITY (OEO)
Publishes information pertaining to opportunities for education and training for everyone.

> Adult Basic Education Program
> Community Action Programs
> Job Corps
> Volunteers in Service to America (VISTA)
> Work Training Programs
> Youth Conservation Corps

DEPARTMENT OF HEALTH, EDUCATION, AND WELFARE (HEW)
Administration on Aging
> Prepares and disseminates educational materials directed primarily at professional aging specialist or the aging population.

Office of Education
> Publishes *American Education,* which includes reports on Federal activities in education—research, services, and grants; summarizes laws affecting education; announces publication.
> Issued ten times a year at an annual cost of $4.50.
> *Earned Degrees Conferred by Higher Educational Institutions,* annual, free.

The Educational Directory, Part I, State Government; Part II, Counties and Cities; Part III, Higher Education; Part IV, Educational Associations; and *Part V, Federal Government.* Names and addresses of principal educational institutions and personnel as well as other vital information is given. Issued annually.

Higher Education includes new publications and current developments in higher education, nine issues a year.

School Life includes new publications and current developments in elementary and secondary education, nine issues a year.

A complete list of publications of the Office of Education is available from the Superintendent of Documents.

Bureau of Adult and Vocational Education
 Division of Adult Education Programs Library Services and Educational Facilities

Office of Disadvantaged and Handicapped

Bureau of Elementary and Secondary Education
 Division of Educational Personnel Training
 Division of Plans and Supplementary Centers
 Division of Program Operations
 Division of School Assistance in Federally Affected Areas
 Division of State Agency Cooperation

Office of Equal Educational Opportunities

Bureau of Higher Education
 Division of College Facilities
 Division of College Support
 Division of Foreign Studies
 Division of Graduate Programs
 Division of Student Financial Aid

National Center for Educational Statistics
 Coordinates information-gathering activities and assists in application and use of automatic data-processing systems and service.

Bureau of Research
 Division of Adult and Vocational Research
 Division of Elementary-Secondary Research
 Division of Higher Education Research
 Division of Laboratories and Research Development
 Division of Research Training and Dissemination

Vocational Rehabilitation Administration
 Administers research and training programs for rehabilitation of individuals.

Welfare Administration
 Children's Bureau

Office of Juvenile Delinquency and Youth Development
  Controls programs to train personnel who work or are preparing to work in the field of juvenile delinquency.

DEPARTMENT OF LABOR
Assistant Secretary for Labor Standards
  Bureau of Labor Standards
    Assists in international exchange of persons and training.
  Women's Bureau
    Concerned with training and skills for women.
Commissioner of Labor Statistics
  Prepares literature relating education and training to the labor force.
  Bureau of Labor Statistics (BLS)
Manpower Administration
  Bureau of Apprenticeship and Training
    Variety of publications relating to apprenticeship and other types of training for skill occupations.
  Bureau of Employment Security
    Training programs supervised, including Manpower Development and Training Act (MDTA).
      United States Employment Service (USES)
  Neighborhood Youth Corps (NYC)

NATIONAL SCIENCE FOUNDATION
Publishes research reports on trends in employment and training of scientific and technical manpower.

DEPARTMENT OF STATE
Bureau of Educational and Cultural Affairs
  Information on opportunities in education in other countries; operates student and teacher exchange programs.
Peace Corps

DEPARTMENT OF THE TREASURY
Coast Guard

VETERANS ADMINISTRATION
Department of Veterans Benefits
  Compensations, pension, and education service to veterans.

Departments, Offices, and Bureaus within various ones of the fifty states are also sources of educational information. A partial list is as follows (specific names of agencies vary from state to state):

DEPARTMENT OF COMMERCE

DEPARTMENT OF EDUCATION OR PUBLIC INSTRUCTION

Division of Counseling and Guidance
Division of Elementary and Secondary Education
Division of Higher Education
Division of Public Personnel
Division of Vocational Education

DEPARTMENT OF HEALTH

DEPARTMENT OF LABOR

Various offices and agencies within the county or local urban areas make educational information available. The extensiveness varies from one geographic area to another, but each counselor should survey the sources and resources available locally. Often the agency will have personnel available to assist in personalizing the information as well as have literature available.

BUSINESSES AND INDUSTRIES. In addition to the three sources of publications—commercial publishers, associations and organizations, and government—businesses and industries are also excellent sources of information concerning their educational and training programs. Counselors can obtain information from businesses and industries located within the area where their counselees usually would be employed. Some companies, however, do supply educational information on a national scale. Examples of businesses and industries (addresses listed in Address Index) that would be sources of material for educational information for national distribution would include:

General Electric Company, Educational Relations Service
General Mills
General Motors
John Hancock Mutual Life Insurance Company
New York Life Insurance Company
Prudential Insurance Company of America
Sun Life Assurance Company of Canada
Westinghouse Electric Corporation

Educational and Training Institutions

Comprehensive information can be obtained directly from the institution involved. As indicated in the first source, people in the educational and training situations can supply much of the information personally. Also information about the educational programs and opportunities, results of surveys, statistics and research findings concerning education, admission policies, characteristics of the student body, and other pertinent facts are obtainable from a variety of printed materials, such as newsletters, catalogues, student handbooks, bulletins, and other special publications for the professional counselor. In addition to people and publications, an individual can gain an impression about the educational or training institution through the various activities within the institution.

Educational and training institutions would include private and public elementary and secondary schools, state and private colleges and universities, specialized schools (for special education students and for specialty-oriented students), military academies, technical schools and area vocational schools, junior and community colleges, apprenticeship training programs, and in-service training programs in business and industry. Names and addresses of particular institutions can be found in various directories, such as those listed in this chapter under reference materials.

In some cases the acquisition of educational information for a given individual is a visit to a campus, an educational building, or a room where the course or program is offered. In other cases, the individual gains information through the image of the institution. As vague as the image is, it does seem to portray something that attracts certain kinds of students as is reported in studies on profiles of educational institutions, i.e., the Astin (1965) study on *Who Goes Where to College*. Other media of educational information from educational or training institutions include grades, test scores, performance record, and personnel ratings of an individual. These media could be the source of information at the third depth—feedback.

The role of the counselor is not one in which he obtains *all* the information for an individual as much as one of helping to determine what sources are available, what kinds of information can be obtained from each, and how it can be acquired. The individual can in some cases assume the responsibility of obtaining information from the original source. Information available through the counselor can supplement the independently acquired information.

Types of Educational Information

The types of educational information that the counselor and/or individual generally comes in contact with are varied in number. The usual ones include training or college catalogues, brochures, handbooks of the school, annuals or school yearbooks, educational or training program description leaflets, literature including recruitment information, posters and charts, articles and reprints, films and filmstrips, audio and video magnetic tapes, phonographic records, cartoons, and comics, library books on education, and reference books.

Types of educational information in the past often have been classified by headings such as book, pamphlet, educational film, catalogue, or brochure. The classification was based primarily on the medium rather than upon the user. If educational information is to be personalized, then the emphasis should not be upon the medium—book, sheet of paper, brochure, or catalogue—but rather the emphasis should be upon the person with whom the information is intended to be used and for what purpose. The individual needs to be exposed not only to different depths but also to different types of material by different techniques of using the information. The individual stands a better chance of finding the approach for personalizing the information when he has available for his use a variety of media at different depths. (See Chapter 8.)

To assist the counselor in obtaining the various types of information for use with the individuals with whom he does or potentially may work, the counselor should depend on receiving information regularly. One type of educational information for the counselor to use with individuals is *reference materials.* These contain specific information that must be updated frequently, thus necessitating frequent replacement with new editions or different publications. A second type would be *subscription service* materials, including periodic reviews of recent materials, bulletins, research studies, and "how to" approaches. A counselor can keep aware of additional and new materials of the third type, *audio-visual,* through catalogues, brochures, and announcements of available materials. A fourth type on which counselors depend for articles, book reviews, and other items of major interest is *professional journals.*

Reference Material

In regards to reference books, one copy of each of several usually are kept in the counselor's office, so that he may obtain specific information at the time he is working with a given individual. In some cases duplicate copies plus possibly other reference books are kept in the library. The kind of reference books depends, of course, upon the persons in the first dimension. Who they are is the determining factor. When a counselor works in a secondary school he usually needs information for college-bound students on junior colleges and degree-granting institutions; such reference books as *American Junior Colleges, American Universities and Colleges,* and *Handbook for College-Bound Students and Their Counselors,* serve this need. In addition the counselor would need reference books for specialty-oriented students, such as books on business schools, trade schools, apprenticeship programs, and so on. The counselor would also need some reference books for those individuals with special needs, such as handicapped students, members of minority groups, and students who are in need of preparatory schools, private schools, summer schools, and summer camps. The counselor also needs reference books for teachers and other professional persons who work with the students.

If the counselor works in the elementary school his reference books probably would have information for individuals with special needs, including physically or mentally handicapped children, academically bright students, parents who want their children to have specialized training, and teachers who work with the children.

If the counselor is working with those individuals who presently are not enrolled in any educational program, the reference books would probably include information on correspondence schools, vocational and trade schools, and information on short-term training programs. The reference books would be pertinent to adults who need or want additional education for retraining, upgrading, or self-fulfillment, and also for youth who have dropped out of school.

No one counselor would probably need all the reference books available, but he would select the ones most helpful to him and the individuals with whom he works. A few reference books, booklets, and pamphlets are listed to illustrate the wide range and variety available. In some cases a short annotation is provided. Addresses of sources are given in the Address Index.

Accredited Institutions of Higher Education, American Council on Education; $2.50 for one year. Issued twice a year, supplement to *American Universities and Colleges* and *American Junior Colleges.*

American Junior Colleges, American Council on Education; $14.00.

American Trade Schools Directory, Croner Publications, annual; $9.95 for one year. Loose-leaf edition with supplements.

American Universities and Colleges, American Council on Education; $15.00.

The ACAC Handbook for College Admissions, Association of College Admissions Counselors; $5.50.

Admissions Schedules of the Member Colleges, College Entrance Examination Board; $0.50.

Barron's Profiles of American Colleges, Barron's Educational Series, Inc.; $3.95.

Catholic Colleges and Universities, Catholic College Bureau; $1.00.

Classrooms in the Military, Bureau of Publications, Teachers College, Columbia University Press; $3.95.

The College Blue Book, College Planning Programs, Ltd., 3 vols., 8 books. Vol. I, Bk. 1, *American Institutions of Higher Education;* Vol. II, Bk. 2, *Majors and Curricula Leading to Collegiate Degrees;* Bk. 3, *Educational Atlas and College Towns;* and Vol. III, Bk. 4, *Financial Aids for American Students and Scholars;* Bk. 5, *Study Abroad;* Bk. 6, *Accreditation and Professional Planning;* Bk. 7, *Organization Register;* Bk. 8, *Secondary Schools, Public and Private of the United States;* $75.00.

College Guide for Jewish Youth, B'nai B'rith Vocational Service; $3.00.

The College Handbook, College Entrance Examination Board; $2.50.

Comparative Guide to American Colleges, Harper & Row, Publishers; paper, $3.95; cloth, $9.95.

Directory of Accredited Private Home Study Schools, National Home Study Council; free.

Directory of Business Schools, United Business Schools Association; free.

Directory for Exceptional Children, Porter Sargent Publishers; $7.00.

Directory, National Association of Trade and Technical Schools; free.

Directory of Post-Secondary Retailing and Marketing Vocational Programs, American Vocational Association, Inc.; free.

Directory of Vocational Training Sources, Science Research Associates, Inc.; $4.40.

Education in the Job Corps Conservation Center, U.S. Government Printing Office. Information on the content of the courses of study.

The Educational Directory, U.S. Office of Education, 5 parts. I, *State Government;* II, *Counties and Cities;* III, *Higher Education;* IV, *Educational Associations;* and V, *Federal Government;* $3.10 a set.

The Gifted: Educational Resources, Porter Sargent Publishers; $4.00.

Guide to American Graduate Schools, The Viking Press, Inc.; paper, $3.95; cloth, $6.95.

A Guide to Graduate Study: Programs Leading to the Ph.D. Degree, American Council on Education; $7.50.

Guide to Summer Camps and Summer Schools, Porter Sargent Publishers; paper, $2.50; cloth, $4.40.

Handbook of Adult Education in the United States, Adult Education Association of the United States; $7.50.

Handbook for College-Bound Students and Their Counselors, Association of College Admissions Counselors; $2.00.

The Handbook of Private Schools, Porter Sargent Publishers; $10.00. Provides information on thousands of private boarding and day elementary and secondary schools.

International Handbook of Universities, American Council on Education; $13.50.

Junior College Directory, American Association of Junior Colleges; $2.00.

Lovejoy's College Guide, Simon and Schuster, Inc.; $3.95.

Lovejoy's Vocational School Guide: A Handbook of Job Training Opportunities, Simon and Schuster, Inc.; $2.95.

Manual of Freshman Class Profiles, College Entrance Examination Board; $5.00.

Need a Lift? Educational Opportunities, The American Legion Education and Scholarship Program; $0.25.

The New American Guide to Colleges, Columbia University Press; $8.95.

The New American Guide to Colleges, The New American Library, Inc.; $0.95.

Nonpublic Secondary Schools Directory, U.S. Government Printing Office; $0.75.

The Official Guide to Catholic Educational Institutions, National Catholic Welfare Conference, annual; $2.95.

Private Independent Schools, Bunting and Lyon, Inc.; $12.00. Directory of boarding, day, and military schools.

Technician Education Yearbook, Prakken Publications; $10.00. Information for nonuniversity-bound students on all phases of technician training, including industrial, health-related, agricultural, and business-related. Directory of public and private institutions.

Undergraduate Study Abroad, Institute of International Education; $2.95.

Subscription Services

Counselors have need for three types of materials that should be received periodically. One type is annotated bibliography of current guidance literature, which also lists the cost and procedure for obtaining copies. The second type is a guidance service that includes recent material applicable to educational information for the individuals to be served. A third type of subscriptions sometimes purchased by counselors is for magazines that have included regularly articles of educational information value. Some of the subscription services in addition to material for the counselor include regularly published material designed for use by persons other than the counselor. A few subscription services of the first two types are listed. The counselor will need to obtain samples for his review before selecting the ones most appropriate for his use.

Chronicle "3-in-1" Guidance Service, Chronicle Guidance Publications, Inc.; $42.50. Offers a package of occupational, educational, and professional guidance material; "Educational Guidance Items" contains booklets, bulletins on college entrance requirements and costs, scholarships, a guide to college majors, and classification of colleges.

College Admissions Data Service, Educational Research Corporation. Revised annually and monthly bulletins issued.

Counselor's Information Service, B'nai B'rith Vocational Service; $7.00. Twenty-four-page annotated bibliography of current literature on educational and vocational guidance issued four times a year.

Guidance Exchange, Guidance Exchange; $15.00. Digest of current guidance literature—books, films, filmstrips, pamphlets, records, and other literature in more than 135 subject categories. Issued four times a year.

SRA Guidance Service, Science Research Associates; $36.50. Issued four times a year, generally contains textbooks(s), reference book(s), booklets, newsletter, research reports, posters, and occupational information.

Selected List of U.S. Government Publications, U.S. Government Printing Office; free. Monthly list.

Guidance Information Kit, Careers, Inc., or National Cash Register Company; $295.00 annual lease. Twelve microfilm transparencies with one reader. Contains various educational information, including catalogues of educational institutions. All transparencies are revised yearly.

Audio-visual

Often in considering educational information for use with individuals, only printed material (frequently identified as educational literature) is included; however, today audio-visual material also is becoming very important. Audio-visual types might be classified under motion pictures, filmstrips, audio and video tapes, and phonograph records. Several companies sell audio-visual materials applicable for educational information. Counselors should obtain lists of available audio-visual materials and select the most appropriate ones for the individuals with whom he expects to work. The names of a few companies are as follows:

Association Films, Inc.
Cathedral Films, Inc.
Coronet Films
Encyclopedia Britannica Films, Inc.
Guidance Associates
International Film Bureau
Jam Handy Organization
McGraw-Hill Book Co., Text-Film Division
Society for Visual Education, Inc.
Sterling Movies, USA, Inc.

New developments in automation and reproducing equipment will probably bring about newer approaches to sources of educational information that will implement a combination of both printed and audiovisual materials. Studies being made in the late 1960's have been successful enough to indicate that in the future more information might be placed onto audio-visual equipment from which an individual might select an education program by simply pushing or dialing combinations of numbers or letters to discover the appropriate resources available to him. The primary resource information may be located in another city, but by means of a communication system, the equipment used by the individual is connected directly with the resource center containing the desired information. If the individual finds the specific information useful and needs a copy for later reference, he will need only to push a button and within seconds he will have a copy. Thus, the trend toward automation of educational information may mean faster scanning, exposure to more information, availability of more comprehensive recent information, and a greater chance that the individual can have the most appropriate information available anywhere at the time when the information may be of maximum benefit in his development. Reproduction of the information for him to keep may enable him to better analyze his own growth and development, thus making it possible for him to be able to assume a larger control of the causal factors in his educational maturation.

Professional Journals

The counselor needs to keep abreast of the developments in education. One of the ways is to read the professional journals. As with all educational information, selection has to be made according to the persons with whom the counselor works. A few of the professional journals are as follows (additional journals that may be pertinent are listed in the occupational area, Chapter 11):

American Educational Research Journal, American Educational Research Association.

The Bulletin of the National Association of Secondary-School Principals, National Association of Secondary School Principals, NEA.

Elementary School Guidance and Counseling, American School Counselors Association.

The Elementary School Journal, University of Chicago Press.

The Journal of College Student Personnel, American College Personnel Association.

Journal of Educational Psychology, American Psychological Association.

The Journal of Higher Education, Ohio State University Press.

The National Elementary Principal, Dept. of Elementary School Principals, NEA.

The Personnel and Guidance Journal, APGA.

Phi Delta Kappan, Phi Delta Kappa.

Rehabilitation Literature, National Society for Crippled Children.

The School Counselor, American School Counselor Association.

Today's Education, NEA.

Evaluative Criteria for Educational Information

An evaluative instrument for educational information has not been developed by a professional organization. If the educational information is to be personalized and is to contribute to the developmental approach, then the evaluative criteria should depend upon two major factors—the potential user and the other educational information that is available or that has been utilized by the individual. With these two factors as basic, information may be selected for complementary and supplementary value in relation to other information and in terms of the depth dimension and educational maturation of the individual at the time.

If educational information is to be evaluated in terms of a potential user, then no national evaluative instrument will be appropriate. Some criteria can be considered and for a basis of developing the criteria locally, the counselor needs to examine what the information is to achieve with or for the user. For a general presentation the definition for educational information used in this book will be the basis. Upon examination of the definition for educational information, the authors included the following: (1) increases awareness of available educational opportunities, successive levels of attainment for continued progress, additional responsibilities to society as additional education is obtained, and possibilities for the individual himself; (2) contributes to the individual's obtaining the skills and capabilities required by society as he takes additional education; and (3) possesses accurate, comprehensive up-to-date data and specific information about the topic—institution, program, course, or whatever—plus trends and their potential effects on the individual. If the sources are people, publishers, and educational and training institutions, then these criteria can be applied to each and to the information from them. Sometimes a specific educational information source in its totality may be considered poor, but if part of it contains information not obtainable otherwise, then the source can be used as a supplement with notations added as to why the information is included. When the information is used, the counselor may need to be more cautious than usual to assure that comprehensive, accurate, up-to-date, personalized information reaches the individual.

The important point is that the potential users become the governing criteria rather than such things as number of pages, kind of paper, or size of print. When two or more sources offer the same information, then style and format may become the deciding factors if only one is to be utilized.

Because individuals often do not know how to evaluate the educational information that they may need, the counselor may need to assist each individual in developing criteria appropriate for him at the time. Review of some points often considered when evaluating an educational institution or program may be helpful:

KIND OF PROGRAM(S) OFFERED
All levels, preschool through adult
elementary-grade levels
secondary-grade levels
specialty school—business, trade, technological, leisure time, recreational
continuing education—age limits
junior or community college
degree-granting programs—including analysis of the kind and extent of degrees offered
Astin (1965) listed six environmental assessments: realistic, scientific, social, conventional, enterprising, and artistic.

CONTROL
tax supported
military
church-related
independent
business and industry
labor unions

LOCATION
commuting distance to place of residence
accessibility—easy, some difficulty, hardship
climate according to individual's standards

relationship to other environment factors desired by individual
urbanization—rural, small city, urban

ADMISSIONS AND RETENTION
criteria for admission
policies regarding remaining in program

COST

ENROLLMENT

STUDENT BODY
male
female
coeducational
factors such as those listed by Astin (1965)
    intellectualism
    aestheticism
    status
    pragmatism
    masculinity

INSTITUTION'S RATING OR STANDING—IN THE PROGRAMS BEING
    CONSIDERED

FACILITIES
buildings(s)—condition, number
equipment—condition and extent in the special program
faculty
    caliber including degrees held
    age
    recognition received
housing and eating facilities

CLASSES
size
hours
means of conducting
    individual
    group
    lecture
    discussion
    laboratory

STUDENT SERVICES
financial assistance
    kind

limitations
availability
placement
    educational placement while in the program in terms of such
        items as class sectioning, advance placement
    part-time job placement while attending
    job placement services offered upon graduation and as alumni
        years later
counseling services availability
health services availability

AWARDS UPON COMPLETION
certificate
diploma
degree
recognized by whom

STUDENT ACTIVITIES
fraternities and/or sororities
clubs and/or student organizations
recreational
cultural

Counselor's Techniques for Obtaining Educational Information

The techniques used for obtaining educational information are somewhat dependent upon the counselor's ingenuity. A review of some practices may serve as a springboard for developing others. The techniques listed are classified under three major approaches for obtaining information: (1) from literature including audio-visual, (2) by observation and participation, and (3) by interaction with people. The three classifications make possible the full utilization of the various sources available.

From Literature Including Audio-visual

To obtain educational information from literature the counselor must, of course, come in contact with a broad scope of educational literature. By *writing* each publisher and requesting a catalogue or brochure of educational information available, plus asking that the counselor's name be added to the mailing list, many pieces of literature will come to the counselor immediately and over an extended period of time as new materials are published. A sample list of publishers was provided earlier in this chapter.

When a counselor *joins professional organizations*, such as American

Personnel and Guidance Association and the state personnel and guidance association, he not only receives their publications, which often contain educational information, he also has his name listed among those interested in professional activities working with persons at certain age levels under given conditions. Interested publishers, who have material for use with the kind of persons served by the counselor, often send material to the professional organization members. The dues-paying membership list applicable to material to be distributed is probably one of the best mailing lists that a company could obtain. Also salesmen and educational representatives use the membership list for identification of people on whom to call.

No better way can be listed than to *read* widely. Magazines, professional journals, newspapers, bulletins, catalogues, brochures, and all other types of literature should be reviewed. Frequent visits to the library with adequate time allotted for reading become a must for the professional counselor. Printed materials are not the only source. Audio and video tapes, phonograph records, films and filmstrips, and other audio-visual media should be reviewed regularly. Often this can be done through the use of the library, whereas in other cases materials will need to be requested, to be sent on approval for review locally.

A counselor needs to have *access to subscriptions* on sources of educational information such as those listed earlier in this chapter. In reviewing the annotated bibliographies the counselor can obtain much of the material free by simply requesting a copy. A form letter can be printed or duplicated to facilitate the *ordering*. A self-addressed gummed label included with the letter may reduce the time lag between request and receipt (Hollis and Hollis, 1965, pp. 287–288).

Some materials from the annotated bibliographies of educational information that were identified as having value for potential users will be available only at a cost. Such materials will need to have a requisition prepared and sent through the proper channels at the counselor's place of employment. A *budget* should be established for the counseling and guidance area and a designated part of that budget should be available for purchasing educational information not only at the regular yearly requisition time but throughout the year as materials are needed and as they become available.

Another technique used by a counselor is one that needs to have his careful consideration—the purchasing of educational information with his own money. If the material is to be used with a counselee, then the employing agency, school, or organization should pay for the material or the individual himself should make the purchase. If the material is to be used for the counselor's own self-improvement and the place of employment has no in-service funds, then the counselor will need to pay the bill. No hard and fast rule can be made in such cases.

By Observation and Participation

By the counselor's keeping his eyes and ears attuned to educational information, he will be able to obtain much information. He can make *visits to educational exhibits,* such as those displayed in stores, fairs, conventions, libraries, and various other places. Educational institutions often set up exhibits to tell the story of their program(s). Usually the exhibit has free literature as well, plus forms for requesting additional information. The exhibit generally is attended by an official of the institution who is willing to supply information.

Field trips associated with education and educational institutions become another technique for obtaining educational information. One of the best ways to gain firsthand impressions and information is to make a visit to the educational or training institution, whether it be an on-the-job training program, one room classroom on main street for specialty students, private boarding school, or university campus. Just as a picture might take the place of a thousand words, a visit might take the place of a two- or three-volume book. Some counselors include educational institutions in many of the trips they take for business and pleasure. Stopping at an educational institution or a college campus may be a welcome change in the trip and often adds much firsthand information.

Counselors can observe and often *participate in meetings, conventions, and workshops* on educational topics. The observations and participation at such meetings can contribute to the educational information that the counselor has and may enable him to help others know the best sources from which to obtain information that will have personal meaning to them.

By Interaction with People

The counselor can and should obtain much educational information from other people directly. As indicated earlier in this chapter the counselor may communicate with different individuals associated with specific educational institutions. *Consultation* with students and alumni, school officials, faculty members, and school representatives serve as a valuable technique for obtaining information. Probably no place else can as complete up-to-date information be obtained as from school personnel. True, the individuals may be biased; but from frequent consultations the counselor can begin to identify those areas and persons where other sources need to be utilized to counterbalance biases.

Interaction with people to gain educational information can be done through consultation, interview, telephone conversation, and correspondence. Such techniques as *follow-up studies and community surveys* of educational opportunities provide a means of gaining educational information. *Panels, forums, symposiums, and speeches* on educational topics are other ways of gaining educational information. Often these are available on radio and TV programs.

Techniques for Individuals and Groups for Obtaining Educational Information

Two things counselors need to recognize are that individuals obtain educational information on their own and that the process has been going on throughout their lifetimes. Counselors do not need to have accumulated all of the information; in fact, if counselors do, they will probably interfere with part of the growth and development processes whereby the individual learns how and where to obtain information needed. Thus, counselors need to assist individuals and groups in obtaining educational information on their own. The techniques for achieving the goal are primarily the same for them as for the counselor. The individual may *write* directly to the sources for copies of literature, *preview* audio and video tapes and phonograph records if such are available, *purchase* materials, and *read* widely in books and magazines.

To obtain educational information by observation and participation, the individual or groups can make *visits to exhibits, take field trips* to educational institutions, and *attend meetings* on educational topics. As for interaction with people, the individual should *visit the educational institutions* where he is considering becoming a student, plus possibly visiting others for comparison. He should *talk with students, alumni, and school officials.* Such visits and interaction with people are a vital part of his educational maturation and preparation for attendance at the institution and participation in the program. In some junior and senior high schools visitations, educational opportunity surveys, and other similar active participation on the part of the young people are encouraged.

Mobilizing and Organizing Resources

To obtain all the sources and types of educational information that potential users may need requires considerable planning. No one counselor can do it all and no counseling and guidance staff should do the job alone. The librarian in the school, community agency, business or industry, or city library needs to be an integral part of the planning. Certainly decisions will need to be made on housing the material, coding, filing, retrieving, checking out (Chapter 7), and utilizing of information (Chapter 8) before an overall plan is complete. Budgets both in time and money (Hollis and Hollis, 1965, pp. 246–270) will need to be established to assure adequate financing and time allocation. Personnel will need to be identified with specific jobs assigned to avoid duplication of labor and to assure continuity and designation of responsibilities.

Identification of appropriate sources for the potential users is a major task in itself, but to make sure that the sources can be utilized is even more complex. The identification of a person who can provide a given individual with educational information that he personally needs is not enough. The person has to be contacted and he has to be willing to supply the information. Personalizing educational information at all three depths throughout an individual's lifetime (developmental) becomes a major undertaking in which he must assume much of the responsibility, with specialized assistance available at times.

The counselor, regardless of his employment setting, has resources that can be utilized to assist him in obtaining and maintaining comprehensive educational information for personalizing the information processes with each individual. Mobilizing and organizing the resources according to the local situation are essential.

Summary

The counselor guided by the 3-D concept can obtain types of educational information from sources—people, publications, and educational and training institutions—that can be personalized for individual users in their search for information on which to base decisions. ERIC, serving as a clearinghouse, facilitates the accessibility of information.

The source—people (interaction with)—includes those persons who are in a position to gain firsthand information, such as educational directors in business and industry, admissions officers of colleges, and other officials and employees. The information may be gained from these persons by consultations, interviews, correspondence, through follow-up studies and community surveys, panels, forums, symposiums, and speeches.

Another source—publications (literature and other canned media) —may be obtained from commercial publishers, associations and organizations, government publishers, and business and industry. Techniques for the counselor to obtain information would include requesting catalogs and brochures, joining a professional organization, subscribing for materials, reading, and purchasing materials. Literature and other canned media would include printed materials, films, filmstrips, audio and video tapes, records, and cartoons.

A third source—educational and training institutions—may be utilized through observation and participation by visits to educational exhibits, field trips, participation in meetings, conventions and workshops, as well as those techniques mentioned under "people (interaction with)."

Evaluative criteria for educational information have not been developed by a professional organization as have been done for occupational materials. In establishing a criterion, the *user* should be the determining factor. The criteria for educational information would include items such as extent to which awareness of educational opportunities are increased, facilitation for obtaining maximum benefit by the individual from education and training, accuracy of information, comprehensiveness, authoritativeness, and up-to-dateness. Specific points to consider are kinds of programs offered, control of such programs, location, admission and retention, cost, enrollment, student body, facilities, classes, student services and activities, and the potential accomplishments.

Mobilizing and organizing the resources for utilization with an individual contribute to effectiveness. Mobilization and organization involve designating responsibilities to certain members of the staff with sufficient time and monies to operate the activities of obtaining, coding, filing, housing, retrieving, and utilizing educational information.

SELECTED REFERENCES

Adams, James F. *Counseling and Guidance, A Summary View.* New York: The Macmillan Company, 1965. Pp. 309–316.

Arbolino, Jack N. *Progress Report February 1966, Council on College-Level Examinations.* New York: College Entrance Examination Board, 1966. 8 pages

Astin, Alexander W. *Who Goes Where to College?* Chicago: Science Research Associates, Inc., 1964. Pp. 319–358.

Guide to College Level Independent Study. Moravia, N.Y.: Chronicle Guidance Publications, Inc., 1967. 239 pages. (Mailed on August 8, 1967)

Hollis, Joseph W., and Lucile U. Hollis. *Organizing for Effective Guidance.* Chicago: Science Research Associates, Inc., 1965. Pp. 246–270, 287–293.

Isaacson, Lee E. *Career Information in Counseling and Teaching.* Boston: Allyn and Bacon, Inc., 1966. Pp. 215–238.

Norris, Willa, Franklin R. Zeran, and Raymond N. Hatch. *The Information Service in Guidance,* 2nd ed. Chicago: Rand McNally & Company, 1966. Pp. 253–258, 297–301, 558–560.

Chapter 7

Making Educational Information
Available to Users

The effectiveness of the information service in counseling and guidance is determined primarily by the extent to which potential users have the right materials available when appropriate.

Unless educational information is available for users and readily accessible to be used according to their needs, the information is not serving the purpose for which educational information in counseling and guidance has a role. The amount of information collected is not the major criterion for evaluation, but rather the extent to which the information is made available and used by those who can benefit from it. Visibility of information that will increase awareness of the information as well as the kind and the extent becomes important in making the information readily available when the individual needs it. The question becomes not one of what kind of information can be collected, but rather the questions: Who are the potential users? What are their present and projected needs? What kinds of information and at what depth will it be beneficial to them? How can the information be made available and readily accessible to them? The guidance staff must consider these questions and then select the personnel, facilities, and the information that will accomplish what individuals need or may need.

Accessibility as a Determinant of Extent of Use

The extent of use will be determined by the accessibility of the educational information. The accessibility, of course, will depend upon where the information is located, how it is filed, and what personnel are available to assist the individual in locating and utilizing materials.

No one best way exists for accomplishing the task of making educational information readily accessible, but rather a compromise choice is necessary (Isaacson, 1966, pp. 317–324). The final decision or compromise choice in place and location will be made on the basis of present and projected needs, skills, intellectual level, and maturity of potential users. Generally speaking, no commercially produced filing system is readily available for processing educational information. The homemade plans that have been devised seem to be as suitable as or more so than commercially produced ones. The file plans being used vary considerably from one school to another, and from one business or commercial agency to another. Frequently, counselors indicate that their homemade educational information filing system serves certain major aspects for which it was designed although falling short in some other areas. Also the record keeping for loaning materials needs to be considered. In some cases the work of loaning and returning materials can be done by the secretary in the counseling offices, whereas in other cases, this job can be done more efficiently and effectively by persons who are well prepared for these functions, such as librarians and their staff. For materials to be considered by the user as being accessible, identifying, locating, retrieving, record keeping, and returning will all need to be accomplished in a minimum amount of time.

Baer and Roeber (1964, p. 375) stated that the effectiveness of the informational resources depends upon two major factors—the professional uses made of the information, and the administrative provisions. Within these two major factors, they include the information being used both in small group counseling and in classroom situations. Information is not housed in a remote location from the individual users, but rather is housed so that it is made an integral part of the educational program and of the guidance services. The administrative provisions of which Baer and Roeber wrote include the personnel to store and service the information, a budget for the information resources, the housing facilities, and the publicity that is provided for the information service. Unless these kinds of provisions can be considered, the information will not be accessible; unless it is accessible, it cannot or will not be used, thus defeating the purpose for gathering and processing it.

The question is not, Where is the educational information located? but, How accessible is the educational information at the time when most applicable for the individual and for those working with him? This consideration does not place location as the prime factor, but rather makes location become a factor in considering accessibility. Location, storage, coding, personnel to assist in obtaining information, and facilities for utilizing it are components of accessibility. Information needs to be accessible for individuals and groups working with or without professional assistance.

Criteria for Housing Educational Material

The location for housing educational material should be determined primarily on the basis of the users and the depth or purposes for which they will use the information. With these factors considered, then in a school setting the extent to which the information is being compiled for direct use by students, teachers, parents, and administrators becomes a major factor. For example, if the information is being collected primarily for teachers to use with students, then the information must be housed where it will be readily available in classrooms or instructional materials center. If the information is being collected for the primary purpose of the counselor's use during the counseling process, then the information must be in the counselor's office or in the adjacent secretarial area. If the information is being collected to be used primarily by individuals at their own leisure, then the library or instructional materials center becomes the major point for consideration.

Another frequent reason for collecting educational information is so that it can be used by groups—generally by specific groups when particular activities are being undertaken, such as group guidance sessions. In that case, the information probably should be kept in special rooms where such group meetings are to be held. Also, certain information may be collected on mobile units for moving from place to place.

Consideration also must be given to the traffic flow as individuals come to identify the information available, to preview and select the appropriate material, and later to return the materials.

In most schools with a comprehensive guidance program, all of the conditions for use—different persons, individually and in groups—will prevail. Some compromise location or locations must be selected to make the information available for potential users.

Consideration of location for educational information for use in a community agency will involve the same two factors as for schools— users and depth of information needed. Probably the most frequent use will be by advisers and counselors with individuals, therefore determining that the information will be located in proximity to the adviser's or counselor's desk or office.

In small agencies of one adviser or counselor, no problem of location exists. In an agency of more than one counselor or adviser, a central location near the offices might facilitate use best. However, if duplicate copies of materials used frequently are located in individual offices, this might contribute to more effective and efficient use.

In state employment agencies, each adviser and counselor may function more effectively and efficiently if frequently used copies of educational materials were located on his desk, with other educational information being located in a central area readily accessible to the various desks.

As previously stated, the depth of the information that is being collected is another factor to be considered in selecting location. If the information collected is primarily classified as first depth, that is, for broadening an individual's warehouse of information, then the information should be housed in a manner and place where it will be most visible to as many individuals as possible. If the information is primarily classified as second depth, that is, as resource and specific information, then the information should be located so that the individual will have an opportunity to make notes of the specific information if he wants to do so. In some cases he may want an exact copy of the information. Facilities should be available for reproducing a copy by one of the various duplicating or copying machines. If the information is classified primarily as the third depth, that is, stimulating feedback to the user, then it should be collected, housed, and available for use in a place that will provide as much visual and auditory privacy as possible in order that the individual can examine himself in light of the information as well as evaluate the information from his perception of himself.

When all factors of location are considered in a comprehensive guidance program that serves the various purposes and consumers, one can readily deduct that no one location is best and probably that no one place will serve all users and all purposes. The educational information probably will be housed in more than one place with a primary location being designated, such as a library or central area, as the major depository. Card indexes will need to be readily available in more than one place so that the user can know what information is available and where he can obtain it.

In a school system with a comprehensive guidance program, the major information depository would be the library, with the specific information most applicable to the kinds of activities conducted by certain teachers located in the classrooms or the instructional materials center where they will use it. Information of the third depth probably will be located in the counseling office, where it can be used with individuals during a counseling session. Some second depth specific and reference materials, such as reference books on colleges, universities, and special schools, probably will be located in the counselor's office. Such a plan will necessitate duplicate copies of certain information because copies will need to be available in the central location as well as in the counselor's office.

A question frequently asked in regard to location is how much space will be needed for the guidance information in the library. The amount of space, of course, is determined by such factors as the present and anticipated maximum size of the collection, the extent to which the information will be used, and the way in which the information is to be used—will it be used primarily by individuals or primarily by groups; primarily within the room or removed to other areas? These factors cannot be stated exactly based on predicted use, but consideration must be given to them before a decision is made on the amount of space required for housing materials. In reality, generally what happens is that the amount of space that is to be designated is determined primarily by the available space in the school. Starting with this factor may, however, be a major deterrent to the effectiveness of the educational information.

Physical Facilities for Housing Educational Material

Besides the alternative locations, such as library, classroom, small rooms, counselor offices, and instructional materials center, consideration also must be given to other kinds of physical facilities for housing educational materials. Because much educational information is in unbound form, the facilities will require filing cabinets and manila folders. For other materials, file boxes and shelves can be used rather than filing cabinets and manila folders.

Information received directly from educational and training institutions often is in booklet or soft-back-bound form, such as catalogues. Because extensive numbers of such materials generally are needed to fulfill the needs of potential users, a considerable quantity of shelf space will be required. In order that users can peruse information and, in some cases, record information in their own notebooks, study tables and chairs will need to be available in the same area as the educational information is housed.

Display racks and bulletin boards become a means for helping individuals to know about new materials. Both are an essential part of the educational information facilities and both require space well located, with special equipment designed for the type of information to be displayed.

Some type of master record system, similar to a central card index in a library, will need to be available for potential users. The master record system enables users to scan by topics all available information even though a specific piece of material may at the time be checked out for use by another person. Physical facilities for housing a master record system will be required.

Physical space requirements for the information service need to be considered from various aspects. Processing of material when first received will necessitate space, not only for the material but for the personnel to work with the material. Some outdated information will be preserved for comparative purposes rather than for regular use, thus necessitating storage space. In other cases, where information will have frequent use and may become shopworn or may disappear, quantities of such materials may be purchased and only a few copies made available at a time, thus necessitating storage cabinets or closets separate from but adjacent to or in the same room with the accessible educational information.

The physical facilities provided should facilitate making the material as visible as possible, as well as accessible. Consideration must be given also to the security of the information, but security should be provided without restricting users who have positive socially acceptable intents and attitudes.

When physical facilities for educational information are maintained as part of a total overall library, generally space becomes more meaningful and useful when one section or corner of the library or materials center can be devoted to educational information. In newly constructed libraries today, reading rooms within the library or materials center are becoming prevalent so that if an individual wants privacy in examining information or if he needs to preview a film or view microfilm, he can do so readily. Some information is most meaningful when used by a small group of individuals working together. This need can be fulfilled when a room can be obtained adjacent to the area where the information is maintained.

Filing Plans—Values and Limitations

Baer and Roeber (1964, p. 374) indicated two major steps in a filing plan—selection of a schematic plan, and development of a cross-reference plan. The selection of the schematic plan is not an easy one because commercial plans are not available for purchase. Instead, a plan must be developed locally for the educational information center.

The criteria for selection of a filing plan include many different items. Norris, Zeran, and Hatch (1966, pp. 399–401) included the following items in the factors for consideration: kinds of materials, purposes of files, type of users, keeper of files (librarian, counselor, student), ease of administering the files (coding, retrieving, refiling, replacing), ease of use, logic of categories, and expandability. Isaacson (1966, pp. 317–324) included also many of the preceding items, and, in addition, facilities for filing and the degree to which the file is adaptable to several different media of materials. Isaacson wrote in terms of the responsibilities and staff available for maintaining the files. He expressed concern in regard to the ease of operation (pp. 315–316, 324).

Hoppock (1967, p. 78) listed eight characteristics of a good file system, which are summarized as follows: furnishes a safe place for housing various types of information, designates one and only one location for each item, contributes to ease of use with a minimum amount of time and effort, brings together like materials, brings together related information, provides for quick filing and locating, expands with ease as the collection grows, and provides for filing and finding related materials.

Whenever a file plan is selected, consideration should be given to what the file plan is to facilitate. Once the objectives have been delineated then a plan can be selected, or probably more realistically a homemade plan can be developed using a composite of several different file plans. The following criteria should be considered in the selection of filing plans.

1. Sophistication of filing is according to projected users. If elementary school children are to obtain the materials directly from the files, the system has to be simple and self-explanatory. However, if the librarian is to maintain the files, then the files can be coded in keeping with local practices.

2. The filing plan facilitates the user's achievement of the purposes for which he consults the information files. The filing plan should assist the individual rather than be a hindrance to his finding the materials. It should be one that is constructed according to purposes rather than according to types of materials. This means that the files should be set up in such a fashion that the individual will be assisted in locating specific information when he wants it, or will enable him to get information that will broaden his knowledge and make him more aware of opportunities if this is his purpose for wanting the material at that time.

3. Logical categories should exist with classifications that make possible filing of related materials in the same place or in close proximity, thus enabling the users to obtain related materials readily.

4. The filing plan should be effective for use with a few items within a classification as well as to handle hundreds of items within a comparable classification. Not only must expansion of the files be feasible as more materials are collected, but probably at all times some classifications or subdivisions will contain numerous materials, whereas other classifications will contain relatively few or perhaps none.

5. Security emphasis is present in the filing plan; however, the purpose of the plan is to ensure that the user will be able to locate the material readily rather than absolute security. Materials are often lost because the filing system does not facilitate refiling them readily. A check-out system needs to be designed for recording who has each item on loan and when he expects to return it. Every effort should be made to prevent a potential user from losing time in searching for material that is loaned, misfiled, or lost.

6. Cross indexing should be expedited easily and should ensure that the user will know or be able to identify related materials.
7. Different media and types of materials within each medium can be filed within the filing plan rather than necessitating adopting different filing plans for each medium, such as films, books, and tapes. The filing plan should enable the user to be concerned more about what he wants rather than the necessity to concentrate upon whether he can find the information in a book or a film or a newspaper. The filing plan should pull together information regardless of the medium or type of material, such as single pages, articles, brochures.
8. The file plan should facilitate the achievement of locally desired outcome, i.e., the plan should be in line with the objectives of the information service in the local school or community agency or business. If, as time passes, the local objectives are modified and the filing plan as originally designed no longer is applicable, the plan should lend itself to modifications without extensive work.

In the homemade filing plans in use, filing of educational information generally is done by one or a combination of two or more of the following four classifications—control of education program (state, private, military, or denominational), programs offered, geographical, or alphabetical. The first two are not used extensively. The last two, geographical and alphabetical, are the two used most frequently. In many school files, a combination of these two types of classifications exist. The information on schools is generally filed alphabetically by names of school or alphabetically by states. In other cases those schools that are within close proximity, or those in which individuals frequently enroll, are filed together in one group and all other schools are filed alphabetically. One limitation that should be noted is that any one or combination of these filing classifications places emphasis upon filing educational information pertaining to training institutions but does not facilitate or encourage collecting and filing other information that does not relate directly with a training institution, but that may be pertinent to the information users.

The second general limitation to these filing classifications is that most of the information filed is of the resource or specific information type, the second depth. Some D-1 (first depth) information of value is obtained, but filing systems are primarily geared to the kind of information normally filed in D-2. Therefore, three general limitations can be listed for all four of the previously mentioned filing classification plans for educational information: (1) they place emphasis on training institutions rather than on the individual and his needs; (2) they are most applicable to the second depth, and therefore they tend to cause the counselors to overlook or not collect other information, thereby increasing the possibility for the counselors to do an inadequate job with educational information for the other two depths; and (3) they lack breadth and adaptability to the scope of educational information.

Additional limitations can be listed for each of the filing classification plans. A specific limitation to filing according to control of the educational program is that control generally is not the major criterion of an individual when he seeks educational information. When educational information is filed according to the programs offered, the limitation is that many educational institutions offer more than one program, thus necessitating an extensive cross-reference card system or the duplication of materials in order for a copy to be filed in all applicable places. The geographical classification presents a limitation to those individuals who do not know the location of all of the educational institutions that might be appropriate for them. The alphabetical classification plan places emphasis upon the individual's knowing the exact name of the institution, and, in some cases, the individual may not even be aware of the names of some institutions that might be applicable to him.

Each of the four classification plans has some values. Filing according to the control of the educational program brings together institutions with common control and thus helps the individual to identify one factor that contributes to the prevailing philosophy in those institutions. Filing according to programs offered brings together institutions according to the kinds of programs that the individual may want, thus enabling the individual at times to become familiar with a number of institutions from which he can select rather than only one or two about which he is aware. Geographical classificatoin brings together institutions in the same locale; and in some cases, this becomes an asset in making the individual aware of the many different institutions offering different programs in the geographical area of interest. The alphabetical system generally is used because of its simplicity and ease of use with a minimum amount of training needed to use it and a minimum amount of supervision needed for obtaining and returning information to the files.

When considering whether or not to adopt a filing classification plan, four important points need to be deliberated. First, at the present time commercially produced file plans are not available; therefore, a local plan must be developed if one is to be used. Second, without some type of file plan, considerable time probably will be wasted each year searching for pieces of materials that have been received. Therefore, a plan should be designed before materials begin to arrive so that they can be coded and filed immediately to facilitate retrieval.

Third, with a file system established, other people can use the material without depending upon a certain person to be present to locate the material. Without a file plan, counselors and secretaries will spend valuable time locating materials for others as well as for themselves. The material possibly could be located by the user himself if an adequate file plan was in operation. Also, with an established file system, two or more counselors may be able to use the same material, therefore eliminating the necessity of duplicate copies. The plan, of course, should be one that facilitates coding, filing, and retrieving.

Fourth, information retrieval often requires a considerable amount of time, which could be reduced by a good file plan designed to facilitate rapid retrieval. Based on recent developments, one might predict that automation will soon invade the counseling and guidance field. If information is essential to the development of an individual, then more and more information needs to be collected and utilized now and in the future; therefore, automation becomes a natural tool. The selection of a file plan might be with the anticipation that the information can be keyed with a minimum of difficulty into automation equipment when available and when the volume of information merits doing so.

Developing Files to Facilitate the 3-D Concept

The 3-D concept starts with the premise that educational information is needed at all three depths and at various reading levels within each. For the different persons in the people dimension the need exists for information applicable at all chronological ages. The implication for the counselor is that he should have educational information available through materials and resource persons for both individuals and people who work with them.

The files maintained should facilitate use of materials; thus files become enablers for using information appropriate for the individual on the topic of his interest at a depth meaningful to him. Files assist in the communication of information and as such must have an organizational plan built upon the same principles used in a counseling and guidance program. The 3-D concept was derived from the combinaton of principles in both communication and counseling and guidance.

If Figure 3-1 in Chapter 3 were redrawn for the *educational area* only, it would show *people and depth* (see Figure 7-1). The *people* dimension would show six different classifications or a total of eighteen divisions. In a local counseling situation more or fewer divisions may be needed. In many cases eighteen different divisions would be sufficient for arranging materials after analyzing them for projected use. However, because of the volume of materials within some or perhaps all of the eighteen different divisions, additional divisions or subdivisions may be needed to increase the ease of filing and retrieving. An example of an existing need for subdivisions would be in a setting where comprehensive collections of college, trade, and technical school catalogues are

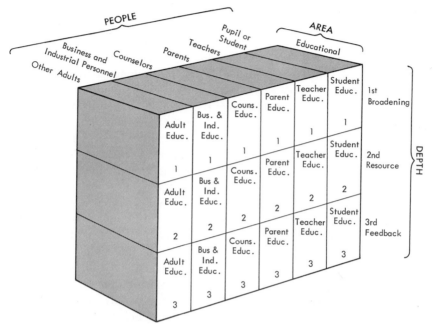

Figure 7-1. SCHEMATIC OF THE 3-D CONCEPT FOR THE EDUCATIONAL IN-
FORMATION AREA.

maintained for second depth information. Within that division additional
subdivisions or coding may be needed to facilitate usability.

Developing files to facilitate the 3-D concept means that advantages
of presently used file plans can be retained. In a specific setting a plan
similar to any one of the four classification plans mentioned in the
previous section may be in use. It can be expanded to arrange materials
according to the depth of information and the individuals for whom the
materials may have projected use.

Analyzing available educational information according to the 3-D
concept will point up divisions containing insufficient educational information. Filling the voids or near voids may make available more types
of information to be communicated and will possibly achieve personalizing
information on as broad a scope as needed for an effective counseling
and guidance program. Related materials will be brought together according to the needs of the individual rather than to be filed unassociated.
Information that should be related is forced together by a filing plan
based upon the 3-D concept whereby emphases are placed upon the
individual and his educational maturation.

The use of the 3-D concept encourages counselors to recognize the
developmental viewpoint and also may enable an individual to obtain
information according to his needs rather than just obtaining all avail-

able information or obtaining information at an inappropriate depth. The 3-D concept classifies information for individuals at any age level who may need the information for any or all three depths—to broaden his perspective of alternatives, to acquire information of a specific nature, and/or to obtain information about himself in a manner that encourages integration of self into the related information to the point where he can accept or reject through both the cognitive and affective processes.

Filing plans presently used tend to cause the counselor to consider educational information as a certain type that must be presented within a given school level—elementary or secondary school, trade or business school, or college—and at no other time, and that a different type of information should be presented at the other educational levels. The 3-D concept takes into consideration that the *development* and *educational maturity* as well as *chronological age* and *grade level* of the individual determine the kind of information he needs at a particular time in order to continue his development. If this point of view is correct, a file plan should be used locally to facilitate the concept.

In some file classification plans, a given piece of material would be filed in one place only, whereas other pieces of materials, because of their broad coverage, would not lend themselves to being filed in just one particular place under the classifications. The 3-D concept places emphasis upon selection of material to serve needs of individuals, thus material can be filed according to the purpose for which it was obtained rather than on the title or major content alone. Analyzing material according to the 3-D concept may assist in identification of information where quality and quantity are insufficient. A piece of literature written primarily on one topic may contain the best information available on another topic; thus the literature may be purchased for the projected use in the topic where the 3-D analysis revealed information lacking. The material can be cross-indexed for inclusion in the other areas.

If at a later date and after working with different individuals and groups, the counselor finds a given piece of material serves better in a different purpose classification, it can be recoded and cross-indexed for the previously coded area. An illustration would be a book about colleges and higher education that has the first one hundred or so pages devoted to general considerations for the individual and his family during the selection of a college or university. The next two hundred or so pages may be detailed information about separate colleges or universities. How would the book be coded? In one secondary school, the book may have been purchased for general reading for senior high students and their parents, to help them recognize the opportunities available to young people and how they can prepare themselves for admission to a college or university. In that school the book probably would be coded for filing in the first depth and cross-indexed for the second depth.

In another secondary school the book may have been purchased as a resource (reference) book because of the specific data on each college and university, with only limited intended use for the first part of the book on general information. Under these conditions the book would be coded for filing in the second depth and cross-indexed in the first depth. If, however, in actual practice the counselor should discover that the book is being used primarily for the general part, rather than the specific information, then the book could be recoded for the first depth and cross-indexed in the second depth.

Probably no one right way exists for filing educational information. The 3-D concept does provide enough format to make a filing plan adaptable to the local situation and to encourage the continuation of filing plans that have been effective for such materials as alphabetical filing of college catalogues.

Filing Code Based on the 3-D Concept

The 3-D concept is designed for personalizing information according to the person, his needs (areas) or potential needs, and the depth appropriate. Thus, a filing code based and developed on the 3-D concept will probably vary from one guidance program or counseling center to another. A suggested schematic plan is presented in which letters and numbers are used for coding. (Table 7-1). Numbers alone could just as well have been used; but in the illustrative material presented, letters and numbers were chosen to facilitate more readily the identification of the symbol with the classification.

In Table 7-1 there is a schematic code plan based on the 3-D concept. This plan is not presented as *the* answer to all filing and coding needs but is provided as one means of keying materials for projected use. Other codes and filing schematisms could be developed based on the 3-D concept; however, only one plan is presented and it only for demonstrating the 3-D concept in using information with individuals. The schematism in Table 7-1 will be used in this book as a vehicle for communicating the kinds and analysis of materials essential to perform the different purposes to be achieved in a comprehensive informational program using the developmental approach. An explanation of the schematism is provided in the following few pages. In using the schematism in a local setting, modifications probably will be needed to formulate a coding system that will facilitate the purpose to be achieved and to place emphasis where needed.

If the person is a pupil or student, then subdivisions probably are needed for the grade placement of the individual. The number of subdivisions needed will depend upon the type and extent of information to be coded. For illustration, eight subdivisions are provided with letters

Table 7-1

SCHEMATIC CODING SYSTEM FOR FILING
INFORMATION BASED UPON 3-D CONCEPT.

*People**	*Area*	*Depth*
S—STUDENT	E—EDUCATIONAL	1—1st—BROADENING
p—pre-kindergarten	c—community offerings	Basic
l—K–3 (elem. lower)	f—foreign study	Concepts
i—4–6 (elem. intermediate)	g—governmental programs	Attitudinal
j—7–9 (jr. high)	i—educ. or training applicable to indiv. with spec. needs	Introductory
s—10–12 (sr. high)		Primary
t—tec–bus–trade	l—local school	Fundamental
d—degree program	n—next educ. setting or step	General
c—continuing education	u—upgrading	
I—INDIVIDUAL WITH SPECIAL NEEDS	O—OCCUPATIONAL	
a—academically talented	d—demography	
d—disadvantaged	f—families & fields of occ. (file alphabetically within)	
c—culturally		
e—educationally		
h—handicapped	j—job placement entry exploratory temporary	2—2nd—RESOURCE
e—emotionally disturbed		Reference
m—mentally retarded	l—law and regulations	Specific
p—physically handicapped	m—maturation (Occ. Dev.)	Answering questions
p—potential drop-outs	s—salary and wages	Statistical
	t—trends and outlook	
P—PARENTS	‡—specific occ. inf. (file according to *D.O.T.*)	
s—self		
†—(working with others)		

Table 7-1 (*continued*)

*People**	*Area*	*Depth*
T—TEACHERS 　s—self 　†—(working with 　　others) C—COUNSELORS 　r—reference 　　material 　s—self 　†—(working with 　　others) B—BUSINESS 　AND INDUSTRY 　s—self 　†—(working with 　　others) A—OTHER ADULTS 　g—general 　r—retraining 　　and/or 　　relocating 　s—senior citizens 　v—veterans 　w—women	P—PERSONAL 　e—etiquette 　f—financial 　　f—financial aid 　　g—general 　　p—planning and 　　　budgeting 　　s—savings & 　　　investments 　g—grooming 　h—health & 　　physical dev. 　l—leisure time 　m—military 　　e—educ. & train- 　　　ing opportu- 　　　nities 　　g—general 　　l—laws, regula- 　　　tions, etc. 　　o—occupational 　　　dev. 　p—psychological 　　development S—SOCIAL 　a—alcohol 　　and drugs 　b—boy-girl 　　relationship 　f—family 　m—marriage 　p—peer 　s—social 　　development	3—3rd—FEEDBACK Means of validating 　self-concept Check on decisions Reality Testing Tryout Exploration

* Code according to major user.
† If material is to be used with others, then add code for that person.
‡ Use the *D.O.T.* File Code wherever applicable.

Sample Codes:　*P – A – D*
　　　　　　　Sj – En– 2
　　　　　　　Ihp – Ol– 2
　　　　　　　Psi – Pp– 3
　　　　　　　CSl – Sf– 1

representing each as follows: *p* for *prekindergarten;* *l* for *lower elementary grades* (kindergarten through third grade); *i* for *intermediate grades* (fourth through sixth); *j* for *junior high school* (seventh through ninth grades); *s* for *senior high school;* *t* for *technical, business, and trade schools;* *d* for *degree-program colleges and universities;* and *c* for *continuing education.* The first part of the code placed on material to be used by a student (*S*) in continuing education (*c*) would be *Sc*. The use of capital and small letters is done to identify major subdivisions (capital letters) and minor subdivisions (small letters).

Educational information centers functioning in settings where extensive quantities of information would be needed for persons with special needs probably would want to have a major subdivision based on special needs of individuals served (*I*). A minor subdivision example within that classification would be *h* for *handicapped,* which could be subdivided further, if needed, as *p* for *physically handicapped,* *m* for *mentally retarded,* and *e* for *emotionally disturbed.* Comparable to the minor subdivision titled *handicapped* would be another minor subdivision, *d* for *disadvantaged individuals,* including *c* for *culturally disadvantaged individuals* and *e* for the *educationally disadvantaged.* Two other examples comparable to the minor subdivision for the handicapped would be the minor subdivision *a* for *academically talented* and the minor subdivision *p* for *potential drop-out.* When the counselor codes the material for the file drawer or manila folder, the first part of the code placed on material to be used by an individual (*I*) who is disadvantaged (*d*) culturally (*c*) would be *Idc*.

Another major subdivision, parents (*P*), is used to classify information for use by parents to achieve two purposes: self-improvement (minor subdivision *s*) and working with others, such as their own children. In the second minor subdivision the coding could be the same letters as used for that person and in the case of his own child use the code for student to classify the information for use by parents with their child according to the school classification. Coding of material for one person working with another person would give two capital letters, i.e., material for use by parents (*P*) in working with own child (*S*), who is in second grade (*l*) would be coded *PSl*.

For teachers (*T*) the major subdivision may be treated the same as for parents: minor subdivision for self-improvement as *s* and when working with others use the capital letter for the person with whom working and any minor subdivision that is needed.

For counselors (*C*) the major subdivision would be treated the same as for parents and teachers except that a minor subdivision coded *r* has been added to provide a coding for the reference materials generally used extensively by counselors.

For business and industrial personnel (B) the suggested classification is the same as for parents and teachers. If the educational information center is in a business or industrial setting, additional minor subdivisions could be developed.

For the major subdivision other adults (A) the additional subdivision (minor) that may be needed, if any, will depend upon the setting. Such ones as w for women, v for veterans, s for senior citizens, and r for retraining and/or relocating may be appropriate.

In the second dimension—area—the major subdivision is educational and training information; the minor subdivisions could be l for information pertaining to the local school setting, n for the next educational setting or step, i for education or training applicable to individuals with special needs, c for community offerings of an educational or training nature, f for foreign study, g for governmental programs, and u for education for upgrading the individual himself.

In the third dimension—depth—the suggested coding would be in numbers ($1, 2,$ or 3) to represent the depth.

Suggestions for writing the total code is always in the People, Area, and Depth order. Thus, information that has potential use by a teacher (T) with a student (S) in college (d) who is concerned about educational information (E) pertaining to foreign study (f) and wants specific data (2) would be coded $TSd–Ef–2$.

To signify that a piece of material also may be significant to an additional person, beneath the original code the other user could be indicated by writing that code. For example, if the piece of material on foreign study is pertinent for the parent working with the student mentioned, the second code would be $PSd–Ef–2$. A cross-reference sheet prepared and filed in the appropriate folder for "Parent" would facilitate locating the piece of material when needed.

Supplies necessary for efficient storing of materials in a vertical file will include guides and folders. The guide and folder tabs may be in various positions. One satisfactory arrangement is to have the main guides and folders in the second or middle position with captions for the major subdivisions of the filing plan—the people and area dimensions. The minor subdivision guides and folders could occupy the third (right) position, with further sub-subdivisions in the first (left) position. An illustration of guides and folders arranged in a file drawer is presented in Figure 7-2.

Sample Materials

In Chapter 6 were listed various sources of educational information. The specific information needed will depend upon the individuals served, with materials being changed as new information becomes available. No

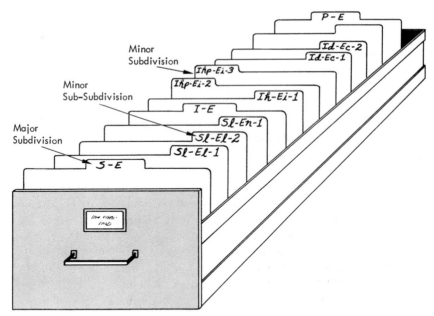

Figure 7-2. ILLUSTRATIVE CAPTIONS FOR FILING EDUCATIONAL INFORMA-
TION IN FILE DRAWER: CODE BASED ON 3-D CONCEPT.

list can be comprehensive nor can any list be used as a model of what
should be available.

For illustrative purposes sample materials for different settings—
elementary school, junior high school, senior high school, and community
agency—are provided. Within the illustrations are provided titles, media,
sources, costs, annotations, potential user, and code based on the 3-D
concept for utilizing information. Addresses for the sources are listed
in the Address Index. The materials listed are only illustrations rather
than a comprehensive list. Each piece of material might have been coded
differently if another counselor had processed it for projected users in
a different setting.

Elementary School Materials

The following were selected from an educational information center
in an elementary school:

Learn How to Study. Booklet. Science Research Associates, Inc.; $0.90. To
help children develop good study habits—reading, report writing, memorizing, and preparing for tests. (For pupils. Code: Si–El–2)

How Quiet Helps at School. Film. Coronet Films; B&W, $60.00; color, $120.00.
Shows how a quiet atmosphere is conducive to working well and reflects
consideration for others. (For teachers to use with pupils. Code: TSl–El–3)

Beginning Responsibility: Doing Things in School. Film. Coronet Films;

B&W, $60.00; color, $120.00. A day in Steve's life—how he learns to do things for himself. (For teachers to use with pupils. Code: TSl–El–3)

Guidance Techniques for Elementary Teachers. Book. Charles E. Merrill Books, Inc.; $7.50. Guidance Book useful for in-service education. (For teachers. Code: Ts–Eu–2)

Directory for Exceptional Children. Book. Porter Sargent Publishers; $7.00. Reference to educational and training facilities for children who require specialized programs, care, or treatment for their development. (Reference for counselor and for use with parents of children who have special needs. Code: CrP–Ei–2)

Analysis of Socio-Economic, Achievement, and Personality Characteristics of Superior Students. Book. McGraw-Hill, Inc. (Reference and for counselor use with superior ability students. Code: CrIa–E–2)

Encouraging Children to Learn: The Encouragement Process. Book. Prentice-Hall, Inc.; $4.25. (For counselor use. Code: Cs–Eu–2)

How to Help Your Child Learn. Booklet. National Education Association; $0.75. For parents of children in kindergarten through sixth grade. (For parent use. Code: PSl–El–1)

Beginning Responsibility: Rules at School. Film. Coronet Films; B&W, $60.00; color, $120.00. Class develops own rules and follows through in application. (For teacher use with pupils. Code: TSi–El–1.

The Handbook of Private Schools. Book. Porter Sargent, Publishers; $10.00. Reference book on independent primary and secondary boarding and day schools. Also directory of summer academic programs in camps. (Reference for counselor and for use with parents. Code: CrPi–El–2)

Junior High School Materials

The following were selected from an educational information center in a junior high school:

Planning My Future. Booklet. Science Research Associates, Inc.; $0.65. Student workbook covering educational and vocational planning and includes self-administered tests and inventories. (For student use. Code: Sj–El–3)

My Educational Plans. Book. Science Research Associates, Inc.; $1.60. Help students plan high school program with them considering their interest, abilities, achievements, and past experience. A manual is available for counselors and teachers. (For student use. Code: Sj–El–3)

Looking Toward High School. Booklet. Science Research Associates, Inc.; $0.80. Assists students in preparation for high school. (For student use. Code: Sj–En–1)

What High School Can Do for You. Booklet. Science Research Associates, Inc.; $0.67. (For student use. Code: Sj–En–2)

Chronicle College Charts. Charts. Chronicle Guidance Publications, Inc.; $5.00. For use on bulletin boards. (For student use. Code: Sj–En–2)

The Bobby G. Text-workbook. McKnight & McKnight Publishing Co.; $1.20. Written for seventh grade use. (For student use. Code: Sj–Eu–3)

When You Visit a College. Sound filmstrip. Guidance Associates; $14.95. (For student use. Code: Ia–Eu–2)

Private Independent Schools. Book. Bunting and Lyon; $12.00. Directory of private schools for boys and girls, including boarding, day, and military schools. (Reference material for counselor to use with parents. Code: CrPj–E–2)

Sargent Guide to Summer Camps and Summer Schools. Book. Porter Sargent Publishers; $4.40. Reference for many summer programs, including camps, schools, and travel for boys and girls throughout the United States, plus a select listing of private camps in Canada. (Reference material for counselor to use with parents. Code: CrPj–E–2)

Stanford Achievement Test. Tests. Harcourt, Brace & World, Inc.; price depends on specific test battery selected. Battery of tests in various subject areas to assist students in knowing their achievement in comparison to others. (For counselor use with students. Code: CSj–El–3)

Starting Junior High. Color filmstrip. McGraw-Hill, Inc.; $6.95. (For student use. Code: Sj–El–1)

Senior High School Materials

The following were selected from an educational information center in a senior high school:

Educational Brochures. Obtained from the educational institution; free. (For student use. Code: Ss–En–1)

Choosing a College. Sound filmstrip. Guidance Associates; $14.95. (For student use. Code Ss–En–2)

College Catalogues. Obtained from the college or university; free. (For student use. Code Ss–En–2)

Your Career—If You're Not Going to College. Booklet. Julian Messner, Inc.; $3.64. Helpful in understanding training facilities of a noncollege nature. (For student use. Code: Ss–En–1)

Who Should Go to a Community College? Sound filmstrip. Guidance Associates; $14.95. (For student use. Code: Ss–En–2)

Who Goes Where to College. Book. Science Research Associates, Inc.; $2.45. Research report on evaluation of college environments. (For student use. Code: Ss–En–2)

How to Visit Colleges. Pamphlet. National Vocational Guidance Association; $0.25. Focuses attention on the need for college visits in the wise choice of a college. (For student use. Code: Ss–En–2)

How to Read a College Catalog. Sound filmstrip. Guidance Associates; $14.95. For student use. Code: Ss–En–2)

The College Entrance View Deck. Illuminated viewer and individual perforated cards. Chronicle Guidance Publications, Inc.; $110.50 to $150.00. Assist students in locating small number of colleges possessing characteristics they have selected as important. Yearly service sold to keep cards on colleges updated. (For student use. Code: Ss–En–3)

Your Child and College. Booklet. National Education Association; 35 for $1.00. Guidance on the selection of colleges, entry requirements, tuition costs. (For parents use with students. Code: PSs–En–1)

Freshman Year at College. Sound filmstrip. Guidance Associates; $14.95. (For student use. Code: Ss–En–3)

High School Course Selection and Your Career. Sound filmstrip, 2 parts. Guidance Associates; $29.95. (For student use. Code: Ss–El–3)

Hung Up on Homework. Sound filmstrip, 2 parts. Guidance Associates; $29.95. A student's guide to effective learning. (For student use. Code: Ss–Eu–3)

What Tests Can Tell Us About Children. Booklet. Science Research Associates, Inc.; $0.67. (For use by parents. Code: Ps–El–2)

Guidance Activities for Secondary School Teachers: Science, Mathematics, Foreign Languages, Social Studies, and English. Five Booklets. Science Research Associates, Inc.; $1.10. Each booklet contains specific guidance activities that the teacher of that subject can introduce in the classroom on educational and vocational guidance. (For teacher use. Code: Ts–El–2)

Guidance Testing and Other Student Appraisal Procedures for Teachers and Counselors. Book. Science Research Associates, $6.00. Contains techniques of studying individuals and how to use the findings. (For counselor use. Code: Cs–Eu–2)

Looking at Private Trade and Correspondence Schools. Booklet. American School Counselor Association; $0.25. A guide for students who are considering continuing their education at a private trade or correspondence school. (For student use. Code: Ss–En–1)

Accredited Institutions of Higher Education. Book. American Council on Education; $2.50 year, two issues. National directory of accredited junior and senior colleges, universities, and professional and specialized schools. Published twice a year so that latest changes are available. (Reference for counselors and for use with students. Code: CrSs–En–2)

Guide to Correspondence Study in Colleges and Universities. Booklet. National University Extension Association; $0.25. (For counselor use with students. Code: CSs–En–2)

American Trade Schools Directory. Loose-leaf book. Croner Publications; $9.95 year. (For counselor use with students. Code: CSs–En–2)

The College Blue Book. Books. The College Blue Book; $75.00 a set. See write-up in Chapter 6. (Reference for counselor and for use with students. Code: CrSs–En–2)

Preliminary Scholastic Aptitude Test. Test. College Entrance Examination Board. Test to help students understand their scholastic aptitude in comparison to others. (For counselor use with students. Code: CSs–El–3)

The National Apprenticeship Program. Booklet. U.S. Government Printing Office; free. Explains in nontechnical language the national apprenticeship program, its aims and organization, and how it operates. (For student use. Code: Ss–Eg–2)

Education in the Job Corps Conservation Center. Booklet. U.S. Government Printing Office. (For counselor use with students. Code: CSs–Eg–2)

Materials for Use in Community Agencies

The following educational information was selected from an education information center in a community agency:

The Second Time Around: Who Should Transfer, When, and Why? Sound filmstrip. Guidance Associates; $14.95. To assist adults who may have stopped college and now are considering re-entry. (For use with adults. Code: Ar–En–3)

Directory, National Association of Trade and Technical Schools. Booklet. National Association of Trade and Technical Schools; free. (Reference for counselor and for use with adults. Code: CrAr–En–2)

Handbook of Adult Education in United States. Book. Adult Education Association of the United States; $7.50. (Reference for counselor and for use with adults. Code: CrAr–En–2)

Classrooms in the Military. Book. Teachers College Press, Columbia University; $3.95. Comprehensive picture of the overall educational program in the Armed Forces. (For use with adults. Code: Ar–En–2)

Directory of Accredited Private Home Study Schools. Pamphlet. National Home Study Council; free. (Reference for counselor and for use with adults. Code: CrAr–En–2)

Guide to College-Level Independent Study. Book. Chronicle Guidance Publications, Inc.; $5.00. Provides information about correspondence study programs available through the sixty-seven accredited colleges and universities in United States and Canada. (Reference for counselor and for use with adults. Code: CrA–En–2)

Education for a Changing World of Work. Book. U.S. Government Printing Office; $1.25. Contains reports by various authorities with topics on vocational training and technical education. (For counselor use. Code: Cs–Eu–2)

Educationally Deficient Adults: Their Education and Training Needs. Booklet. U.S. Government Printing Office. Report of survey on educational and training needs of educationally deficient adults. Guidelines for a plan of action and materials required are provided. (Reference for counselor use. Code: Cr–Ei–2)

Unemployment and Retraining: An Annotated Bibliography of Research. Booklet. U.S. Government Printing Office. An annotated bibliography relating to social psychological factors in job training and hard-core unemployment. (Reference for counselor use. Code: Cr–Ei–2)

Criteria of Educational Maturation

If one develops continuously throughout life, then his educational processes must also go through different stages, steps; thus he is constantly undergoing educational maturation, which is the individual's cumulation or modification in his educational process of bringing, or of coming, to full development. Educational maturity may never completely take place, but educational maturation should and does. The extent and rate of maturation can be affected. Some criteria for determining the extent of maturation need to be formulated. Research is being done on vocational maturity and the data may yield information meaningful for educational material. Information on research and theories is presented in Chapter 9.

The school grade in which an individual is enrolled or has completed may correlate highly with his educational maturity. However, the person's degree of educational maturity will vary from topic to topic, which means that the educational information needed on any one particular topic may be of either the first, second, or third depth, and that each topic may be at a different depth. Development of educational maturity for each person, whether enrolled in school or not, is a lifelong process. An individual's extent of educational maturation on different topics might be determined in comparing him to others; another means may be to examine his readiness for general information, specific information, and relationship of self to information on the topic.

The criterion for determining educational maturation becomes one in determining how much depth he has on a given educational topic. If the individual already has broad general knowledge, then he is placed beyond the first depth in the 3-D concept. In such a case the person would probably be ready for specific or more detailed information on the topic—second depth. In both the first and second depth the information remains somewhat abstract, i.e., outside of extensive personal involvement of the individual. The information is obtained more in terms of awareness, the increasing of knowledge, and relationship to other information already known. In the third depth the information necessitates self-involvement. The individual is ready to examine himself in the light of the information or to examine information in the light of himself. The person who has enough educational maturation to begin to relate himself to the information and the alternative opportunities is at the third depth.

Whenever an individual obtains additional information at any one of the three depths, he may mature to another depth. For example, if he is at the second depth and obtains specific information, he may then recognize that the topic and area of investigation does not meet his needs, so he returns to search for information at the first depth to help him to gain a broader perspective, or, upon obtaining the specific information, to begin to relate it to himself—creating a need for the third depth or feedback with introspection. (See Chapter 3, Figure 3-2.) Maturity of the individual on a given topic, then, is determined by the extent to which he is able to comprehend information in terms of breadth, specifics, and relation to himself.

Educational maturity is not a position to be reached and forgotten but rather is an on-going process that requires continuous maintenance. The world is changing and a person must change as fast to maintain educational maturation.

Relationship of Ease of Checkout of Information to P and D Dimensions

The 3-D concept, if utilized by the counselor, makes his job of retrieving educational information easier as he identifies the information most appropriate to the needs of the person with whom he is working. The 3-D concept enables the identification of information according to the potential user, whether he is seeking the information for himself or plans to use it in working with another individual; i.e., teachers needing information in order to work with students.

Under the people (P) dimension, the classification of the information according to potential users, such as early elementary school child, secondary school child, collegiate level student, parent, teacher, and so on, should enable one to locate appropriate literature and other information readily. The subdivisions can be as minute as needed, thus collecting together information for users rather than necessitating the individual needing to know the various places to search. In having the information collected together the individual may become aware of additional materials that would assist him.

Recognizing that the educational maturity of the individual on a specific topic may be such that he may ask for information at any one of the three depths, the counselor will be able to locate information according to the D dimension at the maturity level for the individual. Using the requested information with the person may immediately help the individual and the counselor to recognize that additional information is needed at a different depth. With the use of the 3-D concept, the counselor will be able to help the individual in identifying the additional information available within that depth or at a different depth that might be useful for him. The coding system will facilitate the individual's becoming aware of additional information that will help him to broaden his horizons, answer specific questions, or to relate himself to the information.

Improving Extensiveness of Use

Because education information is "changing so rapidly, the addition of new material and the retirement of old are necessary to the proper development of informational resources. Material can be added or retired only if adequate provisions have been made for doing so" (Baer and Roeber, 1964, p. 375). If adequate provisions are made to keep the information current and to retire the inappropriate and inadequate information, users will have more confidence in relying upon the information available.

One point frequently misunderstood is the recommendation that information maintained should be based upon the needs of groups of users. Once those needs have been determined, many counselors proceed to update information on the premise that these needs and population groups remain static. However, the groups to use the information do change in composition and a reassessment of needs is necessary to determine if they too have changed. For example, in a junior or senior high school one third or more of the student body changes every year because one class is promoted or graduated, plus additional change in composition from transfer students. Turnover of employees in industry, business, and other community agencies also creates a changing population for counselors and advisers in such positions. A continual search must be made in order to identify needs of present and potential users so that information can be collected according to the current population, the areas in which information is needed, and the depth that is appropriate.

To improve the extensiveness of use, counselors could learn much from the knowledge of business and industry about one effective process on which millions of dollars are spent yearly—that of publicizing their products. The potential users must be made aware of the kinds of information available, the location, the hours available, and the ease of obtaining the information. One emphasis should be upon housing the information so that it is *visible* as well as *available*. Bear and Roeber (1964, p. 377) emphasize that publicity should be through bulletin boards, display racks and tables, and newspaper stories. The techniques of publicizing the educational information are many in number including skits and role-playing, school newspaper, assembly programs, and group meetings (Hollis and Hollis, 1965, pp. 65–69).

The leadership that is furnished for the educational information area will be a major determinant of the extensiveness of use. The person who is in charge of the educational information should be interested and well qualified and should possess a dynamic personality that will enable him to help others to recognize how educational information can be meaningful to them regardless of the stage of their development. Leadership roles should be assumed by all persons involved with establishment, maintenance, and utilization of educational information. This would include all people who will be working with an individual in utilizing the information. In business and industry the personnel people, the president and his administrative staff, and the foremen can help the individual to know about the available information. In schools, counselors, librarians, teachers, principals, and superintendents must take the active role.

The more individuals themselves can be involved in a project, the more they have a tendency to use the available information. Therefore, the person in charge needs to recognize that if he wants to improve the extensiveness of use, he must involve potential users in the area of educational information, i.e., involve them in the development and maintenance of educational information. They can be involved in deciding on kinds of information to be obtained and in evaluating it once obtained. Student assistants can assist in checking out and checking in materials. In some cases student assistants can be helpful in assisting other students in retrieval of appropriate information and certainly in helping them to understand how to use the coding and filing system.

Another means of improving extensiveness of use is to ensure that a potential user gets to review materials that have possibilities for him. Any newly acquired materials or any that have been returned that were on loan at the time of the request could be routed or channeled to the individual. Development of a system for notifying or sending material should be relatively easy.

Baer and Roeber (1964, p. 378) listed some administrative provisions that if followed would improve extensiveness of use. Their list included making sure that the information is readily accessible; available for check-out so that the information can be used at home, at work, or in the classroom; replaceable by means of additional requisition of free material or a budget being available to cover cost of replacement (replacement may be necessary because of loss, of wearing out, or disappearance); easily returned as well as withdrawn from the files; and mobile through the placing of materials on mobile units so that they can be taken to classrooms and other places for utilization. For some materials, several copies will be needed to allow for frequent use and check-out of the material and for placing the material in two or more locations.

In order to make the materials most meaningful, some frequently requested information may need to be purchased in sufficient quantities to give each user a copy, or if the information is such that it can be reproduced by mimeograph or some other means it might be reproduced and available for handouts. With the progress that has been made in automation and new equipment, the counselors should anticipate that in the future information will be retrieved by automation equipment. The use of such equipment will make the information more readily available. With the use of automated equipment the individual can feed into the machine the kinds of information desired; then the automated equipment can retrieve or identify the exact information or where it can be acquired.

The use of microfilm, microfiche, or aperture cards provides a quick visual image of the desired information and in some cases is connected to a reproduction machine so that when the individual finds the specific information he wants, he need not laboriously copy it, but can push a button and have a copy of the information in a matter of only a few seconds. VIEW (see Chapters 3 and 9) in San Diego, California, in cooperation with Minnesota Mining and Manufacturing Company (3M) is an example of a project where local information on jobs, financial aids, and colleges has been recorded on aperture cards, which can be inserted into specialized reader-printer machines to produce regular size print-outs for individuals. College catalogues and other educational information could be placed on aperture cards or microfiche for use in a similar way to VIEW. CAREERS in Largo, Florida, and National Cash Register Company have joined forces to put such information on microfiche and plan to update the material periodically. ERIC, the Educational Resources Information Center for Counseling and Personnel Services at the University of Michigan, is funded through the U.S. Office of Education and is providing much information, part of which is by microfiche.

Complete up-to-date bibliography or index cards housed in different locations in the building will increase the extent of use also. Certainly in the master or primary location, where most of the materials are housed, should be a complete index card file of all information available; and for counselors who use the information with individuals, as is done in a comprehensive guidance program, a complete index card file should be available in the counseling reception area also. The counselor then can help individuals identify educational information applicable to their needs at the appropriate time. On the index cards should be information as to code, location, type, and amount of information.

When educational information is kept visible and accessible, has been collected according to projected users, and obtained to assist them in their present and potential needs, the information will be used. The emphasis should always be upon the individual and his needs.

Methods of Keeping Educational Materials Up-to-Date

Keeping educational information up-to-date is a continuous process. Some organized plan for doing this task should be outlined so that all persons involved in handling educational information will know the procedures. All the information should be dated the day received, thus enabling one to know how recently something has been obtained and which ones among all the materials are the most recent. Some plan should be established for reviewing the material periodically to discard out-of-date information. A schedule that would necessitate all materials being reviewed once a year should be established.

Frequently flyers or additional brochures are received from schools, colleges, universities, and training institutions about changes that have occurred since their last major publication. When such material is obtained, it should be added to the major publication in the files and a note attached to the old publications referring the reader to the more recent information. When an entrance requirement or an effective date is to become a reality, notation should be made on the currently used publication so that individuals referring to the information can make plans accordingly. When counselors write for educational information, they should request that their names be added to the mailing list for any future publications, thus enabling them to receive additional publications as they are produced.

Another factor to ensure that educational information is kept up to date is to organize a procedure for identifying the present and potential users and their needs and then relating these facts to available information. Once having made the check, additional information may need to be obtained, so that materials are meeting present needs and are suitable at the required depth. Equally essential is to check that information available for use by persons who work with other individuals is evaluated and is comprehensive and suitable.

Summary

Effectiveness of educational information is governed by its accessibility, ease of use, and appropriateness of the information for the individual. The 3-D concept serves to help counselors obtain a broad coverage of materials for meeting needs of individuals with whom they work regardless of the setting—school, business, or community agency. Adequate physical facilities and procedures for organizing and utilizing information are important to the users. The location of materials will be controlled by the purpose of use and by the users. Plans for processing educational information will need to be developed on the local scene to meet needs as they exist.

Extensiveness of use of information depends upon the leadership of the personnel who are responsible for the area. Duties and responsibilities need to be identified with the personnel so that the educational information center is maintained efficiently and effectively.

SELECTED REFERENCES

Baer, Max F., and Edward C. Roeber. *Occupational Information: The Dynamics of Its Nature and Use.* Chicago: Science Research Associates, Inc., 1964. Pp. 366–378, 461–474.

Hollis, Joseph W., and Lucile U. Hollis. *Organizing for Effective Guidance.* Chicago: Science Research Associates, Inc., 1965. Pp. 65–69.

Hoppock, Robert. *Occupational Information: Where to Get It and How to*

Use It in Counseling and in Teaching, 3rd ed. New York: McGraw-Hill, Inc., 1967. Pp. 57–83.

Isaacson, Lee E. *Career Information in Counseling and Teaching.* Boston: Allyn and Bacon, Inc., 1966. Pp. 314–331.

Norris, Willa, Franklin R. Zeran, and Raymond N. Hatch. *The Information Service in Guidance,* 2nd ed. Chicago: Rand McNally & Company, 1966. Pp. 396–401.

Chapter 8

Utilizing Educational Information with Individuals and Groups

In the processes of using educational information, the counselor is a service person to the student and often is a catalyst.

Information can be obtained, evaluated, coded, and filed, but unless it is utilized by individuals the information is useless. Individuals should receive assistance in using the information, and steps should be taken to ensure the creation of an educational information environment personalized for each individual to contribute to his educational maturation. At times the information will be utilized in groups and at other times on an individual basis. The objectives for using information with groups and individuals may differ but utilization with both are needed, and if the objectives usually achieved in one setting have not been done than those objectives must be added to the other objectives.

The methods for utilizing educational information with individuals vary with the depth of information needed. Methods and media may be classified as prestructured and fixed, input controlled by individual, simulation of situation, and real situation. Selection of method and medium is based upon the most effective ones for personalizing information.

"Utilizing Information with" As Compared to "Supplying Information to"

Individuals and groups are supplied information from many sources and through various media. Much of the information that an individual or group obtains is in a setting other than that of counseling and guidance. Businesses and industrial organizations supply information to individuals and groups. Professional organizations supply educational information to help individuals recognize the kind of education necessary and where it can be obtained so that an individual might become a member of the profession. Pressure groups and biased individuals supply educational information at various times and frequently aim the information at given individuals or groups. Educational institutions publish various kinds of books, brochures, and so on, in order to make sure that sufficient information is supplied to the public and to people about their programs. Federal, state, and local agencies also supply educational information.

The supplying of information to individuals and groups is done through various media. Mass media, such as radio, television, newspapers, and magazines, are frequently used to make educational information available to different people. Literature is forwarded through the mail or printed in the form of leaflets for distribution. Educational information is placed on billboards, signs, and packages. In many cases information supplying is done on the assumption that a mass coverage of people will enable a given percentage of the group to obtain the information who might use it. In other words, the information is supplied to the individual with the idea that if he can use it, he should take it; and if he wants more, he should ask and the additional information will be supplied. The individual may gain additional information in such a procedure; frequently individuals obtain their first awareness of information in this way, but the result may not bring about the change in behavior or the action that was desired (Bany and Johnson, 1964, p. 294).

"Utilizing information with" an individual or group is done in a manner by which the information can be personalized. Fewer numbers of individuals may receive the same information, but the person who really needs and can use the information is more likely to receive the information in a form that will be meaningful to him. The information is selected with the individual for him personally, rather than being selected without him in mind or without knowing him and then being broadcast to a large number hoping that it will reach those who need it.

The counselor must know the individual as a person in order to "utilize information with." Whereas in "supplying information to" the counselor can assume that the individual is like others and can proceed on the basis of past experiences. The previous statement applies when the counselor is working with a group. In utilizing information with the individual, the counselor must know the individual's educational and occupational maturity in order to know the depth or place to start. One of the postulates in counseling and guidance is that information acquisition is done to make possible growth and development—change—if the individual wants to do so. Such being the case, individual involvement

—utilizing information with—is better than telling or supplying information to. The counselor can and should strive to coordinate methods, materials, and the individual's educational maturation rather than to consider information as a separate entity.

Objectives in Using Information with Groups and Individuals

The general objectives of educational information must be achieved through using information with both groups and individuals. At times, the objectives can best be achieved through working in a group setting, whereas at other times the individual can best be served through working with him alone. In groups an individual can obtain information from other group members as well as from materials; however, on some topics an individual may best obtain the information needed by working outside the group setting. A counselor or other persons assisting the individual or group in obtaining and personalizing information should accept the objective to complement and supplement what has already been done rather than to repeat. The same objective should be supreme when the individual is selecting a group. He should choose a group that will provide an opportunity to continue his growth and development.

The general objectives in using educational information with groups and individuals should be in keeping with the scope of the total information processes as outlined in Chapter 1. The general objectives for educational information would include the following: to facilitate the individual's understanding of the available educational opportunities; to assist the individual in understanding the successive levels of attainment that are necessary for continued progress in the educational program for which he has expectations; to increase the individual's awareness of the possibilities for him to continue his educational development; to help the individual learn how he can obtain the maximum benefits from his present and future educational offerings; to make the individual aware of his increased responsibility to society as he obtains additional education and to help him understand the increased societal expectations commensurate with the educational level attained; to provide an opportunity for the individual to relate information to and with himself; and to provide factual background about American and international educational trends and their effects upon individuals, so that the person may understand changes within the educational structure and their potential affects upon him.

Objectives for educational information in groups could be obtained from books such as those by Walter Lifton, *Working with Groups* (1961); E. C. Glanz, *Groups in Guidance* (1962); and M. E. Bennett, *Guidance in Groups* (1965). Generally speaking, the objectives for using information with groups are to help broaden the educational outlook of the group member and to help him to obtain some techniques for understanding himself in relation to the educational world. The information that is used with the group may be at the second depth as well as the first. Such specific information is most frequently about educational institutions rather than about the individual himself. The group setting does provide an environment for the individual to have a feedback on his own ideas and feelings (Lifton, 1961, pp. 27–28). In some cases, individuals within the group become stimuli to other individuals; thus one of the values of using information with a group is to get the interaction among members so that the information processes will be an opportunity for each individual to become involved.

The objectives for using information with the individual are to a very large extent of the same objectives as those for the group. The use of the information with the individual is not to replace or repeat those objectives previously achieved in the group but rather is to assist the individual in his educational maturation, thus covering those objectives that have not already been accomplished through other means. The objectives for using information with the individual are focused more on the individual and how he relates to the information rather than upon the abstract. For contrast, the differences between objectives for using information with groups and individuals might be stated as follows: *the objectives for using information with a group place emphasis primarily upon ideas, truths, people, relationships between and among information, and materialistic and abstract things, whereas the objectives for using information with an individual place emphasis primarily upon the person and how he relates to ideas, truths, people, and things.* The preceding statement is an oversimplification but is an illustration of how information can and should be utilized with persons during their growth and development in both settings—group and individual—rather than one alone.

Needs as a Determinant of Methods

Frequently in the past, methods were studied and then one method was selected as *the* means of presenting educational information. To a very large extent, the person who was to utilize the information with the individual was the primary determiner of the method that would be used. Today, counselors are better educated and are skillful at using various methods. Counselors are better prepared for considering the individual and the benefits he might receive as a result of using one method over another. In addition the counselor is trying to help the individual to understand his own needs, his own circumstances, and his own state of readiness and then to assist the individual in understanding the method(s) that might be best for him to use in obtaining and utilizing the information appropriate for him. The counselor, together with the individual, considers what information is available and what media—books, tapes, films, and other people—are available for obtaining the necessary information and for assisting in the personalizing processes. The counselor recognizes that one of the individual's needs is that of feeling more secure. Once methods are used that will assist the individual in feeling more secure, then the individual will be better able to accept new and different information (Lifton, 1961, p. 21). Methods are used that will assist the individual to understand not only himself or the educational information, but both of these and the relationships between them.

Berdie and Hood (1965) in a study of the determinants of post-high-school plans expressed the view that the complexity of determinants and duration of their effectiveness can become more understandable if the concept of needs is used. Berdie and Hood identified six needs that appear to be most relevant to the planning of high school graduates. Perhaps these six needs would also be applicable to individuals in their seeking of educational information when they are at ages other than high school seniors. Recognition of these needs within the individual may help the counselor to work better with the person in selecting the method most appropriate for utilizing information. The six needs that individuals have were listed as follows: (1) to do something; (2) for independence; (3) for security; (4) for status, recognition, and acceptance; (5) for learning and for mastering skills; and (6) for role fulfillment (pp. 10–13). A counselor's recognition of these six needs will help him to realize that he should have competence in a variety of methods so that at times the same information may be utilized differently among the persons with whom he works—the information may be the same, but because the needs are different the perception of each will be different.

> *Although a major role of orientation is to provide information, it falls on deaf ears if the hearers have not been helped first to perceive the need for the information and then to face the anxieties the new situations may provoke.* (Lifton, 1966, p. 188).

Method Variation as Depth Dimension Changes

A given method may be very effective in working with an individual at one depth, whereas that same method may not be effective in working with that same individual at another depth. The counselor working with an individual needs to be seeking a variety of methods that will or may be effective with that person. Recognizing which methods are effective at each depth may help the counselor to be more effective in the future with that individual as the topics are changed. The counselor may be able to use some of the same methods on different information and perhaps for different purposes but with the same individual.

At the first depth more group work is suitable, and the counselor will probably look for a variety of methods providing exposures to help broaden the individual and to increase his awareness of the different educational opportunities available. At first the counselor may be helping the individual to perceive the need for the information as well as to gain a broadening concept. The group setting may at this depth help the individual to face anxieties that the new situation may provoke.

At the second depth more opportunity needs to be provided for the individual to study and learn. The time element can be longer because the specific required time to learn is generally increased at the second depth. Methods need to be utilized that will provide not only for additional time exposure to the information, but so that a longer time period can be provided for the individual to learn the information if he so desires.

At the third depth the exposure at a given time may be shorter, e.g., counseling sessions. Because of the need at the third depth for self-understanding and more feedback, the method utilized will need to be one that will help the individual to understand himself and how he can relate the information to himself. Methods may not be identifiable specifically according to the depth of the information, but at least the counselor should give consideration to the depth as he makes his choice and helps the individual to choose what approaches will be used.

Information in Counseling

The counseling session is a period in which the individual has an opportunity to integrate ideas about himself, consider the relationship between concepts, review his thoughts, examine his feelings and attitudes, and explore implications for himself. A counselor may function in different capacities as perceived by the counselee. At times the counselee wants the counselor to assist him in obtaining information so that he can continue his growth and development. The counselor may supply the information, may assist the individual in obtaining the information, and in some instances may refer the individual to another person or other sources.

Another function that may be expected of the counselor by counselees is assistance in interpreting information he has about himself, an occurrence, or other people, things, ideas, and data. The interpretative role may require additional information on the part of the individual or the counselor. Frequently the counselee can make his own interpretation if he can obtain sufficient information. The counselee also may need feedback information to enable him to continue his decision-making processes with the security that will contribute to growth and development.

At times a counselee wants assistance in identification of things that are troubling him or of means for increasing the pace of his development. Diagnostic work can often be done by the counselee if he has sufficient personal information. The individual may benefit from making his own identification and taking steps to utilize the diagnostic information in his decision-making process for continued growth.

Another function often listed for the counselor in a counseling relationship is supportive. The techniques for being supportive vary, but often include additional information being supplied to the counselee. The counselor may supply the information or may assist the individual in obtaining the information from other persons or through another source.

The therapeutic function in counseling often necessitates several counseling sessions. The counselee may explore many ideas, thoughts, feelings, and activities between sessions. At times the counseling sessions may be more beneficial if the individual gains additional information between and/or during the sessions.

Often the information individuals have acquired and the additional information being received is inappropriate or incomplete for the individual to become as thoroughly involved as he would like or to make the decision that should be made. Persons often do not take an active role because they lack sufficient information or at least do not perceive the information as being applicable to them.

Counseling as a face-to-face relationship whether done on an individual or group basis has objectives that include assisting the individual to understand himself, his feelings, values, attitudes, and behavioral patterns; to know better his environment and the persons who have influenced, are influencing and probably will influence his life; to recognize how he may relate better within his environment and how he may use himself and his environment for maximum benefit to both; and to establish and enter upon plans of action that will assist in life fulfillment. To achieve any or all of these objectives requires information not just at one time but frequently throughout life. The counseling sessions may assist the individual in utilizing the information he has and in planning for additional information processes.

Selection of Method

Recognizing that educational muturation is a lifelong process, which probably can be accelerated or retarded by the educational information available and the method by which an individual is exposed to it, then *the selection of methods for utilizing information with individuals and groups should make possible differential and sequential activities with progressive increase in degree of involvement.* To achieve that goal methods of utilizing information must be studied and classified as to the extent to which each method provides or encourages personal involvement by the individual. The 3-D concept depth dimension becomes a basis for consideration—from the simplest *broadening* concept, with the individual having little or no control over the information, to the third depth, *feedback,* where the individual is obtaining a relationship between himself and the educational world. In reality, then, the ongoing personalized education information processes bring about an educational development that means the person knows more about the educational world; but probably equally important, the person also knows about himself, both in cognitive and affective processes, in relation to that world and how he can make decisions that will enable him to have maximum benefits from the opportunities available.

Albert S. Thompson, Professor of Psychology and Education, Teachers College, Columbia University, New York City, made some comments at the U.S. Office of Education's National Conference on Occupational Information in Vocational Guidance, Chicago, Illinois, May 16–18, 1967, pertaining to a classification of methods by which individuals obtain information. He suggested a sequential order from the most prestructured and fixed methods, with the individual having little or no control, through the real situation, where the individual has maximum control. His four classifications and sub-divisions were given for occupational information and were as follows: (1) prestructured and fixed with first subdivision of publications, second as audio-visual aids, and third as planned programs; (2) input controlled by the individual, with the three subdivisions of program instruction, computer-aided instruction, and interviews, (3) simulation of a situation, with the two subdivisions of role-playing and/or career games and synthetic work environment; and (4) the real situation, with the three subdivisions of direct observation, directed exploration, and actual job experience. Thompson's classification could be modified slightly and made applicable to educational information. Table 8-1 contains the revised classification, plus some methods frequently used by individuals in gaining educational information.

Methods of Utilizing Educational Information

Methods of utilizing educational information with a person and methods for helping him obtain the information are important, but far more important is the information transmitted, how it is perceived by the person, and the extent to which he is able to internalize and personalize the information, thus recognizing the implications and being able to use the educational information and the understandings, both

Table 8-1.

SCHEMATIC CLASSIFICATION OF MEDIA AND SPECIFIC METHODS FOR UTILIZING EDUCATIONAL INFORMATION WITH PERSONS ON AN INDIVIDUAL AND GROUP BASIS.

Classifications*	Media*	Specific Methods
PRESTRUCTURED AND FIXED	Publications	Magazines Periodicals Newspaper (school, business, and community) Catalogues and booklets Brochures Student handbook Songs and poems Yearbook Reference books
	Audio-visual aids	Bulletin board Displays, exhibits, and charts Films and filmstrips Audio tapes Video tapes Radio and television Murals—art
	Planned programs	College day or night Panel Parent night Assembly program Educational talk in classes
INPUT CONTROLLED BY THE INDIVIDUAL	Programmed instruction	Educational workbooks College Entrance View-Deck Individually developed projects ("My Educational Goals")
	Computer assisted information	Computer assisted information system VIEW
	Interviews	School or college conference Group discussion Conference with admissions officers or other school officials Interview of enrollees and alumni

Table 8-1 (*continued*)

Classifications*	Media*	Specific Methods
SIMULATION OF SITUATION	Role-playing and/or game methods	Quiz contests Dramatization Brainstorming Role-playing Game theory activities
	Synthetic educational environment	Club (scholarship, college-bound, and so on) Laboratory study Orientation program
REAL SITUATION	Direct observation	Visitation to educational institution (field trips) Foster uncle or aunt
	Directed exploration	Try-outs (introductory and orientation classes)
	Actual educational experience	Enrollment and participation in the program

* Source: Classification and media based on comments by Albert S. Thompson at U.S Office of Education, National Conference on Occupational Information in Vocational Guidance, Chicago, Illinois, May 16–18, 1967.

cognitive and affective, about himself as bases for decisions—future action. Decisions are made by individuals with or without adequate information. Effective educational information processes assist the person in knowing not only more facts but also how to evaluate information and where and how additional information can be obtained. The methods listed here are only some of those used at present. Probably no one person will use all of the methods listed and most counselors are creative enough to modify or formulate new methods when the situation warrants.

The methods presented in this section are the ones listed in Table 8-1 and are according to the suggested classification. References are suggested for additional readings on the various methods.

Prestructured and Fixed Classification

In the classification of prestructured and fixed are three media with the first medium being *publications*, in which are found many of the different types of educational information that are obtained, coded, and filed by counselors. Most of the material is canned and the individual has very little or no control over the information. He can only select from the material and react to it. The information here is primarily to broaden the individual's understanding of the topic and to provide facts about educational programs, institutions, and structure.

The materials in the publication medium would include educational articles in magazines, periodicals, and newspapers (Norris et al., 1966, pp. 469–470; Baer and Roeber, 1964, p. 389). Reading college and university catalogues, booklets, and brochures is often the major method by which individuals gain information about colleges or universities. Reading similar publications issued by other educational and training institutions is probably the major method for finding out about those institutions. Other publications that have influence upon individuals would include student yearbooks (Norris et al., 1966, pp. 470–471; Detjen and Detjen, 1963, pp. 215, 230, 233; Miller, 1961, pp. 196–198), school songs, poems, student handbooks, and educational reference books.

The second medium is *audio-visual aids* that include films and film-strips (Norris et al., 1966, pp. 471–474) about education in general or special educational institutions and their programs. Phonograph records and video and audio tapes (Baer and Roeber, 1964, pp. 389–390, 433–434; Norris et al., 1966, pp. 476–477) are often used as means of obtaining information. Radio and television programs (Norris et al., 1966, pp. 477–480), public service announcements, and commercial advertisements all become a continuous method by which individuals gain information. Often the individual receives information through radio and television unexpectedly because the educational information was sandwiched into another program. Murals and other forms of art often communicate educational information. Art as a method for assisting individuals to gain information may not have been used as extensively for educational information as for occupational and personal-social information. Bulletin boards (Norris et al., 1966, pp. 475–476), displays (Norris et al., 1966, p. 474; Baer and Roeber, 1964, pp. 382–384), exhibits, and charts are frequently used methods for educational information.

The third medium, *planned programs,* would include talks about education in general and specifically those used in regular subject classes and in orientation programs (Norris et al., 1966, pp. 424–425, 460–461; Detjen and Detjen, 1963, pp. 224–234; Ohlsen, 1964, pp. 330–333; Miller, 1961, pp. 194–195; Moser and Moser, 1963, pp. 99–105). Sometimes question-and-answer sessions follow that go beyond the prestructured classification, but primarily talks, panels, assembly programs (Norris et al., 1966, pp. 468–469; Baer and Roeber, 1964, pp. 387–388; Hoppock, 1967, p. 343), college day, college night (Norris et al., 1966, pp. 458–459; Baer and Roeber, 1964, pp. 386–387; Ohlsen, 1964, p. 319; Shertzer and Stone, 1966, p. 286; Hoppock, 1967, p. 343; Miller, 1961, pp. 205–208; Moser and Moser, 1963, pp. 91–93), and parent nights are pre-structured, and the person can only select from the information rather than have any control over what the information is.

Input Controlled by the Individual Classification

In the first medium of *programmed instruction* are some methods that have been used for years, such as projects developed by the individual at various times throughout his schooling. The child or youth is often asked to write themes on topics like "My Educational Goals." Much thought and research often are an integral part of the project and the individual does control primarily the input. Another method that has been used mostly in orientation classes but to some extent by the individual on his own is some form of educational workbook whereby the individual begins to have some control over the contents and must examine himself as well as the abstract information. For assistance in selection of institutions and programs some programmed instructional devices are now being produced where the individual makes certain choices, such as location, tuition, coeducational and majors, and each choice eliminates some schools, thus enabling the person to reduce the number of possibilities to a number that can be investigated in more detail. The *College Entrance View-Deck* produced by Chronicle Guidance Publications is an example of such a device. Another type of program now being offered commercially is a systems approach to group guidance entitled *Counseling Information Service* (CIS) and offered by Follett Publishing Company. In CIS a systems specialist works in the school with students and faculty to develop a sequential system for meeting student needs.

In the second medium—*computer assisted information*—the developments today have been minimal for general use; however, the prospects look bright for the future. See in Chapter 3 the section titled "Systems Development for Information Utilization" for a more detailed write-up. Programs like VIEW, developed at San Diego, California, are gaining in acceptance.

In the third medium—*interviews*—many persons take advantage of opportunities, whereas others do not know the extensiveness of resources nor how to utilize the interview method as a means of gaining educational information. Organizing and systematizing of resources for group discussions could probably improve the amount of quality information gained through conferences with admissions officers or other school officials (Hoppock, 1967, pp. 263–265), interviews with enrollees or alumni, group discussions (Norris et al., 1966, pp. 438–439), and educational conferences in general.

Simulation of Situation Classification

In the simulation of situation the individual has an opportunity to project himself into a situation that is almost like a real one but without the fear or threat normally presented by the true situation. Two media are suggested, with the first one being *role-playing and/or game methods,* which might include dramatization (Norris, et al., 1966, pp. 439–440; Norris, 1963, pp. 70–71; Peters, Shertzer, and Van Hoose, 1965, pp. 59–60; Hoppock, 1967, p. 322), brainstorming, quiz contests (Norris et al., 1966, pp. 465–468), role-playing (Norris et al., 1966, pp. 440; Norris, 1963, p. 70; Peters, Shertzer, and Van Hoose, 1965, pp. 59–60; Bany and Johnson, 1964, pp. 395–396; Hoppock, 1967, pp. 322–323; Glanz, 1962, pp. 228–229), and game theory activities.

In the second medium of *synthetic educational environment* the objective would be to enable the individual to be in a created environment conducive to gaining educational information and contributing to his educational maturation. The methods might include clubs (Baer and Roeber, 1964, pp. 388; Isaacson, 1966, pp. 382–383; Moser and Moser, 1963, pp. 84–85), such as those for scholarship and college-bound students, where the persons themselves create their own environment and produce a stimulus for each other. Orientation programs (Lifton, 1961, pp. 130–135; Miller, 1961, pp. 194–195; Moser and Moser, 1963, pp. 99–105; Stewart and Warnath, 1965, pp. 298–299), in some cases, and laboratory studies are also synthetic educational environments.

Real Situation Classification

Experience and opportunity for growth probably cannot be exceeded beyond that in which the person has the opportunity to be within the real situation. However, the methods for assisting the individual in gaining educational information through the real situation are not the only ways nor at times the best ways for a person. Methods within all the classifications contribute to the incubation period necessary for the creation of readiness for the next depth. The real situation provides an opportunity for feedback; however, for some persons and in many situations the feedback is too fast and in such proportions that the individual is overwhelmed. Real situation methods cannot be used indiscriminately. Each must be personalized in order that the information processes will have maximum meaning for the individual.

In the first medium—*direct observation*—would be included visitations to educational institutions (Norris et al., 1966, pp. 462–465; Baer and Roeber, 1964, pp. 388–389; Isaacson, 1966, pp. 381–382; Miller, 1961, pp. 195–196; Moser and Moser, 1963, pp. 93–94), where the person would have an opportunity to observe firsthand what is happening. Not only the visits to the campus or building, but also to visit classrooms and laboratories and perhaps even sit in on a class session. Another method that may be within the direct observation subdivision would be the foster uncle or aunt method, where a person with an educational attainment similar to the goal of another person agrees to work with that individual pertaining to educational information and implications.

A second medium is *directed exploration,* where the individual can try out some of the real situations without becoming totally committed. Introductory and orientation classes might be within this subdivision.

The third medium is the *actual educational experiences,* where the individual is enrolled and participating in the program. The length of time for this method may be extended over years if the individual is meeting with success.

Summary

Utilizing educational information with persons necessitates both a group and an individual setting. The emphasis is upon *utilizing information with* rather than *supplying to or for.* The counselor avoids working with information; instead he works with individuals and uses information to facilitate their development.

Decisions are made by individuals with or without adequate information. Often the person has a decision to make without being aware (1) that he does not have all the pertinent information, (2) of how to evaluate the adequacy of the information he does have, and/or (3) of from whom and where additional information can be obtained. The information processes of the individual should assist him in building a reservoir in all three areas. The processes necessitate the utilization of information over an extended period of time and recognition that different methods assist in achieving different purposes. The methods need to be classified according to the way in which they assist the individual in gaining educational information. A schematic classification structure together with media and specific methods were provided.

SELECTED REFERENCES

Baer, Max F., and Edward C. Roeber. *Occupational Information: The Dynamics of Its Nature and Use.* Chicago: Science Research Associates, Inc., 1964. Pp. 378, 382–390, 433–434.

Bany, Mary A., and Lois V. Johnson. *Classroom Group Behavior: Group Dynamics in Education.* New York: The Macmillan Company, 1964. Pp. 292–295, 395–396.

Bennett, Margaret E. *Guidance in Groups,* 2nd ed. New York: McGraw-Hill, Inc., 1965.

Berdie, Ralph F., and Albert B. Hood. *Decisions for Tomorrow: Plans of High School Seniors for After Graduation.* Minneapolis: University of Minnesota Press, 1965. Pp. 10–13.

Detjen, Ervin Winfred, and Mary Ford Detjen. *Elementary School Guidance,* 2nd ed. New York: McGraw-Hill, Inc., 1963. Pp. 215, 224–334.

Glanz, Edward C. *Groups in Guidance: The Dynamics of Groups and the Application of Groups in Guidance.* Boston: Allyn and Bacon, Inc., 1962. Pp. 228–229.

Hoppock, Robert. *Occupational Information: Where to Get It and How to Use It in Counseling and in Teaching,* 3rd ed. New York: McGraw-Hill, Inc., 1967. Pp. 263–265, 322–323, 342–343.

Isaacson, Lee E. *Career Information in Counseling and Teaching.* Boston: Allyn and Bacon, Inc., 1966. Pp. 381–383.

Lifton, Walter M. *Working With Groups: Group Process and Individual Growth.* New York: John Wiley & Sons, Inc., 1961. Pp. 21, 27–28, 130–135; 2nd ed., 1966, pp. 26–29, 49–53, 187–192.

Miller Frank W. *Guidance Principles and Services.* Columbus, Ohio: Charles E. Merrill Books, Inc., 1961. Pp. 193–211.

Moser, Leslie E., and Ruth Small Moser. *Counseling and Guidance: An Exploration.* Englewood Cliffs, N.J.: Prentice-Hall, Inc., 1963. Pp. 84–85, 91–94, 99–105.

Norris, Willa. *Occupational Information in the Elementary School.* Chicago: Science Research Associates, Inc., 1963. Pp. 41–45, 51–107.

Norris, Willa, Franklin R. Zeran, and Raymond N. Hatch. *The Information Service in Guidance,* 2nd ed. Chicago: Rand McNally & Company, 1966. Pp. 424–425, 438–440, 458–480.

Ohlsen, Merle M. *Guidance Services in the Modern School.* New York: Harcourt, Brace, and World, Inc., 1964. Pp. 319, 330–333.

Peters, Herman J., Bruce Shertzer, and William Van Hoose. *Guidance in the Elementary Schools.* Chicago: Rand McNally & Company, 1965. Pp. 59–60.

Shertzer, Bruce, and Shelley C. Stone. *Fundamentals of Guidance.* Boston: Houghton Mifflin Company, 1966. P. 286.

Stewart, Lawrence H., and Charles F. Warnath. *The Counselor and Society, A Cultural Approach.* Boston: Houghton Mifflin Company, 1965. Pp. 298–299.

PART III

PERSONALIZING OCCUPATIONAL INFORMATION

Changes in the occupational world have affected workers and have outdated many stereotype ideas about occupations. The average number of occupations and the years spent in each by an individual has been reduced from one occupation of forty to forty-five years to three or more occupations with less than fifteen years each. The number of changes in occupations during a lifetime is sufficient to bring about a need for occupational information to be made a personalized process without a termination point. Even the retiring person is making an occupational change and often has need for extensive personalized information processes.

The theories about occupational development have undergone many changes during this century. The research studies in the area are increasing and data are available that have implications for counselors working with individuals of various ages. The media through which individuals obtain occupational information have changed. The kind of information needed depends upon the individual, his perceptions, his variables, and his stage of development.

The sources and types of occupational information have expanded. The counselor of today can go beyond the counselor of yesterday, who said, "I have occupational information, come see me." Today, the counselor can help the individual obtain the personal information he needs, through a medium meaningful for him, using a technique applicable to the individual. To accomplish the new role counselors need occupational information keyed to the different depths, collated to provide breadth and depth, housed in a retrieval system designed from the users' viewpoint, and utilizable through a variety of media.

Chapter 9

Implications of Recent Research and Occupational Theories for the Counselor

Without a philosophy to serve as a basis, no man can be professional. Theories can be a guide, but the proof must come from research and an interpretation for implications.

Studying various occupational theories and examining research findings are of concern for the counselor. The counselor's role in the occupational, educational, and personal-social information areas is affected by significant findings and by developed theories that stimulate changes in concepts pertaining to the world of work.

Research and Theories as Recent Developments

Historically the viewpoint has focused on "vocational choice" or "decision" with the emphasis for study centered on the *when*—the time—and the conditions under which occupational choices or decisions were made. In the 1940's, however, some examiners began to consider the world of work through a different orientation applying developmental psychological concepts. Researchers began to think not so much in terms of time of choice but began rather to consider stages, patterns, levels, and developmental processes. An individual's entrance into an occupation was no longer considered as a single choice or decision, but rather as processes ongoing over an extended period of time. With the shift of emphasis in the philosophical base, more changes have occurred in the understanding of man in the world of work in the past twenty years than probably in the total preceding twenty centuries.

Many people still believe that one's occupation is a matter of luck. They think of one getting the right job by "the right person at the right

173

time pulling the right strings on the right day." Some people believe that one's occupation is determined by the family into which he is born or marries. This group who believes that one's occupation is determined by his "environmental inheritance" from his family is joined basically in philosophy by another group of people, who believe that one's occupation is determined by the geographic area, i.e., where one lives will determine what one does. These beliefs or theories have been researched, but the studies, in general, have been cross-sectional rather than longitudinal or on a small and often highly select group that is not applicable to the total population. Enough example cases have been identified to perpetuate the theories, but the theories each lack comprehensiveness to include the total population.

The developmental approach places emphasis upon a study over an extended period of time—a longitudinal study. The belief is that many different variables affect an individual's occupation(s) and that his ideas about what he wants to do may be one way at one time and a different way at another time. These changing ideas occur not only in early childhood and in adolescence, but also in adulthood. One's life is an ongoing process of which his occupations are vital and integral parts. With the developmental processes approach, decisions are made; but each of these becomes a forerunner to another. The postulate is held that man must by necessity make decisions, many of them throughout life, and each of the decisions possibly could be made with more security if the individual could have the information pertinent to the topic and intrinsically understood as it applies to him personally. Recent research on the decision-making process has yielded enough significant data to indicate the decision theory may be of major importance to counselors as they work with individuals and groups (Thoresen and Mehrens, 1967; Gelatt and Clarke, 1967).

In textbooks in the area of counseling and guidance and specifically in occupational and educational information, seldom will more than two or three references be made to theories or research studies prior to the 1940's concerning man and his occupation. Most of the references start with Ginzberg, et al., in 1951, which appears to be the beginning of a new era. Research studies are continually being conducted, but the findings are not yet comprehensive enough nor concise enough to answer all questions concerning the individual in the world of work. Findings have been sufficient to indicate a new frontier of knowledge is before us and with it may come new approaches in assisting the individual in the area of occupational information.

Many of the recent research studies are in one way or another primarily based upon the developmental processes approach. The number of persons becoming involved in research and writing in the area of theoretical concepts is increasing. The work began with Parsons, Harper, and Witmer in the early part of the twentieth century. Keller and Viteles gave vocational guidance additional emphasis in the 1920's (Chapter 2). Recent developments in research and theories can be dated from approximately the World War II period. A representative list of researchers and theorists in occupations is provided so that the reader may review in time sequence when they did their work. Interesting to note is that not only have most of the activities occurred in the last twenty-five years, but also that the frequency of research studies and theories development have been increasing during this period of time. The following list is not comprehensive but is representative of persons who have contributed and who have written in publications that can be readily obtained for additional study. The selected references at the end of this chapter contain a bibliographical entry for each of the persons listed. Also in the section on "Theories and Research in Vocational Development and Their Implications," presented later in this chapter, are research studies and the theories associated with a representative sample of these people.

1931	Harold F. Clark
1943	Edward S. Bordin
1949	Abraham A. Brill
1949	F. M. Carp
1949	A. B. Hollingshead
1951	Eli Ginzberg, et al.
1951	D. C. Miller and W. H. Form
1952	Harry Beilin
1953	Joseph Samler
1953	Donald E. Super
1954	Theodore Caplow
1955	William L. Warner and James C. Abegglen
1955	Leona Tyler
1956	Peter M. Blau, et al.
1956	Anne Roe
1957	Donald E. Super
1957	Robert Hoppock
1958	Sidney A. Fine
1959	John L. Holland
1959	Robert L. Thorndike and Elizabeth Hagen
1959	Robert P. O'Hara and David D. Tiedeman
1960	Donald E. Super, et al.
1961	John O. Crites
1964	Warren D. Gribbons, et al.
1965	David V. Tiedeman
1965	Kenneth B. Hoyt

1966   John L. Holland
1966   Dale Tillery
1967   Glen Pierson, et al.
1968   Many research studies in progress

Practitioner's Role in Understanding Research and Theories

As a practitioner, the counselor's alertness to new developments in the field help him keep abreast of changes as they are promulgated in research findings and new theories. Extending his knowledge of results of research and of theories, interpreting the implications, and evaluating them in terms of his area of operation may contribute to his effectiveness by modifying or reinforcing his prevailing philosophy, ideas, and activities within the local situation. The counselor may experience difficulty in attempting to compare theories and research findings and their implications because of the differences that exist among them. No standard for comparison has been developed and no one standard would serve. Research findings and theories potentially offer more than just a "repair job"; some contribute to a foundation for new operative processes.

A counselor, as a practitioner, operates from some philosophical or theoretical base that encompasses his values, feelings, and attitudes. Each counselor, through studying and exploring theories and research findings, may obtain new insights on formulating a new or modified theoretical base for himself. Integrating the knowledge and insights into his perception of the role of the counselor may contribute to a new and revolutionary role. The philosophy one holds primarily determines his perception. "The quality of the perceptive stuff of growth therefore determines the quality of the behavior of the individual" (Kelley, 1962, p. 13). A counselor's understanding of theories, whether or not he approves of or accepts them, should contribute to his reservoir of information for decision-making.

Theories and Research in Vocational Development and Their Implications

Without an understanding of the developmental processes during the times when an individual selects his occupation, a counselor will not be able to meet fully his professional obligation. If counselors were performing as technicians, then they would be expected to hand out material according to some prescribed procedure. But if counselors are professional persons, then they should be able and be expected to understand the philosophical, psychological, anthropological, and sociological implications of what the individual is experiencing as he makes decisions regarding his life. The decision regarding his entry occupation is only one of many major decisions regarding his occupational life. He may change his occupation two, three, or more times during his lifetime; just as some may change wives or husbands two or three times during their lifetime. Decisions about occupational life as well as decisions about personal life are major decisions. The personal-social information (Chapters 14–18) should be interwoven with the educational and occupational information.

If a counselor is to discharge his professional responsibility, he needs to understand what is happening to an individual as he undergoes the processes of developing his attitudes, his decisions, his entry occupation, and his career progression or passing through different occupations. In research and theories since the latter part of the 1940's, increased emphasis has been given to understanding occupational decision processes.

In the pages to follow are selected recent theories and research findings, which are used as illustrations of the ones available. Space limitations allow for only a minimum presentation of different viewpoints and findings. Speculations about the implications of these theories and research studies may vary from one authority to another. Some possible implications are provided. In some cases the implications are made as they apply to the counselor personally, and in other cases the implications are for the whole area of guidance and counseling. The reader should read the entire original report on the theory or research study and then draw his own conclusions.

Comparisons should be made among the different theories and the research data. Very frequently a new understanding of an article can be obtained by reading different points of view and then contrasting the two; thus attention can be focused upon similarities and differences and why they exist. The perception of the reader will determine, as well as what the author wrote, what is gained from the reading. As is often said, an article never says anything to anyone. It's only in terms of what is deducted, as the results of reading the article. In reading about theories, one must create in himself a readiness, a broad enough understanding of the area to be able to detect the specific differences and their meanings. Through reading contrasting views one may be better able to focus his microscope on the fine points of the theories and research data.

One of the first theories on occupations was developed by an economist. Harold F. Clark in a book, *Economic Theory and Correct Occupational Distribution* (1931, p. 1), wrote "Proper information regarding wages, if sufficiently impressed upon people, will lead to correct choice of occupation and correct number, provided barriers to occupations have been removed." This statement is the economic theory of supply and demand as determinants of what people will do. To a very large extent this theory is still believed in America today. Clark did place emphasis upon individuals having "proper information," but his intent by those words may have been different than when used today by counselors. In 1931 when Clark's statement was published perhaps information regarding wages was about all that could be given; however, some thirty-five to forty years later, with many advancements in various disciplines of knowledge, the counselor can assist persons to know themselves, to know different occupational opportunities, to have some understanding of the different qualities in different people that enable them to contribute the most to their occupation, and to understand what and how different occupations would contribute to the fulfillment of one's self-concept. With the counselor assisting individuals, hopefully each will select his occupation on the basis of how the occupation and the opportunities provided are an integral part of his development rather than occupations being filled with just anybody who happens to be available at that time.

The supply and demand of one locality are no longer the determinants because of geographical mobility—both of people and of industries. The young people of today need not be confined to thinking as their grandparents often had to do—that is, to think of the job opportunities in the community. If a young boy, living in a geographical area surrounded only by land and without large lakes or rivers, wants to be captain of a boat, the counselor would probably not be performing in a desirable manner if he said, "Now look around, John, and see, do we have any rivers or large bodies of water around here?" An individual does not necessarily, on basis of geographic location, need to be discouraged from his consideration of becoming a captain of a boat or ship. The counselor may help him explore the possibilities and to consider the additional changes that the boy will need to bring about before the occupation could become a reality for him.

Abraham Arden Brill (1949, p. 268), the first American psychoanalyst, wrote, "The professions of prize fighters, wrestlers, bullfighters, warriors, and mighty hunters are direct descendants of pure sadism, and the need for the sadistic outlet is well shown by the popularity of these vocations." One way of interpreting Brill's statement (hopefully in the psychoanalytic frame of reference) would be to say that the inner drive of the individual, the psychological drives of a person, are the things that will determine the occupation into which he will go. With such an interpretation the occupation becomes an individual's outlet, his release, his way of life.

> It makes no difference whether a man is a financier, preacher, actor, physician, cook, or shoemaker; provided he himself has selected this vocation and was not forced into it by home environments or social conditions, he will find his proper outlet in his work and under normal conditions he will never become fatigued by it or wearied of it. (Brill, 1949, p. 277.)

One viewpoint may be that a person who is happy in his occupation is a person who is in an occupation that provides an outlet of expression of that person as he perceives himself. In other words, identify a person who is happy in his occupation and at the same time you have probably identified a person who is in an occupation from which he gets enjoyment and one in which he sees his occupation as an outlet for his physiological, psychological, and philosophical self. Brill may never have meant that such an interpretation be made, but if the statement is correct, then it begins to have some additional implications. One implication may be that the counselor is to help each individual to understand himself and to develop a philosophy of life (see also Chapter 14). Note should be made of the emphases placed on physiological, psychological, and philosophical life. The counselor not only has to help an individual understand himself but also needs to assist the individual in developing a philosophy of life, without which he may never be able to select an occupation for himself. Without such assistance an individual may drift with the opportunities rather than find an occupation as a part of and a way of life.

Frances M. Carp (1949) did her work with 165 male students, in which she compared the expressed, desired, or probable occupations of the students with the occupations of their fathers and grandfathers. She reported, "The modal occupational level for both 'desired' and 'expected' occupations is that of both the father and the grandfathers" (p. 98). If this statement is true today, then an implication for counselors would be for them to assist young people to broaden the spectrum of occupational considerations so that each young person might include at least consideration of occupations at levels other than those of his father and grandfather. In the final analysis he may choose an occupation at the same level or the identical occupation as that of his father or grandfather, but he should have the opportunity to make that choice for himself. Choices can only be made in terms of the alternatives seen by the individual at the time he makes the choice. If he does not know and understand occupations at levels other than those of his father and grandfather, then his opportunities from which to choose are limited. If, however, the counselor, working cooperatively with teachers and others, assumes the responsibility for broadening each young person's spectrum of awareness about occupations and the opportunities available to him, then the young person will be making choices, making decisions, from more than the narrow spectrum provided by his ancestors.

In a doctoral thesis of 1952, Harry Beilin (Hoppock, 1963, p. 83), who studied occupational choices of a lower socio-economic group, stated, "The most important type of determinant of choices of both the college and noncollege group was reality factors. . . . One fact that stands out is that experience permeates the entire determinant structure. . . ." Beilin has said that for a lower socio-economic group, reality factors are more important than anything else and that the reality factors of this group of people is determined by the experiences they have had. (Also see section on variables in Chapter 14.) When he wrote about lower socio-economic groups he meant groups comparable to those who are included in the Federal Legislation of 1965 and who are referred to as poverty groups. Beilin's statement is, of course, in agreement with statements made by John Dewey, who placed responsibility upon school staff to provide and involve individuals in experiences within the school setting. These experiences may be mental as well as physical.

One implication of Beilin's statement could be that counselors may have major responsibilities of facilitation so individuals in lower socio-economic groups will have a broad spectrum of experiences while in school. *The counselor does not provide the experiences, he assists the individual in identifying and obtaining a wider variety of experiences.* In addition, the counselor may need to help the individual to visualize those experiences, both in and out of school, that have reality for him in his occupational development, i.e., to recognize, understand and evaluate those experiences that have vocational implications for him. The counselor may work with the individual to help him understand the different experiences he is having, the implications of those experiences, and how to evaluate those experiences in order that the implications and the reality factors can be understood.

Beilin's statement when interpreted for implications during the counseling process may have the counselor be concerned not so much with the facts as facts, but rather to place more emphasis on reality factors as perceived by the individual. Probably most persons in the lower socio-economic group come to know reality through their world of experiences, which, when compared to persons in other socio-economic groups, may be limited in scope. The aspirations and expectations of low socio-economic persons also may be determined by their experiences. Young people from poverty homes may obtain their first depth (broadening), second depth (specific), and third depth (feedback or integration of self with information) all from their experiences and their interaction with their environment. For children from high socio-economic homes, such experiences may be considered a third depth with the first and second depth possibly coming through other media. The emphasis, then, needs to be placed upon knowing the person, his needs, theories in occupational development, research findings, and different techniques and materials sufficiently to be able to select and apply these appropriately for the person.

The work of Eli Ginzberg, S. W. Ginsburg, S. Axelrad, and J. L. Herma and their book *Occupational Choice, An Approach to a General Theory* (1951) are well known and often are considered as the begin-

ning of new theories and research in occupations. Ginzberg and his associates indicated that the occupational choice process extends over a
minimum of six to seven, and more frequently, ten or more years. They
emphasized the compromises that occur between the subjective elements
and the opportunities and limitations of reality, thus producing crystallization of occupational choice and decision-making, which then is essentially irreversible. In a later article Ginzberg (1960) stressed the
need for counselors to ensure that information is made available to those
who need it. He believed that "Counselors can never acquire enough
knowledge of the rapidly changing economy and society to become ex-
perts in their own right about all the different facets," but that counselors could elicit the assistance and effective cooperation of those who
do have the specialized competence and information to assist the individual (Ginzberg, 1960, p. 712).

Theodore Caplow (1954, p. 214), a sociologist, wrote, "error and
accident often play a larger part than the subject himself is willing to
concede." If this statement is true, then Caplow was agreeing with the
long-believed concept, from the historical viewpoint of occupational
selection, that it is a matter of being in the right place at the right time
and knowing the right person to pull the right strings for you, otherwise
you don't get the job. In America this viewpoint has long been expressed,
but had the leadership in America operated on that basis, many of the
great advancements might never have been made.

Caplow (1954, p. 220) in another statement said, "Occupational
choices are made at a time when the student is still remote from the
world of work." Certainly curricular choices in schools are forcing this
situation upon young people. They are forced to make a decision about
occupation when the world of work is still remote, when it is still far
in the distance for them. A child in the seventh, eighth, or ninth grade
at an age of twelve to fourteen years often is expected to make an
occupational choice in order that he may choose the correct curricular
track among the many available to him in the comprehensive junior and
senior high schools.

Transporting children by bus, school consolidations, and many other
factors have contributed to making schools comprehensive—to making
several curricular tracks possible. Thus, the child has been forced to
make a curricular choice based to a large extent upon his potential
occupations. In Caplow's words, the child has to make the choice while
he "is still remote from the world of work." Major employment for a
young person will probably be postponed until he has completed high
school and college, if he goes to college; or, if he does not, then major
employment will probably come after his entry occupation. In either
case the occupational choice is being made approximately seven to nine
years "remote from the world of work." When the "seven to nine years

remote" are compared against his junior or early senior high school age, which is at the time of the forced decision, the seven to nine years are as much as 60 per cent of his present age. The time when he will be in his major employment may be as many years into the future as he can even remember about his own life. For that child the decision is being made in terms of a complete lifetime away.

Caplow (1954, p. 220) also wrote, "occupational choices are made in the schoolroom, under the impersonal pressure of the curriculum, and remote from many of the realities of the working situation." In another place he wrote, "Realistic choices typically involve the abandonment of old aspirations in favor of more limited objectives. This is, in some sense, only a temporary abandonment" (p. 228). If Beilin's statements are interwoven with Caplow's, then the implications for the counselor may include helping each child to have a greater variety of experiences and to connect these experiences with reality in life particularly as the experiences relate to the realities of the working situation. If individuals tend to abandon old aspirations in favor of more limited objectives, then the counselor may need to help persons to have not only one goal but also to consider a series of progressive goals, each dependent upon the preceding one and each being a check point for evaluation as to whether or not to continue or to deviate from the long-range goal.

If educational potential is a determinant of job potential (Chapter 4), then the individual needs to evaluate his educational achievement against his occupational aspirations frequently. He needs to identify small goals that will lead to larger ones. Once he has reached one of the subgoals, he needs to know how to evaluate his progress. The achievement of a subgoal will enable him to have more vista, more vision, more opportunity to see than he has had. The individual needs to move progressively toward his goals and to evaluate periodically to determine if his pattern of achievements is moving him toward his original goal and whether or not, in light of new developments in himself and in the world about him, the goal is still realistic for him. An illustration of other changes that may cause abandonment of old aspirations is the development of new occupations. In the world of work today approximately one in every seven job definitions has been added, created, new in the last sixteen years. When a junior high child is asked to decide on an occupation, he must make his decision on the basis of what the occupational world has been or is now like; however, his decision is not for now but rather is for a future occupational world, in which he has no way of knowing the opportunities. Probably 10 to 15 per cent of the occupations that will be available to him at the time of his first major occupation are not even known now. One third to one half of the elementary school children may at some period during their lifetimes work in occupations that do not even exist today.

The results from research done by Warner and Abegglen (1955, p. 176) enabled them to state: "Since 1928 there has been a strong trend away from the influences of the family and an increasing emphasis upon competitive achievement. Birth status does not assure a son of the elite permanent position there." With research data from this longitudinal study supporting such a statement, the counselor may well take note not to overemphasize the occupational inheritance but rather to emphasize the developmental achievements of the individual.

Donald Super (*Psychology of Careers*, 1957, pp. 186–187), stated: "*Vocational maturity is thus defined in terms of types of behavior, whereas vocational adjustment is defined in terms of the outcomes of this behavior.*" He emphasized types of behavior that a person exhibits toward the world of work. Super's statement may be meaningful in determining the extent of an individual's vocational maturity; thus the emphasis is placed upon development rather than adjustment.

If vocational development is a process and maturing takes place, some bench marks should be able to be established as indices of the extent or amount of progress one has made at various times along the road toward maturity. What are these determinants of occupational maturity? One starting point is to think of vocational development as a means of implementing a self-concept. (For additional information on self-concept see Chapter 14.) For the individual a job is a process for finding out whether he can be the kind of person he wants to be, whether the role he has to assume on the job is compatible with his self-concept, and whether he can put into operation his self-concept—thus reality testing (Super, *The Psychology of Careers*, 1957, p. 191).

Super (et al.) wrote in *Vocational Development, A Framework for Research* (1957, p. 58), that two important conditions prevail in determining vocational maturity: "One pertains to vocational developmental tasks and the other concerns time." In order to do the necessary longitudinal research that is required to obtain data on a developmental philosophical base identifying and/or labeling of characteristics is necessary. The book *The Vocational Maturity of Ninth Grade Boys* (Super et al., 1960, Foreword, p. v) "lays the groundwork for the study of career development during the succeeding adolescent years."

A review of the literature seems to reveal that theories and research in the past twenty years have shifted to recognition of man's relation to the world of work, including his attitudes, values, and processes. The contents of Super's book are focused upon how the counselor can utilize information in working with individuals and groups to facilitate attitude and value formation during the vocational development processes.

Robert L. Thorndike and Elizabeth Hagen (1959) made a study of 17,000 men who were given a battery of aptitude tests in 1943. In 1955 and 1956 an attempt was made to locate as many of these men as possible and to obtain information from each about his educational and vocational history. Information was obtained from over 10,000 men, who were at that time out of the Air Force and in the civilian world of work (p. 3). The study included 124 occupational groups in which specific information obtained from the test results were provided. Thorndike and Hagen wrote, "there are some occupations with very distinctive profiles. . . . In addition to the differences in pattern we can point out rather marked differences in level of performance on the test" (p. 26). From an examination of the test results provided in Thorndike and Hagen's longitudinal study, the conclusion can be reached that occupations do have distinctive profiles and that individuals who seemingly go into those occupations have marked differences in level of performance as measured by tests.

Thorndike and Hagen also had available to them, for each of the individuals included in their sample, biographical data, which was obtained at the time the aptitude tests were given. The biographical data included "over 100 independent responses from the respondents, dealing with matters of family background, personal and family education, success in school, hobbies, sports, activities, work experience, and other facts of personal history" (p. 38). The biographical items did tend to discriminate among occupational groups. Some of the items that seemed to have the greatest discrimination were items such as the following: whether or not the man had had some college education before he entered the Air Force, an indication of whether he had a college major when in school, whether he had entered college by the time he had reached eighteen to twenty-six years of age, the amount of education obtained by his mother, extent of success in physics and trigonometry, the number of books in his home at the time he was a youth, and an item pertaining to mechanical nature that inquired about whether he frequently had adjusted a carburetor. The items in the next group in terms of their frequency of discrimination included also a considerable number of items on some type of mechanical activity, either as a work experience or as a free time hobby experience (p. 39). This research study tends to be in agreement with other studies, which indicate that biographical data is significant in helping an individual to examine and understand himself and may give indication of possible occupational implications.

Thorndike and Hagen concluded that "there is no convincing evidence that aptitude tests or biographical information of the type that was available to us can predict degree of success within an occupation insofar as this is represented in the criterion measures that we were able to obtain" (p. 50). This longitudinal study on a large number of people has implications for counselors in that they can use tests and biographical information to help the individual to understand himself, but that counselors should not try to predict the degree of success that an individual can or cannot have within an occupation. The counselor may help the individual to examine what characteristics other persons in an occupation seemingly have, but by recognizing that the individual may change the counselor may avoid the mistake of saying what the individual will do.

Anne Roe and Marvin Siegelman in a booklet, *The Origin of Interests* (1964), wrote about three studies that had implications for Roe's 1957 hypothesis about occupations. The three studies that they commented about were D. Hagen (1960), A. C. Utton (1960), and A. E. Grigg (1959). Roe and Siegelman (1964, p. 9) concluded, "In short these studies offer no support for any general hypothesis of a relationship between early parent-child interaction and specific occupational choice. There are, however, some suggestions of relationships between early parent-child interactions and later attitudes toward persons, and some further suggestions that this has played a part in choice of a few occupations." The implications seem to be that the counselor cannot make the deduction that the relationship between the parent and child will determine the specific occupational choice. These relationships may, however, be significant in helping the individual to examine his attitudes toward other persons and thus may affect his happiness or lack of happiness in working in certain occupations where certain kinds of people might be predominant.

Statewide studies done by state departments of education are also very helpful in understanding the role and change of education and occupations in the lives of young people. One example of such a study was reported in January, 1964, Ohio Guidance Service Section, where 25,541 sophomore and junior students from 96 schools had completed a vocational interest survey. Three of every four (75.6 per cent) students indicated that they desired high school vocational training with one half (41.3 per cent) of all the students indicating they wanted such training and had no plans to go to college, whereas one fourth (24.3 per cent) indicated they wanted the vocational training and also planned to go to college (*Guidance Services in Career Planning*, 1964, p. 1).

John O. Crites has been doing research during the 1960's to develop a standardized test of vocational maturity that is objective and valid (Breyfield and Crites, 1964, pp. 327–334, and Campbell, 1966, pp. 87–90). As part of a project sponsored by the U.S. Office of Education, he has produced the Vocational Development Inventory (VDI), which consists of two subtests: (1) the Competence Test, which was designed to assess the aptitude dimension of vocational development and (2) the Attitude Scale, earlier called Concept Test, which was designed to assess attitude dimension. Experimental forms of the Competence Tests were administered in 1966 to fifth through twelfth graders. The Attitude Scale was administered in 1962. The results from this research and others in the area of assessment of vocational development may begin to provide counselors with new data on which to formulate new procedures in counseling and in personalizing information processes.

In the VDI Competence Test is an attempt to measure the "comprehension and problem-solving abilities as they pertain to the vocational choice process" (Crites, 1965, p. 7). The Competence Test consists of five parts. The Problems Test, where the individual is to use his ability to resolve conflicts in vocational choice factors; the Planning Test, where the individual is to give order to a scrambled series of steps so as to lead to various vocational goals; the Occupational Information Test, which includes test items on future employment opportunities, occupational trends, job duties, and tasks; the Self-Knowledge Test, where the individual's results are compared to standardized test information for accuracy of estimated vocational capabilities; and the Goal Selection Test, where the individual must choose the most realistic occupation for a hypothetical individual presented in the test.

In the VDI Attitude Test is a design "to elicit the attitudinal or dispositional response tendencies in vocational maturity which are non-intellectual in nature, but which may mediate both choice behaviors and choice aptitudes." (Crites, 1965, p. 7). Results from the research with the VDI are interesting. The research is continuing.

David V. Tiedeman and his associates have been since 1952 preparing reports and articles on theories and research in the area of vocational development. Tiedeman, like Super, views the self-concept as the basic part of the career orientation. Tiedeman differs with Warren D. Gribbons (1964), whose work is on vocational readiness planning and with John O. Crites (Brayfield and Crites [1964]), whose work is on a vocational development index, both of whom use the concept of maturation in relation to the task of vocational choosing. In the words of Tiedeman (1965, p. 5):

> Crites and I have important differences in our conceptions of vocational maturity. Crites seemingly believes that vocational maturity must be defined *only* in terms of empirical observations. As I previously noted in my discussion of the paradigm which I find useful in thinking of the science of the personally-determined career, I believe that it is not only possible, but also necessary, to define vocational maturity in terms of an ideal a) which is presented to the person as information, and b) which the subject can then act towards in either a mature or an immature manner as the case may be. I recognize that I use my conception of "maturity" twice as I frame this premise. I use the conception first as the ideal presented to the person and then as the criterion which I, a second party, impose upon his present behavioral repertoire to assess whether it is now mature or not. Thus,

for me, vocational maturity is an *interactional* conception necessarily defined in relation to a person's response to others' expectations for his mature reaction. Crites (1964, 1965) writes as if the conception is *only* empiric and other determined, not personal, but realized in an interpersonal context.

Tiedeman (1967) stated that he was making a "transition from the theory of vocational development to the problem of mediating occupational information" (Tiedeman and Dudley, 1967, p. 4). He stated two central issues regarding mediation of occupational information for the goal of vocational maturation—the media through which the information is modulated and providing the inquirer with personal responsibility for goal delineation. A third issue of timing and supervision was also identified (Tiedeman and Dudley, 1967, p. 7). The implications of work of this kind are many. Until the findings are reported, the specific implications cannot be written.

Tiedeman and his coauthors are doing research on an information system for vocational decisions (ISVD). The implications of computer-assisted information system (CAIS) were presented in Chapter 3. Probably counselors will in the near future have a breakthrough in computer use with information for decision-making. When the breakthrough comes, a new era may be ushered in with individuals receiving much more information at the most appropriate times and information that can be geared to the individual's needs. In contrast to comments frequently made the CAIS *can* make available information that can become more meaningful instead of impersonal. If CAIS can achieve this goal then counselors may use more of their time in depth professional activities that facilitate the personalized information processes.

Another type of research is that done by Kenneth B. Hoyt (1965) to produce materials for students who may seek post-high-school training in institutions other than colleges and universities. Hoyt's work is referred to as the Specialty Oriented Student (SOS) Research Program. Information has been produced for use in counseling with high school students who have or probably should consider in their educational and vocational plans some kind of post-high-school training. The research thus far has been conducted in specialty-oriented schools on the students enrolled in their programs, and a follow-up study on the same students several months after leaving training for employment. Thus the research data are presented about students and are organized on the basic questions frequently asked by high school students and their parents.

Hoyt's research has begun to supply information in a much needed area. He has made counselors more aware of the need for information about post-high-school training institutions, has helped young people think about themselves in terms of their post-high-school educational and vocational plans, and has assisted in crystallizing questions that should be considered prior to the decision-making point for students considering training at a specialty school.

John L. Holland (1966) in studying vocational choice started with a theory of personality types and model environments that was based on some assumptions: (1) people can be characterized according to their resemblance to one or more personality types, (2) environments in which people live can be characterized according to their resemblance to one or more model environments, and (3) several outcomes can be predicted and understood from the knowledge of personality types and environmental models when persons and environments are paired (p. 9). Holland believed that " 'vocational interests' are simply another aspect of personality" (p. 3). With the belief of relationship between vocational interest and personality, he was able to assume that people in a vocational group have similar personalities (p. 6); that one's satisfaction, stability, and achievement in an occupation is dependent upon the congruency between his personality and the other people in the environment where he works (p. 6); and that the stereotypes often associated with vocations have reliable and important psychological and sociological meanings (p. 5).

If Holland's work is interpreted as to meaning for counselors in occupational information, several implications may be made. Counselors may be able now or in the not-too-distant future to help an individual analyze an occupation not so much in the abstraction as in terms of the extent to which the occupation will permit the individual to exercise his skills and abilities, to express his attitudes and values, and to take on agreeable problems and roles (Holland, 1966, p. 11). When counselors practice more extensively this type of counseling and utilizing of occupational information, a need will exist for third depth information to enable the individual to have a feedback to the extent that he can have an understanding of the reality from the intermeshing of himself and occupational considerations. Holland's work on occupations may be similar to Astin's work in educational information (presented in Chapter 4), where the student can obtain a profile of the college and then intermesh his profile for a better feedback of possible implications of the college for him.

Holland's scheme of personality types enables the counselor not to label a person into one of a few categories but rather "allows a simple ordering of a person's resemblance to *each* of the six models provides the possibility of 720 different personality patterns" (Holland, 1966, p. 11). Such a scheme enables the counselor to use a variety of scales and techniques to obtain the information to make the person's profile. If counselors believe that guidance activities or the lack of them make a difference in occupational development, Holland's work may provide a basis for establishing a research study to determine the extent or influence made on occupational development by guidance activities.

Dale Tillery (1966) is conducting a longitudinal research study entitled "School to College: Opportunities for Postsecondary Education" (SCOPE). The study is planned as a five-year investigation of patterns of access to postsecondary education. Research is being done in four different states and the findings may provide fundamental information about the transitions from secondary to postsecondary education. School counselors in secondary education, post-high-school training, and colleges should keep informed of the research findings from the SCOPE study as well as from the Project Talent study that has been conducted for several years.

Studies on situational simulations, including gaming theories and techniques, booklets, and decision-making problems hold possibilities for contributing information about the various media and their effects on assisting individuals in gaining the occupational, educational, and personal-social information necessary for effective growth and development. Some of the people who have done work in this area include James Coleman, Sarane Boocock, Garry Shirts, and Barbara Varenhorst. Each simulation is built around a theoretical model. The situational simulations seem to have potential value in motivating people, assisting them in doing better inquiries, improving the skill of identifying pertinent information for decision-making, increasing understanding about self and some of the important factors in decision-making regarding occupations, relating self into the situation associated with an occupation, and recognition of some attitudes possessed. The materials are not sophisticated enough and the studies are not comprehensive enough to give a clear picture of which ones are most advantageous to use at various times and which ones achieve some values and not others.

Glen Pierson, Richard Hoover, and Edwin Whitfield (1967) have been involved in a different kind of research, in which they have tried to find a means of making more accurate, comprehensive national and local occupational information available to students, counselors, and others. Their study was entitled "Vocational Information for Education and Work" (VIEW). Their work has proven the value of information on microfilms with a means for students and others to scan the material and also obtain a print-out if the information seems pertinent to them.

The study by Pierson, et al., on a system for vocational guidance is only one example of the many studies being conducted. The following is only a partial list of other research studies in progress, for which counselors should be alert for articles and other information from which they may deduct implications for their work: J. F. Cogswell's Exploratory Study of Information Processing Procedures and Computer-Based Technology in Vocational Counseling, December 1965 to May 1969; Educational Testing Services Study of Intellectual Growth and Vocational Development conducted by Thomas L. Hilton, Gerald Halpern, Marion Tyson, Lynn Gaines, Lenora Segal and others, spring, 1965 until an undetermined time; John C. Flanagan and William W. Cooley's Project Talent, 1957 to 1984; Joseph T. Impellitteri's Development and Evaluation of a Pilot Computer Assisted Vocational Guidance Program, January 1966 to April 1968; John D. Krumboltz's Vocational Problem-Solving Experiences for Stimulating Career Exploration and Interest: Phase II, June 1965 to November 1966; Thomas Magoon's four projects, Clear Language Print-Out of Demographic and Psychometric Data Regarding College Students, Educational Information Transmissions via Single Message Repeater Tape, Education Information Transmission via Multiple Message Repeater Tapes, and Effective Problem Solving Model for Educational-Vocational Planning, 1966 to an indefinite time; Ann M. Martin's Multi-Media Approach for Communicating Occupational Information to Non-College Youth, October 1965 to November 1967; Frank J. Minor's Vocational Orientation System (VOS), January 1966 to December 1967; and Robert P. O'Hara, David V. Tiedeman, Russel G. Davis, Allan B. Ellis, and Michael J. Wilson's Harvard-Needs-Newton Information System for Vocational Decisions, June 1966 to June 1969 (Campbell, et al., 1966).

A total listing of all research studies and theories is beyond the scope of this book, but a partial list has been provided to illustrate the vast amount of recent work and the extent to which the research studies are expanding. Regardless of the setting, no counselor can truly refer to himself as professional unless he is keeping abreast with the theories, philosophy, and research studies in his area.

Summary

An understanding of how man becomes involved in an occupation and how he changes from one occupation to another during his vocational career has long been considered. The theories and research developed in the past twenty years have been productive in quality and quantity and have provided information beneficial to counselors. Most of the viewpoints held today are based on a developmental, longitudinal approach extending from early childhood. Most of the theories use the self-concept approach in some form as basic, recognize the socio-psycho-physiological conditions affecting the decision-making processes, and consider the economic-environmental conditions affecting the opportunities. The studies being conducted are also concerned with the media and kind of information necessary for effective occupational development. The timing—pacing and readiness—for information and at what depth seems to be a direction into which some studies are moving.

The early studies seemed to be preoccupied with predicting occupations, whereas the more recent studies have included a larger scope of facilitating vocational maturation with the individual himself assuming a more personal responsibility for his destination. Many of the studies are still in progress and the research findings are too sketchy to determine the implications for counselors; however, findings are beginning to provide information comprehensive enough to suggest that counselors need to question part of their practices in educational, occupational, and personal-social information processes.

SELECTED REFERENCES

Adams, James F., ed. *Counseling and Guidance, A Summary View.* New York: The Macmillan Company, 1965. Pp. 206–249.

Arbuckle, Dugald S. *Pupil Personnel Services in the Modern School.* Boston: Allyn and Bacon, Inc., 1966. Pp. 253–260.

Astin, Helen S. "Patterns of Career Choices over Time," *The Personnel and Guidance Journal,* **45** (September 1966), 37–42.

Barry, Ruth, and Beverly Wolf. *An Epitaph for Vocational Guidance: Myths, Actualities, Implications.* New York: Bureau of Publications, Teachers College, Columbia University, 1962. 241 pages.

Baymur, Feriha B., and C. H. Patterson. "A Comparison of Three Methods of Assisting Underachieving High School Students," *Journal of Counseling Psychology,* **7** (Summer 1960), 83–89.

Beilin, Harry. "The Application of General Developmental Principles to the Vocational Area," *Journal of Counseling Psychology,* **2** (Spring 1955), 53–57.

Beilin, Harry. "Discussion," *The Personnel and Guidance Journal,* **41** (May 1963), 780–782.

Blai, Boris, Jr. "An Occupational Study of Job Satisfaction and Need Satisfaction," *The Journal of Experimental Education,* **32** (Summer 1964), 383–388.

Blau, Peter M., et al. "Occupational Choice: A Conceptual Framework," *Industrial and Labor Relations Review,* **9** (1956), 531–534.

Blum, Lawrence P. "Guidelines for Career Development," in *Guidelines for Guidance: Readings in the Philosophy of Guidance,* Carlton E. Beck, ed. Dubuque, Iowa: Wm. C. Brown Company Publishers, 1966. Article 17, pp. 119–129.

Bordin, Edward S., Barbara Nachmann, and Stanley J. Segal. "An Articulated Framework for Vocational Development," *Journal of Counseling Psychology,* **10** (Summer 1963), 107–117.

Borow, Henry. "Vocational Development Research: Some Problems of Logical and Experimental Form," *The Personnel and Guidance Journal,* **40** (September 1961), 21–25.

Borow, Henry. "An Integral View of Occupational Theory and Research" in *Man in a World at Work,* Henry Borow, ed. Boston: Houghton Mifflin Company, 1964. Chap. 16, pp. 364–386.

Brayfield, Arthur H., and John O. Crites. "Research on Vocational Guidance: Status and Prospect," in *Man in a World at Work*, Henry Borow, ed. Boston: Houghton Mifflin Company, 1964. Pp. 310–340.

Brill, Abraham Arden. *Freud's Principles of Psychoanalysis: Basic Principles of Psychoanalysis*. New York: Garden City Books, Reprint Edition, 1953 by special arrangement with Doubleday & Company, Inc. at the Country Life Press, 1949. Copyright by Rose Brill. Chap. 13, pp. 265–287.

Campbell, Robert E., ed. *Guidance in Vocational Education: Guidelines for Research and Practice*. Columbus, Ohio: The Center for Vocational and Technical Education, The Ohio State University, 1966. 181 pages.

Campbell, Robert E., David V. Tiedeman, and Ann M. Martin, eds. *Systems Under Development for Vocational Guidance*. Columbus, Ohio: The Center for Vocational and Technical Education, 1966. A report of a Research Exchange Conference, August 18 and 19, 1966, held at The Ohio State University, 60 pages. Not copyrighted.

Caplan, Stanley W., Ronald A. Ruble, and David Segel. "A Theory of Educational and Vocational Choice in Junior High School," *The Personnel and Guidance Journal*, 42 (October 1963), 129–135.

Caplow, Theodore. *The Sociology of Work*. Minneapolis: University of Minnesota Press, 1954. Chap. 9, pp. 214–229.

Carp, Francis M. "High School Boys Are Realistic About Occupations," *Occupations*, 28 (November 1949), 97–99.

Clark, Harold F. *Economic Theory and Correct Occupational Distribution*. New York: Bureau of Publications, Teachers College, Columbia University, 1931. 176 pages.

Crites, John O. "A Model for the Measurement of Vocational Maturity," *Journal of Counseling Psychology*, 8 (Fall 1961), 255–259.

Crites, John O. "Symposium: New Research in Vocational Development, Introduction," *The Personnel Guidance Journal*, 41 (May 1963), 766–767.

Crites, John O. "Measurement of Vocational Maturity in Adolescence: 1. Attitude Test of the Vocational Development Inventory," *Psychological Monographs: General and Applied*. Washington, D.C.: American Psychological Association, Inc. 79 (1965), Whole No. 585, 36 pages.

Dictionary of Occupational Titles, 3rd ed. Washington, D.C.: Bureau of Employment Security, Manpower Administration, U.S. Department of Labor, 1965. Vol. I, *Definitions of Titles*; Vol. II, *Occupational Classification*. Also *A Supplement to the Dictionary of Occupational Titles*, 1966.

Dolliver, Robert H. "An Adaptation of the Tyler Vocational Card Sort," *The Personnel and Guidance Journal*, 45 (May 1967), 916–920.

Field, Frank L., Chris D. Kehas, and David V. Tiedeman. "The Self Concept in Career Development: A Construct in Transition," *The Personnel and Guidance Journal*, 41 (May 1963), 767–771.

Fine, Sidney A., and Carl A. Heinz. "The Functional Occupational Classificational Structure," *The Personnel and Guidance Journal*, 37 (November 1958), 180–192.

Gelatt, H. B., and R. B. Clarke. "Role of Subjective Probabilities in the Decision Process," *Journal of Counseling Psychology*, 14 (July 1967), 332–341.

Gerstein, Martin, and Richard Hoover. "VIEW—Vocational Information for Education and Work," *The Personnel and Guidance Journal,* **45** (February 1967), 593–596.

Ginzberg, Eli. "Guidance—Limited or Unlimited," *The Personnel and Guidance Journal,* **38** (May 1960), 707–712.

Ginzberg, Eli. *The Development of Human Resources.* New York: McGraw-Hill, Inc., 1966. 350 pages.

Ginzberg, E., S. W. Ginsburg, S. Axelrad, and J. L. Herma. *Occupational Choice.* New York: Columbia University Press, 1951. 271 pages.

Glick, Peter, Jr. "Preliminary Trial of a Three-Dimensional Classification of Occupations," *Journal of Counseling Psychology,* **11** (Spring 1964), 95–97.

Gribbons, Warren D. "Changes in Readiness for Vocational Planning from the Eighth to the Tenth Grade," *The Personnel and Guidance Journal,* **42** (May 1964), 908–913.

Gribbons, Warren D., and Paul R. Lhones. "Relationships Among Measures of Readiness for Vocational Planning." *Journal of Counseling Psychology,* **11** (Spring 1964), 13–19.

Gribbons, Warren D., and Paul R. Lohnes. "Validation of Vocational Planning Interview Scales," *Journal of Counseling Psychology,* **11** (Spring 1964), 20–25.

"Guidance Services in Career Planning" (Columbus, O.: State Department of Education, Division of Guidance and Testing, Guidance Service Section, January 1964), 1 page.

Hall, Donald W. "The Vocational Development Inventory: A Measure of Vocational Maturity in Adolescence." *The Personnel and Guidance Journal,* **41** (May 1963), 771–775.

Hewer, Vivian H. "What Do Theories of Vocational Choice Mean to a Counselor?" *Journal of Counseling Psychology,* **10** (Summer 1963), 118–125.

Hilton, Thomas L. "Career Decision-Making," *Journal of Counseling Psychology,* **9** (Winter 1962), 291–298.

Holland, John L. "A Theory of Vocational Choice," *Journal of Counseling Psychology,* **6** (Spring 1959), 35–44.

Holland, John L. "Explorations of a Theory of Vocational Choice, Part I: Vocational Images and Choice," *The Vocational Guidance Quarterly,* **11** (Summer 1963), 232–239.

Holland, John L. "Exploration of a Theory of Vocational Choice, Part II: Self-Descriptions and Vocational Preferences; Part III: Coping Behavior, Competencies, and Vocational Preferences," *The Vocational Guidance Quarterly,* **12** (Autumn 1963), 17–21, 21–24.

Holland John L. "Explorations of a Theory of Vocational Choice, Part IV: Vocational Daydreams." *The Vocational Guidance Quarterly,* **12** (Winter 1963– 64), 93–97.

Holland, John L. "Major Programs of Research on Vocational Behavior," in *Man in a World at Work,* Henry Borow, ed. Boston: Houghton Mifflin Company. 1964. Chap. 12, pp. 259–284.

Holland, John L. *The Psychology of Vocational Choice: A Theory of Personality Types and Model Environments.* Waltham, Mass.: Blaisdell Publishing Company, 1966. 132 pages.

Hollingshead, A. B. *Elmtown's Youth*. New York: John Wiley and Sons, Inc., 1949. 480 pages.

Hoppock, Robert. *Occupational Information: Where to Get It and How to Use It in Counseling and in Teaching*, 1st, 2nd, and 3rd eds. New York: McGraw-Hill, Inc., 1957. Pp. 74–85; 1963, pp. 82–133; 1967, pp. 84–130.

Hoyt, Kenneth B. "High School Guidance and the Specialty Oriented Student Research Program." *The Vocational Guidance Quarterly*, 13 (Summer 1965), 229–236.

Isaacson, Lee E. *Career Information in Counseling and Teaching*. Boston: Allyn and Bacon, Inc., 1966. Pp. 19–38.

Katz, Martin. "A Model of Guidance for Career Decision-Making." *The Vocational Guidance Quarterly*, 15 (September 1966), 2–10.

Katzell, Raymond A. "Personal Values, Job Satisfaction, and Job Behavior," in *Man in a World at Work*. Henry Borow, ed. Boston: Houghton Mifflin Company, 1964. Chap. 15, pp. 341–363.

Kelley, Earl C. "The Fully Functioning Self," in *Perceiving, Behaving, Becoming: A New Focus for Education*. Arthur W. Combs, ed. Washington, D.C.: Association for Supervision and Curriculum Development. A department of the National Education Association, Yearbook, 1962, Chap. 2, pp. 9–20.

Kohout, Vernon A., and John W. Rothney. "A Longitudinal Study of the Consistency of Vocational Preferences," *American Educational Research Journal*, 1 (January 1964), 10–21.

Lipsman, Claire K. "Maslow's Theory of Needs in Relation to Vocational Choice by Students from Lower Socio-Economic Levels." *The Vocational Guidance Quarterly*, 15 (June 1967), 283–288.

Meadow, Lloyd. "Toward a Theory of Vocational Choice." *Journal of Counseling Psychology*, 2 (Summer 1955), 108–112.

Miller, Delbert Charles, and William H. Form. *Industrial Sociology: The Sociology of Work Organizations*. New York: Harper & Row, 1951. 873 pages.

Morrison, Richard L. "Self-Concept Implementation in Occupational Choices." *Journal of Counseling Psychology*, 9 (Fall 1962), 255–260.

Norris, Willa. *Occupational Information in the Elementary School*. Chicago: Science Research Associates, Inc., 1963. Pp. 18–34.

O'Hara, Robert P., and David V. Tiedeman. "Vocational Self Concept in Adolescence." *Journal of Counseling Psychology*, 6 (Winter 1959), 292–301.

Osipow, Samuel H., Jefferson D. Ashby, and Harvey W. Wall. "Personality Types and Vocational Choice: A Test of Holland's Theory." *The Personnel and Guidance Journal*, 45 (September 1966), 37–42.

Peters, Herman J., and James C. Hansen. *Vocational Guidance and Career Development: Selected Readings*. New York: The Macmillan Company, 1966. 466 pages.

Pierson, Glen N., Richard Hoover, and Edwin A. Whitfield. "A Regional Career Information Center: Development and Process,"*The Vocational Guidance Quarterly*, 15 (March 1967), 162–169.

Pritchard, David H. "The Occupational Exploration Process: Some Operational Implications," *The Personnel and Guidance Journal*, **40** (April 1962), pp. 674–680.

Robinson, H. Alan, and Ralph P. Connors. "Job Satisfaction Researches of 1962," *The Personnel and Guidance Journal*, **42** (October 1963), 136–142.

Roe, Anne. *The Psychology of Occupations*. New York: John Wiley and Sons, Inc., 1956. 340 pages.

Roe, Anne, and Marvin Siegelman. *The Origin of Interests*. Washington, D.C.: American Personnel and Guidance Association, 1964. 98 pages.

Samler, Joseph. "Toward a Theoretical Base for Vocational Counseling." *The Personnel and Guidance Journal*, **32** (September 1953), 34–35.

Shertzer, Bruce, and Shelley C. Stone. *Fundamentals of Guidance*. Boston: Houghton Mifflin Company, 1966. Pp. 291–323.

Simons, Joseph B. "An Existential View of Vocational Development," *The Personnel and Guidance Journal*, **44** (February 1966), 604–610.

Sinick, Daniel, William E. Gorman, and Robert Hoppock. "Research on the Teaching of Occupations, 1963–1964." *The Personnel and Guidance Journal*, **44** (February 1966), 591–595.

Stefflre, Buford. "Vocational Development: Ten Propositions in Search of a Theory," *The Personnel and Guidance Journal*, **44** (February 1966), 611–616.

Super, Donald E. "A Theory of Vocational Development," *American Psychologist*, **8** (1953), 185–190.

Super, Donald E. "Dimensions and Measurement of Vocational Maturity," *Teachers College Record*, **57** (December 1955), 151–163.

Super, Donald E. *The Psychology of Careers: An Introduction to Vocational Development*. New York: Harper & Brothers, 1957. 362 pages.

Super, Donald E. "Some Unresolved Issues in Vocational Development Research," *The Personnel and Guidance Journal*, **40** (September 1961), 11–15.

Super, Donald E. "The Definition and Measurement of Early Career Behavior: A First Formulation," *The Personnel and Guidance Journal*, **41** (May 1963), 775–780.

Super, Donald E. "A Developmental Approach to Vocation Guidance: Recent Theory and Results," *The Vocational Guidance Quarterly*, **13** (Autumn 1964), 1–10.

Super, Donald E., and Paul B. Bachrach. *Scientific Careers and Vocational Development Theory: A Review, a Critique and Some Recommendations*. New York: Bureau of Publications, Teachers College, Columbia University, 1957. 135 pages.

Super, Donald E., and John O. Crites. *Appraising Vocational Fitness by Means of Psychological Tests*, revised ed. New York: Harper and Row, 1962. 688 pages.

Super, Donald E., et al. *Vocational Development: A Framework for Research*. New York: Bureau of Publications, Teachers College, Columbia University, 1957. 142 pages.

Super, Donald E., and Phoebe L. Overstreet, et al. *The Vocational Maturity of Ninth-Grade Boys*. New York: Bureau of Publications, Teachers College, Columbia University, 1960. 212 pages.

Thompson, Albert S. "A Rationale for Vocational Guidance," *The Personnel and Guidance Journal*, 32 (May 1954), 533–535.

Thoresen, Carl E., and William A. Mehrens. "Decision Theory and Vocational Counseling: Important Concepts and Questions," *The Personnel and Guidance Journal*, 46 (October 1967), 165–172.

Thorndike, Robert L., and Elizabeth Hagen. *Ten Thousand Careers*. New York: John Wiley & Sons, Inc., 1959. 346 pages.

Tiedeman, David V. "Decision and Vocational Development: A Paradigm and Its Implications," *The Personnel and Guidance Journal*, 40 (September 1961), 15–21.

Tiedeman, David V. "The Cultivation of Career in Vocational Development Through Guidance-in-Education," in *Guidance in American Education II: Current Issues and Suggested Actions*. Edward Landy and Arthur M. Kroll, eds. Boston: Harvard Graduate School of Education, 1965. Pp. 280–300.

Tiedeman, David V. *Career Pattern Studies: Current Findings with Possibilities*. Harvard Studies in Career Development, No. 40. Boston: Center for Research in Careers, Graduate School of Education, Harvard University, July 1965. 34 pages.

Tiedeman, David V., and Gordon Dudley. "Prospects for Technology and Commerce in the Mediation of Vocational Development for Vocational Maturity. Outline and Appendices Accompanying Recent Developments and Current Prospects in Occupations Fact Mediation." Mimeographed copy of speech, National Conference on Occupational Information in Vocational Guidance, sponsored by the U.S. Office of Education, Chicago, Illinois, May 17, 1967.

Tillery, Dale (Chief Investigator) et al. *Scope: Four State Profile, Grade Twelve, 1966; California, Illinois, Massachusetts, North Carolina*. New York: College Entrance Examination Board, December 1966. 71 pages.

Tyler, Leona E. "The Development of 'Vocational Interests': I. The Organization of Likes and Dislikes in Ten-Year Old Children," *The Journal of Genetic Psychology*, 86 (1955), 33–44.

"The Unemployed, Portrait in Depth," *Occupational Outlook Quarterly*, 10 (May 1966), 31–32. Based on Special Labor Force Report No. 61. "A Portrait of the Unemployed," reprint 2484 from *Monthly Labor Review*, January 1966.

Venn, Grant, assisted by Theodore J. Marchese, Jr. *Man, Education, and Work: Postsecondary Vocational and Technical Education*. Washington, D.C.: American Council on Education, 1964. 184 pages.

Wall, Harvey W., Samuel H. Osipow, and Jefferson D. Ashby. "SVIB Scores, Occupational Choices, and Holland's Personality Types," *The Vocational Guidance Quarterly*, 15 (March 1967), 201–205.

Walz, Garry. "Who or What is ERIC?" *The School Counselor*, 14 (January 1967), 143.

Warner, William Lloyd, and James C. Abegglen. *Occupational Mobility in*

American Business and Industry, 1928–1952. Minneapolis: University of Minnesota Press, 1955. 315 pages.

Williamson, E. G. *Vocational Counseling: Some Historical, Philosophical, and Theoretical Perspectives.* New York: McGraw-Hill, Inc., 1965. Pp. 153–198.

Wurtz, Robert E., "Vocational Development: Theory and Practice," *The Vocational Guidance Quarterly,* **15** (1966), 127–130.

Chapter 10

Effects of the Occupational
World on the Individual

Probably one half the children in school will during their lifetime be employed in occupations that don't exist today; therefore, instead of emphasis being placed upon an existing occupation more attention should be devoted to understanding the world of work, attitudes toward work, and recognition of the need for continued occupational growth with a realization of potential means to maintain the growth.

The occupational world, its nature, structure, and changes affects the alternatives that an individual has or will have as an employee. The facts about the occupational world are changing and the employees are changing too. The various information about occupations is not so much isolated as related, but often the information is obtained as a fact or without placement within the total context. The counselor needs awareness of conditions and their intra- and inter-dependence upon each other and how these may affect different individuals and their opportunities in different ways.

Changing Nature of World of Work

In the twentieth century have been many scientific discoveries that have affected the world of work. These scientific discoveries and their applications in industry and business technology have changed the organization functions and tasks, and thus shifted the nature of the world of work. As industries change, so do their manpower needs. The number and kinds of new jobs created are large, but also a large number of jobs are replaced or discontinued as a result of scientific discoveries. Data processing alone has in this century given to man a means of computation that is one million times faster at one one-thousandth the cost. As has been seen, even though we can compute at a faster rate and at less cost, thus reducing the need for a number of people to do many of the jobs they were doing, man is now doing additional computations that he never did before and doing those computations routinely.

With the formation of new discoveries, new industries have been created, some industries have been reduced, and others even discontinued. The airplane and the creation of the space age has brought about many new jobs, and particularly new occupations, that have had to be filled by men and women who at the time they were in elementary, secondary, and college preparation were not preparing for these occupations because they did not exist. The world of work is changing, and changing at a faster pace today than ever before, which means that man must also change his occupation and his job more frequently than ever before (*Manpower Implications of Automation,* 1965).

The composition of the labor force has changed from one in which goods-producing industries were foremost to one in which service industries predominate. Moreover, occupational requirements have changed in favor of jobs needing more education and training. Since the middle of the twentieth century, with the increasing use of material-handling processes and automation equipment, the need for highly trained professional and skilled manpower has risen sharply. With a reduction in the need for individuals with little or no skill and a limited amount of education, the ability of the American labor force to respond quickly to job opportunities and to adjust to changing job requirements is basic to the achievement of full employment and full utilization of the labor force. Americans have responded to this changing world of work by a willingness to extend their education and training for a new job, thus a willingness to transfer jobs not only within the local community but also to move geographically to the place where they can find the kind of employment for which they feel they can best qualify either presently or through additional training or education.

A problem arises, however, from the two and one half million people in the United States who cannot read and write and the nearly eight million who have not completed the fifth grade in school. The changing nature of the world of work necessitates a continuing, developing labor force, not only through the addition of new people to the labor force, and the retiring of others, but through the continuing education and training obtained by those who are in the labor force. The necessity for new skills, not necessarily skills that are an upgrading but the necessity for skills to change within a job in order to maintain the same level are needed just as are the additional skills for upgrading. The necessity in the labor force to have built into it an attitude for flexibility is essential, so that individuals may recognize that on the average they may hold, during their lifetime, jobs in different industries and may have six, seven, or more different jobs and employers. The concept, then, needs to change gradually from that in which an individual is trained for a specific occupation or job to one in which an individual is given the kinds of skills and attitudes by which he finds the kind of a job that assists him to have fulfillment of self and at the same time to see the relationship of his present job to a family of jobs into which he might then, as he moves through life, change within his career.

The United States will have about 86 million workers by 1970, which is approximately 20 per cent more than in 1960. The average yearly rate increase in number of workers in the last half of the 1960's will be over 1½ million a year. Women will continue to increase in the labor force with the number of women workers aged twenty-five and over increasing at nearly ½ million a year in the last half of the 1960's, with approximately 4 out of every 5 of these additional women entering into the labor force being forty-five years of age or older. The number of women workers and the percentage of the total work force who are women are increasing each year and the average number of working years for women is also increasing each year (*Highlights from the 1966 Manpower Report*, p. 13).

A shortage of skilled and technical labor has occurred in the labor force. Companies have been unable to employ all the machinists, welders, fitters, riggers, chemical engineers, and other workmen that are needed. (*Business Week*, July 23, 1966, p. 8). The shift in percentage of people in different classifications within the labor force is graphically shown in Figure 10-1, where the professional classification has changed from 4 per cent in 1900 to an estimated 15 per cent in 1975; while the laborers' classification has decreased from 13 per cent in 1900 to 4 per cent of the labor force estimated for 1975. If the farm workers and laborers are placed together, 31 per cent of the labor force in 1900 were in that classification, whereas the anticipated percentage in 1975 will be 6 per cent.

In 1900 about one in five workers had a white-collar (professional, manager, clerical, or sales) job, whereas in 1964 approximately two in every five workers were in white-collar jobs, with approximately one in every two being in white-collar jobs anticipated by 1975 (Campbell, 1966, p. 37).

The employment rate in the United States the latter part of the sixties was high, near 96 per cent; but the unemployment rate was high among teen-agers—approximately three times the overall average. For non-white teen-agers the rate was even higher, approximately six

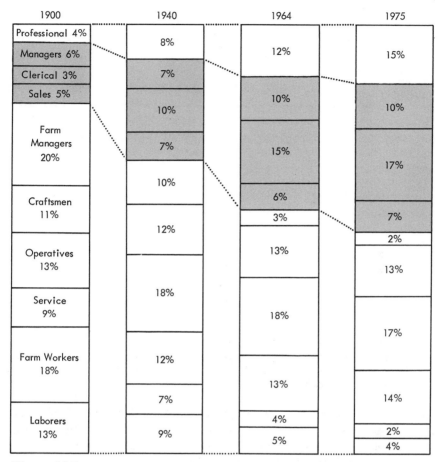

Figure 10-1. PERCENTAGE OF LABOR FORCE IN EACH OCCUPATIONAL GROUP FOR SELECTED YEARS.

Source: Higher Education and Jobs. *Columbus, Ohio: Ohio Board of Regents, Chart 4, p. 9. Primary source of data for the Chart: Data for 1900, 1940, and 1964 from* This U.S.A., Ben J. Wattenberg, Doubleday and Company, Garden City, New York, 1965. Data for 1975 from *Technology and the American Economy—Appendix, Vol. 1, The Outlook for Technological Change and Employment,* Table 2; The National Commission on Technology, Automation, and Economic Progress, U.S. Government Printing Office, 1966.

times the overall unemployment national average. In 1965, of the non-white teen-agers 23 per cent of the boys and 30 per cent of the girls were unemployed. Part of this high percentage for both whites and non-whites was because of school drop-outs, but among the unemployed teen-agers were also some high school graduates who wanted to enter the labor force but were unable to find jobs. (See Figure 10-2) The nature of the world of work did help many young boys and girls to

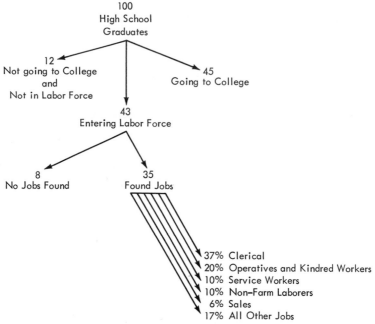

Figure 10-2. NEXT STEPS FOR HIGH SCHOOL GRADUATES IN THE MID-1960's: NUMBERS ARE APPROXIMATES FOR THE NATION.

Source: Based on data released by Bureau of Labor Statistics and Department of Health, Education, and Welfare.

decide to go to college, but about an equal number entered into the labor force in the mid-1960's. Of those who did enter directly into the labor force upon high school graduation, approximately one out of three found work in clerical jobs. (See Figure 10-2)

In today's businesses and industries the cost of materials usually is not the most expensive part of the operation. Instead, labor has become the biggest cost. Thus, today, business and industry is striving to reduce the number of workers without reducing production. The turn to automation and heavy equipment has enabled business and industry to increase production of goods per person to the point where it is at least triple what it was in 1900 by increasing the output per man-hour of work. With the shift to more specialized equipment, and the need for more experience and higher education, the inexperienced person is the one who is handicapped the most in the labor force. To improve the chances of inexperienced persons in obtaining work, schools have increased their function in the preparation of people for work by increasing the amount of experience associated with the schooling so that the person is not totally inexperienced at the time he is ready for full-time employment.

For young people and for older people who want to change occupations, a limited number of opportunities for exploratory experiences while they are in the process of decision-making exist today. *The need for increasing exposure to alternatives with also the opportunity for exploration of consequences continues to be a real challenge in order to help individuals during the decision-making process to find the occupation that might be most nearly suited to their world of work.* The research on decision theory has not been conclusive, but the data available would support the viewpoint that increased exposure (greater experience) with the alternatives would increase the subjective probability information used by the decision-maker. Opportunity for exploration (greater understanding) of the consequences may be a means of increasing the cognitive process in decision-making behavior.

Changing Role of Work in Life of Individual

Change is the only changeless thing. The variety of discoveries and improvements flowing from the minds of men is at a faster rate today than ever before. In 1965 alone more than ninety-four thousand applications for U.S. patents were filed, more than a 13 per cent increase in five years. Stanley Learned, President, Phillips Petroleum Company, on October 19, 1966 (p. 5), stated:

> Other energy affecting developments which the speculators say may unfold over the next 100 years include underground, automated highways but with wheels and road surfaces eventually giving way to hovercraft riding on air; enormous supersonic transport planes; individual propulsion; transportation by ballistic rockets to any place on earth within 40 minutes; permanent space stations; regular trips to the moon; all plastic houses entirely weather conditioned. The next 100 years may also see huge cities entirely enclosed and weather conditioned and served by trains reaching speeds of 1,000 miles an hour; synthetic clothes, and other goods and appliances made to be used and thrown away; teaching machines; automated libraries; facsimile newspapers and magazines; communication with anyone, anywhere at anytime by voice, sight, and written message via satellite telephone, radio, and television; motorized and computerized artificial arms and legs; far more use of elevators and escalators, outdoors and indoors; and chemical control of the aging process extending life by up to 50 years.

The changes that have occurred during the history of man have brought about different concepts about the role of work in the life of an individual. The changes to come may bring about even more concepts and probably will assist in giving a new definition to work.

The ethical, theological, and philosophical outlooks regarding work have changed and, to some extent, traveled parallel with other social, moral, and spiritual concerns. To the Greeks work was a curse, something to be avoided. According to Homer, the gods hated mankind and out of spite condemned men to toil. Xenophon called work the painful price the gods charge for the goods of life.

The Hebrews, like the Greeks, thought of work as drudgery. The human race must work as a duty to expiate the original sin committed in the earthly paradise. Early Christian beliefs followed the tradition of regarding work as a punishment laid on man by God because of man's original sin. To this negative doctrine the Christians added a positive function: to work is necessary not only to earn one's living, asking alms of no man, but above all so that the goods of fortune may be shared with one's needy brothers. St. Thomas Aquinas believed that work was an obligation only insomuch as it is necessary to maintain the individual and the group of which he is a part. If that purpose was fulfilled, then man did not need to work.

During the Renaissance period stress was placed on the importance of work for the benefit of mankind, thus avoiding connection of work to religion. Work can help fulfill a more bountiful life for the ethical and aesthetic man (Tilgher, 1930, pp. 1–50).

Work has come to have different meanings through the ages and as such has had different roles in the lives of individuals. From a physiological viewpoint work has been for survival—food, clothing, and shelter. From an economical viewpoint work has been for bringing financial return so that man may purchase those things he treasures. In the sociological concept work has been for bringing recognition from other members of the group and has been a means for determining one's position or prestige within the group. The philanthropist does work for the love of mankind and the good his efforts, when expanded, will do for all men.

Psychologically, man may now be ready to re-examine his concept about work and *may now perceive work, whether for financial gain or not, as being an integral part of self-expression and self-realization.* Work then need not be considered as a task or drudgery but may be an opportunity for expression, growth, development. Work, in its broadest concept, for some people becomes not a necessity but rather a desire. Some of the research studies have shown that people want to work even when they don't need to do so.

With the changing role of work in the life of an individual the psychological, as well as the physical, conditions involved in work must be considered. (Personal-social information is presented in Part IV.) Job satisfaction involves more than financial return, and job satisfaction is not the same for all persons. For the unskilled and undecided—job jumpers—money does seem to be a major factor in job satisfaction. Other persons seem to be more interested in the happiness and contentment offered by the job than in money and other rewards. Whether or not this is one measurement of occupational maturity is yet to be determined.

If work is beginning to be viewed as an expression of oneself and if one is ever changing, then his job and probably his occupation should change—maybe more frequently during some periods of his life than other stages of his development. Maybe the frame of reference should be one in which a normal development of an ever-maturing individual is a succession of jobs during the course of a lifetime in which each job contributes to his growth and to the improvement of the individual in preparation for the next. "Individuals should be helped to find out what alternatives exist, aided to reach judgments about them, and encouraged to make plans and take appropriate steps to execute them" (*American Women*, 1963, pp. 13–14).

The personal involvement in work, or more so the lack of involvement (unemployment), is a critical part of many individuals' lives. In 1965 "only 58 per cent of the Negro men worked full time the year round compared with 68 per cent of the white men" (Bogan and Swanstrom, 1966, p. 1369). The older worker (ages forty-five to sixty-four) is more likely to be unemployed a number of times during a year than is a worker aged twenty to forty-four. The effect of unemployment, especially when produced involuntarily, upon the life of an individual is often immeasurable. The percentage of the long-term jobless in the mid-1960's was greatest among "nonwhites, unskilled and semi-skilled blue-collar workers, persons last employed in mining and construction, and those without previous work experience" (Holland, 1965, p. 1076). Another group who are influenced by lack of personal involvement in work would be individuals who have retired but who want to work. Vocational development for the unemployed, underemployed, and retired becomes an item that needs major attention if the individual and his development is to remain a central core in the American way of life.

The role of women is changing also. Women are marrying younger, remaining widowed or divorced a fewer number of years between ages fourteen and sixty-five, and working in the labor force more years. More thirty-five years of age or older married women are participating in the labor force than ever before in United States history. A smaller percentage of single women are in the labor force today than at any period in the past twenty-five years; however, a larger percentage of married women are working (Figure 10-3). Approximately one in every three workers today is a woman, compared to one in every five in 1920 (*American Women*, 1963, pp. 6, 11, and 28).

In 1966 the President's Committee on Employment of the Handicapped reported 22.2 million persons in the United States were limited

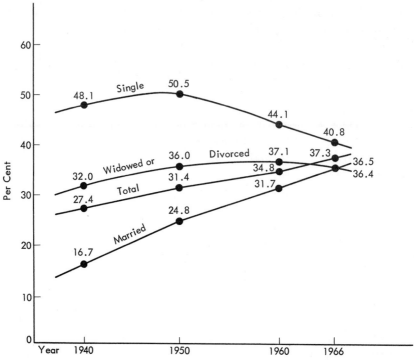

Figure 10-3. FEMALE LABOR FORCE COMPARED TO FEMALE POPULATION SHOWN IN PERCENTAGE FOR TOTAL AND BY MARITAL STATUS (FOURTEEN YEARS OF AGE AND OVER).

Source: Based on data from Statistical Abstract of the United States, 1967, 88th Annual Edition, U.S. Department of Commerce, p. 229.

to some degree in their activities as a result of chronic disease or impairment. The number represents 12.2 per cent of the civilian population not residing in institutions. During the past five years, an annual average of eighty thousand persons received permanent disabilities from work injuries. With work becoming an integral part of the development of an individual, rehabilitation becomes an important part of the American way. For the self-fulfillment of the individual the employment of the handicapped person is as much or more important than employment of persons who possess average or above-average physical and mental abilities.

Multiple job holding is becoming a trend. In a national survey in May, 1963, one in every eighteen workers was a moonlighter—held an extra job. The majority of dual jobholders were wage-and-salary workers on both jobs. A large part of them combined wage work with a profession, business, or farm enterprise. Usually self-employment was the extra job and the wage or salary job was the main one (Bogan and Hamel, 1964, p. 6).

Sociologically, an individual's work is a major device for his identification with his peers, his family, and society in general. When a man loses his job his image changes among his friends and his family and often he is psychologically affected also. Work to an individual is often such an important part of his life that when he is becoming ill—physically or psychologically—he will show the signs of the illness in activities outside of his work before showing the cues at work. His friends know something is wrong before his employer does.

Studies have been reported on the effect of sociological factors in determining the occupational decisions of individuals. Anne Roe and Marvin Siegelman, in *The Origin of Interests* (1964), reported that the farther from the cultural sex stereotype the occupational choice is, the more likely that particular pressures did exist in the early histories that influenced such a choice. More studies are needed to assist in more completely understanding the forces that affect the occupational choice(s) of an individual and the way in which he sees his work as contributing to or interfering with his life.

Technological Advances Necessitate Change in Job and Man

Occupational information today is different in design, or should be, from that of a few years ago. The role of occupational information in the life of an individual has changed. He still needs some of the same types of information his grandparents received, plus information of a more personalized nature over an extended period of time. Technological advancements will by necessity change the jobs and thus change the functions of the men and women who perform the jobs.

Technological advances have changed the labor force and the activities performed and probably have facilitated the entrance of more women into the labor force. Technological changes in the home—automatic ovens, dishwashers, clothes dryers, prepared foods, and so on—have reduced the number of woman-hours required in the home to perform the same duties previously, thus making possible additional hours of work that can be performed outside the home—work that often is for a financial return and thus classified as work performed in the labor force. In April, 1967, the Women's Bureau, U.S. Department of Labor, reported that women worked in all occupations in 1966 with 8.5 million in clerical jobs, 4.1 million in operatives, 4.1 million in service work, and 3.5 million in professional and technical occupations. With the change in clerical jobs and the increase in service work, girls of the future—nine out of ten girls will work at some time during their lifetime—may find that the percentage employed in the different occupations may change and may find they need to extend their education or engage in retraining in order to obtain the job they need for self-fulfillment.

A portrait of the typical worker in a given community today compared with a portrait of twenty years ago may show how the worker and the job structure of the community has changed. The same comparison for the unemployed within a given community may show considerable change also.

Technological revolutions are changing the employment picture, many times without the fanfare to point up the change (Nosow and Form, 1962, pp. 63–87), but both men and women need to receive the personalized occupational information that will not only keep them abreast of the changes, but also ready and prepared for the changes. An interesting point that is often forgotten: *implementation of technological changes can never occur until the labor force is prepared.* America has been fortunate in having a labor force that is flexible, educational and technical training systems that are adaptable, and an attitude that change for improvement is desirable. These same three qualities are not found extensively in underdeveloped countries. The more ready an individual is for consideration of new ideas, methods, training, education, and responsibilities, the more likely he is to have an opportunity for advancement. Technological changes can change man's role in the world of work and similarly man's changes can bring about technological and other changes in the world of work.

No one individual needs information on all occupations, but each individual needs information personalized to the point of assisting him to identify at various times in his life the occupational alternatives that he does have and the steps he might take to expand the alternatives or obtain additional information for making selection or decisions on the alternatives. The decision-making process requires more than just having the facts. Personalized information processes extended over a lifetime provide a backdrop of information that can be expanded when needed and extended beyond the decision-making process to enable evaluation of the decision and the results being received. Personalized information processes continue so that new and different decisions can and will be made as needed.

Geographical Considerations in Occupations

The approximately twenty-two thousand separate occupations are fairly well distributed throughout the United States in the 150 major labor areas that existed in 1966, but most geographic areas are void in certain occupations and have a concentration of certain other occupations. Even though one in six families moves each year and a high percentage of young people leave the community in which they are reared, variables do exist that prevent some individuals from being able to move to the geographical areas where they may have the best chance of employment in selected occupations.

Examples of geographical concentration of occupations would be many. Even though the automobile is manufactured in various parts of the United States, a worker has a better chance, based on the number of automobile workers per thousand in the labor force, of finding employment in the automobile industry in Michigan than in most of the other states. Shipbuilding would be another example in which the chances are better in those states with an ocean coastline, and then in selected areas of those states. Clothing industries would be another example. An interesting one to consider is the fruit and vegetable harvesters. Those individuals who want this type of work must follow the ripening of the crops across several states. The migrant farm worker has received considerable attention in recent years. He moves frequently while working and his place of residence often is occupied during a time of slack employment or unemployment. His children receive minimal education and his living conditions at the places of employment are often very poor. Even though the stay in any one place may be for a short period of time the poor living conditions are often repeated at the next location.

Because of health reasons, family ties, kind of weather desired, personality make-up as to living conditions, and many other variables, an individual often is not at liberty to consider all occupations for which he might be physically and mentally capable. For many individuals the geographic location of some occupations prevents them from being able to consider those occupation(s) within their alternatives.

Coupled with the recognition of increase and decrease in employment in different geographic areas should be an understanding of the research data about who migrates within the labor force. Samuel Saben, U.S. Bureau of Labor Statistics, reported in August, 1964 (p. 873), that unemployed workers were much more likely to migrate than employed workers and that on the average migrants were younger and less well established in job tenure. Jobless men who did migrate in 1962–1963 did better than those who did not move.

The percentage of increase in the projected labor force from 1970 to 1980 varies considerably from state to state. The three states with a projected increase over 30 per cent are Arizona (36.3), New Mexico (35.6), and Florida (33.5). Eight states have from 20 to 29.9 per cent increase projected: Utah (29.2), California (27.8), Colorado (24.5),

Louisiana (24.4), Delaware (22.7), Idaho (21.4), Texas (20.8), and Maryland (20.4). The state with the smallest projected increase is Rhode Island with 7.4 per cent. The total for the United States is a projected 18.1 per cent increase (Johnston and Methee, 1966, p. 1100).

Terminology and Definitions

Vocational development is used frequently to mean the extended growth of a person in his cognitive and affective processes related to vocations. *Occupational development* is sometimes used with the same meaning. Vocational development, rather than a choice or act, is accepted as being the philological framework for studying how individuals become engaged in different occupations. Super, Overstreet, et al., (1960, pp. 31–32) indicated that concepts in developmental psychology help to understand indices in vocational development: "(1) development proceeds from random, undifferentiated activity to goal-directed, specific activity, (2) development is in the direction of increasing awareness and orientation to reality, and (3) development is from dependence to increasing independence." Vocational development extends over many years beginning in early childhood and, for many, extending into retirement.

Career is a word often used in connection with the work one does. The definition is not consistent from one writer to another. In the dictionary *career* is defined as a running, a course of a person's life, especially in some particular pursuit, notable or conspicuous progress or success in one's chosen calling. Edward Gross uses the term "to refer to a succession of positions which have a pattern which is, to some extent, predictable and controllable" (Campbell, 1966, p. 55). *Career* generally refers to the long-time or life pursuit of a person. The term *career* is receiving increased use in counseling and guidance literature and is beginning to take on the meaning of the total sequence of activities, occupations, and positions associated with one's work throughout his lifetime.

Vocation, according to English and English in *A Comprehensive Dictionary of Psychological and Psychoanalytical Terms* (1958, p. 586), was "originally, a task in life to which one was 'called' either by Providence or by Nature." Today the term is used to refer to the way in which one earns his living and, as such, is often used interchangeably with the term *occupation. Vocation,* in general use, carries a connotation of lifelong, whereas *occupation* may more frequently refer to the ongoing activities in which one is engaged. Anne Roe (1956, p. 3) defined *occupation* as "whatever an adult spends most of his time doing . . . the major focus of a person's activities, and usually of his thoughts."

Work, as indicated earlier in this chapter, has different meanings depending upon the viewpoint taken. Work, as previously perceived, as drudgery and something to be avoided, is becoming an archive of today's generation. *Work* is taking on new social and psychological concepts and, as such, may be defined as a way of life in which one can find self-expression and self-fulfillment, whether the work activity is studying, singing, manual activities, traveling, or any other kind of activity in which the person sees his expenditure of energy as purposeful, useful, and self-rewarding, which in most cases will include benefit to society. *Work* for many has not achieved this new meaning and some people do not even believe the new meaning is within the realm of reality.

Job is "a group of similar positions in a single plant, business establishment, educational institution, or other organization" (Shartle, 1959, p. 23). The job differs from the position in that *position* refers to what one person does, thus making as many positions as employees. The confusion more frequently is between the usage of *occupation* and *job*, especially since the *Dictionary of Occupational Titles*, 1965, lists 21,741 separate occupations, which are "arranged alphabetically according to the job titles" (p. xv). Thus *occupation* is the broader term used to refer to similar jobs found in several establishments, whereas the term *job* generally refers to similar kinds of work within one establishment.

Employed persons, as reflected in the U.S. Bureau of Labor Statistics, include those (1) who work for pay or profit, (2) who work without pay for fifteen hours or more on a family farm or business, and (3) who do not work and are not seeking work but have a job or business from which they are temporarily absent because of vacation, illness, industrial dispute, bad weather, or taking time off for various other reasons. The unemployed persons include those (1) who are not working and are seeking work, (2) who are laid off or are to report to a new wage or salary job, and (3) who are not working and would be seeking employment except for temporary illness or because no work is available within the community for which they are qualified. The labor force is the composite of the persons included in the employed and unemployed classifications.

Classification Structures for Occupations

The classifications for occupations vary according to the purpose(s) for which the codification is used. Shartle presented four kinds of occupational classifications, including industrial, socio-economic, job characteristic, and worker characteristic (Borow, 1964, pp. 295–306). In general the Government uses the industry or the job characteristic as the basis for coding. The current *D.O.T.* does use the workers' characteristics more than previously.

Another way of grouping different occupational classifications would be their origins. One origin of classification is the *Federal Government*, which uses the Standard Industrial Classification, the Bureau of the Census Classification, the Department of Labor Classification (*Dictionary of Occupational Titles*), and military classifications. Another origin for classifying occupations is *society*, which according to sociological studies has been prestige, income, and other socio-economic classifications (Caplow, 1954; Centers, 1949; Nosow and Form, 1962, pp. 263–283). The *individual* himself throughout history has classified occupations on the basis of such factors as interest, skill, and ability. During this century another kind of classification has been added—one which has its origin in theory. Anne Roe's two-way classification of occupations (Roe, 1956, pp. 149–152) and Donald Super's three-dimensional classification of occupations (Super, 1957, pp. 48–50) are examples of the theorical classifications. (See Chapter 9.)

From the individual's viewpoint the classification that probably affects him the most is the *D.O.T.* Public and private employment offices use the *D.O.T.* code for assigning numbers to what work he has done and for considering him for referrals to new jobs. Unemployment insurance and physical disability claims are often keyed to the *D.O.T.* classification. In Chapter 12 is a description of the *D.O.T.* and the method used for coding occupations. If the person is in the military services, then the classification used by the armed forces becomes significant for the individal. The relationship between military and civilian occupations is important at time of entry or separation from the armed forces.

From the counselor's viewpoint the *D.O.T.* and possibly the military classifications will be the most used. However, for trends and comparative purposes the Bureau of Census Classification will be meaningful. The major eleven categories used in the Census Classification are listed in Figure 4-2 and Table 10-2. The Census Bureau and the *D.O.T.* classification systems differ significantly. The former is occupational and the latter is more worker oriented. For assisting individuals in understanding different occupational requirements and values the interest, skill, and ability classifications will be helpful, for which the 1966 *Supplement to the D.O.T.* may be a major reference. The counselor cannot afford to overlook the importance of societal factors, like prestige, income, and social rigidity, to a major occupational shift for an individual.

The classifications are each meaningful for the purposes designed, but often provide data that cannot be compared from one classification directly to another. The counselor's knowledge of the classifications would need to be extensive enough to enable him to determine the implications of the information for an individual. In the role and setting of most counselors, no need will exist for referring directly to the intricate details of each classification, but he should review regularly the information obtained on occupations irrespective of the classification system used in compiling the data.

Sociological Implications of Occupation

What one does as an occupation has sociological and psychological implications. Sociologists and social psychologists have completed studies on the social status of occupations and their change over a period of time. The main factors that seem to make a difference in the prestige of an occupation are two: (1) the amount of highly specialized training required for the occupation and (2) the extent of responsibility for the public welfare (Nosow and Form, 1962, p. 277). Studies conducted as much as a quarter of a century apart show a high degree of similarity in the ranking of different occupations.

For some persons the social acceptance and prestige of an occupation is of primary concern in determining whether or not they would be happy as an employee doing that kind of work. Decision-making based primarily on occupational ranking may, however, lead to more problems for the individual. Of course, skill and ability need to be considered; however, an individual who has a psychological need for recognition may find that of the two or three occupations he is considering his ability may enable him to gain more recognition from his peers in an occupation that is not as high in the prestige ranking. In other words, recognition may come more from one's peers and occupational associates than from society in general, which is the basis of the prestige ranking of occupations. Figure 10-4 is a schematic comparison of two approaches to considering prestige—interoccupational ranking and intra-inter-occupational ranking. In the latter consideration is given to prestige among the members within a given occupation. Thus, a person may find that in one occupation he would be high on the scale of recognition and prestige given by his peers, whereas in another occupation, which is higher in the interoccupational ranking, he would be lower in the scale of recognition and prestige received from his peers and occupational associates. The realization of this may help some persons to develop occupational aspirations in keeping with levels of expectations. On the other hand, the realization of possible lower recognition in a so-called higher prestige job may be what prevents some persons from being as flexible in occupational mobility as other persons. The individual's perception of prestige ranking and his use of it in his decision-making behavior may be important enough to give additional consideration in future decision-theory research as applied to occupational development.

PERSONALIZING OCCUPATIONAL INFORMATION

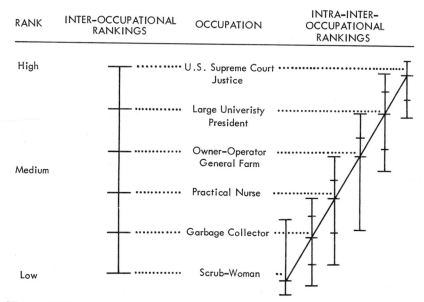

Figure 10-4. SCHEMATIC COMPARISON OF TWO DIFFERENT APPROACHES TO CONSIDERING PRESTIGE OF OCCUPATIONS—INTEROCCUPATIONAL RANKINGS AND INTRA-INTER-OCCUPATIONAL RANKINGS.

Demographic Factors

Demography means the statistical study of populations as to birth, marriages, mortality, health, and so on. The demographic data can have significant meaning in the study of occupations and the possibilities available in certain occupations as compared to other occupations for given individuals.

The population increase in the United States in any given period of time will have an effect upon the percentage of workers within given age brackets over the next one-half century. In 1960 the population of the United States was 181 million; projected figures for 1970 are 209 million, and for 1975, 226 million. The increase is at a rate of nearly 3 million a year in the 1960's and over 3 million a year in the first half of the 1970's. By 1975 the number of persons under fifteen years of age is estimated to be 64 million. Table 10-1 contains the percentage of change in the labor force by age by decades. The young fourteen- to twenty-four-year-old worker increased at a rate four times faster than the next highest during the 1960's. This large increase will move into the twenty-five- to thirty-four-year-old bracket during the 1970's.

The employment and unemployment rates and trends by occupa-

Table 10-1

PERCENTAGE CHANGE IN LABOR FORCE BY AGE (FOUR-
TEEN AND OVER) BY DECADES. ACTUAL 1950 AND 1960
AND PROJECTED 1970 AND 1980 LABOR FORCE DATA
USED FOR DETERMINING PERCENTAGES.

Age	From 1950 to 1960	From 1960 to 1970	From 1970 to 1980
14–24	2.7	48.2	18.3
25–34	−0.3	12.3	47.1
35–44	18.3	−1.8	12.0
45 and over	24.1	17.3	5.4
Total	12.9	17.7	17.9

Source: Based on material in *Education and Training:
The Bridge Between Man and His Work*, U.S. Department
of Health, Education, and Welfare, p. 4.

tional groups are important. The U.S. Department of Labor and Bureau
of the Census supply information regularly to assist in understanding
the changes. The occupational group with the largest number of workers
is the operatives and kindred workers (Figure 10-5), with approximately
seven out of ten of the workers being men. This group also has the
highest percentage of unemployed workers among both the white and
nonwhite labor force (Table 10-2). The second largest occupational
group as far as number of workers is clerical and kindred workers,
where seven out of ten workers are women. Approximately one third
of the white women are employed in the clerical group but only 11.8
per cent of the nonwhite. The clerical occupation group ranks first in
number of white women employed but ranks fourth in number of
nonwhite women employed. In unemployment the clerical occupation
group ranks second in number of white persons unemployed with work
experience within the group and ranks sixth for nonwhite persons.

In April, 1962, the U.S. Department of Labor made a detailed
survey of the characteristics of the unemployed (Stein, 1963, pp. 1407
and 1413). The reported figures were that one fifth of the labor force
experiences unemployment each year and that only one third of the labor
force was able to span a three-year period without unemployment. The
unemployment caused insufficient income to maintain living standards
and almost one half of the families in the unemployed group withdrew
funds from savings and nearly one quarter of the families borrowed
money. Many turned to friends and relatives for help. In 1966, the U.S.

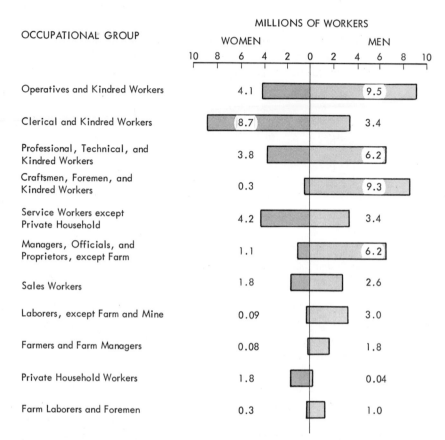

Figure 10-5. EMPLOYED PERSONS FOURTEEN YEARS OF AGE AND OVER BY MAJOR OCCUPATIONAL GROUP AND SEX, MARCH, 1967.

Source: Based upon data from Statistical Abstract of the United States, *1967, 88th annual edition, U.S. Department of Commerce, p. 230.*

Department of Labor reported about two-thirds of the male work force had year-round full-time jobs, whereas only 38 per cent of the women did (Hodge, 1966, p. 746).

The composition of the unemployed varies with the season. An approximation can be obtained through averaging survey results obtained at different times during the year. In 1965 and 1966, during a period of rapid economic expansion, four surveys were made. The approximate composition of the unemployed and the reasons why the unemployed looked for work were as follows: 40 per cent had lost their previous jobs, 15 per cent had quit their last jobs, 25 per cent were re-entering the labor force after a period of absence, and 20 per cent were new entrants who had never held a full-time job (Hoyle, 1967, p. 32).

Table 10-2

PERCENTAGE DISTRIBUTION OF EMPLOYED AND UNEMPLOYED PERSONS BY OCCUPATIONAL GROUP FOR 1965; PERCENTAGE SHOWN BY COLOR AND SEX FOR EMPLOYED PERSONS AND BY COLOR FOR UNEMPLOYED PERSONS.

Occupational Group	Employed*						Unemployed**	
	WHITE			NONWHITE			WHITE	NONWHITE
	BOTH SEXES	MALE	FEMALE	BOTH SEXES	MALE	FEMALE		
Operatives and kindred workers	18.2	19.8	15.1	21.3	26.1	14.4	23.3	18.7
Clerical and kindred workers	16.3	7.1	34.1	8.2	5.7	11.8	12.3	5.1
Craftsmen, foremen, and kindred workers	13.5	19.9	1.1	6.7	10.9	0.7	11.3	4.7
Professional, technical, and kindred workers	13.0	12.6	13.7	6.8	5.6	8.4	4.3	2.0
Managers, officials, and proprietors, except farm	11.1	14.3	4.8	2.6	3.4	1.5	2.9	0.6
Service workers, except private household	8.7	6.0	14.0	19.0	15.1	24.5	10.4	17.8
Sales workers	7.1	6.5	8.2	1.9	1.8	2.0	5.5	1.6
Laborers, except farm and mine	4.5	6.5	0.4	12.7	21.1	0.7	8.9	15.1
Farmers and farm managers	3.3	4.7	0.5	1.8	2.7	0.5	0.3	0.1
Farm laborers and foremen	2.4	2.4	2.3	6.3	7.2	5.1	2.3	5.7
Private household workers	2.0	0.1	5.6	12.7	0.4	30.3	1.3	8.8
Unemployed persons who never held a full-time job							17.2	19.8
Total	100.0	100.0	100.0	100.0	100.0	100.0	100.0	100.0

Source: "Labor Force and Employment in 1965," *Special Labor Force Report* No. 69, U.S. Department of Labor, Reprint No. 2494, 1966.

* C-7, p. A-22
** Table F-5, p. A-37

Employees stayed with the same job or employer on an average of 4.2 years in 1966, which was a decline from 4.6 years in 1963 (Hamel, 1967, p. 31). The reasons for change may in part be because of a rise in the proportion of young workers in the labor force or to rapid economic expansion, which enabled workers to make job shifts to improve their economic status. The decrease may reflect a trend of employees remaining on one job or with a given employer a shorter period of time, thus emphasizing the need, more frequently, for personalized occupational information to assist the individual in his progress evaluation as he implements previous decisions and to assist in the new decision-making process that concerns occupations and jobs appropriate for him.

Over 90 per cent of the men between the ages of eighteen and sixty-four were in the labor force in 1966, thus four and a half million men of the civilian, noninstitutionalized population of that age range were outside the labor force in 1966. Of this group the proportionate number was higher for nonwhites than whites, with 6½ per cent of the nonwhite men aged twenty-five to fifty-four and 3 per cent of the white men in the same age group neither working nor seeking work. The reasons for remaining outside the labor force include 1.9 million who were going to school, 1.1 who were unable to work because of long-term physical or mental disability, and the remaining number, who were in such classifications as early retirees, waiting to return to school or enter the Armed Forces, expecting to move to another community, or undecided as to what to do after having quit a job. Approximately 2.9 million of the 4.5 million men out of the labor force were living in families, and over one half of the 2.9 million were heads of families (Holland, 1967, pp. 5–7).

Impediments to Occupational Mobility

Even when the economy is rapidly expanding impediments exist to an individual's occupational mobility. In counseling with individuals, counselors often find many of them desire to improve and are willing to change, except conditions prevail over which they have limited or no control, which therefore prevent occupational mobility. Family ties are one of the conditions. The family ties are generally impediments only when the change in occupation would necessitate a geographic move.

Today the fringe benefits often increase with the length of time an employee has worked with an employer; thus, if occupational improvement would necessitate a change in employer, the person may feel that the loss in fringe benefits is greater than the gain in occupational position. Fringe benefits may be one of the reasons for more frequent change in jobs and employers among young workers than among older employees.

Race, color, and creed are supposed to be outlawed as a basis for considering one applicant over another. The practice may be hard to prove in court, but those of a race, color, or creed different from the other employees within a given employment setting often have reason to believe that these conditions are impediments to their equal consideration. Much has been done to remove as a barrier race, color, or creed.

Table 10-3

PERCENTAGE OF UNEMPLOYMENT FOR 1950 AND 1962 AND PERCENTAGE CHANGE IN UNEMPLOYMENT ACCORDING TO YEARS OF SCHOOLING COMPLETED.

Years of Schooling Completed	Percentage Unemployment 1950	1962	Percentage Change in Unemployment 1950 to 1962
0–7	8.4	9.2	+9.5
8	6.6	7.5	+13.6
9–11	6.9	7.3	+5.8
12	4.6	4.8	+4.4
13–15	4.1	4.0	−2.4
16 or more	2.2	1.4	−36.4
All Groups	6.2	6.0	−3.5

Reports such as *Company Experience with Negro Employment*, by Habbe, are becoming available on the practices, and counselors need to keep informed.

The average educational level of the labor force is increasing annually, as was indicated in the educational information part of this book. A study of the educational level of the unemployed shows how the percentage of unemployed increased for those possessing a low educational level and reduced for those with more education. In Table 10–3 are the percentages of unemployment for 1950 and 1962, shown according to the years of schooling completed. The lack of adequate education and training becomes a limiting factor to the number of occupations and industries in which an individual can be considered for employment; thus, even if he is employed once, his chances of being re-employed if ever out of work are reduced if he has limited schooling.

Another impediment is the attitude of the worker. Once in a job and having satisfactory experience he often tends to gain in a feeling of security. A change in job means possibly insecurity to many and thus becomes a reason for not changing jobs. To offset the feeling of insecurity there must be benefits from the employee's vantage point, such as income increase, fringe benefits, higher prestige, better working conditions, or other benefits that the employee considers important. Personal-social information (Chapters 14–18) is an important part of the occupational considerations of an individual and should be interwoven with the educational and occupational information.

People often are able to move from one occupation to another, but the conditions necessary for doing so vary with the occupation and with the individual. Research studies have provided valuable information but have not revealed the exact methods for effectively moving from one occupation to another; however, from the literature one can identify some general guidelines as to the characteristics individuals frequently possess who do make upward occupational mobility. First, the person should possess *communication skills*. Employees are becoming more involved as members of a team rather than as isolated workers, thus requiring better communication skills to be able to work with other employees. Second, the person should have a *positive attitude*. The new job has to be one into which the employee wants to move and one in which he has a positive attitude about himself as an employee in it. Third, the person should possess an *educational potential*. Jobs today often require additional education or training before an individual can start on the job. Some jobs necessitate that periodically the employee obtain additional training as the tools, equipment, or material used changes; thus the employee has to have an educational potential. Fourth, the person should have the *willingness and the self-security* that seems to be necessary for change.

Influence of Labor Unions and Collective Bargaining

Labor organizations are an integral part of the industrial society and must be considered within the occupational information of many occupations. The objectives of labor unions generally include protection of workers from arbitrary or discriminatory decisions of management, improving employees' peace of mind through greater job security, and raising the level of dignity and respect with which wage earners are treated. The number of United States workers with membership in unions in 1964 was 16.8 million with five states having nearly one half the members—New York, California, Pennsylvania, Illinois, and Ohio. The union membership has varied between one fourth and one fifth of the total labor force throughout the last quarter of a century. The proportion has been one third or less of the nonagricultural employment (*Statistical Abstract of the United States*, 1966, p. 246).

Workers in the past identified with the business or industry where they worked. Today workers belonging to a union often identify with the union as much as or more than with the business or industrial concern where they work. Workers in occupational groups high in union membership often must surrender the freedom to manage their own affairs except as they influence the decisions of the union. The worker is often discouraged from displaying initiative beyond that required by the job because in many businesses and industries where union contracts exist, promotions to better paying jobs depend upon impersonal seniority rules (Packard, 1959, p. 300).

Labor unions and collective bargaining are important considerations in today's occupational world, and the counselor has the responsibility of assisting individuals to obtain personalized, comprehensive, reliable information on unions. The unions potentially affect the individual and his occupational world whether he becomes a union member or not.

The counselor probably will not be competent in knowing all of the labor union information a given person may need, but the counselor can facilitate the information-obtaining process for the individual and the counselor can assist in identification of information that will have personal meaning. The counselor also can assist in bringing about an integration of information in all three areas—educational (Chapters 4–8), occupational (Chapters 9–13), and personal-social (Chapters 14–18).

Governmental Influence in World of Work

The Federal, state, and local governments are becoming more influential in the world of work each year. The extent of influence of the Federal Government alone is probably too comprehensive for any one counselor to know and understand completely. Each counselor can and should have general governmental information pertinent to his clientele. For more specific or related information, he should know where it can be obtained or to whom he can refer an individual for such information.

Governmental influence is felt by both the employer and the employee. A discussion of the Federal laws that affect the world of work is beyond the scope of this book; however, the counselor may want to become familiar with the Taft-Hartley Act, the Right-to-Work Laws, the Minimum Wage Laws, the Civil Rights Acts, the Antitrust Act, price control legislation, the Economic Act, housing laws (where people can rent or buy), the Equal Opportunity Act, the Vocational Education Act, the Manpower Development and Training Act, and many more.

Summary

The world and the jobs in it are changing today at a faster rate than ever before in history. These changes affect what the worker does and how he does it. Who works, at what age, and how much schooling he possesses are different today than in the last century or even ten years ago; thus, work in the life of an individual takes on a new and different role.

Geographic considerations become important as the extensiveness of occupational openings and kind of jobs are related to geographic regions of the country. Some persons can move to the jobs, whereas others cannot move; or if they can, the move is restricted to certain geographic regions. Some workers want to be migrants or move every few years, whereas others prefer to or must remain in a given part of the country, thus making it necessary for them to engage in whatever job(s) is (are) available.

Terms such as *career, vocation,* and *occupation* have different meanings to different authors. The term *vocational development* is being used rather consistently to mean the extended growth of a person in his cognitive and affective processes related to vocations. *Work* is a word used by professionals and laymen to mean different things at different times, but many people today are beginning to see work as an integral, expressive part of life, necessary for self-fulfillment.

Occupations are classified by different means for different purposes and the counselor needs to be able to interpret the information and its implications regardless of the classification system used. Much of the information has sociological and psychological implications that often are not understood by the person. Helping an individual obtain demographic data and other essential information so as to be meaningful and useful for the individual is an essential part of personalizing occupational information processes, not only prior to his first job, but also at various times throughout life, to enable him to have maximum occupational mobility at the most opportune times.

SELECTED REFERENCES

American Women, Report of the President's Commission on the Status of Women, 1963. Washington, D.C.: Superintendent of Documents, 1963, 86 pages.

Baer, Max F., and Edward C. Roeber. Occupational Information: the Dynamics of Its Nature and Use. Chicago: Science Research Associates, Inc., 1964. Pp. 15–90, 162–228, 229–256, 408–417.

Bogan, Forrest A., and Harvey R. Hamel. "Multiple Jobholders in May, 1963," *Monthly Labor Review,* March 1964, and Special Labor Force Report No. 39, pp. 1–9, plus A-1 through A-9.

Bogan, Forrest A., and Thomas E., Swanstrom. "Work Experience of the Population in 1965," *Monthly Labor Review,* December 1966, pp. 1369–1377.

Borow, Henry, ed. *Man in a World at Work.* Boston: Houghton Mifflin Company, 1964. Pp. 96–173; 285–309.

Brickman, William W., and Stanley Lehrer, eds. *Automation, Education, and Human Values.* New York: School and Society Books, 1966. 419 pages.

Business Week, July 23, 1966, p. 8.

Campbell, Robert E., ed. *Guidance in Vocational Education: Guidelines for Research and Practice.* Columbus, O.: The Center for Vocational and Technical Education, The Ohio State University, 1966. 181 pages.

Caplow, Theodore. *The Sociology of Work.* Minneapolis: University of Minnesota Press, 1954. 330 pages.

Census, Bureau of the, *Statistical Abstract of the United States, 1967,* 88th annual edition. Washington, D.C.: U.S. Department of Commerce, 1967. 1050 pages.

Centers, Richard. *The Psychology of Social Classes.* Princeton, N.J.: Princeton University Press, 1949. 244 pages.

Dictionary of Occupational Titles, 3rd ed. Washington, D.C.: Bureau of Employment Security, Manpower Administration, U.S. Department of Labor, 1965. Vol. I, *Definitions of Titles;* Vol. II, *Occupational Classification.* Also *A Supplement to the Dictionary of Occupational Titles,* 1966.

Ginzberg, Eli. *The Development of Human Resources.* New York: McGraw-Hill, Inc., 1966. 350 pages.

Glick, Peter, Jr. "Three-Dimensional Classification of the Occupations of College Graduates," *The Vocational Guidance Quarterly,* **14** (Spring 1966), 130–135.

Gross, Edward. "A Sociological Approach to the Analysis of Preparation for Work Life," *The Personnel and Guidance Journal,* **45** (January 1967), 416–423.

Habbe, Stephen. *Company Experience with Negro Employment,* Studies in Personnel Policy, No. 201, Vol. 1. New York: Service Extension Division, National Industrial Conference Board, Inc., 1966. 177 pages.

Hamel, Harvey R. "Job Tenure of Workers, January 1966," *Monthly Labor Review,* January 1967, pp. 31–37. Also see *Special Labor Force Report* No. 77, Reprint No. 2513, pp. 31–37, plus pp. A-1 through A-14.

Herzberg, Frederick. *Work and the Nature of Man.* Cleveland: The World Publishing Company, 1966. 224 pages.

Higher Education and Jobs. Columbus, O.: Ohio Board of Regents, no date. 19 pages.

Highlights from the 1966 Manpower Report, A Summary of the Report Transmitted to the Congress, Washington, D.C.: U.S. Department of Labor, 1966. O-221-349. 40 pages.

Hodge, Claire. "The Effects of Employment Redistribution on Earnings," *Monthly Labor Review,* July 1966, pp. 744–748. Also see *Special Labor Force Report* No. 70, Reprint No. 2496, pp. 744–748 plus pp. A-1 through A-5.

Holland, Susan S. "Adult Men Not in the Labor Force," *Monthly Labor Review,* March 1967, pp. 5–15. Also see *Special Labor Force Report* No. 79, Reprint No. 2520, pp. 5–15.

Holland, Susan S. "Long-Term Unemployment in the 1960's," *Monthly Labor*

Review, September 1965, pp. 1069–1076. Also see *Special Labor Force Report* No. 58, Reprint No. 2475, pp. 1069–1076, plus pp. A-1 through A-7.

Hoppock, Robert. *Occupational Information: Where to Get It and How to Use It in Counseling and in Teaching.* 3rd ed. New York: McGraw-Hill Inc., 1967. Pp. 148–164; 481–500.

Hoyle, Kathryn D. "Why the Unemployed Look for Work," *Monthly Labor Review,* February 1967, pp. 32–38. See also *Special Labor Force Report* No. 78, Reprint No. 2518, pp. 32–38.

Isaacson, Lee E. *Career Information in Counseling and Teaching.* Boston: Allyn and Bacon, Inc., 1966. Pp. 41–101, 166–174, 185–211.

Johnston, Denis F., and George R. Methee. "Labor Force Projections by State, 1970 and 1980," *Monthly Labor Review,* October 1966, pp. 1098–1175. Also see *Special Labor Force Report* No. 74, pp. 1098–1175.

Kaufman, Jacob J., et al. *The Role of the Secondary Schools in the Preparation of Youth for Employment: A Comparative Study of the Vocational, Academic, and General Curricula.* University Park, Pa.: Institute for Research on Human Resources, The Pennsylvania State University, 1967.

Labor, U.S. Dept. of, Bureau of Labor Statistics, "Labor Force and Employment in 1965," *Special Labor Force Report* No. 69, Reprint No. 2494. 40 pages.

Learned, Stanley. *An Oilman's Glimpse at the Next 100 Years.* Bartlesville, Okla.: Public Relations Division, Phillips Petroleum Company, 1966. 12 pages.

Mann, Floyd C., and L. R. Hoffman. *Automation and the Worker.* New York: Holt, Rinehart and Winston, Inc., 1960. 272 pages.

Manpower Implications of Automation. Papers Presented by the U.S. Department of Labor at the Organization for Economic Cooperation and Development North American Regional Conference, December 8–10, 1964. Washington, D.C.: Office of Manpower, Automation, and Training, U.S. Department of Labor, September 1965. 86 pages.

Norris, Willa. *Occupational Information in the Elementary School.* Chicago: Science Research Associates, Inc., 1963. Pp. 108–116.

Norris, Willa, Franklin R. Zeran, and Raymond N. Hatch. *The Information Service in Guidance,* 2nd ed. Chicago: Rand McNally & Company, 1966. Pp. 31–56, 65–148.

Nosow, Sigmund and William H. Form. eds. *Man, Work, and Society: A Reader in the Sociology of Occupations.* New York: Basic Books, Inc., 1962. 612 pages.

Office of Education. *Educationally Deficient Adults, Their Education and Training Needs.* A report of a survey conducted by the Information and Training Service, A Division of McGraw-Hill, Inc., New York, N.Y. Washington, D.C.: U.S. Government Printing Office, 1965. 60 pages.

Packard, Vance. *The Status Seekers: An Exploration of Class Behavior in America and the Hidden Barriers That Affect You, Your Community, Your Future.* New York: David McKay Co., Inc., 1959. 376 pages.

Patterson, Cecil H. "Occupational Information in School Counseling." *The*

Counselor in the School: Selected Readings. New York: McGraw-Hill, Inc. 1967. Part VII, pp. 305–316.

Reiss, Albert J., et al. *Occupations and Social Status.* New York: The Free Press of Glencoe, Inc., 1961. 305 pages.

Roe, Anne. *The Psychology of Occupations.* New York: John Wiley & Sons, Inc., 1956. 340 pages.

Roe, Anne, and Marvin Siegelman. *The Origin of Interests.* Washington, D.C.: American Personnel and Guidance Association, 1964. 98 pages.

Saben, Samuel. "Geographic Mobility and Employment Status, March 1962–March 1963," *Monthly Labor Review,* August 1964, pp. 873–881. Also see *Special Labor Force Report* No. 44, pp. 873–881 plus A-1 through A-13.

Samler, Joseph. "Psycho-Social Aspects of Work: A Critique of Occupational Information," in *The Counselor in the School: Selected Readings,* Cecil H. Patterson, ed. New York: McGraw-Hill, Inc., 1967. Chap. 37, pp. 305–316.

Shartle, Carroll L. *Occupational Information: Its Development and Application,* 3rd ed. Englewood Cliffs, N.J.: Prentice-Hall, Inc., 1959. Pp. 23, 62–75, 83–89, 135–168, 341–352.

Sheppard, Harold L., and A. Harvey Belitsky. *The Job Hunt: Job-Seeking Behavior of Unemployed Workers in a Local Economy.* Baltimore, Md.: The Johns Hopkins Press, 1966. 270 pages.

Shostak, Arthur B., and William Gomberg, eds. *Blue-Collar World: Studies of the American Worker.* Englewood Cliffs, N.J.: Prentice-Hall, Inc., 1964. 622 pages.

Stein, Robert L. "Work History, Attitudes, and Income of the Unemployed," *Monthly Labor Review,* December 1963, pp. 1405–1413. Also see *Special Labor Force Report* No. 37, Reprint No. 2430, pp. 1405–1413 plus A-1 through A-7.

Stoodley, Bartlett H. ed. *Society and Self.* New York: The Free Press, 1962. 713 pages.

Super, Donald E. *The Psychology of Careers: An Introduction to Vocational Development.* New York: Harper & Row, 1957. 362 pages.

Super, Donald E., and Phoebe L. Overstreet, et al. *The Vocational Maturity of Ninth-Grade Boys.* New York: Bureau of Publications, Teachers College, Columbia University, 1960. 212 pages.

Tennyson, W. Wesley, Thomas A. Soldahl, and Charlotte Mueller. *The Teacher's Role in Career Development.* Washington, D.C.: National Vocational Guidance Association, 1965 Revision. Pp. 28–42.

Thomas, Lawrence G. *The Occupational Structure and Education.* Englewood Cliffs, N.J.: Prentice-Hall, Inc., 1956. 502 pages.

Tilgher, Adriano. *Work: What It Has Meant to Men Through the Ages.* New York: Harcourt, Brace and Company, 1930. 225 pages.

Venn, Grant, assisted by Theodore J. Marchese, Jr. *Man, Education, and Work: Post-Secondary Vocational and Technical Education.* Washington, D.C.: American Council on Education, 1964. 184 pages.

Williamson, E. G. *Vocational Counseling: Some Historical, Philosophical, and Theoretical Perspectives.* New York: McGraw-Hill, Inc., 1965. Pp. 15–43.

Wolfbein, Seymour L. *Employment and Unemployment in the United States: A Study of the American Labor Force.* Chicago: Science Research Associates, Inc., 1964. 339 pages.

Women's Bureau. *1965 Handbook on Women Workers,* Bulletin No. 290. Washington, D.C.: U.S. Department of Labor, 1966. 321 pages.

Women's Bureau. *Expanding Opportunities for Girls: Their Special Counseling Needs.* Washington, D.C.: U.S. Department of Labor, April, 1967, WB67–281. 4 pages.

Chapter 11

Sources and Types of

Occupational Information

The occupational world is a world in transition and the counselor will have to keep pace with this transition if he wishes to conduct high caliber vocational counseling.—ADAMS, 1965, p. 364.

Counselors need to become aware of the breadth and depth of occupational information and to improve effectiveness and efficiency in obtaining information that will assist an individual's development on an individual and group basis. Occupational information sources will need to include people, literature, and places of employment and to consider the various occupational information types that are available from each source. As sources are identified, criteria will need to be used for selecting the most appropriate sources and types for each person so that he may achieve his objectives at that time and to recognize that as he develops over time different sources and types of occupational information may be needed.

Occupational Information for a Developmental Approach

Occupational information is a continuous facet of development for an individual. No stopping point exists if the individual is to continue his vocational development throughout his lifetime. As a youngster, he gets his information from persons, ideas, and things involved in the home environment, then later branches out into the neighborhood, the community, the schools, and today's total society, which, to some extent, means ultimately into international settings. Today, exposure by television and travel to national, international, and world affairs may enable the individual to operate in a much larger circle of experiences and he may become concerned about vocational topics on a national level before locally. The human being is surrounded with information, but the important point is that information be in a form that will or does have meaning to him. *Pacing* and *readiness* should receive prominent consideration; if not, even though the individual may be surrounded by information and experiences, he may perceive only limited significance to himself.

Occupational maturity is a longitudinal process, with information contributing to an individual's development both upward (vertically) and outward, broadening (horizontally). An individual begins in a limited sphere consisting of the home environment as his world. As information and experiences broaden, including a larger sphere of people, ideas, and things in his environment, he may advance in occupational maturity (Figure 11-1).

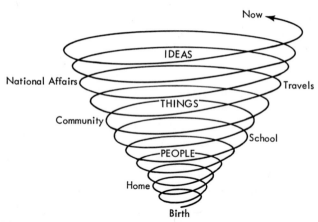

Figure 11-1. DIAGRAMMATIC REPRESENTATION OF HOW OCCUPATIONAL IN-FORMATION PLUS EXPERIENCES CONTRIBUTE TO AN UPWARD (VERTICAL) AND OUTWARD, BROADENING (HORIZONTAL) DEVELOPMENT, THUS ADVANCING THE INDIVIDUAL'S OCCUPATIONAL MATURATION.

Each circle or sphere does not replace the previous one but does expand scope so that an individual can potentially become more involved, thus influencing both his cognitive and affective processes in relation to the occupational world. Without the expanding sphere of people, ideas, and things an individual may never develop occupationally. An extreme example would be a handicapped individual who is sheltered within the home to such an extent that he is not permitted outside of the home except within the immediate neighborhood and then only when accompanied by a member of the family, not allowed to participate in school or community activities, nor to see and hear radio and television. To such a person the occupational world would be very small. However, the reverse could be true if this individual receives pertinent information and experiences to encourage his development to the fullest potential. His world of occupational understanding would continually grow and enlarge throughout his lifetime and he might become a contributing member of society, in which his work becomes an important part of his life fulfillment. For each individual, then, occupational information must be based upon his perceived world (Chapter 14) in order to contribute to his development.

Occupational Information for the 3-D Concept

Occupational information processes needs to be personalized, which includes systematizing so that the individual can understand and use the information, pacing information at a rate and depth harmonious with the individual's development, and facilitating selection of pertinent information to enable internalizing by the individual. Selection and perception are both major concerns in personalizing occupational information, and probably equally important is integration—the extent to which the individual interweaves attitudes about himself and the external occupational information. At the point of integration he begins perceiving his potential utilization of the information, possibly requiring additional information about self or the world of work, carrying through assimilation and integration into his own private world, exploring new ideas or feelings stimulated as a result of gaining the information, and/or taking action, possibly including preparation for or actual decision-making as a result of the information. Personal-social information (see Chapters 14–18) is an integral part of the decision-making process.

As a counselor seeks sources of occupational information, he must be concerned with various media. To serve some individuals he will need to use his ingenuity and creativity to find sources that will assist the individual in progressing to the third depth—feedback—so the person can continue his occupational maturation at as rapid a pace as possible for him at the time. Occupational information should serve to enlarge and enrich one's images about the world of work and himself as an integral part of it. For some, the experiences must come from firsthand involvement with work—primary experiences—whereas for others the major portion of the information can come through other media, such as publications, audio-visual aids, computerized occupational information, interviews, role-playing, and simulated occupational environments that are secondary experiences, or what Calia (1966, pp. 322–323) called "vicarious explorations." The 3-D concept emphasizes the information's being personalized in an area and at a depth at which the person can internalize and utilize the information. Another emphasis in the 3-D concept is the continuity of information—fluctuation in depth according to the development of the individual. Sources are identified not to submit information to but rather to have resources from which selections could be made of various kinds of information and media.

Sources of Occupational Information

Today, with the rapid increase in information and the facilities to reproduce copies, selectivity becomes a major factor in obtaining the most pertinent information for individuals in a particular setting. A counselor has almost unlimited sources from which to obtain or to which to refer individuals for occupational information that will meet present or potential needs.

In a school setting, occupational information becomes an important contribution to individual development, whether in the elementary, junior high, senior high, or post-high-school—occupational information either for the student or for those who work with the students. The information must be appropriate for the level of understanding of each individual regardless of the chronological age or school grade.

In settings other than schools, such as employment services and rehabilitation centers, occupational information applicable to the clientele must be available at the occupational maturity and reading levels needed. The varying types of individuals in such settings in regard to age, educational maturity, abilities, interests, understanding, and other variables (see Chapter 14) create a need for a wider range of variety of information on all three depths—broadening, specific, and feedback— as well as for information within each depth geared to the variable characteristics of individuals. Such settings perhaps will involve a greater diversity of individuals than a setting in an elementary school or another particular school setting. However, information in the particular school setting will need to be available at all three depths and at different levels of comprehension and maturity within each depth, as is true for information for other settings, but the varying types of individuals probably will be more restricted in range because of a certain commonality within the situation.

Sources of occupational information may be classified under similar headings to those of the educational information sources, with one modification. Because of concern for occupational information rather than educational information, a change is made from "educational and training institutions" to *"places of employment"* as a major source classification. The other two classifications were *people* (interaction with) and *publications* (literature and other canned media), which may remain the same in occupations as in education.

People—Interaction With

An individual's home environment and the persons involved in it—parents, siblings, grandparents, and other relatives (see Chapters 15 and 17)—becomes probably his first source of information concerning the world of work. His work world at first is the home life—mother involved in household chores and/or outside employment, father working outside the home, as well as older brothers or sisters and other relatives. Their attitudes, their satisfaction or dissatisfaction, and other information conveyed about their work begins the individual's perception of the occupational world—attitude formation and general information. Later, neighbors, the groceryman, the milkman, and other employed persons involved in the life of the child expand his information about the world of work. Radio, television, and his travel also broaden his contact and are factors in formation of attitudes about the world of work.

As the counselor begins to work with an individual in the area of occupational information, he needs to recognize that the individual has integrated previous information into his frame of reference as he perceived it, not necessarily realistically nor as others perceive it, however. Involving an individual with other persons who potentially can supply occupational information will enable the individual to obtain "structured information" according to the perception of those persons. The individual then needs assistance in developing the ability to analyze different information and implications as they apply to him.

A list can be compiled of persons who potentially can serve as a source of occupational information, beginning with persons involved in the limits of the home environment of the young child and continuing through his lifetime. The individual may contact persons who know about but are not actively involved in the particular work activity (interinformation) or who are participants within the occupational setting (intrainformation). Some of the persons listed would remain sources of occupational information throughout the lifetime of the individual, whereas others would be for single contacts or of limited duration.

The roles different persons serve as they assist an individual in obtaining and integrating occupational information vary from one time to another and from one individual to another who is to receive the information. At times an individual may be consulting several source people and replacing or extending the sources of one by another. A counselor, considering his employment setting, would attempt to identify persons as occupational sources who would be most appropriate for serving the needs of individuals to be referred. A partial list of potential people for supplying information may include the following:

PEOPLE ASSOCIATED WITH SCHOOLS
teachers
principals and other administrative officials
counselors
school nurse
social worker
psychologist
secretaries
cafeteria and other auxiliary personnel
guest speakers at the school
school alumni
parents of students
other students, particularly the ones employed

BUSINESS AND INDUSTRY PERSONNEL
personnel directors
educational or training director of respective business or industry
officers of businesses or industrial plants
officials and members of labor unions
other employees of respective firms—sales personnel, cashiers, fore-
    men, skilled or semiskilled employees, laborers, and so on
coworkers (if the individual wanting information is already em-
    ployed)

FRIENDS AND ASSOCIATES
parents
friends
brothers and sisters
other relatives
other associates

OTHER COMMUNITY PERSONS
ministers and other church or synagogue employees
lay workers in church or synagogue, such as Sunday school teachers
family insurance agent
physicians
dentists
lawyers
bankers
policemen
garage and service station attendants
YMCA, YWCA, and other organization personnel
accountants and representatives from other occupations
government officials (local, state, national, international)
employment agency personnel

A total list of persons who could potentially supply information is practically inexhaustible; however, a counselor would attempt to identify those who could be contacted by an individual who needs pertinent occupational information. Willingness to be contacted on the part of the person identified should be established by the counselor prior to his recommending that an individual contact a certain person.

Publications—Literature and Other Canned Media

(Also see Chapter 6.) Publications as a source for occupational information are more extensive than for either educational information or personal-social information. Classifications of sources as used for educational information can be applied for occupational information—*commercial publishers, tests and test information, associations and organizations, government publishers, businesses and industries,* and *educational and training institutions.* Some publication sources because of the scope of their many publications will be listed in both educational and occupational information. Generally the counselor needs only to write asking that his name be placed on the publisher's mailing list to receive notification of counseling and guidance material and, as such, usually receive notifications of materials in all areas. For convenient references some of the more frequently used publication sources are listed.

COMMERCIAL PUBLISHERS. The setting in which a counselor works would determine his potential users and the kind of occupational information that would be beneficial. He would select only those commercial publishers who could supply pertinent information for individuals in the particular setting. The following list should be supplemented as the counselor identifies other sources. For additional information on each source given see the Address Index.

Academic Press, Inc.
Allyn and Bacon, Inc.
ALP Publications, Inc.
American Guidance Services, Inc.
Associated Publishers
Bellman Publishing Company
B'nai B'rith Vocational Service
W. C. Brown Company, Publishers
The Bruce Publishing Company
Careers
The Center for Applied Research in Education, Inc.
Children's Press, Inc.
Chronicle Guidance Publications, Inc.
Condé Nast Publications, Inc.
Doubleday & Company, Inc.

Educators Progress Service
Edu-Craft Incorporated
Finney Company
Free Press of Glencoe
Golden Press, Inc.
Gregg Division, McGraw-Hill, Inc.
Guidance Associates
Guidance Publications Center
E. M. Hale and Company
Harcourt, Brace & World, Inc.
Harper & Row, Publishers
D. C. Heath and Company
Holt, Rinehart, and Winston, Inc.
Houghton Mifflin Company
Alfred A. Knopf, Inc.
J. B. Lippincott Company
Little, Brown and Company
Lothrop, Lee & Shepard Company, Inc.
The Macmillan Company
Maco Publishing Company, Inc.
Macrae Smith Company
McGraw-Hill, Inc.
McKnight & McKnight Publishing Company
David McKay Co., Inc.
Julian Messner, Inc.
William Morrow and Company, Inc.
National Directory Service
National Industrial Conference Board, Inc.
Thomas Nelson & Sons
The Odyssey Press, Inc.
Pitman Publishing Corporation
Prentice-Hall, Inc.
The Psychological Corporation
G. P. Putnam's Sons
Rand McNally & Company
Randall Publishing Co.
Random House, Inc.
Research Publishing Co.
Richard Rosen Press, Inc.
Science Research Associates, Inc.
Scott, Foresman and Company
Simon and Schuster, Inc.
South-Western Publishing Company
The United Educators, Inc.

Vantage Press
Vocational Guidance Manuals
Henry A. Walck, Inc.
Franklin Watts, Inc.
Wayne Publishers
John Wiley & Sons, Inc.
H. W. Wilson Company
World Trade Academy Press

Tests and Test Information. Tests and test information in the area
of occupational information are essential for a comprehensive coverage
of the area. As in the educational information area, test results may serve
as a source for feedback. Tests and information about tests may be needed
by other persons working with an individual, such as a teacher, as well
as by the individual and the counselor. A list of publishers of tests and
test information would include the following and should be modified to
include other tests and test information sources to provide the resources
needed in the local setting. Addresses are provided in the Address Index.

American Guidance Service, Inc.
California Test Bureau
Educational Testing Service
Harcourt, Brace, & World, Inc.
Personnel Press, Inc.
The Psychological Corporation
Science Research Associates, Inc.
Stanford University Press
U.S. Employment Service

Associations and Organizations. Publications are produced by
associations and organizations to serve at least two purposes and maybe
three: (1) for the association or organization for a perpetuation of its
purposes and for recruitment; (2) for users of the publications, other
than members of the association or organization, a source of occupational
information, biased to some extent, but pertinent to the individual in his
occupational development; and (3) for some associations and organizations publications are produced as a service to the public.

The following list contains examples of associations and organizations
from which occupational information may be acquired by the counselor
and/or by the individual desiring information. Addresses are provided
in the Address Index.

Alumnae Advisory Center, Inc.
American Association of Advertising Agencies
American Astronomical Society
American Bakers Association

American Baptist Convention
American Chemical Society
American Council on Education
American Dental Association
The American Dietetic Association
American Foot Health Foundation
AFL-CIO
American Home Economics Association
American Hospital Association
American Hotel and Motel Association
American Institute of Certified Public Accountants
American Iron and Steel Institute
American Library Association
The American Lutheran Church
American Medical Association
American Nurses' Association
American Personnel and Guidance Association
American Psychological Association
American School Counselor Association
American Society of Biological Chemists, Inc.
American Society of Traffic and Transportation
American Veterinary Medical Association
Associated Master Barbers and Beauticians of America
Association of American Railroads
Chamber of Commerce (local)
College Entrance Examination Board
Council for Church and Ministry
Council of Student Personnel Associations in Higher Education
Engineers' Council for Professional Development
Interagency Committee on Church Vocation
Kiwanis Club (local)
National Association of Manufacturers
National Association for Retarded Children
National Commission for Social Work Careers
National Committee for Children and Youth
National Education Association
National Vocational Guidance Association
Recreation Association
Special Libraries Association
United Engineering Center
United Presbyterian Church

GOVERNMENT. From governmental units (local, state, and national) vast amounts of occupational information may be procured as well as the educational information discussed in Chapter 6. Surveys and research projects conducted under the auspices of some governmental units yield pertinent occupational information that is almost nonexistent from other sources on such a major scale. This information would include demography, trends, statistics on employment and unemployment, minority groups, and occupations, such as information supplied in Chapter 9, as well as actual descriptions of occupations and jobs.

A list of examples of governmental units involved in the publication of occupational information would include the following. Some are annotated. (See Address Index.)

DEPARTMENT OF AGRICULTURE
Various publications are available pertaining to farm and agri-business occupations.

CIVIL SERVICE COMMISSION
Prepares literature about occupations in civil service.

DEPARTMENT OF COMMERCE
Office of Business Economics
Bureau of the Census
Produces various publications on census of population and manufactures.
Economic Development Administration (EDA)
The primary function is long-range economic development and programming for areas and regions of substantial and persistent unemployment and underemployment and low family incomes through creation of new employment opportunities.

DEPARTMENT OF DEFENSE
Department of the Air Force
Department of the Army
Deparment of the Navy
Marine Corps (Department of Navy)

OFFICE OF ECONOMIC OPPORTUNITY (OEO)
Youth Programs
Job Corps
Work-Training Programs (administered by Neighborhood Youth Corps)
Youth Conservation Corps
Urban and Rural Community Action Program
Adult Basic Education Program
General Community Action Programs
Work Experience Programs
Volunteers in Service to America (VISTA)

DEPARTMENT OF HEALTH, EDUCATION, AND WELFARE (HEW)
Administration on Aging
Office of Education (for Offices and Bureaus see Chapter 6)
Vocational Rehabilitation Administration
Produces *Rehabilitation Record,* bimonthly, $1.75 a year.
Welfare Administration
Children's Bureau
Bureau of Family Services
Administers Economic Opportunity Act of 1964, Title V, work
experience and training program to help unemployed persons.

DEPARTMENT OF LABOR
Assistant Secretary for Labor Standards
Bureau of Labor Standards
Develops the publication *Safety Standards,* bimonthly. $1.00 a
year.
Women's Bureau
Produces various publications, including *Handbook on Women
Workers.*
Commissioner of Labor Statistics
Bureau of Labor Statistics (BLS)
Develops various publications, including:
Current Wage Developments, monthly.
*Employment and Earnings and Monthly Report on the
Labor Force,* monthly, $7.00 a year.
Industry Wage Surveys, approximately twenty bulletins
annually, titles and prices vary.
Labor Developments Abroad, monthly.
Monthly Labor Review, $7.50 a year.
Occupational Outlook Handbook, biennial, $5.00.
Occupational Outlook Quarterly, $1.25 a year.
Occupational Wage Surveys, eighty bulletins annually,
titles and prices vary
Special Labor Force Reports, free.
Union Wages and Hours, four bulletins annually.
Manpower Administration
Bureau of Apprenticeship and Training
Bureau of Employment Security
Produces various publications, including:
Area Trends in Employment and Unemployment, monthly.
Career Guide for Demand Occupations (1965), $.30.
*The Current Employment Market for Engineers, Scientists,
and Technical Personnel,* semiannual.

Dictionary of Occupational Titles, Vol. 1, $5.00; Vol II, $4.25; Supplement, $2.75.
Employment Service Review, monthly, $4.50.
Farm Labor Developments, monthly during season.
Health Career Guidebook, $1.50.
Job Guide for Young Workers, biennial, $.45.
   United States Employment Services (USES)
   Neighborhood Youth Corps (NYC)
National Labor Relations Board (NLRB)

DEPARTMENT OF STATE
Peace Corps

DEPARTMENT OF THE TREASURY
Coast Guard
Internal Revenue Service

From the Superintendent of Documents, U.S. Government Printing Office, can be obtained complete price lists for areas applicable to occupational information. Examples of areas and their respective code numbers are Labor, No. 33; Occupations, No. 33A; Government Periodical and Subscription Services, No. 36; Census, No. 70; and Children's Bureau, No. 71.

Within each of the fifty states are departments, offices, and bureaus that are sources of occupational information.. A partial list is as follows (specific names may vary from state to state):

Employment Security Division
Department of Labor
State Public Health Division
State Rehabilitation Office

BUSINESS AND INDUSTRY. Businesses and industries are a major source of occupational information literature also. Publications are issued for similar reasons as those of associations and organizations—recruitment and/or services to readers. Many firms publish materials concerning occupations within their own company. In addition to these firms, however, are those with established services for publishing occupational information of a broader coverage than just their own occupations. New York Life Insurance is an example of such a company.

A list of other examples of businesses and industries as sources of occupational information would include (see Address Index):

Allis-Chalmers Manufacturing Company
Aluminum Company of America

American Iron and Steel Institute
American Petroleum Institute
Armstrong Cork Company
Eastman Kodak Company
Equitable Life Assurance Society of the United States
Ford Motor Company
General Electric Company
General Motors Corporation
Metropolitan Life Insurance Company
National Broadcasting Company
National Cash Register Company
New York Life Insurance Company
Prudential Insurance Company
Sun Life Assurance Company of Canada

EDUCATION AND TRAINING INSTITUTIONS. Occupational information as well as educational information is often published by educational institutions and by many of the training institutions involved in training for specialized occupations. On the part of some of the institutions the purpose of the publication is recruitment or enrollment; but some institutions do offer the informational publications as a service. Some occupational information from these sources may be based on research studies and projects performed by personnel of the institution. A partial list of educational and training institutions where publications containing occupational information have been produced is as follows (see Address Index):

Athenaeum and Mechanics Institute
Columbia University Press
Illinois Institute of Technology
University of Iowa
Massachusettes Institute of Technology
University of Michigan Press
University of North Carolina Press
Saint Francis College in New York
Simmons College
Syracuse University

In addition to publications, the education and training institutions are sources of occupational information in other ways, including exhibits, laboratories, special projects, speakers, displays, and various other activities. The relationship between schooling and occupations is becoming more and more intertwined, to the point that education and training institutions become an interweaving source of occupational information.

Places of Employment

A third major classification of sources of occupational information is places of employment. In addition to the publishers, places of employment have much occupational information to offer. Through visitations, tours, exhibits, and various other media, places of employment are sources for the counselor and the person. Some places of employment provide short-term exploratory work experiences to assist individuals in getting to know their organizations and the opportunities available.

Places of employment are taking an active role in the recruitment of employees, with some soft-sell procedures starting long before the individual is ready to consider employment. The recruitment procedures vary with establishments and so does the quality of occupational information. Most places of employment are interested in providing accurate, meaningful information, and, if they aren't, they probably would welcome an opportunity to evaluate with the purpose of improvement.

To obtain the pertinent information on specific jobs and positions, places of employment become the major source. Often the information is not something recorded on paper so that it will file neatly. Instead, the information probably can best be obtained through such activities as interviews, visitations, and other media that provide firsthand information through an involvement experience on behalf of the person who wants the information.

Occupational information from the different sources—people, commercial publishers, tests and test information, associations and organizations, government, business and industry, educational and training institutions, and places of employment can serve to formulate a comprehensive picture. Information from the various sources can reinforce, expand, and cause questioning of certain other information. Pertinent occupational information from all of these sources should be available to an individual, but he may not use all of them at one given time.

Types of Occupational Information

A taxonomy for types of occupational information may be based upon the material (the most common taxonomy), the producer or source, the projected uses, or various other bases. If the information is obtained to assist the person and if the information is to be personalized, then development of a taxonomy that includes projected uses would seem advisable.

A taxonomy for types based on uses might include the following: *literature* for individual reading; *tests* (standardized and nonstandardized) for the individual's self-administration or for professional administration; *audio-visual information* for viewing and listening; *reference materials* for use with an individual or for an individual to use on his own; *contractual service* for providing current material, programmed information, or an elaborate information service; and *journals* for counselors and other professional personnel to keep informed about research, techniques, and trends in the area. Within each of these types may be additional taxonomy for ease of communication, coding, and filing.

Sources for each of the occupational information classifications will need to be identified so that resources will be available for the projected uses. As the media (see Chapters 6 and 13) increase, including game methods, simulated environments, programmed instruction, and others, the taxonomy will need to be expanded and/or modified to include these types of occupational information.

Literature

Probably the most accepted classification of types of printed occupational literature is that adapted by the National Vocational Guidance Association's Information Review Service Committee in a publication entitled *NVGS Bibliography of Current Occupational Literature, 1956.* The classification is used by the Committee as the members review and rate current occupational literature for each issue of *The Vocational Guidance Quarterly.*

Sources of occupational literature were provided in the preceding part of this chapter under "Publications." Examples of the different types can be found in the back of any recent issue of *The Vocational Guidance Quarterly* under "Current Occupational Literature: Career Information Review Service."

The types of publications, definitions, and recommendations as listed in the 1956 publication (pp. 7–8), are as follows:

TYPES OF PUBLICATIONS:

A—*Career Fiction:* An account, portrayed through the experiences of one or more fictional characters, of an occupation which may encompass duties, qualifications, preparations, conditions and nature of work and advancement.

B—*Biography:* An account of the life of a successful man or woman in a given field of endeavor portraying the problems faced by these people in preparing for and advancing in their careers.

C—*Occupational Monograph:* (about 4,000–8,000 words) Extensive coverage of all phases of an occupation. A detailed, comprehensive analysis of a field of work and its related occupations.

D—*Occupational Brief:* (about 3,000 words) Covers the various types of specialization in an occupational field in general terms.

Not as extensive as a Monograph, yet describes all phases of the various job opportunities. Usually prose style.

E—*Occupational Abstract:* (about 1500 words) A concise summary of a job in an occupational area citing the duties and nature of employment, etc., in general terms. May be in prose or outline form.

F—*Occupational Guide:* Brief facts about various phases of an occupational title. Contains general information about the occupation but does not describe any particular job. May be in outline form. Often a booklet or leaflet.

G—*Job Series:* Broad coverage of an entire occupational area giving brief accounts of all job opportunities in the field. May be book, manual or article.

H—*Business and industrial descriptive literature:* Describes a particular business or industry. May show scope and pattern of occupational opportunities.

I—*Occupational or industrial description:* Describes the principal opportunities of an occupation in *one* industry or *one* occupation in several industries. Discusses an occupation as it relates to employment opportunities in industry. May include a brief account of the industry or industries.

J—*Recruitment literature:* Descriptive promotional information pointed toward recruiting young men and women in an occupation or career field. Brief coverage of facts.

K—*Poster or chart:* Occupational information presented by pictures, graphs, tables, etc., in black and white or color, portraying information about jobs, opportunities, trends, qualifications and preparation. Data in concise summarized form permitting a quick review of or stimulating an interest in a major occupational group.

L—*Article or reprint:* An account of an occupation, a phase of an occupation or a person performing the occupation. Covers most phases of the job. Varies in length and degree of coverage. May also be a fact sheet, series of tables, etc. Usually, but not necessarily, in prose style. May be newspaper, magazine or other publication.

M—*Community survey, economic report, job analysis:* Very accurate, highly statistical, comprehensive reports made as the result of local, national or industrial studies. Professional studies not easily adapted to student use.

N—*Other:* Specialized occupational studies, general occupational reviews, technical reports or portions thereof, if applicable, and other miscellaneous occupational information. Information presented by types other than those listed above should be accounted for here. Includes occupations in relation to specific college curricula.

RECOMMENDATION:

1—*Highly recommended:* Maximum adherence to NVGA Standards. Adequately meets most of the points outlined. A very high caliber publication—comprehensive, authentic, objective, readable, and up-to-date.

2—*Recommended:* General adherence to NVGA Standards. Adequately meets more than half the points outlined. A high caliber publication—authentic, objective, readable, up-to-date but not necessarily as comprehensive.

3—*Useful:* Does not adequately meet NVGA Standards because limited in scope. However, contains information helpful to students making it worth including in an occupational file or library. In all cases, applicable information is authentic, objective, readable and timely.

4—*Not recommended:* Does not adhere to NVGA Standards or appear to have value for students. Not listed. No undated material is listed.

Tests

The types of tests have been fairly well established in terminology as they apply to information for occupations. The standardized tests generally include aptitude, ability, achievement, interest inventory, and personality measurements. The standardized tests generally are constructed for administration by a person who has a background in tests and measurement; some of the instruments require considerably more specialized training than others.

In addition to the standardized tests are self-administering instruments that may be helpful to an individual in understanding himself and in some cases his potential in certain areas of work. Many of these are not reliable. Magazines, pocket-books, newspapers, and nonprofessional publications often carry nonstandardized self-administering instruments that are used by the individual, who then formulates attitudes based on the results. With the instruments receiving wide use, perhaps counselors need to be more concerned with why they are used and perhaps assist individuals to obtain the kind of information they need but from a more reliable source. Counselors need to be aware of the scope and use being made of such instruments and in so doing may be able to assist individuals to obtain the information in a professional manner that may overcome many negative points that can be made about the present practices of nonstandardized instruments with indiscriminate use.

Audio-Visual

Occupational information often is available on films, filmstrips, slides, phonographic records, magnetic tapes, video tapes, microfiche, microfilms, aperture cards, exhibits, dramatizations, trips, tours, radio, television, and other audio-visual media. Because some of the audio-visual media do not readily adapt to file plans presently used, the extent of occupational information available through these types is not always fully considered by the potential user. Each counselor who is concerned about personalizing information should consider audio-visual as a type of occupational information that may be effective for some individuals.

To consider the various audio-visual occupational information available the counselor should contact various sources. Places to write for audio-visual occupational information would include the following (addresses are listed in the Address Index):

American Personnel and Guidance Association
Associated Films, Inc.
Audio-Visual Center
Bell Telephone Company
B'nai B'rith Vocation Service Bureau
Bureau of Labor Statistics
Coronet Films
T. S. Denison Company
Encyclopedia Britannica Films
J. G. Ferguson Publishing Company
General Mills, Inc.
Guidance Associates
International Film Bureau, Inc.
Jam Handy Organization
Job Corps
Modern Talking Picture Service
Railroad Association of America
Science Research Associates, Inc.
Society for Visual Education, Inc.
Sound Seminars
Sterling-Movies U.S.A., Inc.
Vocational Films

Reference Material

One type of information that has meaning to the user is reference material, which generally contains the specific information in condensed form. A reference book often is used by a counselor with a person or may be used by the individual to obtain the specific information needed. Reference material often is in the counselor's office or immediate area, with another copy located in the library area. In school settings the number of copies would be determined by frequency of use of the reference material.

Examples of occupational information reference material would include the following:

Career Facts: 1966/67, Addison-Wesley Publishing Company, Inc.; $3.95. Describes over four hundred career positions: what they are; where to find them; and how much they pay.

Educators Guide to Free Guidance Materials, Educators Progress Service; $6.00 annually. Listing of free printed, taped, and filmed materials.

The Encyclopedia of Careers and Vocational Guidance, J. G. Ferguson Publishing Company; $19.95. In two volumes. Describes 71 major career fields and 650 jobs.

Handbook of Job Facts, Science Research Associates, Inc.; $4.69. Convenient listing of 237 major occupations with information on education and training required, personal requirements, pay range, ways of getting started, possibilities for advancement, locations, numbers of persons employed in the field, and future outlook.

Dictionary of Occupational Titles, 3rd ed. U.S. Employment Service, Bureau of Employment Security; Vol. I, $5.00; Vol. II, $4.25; Supplement, $2.75.

Occupational Literature: An Annotated Bibliography, Gertrude Forrester, H. W. Wilson Company; $8.50. Includes 6,650 references to occupational literature, career planning, college information, scholarships, job seeking and related topics.

Counselor's Guide to Occupational and Other Manpower Information, Bulletin No. 1421, Bureau of Labor Statistics; $.50. An annotated bibliography of selected Government publications.

Occupational Outlook Handbook, U.S. Department of Labor, Bureau of Labor Statistics; $5.00. Information on employment outlook, nature of work, earnings and working conditions, training and education, and prospects for promotion. Profiles of seven hundred occupations and thirty major industries.

NVGA Bibliography of Current Occupational Literature; $1.00. Contains compilation of ratings of literature included in previous issues of *Vocational Guidance Quarterly*, along with some new materials. Last published in 1966 with plans for new issues every two years.

Contractual Service

Supplying of occupational information to counseling centers has expanded to the extent that most counseling centers and information centers are purchasing some service from another source. The extent and kind of service purchased depends upon the potential needs of the center.

Almost all centers subscribe to one or more subscription services that periodically send occupational information plus summaries of other studies and often include lists of occupational information produced by other sources. Examples of subscription services would include the following:

American Youth, General Motors Corporation. Contains articles about future vocations and occupations.

Changing Times, Kiplinger Washington Editors, Inc.; $6.00.

Counselor's Information Service, B'nai B'rith; $7.00. Quarterly. Annotated bibliography of current literature on educational and vocational guidance.

Career Guidance Index, Careers; $6.00 for one year. Monthly (October through May). Annotated bibliography.

Chronicle Guidance "3-in-1" Service, Chronicle Guidance Publications, Inc.; $42.50.

Employment Service Review, U.S. Department of Labor, Bureau of Employment Security, U.S. Employment Services; $4.50. Monthly journal of Federal-State programs and operations.

Guidance Exchange, Guidance Exchange; $15.00. Four issues.

Monthly Labor Review, Bureau of Labor Statistics; $7.50.

Job Information Service, National Association of Manufacturers.

NVGA Bibliography of Current Occupational Literature, National Vocational Guidance Association; $1.00.

Occupational Index, Personnel Service, Inc.

Occupational Outlook Quarterly, Bureau of Labor Statistics; $2.50 for two year subscription. Published September, December, February and May. Timely articles on Government and research findings in the demographic, educational, and technical fields.

SRA Guidance Service, Science Research Associates, Inc.; $36.50.

In addition to the subscription services are other types of contractural arrangements to assist in occupational information. One such contract would be with a computer-assisted information system where by contract a local information center would make possible the use of a console in the local setting by an individual so that he could gain information stored in a computer at some other location.

Another contractual arrangement might be where two or more local centers have purchased the services of another person or agency to keep the local occupational information current and comprehensive. Consultative work to the local center would also be within this classification of occupational information types.

Professional Journals

A type of occupational information used by all counselors would be professional journals. Some of the journals provide articles on research, theories, and ideas, whereas other journals report specific and broadening information about different occupations. Some of the professional journals that would be included are as follows:

American Educational Research Journal, American Educational Research Association; $6.00 annually.

Journal of Counseling Psychology, American Psychological Association; $10.00.

The Personnel and Guidance Journal, American Personnel and Guidance Association; $10.00.

The School Counselor, American School Counselor Association; $5.00.

The Vocational Guidance Quarterly, National Vocational Guidance Association; $4.00.

Evaluative Criteria for Occupational Information

Professional evaluative instruments for occupational information have been constantly evolving over an extended period of time. In 1924 the National Vocational Guidance Association formed a Committee on Occupational Research. In 1926, May Rogers Lane wrote an article, "The Content, Volume, and Uses of Occupational Studies" (pp. 326–333), and in 1931, she wrote "Outlines Used in Preparing Occupational Studies" (pp. 356–359). In 1939 the Committee on Occupational Research published "Distinguishing Marks of a Good Occupational Monograph" (1939, pp. 129–130), and in 1940 they published "Content of a Good Occupational Monograph—The Basic Outline" (1940, pp. 20–23). In celebrating the twenty-fifth anniversary of the Committee on Occupational Research, NVGA proposed that an entirely new document be produced to combine the previous information into a single guide, which was developed as the NVGA "Standards for Use in Preparing and Evaluating Occupational Literature" (1950, pp. 319–324). The material was revised as the "Guidelines for Preparing and Evaluating Occupational Materials, 1964" (pp. 217–227). The publication can be purchased from NVGA. The following are highlights from the publication:

Basic Concepts

1. A basic standard for any occupational publication should be the inclusion of a clear statement as to its purpose and the group to whom it is directed.

2. Occupational information should be related to developmental levels which will vary with age, educational attainment, social, and economic backgrounds.

3. Consideration should be given to the implications of the material for all groups in our society.

4. The description of an occupation should be an accurate and balanced appraisal of opportunities and working conditions which should not be influenced by recruiting, advertising, or other special interests.

5. Occupational information should include the nature of personal

satisfactions provided, the kinds of demands made, and the possible effects on an individual's way of life.

Guidelines for Content

The quality and specificity of detail in occupational materials will vary with the intended use of the publication.

Definition of the occupation as given in the *Dictionary of Occupational Titles* or as determined by the U.S. Employment Service.

History and development of the occupation including its social and economic relationships.

Nature of the work such as duties performed, tools or equipment used, relationships to other occupations, possible work settings and fields of specialization.

Requirements such as education and training, aptitudes, temperaments, interests, physical capacities, and working conditions.

Special requirements such as licensure or certification imposed by law or official organizations.

Methods of entering the occupation such as direct application, personal reference, examination, apprenticeship.

Opportunities for experience and exploration through summer and part-time employment, work study programs, programs of the Armed Forces or voluntary agencies such as the Peace Corps, youth organizations and community services.

Description of usual lines for advancement or possibilities for transfer to related occupations either through seniority, experience, on-the-job or in-service training, additional education, and examinations.

Employment outlook as suggested by trends likely to affect employment the next five, ten, or twenty years.

Earnings, both beginning and average wage or salary according to setting, locality and other significant factors as well as supplementary income and fringe benefits such as commissions, tips, overtime, bonuses, meals, housing, hospitalization, vacations, insurance and retirement plans.

Conditions of work and their implications for the individual's way of life, including where significant, daily and weekly time schedules, overtime, seasonality, physical conditions such as travel required, setting—indoor or outdoor, noise, confusion, temperature, health hazards, and strength demands.

Social and psychological factors such as work satisfactions, patterns of relationships with supervisors and other workers, and with unions, associations, or other organizations in which membership may be required or desirable.

Sources of additional information such as books, pamphlets, trade and professional journals, motion pictures, slides and other visual aids, pertinent literature provided by government agencies, unions, associations, industry, schools, colleges and universities.

Criteria for Style and Format

The intended use of the occupational material will be a critical factor in the consideration of style and format.

Style should be clear, concise, interesting, and adapted to the readers for whom the material is intended.

Publishers are encouraged to be creative and imaginative in presenting factual information in a stimulating fashion.

Charts, graphs, or statistical tables should be properly titled and interpreted. Sources and dates of basic data should be given.

The occupational book or pamphlet should state specifically, the publisher, date of publication, the sponsoring organization, group or individual and the author.

In view of the changing nature of occupations, it is important that information be kept up-to-date. Provision should be made for reviews and revision when the original publication is issued and new editions should state whether or not contents have been revised.

In addition to the preceding information the same brochure contains a "Guide for Preparing Industrial Careers Brochures," which includes "A Suggested Brochure Outline."

In 1966 *The Ohio University Check List and Rating Device for Evaluating Occupational Literature* was published (Hill, 1966, pp. 272–276). The rating device was designed over a fifteen-year period for use in evaluating occupational literature that is comprehensive enough that expectations would be for a complete description of an occupation or job family.

In 1966 NVGA prepared a brochure, "Guidelines to Preparation and Evaluation of Occupational Films" (1966, pp. 1–7). This was the first NVGA standard produced for evaluation of films. The brochure may be purchased from NVGA. Highlights from the brochure include the following:

Content

The following occupational characteristics form criteria for selection of significant content.

1. The interdependence of related occupations.
2. Activities of the worker.
3. The setting of the work.
4. Preparation required.
5. Contribution of the occupation to society.
6. Excellence of workmanship.
7. Levels of occupational opportunities.
8. Personal rewards of the occupation.
9. Organizations related to occupations.
10. Factors affecting growth of the occupation.

Style and Format

The effectiveness of a film is frequently determined by its style and format. Teachers and counselors are concerned with the following factors:

1. Length of the occupation film.
2. Implications for motivation.
3. Implications for social and ethnic groups.
4. Basic information.
5. Credits.

As was stated in both of the NVGA brochures the evaluation of occupational information depends upon the projected uses to be made of the materials. The major considerations are based upon the user or potential user and through such constant evaluation the information will become personalized. Material inappropriate for one user may be excellent information for another user.

Counselor's Techniques for Obtaining Occupational Information

A counselor may obtain occupational information by techniques very similar to those used in obtaining educational information, which were presented in Chapter 6. The techniques will vary from counselor to counselor and will depend upon the projected use to be made of information and upon the availability of other occupational information on the topic.

Three major approaches were used to classify the techniques: from literature including audio-visual, by observation and participation, and by interaction with people. Techniques for use in obtaining occupational information from literature would include *joining professional organizations* so as to receive the literature periodically for review, *writing* to publishers and producers for copies, *reading* in various sources, *establishing a budget* with a line entry for occupational information for enabling the requisitioning of materials, and *purchasing materials* as part of the expenses associated with professional growth. Most of the material purchased should be paid for from the budget of the organization or school where the counselor is employed rather than from his own personal funds.

Techniques used in obtaining occupational information by observation and participation would include *visitations* to different places of employment, such as those made possible through B-I-E Days, field trips, and plant and business establishment tours. Often the counselor can gain much occupational information from *exhibits* produced by businesses, industries, governmental agencies, libraries, museums, and community agencies. Some communities have undertaken a program to assure counselors, who want to participate, *summer or part-time employment* as a means of facilitating counselor firsthand experience in a setting different from that in which he usually is. Some vocational schools are sponsoring workshops for counselors to learn firsthand about occupations and the education or training associated with each.

The counselor can gain much occupational information by interaction with people. Some of the techniques would include the following: *consultation or interviews* with employers, personnel officers, and employees; *follow-up studies* of former persons associated with the setting in which the counselor is working, such as school alumni or community agency participants; *community surveys* of jobs in different businesses, industries, and other places of local employment; *correspondence* with different persons who are engaged in a specific occupation or with an authority within the field; and interaction with different people through *panels, forums, symposiums, and speeches.*

Techniques for Individuals and Groups for Obtaining Occupational Information

Individuals will on their own obtain much occupational information. The process of living will in itself bring about interaction with people, ideas, and things that will enable the individual to gain occupational information. At times individuals join with others to obtain occupational information. Counselors can facilitate on an individual or group basis a person's obtaining occupational information at the most appropriate time and at a pace in keeping with the individual's needs. Techniques listed in the section in Chapter 6 on "Techniques for Individuals and Groups for Obtaining Educational Information" are applicable to occupational information also.

Summary

Sources of occupational information can be grouped under three classifications—people, publications, and places of employment. Occupational information is needed by an individual from early childhood throughout life to ensure him of maximum occupational development. The information probably will need to be highlighted at certain times in order that he may have the necessary information prior to each of the many decision-making times in his life. The various sources contribute information that enables an individual to integrate occupational information with himself so that the transfer from one occupation to another is a normal expectation in the individual's career pattern rather than a haphazard, unrelated sequence of events.

Literature, tests, audio-visual material, references, contractual services, and journals are different types of occupational information. In addition NVGA classifies occupational literature as occupational monographs, briefs, abstracts, and guides: job series; posters or charts; articles or reprints; business and industrial descriptive literature; occupational or industrial descriptive literature; recruitment literature; community survey economic report; job analysis; biography; and career fiction.

Evaluation criteria for occupational information have been evolving over the past forty-five years, with NVGA taking the leadership role. Two guidelines have been issued recently for preparing and evaluating occupational information—one for occupational materials and the other for occupational films. The quality and specificity of detail as well as format and style in occupational materials will vary with the intended use; thus the criteria are dependent upon the user and each source and specific occupational information material should be selected to assist in personalizing the occupational information processes.

The counselor uses techniques that help him obtain occupational information from literature, by observation and participation, and by interaction with people. He also assists persons on an individual or group basis to obtain occupational information.

Some sources of occupational information are the same as for educational information because they contribute to both areas. Whether or not a counselor or an individual obtains all information or only some from a particular source is determined by the pertinence of the information to the potential user.

SELECTED REFERENCES

Adams, James F. ed. *Counseling and Guidance, A Summary View.* New York: The Macmillan Company, 1965. Pp. 362–364.

Arbuckle, Dugald S. "Occupational Information in the Elementary School," *The Vocational Guidance Quarterly,* **12** (Winter 1963–64), 77–84.

Baer, Max F., and Edward C. Roeber. *Occupational Information: The Dynamics of Its Nature and Use.* Chicago: Science Research Associates, Inc., 1964. Pp. 136–161, 268–318, 338–358, 365–366.

Burchill, George W. *Work-Study Programs for Alienated Youth.* Chicago: Science Research Associates, Inc., 1962. 265 pages.

Calia, Vincent F. "Vocational Guidance: After the Fall," *The Personnel and Guidance Journal,* **45** (December 1966), 320–327.

Clark, Florence E., et al. "Distinguishing Marks of a Good Occupational Monograph," *Occupations,* **18** (November 1939), 129–130.

"Content of a Good Occupational Monograph—The Basic Outline," *Occupations,* **19** (October 1940), 20–23.

Crow, Lester D., and Alice Crow. *Organization and Conduct of Guidance Services.* New York: David McKay Company, Inc., 1965. Pp. 282–285.

Dictionary of Occupational Titles, 3rd ed. Washington, D.C.: Bureau of

Employment Security, Manpower Administration, U.S. Department of Labor, 1965. Vol. I, *Definitions of Titles;* Vol. II, *Occupational Classification.* Also *A Supplement to the Dictionary of Occupational Titles,* 1966.

"Distinguishing Marks of a Good Occupational Monograph," Publishers Committee, NVGA Occupational Research Section, *Occupations,* 18 (November 1939), 129–130.

Ehrle, Raymond A. "Vocational Planning Information Available to Employment Service Counselors," *The Vocational Guidance Quarterly,* 13 (Winter 1964–1965), 91–94.

Feingold, S. Norman. *The Job Finder.* Cambridge, Mass.: Bellmann Publishing Company, 1966.

Ferguson, Robert H. *Unemployment: Its Scope, Measurement, and Effect on Poverty.* Ithaca, N.Y.: New York State School of Industrial and Labor Relations, Cornell University, Bulletin 53–2, May 1965. 76 pages.

Forrester, Gertrude. *Occupational Literature: An Annotated Bibliography.* New York: H. W. Wilson Company, 1964. 675 pages.

Hill, George E. "The Evaluation of Occupational Literature, A Guide for Use by Counselors and Librarians," *The Vocational Guidance Quarterly,* 14 (Summer 1966), 271–277.

Hopke, William E. "A New Look at Occupational Literature," *The Vocational Guidance Quarterly,* 15 (September 1966), 18–25.

Hoppock, Robert. *Occupational Information: Where to Get It and How to Use It in Counseling and in Teaching,* 3rd ed. New York: McGraw-Hill, Inc., 1967. Pp. 27–43, 204–251, 273–285, 401–402.

Isaacson, Lee E. *Career Information in Counseling and Teaching.* Boston: Allyn and Bacon, Inc., 1966. Pp. 215–255.

Kaback, Goldie Ruth. "Automation, Work, and Leisure: Implications for Elementary Education," *The Vocational Guidance Quarterly,* 13 (Spring 1965), 202–206.

Kell, Bill L., and William J. Mueller. *Impact and Change.* Des Moines, Ia.: Appleton-Century-Crofts, 1966. 148 pages.

Lane, May Rogers. "The Content, Volume, and Uses of Occupational Studies," *The Vocational Guidance Magazine,* 4 (April 1926), 326–333.

Lane, May Rogers. "Outlines Used in Preparing Occupational Studies," *The Vocational Guidance Magazine,* 9 (May 1931), 356–359.

Moser, Leslie E., and Ruth Small Moser. *Counseling and Guidance: An Exploration.* Englewood Cliffs, N.J.: Prentice-Hall, Inc., 1963. Pp. 52–55.

NVGA, "Standards for Use in Preparing and Evaluating Occupational Literature," *Occupations, The Vocational Guidance Journal,* 28 (February 1950), 319–324.

NVGA, *Bibliography of Current Occupational Literature,* Compiled by the National Vocational Guidance Association's Guidance Information Review Service Committee, Dora Peterson, Chairman. Washington, D.C.: National Vocational Guidance Association, 1956. 40 pages.

NVGA, *Guidelines for Preparing and Evaluation Occupational Materials.* Washington, D.C.: National Vocational Guidance Association, 1964. Reprint from *The Vocational Guidance Quarterly,* 12 (Spring 1964), 217–227.

NVGA, *Guidelines to Preparation and Evaluation of Occupational Films.*

Washington, D.C.: National Vocational Guidance Association, 1966. 7 pages.

Norris, Willa. *Occupational Information in the Elementary School.* Chicago: Science Research Associates, Inc., 1963. Pp. 150–243.

Norris, Willa, Franklin R. Zeran, and Raymond N. Hatch. *The Information Service in Guidance,* 2nd ed. Chicago: Rand McNally & Company, 1966. Pp. 56–64, 148–160, 239–253, 263–297, 301–368, 480–484, 550–558, 571–575.

"Outlines Used in Preparing Occupational Studies," *The Vocational Guidance Magazine,* 9 (May 1931), 356–359.

Patton, Evelyn D., and Dora W. Steiner. *Let's Look at Your Future.* New York: Scarecrow Press, 1966. 247 pages.

Shartle, Carroll L. *Occupational Information: Its Development and Application,* 3rd ed. Englewood Cliffs, N.J.: Prentice-Hall, Inc., 1959. Pp. 94–134, 169–180.

Smith, Margaret Ruth, ed. *Guidance-Personnel Work: Future Tense.* New York: Teachers College Press, Columbia University, 1966. 176 pages.

Tennyson, W. Wesley, and Lawrence P. Monnens. "The World of Work Through Elementary Readers," *The Vocational Guidance Quarterly,* 12 (Winter 1963–64), 85–88.

Tennyson, W. Wesley, Thomas A. Soldahl, and Charlotte Mueller. *The Teacher's Role in Career Development.* Washington, D.C.: National Vocational Guidance Association, 1965 Revision. Pp. 48–56.

Chapter 12

Making Occupational

Information

Available to Users

No system of tests or of occupational classifications, no machinery of collecting or tabulating or charting or filing, can take the place of the personal integrity, the individual capacity, and the basic common sense of the counselor.—"About Guiding Young People." *The Royal Bank of Canada Monthly Letter,* Montreal, Canada. Volume 44, Number 9, September, 1963.

In addition to selecting and obtaining various occupational materials, many major decisions must be made in determining the most appropriate ways to make occupational information available to users. Decisions on making materials readily available and accessible to users would entail examining the effects of the location of information for users; determining and providing the facilities necessary; exploring alternatives in arranging materials for effectiveness; examining different classification systems, their values and limitations; selecting and perhaps developing a classification and code system for a particular setting; and maintaining files and materials to facilitate utilization.

Needs Determine Use

In counseling and guidance, occupational information is obtained, coded, and filed for potential use rather than for historical purposes; thus, the occupational information obtained is determined by the projected uses that may be made of it. The needs, present and potential, are the bases for determining use.

256

All occupational information used in counseling and guidance is not for the purpose of answering questions or satisfying all needs, but rather some information is used to broaden the horizon, increase curiosity, stimulate imagination, amplify inquisitiveness, and intensify the thirst for additional knowledge. The individual, who is unaware of the opportunities available in some occupations that may be within his sphere of potential consideration, may need occupational information on the first depth to broaden his realm of consideration. Such an individual may be in the elementary school or at any other age throughout his life.

If need determines use, then the occupational information center has to be housed in an area where users can readily obtain information, which is coded and filed primarily in a manner related to people and their needs. Occupational information has to be constantly evaluated to ensure appropriateness for the intended use; but equally important is a frequent study of the availability of the occupational information to users at the most essential times.

Considerations for Filing Educational and Occupational Information Separately

Education and occupations are becoming so interwoven that some people believe the information should be treated as one rather than as two separate ones. Others visualize education as having a primary function other than for the world of work and thus feel that a very definite separation should be made between educational information and occupational information.

At times an individual wants information about the world of work and about the preparation needed to enter and progress within certain occupations. Frequently such a request requires a consideration of both occupational information and educational information. Other persons may not be interested in obtaining additional education or training, but do want occupational information that will facilitate their occupational mobility. Also, frequently a person may want additional education for reasons not associated directly with his work but for his personal and social development. The three areas—educational, occupational, and personal-social—should all be developed throughout life with the recognition that the growth of each is dependent on and interwoven with the others.

Probably no one filing system will be ideal for all persons; however, the housing of the information center and the filing plan selected should be done on the basis of what will be most appropriate for the users in that situation. For most information centers probably the educational, occupational, and personal-social information will be filed separately;

however, they could be filed within the same geographic location so that the user, if he chooses to do so, can use all three at the same time. For better utilization consideration should be given to filing educational and occupational information under a filing system that would be compatible rather than treating each as a distinct and separate area without relationship to the other. If possible the same plan should be used in filing personal-social information. In Chapters 14–18 suggestions are made on filing such information.

Criteria for Location of Occupational Material

Morris LeMay and Charles Warnath (1967, pp. 821–823) made a questionnaire survey of student opinion on the location of occupational information on a university campus and found that almost nine out of ten students wanted a central occupational library, approximately two out of five wanted it located in the Student Union, and one out of four named the university library as the best location. The authors stated that the findings tend to reinforce the feeling that ". . . services need to be taken to these locations where students carry on their normal activities if these services are to be of maximum value on campus."

In Chapter 7 under "Criteria for Housing Educational Material" were presented some criteria that apply to occupational information as well as to educational information. A point stressed was that one location alone may be insufficient and that consideration should be given to the purposes for the information, because the purposes to be achieved do affect the depth of information and the most appropriate location. If the potential user considers occupational information primarily for the purposes of broadening his warehouse of information, then he probably will want the information in a casual, informal location, where he can obtain the information at his leisure, or, if possible, he seems to want the information to become an integral part of his environmental surroundings, which will contribute to his breadth of knowledge with a minimum expenditure of energy. If the potential user views the information as resource and specific information, then he may want the information located where he will be able to make notes, use a copying machine for obtaining an exact copy of the information needed, or concentrate while reading, viewing, or listening. Such purposes would necessitate locating the information away from noise and heavy traffic flow, and near tables, chairs, and reading areas. The library may be such a location. If the potential user wants to use the information at the third depth, where it will stimulate feedback, he probably will desire as much visual and auditory privacy as possible. Such differences in purposes may help interpret the suggestions for different locations obtained by LeMay and Warnath in the survey of students. The students surveyed may have viewed information primarily for a broadening experience; thus the student union or the library may be from the students' standpoint a very vital and realistic location.

Location per se is not the prime factor but rather having appropriate information accessible when needed is; therefore, location is only one factor in the consideration of accessibility. Therefore, one determines purposes to be achieved by the occupational information and then selects the location(s) of the information that will best serve the purposes at the depth for which the user will use the information.

The counseling offices and waiting room should contain occupational information. The amount and different depths of information will depend upon the philosophy prevailing in the counseling center. Duplicate copies of some occupational information will be needed in order that the material may be placed in different locations and also to supply the demand for the more frequently used materials. In Chapter 7 were suggested different locations, depending upon the setting.

Physical Facilities for Housing Occupational Material

In addition to the consideration of different locations, such as the counselor's office, his waiting room, the library, the student union, classrooms, a special center, and other select places, attention must be given to the housing of the materials, such as file cabinets with manila folders for unbound materials, bookshelves, tape and record cabinets, aperture-card file drawers, and other specifically designed equipment.

The chances are better that all available appropriate material will be reviewed by a potential user if all types of material (monographs, briefs, books, and so on) are filed together rather than each type being filed separately. Filing all types together creates problems because some materials do not lend themselves to being housed together with other materials, such as aperture cards being filed with hardback books. Problems of one kind or another are present in any filing or storage of different types of material. Cross-indexing and ingenuity will help in filing. When trying to collect material in a location and under a classification system that will be meaningful, the counselor considers the use to be made of the information with a given person rather than starting with a consideration of the type of material. The latter forces filing similar types together rather than filing so that different types and media can be supplementary and complementary to each other.

In Chapter 7 under "Physical Facilities for Housing Educational Material" were presented points that are appropriate for occupational information also and that should be considered. If at all possible, the educational, occupational, and personal-social information should be physically located and housed together. Space will need to be large enough to accommodate not only the housing of the material, but also the *activities associated with the uses of the material,* i.e., individual reading and studying; small group discussions while using the material; the viewing of motion-picture films, slides, and microfilm; listening to audio tapes and phonographic records; viewing plus listening to video tapes; reproducing material by use of a copying machine; and any other activities that users may need to benefit fully from the information.

Codification and Filing Plans—Values and Limitations

Criteria for selection of filing plans were presented in Chapter 7 under "Filing Plans—Values and Limitations." Several different plans exist for filing occupational information. Each plan has values and limitations. From a study of different plans one can be adopted or possibly two or more combined and adapted to the local situation. Some of the more frequently listed plans are presented in summary form, together with some of the values and limitations.

Alphabetical

For filing unbound occupational information in vertical files the alphabetical method often is used. The alphabetical plan has value because it is easy to use, seems logical, can be used by lay people as well as professionals, can be used in elementary schools, is adjustable to local conditions, can contain a variable number of folders depending on need, has no need for a key or index to use it, has simplicity in initiation of the plan, and is efficient for small amounts of material up to one or two file drawers.

The alphabetical plan has some disadvantages, including reduced efficiency as the amount of material increases, greater possibility of filing material where it will not be relocated (especially true when the volume of material is more than one to two file drawers), lacks means of providing for both occupational families and for individual occupations, and related occupational information often is filed far apart because of the alphabetical order. The alphabetical plan has the limitation of being useful primarily on a small amount of material and does not take into account natural groupings of occupations.

A modified alphabetical plan is the one developed by Wilma Bennett, variously referred to as the *Michigan Plan. Occupations Filing Plan and Bibliography, NVGA Plan,* or *Bennett Occupations Filing Plan.* NVGA uses the subject headings in the listing of "Current Occupational Literature" in each issue of the *Vocational Guidance Quarterly.* The plan is primarily for filing unbound literature in manila folders, but the captions can be used for films, books, and other kinds of occupational information. The 270 subject headings (printed in red) are adapted from subject areas in the *D.O.T.* Cross references are provided on 501 blue-tabbed cards the same size as the folders. In addition, 58 black-tabbed folders are provided for supplementary related materials. One value is that any or all of the 829 labels can be used, thus allowing for increasing the size as needed; however the counselor probably will want to use all of them from the start. The plan has been used for some time and found satisfactory in some settings. One limitation of this plan is that it forces classification according to a prepublished plan, and the counselor must examine the material and then search the printed list of headings for the one most appropriate. The emphasis is upon the plan and the material, not upon the projected use or potential user. The plan precludes an overall view of the world of work and tends to ignore the ability and interest of the potential user.

Interest

In some junior and senior high schools occupational information is filed according to interest, generally using the headings on the Kuder Preference Record, Vocational, Form C. The plan relates the occupational information to another activity and places emphasis upon occupational information as well as upon the preference record. One of the disadvantages is the tendency to cause the user to place undue emphasis on scores received on an interest inventory for which usually no validity correlation coefficient is provided. Another disadvantage is that interest is not the most convenient way of classifying occupations. Most fields of work do not have statistically proven unique interest patterns.

School Subject

In secondary schools some counselors have filed occupational information according to school subjects. Such a plan has been developed by Edward C. Roeber in 1950, often referred to as the *Missouri Filing Plan*. The plan used 325 subject headings under 11 school subjects, including agriculture, art and drawing, commercial, home economics, industrial arts, language arts, mathematics, music, physical education, science, and social science. The plan was designed for unbound materials to be placed in vertical file folders, which could be prepared in advance or as needed. Additional folders can be added easily. One of the values is in assisting students to relate school subjects to the world of work. The limitations of the plan have made its use minimal. Many occupations do not seem to relate directly to any school subjects, whereas others relate to many and necessitate many cross references in the Missouri Filing Plan.

Industry

In some placement offices, such as college placement offices, occupational information may be filed by industries. The material generally placed in such a file includes brochures and other material published by a business or industry. Other settings, in addition to placement offices, sometimes use an industrial file plan for part of the occupational information. Such a plan is necessitated because many pieces of occupational literature do not lend themselves to one occupation but more to an industry. In establishing an industrial file system, usually as part of another system, the *Standard Industrial Classification Manual* is probably the best source. Nine major classifications of industries are used with seventy-nine major groups. The seventy-nine groups may be sufficient divisions for use in occupational file plans in most situations; however, the manual provides codes for five hundred subdivisions of the seventy-nine groups. The five hundred subdivisions are for closely related industries, which are subdivided into approximately fifteen hundred industries. The limitations for using this file plan as the only one would include the following: many occupations are associated with more than one industry, not developed according to the usual way of considering occupations, and emphasis is placed on the industry rather than upon the worker and what he does.

California Plan

Barbara Kirk and Marjorie Michels (1964) developed the *California Plan* (Table 12–1) for filing information for counseling. Its advantages include the following: retains simplicity of alphabetical plans, groups material by subject based on interest and ability, uses a simplified

Table 12-1

THE CALIFORNIA FILE PLAN DEVELOPED BY KIRK AND MICHELS.

Shown are the three major divisions, all subdivisions, and the arabic numbered sections. Each numbered section has two additional classifications, which are not shown.

I. Vocational	II. Educational
A. Occupations	A. Status and Trends
1. Agriculture and home economics	1. Higher education
2. Arts and letters	2. Secondary and primary education
3. Graduate/research	3. Special education
4. Education and welfare	4. Vocational education
5. Engineering and architecture	5. Adult education
6. Government and law	6. Foreign study

Table 12-1 (*continued*)

I. Vocational	*II. Educational*
7. Health	*B. Schools, Colleges and Universities*
8. Industrial, trade, and service	1. Directories
9. Science	2. College and university catalogues
B. Trends and Outlook	3. Professional–vocational school bulletins
1. Population and migration	4. Adult and continuation school announcements
2. Business and industrial	5. Preparatory, remedial and special school announcements
3. Occupational and employment	
4. Salary and wage	
5. Labor movement	
C. Legislation	*C. Scholarships, Fellowships, Grants, and Loans*
1. Labor	1. Directories
2. Licensing	2. Undergraduate
D. Special Groups	3. Graduate/research
1. Handicapped	4. Foreign study
2. Minorities	
3. Veterans	
4. Women	
5. Youth	
6. Over 40	
E. Job Training	
1. Apprenticeship	*III. Personal*
2. Informal	
3. Work-study	*A. Planning*
4. Retraining	1. Career
F. Employment	2. Education/training
1. Directories	3. Employment
2. Business and industry	*B. Adjustment*
3. Government	1. School
4. Agency, organization and institution	2. Work
5. Home and sheltered workshop	3. Family
6. Self-employment	4. Social
	5. Health

numbering system that can be omitted, contains no miscellaneous categories, uses a minimum number of cross references, is expandable, and can be used with any size collection. The format of the coding is three major divisions, identified by Roman numerals. Within each major division are subdivisions of broad subject categories, identified by capital letters. Each subdivision is further divided into additional headings, identified by Arabic numbers, which can be further divided by headings, identified by small letters. Additional division is done on an alphabetical basis (see Table 12–1). For example, *airline hostess* would be classified as *I.A.8.r.,* where the code representations are as follows: *I,* Vocational; *A,* Occupations; *8.* Industrial, Trade, and Service; *r,* Travel and Transportation Industries and Related Services; and a folder within that section for filing is labeled *Air Hostess and Steward.* The limitations to the plan may be that it is too limited in the "personal" classification, which is one of the three major divisions; folders marked *general* may become too large and just be a replacement for "miscellaneous"; no recognition of the type of person with whom material is to be used, no provision for designating the age, grade or comprehension level of potential user; and no consideration given to different depths of information.

Dictionary of Occupational Titles

The Federal Government has produced three classification systems: *Standard Industrial Classification Manual* (described in this section earlier), classification plan used by the Bureau of the Census, and the *Dictionary of Occupational Titles* (*D.O.T.*). None of the three Federal classification systems were designed for filing occupational information but each of them has been used by counselors for that purpose. The Standard Industrial and the Bureau of Census Classifications were, in the past, used more than presently by counselors as a basis for file plans. The *D.O.T.* has been used frequently and has been the basis for some commercial filing plans. The earlier editions, 1939 and 1949, of the *D.O.T.* used a different coding system than the 1965 edition.

The skilled, semiskilled, and unskilled classifications were discontinued in the 1965 edition and were replaced by other occupational groupings. The coding in the latest edition uses nine major occupational categories, identified by the numbers 0 through 9, and used as the first digit of the code number:

0 and 1. Professional, technical, and managerial occupations.
      2. Clerical and sales occupations.
      3. Service occupations.
      4. Farming, fishery, forestry, and related occupations.
      5. Processing occupations.
      6. Machine trades occupations.
      7. Bench work occupations.
      8. Structural work occupations.
      9. Miscellaneous occupations.

The nine major categories are divided into eighty-four two-digit divisions (Volume II, pp. 1–2), and the divisions, in turn, are subdivided into 603 distinctive three-digit groups (Volume II, pp. 3–24). Definitions for each category, division, and group are presented in the *D.O.T.* (Volume II, pp. 33–213), following the introduction of each of the classifications.

The last three digits of the *D.O.T.* code number are based on research done by the U.S. Employment Service in regard to how each job requires the worker to function in relation to *Data* (fourth digit), *People* (fifth digit), and *Things* (sixth digit). Functions have been arranged in a hierarchy relationship to each of the three digits and then numbers, 0 through 8, assigned to the functions for each digit. Taken together, the last three digits of the code number can express the total level of complexity at which the job requires the worker to function. The worker-function hierarchy used in the code for the last three digits as shown in Volume I, p. xviii, is as follows (for application see Figure 12–1):

DATA (4TH DIGIT)	PEOPLE (5TH DIGIT)	THINGS (6TH DIGIT)
0 Synthesizing	0 Mentoring	0 Setting-up
1 Coordinating	1 Negotiating	1 Precision working
2 Analyzing	2 Instruction	2 Operating–controlling
3 Compiling	3 Supervising	3 Driving–operating
4 Computing	4 Diverting	4 Manipulating
5 Copying	5 Persuading	5 Tending
6 Comparing	6 Speaking–Signaling	6 Feeding–offbearing
7 ⎫ No significant 8 ⎭ relationship	7 Serving	7 Handling
	8 No significant relationship	8 No significant relationship

The *D.O.T.* provides a grouping (114 such workers' trait groups) of jobs according to some combination of required general educational development, specific vocational preparation, aptitudes, interests, temperaments, and physical demands. The 1966 *A Supplement to the D.O.T.* listed individual physical demands, working conditions, and training-time data for each job defined in Volume I. The code and related material provides a wealth of material, but to use it as a file code often necessitates a trained person to assist others in the use of the files.

Several file plans have been developed using the *D.O.T.* as the basis. A counselor or librarian could develop his own designations using the *D.O.T.* and need not purchase any other plan. Two commercially produced plans, including folders and occupational information, are the "Chronicle Plan," produced by Chronicle Guidance Publications, and the "Desk-Top Kit," produced by Careers.

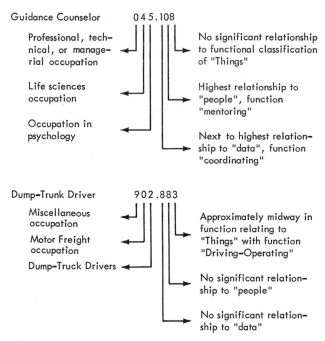

Figure 12-1. D.O.T. CODES FOR TWO OCCUPATIONS WITH CODE EXPLANATION.

The "Chronicle Plan" is based on the *D.O.T.* and is designed for filing unbound occupational information in a vertical occupation file, using manila folders with one-third tab cuts. The vertical file is for pamphlets, clippings, magazine articles, mimeographed papers, and other types of occupational information that is on paper with a minimal number of pages. The titles and codes are printed on the tabs in a different color for each division of the file. The plan classifies all occupations under 10 major groups, subdivided into 130 occupational divisions, which are further divided into 210 specific occupations. In addition to the 350 tabbed folders and their contents are directions, an outline of the codes used, and cross references, all printed on manila-weight cards for assistance in using the "Chronicle Plan." The values of such a plan include being based on a nationally used classification system; utilization in various settings, such as schools, employment offices, armed services, and industry; coding is already done and printed on some occupational information as received from various sources; and flexibility offered through expanding areas as material increases in amount. Another value is that a guidance service subscription is sold on a yearly basis to help keep the file of information current. The limitations seem to be centered around such criticisms as that the coding requires special training; lay persons cannot use the files on their own without instruction first; the file tends to separate occupations rather than show relationships; and emphasis is on the world of work rather than the worker.

The "Desk-Top Kit" is based on the *D.O.T.*, arranged in an open-top metal box six inches by nine inches by nineteen inches and designed to be placed on a desk or table top. The kit is easily carried from place to place, and the materials on six-inch by nine-inch cards are convenient to use. Two kits are available, one for junior high and the other for senior high schools. Each has a yearly service to help keep the material up-to-date. The values include ease of use, short thumbnail sketches, and a wide variety of information. The limitations include all those listed for the "Chronicle Plan," plus the information is too condensed for many uses, cards or stiff paper seem to be the only weight of paper that is satisfactory, the size is restrictive and is not convenient for filing material from other sources, and the plan is not as flexible as some situations would warrant.

Other Occupational Kits

One commercially produced file plan, the "SRA Career Information Kit," is based on a numeric coding classification. The filing system reflects major job areas and job families. The kit includes approximately two hundred manila folders categorized into ten major groups. Easy reference is provided to specific job titles as the information is coded and filed by job category within related job areas. A second section of the kit provides selected publications for the counselor and the student. A manual and an index pertaining to the kit are both published. The values seem to be the relation of an occupation to a series of other jobs and a coding system that tends to group together job families. The limitations are the use of a special numeric coding, which is not commonly used in classifying occupational information; the material is to a large extent dependent upon publications from one publisher; and training is needed to use the plan.

SRA produces a junior high kit entitled the "Widening Occupational Roles Kit" (WORK), which includes 400 job briefs related to the field of work, 5 junior high guidance booklets, student workbooks, 5 color filmstrips, and a teacher's manual. The kit is designed to help students explore careers on their own. The interdependence of occupations and the need for different types of education is provided.

For the senior high school the "SRA Occupational Exploration Kit" (OEK) includes an occupational scanner to help students explore jobs based on their own educational aspirations, abilities, and interests; 360 occupational briefs; 16 job family booklets; 8 guidance series books; student record books; and a guide for counselors and teachers. The kit is designed to assist each senior high school student in looking at jobs beyond the limiting experience of his immediate environment.

For students who finish high school but who do not plan on finishing college, two kits are available. SRA "Careers for High School Graduates" contains 116 appropriate occupational briefs, a book for student use, four posters, and an instructor's guide. The second kit is the "SOS Guidance Research Information Booklets" kit, which contains 43 booklets, 6 inches by 9 inches in size and a counselor's manual, all of which is in a set-up box for ease of use. The material is for high school students who plan on entering a vocation necessitating post-high-school training. The kit is available from the Bureau of Educational Research and Service, The University of Iowa.

"Career Exploratory Kit," produced by Careers, contains 450 career briefs and summaries in a file with alphabetical tab cards. The cards are 6 inches by 9 inches and are contained in a lightweight cardboard box for ease of moving from one location to another.

Development of Files to Facilitate 3-D Concept

In the file plans presented in the preceding section, focus either was upon the literature or the occupational classification. To personalize information and to facilitate it as a process instead of an act, the focus needs to be upon the potential user and how the information may assist him. These two are fundamental to the 3-D concept in utilizing information, plus consideration of the communication process and the developmental approach in counseling and guidance.

File plans in occupational information are much better developed than in either educational or personal-social information areas. The occupational information file plans are excellent for the purposes for which they are designed, and when they are used within that framework they do fulfill a need in counseling and guidance. Every effort should be made to retain the functional plans and to expand them beyond just filing available information from which individuals can select materials. The files should facilitate a broader scope of personalized information processes.

File plans based on the *D.O.T.* enable the filing of occupational briefs, abstracts, and similar vertical file materials. The *D.O.T.* codes are primarily for literature written on a specific occupation, which by its content is applicable at the second depth. The difficulty often occurs in the use of *D.O.T.* codes when material is of broad coverage or when it is of a feedback, personal nature. This limitation is to be expected because the *D.O.T.* was not developed for filing occupational information, but rather as an occupational classification. The Federal Government has three different coding systems in the occupational area—*D.O.T.*, the Bureau of the Census, and the Standard Industrial Classification. Three coding systems were needed because different objectives were to be achieved. Counselors need a file plan for occupational information that has been developed to facilitate achieving counseling and guidance objectives rather than being limited by a file system developed for another purpose.

The 3-D concept is applicable for children, youth, and adults, as well as for recognition of three depths of information for each. A suggested schematic code system (see Table 7-1) contained codes within the occupational area for such information as demography, families and fields of occupations, job placement, laws and regulations affecting occupations, maturation or occupational development, salaries and wages, trends and outlook, and specific occupational information. To make use of plans presently in operation, the suggestion was made to use within the 3-D schematic code the *D.O.T.* numbers for filing specific occupational groups, such as occupational families and fields, and to use subdivisions where needed, such as entry, exploratory, and temporary job placement. Examples of coding are provided later in this chapter.

In the 3-D schematic code system given for specific occupational materials, no subdivisions other than the *D.O.T.* were provided. The *D.O.T.* seems to be operative for most settings for specific occupational information (second depth) and does provide a widely accepted plan for subdividing and classifying the bulk of the presently published occupational information. Many pieces of literature have the *D.O.T.* number, when applicable, printed on them. Using the 3-D concept in connection with the *D.O.T.* code would necessitate analyzing the material in terms of people with whom it may be used and at what depth. These two entries could be added to the *D.O.T.* code. An example would be literature on a varitypist (203.532) that is applicable for a senior high school student (Ss) and contains specific information (second depth). The total code would be Ss–203.582–2.

In the case of literature written on broad occupational fields or occupational families, the *D.O.T.* numbers are not applicable. Probably the most frequent plan is to file this material alphabetically. The 3-D code will, however, integrate such material into the total file rather than separating the broad coverage materials from the balance of the occupational information.

In elementary schools the occupational information materials that are filed for use by the children and are for them to select often cannot be filed by a numbering system such as the *D.O.T.* Use of either family, field, or industry designation with alphabetical filing of the classification and then alphabetical filing within the classification probably will be more satisfactory. The *D.O.T.* (Volume II, pp. 637–639) provides an industry index consisting of 229 different industries and an alphabetical listing (pp. 531–635) of all jobs according to the industries in which they are usually found. The 229 different industries are fundamentally those listed in the *Standard Industrial Classification Manual* (1957) with some modifications. In the *D.O.T.*, Volume I, following each job title is the industry in which that job is found. When the children are to obtain the information on their own, the file plan should be kept as simple as possible. The 3-D code would not be applicable in lower grades. If the teachers are to obtain the material and use it with the children, then the 3-D code may be meaningful.

In high schools, colleges, and many other information centers much of the occupational information used cannot be filed by a *D.O.T.* number because the material often is inappropriate for a specific occupation. A career leaflet like *Scientific Careers in Plant Pest Control*, prepared by U.S. Agricultural Research Service, is an example. The material could be filed in the 3-D system under the industry of agriculture. Other examples of useful occupational information that need additional consideration for filing beyond the *D.O.T.* filing system would be *Army Occupations and You, Adjustments to the Introduction of Office Automation, Tips For Handicapped Job Seekers,* and *Comparative Job Performance by Age: Office Workers,* all of which can be obtained from the Superintendent of Documents, U.S. Government Printing Office. Some occupational information materials are of the first depth, whereas other materials are of the second and third depths. The counselor will need to consider a filing plan that will facilitate filing broad coverage information and different media, i.e., films, pamphlets, books, leaflets, and so on.

Use of the 3-D concept, whether a filing system is developed on the basis of it or not, will facilitate consideration of different occupational information and the identification of information by people (potential users) and by depth. In using the 3-D concept for determining scope of coverage, the counselor may find some information of insufficient quantity to achieve the goals established for the occupational information center. The application of the 3-D concept will tend to encourage obtaining and using a wider scope of information, different types of occupational information, and a greater number of media.

Many file plans are developed for a special medium—unbound occupational information—also with no consideration given to other media. Another emphasis placed in many file plans is upon the industry, the specific occupation, the interest, or some other single theme, whereas the counselor and the coordinator of a comprehensive occupational information center should be more concerned with the wide scope of information that has potential value to the clientele, the many different media, and the great number of different types of occupational information. No longer can a professional counselor think of facilitating the occupational information processes over an extended period of time through the media of unbound literature only.

The developmental approach has enabled counselors to recognize multifarious media, an extended time period, and multiple depths as essential in the consideration of occupational information. The counselor is in need of a file plan that will pull together the multifarious media at multiple depths so that potential users, as well as the counselor, can spend more time on utilization and interpretation and less time on wondering if the information might possibly be filed someplace else because of its being available in a different medium.

The 3-D concept is applicable to all three information areas—educational, occupational, and personal-social—in counseling and guidance, rather than being restricted to occupational information alone. The application of a 3-D concept tends to show the relationships among the three areas, which, if used with individuals, may assist them in thinking of a broader range and facilitate their growth and development. The 3-D concept focuses attention upon the need for a comprehensive overall file system. Whether the schematic file plan suggested is appropriate or not for a local situation, each counselor will need to determine; but the application of the 3-D concept can be useful in the selection of a file plan.

Sample Materials

For illustrative purposes the following occupational materials, applicable to different settings, are presented, together with titles, media, publishers and sources, costs, annotations, potential users, and possible file codes based on the 3-D system. The materials were selected from different settings—elementary, junior high, and senior high schools and community agencies serving adults. Some of the materials would have been applicable in more than one setting, but for illustrative purposes were only listed once. The lists are illustrative rather than comprehensive in scope.

Elementary School Materials

The following would be illustrative of materials applicable in an elementary school setting:

I Want to Be a Ship Captain. Book. Children's Press, Inc.; $1.88. Pictures and large print for primary grades. (For pupils' use. Code: S1–197.168–1)

I Want to Be a Dentist. Book. Children's Press, Inc.; $1.88. Pictures and large print for primary grades. (For pupils' use. Code: S1–072.108–1)

You and Transportation. Book. Children's Press, Inc.; $1.88. Illustrated book on transportation written at fifth grade reading level. (For pupils' use. Code: S1–Of–1, Transportation)

Let's Go to a Weather Station. Book. G. P. Putnam's Sons; $1.97. (For pupils' use. Code: S1–Of–1, Weather Station)

What Could I Be. Book. Science Research Associates, Inc.; $0.75. Illustrated book designed to broaden knowledge of occupational areas for boys and girls. (For pupils' use. Code: Si–Om–3)

Let's Go to a Post Office. Book. G. P. Putnam's Sons; $1.97. (For pupils' use. Code: Si–Of–1, Post Office)

Fiction and Non-Fiction Literature. Publishers listed in Chapter 11. Literature can be used as reading material for individuals or in classroom work. (Mostly designed for pupil use, but some may be for teacher or counselor to use with pupils. Code according to projected use. The 3–D concept may be helpful in analyzing material and in keying for storage and retrieval.)

"W. O. W. Series." Filmstrips, records, and teaching guides. Edu-Craft Incorporated. Contains film strips with accompanying records for purpose of prevocational information. Written on three levels: kindergarten through third grade with eleven filmstrips, $138.00; grades four through six with thirteen filmstrips, $162.00; and grades seven through nine with twenty-six filmstrips, $318.00.

Junior High School Materials

The following materials were selected from a junior high school counseling and guidance information center:

Behind the Scenes at the Post Office. Book. Dodd, Mead, & Company; $2.79. General material on occupations in the Post Office. (For student use. Code: Sj–Of–1, Post Office)

Find a Career in Law Enforcement. Book. G. P. Putnam's Sons; $2.95. General information on law enforcement occupations. (For student use. Code: Sj–Of–1, Law Enforcement)

The Teacher's Role in Career Development. Book. National Vocational Guidance Association; $1.00. Presents viewpoints on how the teacher helps students in career development. (For teacher use. Code: Ts–Om–2)

Career Development: Self-concept Theory. Book. College Entrance Examination Board; $2.50. Useful for in-service education. Explains Super's self-concept theory. (For teacher use. Code: Ts–Om–2)

Automation and Your Child's Future. Leaflet. National Education Association; 35 for $1.00. For parents' use. Code: Ps–Om–1)

Factbook on the School Dropout in the World of Work. Booklet. Bureau of Labor Statistics; free. Information on drop-outs. Compares earnings of drop-outs and high school graduates. Gives general characteristics of drop-out. (For counselor use with potential drop-outs. Code: CIp–Os–2)

Bibliography of Current Occupational Literature. Booklet. National Vocational Guidance Association; $1.00. (Reference book for counselor. Code Cr–O–2)

You Want to Be a Tool and Die or Mold Maker. Film. Vocational Films; B&W $60.00; color, $120.00. Specific occupational information. Applicable for potential early school leavers. (For counselor use with potential drop-outs. Code: CIp–601.280–2)

"Widening Occupational Roles Kit." Briefs, booklets, workbooks, Manual, and Filmstrips. Science Research Associates, Inc.; $135.00 See write-up in preceding section of this chapter. (Use code supplied by manufacturer.)

"Desk-Top Kit." Briefs. Careers; $92.50. One is published for junior high and another for senior high schools. See write-up in preceding section of this chapter. (Use code supplied by publisher.)

"Careers for Women." Briefs, booklets, and posters. Science Research Associates, Inc.; $32.50. Contains eighty-five junior occupational briefs, five job family booklets, guidance series booklet, and guidance posters designed for girls in grades seven through ten. (Use code supplied by publisher. May want to integrate into total informational file, then will need to add local file code.)

Occupational Information. Sources were listed in Chapter 11. (File according to local plan or *D.O.T.* code. Could use *D.O.T.* code plus the 3–D system. If material is not on specific occupation but is on family of occupations or general information, the *D.O.T.* code may not be applicable. The 3–D concept may be helpful in keying for storage and retrieval.)

Senior High School Materials

The following were selected from a senior high school counseling and guidance information center:

Your Future as an Airline Stewardess. Book. Richard Rosen Press, Inc.; $2.95. (For student use. Code: Ss–352.878–2)

The Profession of Teaching. Book. Odyssey Press, Inc.; $4.00. (For student use. Code: Ss–Of–2, Teaching)

Opportunities in VISTA. Booklet. B'nai B'rith; free. Explains the VISTA program and is written for students who are interested in becoming VISTA volunteers. (For student use. Code: Ss–Of–2, VISTA)

The Job Finder: It Pays to Advertise. Booklet. Bellman Publishing Co., $2.25. (For student use. Code: Ss–Oj–2)

The High School Student's Guide to Summer Jobs. Booklet. Maco Publishing Company, Inc.; $0.95. (For student use. Code: Ss–Oj–2)

Know Your Employment Rights Under Law. Booklet. U.S. Government Printing Office; $0.15. (For student use. Code: Ss–O1–2)

American Best Source of Guidance Material Bibliographical Catalogue. Book. Associated Publishers. (Reference book for counselor use. Code: Cr–O–2)

Counselor's Guide to Occupational and Other Manpower Information: An Annotated Bibliography of Selected Government Publications. Booklet. U.S. Government Printing Office, $0.50. (Reference material for counselor use. Code: Cr–O–2)

Occupational Outlook Handbook. Book. U.S. Government Printing Office; $4.75. Contains information on several different occupations with latest trends and outlooks in each. (Reference for counselor and material for student use. Code: CrSs–O–2)

Man, Education, and Work. Book. American Council on Education; $1.50. Information on trends and development in the world today. (For counselor use. Code: Cs–Ot–2)

Attitudes and Occupations. Film. Coronet Films; $60.00. (For counselor use with students. Code: CSs–Om–1)

Tips for Handicapped Job Seeker: Some Do's and Don'ts When Applying for Work. Booklet. President's Committee on Employment of the Handicapped; free. (For counselor use with handicapped students. Code: CIh–Oj–2)

Planning My Future. Book. American Guidance Service, Inc.; $4.20. Designed for use in group work. (For teacher use with students. Code: TSs–Om–3)

Social Science and Your Career. Booklet. Bureau of Labor Statistics; $0.10. Useful for classroom use in social science classes. (For teacher use with students. Code: TSs–Of–2, Social Science)

Job Horizons for College Women in the 1960's. Booklet. Women's Bureau; $0.30. Presents the role of women in the world of work, particularly for college women. (For teacher use with students. Code: TSs–Ot–1)

Job Guide for Young Workers. Booklet. U.S. Government Printing Office; $0.45. Provides information about employment prospects, qualifications for jobs, opportunities for advancement, how and where job is obtained, and characteristics of jobs frequently held by young people leaving high school. (For counselor use with potential drop-outs. Code: CIp–Oj–2)

Occupational Briefs and Monographs. See list of Commercial Publishers in Chapter 11. (For use mostly by students. Code according to *D.O.T.*, plus possibly the 3–D code.)

"Occupational Exploration Kit." Scanner, briefs, booklets, books, and guides. Science Research Associates, Inc.; $87.50. Useful for grades nine through twelve. See write-up in preceding section of this chapter. (Use Code supplied by publisher.)

"Career Exploratory Kit." Briefs. Careers; $65.00. See write-up in preceding section of this chapter. (Use code supplied by publisher.)

"SRA Career Information Kit." Briefs and folders. Science Research Associates, Inc.; $179.50. See write-up in preceding section of this chapter. (Use code supplied by publisher. If the material is integrated into total information files, then add local file code.)

"Desk-Top Kit." Briefs. Careers; $97.50. See write-up in preceding section of this chapter. (Use code supplied by publisher.)

"Chronicle Occupational Library." Briefs, folders, and posters. Chronicle Guidance Publications; $160.00. Contains 325 Occupational Briefs, 250 reprints from trade and technical publications, 100 job publications, 30 posters, and 2 direction cards. Can be obtained in mobile file cabinet. (Code is based on *D.O.T.* Could have 3–D code added.)

Occupational Information. List of sources supplied in Chapter 11. (If material is specific occupational information, file according to *D.O.T.* or local plan. If *D.O.T.* or local file plans are not applicable, then the 3–D concept may be beneficial in keying for storage and retrieval.)

"A Man's Work." Fifty long-play records plus instructor's guide. McGraw-Hill, Inc.; $258.50. Contains one hundred recorded on-the-scene interviews with men talking about their jobs as they work. Each record has seventeen to twenty-two minutes' play time. (For student use. Code according to the different occupations or may be left in the box in which received if a record playing room is available.)

Materials for Use in Community Agencies

The following were selected from materials used in counseling and guidance in a community agency:

Occupations for Men and Women After 45. Book. World Trade Publishing Co.; $12.50. For adults over forty-five who need to enter, retrain, or relocate in an occupation. (For adults. Code: Ar–Om–1)

Counselor's Guide: How to Find Employment and Place Blind Persons on Jobs of an Industrial Character in Nonindustrial Areas. Book. Vocational Rehabilitation Administration. (For counselor use with handicapped person. Code: CAIhp–Oj–2)

Occupational Literature. Publishers are listed in Chapter 11. (Most of the literature can be used by an adult by himself or in conjunction with a counselor. Code according to *D.O.T.* or local file plan if literature is on specific occupations. If material cannot be coded according to *D.O.T.*, then the 3–D analysis concept and code provided in Table 7-1 may be helpful.)

Criteria of Occupational Maturity

The criteria for determining occupational maturity or the extent of occupational maturation have received considerable attention in the past twenty years, but agreement upon them has not been reached. Super and Overstreet (1960, pp. 33–34) used five dimensions of vocational maturity: orientation to vocational choice, information and planning about the preferred occupation, consistency of vocational preferences, crystallization of traits, and wisdom of vocational preferences. John Crites, a former associate of Donald Super, has developed a Vocational Development Inventory (VDI), which has been used as an assessment of vocational development (see Chapter 9). Agreement has not been reached as to whether vocational maturity should be determined by expected behavior of a person at a given stage in development and by actual behavior shown in handling developmental tasks (Super and Overstreet, 1960, pp. 8–9) or whether in addition to performance (behavior) consideration should be given to intellectual, attitudinal, feeling, and emotional—cognitive and affective—processes. Consideration of cognitive and affective processes in addition to performance will necessitate many additional criteria being included. In Chapter 3, Table 3-2, was presented a schematism for occupational development, subdivided according to occupational understandings developed, meanings acquired, and attitudes formulated, which does place attention upon both cognitive and affective processes.

Much of the literature pertaining to theories and research in the occupational maturation area might be summarized as placing emphasis upon psycho-social-philosophical considerations. If occupational development can be affected by environmental conditions, including people, things, and ideas, then more consideration needs to be given to criteria for the assessment of progress. Occupational information, whether from people or things, becomes an important part of the environmental conditions, thus better assessments of the effect of occupational information needs to be made. Assessments depend upon criteria. Additional research is needed before criteria of occupational maturity and landmarks of occupational maturation can be identified.

Improving Extensiveness of Use

Occupational information in counseling and guidance has value only when it becomes useful to individuals. Therefore, improving the extensiveness of use becomes an item for major attention. The information must be pertinent to the needs of the potential users or they will use it only when forced to do so. A counselor or the information center director must be constantly determining needs among potential users and seeking appropriate information. Then the potential user must become aware of at least three things: the value of additional information to him, the places where the information is located, and the means by which the information can be made available to him.

Awareness of material can be increased through displays, newspaper articles, radio and television spot announcements on programs, bulletin boards, and many other techniques. The location of materials becomes a determinant of availability and a major determinant of extent of use. The central storage place may not be the major place for use; thus consideration should be given to seeking means of taking appropriate occupational information to places where potential users can utilize the material. Mobile files, decentralization of some materials, multiple copies of some frequently used materials, a check-out system for borrowing material, and easy return of borrowed materials are all means of assuring potential users that the occupational information most appropriate for their use can be moved to other facilities when necessary to promote accessibility and utilization.

The person in charge of the central information center must be well qualified and must possess an interest not only in materials but also in people. His leadership and the pace he establishes for forward thinking, information obtaining, equipment utilization, and personnel performance will definitely affect the extensiveness of use. He must involve potential users so that the third depth—feedback—becomes a reality for the user. He needs to work with users and must see his role primarily in facilitating occupational information utilization while seeing the other tasks—ordering, coding, filing, retrieving—as essential components rather than the focal points.

Automated equipment is now developed to the point that a comprehensive information center should include use of automated equipment. The kind to include depends upon the goals set for the information center; but primarily the purposes for use of automated equipment in information centers should be to save the users' time, increase the kind and amount of information available, and provide better service.

If the emphases are kept upon the values to users rather than completeness and perfection of material, the extensiveness of use will be high. Personalizing the occupational information possessed is more important than cumulation of occupational information material, but recognition should be made of the fact that one probably cannot be achieved without the other.

Methods of Keeping Occupational Information Up-to-Date

To keep occupational information up-to-date someone has to work at it, has to work hard at it. No easy short cuts are available. What is needed in one setting may not be, and often is not, appropriate for another setting, thus preventing the development of a state or national centrally controlled system from doing the work necessary for keeping occupational information up-to-date in all local centers.

A few general guidelines can be stated for occupational information as was done in the last part of Chapter 7 for educational information. Material should be dated when received so as to show how recently it was received and to show if it may be the latest available material even if the issue date is old. The material should be reviewed regularly, at least once a year, marking outdated sections as such if the material is to be kept for other sections, destroying outdated and useless material, and marking but saving selected materials for comparative purposes to study trends and modifications.

One helpful technique for knowing about and being able to order recent materials is to subscribe to and use a periodic review service, such as those supplied by B'nai B'rith, Chronicle, Guidance Exchange, Personnel Service, and SRA (see section on "Contractual Service" in Chapter 11). In addition publications are issued regularly that contain lists of recently produced materials including those by National Vocational Guidance Association (each issue of *Vocational Guidance Quarterly* and current issues of the *Bibliography of Current Occupational Literature*) and the Superintendent of Documents, U.S. Government Printing Office (biweekly issues of the bulletin entitled *Selected United States Government Publications*).

Summary

The users' or potential users' needs and the goals established for the occupational information center become major items in a criterion for determining the location and the facilities necessary for making occupational information available. Recognition of many purposes and the wide scope of needs possessed by users may necessitate occupational information being made available in more than one location. Educational and occupational information probably will be housed in the same geographic area, but the selection of the codification and file plan will determine whether or not educational and occupational information will be housed together and the extent to which users may see them as supplemental and complementary to each other.

Several codification and filing plans are available for consideration, including the alphabetical system, the *Bennett Occupations Filing Plan*, interests, school subjects (the *Missouri Filing Plan*), industry (the *Standard Industrial Classification Manual*), the *California Plan*, and the *D.O.T.* classification system. In addition certain occupational kits and files of materials have been marketed by various companies—the "Desk-Top Kit," the "Career Information Kit," the "Widening Occupational Roles Kit" (WORK), the "Occupational Exploration Kit," "Careers for High School Graduates," "SOS Guidance Research Information Booklets," and the "Career Exploratory Kit."

The 3-D concept when utilized with occupational information helps the counselor to consider the many different people for whom information may be needed and to consider the different depths of information needed over an extended period of time. With the 3-D concept as a backdrop in evaluating the occupational information possessed in the information center, the counselor may be able to identify where the information materials and resources are insufficient for meeting individuals' needs and goals.

Identification, coding, and filing are secondary to the main purpose of utilizing occupational information as a facilitator of occupational maturation. The emphasis is not on what file plan, which piece of material, or where located but rather is on the utilization of information by users. The counselor and the coordinator of the information center must constantly strive to improve the availability of the appropriate information at each and every pertinent time. If the information can be available when and where needed, the extensiveness of use will be great. To achieve the availability desired, attention will need also to be given to occupational maturation and the personalizing of occupational information to assist in the process. As has been emphasized in the 3-D concept, to achieve the personalization necessary the attention must be upon the user, his needs, and his occupational development.

SELECTED REFERENCES

Baer, Max F., and Edward C. Roeber. *Occupational Information: The Dynamics of Its Nature and Use.* Chicago: Science Research Associates, Inc., 1964. Pp. 366–374.

Dictionary of Occupational Titles, 3rd ed. Washington, D.C.: Bureau of Employment Security, Manpower Administration. U.S. Department of Labor, 1965. Vol. I, *Definitions of Titles;* Vol. II, *Occupational Classification.* Also *A Supplement to the Dictionary of Occupational Titles,* 1966.

Eckerson, A. B. "The New Dictionary of Occupational Titles," *The Vocational Guidance Quarterly,* 12 (Autumn 1963), 40–42.

Fine, Sidney A., and Carl A. Heinz. "The Functional Occupational Classification Structure," *The Personnel and Guidance Journal,* 37 (November 1958), 180–192.

Forrester, Gertrude. *Occupational Literature: An Annotated Bibliography,* 1964 ed. New York: The H. W. Wilson Company, 1964. 675 pages.

Hoppock, Robert. *Occupational Information: Where to Get It and How to Use It in Counseling and in Teaching,* 3rd ed. New York: McGraw-Hill, Inc., 1967. Pp. 44–83.

Impellitteri, Joseph T. "A Computerized Occupational Information System," *The Vocational Guidance Quarterly,* 15 (June 1967), 262–264.

Isaacson, Lee E. *Career Information in Counseling and Teaching.* Boston: Allyn and Bacon, Inc., 1966. Pp. 314–332.

Kirk, Barbara A., and Marjorie E. Michels. *Occupational Information in Counseling: Use and Classification.* Berkeley, Calif. Consulting Psychologists Press, Inc., 1964. 80 pages.

LeMay, Morris L. "An Inexpensive Address File for Occupational Information," *The Vocational Guidance Quarterly,* 14 (Autumn 1965), 55.

LeMay, Morris L., and Charles F. Warnath. "Student Opinion on the Location of Occupational Information on a University Campus." *The Personnel and Guidance Journal,* 45 (April 1967), 821–823.

Norris, Willa, Franklin R. Zeran, and Raymond N. Hatch. *The Information Service in Guidance,* 2nd ed. Chicago: Rand McNally & Company, 1966. Pp. 384–402.

Ohlsen, Merle M. *Guidance Services in the Modern School.* New York: Harcourt, Brace, & World, Inc., 1964. Pp. 307–309.

Roeber, Edward C. *Missouri Filing Plan for Unbound Materials on Occupations.* Columbia, Mo.: College of Education, University of Missouri, 1950. Mimeographed, 26 pages.

Rusalem, Herbert. "New Insights on the Role of Occupational Information in Counseling," in *The Counselor in the School: Selected Readings.* Cecil H. Patterson, ed. New York: McGraw-Hill, Inc., 1967. Chap. 39, pp. 321–327.

Shartle, Carroll L. *Occupational Information: Its Development and Applica-cation*, 3rd ed. Englewood Cliffs, N.J.: Prentice-Hall, Inc., 1959. Pp. 135–168, 192–195.

Super, Donald E., Phoebe L. Overstreet, et al. *The Vocational Maturity of Ninth-Grade Boys*. New York: Bureau of Publications, Teachers College, Columbia University, 1960. 212 pages.

United States Technical Committee on Industrial Classification, Office of Statistical Standards. *Standard Industrial Classification Manual*. Washington, D.C.: U.S. Government Printing Office, 1957.

Chapter 13

Utilizing Occupational

Information with

Individuals and Groups

Counselors-in-training must learn to view the student's emerging vocational motives through a developmental prism.

—BOROW, 1966, p. 84.

Counselors are today using a wider variety of methods than ever before, and new methods for utilizing occupational information are becoming available. Some methods have application with groups, whereas others can be used primarily on an individual basis. Counselors will need to study the values and limitations of different methods to determine which ones will be most effective in the local situation and which ones might help achieve an ongoing longitudinal, developmental concept. The information center is no longer serving in the almost single function of an occupational information dispenser, but rather the information center personnel and specifically the counselor are assisting individuals in utilizing occupational information in their growth and development. Other members of the professional staff are also assisting in utilizing occupational information and, as this assistance develops, the team approach will be more beneficial than if each staff member works independently. Occupational information in its broadest connotation will be useful in the counseling sessions.

A Point of View

Purposes for using information in counseling and guidance often are identified as (1) to answer questions and (2) to increase the individual's knowledge about occupational, educational, and personal-social information. However, a broader concept is becoming prevalent today that encompasses these two purposes while also extending and increasing the purposes. The expansion is based upon the developmental approach and upon creating sequential activities that contribute to personalizing information processes.

The utilization of occupational information is dependent upon the limits established by the viewpoint contained within the purposes. If the point of view is that the information is only for the purposes of answering questions and increasing knowledge, the information can be shown to individuals, placed on display, or paraded by with exposure being a major point for consideration. If the purposes are extended on the developmental concept, the emphasis is placed on meaningful, personally useful information. The information is more for individualized coverage with an ongoing development that produces openness, thus increasing exposure to new and different concepts, facts, and understanding. Without the developmental personalizing concept, the information is more for broad coverage and results in being more nonpersonalized, and thus frequently is less effective because of the way the individual perceives the information available.

When the information to be used, both in content and medium, is dependent upon the individual, the extent of use is different and the effectiveness changes as compared to content and medium being determined by the counselor or someone other than the person himself. When the media are selected by someone else, the individual often centers attention on media rather than on the information and its value to him. The individual, in such cases, may make decisions based upon the type of presentation, and in so doing may make the decisions with insufficient and inadequate information.

If information for use in counseling and guidance is designed to answer questions and to increase an individual's knowledge about occupational information, then the material collected is primarily group oriented rather than being information related to the individual, his concepts, his goals, and his needs. The information contains valid, comprehensive, and usable data about the world of work, including duties, working conditions, entrance requirements, pay, advancement patterns, number of jobs, and distribution of workers. In listing additional purposes for the information and taking the point of view expressed in this book, the preceding information contents are still needed, but work is seen more as an expression of self, and occupational information becomes related to the individual and his aspirations with valid, comprehensive coverage being for the purpose of the individual's having more integration of self and information about the world of work. The information center operated under the expanded point of view still places emphasis upon the quality and quantity of material, but emphasis is placed even more upon information being collected for projected use with individuals; therefore, only a minimum amount of information is stored that is not applicable to individuals. The information is collected for use in assisting the individual in his growth and development and may be used on an individual or group basis.

With the purposes listed in the past for information, the personnel who worked with the information needed to be trained in library techniques and methods for handling materials. Any personnel using information with individuals will need to know to some extent such techniques and methods; however, if the purposes are more in a developmental concept, the personnel will need to be well qualified in human dynamics and the utilization of information with individuals in facilitating their development and their decision-making processes. Since World War II, use of occupational information has been undergoing a very definite change, which might be summarized but admittedly oversimplified by saying *a change from occupational information dissemination to personalizing the occupational information processes.* Such a change necessitates personnel with different and more extensive preparation in counseling and guidance, psychology, and sociology.

In the past an individual has been expected to know himself and his needs well enough so that he could select the best information without assistance. As Leona Tyler (1961, p. 154) wrote, "Experience has taught us that a person is likely to be as ignorant of his own assets and liabilities as he is of job characteristics." Today occupational information can be personalized and should be used more with the person; thus emphasis is placed on the third depth, where a feedback can be obtained. Abstract occupational information about the external world becomes an integral part of the subjectively perceived self, together with an understanding and integration of objective data about self into the total picture. Information is used throughout life, with occupational information starting in early childhood instead of being delayed until secondary school or until questions are raised. The emphasis is placed on the total individual, the conceptual self, and the information is an important part of self-development rather than stress upon the materialistic, abstract, factual presentation. Occupational information becomes internalized instead of being seen by the individual as external or something not applicable to him at this time. Personal-social information processes are considered in greater detail in Part IV, Chapters 14–18.

When the supply and demand or economic theory of occupational choice prevailed, supplying occupational information to answer questions and increase the individual's knowledge about occupational information was believed to be the predominant purpose. With prevailing theories (Chapter 9) changing to those based on developmental concepts, the purposes had to be expanded. Occupational choice is no longer seen as a single choice for life; rather, during a lifetime one will probably have a multiple number of jobs and occupations, and occupational information is longitudinal—extended over many years—instead of being given at a specific time of short duration. The decision-making processes are more than just the intellectualizing of information; instead, the information is integrated into one's perceived self by both the cognitive and affective processes. Occupational information today is utilized in such a manner that the development of the individual is assisted and that openness rather than closure is encouraged. Occupational information now is utilized to maximize human freedom and effectiveness, not to close doors and maintain the status quo.

The methods selected for utilizing occupational information are to achieve the new purposes as well as the purposes of long standing. One is not done at the expense of the other; rather, materials, technology, skills, tools, theories, research, and philosophical orientation have all advanced enough so that the counselor of today can be expected to utilize occupational information based on the concept of the developmental approach and used to contribute to personalizing information processes.

Interrelationship of Roles

To achieve a developmental approach many professional personnel must be involved as a team on a longitudinal basis extending from early childhood throughout life (Peters and Farwell, 1967, p. 501). Each individual is considered unique, and the professional personnel attempt to help the individual understand his own uniqueness as well as the professional personnel understanding the uniqueness so that they can work more effectively with him. Recognizing that he is dynamic, growing and developing, the uniquenesses may also change. One member of a professional team may detect the change in the bud and through his work with the individual and the other professional team members may assist the individual in making the change and in understanding how the change was initiated, developed, and dependent upon other conditions. Every effort is to be made to establish productive working relationships among the professional team members in schools and community agencies (Gray, 1963, p. 253). The team approach must exist within the setting, such as in a school where teachers, counselors, psychologists, administrators, social workers, and nurses often function within the same building. Each of them with his own competencies can work conjointly with the other team members so that the individual receives the maximum benefits as they complement and supplement each other. The team approach must also exist between settings, such as employment offices, rehabilitation offices, personnel offices in business and industry, family service offices, and child guidance clinics.

A team approach is sometimes considered to be two or more persons of the same profession working together; e.g., two counselors working with the same person or one of them working with the individual and consulting with the other. That type of team approach is needed and probably should be used more extensively than it is. A second type of team approach is when one professional person recognizes the need for the individual to work with another professional person and makes a referral to him. The number of different kinds of professional persons within a given locality is increasing and the number of referrals is also increasing. The individual generally is benefited by a referral. A third type of team approach is becoming more prominent, in which different professional persons work in a *conjoint relationship*. The members share their ideas, findings, procedures, and results together as they plan their responsibilities in working with the individual. An interrelationship of roles can be achieved through a conjoint relationship with the professional members, using their different skills, techniques, and competencies for a common purpose—assistance to the individual. The team approach can be and often is extended over a long period of time.

The counselor cannot and should not, even if he could, provide all the occupational information. The individual begins to gain occupational information when he first begins to react to people and what they do. He learns from members of his family attitudes about work. He formulates attitudes of his own as a result of being without his mother or father during their working hours. Occupational information is achieved from many sources, and human experiences are continuous in an unsegmented stream, with each experience potentially contributing to the growth and development of the individual (Weitz, 1964, p. 1). Each event is associated with another and the composite occupational information perceived by the individual cannot be attributed to any one person, thing, or idea, nor can the occupational information possessed by an individual be summarized for simple identification of where an individual is on a continuum toward vocational maturity. The complexity of the individual, the multimedia through which occupational information is obtained, and the developmental approach to occupational information necessitate a team concept with all professional personnel recognizing they have a role.

Vocational maturity as defined by Super and Overstreet (1960, pp. 8–9) is primarily determined by behavior, either by the individual compared to the group or by what the individual does in relation to a given task. Occupational maturation as used in this book has used Super and Overstreet's behavior indices plus two other areas—knowledge and attitude or feelings. With the broad concept of occupational maturation and the dependency upon behavior, knowledge, and attitudes, many professional personnel become involved, and their disciplines, specialized education, and competencies can contribute to the occupational maturation of each individual.

As pointed out by Tennyson, Soldahl, and Mueller (1965), the teacher has a definite role in career development. Many of the methods for utilizing occupational information identified in this chapter will be methods used extensively by teachers. The teacher working alone with the child may not be as effective as the teacher with team assistance from the counselor and others.

The occupational maturation of an individual is dependent upon his understanding about himself as well as about the world of work. Psychologists and psychometrists can be important team members in assisting the individual in understanding himself. The social worker can contribute much sociological information to assist the individual and those who work with him. The nurse, physician, and other health-service personnel can contribute information about the physical development of the individual. The counselor in a guidance service role can assist the individual in frequently obtaining appropriate occupational information. The counselor in a counseling session can help the individual evaluate, integrate, and internalize much of the information from various sources. The professional personnel have interrelative roles in assisting the individual in his occupational maturation.

Using Occupational Information in a Counseling Relationship

Baer and Roeber (1964, p. 425) have pointed out two opposing points of view that exist about the use of occupational information in a counseling relationship. One group of counselors would hold that information should be given in the counseling session and that the counselor should help the individual to know and understand occupational information. Another group of counselors believes that giving information will be harmful to the counseling relationship. The views held depend upon what the counselor believes to be the functions of a counseling relationship. If vocational development is an integral part of self-expression and if the counseling relationship is concerned with the individual, then the counseling interviews at times will be focused upon vocational development, of which occupational information is a vital part. As Margaret Bennett (1964, p. 460) wrote, "Realistic vocational goals and aspirations are now seen as stemming from basic life values and motives, and from growing awareness both of personal potentialities and of opportunities in the socio-economic order." Occupational information will be, therefore, an integral part of many, not all, counseling relationships.

Lee Isaacson (1966, pp. 400–407) summarized the various functions of career information in counseling. He listed four functions: *motivational* uses "to arouse or to stimulate the counselee," *instructional* uses "to inform or teach the client about the occupation being discussed," *adjustive* uses "to assist the counselee in developing a more appropriate balance between himself and his tentative career plans," and *distributive* uses to basically focus "upon entrance into employment or the placement activity."

Walter Lifton (1964–1965, p. 77) stated that the profession has fairly well accepted the concept that information can be used by clients and will be incorporated if certain conditions prevail. Lifton stated that clients will incorporate information when:

1. the information is presented in a way which enables them to use the facts with a minimum of transfer.
2. they are secure enough to allow themselves to perceive the situation broadly, rather than using tunnel vision to protect themselves from seeing potentially threatening situations.
3. they have perceived a need for this information to achieve a goal important to themselves.

If recognition is made of the three phases of guidance and counseling —*corrective or remedial, preventive or adjustive,* and *developmental or facilitating*—more than one purpose and many different methods of using occupational information can be identified (Hollis and Hollis, 1965, pp. 12–14). If the major purpose of a counseling session is to remedy a poor occupational placement, then occupational information may be provided to assist the individual in the recognition of alternatives. The occupational information may assist the individual in knowing about occupations into which he may change and the resources available to assist him. If the purpose of a counseling session is to prevent a potentially undesirable vocational situation, the occupational information may be for instructional uses, planning, and exploration. The third phase of development is, as Peters and Farwell (1967, p. 501) stated, to understand the uniqueness of the individual, focus on his strengths, give meaning to his potentialities, and clarify "experiences to the point of achieving a deeply personal meaning that has continuity." If developmental counseling includes these things, occupational information has many functions. The individual needs to have early involvement and to have a continuous feedback (Loughary, 1961, pp. 41–43) whereby he can obtain positive and negative inferences that have meanings for him.

The following are uses for occupational information in the counseling relationship. Not every counseling session, but some, will use occupational information and then for only part of the purposes listed. No attempt has been made to provide an exhaustive list, but rather to select samples of uses (references are to authors where additional information can be found):

1. To help clarify the picture and obtain information pertinent to the topic, thus eliminating vague anxieties over the unknown (Coleman, 1960, p. 387).
2. To provide a backdrop for considering one's own values, feelings, and attitudes. The individual may come to the counseling session with enough occupational information to examine his own values, feelings, and attitudes, or he may need additional occupational information before he can consider his. Comprehensive, pertinent, accurate occupational information is essential at times for an examination of one's own internal beliefs. Counseling relationships have as goals the examination of one's values, feelings, and attitudes, and occupational information may be background for such considerations.
3. To assist in exploration and formulation of alternatives (Tyler, 1961, pp. 155–156).
4. To aid in identifying avenues of approaches toward reaching goals or for testing tentative choices. Exploratory and entry jobs may be examples as well as simulated situations.
5. To build up competencies by knowing information and by identifying means of obtaining necessary skills or resources (Coleman, 1960, p. 387).
6. To serve as stimuli for the individual's own creative cognitive and affective processes.
7. To place various to-be-made decisions in proper perspective in terms of long-range goals, time sequence, and the importance of one to the other (Coleman, 1960, p. 387). The individual may have sufficient information to make an immediate decision as far as he knows, but he may lack information on implications of the decision for the future.
8. To provide a base for making a choice or decision (Tyler, 1961, p. 157).
9. To supply information for planning (Tyler, 1961, p. 157).
10. To have a feedback (Loughary, 1961, pp. 41–43) between subjective self-concepts and the objective data of the occupational world of reality.
11. To discuss from the counselee's viewpoint with someone, the counselor, who is as unbiased as possible and who knows and understands him as well as anyone. The counselor provides an opportunity for the individual to integrate information that previously may have been understood but not internally utilized (Loughary, 1961, p. 87).
12. To utilize occupational information with the counselee rather than to give information to him.

Occupational, educational, and personal-social information does have a place in the counseling relationship. If the philosophy expressed in this book is to be achieved, then counselors need to perceive information in the broader concept and to recognize new and different purposes for information. If information surrounds the individual and if one of his tasks is to personalize information, then the counseling relationship becomes an important part of the personalized information processes. The methods and techniques suggested in this chapter plus those in Chapter 8 on educational information and within each chapter in personal-social information should be considered as potentially having use for the counseling relationship or as complements to it. The methods and techniques if not used in the counseling relationship may be used between counseling sessions as a continuation of the personalized information processes.

Contribution of Group Work to Individual

As Margaret Bennett (1963, p. 8) stated, group and individual procedures are each an implement and supplement of the other and both are essential. In an effective counseling and guidance program, occupational information is utilized in group settings and on an individual basis. Group work in personalizing occupational information has advantages and limitations. With an understanding of when and under what conditions the advantages and the limitations occur, the advantages probably can be accented and the limitations minimized.

Many methods for utilizing occupational information often can be used effectively in group settings, such as in a classroom in an elementary, junior high, and senior high school; colleges and universities; and trade, business, and vocational schools. Working in groups tends to assist the individual in areas that will be more difficult for him to achieve in working alone. As was pointed out in Chapter 8, some of the same objectives can be achieved by either group or individual work, but recognition of the ways each complements and supplements the other, the objectives most effectively achieved by each, and the focal points of each will enable a counselor to work more effectively and efficiently with persons who can benefit from occupational information.

Group work by its very nature tends to emphasize ideas, truths, people, and to examine relationships between and among information, often with the individual sharing his reactions. Contribution can be made by assisting the individual in considering various viewpoints about occupations and himself, viewpoints that may never have been considered if he had worked alone. Self-perception of the perceived occupational world may look different when viewed with feedback from peers or other individuals in a group setting than if viewed alone. The group work may lead to an increased need for individual work with a counselor.

Through group work members of the professional team may help create readiness for occupational information, may sense the timing when utilizing occupational information would be most appropriate, and may determine the depth, kind, and media of occupational information for use with each individual, thus assisting in the developmental approach through personalized occupational information. Group work with occupational information should assist the individual in obtaining skills for studying himself and the world of work so that he may become more self-directed. Baer and Roeber (1964, pp. 428–429) indicated that a primary goal in counseling (and equally true in group work) is to help counselees become increasingly self-directive. As they pointed out, *"Group methods focus on reactions to information, not simply on the imparting of information"* (p. 381). With group work in occupational information focusing on reactions and stressing self-direction, the method does contribute to the individual.

For most individuals, group work can increase their reservoir of experiences and for some can even provide enough experiences so that they will no longer be classified in the poverty of experiences. To make decisions, to grow and develop, one needs to have experiences. Group work is one approach for providing experiences, and often the experiences can be provided in a nurtured environment or in a simulated situation to the extent that the individual can achieve the experience without all of the psychosocial dynamics and insecurities that may prevent growth and development. Once having had the experience within such a situation, the security, through feedback, may be sufficient for him to take the next step toward real total situational involvement.

The individual needs to learn skills for utilizing information in relation to himself. These can be learned in many group situations. The skills learned will be used at various times throughout life (Baer and Roeber, 1964, p. 429). The individual needs skills in order to progress in his occupational maturation. He also needs skills for utilizing information in relation to himself just to help him keep abreast with the occupational world of perpetual surprises—where the changes often come as a surprise to the individual. Changes in the occupational world produce insecurity for many, and one of the functions for utilizing occupational information with individuals is to help them learn skills for flexibility, expectation of change, and growing and developing.

Selection of Method

David Tiedeman (Tiedeman and Dudley, 1967) stated that the "media massages imagination." If so, then the media become an important part of occupational information just as well as does the content. Recognizing that individuals are different and so are their needs, then the use of a variety of learning media will be advantageous (Baer and Roeber, 1964, p. 381). The individual changes as time passes and the media that massage his imagination at one time may no longer be appropriate. The selection of methods for utilizing occupational information becomes a major item; constant consideration of modifications and variety in methods should be the accepted practice rather than the unusual.

New methods for using occupational information are being developed and counselors need to become familiar with them as well as the advantages and limitations of each. One of the weaknesses pertaining to methods that have existed is a lack of a philosophical and theoretical base for sequential experiences and information necessary for occupational maturation. Without such a framework each method tends to be evaluated alone rather than being viewed as an integral part of contributing to an overall progressive development of the individual. Research, limited as it is, seems to support the developmental theories of occupations. If these theories are to have an impact on the counseling and guidance movement, then methods of using occupational information must be considered in terms of their possible position within the development. In Chapter 8 was provided a schematism for considering methods according to the involvement of the individual. A similar schematism for occupational information methods is presented in Table 13-1.

Differential selection of occupational information must be made according to the individual, his needs, and readiness, The method for using the information will also need differential selection according to the depth, degree of individual involvement, and extent of control the individual is to have over the kind of information obtained. As Vincent Calia (1966, p. 322) wrote, "primary experiences can be as misleading as reading faulty occupational brochures. Intimate contacts are likely to be more *potent* but *not* necessarily *more valid*. Primary experience may have a more profound impact on career thinking and planning than reading an occupational pamphlet but this has nothing to do with its validity." As Calia (p. 323) pointed out, "some people use these experiences by personalizing them; others simply accumulate them." Selection of the method should be made in terms of the individual with whom it is to be used.

Literature has in recent years contained statements that seem to indicate that environmental conditions, including people, things, and ideas, do affect the rate of occupational maturation. Research studies as to which conditions and what the rate of effect is on the elementary-school-age child are very limited, but the few studies available do sup-

Table 13-1

SCHEMATIC CLASSIFICATION OF MEDIA AND SPECIFIC METHODS FOR UTILIZING OCCUPATIONAL INFORMATION WITH PERSONS ON AN INDIVIDUAL AND GROUP BASIS.

Classifications*	Media*	Specific Methods
PRESTRUCTURED AND FIXED	Publications	Biographies Magazines and periodicals Newspaper (school, business, and community) Booklets and brochures Reference books Career fiction Songs and Poems Occupational brief, abstract, monograph, and guide
	Audio-visual aids	Bulletin board, display, exhibits, posters, and charts Murals and art Phonograph, video tapes, and tape recordings Radio and television "Show and Tell" Slides, films, and filmstrips
	Planned programs	Assembly programs Career day Panels and career talks
INPUT CONTROLLED BY THE INDIVIDUAL	Programmed instruction	Vocational workbook Reports by individual Occupational exploration kits
	Computer-assisted information	VIEW Computer-assisted information systems
	Interview	Conferences with workers and personnel officers Making a job analysis Group discussions Job clinic Career conferences

Table 13-1 (*continued*)

Classifications*	Media*	Specific Methods
SIMULATION OF SITUATION	Role-playing and/or games	Quiz contest Dramatization and role-playing Practice job interview Game theory activities Brainstorming
	Synthetic occupational environment	Clubs (career) Laboratory study
REAL SITUATION	Direct observation	Visitation to places of work (plant tours, field trips) Foster uncle and aunt
	Directed exploration	Occupational units Occupational courses Occupational curriculums Exploratory job
	Actual occupational experience	Work experience programs On-the-job training Temporary job Entry job

* Source: "Classification" and "Media" based on comments by Albert S. Thompson at U.S. Office of Education, National Conference on Occupational Information in Vocational Guidance. Chicago, Illinois, May 16–18, 1967.

port use of occupational information in early childhood years. Much more research needs to be done, particularly in early occupational maturation, before differentiation among methods can be made with objective data to support the choice.

Individuals who have never held a full-time job and individuals who are changing jobs often want occupational information pertaining to such items as the dress for an interview with the potential employer, the kinds of information needed for completing application blanks, suggestions for writing application letters, typical interview questions, and means of finding out about the firm and the people who work there. Methods used to assist individuals with information of these types may be considerably different from methods used to assist an individual in examining himself, his desires, his strengths and weaknesses in terms of whether or not a specific occupation will provide expression of himself.

Methods of Utilizing Occupational Information

Kenneth Hoyt, in a speech presented May 17, 1967, at the U.S. Office of Education's National Conference on Occupational Information in

Vocational Guidance held in Chicago, stated that practices and methods used grow out of need and existing programs; therefore, no one program could or should use all of the methods existing today, not even all of the good ones. Different methods often develop within divergent programs formulated on different concepts and philosophical bases. Each counselor must review carefully each method in terms of the individual with whom it is to be used and the objectives to be achieved before selection of any one method or combination of methods.

Many more methods of using occupational information are available than space within this book will permit reporting in detail. The ones listed in Table 13-1 are used as a representative sample of those more frequently utilized. In some cases additional references are provided to facilitate review of comments made by other authors about the method. A resourceful, creative counselor will go beyond the methods listed whenever the situation warrants and the person with whom he is working needs assistance that can be provided better by another method.

Prestructured and Fixed Classification

In the classification of prestructured and fixed are three media—*publications, audio-visual aids,* and *planned programs.* In the *publications* medium materials are available and are used in gaining occupational information. Magazines, periodicals, and newspapers often contain articles, advertisements, and pictures that communicate occupational information. Books, such as biographies and career fiction (Norris et al., 1966, pp. 149–151), are often read not so much for the occupational information as for other purposes. Career books may be an effective method for some individuals. Many persons obtain career information from fiction and nonfiction storybooks. Often the occupational information is obtained without the individual's being fully aware of the extent of the occupational information he is obtaining. Other types of publications include booklets and brochures on occupations, which are frequently used. Reference books such as those listed in Chapter 11 are used to obtain specific, generally second depth, information. Songs and poems (Norris, 1963, pp. 74–75) may be used, particularly at the elementary school level. Most secondary-school-age and adult information center libraries will have various kinds of occupational literature, including occupational briefs, abstracts, monographs, and guides.

Items in the *audio-visual* medium would include guidance bulletin boards, displays, exhibits, posters, and charts (Isaacson, 1966, p. 347; Norris, et al., 1966, pp. 154–155 and 475–476; Hoppock, 1967, pp. 315–317; Norris, 1963, pp. 51–52; Baer and Roeber, 1964, pp. 382–384; and Hollis and Hollis, 1965, p. 295). In the lower grades of the elementary school the "show and tell" time often includes occupational information as the children show pictures of where their parents work and tell about the places where they have been. Slides, filmstrips, and films (Isaacson, 1966, pp. 344–346; Hoppock, 1967, pp. 317–320; Norris, 1963, pp. 52–54; and Peters, et al., 1965, pp. 60–61) are means of communicating more than words alone may do. Pictures may help the individual obtain an understanding about the physical environment in which the person works, the kinds of activities he does, the way he dresses, and the kind of machinery and tools with which he works. Pictures are often combined with other methods, and motion pictures or a series of pictures are often very helpful. Murals and art work (Norris, 1963, pp. 76–77, and Crow and Crow, 1965, p. 280) would be in a similar group with pictures and films. Voice recordings, such as phonograph and tape recordings (Norris et al., 1966, pp. 476–477; Baer and Roeber, 1964, pp. 433–434; Norris, 1963, pp. 53–54; and Hoppock, 1967, pp. 313–314), are excellent means of helping individuals hear people who are in the occupation talk about some of their experiences. Some schools have the young people interview workers and make tape recordings. Such a procedure combines the next classification "Input controlled by the individual" with the prestructured classification. The tapes can be saved and used by other individuals. With the development of television and its application in various settings, video tapes can be made and used similarly to the way audio tapes are.

In the *planned programs* medium at the secondary school level, career days and assembly programs (Norris et al., 1966, pp. 451–458 and 468–469; Ohlsen, 1964, pp. 320–321; Hoppock, 1967. pp. 339–442; Isaacson, 1966, pp. 370–375; Crow and Crow, 1965, pp. 291–298; Glanz, 1962, pp. 259–260; Arbuckle, 1966, pp. 279–280; and Baer and Roeber, 1964, pp. 387–388) are means of helping young people learn about occupations. Panels and career talks (Peters et al., 1965, p. 62, and Norris, 1963, pp. 80–86) in classes are also frequently used. One of the ways to emphasize the occupational implications of a school subject is to have speakers talk in the class about occupations that are most appropriate for the people enrolled in that subject. In the planned program methods the individual is often provided the opportunity to ask questions after the presentation is given. When the individuals begin to interact with the presenters, the input then begins to be controlled by the individuals, a medium in the next classification.

Input Controlled by the Individual Classification

In this classification of methods the individual controls part or all of the information requested and to some extent has an opportunity to react to information; thus self-involvement is encouraged more in these media than in the publications and the audio-visual media. The first medium is *programmed instruction,* where methods such as the "Occupational Exploration Kit" described in Chapter 12 would be used. Vocational workbooks (Hoppock, 1967, pp. 333–335) have use in helping individuals learn about occupations. Several commercially produced vocational workbooks are available. In some school settings students are required to write reports on an occupation of their choice (Norris et al., 1966, p. 438; Glanz, 1962, p. 259; Norris, 1963, p. 47; and Hollis and Hollis, 1965, p. 295). The report gives the student an opportunity to study in detail various facets of an occupation. Often the student changes his mind about his projected full-time occupational desires once he has studied an area in detail and has had the opportunity to work with other students as they study different areas.

The second medium—*computer-assisted instruction*—is just beginning to make contributions. Research work done with computer-assisted information systems (CAIS), of which several were reported in Chapters 3 and 9, seems to hold much promise for the future. VIEW at San Diego is probably as well developed and as ready for general use as any at this time. Contractual arrangements for individual work stations in local settings connected to a computer with a wide variety of occupational information is now possible and probably will soon be a reality for many local information centers.

The third medium of *interviews* has several methods that have been used by individuals and counselors. Conferences with workers and with personnel officers often reveal new information or place new meaning on information obtained from other sources. Making a job analysis often sharpens one's ability to see other jobs in more detail. As much as possible the individual should do the job analysis on an occupation in which he has considerable interest. Group discussions (Norris et al., 1966, pp. 38–39; Hollis and Hollis, 1965, p. 295; Peters et al., 1965, pp. 164–178; and Ohlsen, 1964, pp. 326–327) about different occupations provide an opportunity for the individual to become involved in and to examine himself in relation to the occupation as it is discussed. Two other methods are also in this same medium: job clinics (Hoppock, 1967, p. 326) and career conferences (Isaacson, 1966, pp. 375–377; Baer and Roeber, 1964, pp. 384–386; Crow and Crow, 1965, p. 300; and Shertzer and Stone, 1966, pp. 285–286).

Simulation of Situation Classification

To help the individual get the feel of an occupation and to get cognitive and affective processes both involved, methods should be considered that will simulate the real situation while providing the opportunity for the individual to sample the experience without having the total psychosocial insecurity. In simulated situations the individual can experience many of the situational psychosocial conditions without having to place, to such an extent, his entire future or success in the situation as he would if he actually took a full-time job in the situation.

Role-playing and game medium consists of methods such as quiz contests (Norris, 1963, pp. 86–88), the dramatization of occupations, and role-playing (Norris et al., 1966, pp. 439–440; Hoppock, 1967, pp. 322–323; Glanz, 1962, p. 256; Norris, 1963, pp. 70–74; and Peters et al., 1965, pp. 59–60). For young people going for their first job interview, a type of role-playing referred to as a "practice job interview" (Hoppock, 1967, pp. 323–325) seems to be very helpful. Brainstorming as a technique may also be used as individuals in a group session brainstorm ideas about an occupation without value judgments necessarily being attached. After the individual participates in the group he often views the occupation differently than previously. Game theory and work done by S. S. Boocock et al., hold many possibilities for creating activities by which the individual can become involved in a simulated situation. The involvement can be extensive enough to enable a projection of self into the situation without having the consequences if the projection is not in keeping with self-fulfillment. Game theory activities enable the individual to have a broad coverage of experiences in a relatively short period of time. Simulated experiences may prove extremely important in the decision-making process.

Synthetic occupational environment medium has in some places been successful, but the extent of use has been limited. Career clubs (Isaacson, 1966, pp. 382–383; Norris et al., 1966, pp. 65–67; Ohlsen, 1964, p. 321; Hoppock, 1967, p. 339; Baer and Roeber, 1964, p. 388; Crow and Crow, 1965, p. 300; and Peters et al., 1965, p. 61) have been used probably as extensively as any. A modification of the career club that is recently nationally recognized is the Junior Achievement Club where businessmen and women assist young people to formulate a small corporation, produce a product and market it. The program has been successful and is growing. Another synthetic method is the laboratory study, such as in an industrial arts class, where a synthetic production line is established for producing a given item and each student makes only a small part of the total item but produces several parts exactly alike and assembles them onto the major project. In home economics classes similar synthetic projects are established in cooking units.

Real Situation Classification

Experiencing the real situation has no substitute, but the real situation experienced may not be representative of all nor of the potential situation where the individual may be employed. The real situation often does help broaden the frontiers of thinking for many persons, and consideration should be given to methods for achieving real or primary experiences with the occupational situation.

One medium is *direct observation*. The individual could make visitations to places where workers are engaged in their activities. In guidance books the methods are generally referred to as *plant tours* and *field trips* (Peters et al., 1965, p. 60; Isaacson, 1966, pp. 379–381; Baer and Roeber, 1964, p. 388; Arbuckle, 1966, p. 280; Glanz, 1962, p. 259; Norris et al., 1966, pp. 462–465; Norris, 1963, pp. 47–51, 101, and 125–128). Some individuals will be interested in jobs connected with civil service, community organizations, and small private practices or establishments. All places of work should be considered for visitation. A foster uncle or aunt is a means of having a young person identified with a worker who is willing to share his experiences and time with the young person. Some service clubs will help establish such an arrangement whereby a businessman or woman will take a young person for a month or so as his "nephew" or "niece."

Direct exploration is another medium. Occupational units (Norris, 1963, pp. 40–45, 60–70, 78–79, 88–100, and 116–125; Hollis and Hollis, 1965, p. 294; Peters et al., 1965, p. 58; and Norris et al., 1966, pp. 564–570) are frequently used in schools. Occupational courses generally extend for one semester (Arbuckle, 1966, p. 268–277; Shertzer and Stone, 1966, pp. 284–285; Crow and Crow, 1965, pp. 280 and 299; Baer and Roeber, 1964, pp. 474–482; Norris et al., 1966, pp. 414–427; and Ohlsen, 1964, pp. 311–317). Today schools are recognizing that some students have a need for more occupationally oriented curriculums; thus some schools are developing sequential occupational curriculums, whereby the student can have greater exploration for occupational development. An exploratory job is another method of helping an individual become acquainted with the occupation and does provide for direct exploration.

The *actual occupational experience medium* can be illustrated by various methods such as work experience programs, which seem to be on the increase (Norris et al., 1966, pp. 333–345; Ohlsen, 1964, pp. 287–289 and 359–360; Hoppock, 1967, pp. 327–330; Baer and Roeber, 1964, pp. 394–395; and Arbuckle, 1966, pp. 277–279). On-the-job training is another real and actual experience, which provides both job and training experience prior to total commitment to either one by the individual (Crow and Crow, 1965, p. 300; Isaacson, 1966, pp. 243–250; and Norris et al., 1966, pp. 172–173). Temporary jobs and entry jobs are also methods for helping individuals obtain actual experience.

Summary

The purposes for occupational information have been extended beyond answering questions and increasing knowledge to include the developmental concept. With the broader purposes, the utilization of information may retain previous methods and add new ones, with emphasis being placed on those that personalized the information processes over an extended period of time. The methods should help the individual find answers and increase his awareness, but even more important he should become secure enough so that he wants and looks forward to obtaining even more information with new and different concepts, facts, and understanding.

To achieve the broader purposes for utilizing occupational information other professional personnel will need to work with the individual and his counselor. The team approach and particularly a conjoint relationship among the professional members becomes a necessity and in so doing the individual is the one who stands to gain the most. The team members each contribute what they are most competent in doing and the work of each complements and supplements the work of the others, making each more effective than if working alone. With the team approach rather than the loner approach, the duplication of effort should be reduced, thus making possible more professional assistance by reducing the time spent unnecessarily.

Occupational information is used in many different situations. With the purposes broadened to a developmental approach with emphasis on personalizing the processes, using occupational information in counseling relationships becomes meaningful. In all counseling sessions a concern or an emphasis will not be placed on integration of self into the occupational world; therefore, occupational information may not be appropriate in such sessions. Yet, in other counseling sessions, perhaps with the same person, the concern will be with the expression of himself through work and the role that work plays in his life. Occupational information does serve many functions in counseling sessions.

To assist individuals in viewing themselves and the world of work, group work may be one of the most effective means for some phases of the total picture. Studies seem to support the belief that group work contributes to the growth of the individual, but often the group work increases the need for individual work rather than replacing it.

The methods for using occupational information are varied from those requiring a minimum amount of ego involvement to those requiring considerable involvement on the part of the individual. Probably for most individuals a variety of methods with one or more from each classification would be helpful in their occupational maturation. The timing or readiness of the individual may place more emphasis on methods in one medium than those in other media.

SELECTED REFERENCES

Arbuckle, Dugald S. *Pupil Personnel Services in the Modern School.* Boston: Allyn and Bacon, Inc., 1966. Pp. 113–124, 143–180, 192–202, 260–281, 335–360.

Baer, Max F., and Edward C. Roeber. *Occupational Information: The Dy-*

namics of Its Nature and Use. Chicago: Science Research Associates, Inc., 1964. Pp. 380–402, 418–452, 474–482.

Barbarosh, Benjamin. "Developing a Community Vocational Resource Directory," *The Vocational Guidance Quarterly*, 14 (Spring 1966), 179.

Bennett, Margaret E. *Guidance and Counseling in Groups*. 2nd ed. New York: McGraw-Hill, Inc., 1963. 421 pages.

Bennett, Margaret E. "Strategies of Vocational Guidance in Groups," in *Man in a World of Work*. Boston: Houghton Mifflin Company, 1964. Pp. 460–486.

Borow, Henry. "Research in Vocational Development: Implications for the Vocational Aspects of Counselor Education," in *Conference on Vocational Aspects of Counselor Education*, Carl McDaniels, ed. Washington, D.C.: Department of Health, Education, and Welfare, Office of Education Bureau of Research, 1966. Pp. 70–92.

Burchill, George W. *Work-Study Programs for Alienated Youth*. Chicago: Science Research Associates, Inc., 1962. 265 pages.

Calia, Vincent F. "Vocational Guidance: After the Fall," *The Personnel and Guidance Journal*, 45 (December 1966), 320–327.

Coleman, James C. *Personality Dynamics and Effective Behavior*. Chicago: Scott, Foresman and Company, 1960. Pp. 385–497.

Crow, Lester D., and Alice Crow. *Organization and Conduct of Guidance Services*. New York: David McKay Company, Inc., 1965. Pp. 279–281, 285–301.

Detjen, Ervin Winfred, and Mary Ford Detjen. *Elementary School Guidance*, 2nd ed. New York: McGraw-Hill, Inc., 1963. Pp. 202–205.

Ginzberg, Eli, and Berman Hyman. *The American Worker in the Twentieth Century, A History Through Autobiographies*. New York: Free Press of Glencoe, 1963. 368 pages.

Glanz, Edward C. *Groups in Guidance: The Dynamics of Groups and the Application of Groups in Guidance*. Boston: Allyn & Bacon, Inc., 1962. Pp. 255–261.

Gray, Susan W. *The Psychologist in the Schools*. Chicago: Holt, Rinehart, and Winston, Inc., 1963. Pp. 253–279.

Gregory, Robert J. "The Application for Employment," *The Vocational Guidance Quarterly*, 15 (December 1966), 131–132.

Gutsch, Kenneth U., and Richard H. Logan, III. "Newspapers as a Means of Disseminating Occupation Information," *The Vocational Guidance Quarterly*, 15 (March 1967), 186–190.

Hill, George E. *Management and Improvement of Guidance*. New York: Appleton-Century-Crofts, 1965. Pp. 278–285.

Hollis, Joseph W., and Lucile U. Hollis. *Organizing for Effective Guidance*. Chicago: Science Research Associates, Inc., 1965. Pp. 12–14, 294–297.

Hoppock, Robert. *Occupational Information: Where to Get It and How to Use It in Counseling and in Teaching*, 3rd ed. New York: McGraw-Hill, Inc., 1967. Pp. 133–142, 165–203, 252–272, 286–303, 313–347, 425–477.

Hughes, Roland G., Jr. "See for Yourself: A Doing Approach to Vocational Guidance," *The Vocational Guidance Quarterly*, 13 (Summer 1965), 283–286.

Isaacson, Lee E. *Career Information in Counseling and Teaching.* Boston: Allyn and Bacon, Inc., 1966. Pp. 243–250, 335–338, 398–415.

Kaback, Goldie Ruth, "Occupational Information for Groups of Elementary School Children," *The Vocational Guidance Quarterly,* 14 (Spring 1966), 163–168.

Kaufman, Jacob J., et al. *The Role of the Secondary Schools in the Preparation of Youth for Employment: A Comparative Study of the Vocational, Academic, and General Curricula.* University Park, Pa.: Institute for Research on Human Resources, the Pennsylvania State University, 1967.

Lifton, Walter M. *Working with Groups: Group Process and Individual Growth.* New York: John Wiley & Sons, Inc., 1961. Pp. 21, 27–38, 130–135.

Lifton, Walter M. "Counseling Theory and the Use of Educational Media," *The Vocational Guidance Quarterly,* 13 (Winter 1964–65), 77–82.

Lifton, Walter M. *Working with Groups: Group Process and Individual Growth,* 2nd ed. New York: John Wiley & Sons, Inc., 1966. 288 pages.

Loughary, John W. *Counseling in Secondary Schools: A Frame of Reference.* New York: Harper and Brothers, Publishers, 1961. Pp. 37–43, 86–95.

Moser, Leslie E., and Ruth Small Moser. *Counseling and Guidance: An Exploration.* Englewood Cliffs, N.J.: Prentice-Hall, Inc., 1963. Pp. 79–99.

Munger, Daniel I. "The Occupational Information Speakers' Bureau," *The Vocational Guidance Quarterly,* 15 (June 1967), 265–266.

Murk, Virgil. "A Tour Plan to Interpret Occupations Serving Handicapped Children," *The Vocational Guidance Quarterly,* 12 (Spring 1964), 169–171.

Norris, Willa. *Occupational Information in the Elementary School.* Chicago: Science Research Associates, Inc., 1963. Pp. 40–56, 66–107, 116–141.

Norris, Willa, Franklin R. Zeran, and Raymond N. Hatch. *The Information Service in Guidance,* 2nd ed. Chicago: Rand McNally & Company, 1966. Pp. 38–39, 65–67, 149–155, 172–173, 333–345, 414–428, 438–440, 450–458, 462–465, 468–469, 474–480, 564–570.

Odle, S. Gene. "The Student Information Center as an Educational Resource," *The Vocational Guidance Quarterly,* 15· (March 1967), 217–220.

Ohlsen, Merle M. *Guidance Services in the Modern School.* New York: Harcourt, Brace, and World, Inc., 1964. Pp. 287–289, 311–333, 359–360.

Peters, Herman J., and Gail F. Farwell. *Guidance: A Developmental Approach,* 2nd ed. Chicago: Rand McNally & Company, 1967. Pp. 501–509.

Peters, Herman J., and James C. Hansen. *Vocational Guidance and Career Development: Selected Readings.* New York: The Macmillan Company. 1966. Pp. 196–226, 276–312.

Peters, Herman J., Bruce Shertzer, and William Van Hoose. *Guidance in the Elementary Schools.* Chicago: Rand McNally and Company, 1965. Pp. 58–65, 164–178.

Shertzer, Bruce, and Shelley C. Stone. *Fundamentals of Guidance.* Boston: Houghton Mifflin Company, 1966. Pp. 284–286.

Super, Donald E., and Phoebe L. Overstreet, et al., *The Vocational Maturity of Ninth-Grade Boys.* New York: Bureau of Publications, Teachers College, Columbia University, 1960. 212 pages.

Tennyson, W. Wesley, Thomas A. Soldahl, and Charlotte Mueller. *The Teacher's Role in Career Development.* Washington, D.C.: National Vocational Guidance Association, 1965 revision. 107 pages.

Tiedeman, David V., and Gordon Dudley. "Prospects for Technology and Commerce in the Mediation of Vocational Development for Vocational Maturity; Outline and Appendices Accompanying Recent Developments and Current Prospects in Occupations Fact Mediation." Mimeographed copy of Speech, National Conference on Occupational Information in Vocational Guidance sponsored by the U.S. Office of Education, Chicago, Illinois, May 17, 1967.

Tyler, Leona E. *The Work of the Counselor,* 2nd ed. New York: Appleton-Century-Crofts, Inc., 1961. Pp. 153–219.

Weitz, Henry. *Behavior Change Through Guidance.* New York: John Wiley & Sons, Inc., 1964. 225 pages.

Wellington, John A., and Nan Olechowski. "Attitudes Toward the World of Work in Elementary School," *The Vocational Guidance Quarterly,* **14** (Spring 1966), 160–162.

PART IV

PERSONAL-SOCIAL INFORMATION FOR THE INDIVIDUAL

The individual is an emerging, becoming physical and psychological being different from any other and always in a state of flux. He lives in a world composed of people, affected by economic conditions, and influenced by societal evolution. He seeks his own identity, strives for self-actualization, searches for other person(s) with whom he can share life, and ventures for opportunities of self-expression. Information about himself and the existing and possible social environment(s) becomes essential for an individual to approach fulfillment of his potential or to expand his horizons.

Personal-social information is indispensable at every step of life's pathway. Personal-social information may surround the individual but it may lack meaning to him until he is able to perceive personal implications. He needs an exploration and a feedback for integration of information into a self-concept. Goals, aspirations, and future projections of self are an evolution that is an outgrowth of information utilization by the individual. Increasing and personalizing personal-social information processes should enable the individual to push forward into frontiers meaningful to him.

Chapter 14

Integrating Physical and
Psychological Information

From Freud we learned that the past exists *now* in the person. Now we must learn, from growth theory and self-actualization theory, that the future also *now* exists in the person in the form of ideals, hopes, goals, unrealized potentials, mission, fate, destiny, etc.—MASLOW, 1962, p. 48.

The individual's physical and psychological development is as major a concern as his educational and occupational development. An individual is the composition of many variables; the combination of these variables make him unique. Because each variable is subject to change and often is changing, the person is becoming a different person, even unique to himself. The direction and pace of change is in part determined by his own decisions; thus, the future is determined to a major extent by the ongoing evolving decisions. What one chooses is a matter of what alternatives are available and the information processed about each alternative and about one's own self.

Variables Involved in Working with Individuals

The individual is a living, acting organism, similar to but different from all other individuals. Some of the variables that create differences are values, attitudes, motivations, abilities, experiences, environments, wants, needs, desires, expectations, aspirations, conformity, health (mental and physical), knowledge, skills, and concepts of self-identity, self-image, and self-decisions. Understanding the individual within his perceived world involves understanding the interrelation of these variables. The perceived self formulates reactions and interactions with people, ideas, and things. Within the realm of the real world of the individual, which may or may not resemble his perceived world, the individual functions in the pattern of his perception of the world. As the counselor works with the individual, he strives to understand both worlds of the individual, the perceived and the real. The counselor needs to realize that his own interpretation and understanding can only be formulated through his own perceived world.

Consideration of the individual's variables and the effect of the inter-relation of these is necessary for understanding decisions and reactions of the individual. The individual is encompassed by his perceived world —a wall built by the total variables of each individual. The degree of rigidity of the individual determines the closure to new ideas, people, and things. Openness for development and change in relation to actions and decisions is based upon the individual's pattern developed through interrelations of all the variables. These variables can be discussed one at a time, but their importance in understanding an individual and his reactions is based on the blending of the interrelations among them to create the operative structural pattern of the individual.

Needs

Each individual strives to satisfy basic needs, such as hunger, survival, love, and security. Concentrated energy and effort of the individual is expended toward the satisfaction of the most pressuring needs at a given time. Once certain needs are quieted, then a redirection of effort and energy may take place. However, if an individual strives for certain satisfactions and none of his attempts bring satisfaction, the individual may be unable to withstand the pressure and may resort to abnormal behavior; or he may with help discover new alternatives for achieving the satisfaction of his needs and therefore continue to develop and function successfully within his world.

A starving person expends his energy in an effort to obtain food. A number of alternatives may be open to him: (1) work to buy food; (2) ask a relative or friend; (3) beg on the street or from door to door; (4) steal; or (5) starve. Which alternative will he select to try first? His decision will be a result of his total structural pattern, created by the interrelations of all variables—his values, environment, knowledge, skills, and others—at the time of his decision. Stealing may be the accepted decision in his cultural group and according to his values also. However, even though he may make this decision, the implementation of it may not take place if it can be replaced by another alternative possible through new insight stimulated by additional concepts, information, and/or skills. Increasing the individual's reservoir of information may reinforce his original decision or change it in order for him to enhance himself.

Values and Attitudes

The counselor's role in helping the individual to interpret information and to make inferences that go beyond it often involves the counselor's understanding the individual's value system(s). Each individual is entrapped by his value system(s) of that moment. When an individual decides whether he will or will not do something, his decision involves his values and beliefs, which in themselves are a part of his total operative structural pattern interwoven by all variables. A change in any or all values may alter the decision and drive for implementation of that decision. Also the total structural pattern may be modified through a change in the value system. The development as a result of the modification will be governed by all other variables such as motivation, cultural environment, ability, knowledge and skills.

Values of an individual are self-determined, but are influenced by pressures within the world of the individual. Satisfaction achieved through experiences develops and reinforces values of the individual within his cultural existence. When an individual steps outside his cultural environment, his values system(s) may make him a misfit within the new societal pattern. Helping the individual to make the transition from one environment to another is one reason for Head Start and other programs for culturally deprived and disadvantaged persons.

An individual's values are expressed not only by what he says, but also by how he acts. The individual's value system(s) establishes priorities in his life—gives him the basis for choosing what seems the most important to him at the time. His value system(s) serves as his framework of action.

Motivation

Motivation as a variable effects all other variables and in turn is affected by others. Individuals are always motivated. They have an internal need to develop and mature, and the need pressures to be expressed. The individual's motives basically assist him in maintaining a drive to become the best person he can. James Coleman (1960, p. 145) classified "all human motives as striving toward (1) physical and psychological self-maintenance or (2) improvement of oneself and one's situation through growth, fulfillment, and richer satisfactions." To an outsider the individual may seem unmotivated, but the goals established by the person himself may not be the ones an outsider would consider. What an individual desires to achieve and what an outsider thinks that the individual should achieve are not necessarily compatible. Motivation of the individual is governed by his perception. The counselor's role is not necessarily to motivate an individual to change, but may be to work with him to change his perception of himself and his world, thus facilitating the continuous process of development. Motivation is intrinsically produced rather than extrinsically; thus the individual's motivations are an outgrowth of his perceptions.

Environment

James Coleman (1960, p. 52) has stated, "At any given moment an individual is the product of countless interactions between his genetic endowment and his physical and sociocultural environment." An individual is influenced by the past, but he is also capable of moving forward. He has both responsibility for change and choice within his physical and cultural environments. The experiences and all other variables interacting create the operative framework for the individual. He is unique in his reactions because no two individuals interpret or integrate the same information or experiences exactly alike. Physical and cultural environments do limit or slant to a degree the experiences and information available to the individual. (See Chapter 15 for material on subgroups and cultures.)

The counselor working with an individual must be able to assess the environmental influences in the operative structural framework of the individual in order to understand the individual's response and reactions. Even though research findings reveal certain cues and information, exactly how an individual perceives influences is unique with each individual. A counselor can be more effective in his working relationship with the individual if he is knowledgeable about the possible cues and influences of the environment. A caution is necessary in that the individual does not live in just one environment but many sub-environments. Also, care must be taken to ensure recognition of an environment as only one of the many variables, and the focal point as being the interweaving of all variables to create the perceived world of the individual.

Interest

In writings, stress has been placed on the significance of interest of an individual in his choice of an occupation. Interest is one of many variables and should be considered only in the composite of all variables in the operative structural pattern for *each* individual. Interest inventories may be useful as a technique to stimulate feedback with an individual, but the results of the inventory should not be overstressed in its importance to aid an individual in his vocational choice.

John Holland (1966, p. 4) stated that the evidence is now available to show that what have been called vocational interest inventories are really personality inventories. Other writers do not agree with Holland, but in either case the inventories are only part of the total picture and should be used only as stimulators or backdrops for assistance in viewing other variables. Most writers do agree that people search for environments—physically, socially, and occupationally—that enable them to express themselves and to continue their growth and development. The individual's interests and personality are important variables in the environmental search.

Aptitudes and Abilities

For an individual to attain success and personal satisfaction in a task, his interest, aptitudes, and abilities and the task requirements must be somewhat compatible. If the demands of a task exceed the aptitudes and abilities of the individual, he is more likely to become dissatisfied and possibly maladjusted than if the task and aptitudes and abilities are compatible. However, effects of other variables may compensate or determine the maladjustment. For example, W. A. Pemberton (1963, p. 32) stated, "Achievement is affected not merely by *amount* of drive, but the *direction* of orientation or kinds of values." Therefore, the composite effect of all variables of an individual must be considered in order for the counselor to work with him understandingly.

The role of the counselor in the information process, then, is effective only to the extent that he is able to help the individual work with information that will contribute to his development. What area of information? What level of information? These questions can be answered only in relation to the individual and the total effect of all variables in forming the individual's perceived world.

Intelligence is only one variable; if it is considered as an isolated one no particular action or decision can be made. Only as it is interwoven with values, motivation, and all other variables does intelligence become a significant contributing factor. For example, an individual of above-average intelligence may need certain information. If the counselor relies on this factor alone, then material with a reading level for an above-average person could be used. What, for example, if the individual has never learned to read? The information may be meaningless unless someone reads the material to him. All variables then must be considered in a total pattern by the counselor as he works with each individual in the information area.

Experiences

His physical and personal-social environments are the settings for the experiences of an individual. Experiences affect the individual in terms of his own enhancement in his perceived world. He elects to participate in those experiences that promise fulfillment within his own realm of perception. An individual is not always in control of whether he will participate or not in certain experiences, but rather is often integrated into happenings through no choice of his own. E. C. Kelley (1962, p. 14) stated that one fact about perception is that it is *selective* and the individual therefore *chooses* that which the self feeds upon. The growth of the self depends upon those choices.

In a nurtured environment that facilitates experiences for an individual's self-enhancement, growth toward a positive direction is promoted. However, if an individual is entrapped in an environment in which experiences do not contribute to growth, his continual blockage from certain experiences may create a barrier to information that would contribute to his development. The role of the counselor for such a person would involve creating a facilitating climate in which the individual could gain supportive experience that would reduce the blockage created by the previous adverse environment. John Holland (1966, p. 12) stated, "*A person's behavior can be explained by the interaction of his personality pattern and his environment.*" The counselor's role with an individual involves working with him in his environment (perceived and real) and in relation to his experiences.

Experience is a continuous stream of behavior in that each event is united with and derived from every earlier act and that, as each experience occurs, it establishes itself as an element in some future experience (Weitz, 1964, p. 1). If one considers an educationally disadvantaged individual, approaches or techniques to aid him are determined by his environment, experiences, and all other various interwoven affects. The facilitative climate for learning must be designed upon the background of that individual. This fact would be true in working with talented youngsters, slow learners, or any other classification one might use to signify uniqueness of individuals.

The Emerging Self

From conception to death the individual is emerging, becoming, developing. If the individual can perceive his environment as a place where he can have opportunities and can perceive himself positively, then he may make great strides. As Carl Rogers (1962, p. 32) stated, the use of terms such as *happy, contented,* and *enjoyable* may not be nearly as expressive of a self-enhancing individual as use of the terms *enriching, exciting, rewarding, challenging,* and *meaningful.* The individual is constantly emerging and as an emerging self must be open to experiences, which can best be done when he can trust himself and others. The information processes may help him learn how.

Obtaining and using information over an extended period of time, fully utilizing the information processes, should help one launch himself into the stream of life, to become more and more of one's potentialities

(Rogers, 1962, p. 32). *The development should be primarily sequential rather than accidental and should spiral upward with an ever-increasing radius of openness instead of closure.* The information that contributes most to the emerging self is an integral part of the processes of absorption, individualization, and internalizing so that the person perceives meaning in the information for himself and will not reject essential information as applicable only to others, if at all.

In the beginning the individual lacks a self-concept and a self-identity. Then, as he physically grows, he also begins to emerge as an individual psychologically. Some people believe that the individual is a product of his parents; others believe he is the result of his environment; whereas many hold that he is the product of the interaction between heredity and environment. Developmental psychologists are causing counselors to re-examine their concepts and are suggesting that the emerging, developing person may be more than what can be determined from heredity and environment alone. The way a person perceives his world and the way he reacts to it, plus some self-*energizing,* may over a period of time unveil an individual not only unique but one who is continually becoming. The individual cannot be studied or evaluated totally objectively or in the abstract but must himself become an important member of any meaningful study, a study that yields results that are themselves in a state of flux, emerging, changing, becoming.

The emerging self often is a self-actualizing self who, as Maslow (1962, p. 36) wrote, is an "acceptance and expression of the inner core or self." Arthur Combs (1962, p. 51) in writing about self-actualization expressed the belief that such "persons seem to be characterized by an essentially positive view of self." If the positive view of self is necessary and if acceptance and expression of the inner core of self are essential, then the question emerges as to how information processes may contribute and what the counselor's role(s) may be. No one right way exists, but in general a philosophical position can be taken and may be stated as follows: a self-actualizing individual has need over an extended period of time for personal and social information about and for himself that is applicable at his *depth* of development and is *paced* at his rate of growth.

In a democratic society the emerging self hopefully expands his own horizons, develops himself to the fullest potential, and utilizes his capabilities in weighing alternatives so as to bring about self-enhancement and social improvement. In so doing each emerging self becomes different from all other individuals. The goals and aspirations of one period in development will give rise to the new goals and new aspirations of another period. The perceived world may change as the emerging self develops.

Perception—The Perceived World

Phenomenologists have in recent years attempted to study human behavior from the point of view of the individual. The viewpoint starts with a belief that the individual has values, attitudes, and concepts about himself and others that may not be the same as those held by other people. The perceptions he holds about himself, generally referred to as *self-concept,* and the way in which he perceives the world about him and the alternatives available will determine his behavior.

The way in which an individual perceives himself is to a large extent learned from those with whom he interacts. Combs and Soper (1963) found in their research that kindergarten children learned a self-concept from others and that the children's self-concepts were predictive of their academic achievement in the first and second grades. Children from culturally disadvantaged environments have a tendency to perceive themselves negatively and to believe that others also perceive them negatively. Negative perceptions tend to interfere with positive academic growth in children.

"One of the most revealing facts about perception is that it is *selective*" (Kelley, 1962, p. 65). Stated another way, ". . . we cannot see all that our senses report, but only the things which fit the picture we have" (Carl Rogers, 1956, p. 203). If one has no previous experience in an area and has not previously formed a picture, he can be more open to perception. On the other hand, if one has been somewhat prepared for what to look, one may perceive with more meaning and may have longer retention. The perceptions that one will obtain from the world about him are influenced by his concepts and by prior perceptions from previous experiences: ". . . the person's orientation, organizes and directs behavior" (Erb and Hooker, 1967, p. 28). A person modifies his behavior through conditioning and also through developing new perceptions, increased awareness, new or different insights and reorientation of himself and the relationships among different kinds of knowledge. The person is constantly becoming, changing, growing, but changes take place only in a few variables at a time, relatively, rather than in every one at once. The individual seeks self-congruence, while also striving for self-enhancement. A change in one thing may achieve to some extent self-enhancement but may distort self-congruence or produce incongruence. Change is essential, but the change has to take place in a setting that fosters growth and that encourages reorientation for self-congruence. If the self-concept is learned primarily from others, then growth may be accelerated by change occurring in the individual when he is among people who will provide him an opportunity to perceive what the change may mean. A positive feedback may increase the pace toward the total orientation of the individual's having congruence again or what may be called "orientational congruences" (term used by Erb and Hooker, 1967). Once having achieved orientational congruence, the individual may be secure enough to try another change. Each change produces growth and increases the dimensions of the picture. The frame for the picture or the total frame of reference is expanded as the picture grows; thus receptiveness to new experiences and knowledge can be increased.

What one perceives may or may not be reality. What one hears and the interpretation made may be distorted or may be what the speaker intended. What one sees may be a comprehensive view, or one may obtain enough different views to give an inclusive picture of the situation, or one may look without perceiving the items that produce the essential reality. To ensure that perception of an individual is a reality of the situation is impossible. First of all, perception of total reality of any situation probably is impossible. Reality for the individual may not be reality as viewed by another person or as measured by another means. Second, words are inadequate and too slow to describe one's total perception. If words were used, their meanings would have such variance that a check for reality of the situation may be impossible. What the counselor can do is to assist the individual in having a variety of experiences meaningful for him and as much as possible experiences consisting of sequential, purposeful activities.

The information processes of the individual and the counselor's role in them need to be under continuous review. Perceptions do vary not only among individuals, but also between groups. The culturally deprived will view things differently from those who have had so-called desirable cultural opportunities. For example, education and the school system are seen by the middle class as a road to better things, whereas the culturally disadvantaged often see the school as an obstacle course or a trap until they can leave it. In another example, society is something to which the middle class try to conform, whereas the culturally disadvantaged see it as a demand or at times as an enemy. For the counselor, who may himself hold middle-class values, the differences in the perceived world from one individual to another are very significant and the counselor may have difficulty in understanding the perceived world of one who has a different cultural system. The perceived world and the perception of one's own physical and psychological self may be the bases of behavior and certainly are controllers of informational processes.

Tomorrow Is Sculptured Today

Today is yesterday's future and tomorrow's history. Man and time are locked into a continuous flow, in which the future holds the potential, the past provides the experiences for value formation, and the present, even though ever so short, is when the plans are made or revised for goal establishment, directional orientation, self-enhancement, self-expression, creativity and curiosity exploration, societal and environmental interactions, and self-model formation with implications for self within a social setting.

Plan making or revising necessitates decisions, but decisions are not isolated. Instead decisions should be viewed as expressions of the value systems of the individual as he implements them within the many variables and his perception of them. Life is filled with decisions, each of which needs to be seen not as separate but rather as only one in a sequence of decisions. A decision is the implementational beginning of a plan that to the individual is the best available considering the pressures of the moment. A little later, tomorrow or next year, conditions may change, and when they do, the individual may attempt to change his previous decision. The processes by which decisions are made or changed are important to the counselor and are fundamental to the information processes as being developmental, extended over a lifetime.

The teaching done in a home or school is primarily pertaining to how adjustments are and have been made for things that are happening and have happened; however, what each person really wants personally is an understanding of how to orient himself for what he is or may face —a world that will be different from today and yesterday; a world that will be filled with people, things, and ideas that currently cannot be identified, or, in other words, a world of unknowns. The individual has today to sculpture tomorrow, but he cannot use today's time in such a manner unless he can be within a physical and social environment conducive to a positive developmental outlook. Counseling and guidance may assist in the establishment of such an environment, in the individual's identifying potential avenues for becoming part of such an environment, or in the individual's identifying potential avenues for becoming part of such environments.

Man primarily is the creator and controller of his future. His future is controlled by the sequence of decisions he makes among the alternatives as they occur; therefore, his decisions control his experiences. The experiences he has, both within himself and within his environment as a result of living, become major creators of the man. The experiences help generate new ideas. One's ideas do have force and can affect the future. Ideas are not formulated in a vacuum; rather, they are an expression of the individual's creativity as a result of understanding the interrelationship of information. A person who generates ideas is one who obtains additional information and perceives information as not a closure but as a means to open new avenues, information as not isolated but as interrelated, and information as essential for growth, with growth being a sequential progression instead of being haphazard and unoriented.

Frequently in the past the evaluation of information has been done by others and the "good" information plus the evaluation has been given to the individual. In such cases the individual is left with the job of memorizing the information *or* of rejecting the information, which in affect is a rejection of the person giving him the information and of those who evaluated it. The opportunity to be an integral member of the evaluation processes may be essential for internalizing and personalizing information. *Evaluation and projection of self into information, situations, environments, and social groups may be indispensable for man's developing his own identity.* Not that all evaluations and decisions will be right or wrong, but that man has the opportunity to engage in the processes and that he learns how to obtain information vital to the processes. The extension of self, the reorientation of concepts, the approaching of new challenges with an open mind, and a willingness to change are not learned through a single act but can be acquired over a period of time. The acquisition can be made when today's information can be utilized with the individual and in recognition of his many variables so as to assist him in sculpturing a tomorrow meaningful for him. When the utilizing of today's information can be repeated day after day to sculpture a tomorrow of his choice, a developmental, positive-viewing individual will be the outcome.

The individual's aspirations and expectations will in part determine his tomorrow. For those whose social and physical environments lack encouragement for building meaningful aspirations, development will be hampered. Information processes can, over an extended period of time, help to overcome some of the individual's social, physical, and economical conditions. For those who have had a wide variety of experiences and have been assisted in making those experiences meaningful, the information processes can facilitate the continuation of their growth. For many children, youth, and adults the length of time is too long between an idea, dream, or aspiration and the opportunity to test the reality of all or any part of it. The information processes and the counselor's role in working with an individual may include the objective of reducing the time span between an idea and reality testing. Personal physical and psychological information integration into the self-concept and frequent evaluations throughout life are needed in order that the individual can day after day sculpture a meaningful future.

Counselor's Role in Personal Information

Personal information as well as educational and occupational information is needed throughout life by the individual. Personal information should aid the individual in gaining insight into his present physical and social environments, the possibilities in potential environments, and the comparative values of each in relation to his current self-concept. Personal information should help the person perceive himself as he has been, as he is, and as he may become through projection of himself into each available alternative. Personalizing information processes become more than an intellectual understanding. They include a uniting of applicable information into the person's total cognitive and affective processes so as to form a more complete or perfect whole than was present without the information. Some reorientation of previously acquired information may need to take place, and attitudes, feelings, and value systems may be modified. Personalized information and specifically personal physical and psychological information become vital components in planning for the future; thus personal information is in part a determinant of growth, direction, and pace.

Acquiring personal information has often in the past been left to chance. In some schools, units or courses have been added to assure exposure to "essential" information. The teaching of personal information in school has in many cases been beneficial; however, school officials reflect the feeling that what is being done is inadequate for the total need. One of the reasons for units and courses being inadequate is the lack of being able to personalize the information—content frequently is determined by a course of study or by persons other than those taking the class; a course or unit is scheduled in the school program rather than having the needed assistance available at times when the information would be most meaningful; and the information is taught in a way that has resulted in students' often considering the information as something to learn for a test rather than being viewed as information of personal value that can be integrated into self-concepts and value systems.

The counselor can assist the individual in obtaining personal information throughout life and can help the person to increase the emphasis on personal information at times when most appropriate for him. One individual will have need for one kind of personal—physical and psychological—information at one time and a different need at another time. Another person will have needs considerably different; thus the counselor can assist in personalizing the information. In addition the counselor can help the individual interrelate personal information with educational, occupational, and social information. Personalizing the information processes necessitates the counselor's being able to assist the person in bringing into focus all pertinent information; in understanding the reciprocal dependence among the different pieces and kinds of information; and to internalize the information with an integration, where appropriate, into the personal frame of reference. Then the additional information and the modification of previous information can become a framework for future actions and a basis for additional growth and development.

As Peter G. Peterson (1966, p. 11), President of Bell and Howell Company, stated, "Apparently, knowledge, however important, is simply not enough." People learn facts without altering their conclusions or behavior. The transmitting of knowledge no longer remains the challenge. The counselor's role is a very active one in a new frontier where individuals would like to break out of their environmental prisons—three generations of unemployment, inner city slums, societal conformities, keeping up with the Joneses, country club whirlwind, or Wall Street living style. Personal information may assist the individual in becoming secure enough to be flexible, to have ideas of his own, and to be a creator of a new environment. Change rather than rigidity is essential. An individual with no information—ignorant—may be able to change more readily than one with partial or inaccurate information that has been reinforced. The counselor can assist the individual in obtaining information of personal value that can be internalized with positive reinforcements lending support toward development—flexibility, originality, creativeness, and self-expression.

Developing a Philosophy of Life

A mentally healthy, productive individual is more than a drifter without purpose. He not only has insights into himself and his onward changing self but he also has developed a way of life, a philosophy of life. One is not born with a philosophy of life but may develop one from his life experiences and his socio-cultural environment, which influence the unfolding, projecting self. The counselor who desires to promote the growth and development of his counselees must guard against superimposing his own value systems upon them. Educational, occupational, and personal-social information is to be used to facilitate the individual's learning about himself, his present and potential environments, and some of the means by which he can make changes.

Youth have major choices to make in three different areas. One area is concerned with the *why of life*, including the values and philosophy of life. Without adequate information, various life experiences, and opportunities for sensing different socio-cultural environments, the young person, or for that matter the older person, may not be able to develop a philosophy of life that will enable and facilitate a fully functioning, unfolding, projecting self.

Another area to which youth must give attention and where choices must be made is *with whom life will be shared*. The selection of associates and close friends is of major concern to most youth. The loss of close friends, whether through death, moving, or differences developing that cause them no longer to associate, produces major problems in some youth and often in older people. The choosing of a mate and the decisions associated with the sharing of oneself with another deserve careful consideration and expenditure of time and energy to obtain all the information and help needed to arrive at self-satisfactory conclusions.

The third area with which youth must be concerned is *life's career*. This area has been emphasized in the preceding educational and occupational information parts of this book. The three areas—the why of life, with whom life will be shared, and life's career—are so interwoven and dependent upon each other in American society that they must be considered together. Two of the three areas are included in personal-social information.

The development of a way of life, a philosophy of life, is not easy. Suicide is the number two cause of death among college students. Among the high-school-aged and immediately following, ages fifteen to nineteen years, suicide is the number three cause of death. Edwin S. Shneidman, nationally known consultant in the field of suicide prevention, indicated that the five categories of problems most troubling to adolescents are parents, poverty, peers, broken romances, and pregnancy. (*Globe-Democrat*, St. Louis, Missouri, November 9, 1966, Section C, p. 1.) The counselor has a role in assisting individuals in developing a philosophy of life to assist them in their most trying times.

Leisure Time *or* Self-Expressive Time

What is work and what is leisure time? For one person a given activity is work, whereas for another person the same activity may be considered as the time that remains in a day, week, or year after subtracting the employment time (work-for-pay) and the time required for the ongoing necessities of life, including sleeping, eating, and so on. For the retired person leisure time becomes his entire life other than the time for the necessities of life, which also may require a minimum amount of time.

The demand for shorter hours has been a bargaining and legislative issue since the Revolutionary War. Earlier demands for a ten-hour workday after being achieved, were changed to an eight-hour workday and then to a five-day week. During the first one third of the twentieth century the generally prevailing full-time workweek was shortened approximately twenty hours, from sixty hours per week to forty. Since about the mid-1930's, the forty-hour workweek has become standard and very little progress has been made in reducing the average number of hours a week (see Table 14-1). Progress has been made in increasing the number of paid holidays and the length of paid vacations. Averaged over the year, present levels of paid vacations and holidays are in a ratio of one hour to approximately each sixteen hours of work. In 1966, 95 per cent of the office workers and 88 per cent of the plant workers

Table 14-1.

AVERAGE WEEKLY HOURS OF EM-
PLOYMENT FOR SELECTED YEARS.

Year	Average Weekly Hours
1940	38.1
1945	43.5
1950	40.5
1955	40.7
1960	39.7
1962	40.4
1963	40.5
1964	40.7
1965	41.2
1966	41.3
1967 (March)	40.3

Source: Based upon data from *Statistical Abstract of the United States, 1967,* 88th annual edition, U.S. Department of Commerce, p. 237, and *1966,* 87th annual edition, p. 238.

had six or more paid holidays a year, and 99 per cent of the office workers and 94 per cent of the plant workers had two weeks or more of paid vacation after five years of employment (see Table 14-2). The increase in number of paid vacation days has provided sufficient blocks of time for persons to engage in lesiure-time activities for longer durations. The time away from employment and beyond the time required for the essentials of life can no longer be ignored or left to chance alone. The time frequently referred to as *leisure time* is of sufficient importance in one's life to warrant careful planning, just as does educational and occupational planning.

During leisure time today many alternatives are available. The individual must allot his time and determine his priority of leisure-time activities. The leisure-time activities may be for recreation, variety in life, cultural enrichment, physical or mental exercise, creativity, unwinding or recharging the battery, or service to fellow man. Often the

Table 14-2.

PERCENTAGE OF OFFICE WORKERS AND PLANT WORKERS WHO RECEIVED PAID HOLIDAYS AND PAID VACATIONS ANNUALLY IN 1966.

Type of Benefit	Office Workers Per Cent	Plant Workers Per Cent
PAID HOLIDAYS		
No paid holidays	Less than 0.5	5
6 or more days	95	88
7 or more days	78	70
8 or more days	56	43
9 or more days	32	19
10 or more days	17	5
11 or more days	11	2
12 or more days	4	1
PAID VACATIONS		
2 weeks or more:		
After 1 year of service	78	22
After 5 years of service	99	94
3 weeks or more:		
After 5 years of service	14	10
After 10 years of service	66	52
After 15 years of service	87	78
4 weeks or more:		
After 20 years of service	39	31
After 25 years of service	61	49

Source: *Statistical Abstract of the United States, 1967,* 88th annual edition, U.S. Department of Commerce, p. 241.

individual considers his hours away from employment as a time when he can be himself, can try out ideas, and can express himself. For the person who lacks challenge in his employment, who views his work as affording no opportunity for projecting himself, and who believes his job is a dead-end with no opportunities, time away from employment becomes time away from the prison and an opportunity to express himself. How tragic but how true that push-button jobs with time-clock precision have dealt the humanist out, and man must turn to nonemployment activities to find expression. We, society as a group, may be moving rapidly toward the day when advancements come not from what man does on his job but what man does for his kicks.

The individual may use leisure time to explore himself and his present or potential environments. The person may explore during leisure time ideas, aspirations, untried models of himself, hopes, and dreams, which if the feedback is positive may later be applied to his world of work through possibly a change in job or occupation. If man is going to change occupations three or more times in life, some means of building in security may need to be identified. Leisure-time activities for many persons may be used more and more for self-expressive activities. If so, then information will be needed to assist individuals in understanding potentialities.

Leisure-time information is pertinent for persons of all ages—young, middle age, and older. For many persons the time they have outside of employment is minimal, as they view it, but many of them, including retired persons, do want assistance in utlizing their time as an expression of themselves. The individual's social-cultural environment may cause him to value work and leisure time differently than the values held by middle-class persons, a value system often held by the counselor. As Donald Zytowski (1965, p. 750) stated, "At the very lowest social-class status, work seems only to satisfy certain biological needs, and psychological satisfaction is gained from other, non-work, involvements. The highest social class level may produce individuals whose 'vocations' do not include that essence of toil or asceticism which the middle class believes necessary to their work."

Team Work

Three areas exist in education in which professional people are working together to assist the child. The three areas are *instruction,* including all special and general classroom teachers; *administration,* including principals, deans, and superintendents; and *pupil personnel services,* in elementary and secondary schools, and *student personnel services* in higher education. These services may include counselors, social workers, attendance officers, visiting teachers, psychometrists, psychologists, speech and hearing therapists, nurses, physicians, psychiatrists, and dentists. Each of the professional members may work with the child, youth, or adult, but none of them are working totally independently of other professional people. Each has the goal of assisting the individual but each recognizes that to do so the cooperative assistance among different professional people is needed frequently.

In addition to personnel in the school or institution of higher education, the community often has several different professional people engaged in private practice or within community agencies or who are available to work with individuals. The community agency personnel are also engaged in assisting individuals in obtaining either physical or psychological personal information or both. The counselor cannot and should not be the total source of personal information. The counselor may need to help the individual to achieve the maximum benefits from other professional people—through referrals, team use of professional services, and arrangements whereby available materials and resources are utilized at the most appropriate times.

Personal information about drugs, alcohol, tobacco, and narcotics may be essential to the development of the individual, but persons in the health professions are in a better position to provide this information than are most counselors. The counselor can assist the individual in obtaining the information and in some cases the counselor may obtain the information directly for the individual. Generally, first depth information about drugs, alcohol, tobacco, and narcotics may be available through the usual information processes. Some second depth, specific information, may also be available; but in terms of third depth, internalized implications, a referral may be needed.

The individual's physical development is of prime importance and his understanding of his own physical development and its implications are essential for self-concept formation. Persons in health professions can be of a tremendous assistance to the individual and to the counselor. Teamwork must become an existing reality.

The need for teamwork today, a true conjoint relationship among professional people, may exceed that of any time in our history. One reason would be the vast amount of knowledge and special know-how, which are increasing daily. Another reason may be that, as Burchill (1962, p. 156) pointed out, youth of today have a more difficult time of finding ways to gain adult status. At the turn of the century and even through World War II, youth who lacked interest or ability for academic progression could achieve recognition and adult status through entering the world of work. Today's drop-outs have a difficult time of finding any employment; and if they do, their jobs are often ones that instead of bringing them positive recognition often cause them to be alienated from society. Such persons are not living in a socio-physical environment that produces nourishment for positive development (Carkhuff and Berenson, 1967, pp. 3–11). The remedy for or prevention of such conditions probably cannot be done by one professional person alone, but possibly could be achieved through the information processes when the team approach is utilized among persons from several professions.

Tests as a Source of Physical and Psychological Information

For almost a half century standardized tests have been a source of physical and psychological information. The construction and supportive research for tests are improving. The validity and reliability are not perfect, but on many tests they are sufficient to warrant use as a source, although not the only source, of physical or psychological information.

Throughout the individual's development he needs information about himself. At times one of the best sources may be a standardized test. The kind of information needed will vary and so will the kind of information furnished by the test. Some tests can be used to provide general and broadening information about self. Other tests are designed to provide specific information and may furnish data for particular aspects of the individual for which additional information is needed. Tests may have the greatest value to the individual if a sequence of tests can be administered over an extended period of time, with the person having the opportunity to use the test results from time to time as a feedback. Test data may provide a reference point in comparison of self to other people, which is impossible or difficult to obtain in another way. Without comparative physical and psychological information, development of either a self-concept or a self-relationship to potential environments may be severely restricted.

Coding and Filing Physical and Psychological Information

Commercially produced coding and filing plans for physical and psychological information are needed. At present counselors as a group have not accepted a particular file plan. In general, counselors have found materials in this area difficult to code and file. Use of regular library coding is satisfactory for books but frequently is inadequate for vertical file materials. The plan probably most frequently used is an alphabetical arrangement, which by its very nature has many limitations. Modifications in the alphabetical arrangement can be made to overcome some of the disadvantages. Studying areas of need by clientele served will provide major headings for grouping information. Using these major headings will assist the grouping of information for similar purposes, which by alphabetical arrangement without major headings would separate materials to the point where the individual might never locate the materials most essential for him.

Consideration should be given to the appropriateness of the information for the different clientele served. The 3-D concept could be used for analyzing the appropriateness of materials. As the material is obtained, evaluations can be made to determine whether the information is of a general, specific, or feedback nature and how it may be used with different persons. Too many bookshelves and file drawers have wonderful information that has had limited use and has become outdated or inappropriate without its true value ever having been tested in the hands of individuals who potentially could benefit by it.

Coding and filing plans have only two major purposes: (1) grouping materials for the most effective use by the people who may use them, and (2) locating and storing materials where they can be easily retrieved and used. Regardless of the plan selected, the two purposes must become primary criteria. As much as possible the coding and filing plan selected should assist the individual in understanding the relationships among all areas—educational, occupational, and personal-social.

In the next section are given sample materials with an analysis code supplied for each. The code may be beneficial in filing but it is even more beneficial for analyzing materials to determine the adequacy of the information for the clientele served—adequacy from the standpoint of both breadth and depth.

Sample Materials and Sources

The materials pertinent for use in the physical and psychological development of individuals will depend upon the setting and the clientele served. Materials can be obtained from various sources and often are incorporated with educational and occupational information, which may necessitate cross-indexing or obtaining duplicate copies.

The following examples are not all-inclusive but are illustrative of materials available from sources frequently used by counselors. Each illustration contains the title, type of material (such as filmstrip or booklet), source, suggested use, and the 3-D analysis code based on projected use. (For 3-D code see Table 7-1.) In addition, annotations and prices are given for some samples. The illustrations are classified according to preschool; elementary, junior high, and senior high schools; and adults. In some cases the material would be applicable to more than one school level, but for illustrative purposes the material is coded for only one level. Addresses of sources are listed in the Address Index of this book.

PRESCHOOL MATERIALS

Infant and Child in the Culture Today. Book. Western Psychological Services; $6.50. Emphasizes developmental characteristics, birth to elementary school age. (For the counselor to use with parents of preschool age children. Code: CPp–Pp–1)

The First Five Years of Life: The Preschool Years. Book. Western Psychological Services; $6.50. Concerns mental growth patterns. (For counselor's use with parents. Code: CPp–Pp–1)

Parenthood in a Free Nation, Volume I: Basic Concepts for Parents. Book. The Macmillan Company; $2.00. (For counselor's use with parents. Code: CPp–Pp–2)

Frustrating Fours and Fascinating Fives. Film. McGraw-Hill, Inc.: B&W, $120.00; color, $195.00. Portrays a four-year-old and his behavior and again at the age of five. (For counselor's use with parents. Code: CPp–Pp–1)

ELEMENTARY SCHOOL MATERIALS

Susie Went Hunting. Filmstrip, one in a set of six. McGraw-Hill, Inc.; $60.00 a set. Stresses neatness. (For teacher working with intermediate grade pupils. Code: TSi–Pg–1)

Barrie Didn't Report. Filmstrip, one in a set of six. McGraw-Hill, Inc.; $60.00 a set. Concerns perseverance. (For teacher working with intermediate grade pupils. Code: Tsi–Pp–1)

What to Do About Upset Feelings. Film. Coronet Instructional Films; B&W, $60.00; color, $120.00. (For teacher working with intermediate grade pupils. Code: TSi–Pp–1)

Seeing Ourselves. Book. American Guidance Services, Inc.; $3.96. Written to help elementary school children see themselves as they develop in six areas—self-understanding; about school; about family; about friends; about groups; about vocations. (For teacher working with sixth grade pupils. Code: TSi–Pp–2)

Diagnosing Classroom Learning Environments. Booklet. Science Research Associates, Inc.; $2.70. Ten chapters including "The Pupil's Concept of Himself." (For counselor working with teachers. Code: CTi–Pp–2)

Building Self-Confidence in Children. Book. Science Research Associates, Inc.; $0.65. (For counselor working with teachers. Code: CTi–Pp–1)

The Child from Five to Ten. Book. Western Psychological Services; $6.50. (For counselor's use in working with parents. Code: CPk–Pp–1)

Best Friend. Book. Lothrop, Lee and Shepard Co., Inc.; $3.35. Character study portrayed in a simple manner. (For students. Code: Si–Pp–1)

JUNIOR HIGH SCHOOL MATERIALS

Youth: The Years from Ten to Sixteen. Book. Western Psychological Services; $8.00. (For use of counselor with parents. Code: CPj–Pp–1)

Discovering Yourself. Booklet. Science Research Associates, Inc.; $3.67. (For student use. Code: Sj–Pp–1)

Finding Out About Ourselves. Booklet. Science Research Associates, Inc.; $0.65. (For student use. Code: Sj–Pp–1)

Parenthood in a Free Nation; Volume II: Early and Middle Childhood. Book. The Macmillan Company; $2.75. (For counselor's use with parents. Code: CPj–Pp–2)

Adventure for Newcomers. Filmstrip. American Guidance Associates; $4.50. Emphasizes orientation and adjustment to change. (For counselor's use with students. Code: CSj–Pp–1)

Junior High—A Time of Change. Film. McGraw-Hill, Inc.; $65.00. Defines some of the problems that will arise in junior high; encourages students to look at themselves and their place in junior high. (For counselor's use with students. Code: CSj–Pp–1)

Your Junior High Days. Film. McGraw-Hill, Inc.; $70.00. Concerns learning to adjust to many different kinds of people and situations. To face competition, to develop a self-reliance never before required, and to accept responsibility. (For counselor's use with student. Code: CSj–Pp–1)

Attitudes and Health. Film. Coronet Instructional Films; B&W, $45.00; color, $90.00. Portrays that self-confidence and attitudes are important to health. (For counselor's use with student. Code: CSj–Ph–1)

Developing Self-Reliance. Film. Coronet Instructional Films; B&W, $50.00; color, $100.00. Emphasizes that self-reliance is essential to success. (For counselor's use with students. Code: CSj–Pp–1)

Guide to Good Manners. Booklet. Science Research Associates, Inc.; $0.90. (Student's use. Code: Sg–Se–2)

The Summer I Was Lost. Book, fiction. The John Day Company, Inc.; $2.81. Concerns development of a boy's sense of individuality and maturity. (For students. Code: Sj–Pp–1)

SECONDARY SCHOOL MATERIALS

Toward Adult Living. Book. American Guidance Service, Inc.; $4.07. Describes responsibilities and privileges involved as one approaches adulthood. (For teacher's use with students. Code: TSs–Pp–2)

Becoming the Complete Adult. Book. Family Life Publications, Inc.; $4.50. Ten experts help youth assess the total self, goals, maturity, and readiness for adulthood. (Student's use. Code: Ss–Pp–2)

About You. Booklet. Science Research Associates, Inc.; $1.88. To help one learn to understand himself better. (Student's use. Code: Ss–Ph–1)

Human Behavior. Book. Harcourt, Brace & World, Inc.; $9.95. Scientific findings relating to factors that influence human behavior. (Counselor's use with teachers. Code: CTs–Pp–2)

Your Personality and You. Book. Julian Messner, Inc.; $3.64. Discusses and explains to students the effect of personality development on life. Designed to help young people achieve self-understanding. (Student's use. Code: Ss–Pp–2)

Building Your Life. Book. Prentice-Hall, Inc.; $5.96. Describes ways of achieving self-understanding and self-acceptance. (Student's use. Code: Ss–Pp–2)

Identity. Book. The Bruce Publishing Company; $2.00. Centers on teen-age problems of role and identity. (Student's use. Code: Ss–Pp–2)

Parenthood in a Free Nation, Volume III: Later Childhood. The Macmillan Company; $3.00. (Counselor's use with parents. Code: CPs–Pp–2)

Failure: A Step Toward Growth. Film. Guidance Associates; $35.00. Suggests specific ways to face and learn from failure. (Counselor's use with students. Code: CSs–Pp–2)

Preface to a Life. Film. United World Films; B&W, $35.85. Shows environmental influences upon an individual. (Counselor's use with students. Code: CSs–Pp–1)

You and Your Attitudes. Film. Associated Films, Inc.; B&W, $45.00; color, $90.00. An aid to help gain better self-understanding. (Counselor's use with students. Code: CSs–Pp–1)

Somebody's Cheating. Film. Guidance Associates; $35.00. Discusses moral and practical questions from many viewpoints. (Counselor's use with students. Code: CSs–Pp–1)

You're No Good. Film. McGraw-Hill, Inc.; $160.00. Presents a series of episodes that reflect the attitudes, emotions, and actions of a fatherless and confused eighteen-year-old school drop-out. (For counselor's use with students. Code: CSs–Pp–1)

Better Use of Leisure Time. Film. Coronet Instructional Films; B&W $50.00; color, $100.00. Guide to development of attitudes toward leisure time. (For counselor's use with students. Code: CSs–Pl–1)

Enjoying Leisure Time. Book. Science Research Associates, Inc.; $0.65. (For students. Code: Ss–Pl–1)

Exploring Your Personality. Book. Science Research Associates, Inc.; $0.65. (For students. Code: Ss–Pp–1)

Betty Cornell's Glamour Guide for Teens. Book. Pocket Books, Inc.; $0.35. Guide for girls on improving personal appearance. (For students. Code: Ss–Pg–2)

ADULTS

Planning Ahead After Forty: The Process of Psychoevaluation. Book. Western Psychological Services; $4.95. Presents basic materials on values, aptitudes, and other variables. Considers common problems and approaches to solutions of the normal, mature, middle-aged, and aging adult. New concepts for planning, orienting, and adjusting to the years ahead. (Adult use. Code: Ag–Pp–1)

How to Be Healthy and Happy After Sixty. Book. Abelard-Schuman Limited; $4.50. (For adults. Code: As–Ph–1)

Work Attitudes and Retirement Adjustment. Book. University of Wisconsin Press. (Code: As–Pp–1)

Utilizing Physical and Psychological Information

The methods for utilizing physical and psychological information are primarily the same ones used for educational information (see Table 8-1) and occupational information (see Table 13-1). As the individual considers the educational and occupational information applicable to him, consideration on each occasion must be given to his own physical-psychological self. Because man is in a state of flux, change, becoming, or onward striving even when retreating, he needs information periodically. The information will help him not only understand himself but also understand the conditions that have enabled him to change and how he may utilize the information and conditions to bring about positive changes that will facilitate his becoming the person he hopes to and potentially can be.

Methods used should enable the individual to have self-exploration without producing insecurities beyond the threshold of reality recognition. The individual needs a chance to explore ideas, physical strength, and psychological feelings. An overprotective or sheltered life will prevent projecting self, thus thwarting the individual's normal growth and development. For some individuals, methods in physical-psychological information will be needed that will not be needed with other individuals. The more the information is personalized, the more the methods of utilization must be selected according to the person at that time and situation.

Standardized tests are one method of helping the individual to know about himself in comparison to others; however, the limitations should be recognized. Tests often provide a feedback quickly and to a large extent objectively. Role-playing is another method that can be used effectively under certain conditions to enable a person to project himself into a role and situation that may be meaningful to him. The individual's involvement in role-playing may provide a psychological feeling strong enough to assist him in knowing how he might react under the same conditions in reality. Indiscriminate use of role-playing may produce negative results. Role-playing may appear as a simple method, but to be used effectively it should be under the leadership of a qualified person.

Some personality units, courses, games, and questionnaires are meaningful methods for assisting the individual in gaining psychological information. Which one is to be used and when will depend upon two things: the depth of information needed and the extent of the person's involvement desired. As outlined in Chapters 8 and 13, methods can be classified according to the extent of the person's involvement and the control he is to have over the conditions or situations presented to him. In a class that is primarily a lecture, the content is prestructured and the person has little or no control. In a role-playing situation, the person does have some control over what he puts into it and is able to have cognitive and affective processes involvement. In the real life situation he has opportunity for even more involvement.

Research studies seem to indicate that for culturally and/or educationally deprived persons, methods should be selected that include a high degree of personal involvement and immediate feedback. For the academically talented, the methods can be more of the prestructured, intellectually oriented type.

Summary

An individual's characteristic variables and the changes frequently occurring in them make an emerging self an ongoing continuous process, in which the individual has a major role in creating and controlling his future. The perceptions of himself, the world about him, and others' view of him will affect the individual's behavior. Man needs from early childhood throughout life information processes that will enable him to obtain, understand, and integrate a comprehensive perception of himself, those about him, and the potential as well as present environments.

Decisions about the why of life, the person(s) with whom life will be shared, and the occupation(s) to follow are major ones. Often, too, once the decisions have been made and the plans of action followed for some time, one or more of the decisions will be challenged. Changing any one of the three major decisions will require a re-evaluation of one's philosophy of life and may change the direction and rate of becoming. The information processes will be a necessity throughout life with a probable need for professional workers to join together as a team to provide the resources required to perform an adequate job.

In the emerging, ever-changing, developing person, the future is now. Unless sufficient physical and psychological information about self can be obtained in an area of exploration, freedom, and integration, then new ideas, hopes, and goals can never be formed. Without these the future is empty. Now is when the future is formulated. As man changes so must his information and his information processes. Keeping pace, depth, and direction are challenges for each counselor.

SELECTED REFERENCES

Anderson, Kenneth E., ed. *Research on the Academically Talented Student* Washington, D.C.; National Education Association, 1961. 92 pages.

Babbott, Edward F. and Claude W. Grant. "I.Q. as One of Several Variables in Predicting Academic Success," *The School Counselor*, 12 (October 1964), 18–21.

Baer, Max F., and Edward C. Roeber. *Occupational Information: The Dynamics of Its Nature and Use.* Chicago: Science Research Associates, Inc., 1964. Pp. 402–407.

Brough, James R. "The Junior High Schooler: His Concerns and Sources of Help," *The School Counselor*, 13 (December 1965), 71–76.

Burchill, George W. *Work-Study Programs for Alienated Youth, A Casebook.* Chicago: Science Research Associates, Inc., 1962. 265 pages.

Burton, Robert L. "An Experimental Study on Communicating Test Results to Tenth Grade Students," *The School Counselor*, 14 (September 1966), 26–32.

Carkhuff, Robert R., and Bernard G. Berenson. "Man and His Nourishment," *Beyond Counseling and Therapy.* New York: Holt, Rinehart and Winston, Inc., 1967. Chap. 1, pp. 3–19.

Coleman, James C. *Personality Dynamics and Effective Behavior.* Chicago: Scott, Foresman and Company, 1960. 566 pages.

Combs, Arthur W., ed. *Perceiving, Behaving, Becoming: A New Focus for Education.* Washington, D.C.: Association for Supervision and Curriculum Development, A Department of the National Education Association, Yearbook, 1962. 256 pages.

Combs, Arthur W., and D. W. Soper. *The Relationship of Child Perceptions to Achievement and Behavior in the Early Years*. Cooperative Research Project No. 814, U.S. Office of Education, University of Florida, 1963.

Crow, Lester D. *Psychology of Human Adjustment*. New York: Alfred A. Knopf, Inc., 1967. Pp. 578–605.

Edgar, Thomas. "Wistful Wish: Evaluation Without Values," *The Personnel and Guidance Journal*, 44 (June 1966), 1025–1029.

Erb, Everett D., and Douglas Hooker. *The Psychology of the Emerging Self, An Integrated Interpretation of Goal-Directed Behavior*. Philadelphia: F. A. Davis Company, 1967. 289 pages.

Gardner, John W. *Self-Renewal: The Individual and the Innovative Society*. New York: Harper & Row, Publishers, 1964. 141 pages.

Garry, Ralph. *Guidance Techniques for Elementary Teachers*. Columbus, Ohio: Charles E. Merrill Books, Inc., 1963. Pp. 273–382.

Gutsch, Kenneth U., and William D. Bellamy. "Effectiveness of an Attitudinal Group Approach as a Behavior Determinant," *The School Counselor*, 14 (September 1966), 40–43.

Holland, John L. *The Psychology of Vocational Choice: A Theory of Personality Types and Model Environments*. Waltham, Mass.: Blaisdell Publishing Company, 1966. 132 pages.

Hood, Elizabeth. "Group Guidance for Aggressive Junior High School Girls," *The School Counselor*, 11 (May 1964), 196–199.

Hoppock, Robert. *Occupational Information: Where to Get It and How to Use It in Counseling and in Teaching*, 3rd ed. New York: McGraw-Hill, Inc., 1967. Pp. 144–147; 304–312.

Humphreys, J. Anthony, Arthur E. Traxler, and Robert D. North. *Guidance Services*, 3rd ed. Chicago: Science Research Associates, Inc., 1967. Pp. 73–91; 310–317.

Isaacson, Lee E. *Career Information in Counseling and Teaching*. Boston: Allyn and Bacon, Inc., 1966. Pp. 105–143.

Kelley, Earl C. "The Fully Functioning Self," in *Perceiving, Behaving, Becoming: A New Focus for Education*, Arthur W. Combs, ed. Washington, D.C.: Association for Supervision and Curriculum Development, A Department of the National Education Association, Yearbook, 1962. Chap. 2, pp. 9–20; 65.

Ladato, Francis J., Martin A. Sokoloff, and Lester J. Schwartz. "Group Counseling as a Method of Modifying Attitudes in Slow Learners," *The School Counselor*, 12 (October 1964), 27–29.

Lister, James L. "The Relationship of Student Motivation and Intelligence to Accuracy of Self-Estimates," *The School Counselor*, 13 (March 1966). Pp. 173–176.

Maslow, A. H. "Some Basic Propositions of a Growth and Self-Actualization Psychology," in *Perceiving, Behaving, Becoming: A New Focus for Education*, Arthur W. Combs, ed. Washington, D.C.: Association for Supervision and Curriculum Development, A Department of the National Education Association, Yearbook, 1962. Chap. 4, pp. 34–49.

Norris, Willa, Franklin R. Zeran, and Raymond N. Hatch. *The Information*

Service in Guidance, 2nd ed. Chicago: Rand McNally & Company, 1966. Pp. 206–211, 224–231, 569–570.

Pemberton, W. A. *Ability, Values, and College Achievement.* Newark, Del.: University of Delaware, 1963. 77 pages.

Peterson, Peter G. "The Class of 1984 . . . Where Is It Going?" Washington, D.C.: National Committee for Support of the Public Schools, 1966. 17 pages.

Rogers, Carl R. "What It Means to Become a Person," in *The Self: Explorations in Personal Growth,* Clark E. Moustakas, ed. New York: Harper & Row, Publishers, 1956. Chap. 15, pp. 195–211.

Rogers, Carl R. "Toward Becoming a Fully Functioning Person," in *Perceiving, Behaving, Becoming: A New Focus for Education,* Arthur W. Combs, ed. Washington, D.C.: Association for Supervision and Curriculum Development, A Department of the National Education Association, Yearbook, 1962. Chap. 3, pp. 21–33.

Slinger, George E. "Values and the Counseling Relationship in the High School," *The Vocational Guidance Quarterly,* **15** (September 1966), 11–17.

Smart, Mollie S., and Russell C. Smart. *Children: Development and Relationships.* New York: The Macmillan Company, 1967. 582 pages.

Weitz, Henry. *Behavior Change Through Guidance.* New York: John Wiley & Sons, Inc., 1964. Pp. 1–61.

Zytowski, Donald G. "Avoidance Behavior in Vocational Motivation," *The Personnel and Guidance Journal,* **43** (April 1965), 746–750.

Chapter 15

Personalizing

Social Information

Social information surrounds man but without assistance he may never perceive its importance and implications for himself. Children, youth, and adults need information applicable to them about their own social group and other groups of which they may potentially become members.

Socialization processes and the effect of culture begin for an individual at birth and cannot be postponed until some later date. Man is a social being and each person is a member of a social group rather than a hermit. Social information, therefore, becomes important to each individual with whom a counselor works.

The individual, to some extent, has control over part of his social climate, whereas other parts are forced upon him. The image is often given of man being determined by society and culture. Another view is one of man being determined primarily by his biological inheritance. Probably a more realistic recognition of man's development would be to view man as a result of the interactions among society, culture, and cognitive and affective processes within the biological inheritance limits, although recognizing that even these limits may be modified by the advancements of the scientific age, its medical drugs, and its technical know-how. As pointed out by William Kolb (1962, p. 633), the actual ability of an individual to transcend the clutches of culture is restricted to a few. Those few may make major contributions to the advancement of civilization. Hopefully, counselors may facilitate social information becoming personalized to the extent that individuals who want to do so may change.

If man is to be an integral part of a social group, then throughout life he is seeking information about his own group, about other groups with which he has only casual acquaintance, about groups he does not know, and particularly about groups that he has the potential for or the aspirations of making his group. To leave to chance that man will be able to obtain the information on his own in each and every instance or that he will obtain it through structured courses in the social sciences in elementary, secondary, or higher education is probably not accurate. At times the individual will need personalized social information that can best be utilized with him, not just given to him, by the counselor. Obtaining social information is more than the acquiring of facts. It is an ongoing process in which the individual is integrating information into his self-concept, value systems, hopes, and plans, which become involved in his exploratory tryouts in social settings.

Regardless of man's age he has a need for social information, but he does not need all available social information. He wants the social information that has or may have personal meaning to him. Social groups as well as the individual are changing; therefore, additional recent information becomes necessary. In today's mobile society, the need for personalized social information is greater than ever before. One of the problems is in knowing the bias of the person or group who has provided the social information available. Another problem comes in finding the social information that has meaning at the time the individual needs it. Some social information having personal meaning can be filed, stored on bookshelves, or captured on film and tape recordings, but most of it cannot. Personalized social information is not something to be taught and stored in the brain's memory cells.

The individual is an integral member of one or more social groups and in the future may be a member of different groups. The diverse values and conflicting interests of groups will and should affect not only his development but also his potential opportunities, including self-expression. Ethnic, racial, religious, regional, and urban-rural differences provide uniqueness while also providing cross currents and subgroups where the individual may to some extent lose himself or use the subgroups as fertile soil for growth and development. Thus, self-understanding is not enough—the individual must know different groups and social environments where the interactions among ideas, feelings, values, feedbacks, and so on, can be explored for his own growth, security, and dream formation within a world of potential reality. Interaction with people is essential for one's social development.

Purposes of Personalized Social Information and Counselor's Role

Human beings today live in a social environment whether they want to or not. The population of the United States reached 200 million on November 22, 1967, and at that time was increasing at the rate of one additional person every fourteen and one half seconds. Individuals grow and develop not as isolates but as individuals within a social setting. Very often skills and confidence can be gained only by obtaining reactions of other people. Knowing and understanding others is essential for the interpretation of feedback from them.

Social information becomes important for the individual to find groups, conditions, and times when he may explore his own ideas, dreams, feelings, and inner self. Perhaps what is being stated is that for positive mental health one needs social settings for self-expression. With the exception of the hermit, self-fulfillment depends upon a social interaction—to be a contributor, possibly influencing change. Purposeful constructive social interaction can be more meaningful by understanding social information, which is the basis for requiring the teaching of social studies in schools. When effective, the teaching of social studies increases the individual's desire for understanding more about the social information that has personal implications for him. He also wants to integrate the information into his own orientation, value systems, plans, and factual backdrop for future decision-making.

In social information the counselor can assist the individual in intermeshing his own life into society. The role is more than an understanding of society, something in addition to the learning of facts; it is also a process extended over a lifetime, where the individual sees himself as able, in part, to select his friends and associates, who will provide much of the fertile soil for becoming. Though the groups in which he participates will probably determine his future, he is able in a democratic society to choose his associates; and secondly, he is able to affect them. They too are becoming. Man does have a voice in his future; at the very least he can select among those around him whom he will use as reference sets for the feedback he needs in developing his own self-concepts, social concepts, and aspirations.

Sociologists and social psychologists, in general, agree that in America social classes do exist. Total agreement has not and probably will not be reached on the characteristics of each class. However, enough research data are available to draw the conclusion that social class determines to a great extent such matters as where and how one will live, including the kind of house, furnishings in the house or apartment, clothes worn; values and attitudes held; amount and kind of education obtained; aspirations and ambitions; kinds of leisure-time and self-expressive activities in which one will engage; friends and associates; and even the person taken as a spouse. These are personal things and, as such, social information must be more than mass information about society—it must be personalized social information.

In summary, the purposes of personalized social information include the following:

1. Increase awareness on the part of the individual of society, its subgroups, cultures, and the effects of each.
2. Stimulate utilization of additional knowledge through integration into the individual's orientation, value systems, and plans to further his development.
3. Create understanding of present and potential groups in which an individual can find or extend self-expression and self-fulfillment.
4. Enable the individual to consider alternative groups and cultures for personal-social vertical and horizontal mobility, and for laying aside the shackles of present situations.
5. Motivate the individual to contribute to change in social patterns and problems.
6. Assist the individual in understanding others to the extent that he can make decisions about the potential persons necessary for the kinds of interaction desired.
7. Help an individual through knowledge and understanding to translate his experiences in relation to his social development.
8. Assist the individual in identifying groups in which he can explore and test a perceived self as he is and as he is becoming.
9. Supply the necessary information for the individual to interpret and evaluate feedback from other individuals within a social setting.
10. Facilitate social maturity of the individual.

Subgroups and Cultures

Society is a composite of subgroups and cultures—little societies. Each individual is a part of the total society as well as of his immediate subgroup(s) and culture(s). In order for the individual to become a fully functioning person, he needs to understand himself. A counselor working with the individual in the areas of educational, occupational, and personal-social information can work more effectively if he has an understanding of the individual's perception of himself, of others, and of the world of work.

Subgroups may be categorized for discussion into such groups as disadvantaged, academically talented, handicapped, drop-outs, under-privileged, alienated, delinquents, and senior citizens. A danger exists in the possibility of too much generalization concerning each group. Some basic characteristics exist in a culture, and the potential effect on the individual can be surmised; however, only by actually working with an individual can one know his perceptions, because each individual reacts uniquely to a given stimulus and experience.

Each subgroup and culture within the geographical area served by the counelor should be studied in detail. Space in this book limits presentations; therefore, a brief summary of one subgroup—the disadvantaged—is presented as an illustration of the kinds of social information essential for the counselor and the counselee who is in that subgroup or who is considering entering the subgroup.

The Disadvantaged

The disadvantaged, the drop-out, the underprivileged, the alienated, and the delinquent are closely related as products of their environments and experiences. Even though an individual lives within a subgroup, one should exert caution not to hang a label on him or to assume that he is like any other individual within his subgroup. Research has revealed some potential characteristics that may develop within certain subgroups. An awareness of these potential developments is helpful to counselors and other persons working with an individual from that group.

Disadvantaged may be used to refer to individuals who are culturally deprived, educationally deprived, economically deprived, alienated, or any individual who is deterred in his growth and development toward becoming a fully functioning individual. A disadvantaged individual is ageless—however most printed information concerning the disadvantaged concentrates on youth. The information in this section will attempt to create an awareness of the importance of understanding subgroups and cultures, thereby stimulating the reader to do further reading, studying, and research for the particular groups with whom he is immediately concerned. Understanding subgroups will be important in assisting the individual in both his physical and psychological development and his social development.

Generalized Characteristics of Disadvantaged Individuals

Even though disadvantaged individuals may be found within any culture or setting, most emphasis today is on individuals within a low-income bracket who live in substandard, overcrowded housing. Characteristics of the setting and people within the group would include

1. Large families with relatives residing within the family unit in inadequate living space and poor sanitary conditions.
2. Unemployment, dependence on welfare, and inadequate education and skills to compete for gainful employment contribute to perpetuating the prevailing conditions of the subpar living.
3. Nonmarital sexual relationships, illegitimate children, alcoholism, dope addiction, and violence are marked results of the environment.

Summarizing from Frank Reissman's book, *The Culturally Deprived Child* (1962, pp. 26–30), other characteristics of the individual are that he is patriarchal (except in a major section of the Negro subculture, which is matriarchal), superstitious, and somewhat religious; reads ineffectively and is poorly informed in many areas; holds attitudes related to his traditional orientation that are not open to reason or flexible opinions; feels alienated, not fully a part of society; is not individualistic, introspective, self-oriented, or concerned with self-expression; holds the world responsible for his plight rather than himself; has a need for getting by rather than ahead; prefers jobs that are secure; tends to favor the underdog; is strongly anticommunist, likes strong leaders; is prejudiced and intolerant; sets great store by his family and his personal comforts; likes excitement; is pragmatic and anti-intellectual; appears to learn more by the physical or motor fashion; admires strength and endurance; and emphasizes masculinity.

Certain positive characteristics are developed within these cultures that should be understood and appreciated by the counselor and the individual in order to enhance the development of the individual. The stamina required for an individual to survive in such an environment forces the development of a person who adapts to a way of life, who is self-reliant and independent, and who fights to fulfill needs for necessities. He is aggressive toward what he wants and toward fulfilling his commitments. These characteristics influence the total operative structural pattern of the individual and his ability to obtain and integrate personal, social, educational, and occupational information for enhancement of his development.

Eugene McCreary (1966, p. 47) stated, "The socially disadvantaged are not lacking in knowledge, culture, and skills, but possess somewhat different understandings and abilities because of the circumstances of their lives." These individuals live in a world of practical knowledge and experiences and therefore appear to learn better through physical-motor processes. They may learn at a slower pace than an individual who has had an opportunity to develop in an academic climate, but they have the capability of learning. Often within the formal learning climate, because they are slow to learn, persons working with them consider them stupid or noneducable rather than helping them to develop to their potential level educationally, occupationally, personally, and socially.

These individuals are often considered slow learners because of scores on the popular intelligence tests used to measure ability. Most of the intelligence tests are based on reading skill; therefore, because the individuals are poor readers or nonreaders, these tests are no indicator for these individuals. They lack a supportive environment for education that aids development of reading and communicative skills. Within the environment of a noisy, shouting, fighting atmosphere, no privacy for studying exists. Many individuals have an auditory deficiency; they are able to hear but lack the ability to listen and comprehend. They are unable to compete in a formal school situation because of their lack of reading and communicative skills, their lack of auditory attention, their suspicions of the school and teachers, and their lack of school know-how. A counselor working with the disadvantaged individual to foster development and overcome deficiencies will need to help the individual to understand his psychological and physical self and also to work with other persons such as teachers and parents involved with the individual.

Within an environment in which parents have attended schools, the rudiments of school know-how are learned by association to a degree. But within the society of the disadvantaged person, where few have successfully attended schools, the individual lacks the knowledge of the simplest routines and skills that most teachers take for granted in children attending school. Not only disadvantaged children but also disadvantaged adults who may take part in an educational program lack the know-how of school—how to study, how to work with others, and how to promote good teacher-student relations.

Working with the Disadvantaged Individual

Working with the disadvantaged in the area of personal development involves consideration of the characteristics of the culture (both positive and noncontributing) and their effect upon the individual. Since an individual develops a self-concept through his experiences and interactions with others, the influences of the environment either enhance or retard it. The disadvantaged person, through understanding these influences, can help in his own development toward becoming a responsible person in the overall society if he can escape some of the shackles of his setting and build upon the contributing factors. Many disadvantaged individuals are deprived of expressions that create a feeling of adequacy. The disadvantaged person may develop a feeling of indifference and lack a desire to advance because his experiences of repeated failure, as he perceives them, result in a feeling of hopelessness.

Because of the lack of aspirations, he does not respond to the usual stimuli of motivation.

Parents are a key to working with disadvantaged children. The counselor can work with parents to change attitudes and to create an approval and acceptance for learning—a supportive climate for learning and change. These persons usually favor and appreciate the advantages of an education, but they are against formal schools and teachers because of the failure experiences encountered for generations in schools that have not been structured to meet their needs or to build upon concepts that contribute to meeting their particular needs and to overcoming deficiencies. Beginning to work with these individuals at their level rather than assuming that they fit the pattern of middle-class mores can contribute to their development. These individuals need to participate in planned experiences that will lead to successful responses. A planned sequence of successes must override the previous failure pattern sequence experienced by these individuals.

Teachers and other persons working with the disadvantaged individual affect his achievement by their aspiration and expectation levels for him. This effect is not limited only to the disadvantaged. All persons respond to this effect, but since this presentation concerns the disadvantaged it is considered with them. The disadvantaged individual responds to persons who genuinely respect him as an individual and who are interested in his achievement. Experience has taught him to be suspicious of attention, to be belligerent, independent, and self-reliant. He needs standards and rules established for operation, consistency in administering these regulations, and fairness in consideration free from prejudices. He is unable to work in a flexible, permissive atmosphere until he has modified the pattern of behavior learned in the rigors of his environment.

Help boys and girls to have opportunities where they can develop toward becoming workers, successful parents, law-abiding citizens, and happy persons; then they will also be developing toward becoming competent adults (Burchill, 1962, p. 149). Working with these individuals to accomplish these goals means starting with the positive characteristics and overcoming blockages to learning and functioning created by their experiences. Working with them in relation to the interactions of the total variables of the individual and his environment involves self-concept, abilities, aptitudes, values, motivations, knowledge, skills, aspirations and expectations, needs and wants, and experiences.

George Burchill (1962, p. 155) indicated that an essential problem of the alienated group is their failure to find a satisfactory avenue or channel of growth toward adult competence. Since they are failing in school, they cannot grow up in the school pattern. They need alternative pathways. Opportunities to work while in school on cooperative or work-study programs have been facilitated by governmental legislation in such acts as the Vocational Education Act, the Manpower Development Act, and the Economic Opportunities Act (refer to Chapter 2). Work-study programs in the secondary schools can meet the needs of some of these individuals to adjust to successful participation in school and in the world of work. However, a successful program must include social and community successes on the part of the participants.

Working with a disadvantaged individual entails understanding his needs, perceptions, and potentials. Since these individuals are practical and vocationally oriented, a trend is to let them cling to their anti-intellectual attitudes and to remain in vocational and trade schools. This route is easier for all concerned—the individual and those working with him. However, a great loss of human resources occurs because the superior ability individual, as well as others, is not encouraged to develop potentially, educationally, and vocationally.

This presentation on a topic, on which books have been written, is limited. It is presented to indicate that awareness of this impact of subgroup(s) and culture(s) on an individual is essential to the effectiveness of the counselor. Knowledge and understanding of subgroups and cultures are important to the counselor in helping the individual to understand himself and to develop personally, socially, educationally, and vocationally to his fullest potentials. Utilization of information involves the perception of an individual regardless of his subgroup(s) and culture(s); therefore utilization is a personalized process for each individual.

Understanding Others to the Extent of Participation

An individual in his own frame of reference becomes a member of a group or of two or more groups rather than of the total society. He can relate himself to a specific group or groups, but society, in general, is too large, too indefinite. A person wants to be able to participate. To do so he must begin by identifying with a small enough segment of society so that he can have an awareness of the functions and expectations of the other persons in relation to himself. For participation to be facilitated, the individual may need to know only a limited amount of information about the others and will add to his information as he interacts with them.

As the individual becomes a member of one group, the characteristics of that group will elicit certain behavior patterns from him. He may like what he sees in himself and formulate attitudes based upon his behavior, or he may dislike his image as he interprets feedback from the group and then may attempt to modify some things about himself.

He may choose to withdraw or to suppress those things about himself. For effective participation one needs to know how he is like others but, equally important, he needs to know how he differs from others.

An individual is generally a member of several groups rather than just one. Each group will elicit behavior from the individual; some behavior will be the same from group to group, whereas other behavior may be different. The difference in his own behavior patterns as he participates in the different groups may create an awareness of conflict in himself or a realization of the behavioral expectations of different groups. Such recognitions are an integral part of growth; but, to make the development, he wants assistance at these times. He may need information about the groups as they relate to him, assistance in understanding himself, and personalized social information of the type that will enable him to facilitate a different participative self.

Social information desired by the individual often requires emphasis on the group's characteristics rather than upon the specific understanding of each member. An individual does not want to know everything about everybody. He does need, however, to know enough about others to find people who can supplement and complement him as a person, encourage participation and interaction, provide a sounding board or reference set for exploration of himself, and encourage his extension into the new frontiers where he desires to go but lacks the confidence to venture without the assurance of another person. A person doesn't "psych-out" every person he meets; if he did, he probably would not be accepted. One does need to know, understand, and feel that he can trust others. The more one ventures, the more one finds out about himself. The questions may be ones such as the following: How secure am I? Can I afford to venture under these conditions? Do the group members provide a nurtured environment for my exploration?

The more one shares his inner self with a group, the more one needs to feel that he knows and accepts those with whom he shares. The extent to which one needs to understand others is determined by the kind and depth of self-involvement. Personalized social information would mean that not only do needs differ from one person to another but that the social information needed by the individual differs from time to time depending upon his anticipated participation and involvement. Explorations in one's own reference group may be the bases of attitude formation; thus the reference group may extend or constrict the individual's growth.

The Individual in Relation to the Modern World

Man often exhibits behavior patterns not as he wants them to be but as he perceives they must be for the group. In spite of all the emphasis upon man as an individual, he often is prevented from being his inner self because he reasons that he must conform to the group and its expectations rather than show his individuality. Society requires that man perform his particular social function and, if he does, society will leave the rest of the man alone. Here is where the trouble often lies. Man is left alone, outside of his social function, to subsist as best he can. Some people find another person or a few selected people with whom they can share their inner self and obtain interaction for feedback. Others do not find another person with whom they can share their innermost personal feelings, ideas, and psychic energies. In such cases the inner self may be suppressed below the surface of consciousness and forgotten. Modern society encourages this. Man's position in society may preclude him from doing some of the things essential for his understanding and from being able to handle his own emotions and feelings. He may be prevented from doing the activities necessary for his own positive mental health. The preclusions may be more a result of his own perceptions than of the group's expectations, but in either case they are real to him. The preclusions in time may be extensive enough to alienate the person from his "true" self.

Conformity versus Individuality

The social structure exerts a pressure upon each individual. He has a struggle of many ideas, behavior patterns, desires, and so on, as to whether he will let the value system of the group as he perceives it prevail or whether he will let his own individuality predominate. Conformity often is seen as the road of least resistance and the safest one. Individuality has a price tag on it, and often the extent of the price tag is not or cannot be determined prior to exhibiting the individuality.

Total conformity causes man to lose his identity and reduces him below the level of effective maximum participation. On the other hand, total individuality will probably alienate the person from the group. Therefore, for man's own mental health and possibly for the good of the group, he must find those things with which he can be comfortable in conforming and at the same time must identify those things with which he needs to be an individualist and to express himself. Personal-social information of this kind is not something one reads in an article or is told in an interview. Such information is essential and is a process extending over a lifetime. The implications for the individual's counselor are tremendous.

Social Maturity

Just as one grows toward physical maturity and occupational maturity, so does one have the potential for developing social maturity. Just as the authorities differ on what is physical maturity and what is occupational maturity, so do authorities differ on what is social maturity. V. Clyde Arnspiger (1961, pp. 24–26), in writing about a mature person in a free society, included the person's having extensive practice in facing problems realistically, in freeing himself from having unrealistic fears, in appraising the status he has reached, in establishing realistic goals, in becoming aware of social value categories, and in understanding the conscious and unconscious motivations that guide the actions of people.

Social maturity is probably not something one gains and then retains forever. A person may be socially mature in one group and socially immature in another. Because of the extent of similarities among the different groups to which one belongs or comes in contact, much of the social maturity is applicable from one group to another. Social maturity within a group is probably more than just learning about oneself and about people in general. It includes understanding the value system and its implications for the specific group. Social maturity within a group also may be lost if the person does not keep abreast of changes in the group members. Personalized social information may assist the individual in his development toward social maturity and his understanding of how to obtain social maturity.

Masculine and Feminine Roles

Societal role expectations of men and women are changing. Once woman's place was considered to be in the home rearing children. Today society accepts women who work outside the home. At first women could work outside the home if they were secretaries, clerks, or elementary school teachers, or worked in other select occupations. Today the range of jobs open to women is almost identical to that for men. The state laws prohibiting women from doing certain kinds of work have mostly disappeared. Men have been able to accept positions that once were considered only for women. Society's values in general have changed in regard to role expectations in work, but some still have different role expectations for men and women.

Social information for women often is highlighted in childhood, adolescence, and early marriage; but it is needed also immediately following the time when their children have become old enough for the mothers to assume a new social role. The percentage of women of this classification who are entering the labor market is increasing yearly. Many others are assuming unique and different roles in society. During the child-rearing age women often live in a neighborhood of families with small children, a neighborhood characterized by females, toys, children, and pet animals (Useem, 1960–1961). This life is woven around children and their needs. Then comes another life—a new relationship to other people. The relationship between husband and wife has an opportunity for change. The masculine-feminine roles within the home may take on new dimensions.

Individuals at various ages from early childhood through retirement have need for social information that will provide them a basis for understanding their masculine-feminine roles in society. Many people do not recognize the change in those roles as culture and society change, as they change groups or occupations, and as they change in age.

Social Mobility—Vertical and Horizontal

Society makes laws and regulations to govern and protect itself. Some of the laws tend to force people to be neighbors with others who are of a similar class. Building codes restrict one's neighbors and often his associates, including those in schools, shopping centers, churches, and recreation areas. The opportunities that did exist for gaining different social orientations may be decreasing, thus adding a new dimension for needed social information.

Social mobility may occur horizontally when one changes groups but does not change class. Vertical mobility, either up or down, may occur as one changes groups. Sociologists have found that vertical mobility is frequently facilitated by one or more vehicles, including marriage, additional education, change in occupation, change or acceptance of religion, or a move geographically. Social mobility may not result from any one factor but from an interweaving of factors, each dependent upon the others. A job may provide opportunity for more active social participation, which may provide opportunity for job mobility, and this may result in a new self-concept, which could develop a change in mobility orientation.

In the past and to a large extent still today, education has been the key to social mobility. As indicated in Part II, "Personalizing Educational Information," the amount of education that one possesses may not be as much of a criterion as educational potential and attitude toward education. These two conditions plus a positive mobility orientation may enable a person to make meaningful changes. Education and occupation are important considerations in one's social relations. One's work often determines his mainstream of social life. As Wilensky (1961) pointed out, one's participation in community life is a natural extension of his participation in work. The occupation alone may not be as much of a determinant as the total work milieu. One's place of work and one's associates may be as important as or more important in determining social class than one's occupation. Once having recognized some of the conditions affecting one's life, one may develop new aspirations, which may be fulfilled through social mobility—vertical or horizontal. Generally social mobility may be accomplished through changing groups, but also may be done through assisting one's own group to make changes. His educational potential, his attitude toward his fellow man, his self-concept, his mobility orientation, and his beliefs in his own potentials for becoming may be determining conditions for what one will do for himself and for society.

The American family structure is in a process of change. Many families move each year, and often these moves are to better oneself. In one year, March, 1964, to March, 1965, one person in every five in the United States had moved, with two out of three of those who moved taking residence in another house in the same county. However, one in every six of the movers relocated in another state. As might be expected, the median age for movers was in the early-twenty-year-old group for both men and women, whereas the median age for nonmovers was in the early-thirty-year-old group for both men and women. The white population moved less frequently (20.0 per cent moved) than Negroes (25.7 per cent) and others (27.5 per cent) (*Statistical Abstract of the United States, 1966*, p. 32). If a move geographically is one of the items generally associated with social mobility, then Americans have a potential for social mobility. Another way of interpreting the data is to help the individual recognize that moving from one location to another does not in and of itself assure vertical social mobility, nor does the move necessarily have a stigma or prestige associated with it. A geographic move often is the result of one or more members of the family changing jobs and sometimes even occupations. The change in jobs then results in either horizontal or vertical mobility, which seems reason enough to indicate the need for social information prior to and following job or occupational mobility.

Avenues for mobility for persons in poverty have in the past been through additional education, through entering the unskilled labor market and working upward, or through entrepreneurial enterprises where small capital and limited education were required. All three avenues have been reduced, primarily because of technology for the last two and because of additional educational requirements with hidden costs for the first (Pearl, 1965, pp. 91–92). Another problem is also developing for the poor. The closing of the unskilled labor market and the need for additional education are causing many of them to take vocational education, which may lock them into a job classification that causes vertical social immobility. Vocational education is meaningful to the individual and does assist him in obtaining gainful employment; however, it does tend to prepare for the immediate occupation and often lacks the breadth and general education required for making occupational mobility that may result in social vertical mobility.

Occupational mobility is not always for the purpose of vertical social mobility. Intraoccupational mobility, where the individual changes places of work or moves in rank within the occupation, may be characterized by increasing security or may result in new associates, thus horizontal social mobility. Interoccupational mobility often means greater risk for the individual and does hold the possibility of vertical mobility, though that may not be a result (Hatt, 1962, p. 246). Personal information often is needed by the individual in order that he may understand the potentials in the occupational mobilities open to him now and in the future.

Social Problems of Life

Tools for evaluation tend to be out-of-date with the problems. As changes occur, new tools must be designed. By the time evaluative tools are standardized, however, the problem may have changed. Evaluating today's problems with yesterday's tools may be analogous to performing tomorrow's occupations with yesterday's training. The problems created in each new generation may, in part, be because of an adult population endeavoring to superimpose values and evaluate with a value system that was suitable for yesterday's society but is not applicable to the present generation. Research data seem to support the conclusion that adolescents and parents often do not disagree on basic values, but conflict occurs on implementation of values and on such superficial things as dance and dress.

One's self-concept may serve as an insulator against absorbing social problems or becoming one (Reckless, et al., 1962, pp. 43–47). The presence of a socially acceptable concept of self may prevent a person from becoming engaged in or of contributing to the social problems of the times even though he may be living in and surrounded by the problems. The counselor, in assisting the individual in his development, may find that one of his most important roles is in the development of a socially acceptable concept of self and recognition of ways the individual may live without becoming absorbed in social problems. The individual, with his positive self-concept, may be a contributor to the changing of societal problems.

To elaborate upon each social problem of life is beyond the scope of this book, but individuals do need personal information to assist them in recognizing, avoiding, overcoming, and developing beyond social problems. Riots, parades, strikes, protest marches, and other similar activities are only signs of the difference in value systems held by two or more groups of people. Each overt activity is an exhibit against an existing social problem for which one group feels it has an answer—but an answer that has not been accepted by another group. Other social problems exist and are recognized for which seemingly no group of people can agree to the extent that they are willing to try to force a solution.

Social problems of life, such as alcoholism, drug addiction, crime, delinquency, and immorality are included in the topics of major personal concern to individuals with whom counselors work. The setting in which the counselor works may determine the extent of the problems and the kind of social information maintained. For many counselors referral or consultative sources may be the way in which assistance is obtained.

Sex, the population explosion, and the pill are all frequently in head-line articles on social problems. Today's society may be undergoing a revision of the sex code and may even be changing attitudes toward the role of sex in love and the family relationship. If such is the case, the counselor of tomorrow may find that his information of today is out-of-step.

Social Activities Contribute to Development

Social activities provide opportunities in which an individual can explore different roles. A person needs to develop for himself appropri-ate roles in relation to his self-concept as it emerges from social inter-action. Participation in groups is not only a means of finding out about himself as he is and has been but is also a means of extending himself, of projecting himself into ideas, activities, and thoughts that may never occur otherwise.

One's perception of approval and disapproval in a group setting con-tributes to his continuation or modification of behavior and frequently stimulates the addition of new activities. Social activities contribute to an individual's development. If he could become conscious of the dif-ferent ways in which groups can contribute to his development, then perhaps he could more readily identify the time, place, and kind of so-cial activities needed to assist him in his development now. Later he could select different social activities.

Social Agencies for Referrals and Consultation

No counselor can obtain all of the competencies necessary for pro-viding the personalized social information processes that may be needed by the many different counselees with whom he may work. The recog-nition of that statement may cause a counselor to perceive that he has at least three alternatives: continue to learn but recognize he cannot serve all; try to disprove the statement by performing additional activi-ties so that he will be able to provide the necessary social information; or consider himself a team member with other persons in the community who may assist the different individuals.

To become a team member with other persons in the community necessitates the establishment of a relationship whereby referrals and consultations can be made. A working relationship cannot be assumed;

it must be established. One agency or person may want referrals made one way and another agency or person may want a different procedure followed. The fees may vary not only from agency to agency but also from one counselee to another within the same agency. The personnel available and their competencies may vary from community to community and from time to time within the same community. Each counselor will need to develop for himself a community resources directory that can be changed easily as additional information becomes available (Hollis and Hollis, 1965).

Social agency personnel can be excellent sources for feedback—third depth—information to the individual and to the counselor. Many social agency personnel are facilitators for individuals' growth and can assist persons in readily obtaining a feedback to themselves. Often social agency personnel can provide the environment for the feedback, which in many cases may be difficult for a counselor to provide alone. General or breadth information—first depth—is available in many social agencies and can be obtained by the counselor, or perhaps the maximum growth could be accomplished by the individual's obtaining it on his own. The same thing may be true with second depth—resource or specific—information. The recognition of social agencies as available for and allies in personalizing social information means that each referral or consultation should be completed with the purposes as clearly understood as possible.

The list of social agencies and other persons available in a community to assist in personalizing social information will vary from community to community. The following is a partial list of those agencies that may be available:

Business and industrial personnel offices

Chamber of Commerce

Character building agencies—Boy Scouts, Girl Scouts, Campfire Girls, YMCA, and YWCA

Educational institutions—public and private schools, YMCA and YWCA, classrooms on main street, colleges and universities

Employment offices—public, private, business, and industry

Family relation agencies—social workers, Family Service Bureau

Financial and material assistance agencies—Children's Aid Society, Salvation Army, Red Cross, social welfare, service clubs

Labor unions

Legal agencies—courts, lawyers, law-enforcement officials, public defenders, probation officers

Military services—recruitment offices, military bases

Physical health agencies—physicians, osteopaths, chiropractors, nurses, and the many other health improvement personnel

Psychological and psychiatric assistance—child guidance clinics, mental health agencies and institutions, psychiatrists, psychoanalysts, psychologists, psychometrists, counselors

Recreational agencies

Religious agencies—church and synagogue employees and lay workers, missions

Coding, Filing, Storing, and Retrieving Social Information

Once social information has been obtained it needs to be coded according to a file system that will facilitate its use. No one coding system seems to be used universally. Instead, the coding of social information by counselors, in many instances, is not a developed plan that encourages counselees to seek and utilize the information available. Counselors generally are not experienced librarians, nor have they become acquainted with the philosophical framework for filing. Counselors visualize their role as helping people primarily through working directly with them rather than as material organizers. As a result, counselors often comment, "Give me a good file system and I'll use it. I don't care about the theory on which it is based." The difficulty is that no good file system for social information for counseling and guidance has been developed.

Some suggestions can be made to assist counselors in coding, filing, storing, and retrieving social information. First, recognize that the organization of the materials should be for communication as well as for storage; i.e., organize so that an individual using the materials may have his viewpoint broadened in the area while also obtaining readily the exact information desired. Related materials can be grouped together by means of a coding and filing system in a manner that will enable persons to identify other materials that may be meaningful to them. Often a person may find material that will help project his thoughts far ahead.

Second, recognize that a coding and filing system can be an asset in evaluating the quantity and quality of material available if the system is selected with that purpose as one of the criteria. The 3-D concept (Chapter 3) may be used as a means of considering the different people for whom information may be needed and also the different depths. If the materials can be grouped according to those two dimensions and also subdivided according to the different kinds of social information, then quantity can be easily determined. The quality of material will require another kind of evaluation. The 3-D concept may, however, assist in identifying whether or not materials are available for each of the proposed purposes of the information service in the social information area.

Third, recognize that social information that is applicable to one person or group may not be applicable for another. Social information has to be collected and organized for the persons to be served rather than just any and all available materials, being collected. The selection of a coding and filing system should assist in identifying kinds of information desired rather than first coding and filing, and then waiting to see if someone will use it.

Fourth, the storage of materials will depend upon the facilities available, the counselors and their competencies, the traffic patterns of potential users, the location of other personalized information, and various other conditions prevailing in the local situation. Generally some, if not all, of the personalized social information will be housed in an area close to or within the counseling facilities. The waiting room or guidance reading room is generally a good location if someone is available to assist individuals when and if they need help. The storage location should be close to but just outside of usual traffic patterns so that information can be obtained with a minimum of difficulty.

Retrieval must become an integral part of any information system. Much information seems to be gathered, but making the right information available at the appropriate time is becoming more and more of a skill. The fifth suggestion is to select the code, file, and storage place that seems to be the best for retrieval by the potential users of the system. A detailed coding and filing system may prevent potential users from actually using the information instead of encouraging them. *The user is more concerned with retrieval than he is with filing and storing.* Therefore, the coding and filing system needs to be selected with the potential users' viewpoints considered and, specifically, with the intent that the system lend itself to assisting an inexperienced person, who may be confused and puzzled about the topic, in discovering and locating quickly (retrieving) information that may be beneficial.

Sample Materials and Sources

Actual materials pertinent to a particular setting must be determined by the needs of the clientele to be served. Counselors can reach decisions on materials from past experiences in working with individuals in personalizing information. However, if a counselor relies on only past experiences of the utilization of materials, the material will become obsolete for the everchanging groups for which the information is to be made available. The counselor must project potential future users' needs in a changing society.

The following samples of materials are not all-inclusive but are some that may contribute to social development information in certain settings. Such information does not lend itself to ease of coding for drawing related materials together for effective use. However, analyzing the samples by the 3-D concept according to potential users, areas, and depth will help organize related materials for users. In addition to the title of the material, the type, and the source, a code is completed according to the 3-D concept (see Table 7-1 for the code). If a counselor has not already developed his own effective coding for organizing material, he may find that the 3-D concept, modified for his own clientele, will contribute to facilitating utilization.

The samples are classified under preschool; elementary, junior high, and senior high schools; and adults. In general practice, counselors serve clientele who are a segment of the population rather than the total. The sample material presented in this section is illustrative of information for a wide population rather than for one counselor or one setting.

PRESCHOOL MATERIALS

Your Child from One to Six. Booklet. U.S. Government Printing Office; $0.20. Provides helpful suggestions for mental, emotional, and social development. (For parents. Code: P–Ss–2)

Race Awareness in Young Children. Book. The Macmillan Company; $1.50. (For parents. Code: P–Ss–1)

The Day Everybody Cried. Booklet, fiction. The Viking Press, Inc.; $2.57. Story for children three to five years old about crying with someone and the special kind of feeling one has. (For parents to read and show to small children. Code: P–Ss–1)

ELEMENTARY SCHOOL MATERIALS

New Friends in Shepherd's Meadow. Book. Lothrop, Lee, & Shepard, Company, Inc.; $3.25. A story about making new friends and adaptability. (For teacher to use with children. Code: TSk–Ss–1)

Social Development. Film. McGraw-Hill, Inc.; B&W, $80.00. Presents social behavior patterns of children at various stages of development. (For counselors and teachers. Code: CT–Ss–2)

Myeko's Gift. Book. Abelard-Schuman Limited; $3.50. Story of a Japanese child's adaptation and acceptance into an American school and way of life. (For teachers working with pupils. Code: TSi–Sp–1)

Trust a City Kid. Book. Lothrop, Lee, & Shepard Company, Inc.; $3.52. A twelve-year-old Harlem lad learns to adjust and live in an unfamiliar situation. (For students. Code: Si–Ss–1)

Guiding Children's Social Growth. Booklet. SRA; $0.65. (For teachers working with elementary school pupils. Code: TSe–Ss–2)

What to Tell Your Child. Book. Pocket Books, Inc.; $0.50. Helps to answer questions about birth, death, illness, divorce, and other family crises. (For parents. Code: P–Sf–2)

What to Tell Your Child About Sex. Book. Pocket Books, Inc.; $0.50. Concerns child development and frequently asked questions. (For parents. Code: P–Sb–2)

JUNIOR HIGH SCHOOL MATERIALS

What You Should Know About Smoking and Drinking. Booklet. SRA; $0.90. (Student Use. Code: Sj–Sa–1)

Role-playing Methods in the Classroom. SRA; $2.00. Gives step-by-step discussion of how to use role-playing in the classroom. (For teachers. Code: Tsi–Ss–2)

About Growing Up. Book. American Guidance Service, Inc.; $3.27. Emphasizes study habits, sportsmanship, attitudes toward activities, and participation in family and group life. (For students. Sj–Ss–2)

The Savage. Book, fiction. Abelard-Schuman Limited; $3.00. Exciting story of gangs and delinquency in a medium-sized American city high school. Friendships of intelligent classmates result in a happy situation. (For students. Code: Sj–Ss–1)

Stepchild in the Family. Book. Pocket Books, Inc.; $0.75. (For parents. Code: P–Sf–2)

First Party. Book, fiction. Hastings House, Publishers, Inc.; $3.75. The story of a girl who decides to have her first real party—a girl-boy party. (For students. Code: Sj–Sb–1)

Fifteen. Book, fiction. William Morrow and Company, Inc; $3.50. Boy-girl relationships. Enjoyable story. (For students. Code: Sj–Sb–1)

SENIOR HIGH SCHOOL MATERIALS

Facts About Alcohol. Booklet. SRA; $0.90. Effects of alcohol on the system and drinking habits of an alcoholic. (Student use. Code: Ss–Sd–2)

Facts About Narcotics. Booklet. SRA; $0.90. Drug addiction and its effect on the body. (Student use. Code: Ss–Sd–2)

Timid Teen. Playlet. Methods and Materials Press; set of 6 copies, $2.40. Shyness hampers students' social activities. (For teachers use with students. Code: TSs–Ss–3)

Think of Others First. Film. Guidance Associates; $35.00. Some practical guidelines to social interaction. (For counselor working with students. Code: CSs–Ss–1)

I Never Looked at It That Way Before. Film. Guidance Associates; $35.00. Insights into tobacco, alcohol, sex and narcotics. (For students. Code: Ss–Sa–2)

Tonight Is Too Late. Film. Paul S. Erickson, Inc.; $4.95. Discussion of various problems of youth and suggestions of approaches and answers—drugs, sex, venereal disease, and drinking. (For counselor working with parents. Code: CP–Sa–2)

Dignity of Their Own: Helping the Disadvantaged Become First-Class Citizens. Book. Friendship Press; $1.95. Techniques of helping "low status" members of a community achieve a sense of dignity. (For counselor working with culturally disadvantaged youth. Code: CIdc–Ss–2)

How to Be an Adolescent . . . and Survive. Book. Richard Rosen Press; $2.79. (For students. Code: Ss–Ss–1)

The Young Americans: Understanding the "Upbeat" Generation. Book. Time Inc. Book Division. Profile of youth in America—feelings, goals, strengths, and weaknesses of modern young people dramatized through interviews. (For students. Code: Ss–Ss–2)

All About Boys. Book. Pocket Books, Inc.; $0.35. Guide for girls on how to be popular with boys. (For students. Code: Ss–Sb–1)

MATERIALS FOR ADULTS

Alcoholism: Behavior Research, Therapeutic Approaches. Book. Springer Publishing Company, Inc.; $7.50. (For counselor use with adults. Code: CA–Sa–2)

Utilizing Social Information

Methods for utilizing personalized social information are still in their infancy and much research needs to be done. For some people realistic participation is one of the most effective means, whereas for others it constitutes too strong a threat (Allport, 1960, p. 245). One principle that seems to hold true most of the time is the pyramiding of stimulations (Allport, 1960, p. 249), where repeated efforts using several methods, each building on the preceding ones, seem to be more important than a single method. If possible, the methods should be sequential, with enough frequency at each level to assist the individual's maturation. The experiences should be pyramidal for continuous, long-term growth.

Schmuck, Chester, and Lippitt (1966, p. 66) emphasized that ". . . very often skill and confidence can be gained only by getting the reactions of other people." Therefore, the authors stressed the need for rapid and often continuous feedback. If possible, a method should be used that will result in a shared commitment with others. The individual is more likely to take action if a shared commitment does exist because of support during the early stages of the development, a motivating force of having committed oneself to another, and the feedback that provides immediate opportunity for evaluation and modification. As much as possible, create an open communication atmosphere so that social information becomes meaningful and can be explored in a social context.

As Gordon Allport (1960, p. 243) wrote, "Information seldom sticks unless mixed with attitudinal glue. Facts themselves are inhuman; only attitudes are human." Recognizing and utilizing Allport's statement means that methods for social information cannot be just ones that produce items of knowledge to tack on but must be ones that provide an opportunity for attitudinal change. Publications, such as magazines, periodicals, brochures, and handbooks, along with audio-visual aids, such as bulletin board materials, displays, exhibits, charts, panels, films, filmstrips, audio and video tapes, and speeches by authorities, are meaningful and good; but these alone may be inadequate. Publications and audio-visual aids are prestructured and often prevent the social interaction and feedback so desperately needed by many individuals.

In schools opportunities such as social information workbooks, special reports or units on social behavior, group discussions, conferences with social group leaders aud officers, and interview techniques are available for use of materials. All of these methods are within a classification of *input controlled by the individual* and do provide more of an opportunity for the person to extend himself into the process and to control the situation partially.

Sociodrama, debates, group dynamics, dramatization, brainstorming, role-playing, and role reversal are methods that can be used to produce *simulation of situations* and assist individuals in obtaining personalized social information. Examples of situations for use in sociodrama can be found in various books, such as one by Thomas (1965, pp. 157–188), which emphasizes social-class, ethnic, and religious problems.

Opportunities for *real situation* exploration do exist in social information. The individual is already a member of one or more groups in which he is and can probably become more of a participant. In addition, many community programs and social agencies provide an excellent environment for in-depth involvement with rapid and continuous feedback over an extended period of time. One of the difficulties that occur in using social information methods is the follow-through to enable the individual not only to understand but be able to be wrapped into the information to the point of attitude evaluation with crystallization or modification.

Summary

Personalized social information can have several purposes and serve many functions for the individual. Each person is a member of one or more subgroups and cultures, and each of these produces pressures upon him that may cause him to have different behavior patterns within different groups. Some groups provide opportunities for explorations and development of positive self-concepts, whereas other groups tend to make the individual insecure and to inhibit his social development. Man needs to explore different thoughts and ideas about himself and society, but these thoughts and ideas need to be considered in a social context.

Society is changing and the role expectations within social groups are changing also. Individuals need personalized social information to assist them in understanding and utilizing social expectations and in integrating the self-concept into a social setting. The interaction of the individual within a group and the perceived feedback provide the bases for attitudinal crystallization or modification.

The changing of jobs or occupations often results in a change in associates and may result in vertical or horizontal social mobility. At the time of readiness for a change in job or occupation assistance to the individual, including information regarding potential social mobility, should be available. Either inter- or intraoccupational change may produce new associates and perhaps a new geographic location. Additional education may also bring about new associates and holds the potential for other social changes.

One's self-concept may insulate him against absorption of social problems and may blind him to social perceptions that might have been possible with a different self-concept. Social information having personal value will assist the individual in integrating himself into society. In some cases the individual will be affected by the social group and in other cases he will affect the group. Environment does have a major role in the individual's development, but he too helps shape his environment; therefore, social information is needed to help the individual locate and be productive in social groups to which he can give and from which he can receive. Social information cannot be facts alone, but must be assimilated through interaction with others. Attitudes toward self and others may be the result of feedback from interactions in a social context.

SELECTED REFERENCES

Allport, Gordon W. "Techniques for Reducing Group Prejudice," *Personality And Social Encounter: Selected Essays*. Boston: Beacon Press, 1960. Chap. 15, pp. 237–256.

Arnspiger, V. Clyde. *Personality in Social Process, Values, and Strategies of Individuals in a Free Society*. Chicago: Follett Publishing Company, 1961. 361 pages.

Barclay, James R. "Interest Patterns Associated with Measures of Social Desirability," *The Personnel and Guidance Journal*, 45 (September 1966), 56–60.

Borow, Henry, ed. *Man in a World at Work*. Boston: Houghton Mifflin Company, 1964. Pp. 67–95, 237–256, 534–556.

Brown, Roger. *Social Psychology*. New York: The Free Press, 1965. 785 pages.

Burchill, George W. *Work-Study Programs for Alienated Youth, A Casebook*. Chicago: Science Research Associates, Inc., 1962. Pp. 149–165.

The Challenge of Crime in a Free Society: A Report by the President's Commission on Law Enforcement and Administration of Justice. Washington, D.C.: U.S. Government Printing Office, February, 1967. 340 pages.

Coleman, James S. *The Adolescent Society*. New York: The Free Press of Glencoe, 1961. 368 pages.

Coleman, James S., with the assistance of Kurt Jonassohn and John W. C. Johnstone, *Social Climates in High School*. Washington, D.C.: U.S. Government Printing Office, 1961. 75 pages.

Conant, James B. *Slums and Suburbs: A Commentary on Schools in Metropolitan Areas*. New York: McGraw-Hill, Inc., 1961. 157 pages.

Crow, Lester D., Walter I. Murray, and Hugh H. Smythe. *Educating the Culturally Disadvantaged Child: Principles and Programs*. New York: David McKay Company, Inc., 1966. 306 pages.

Dunn, Lloyd M. *Exceptional Children in the Schools.* New York: Holt, Rinehart and Winston, Inc., 1963. 580 pages.

Frost, Joe L., and Glenn R. Hawkes, eds. *The Disadvantaged Child: Issues and Innovations.* Boston: Houghton Mifflin Company, 1966. 445 pages.

Fullmer, Daniel, and Harold Bernard. *Counseling: Content and* Process. Chicago: Science Research Associates, Inc., 1964. Pp. 42–46, 51–75.

Garry, Ralph. *Guidance Techniques for Elementary Teachers.* Columbus, O.: Charles E. Merrill Books, Inc., 1933. Pp. 387–461.

Hatt, Paul K. "Occupation and Social Stratification," in *Man, Work, and Society: A Reader in the Sociology of Occupations,* Sigmund Nosow and William H. Form, eds. New York: Basic Books, Inc., 1962. Pp. 238–249.

Havighurst, Robert J., Bernice L. Neugarten, and Jacqueline M. Falk, with the assistance of James E. Gorney. *Society and Education: A Book of Readings.* Boston: Allyn and Bacon, Inc., 1967. 364 pages.

Henderson, George. "Occupational Aspirations of Poverty-Stricken Negro Students," *The Vocational Guidance Quarterly,* **15** (September 1966) 41–45.

Hollis, Joseph W. and Lucile U. Hollis. *Organizing for Effective Guidance.* Chicago: Science Research Associates, Inc., 1965. Pp. 217–245.

Humphreys, J. Anthony, Arthur E. Traxler, and Robert D. North. *Guidance Services,* 3rd ed. Chicago: Science Research Associates, Inc., 1967. Pp. 326–355.

Isaacson, Lee E. *Career Information in Counseling and Teaching.* Boston: Allyn and Bacon, Inc., 1966. Pp. 144–166.

Johnstone, John W. C., and Ramon J. Rivera. *Volunteers for Learning, A Study of the Educational Pursuits of American Adults.* Chicago: Aldine Publishing Company, 1965. 624 pages.

Kolb, William L. "Images of Man and Sociology of Religion," in *Society and Self,* Bartlett H. Stoodley, ed. New York: The Free Press of Glencoe, A Division of the Macmillan Company, 1962. Pp. 630–645.

McCreary, Eugene, "Some Positive Characteristics of Disadvantaged Learners and Their Implications for Education," in *Knowing the Disadvantaged: Part I of the Disadvantaged Learner,* Staten W. Webster, ed. San Francisco: Chandler Publishing Company, 1966. Pp. 47–52.

Merton, Robert K. *Social Theory and Social Structure.* New York: The Free Press, 1957. 645 pages.

National Education Association of the United States. *Administration: Procedures and School Practices for the Academically Talented Student in the Secondary School.* Washington, D.C.: National Education Association, 1960. 223 pages.

Norris, Willa, Franklin R. Zeran, and Raymond N. Hatch. *The Information Service in Guidance,* 2nd ed. Chicago: Rand McNally & Company, 1966. Pp. 201–206, 212–214, 253–258, 560–563.

Nosow, Sigmund, and William H. Form. eds. *Man, Work, and Society: A Reader in the Sociology of Occupations.* New York: Basic Books, Inc., 1962. 612 pages.

Pearl, Arthur. "Youth in Lower Class Settings," in *Problems of Youth: Transition to Adulthood in a Changing World,* Mazafer Sherif and Carolyn W. Sherif, eds. Chicago: Aldine Publishing Company, 1965. Pp. 89–109.

Peters, Herman J., and James C. Hansen. *Vocational Guidance and Career Development: Selected Readings.* New York: The Macmillan Company, 1966. Pp. 20–29, 41–90, 398–425.

Peterson, Ronald A. "Rehabilitation of the Culturally Different: A Model of the Individual in Cultural Change," *The Personnel and Guidance Journal,* **45** (June 1967), 1001–1007.

Reckless, Walter C., Simon Dinitz, and Ellen Murray. "Self Concept as an Insulator Against Delinquency," *American Sociological Review,* **21** (December 1956), 744–746. Reprinted in Bartlett H. Stoodley, ed., *Society and Self: A Reader in Social Psychology.* New York: The Free Press, 1962. Pp. 43–47.

Riessman, Frank. *The Culturally Deprived Child.* New York: Harper & Row, Publishers, 1962. 140 pages.

Rosenfeld, Reba. "Junior High Programs for Potential Dropouts," *The School Counselor,* **12** (March 1965), 167–172.

Schmuck, Richard, Mark Chesler, and Ronald Lippitt. *Problem Solving to Improve Classroom Learning.* Chicago: Science Research Associates, Inc., 1966. Pp. 63–76.

Staton, Thomas F. *Dynamics of Adolescent Adjustment.* New York: The Macmillan Company, 1963. 532 pages.

Stiller, Alfred. "Social Pressures and the Guidance Function," *The School Counselor,* **11** (May 1964), 233–237.

Stoodley, Bartlett H., ed. *Society and Self.* New York: The Free Press, 1962. 713 pages.

Thomas, R. Murray. "Sociodrama," *Social Differences in the Classroom: Social-Class, Ethnic, and Religious Problems.* New York: David McKay Company, Inc., 1965. Chap. 12, pp. 157–188.

Useem, Ruth Hill. "Changing Cultural Concepts in Women's Lives," *Journal of the National Association of Women Deans and Counselors,* **24** (1960–1961), pp. 29–34. Reprinted in Herman J. Peters and James C. Hansen. *Vocational Guidance and Career Development: Selected Readings.* New York: The Macmillan Company, 1966. Pp. 61–67.

Webster, Staten W., ed. *Knowing the Disadvantaged: Part I of the Disadvantaged Learner.* San Francisco: Chandler Publishing Company, 1966. 252 pages.

Webster, Staten W., ed. *Educating the Disadvantaged Learner, Part III of the Disadvantaged Learner.* San Francisco: Chandler Publishing Company, 1966. Pp. 386–644.

Weinberg, Carl, and Rodney Skager. "Social Status and Guidance Involvement," *The Personnel and Guidance Journal,* **44** (February 1966), 586–590.

Wilensky, Harold L. "Orderly Careers and Social Participation: The Impact of Work History on Social Integration in the Middle Mass," *American*

Sociological Review, **26** (1961), 521–539. Reprinted in Herman J. Peters and James C. Hansen, *Vocational Guidance and Career Development: Selected Readings.* New York: The Macmillan Company, 1966. Pp. 398–425.

Women's Bureau. *Counseling Girls Toward New Perspectives.* Washington, D.C.: U.S. Government Printing Office, 1966, 88 pages.

Chapter 16

Relationship of Economic

Conditions to the Individual

Economic conditions tend to expand or constrict man's opportunities and often do affect the implementation of his decisions.

Man is surrounded by an economic atmosphere that, like man himself, is in a state of flux. What alternatives are open are in part a reflection of the prevailing economic conditions. The choices one will make may be determined by his economic self-aspirations, which are an outgrowth of economic information integrated into the total self-concept.

Financial planning is more than budgeting the anticipated available dollars. It requires integrating occupational, educational, and financial considerations into short-term and long-range goals that seem to be in keeping with the self-concept. No mass-produced financial plan will fit the needs of all persons; rather, each person must develop for himself financial plans that under prevailing conditions and information seem to be realistic. The plans must be re-evaluated periodically, updated, and modified to take advantage of the expanded information and the changes that have occurred.

To obtain the education or training needed, individuals may need financial assistance. Likewise financial assistance may be needed if the individual is starting into business for himself or is trying to relocate himself in order that he may take advantage of another job. Often the persons most in need of financial assistance are the ones least informed about how and where to obtain it.

As leisure time becomes more important, the question of how to afford it economically is of major concern. Leisure time is becoming an expensive time, which can no longer be left to chance but must be included in overall economic self-aspirations and plans.

Purposes of Personalized Economic Information

Society operates within an economic atmosphere that affects each individual and his opportunities. Economic conditions not only influence his food, shelter, and clothing but also his educational setting, occupational life, leisure time, and self-expressive time. If economic conditions affect each person in many ways, then economic information is needed on a personal basis by each.

Personal economic information will assist an individual in obtaining economic understanding of his present social group and of those groups into which he may enter. The economic conditions surrounding a person have affects upon the attitude formations and the aspirations that he develops. Understanding these effects and recognizing in other groups economic conditions that exist and those that may become reality if and when he joins those groups may assist the individual in modifying his outlook on life, changing his aspirations, and providing another substructure for the continuing construction of his becoming.

As indicated earlier in Part II, education and one's potential for education has become an integral part of one's life throughout life. The amount and kind of education received has potential for affecting the economic returns of a person. The cost of education and training is determined in part by the educational setting. The financial assistance that may be obtained while receiving the education or training will, in many cases, vary with the setting. Personalized economic information should assist an individual in knowing and integrating the economic realities of different educational settings with the other facts, attitudes, and dreams of his life.

The financial income for many people is dependent primarily upon salary or wages. Different occupations have different financial rewards and the same occupations in different locations will have different pay. The standard of living and financial obligations associated with different jobs vary considerably. Societal expectations of people in certain jobs tend to place economic limits on those people and to a large extent determine the standard of living they must maintain. Prior to commitment to an occupation an individual should have an operative understanding of the economic conditions associated not only with each occupation but also with its setting. Personalized economic information may assist the individual even in his long-range planning for the world of work.

The utilization of economic information associated with educational and occupational settings may help each person to integrate his total life rather than to departmentalize it and consider education and occupation separately. One's leisure-time and self-expressive activities will affect his economic life as well as his economic life affecting them. Therefore, personalized economic information should assist the individual in economic expectations under conditions similar to his role expectations at the different times in his life.

Economic Self-Aspiration

Sherif and Sherif (1965, pp. 316–321) found in studying three economic levels (low, lower-middle, and upper-middle) that youth tend to set levels for personal goals according to the socio-economic level of the neighborhood and to have differences in goals according to different conceptions of achievement. The same study also revealed that youth in low and lower-middle-rank areas have greater heterogeneity in values and goals than those in upper-middle-rank areas. The amount of educacation desired had a large range in all areas, but the average education desired increased with each economic level. From this study the conclusion can be reached that variations of goals and values are great enough so that no one child or youth can be said to have a given goal or value because he or she lives in a given neighborhood. Another conclusion would be that his economic self-aspiration may be an outgrowth of the economic level in which the person was reared.

Berdie and Hood (1965, pp. 44–46) pointed out economic changes over the decade between 1950 and 1960 that influenced students. With only minor modifications, the list would remain the same for the last one half of the 1960's. The list today might include the population explosion and the increasing number of new pressures resulting from it, the rapid economic expansion within the nations, rising materialistic and leisure-time expectations, the yearly upward number of average years of school completed, scientific developments occurring so rapidly that even science-fiction writers visit industry to get ideas, the sociological changes resulting from social actions such as racial integration, and technological advancements that change work and play. These and other more personal happenings have a bearing upon the economic future of an individual and the *economic self-aspiration* that he may formulate.

The distribution of economic wealth is changing in the United States. The role of the middle class in Wall Street is considerably different from that at the turn of the century. A larger percentage of the population own stocks today than ever before. The general public has a greater share of many different enterprises than ever before. Life insurance has become a commonplace "necessity"; so have savings accounts. A trend seems to be toward mutual funds or buying into a syndicate. These economic activities are now becoming common enough so that they have a place in consideration during the formation of the economic self-aspirations of each person. Most counselors would probably not be competent in many of the economic areas, but if these activities are within the realm of reality planning then resource persons may need to be identified for referral and consultation.

Economics is materialistically oriented and is something that exists externally, but surrounds the individual. Many of the other concepts held by a person are internally oriented and for viewing and working with other persons must be projected outward. The intense striving by some people for materialistic goals is brought about by their inability to project themselves to gain recognition and approval of others. Helping individuals to evaluate materialistic goals with and against other goals and self-concepts often necessitates counseling and extensive personalized personal-social information. Integrating educational potential, occupational expectations, social orientation, and self-concepts does necessitate time, personal information, and often personal help. For many persons economic self-aspirations may be better motivators than economic reality.

Achieving economic self-aspiration is not instantaneous but generally requires planning, decision-making, and many activities. Realistic planning involving sequences of events is necessary and includes more than just economic considerations. Planning for achievement of economic aspirations requires a projection of the total self into the future and into various social and physical settings. An individual needs personalized information pertaining to many areas of which personal economic information is one.

Financial Income

Wages and salaries are often thought of as the means of personal income for Americans. According to the U.S. Department of Commerce (*Statistical Abstract of the United States*, 1966, p. 327), in 1965 wages, salaries, and other labor income accounted for 70.8 per cent of personal income. The other sources are classified under proprietors' income (10.3 per cent), rental income (3.5 per cent), dividends (3.6 per cent), personal interest (7.0 per cent), and transfer payments (7.4 per cent), including old-age survivors' insurance benefits, state unemployment insurance benefits, veterans' benefits, and other. From these incomes must be subtracted contributions for social insurance (2.5 per cent in 1965). The sources of financial income vary considerably from one individual to another. The dreams of financial income sources and their proportionate parts in one's total personal income may have a major role in his motivation toward education, occupations, leisure time, and self-expressive activities.

Education

The difference in financial income average between those who complete elementary school (eighth grade) and those who complete high school is often shown. Figure 16-1 is a graphic representation of median

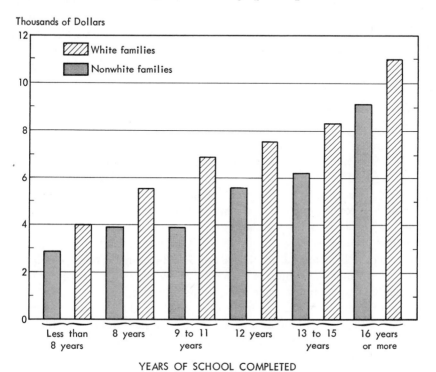

Thousands of Dollars

YEARS OF SCHOOL COMPLETED

Figure 16-1. MEDIAN MONEY INCOME OF FAMILIES, BY YEARS OF SCHOOL COMPLETED AND BY WHITE AND NONWHITE FAMILIES IN 1965.

Source: Statistical Abstract of the United States, 1967, *88th annual edition, U.S. Department of Commerce, p. 318.*

money income of families by years of school completed and by white and nonwhite families. The white families compared to the nonwhite families had a higher median money income at every level shown. Schooling does make a difference but other factors, such as color, may be as much or more of a factor. Another condition not revealed by the graph is that comparison of income by years of school completed does not correct or take into account the ability levels of the groups compared. To say that years of schooling completed is what makes the difference is probably inaccurate. The average ability of those who completed sixteen years or more of schooling compared to those who completed less than eight years is probably considerably more. The people with sixteen years or more of school would probably have made more money than the other group even if they had dropped out of school earlier. The people who completed high school or beyond probably had home backgrounds that also were influential in helping them obtain the additional education and in making more money. Factors in the home backgrounds that may have contributed were such things as "connections," motivation, financial backing, and educational sophistication. Counselors must assist individuals in interpreting statistical data and particularly in personalizing the information. The individual needs to assess his situation and to assimilate the information into the total picture of himself rather than formulate major decisions on isolated data.

Race, Sex, and Age

Race and sex discrimination may not exist in the minds of some, but the difference in financial income is sufficient to warrant consideration. In 1965, 91.5 per cent of the male population over fourteen years of age had income, but of the nonwhite male population the figure was 87.7 per cent. The total female population of comparable age had 59.5 per cent with income and 66.8 per cent of the nonwhites. The median income for the total male population with income was considerably more than the nonwhites (see Table 16-1). Also interesting to note is that when income is arranged in intervals of $1,000 the male total population was fairly evenly distributed in each interval, whereas the nonwhites were with highest percentages in the low-income intervals.

Age of persons on an average does make a difference in financial income, with the median income of male recipients increasing in each ten-year interval, reaching a maximum in the thirty-five to forty-four age interval, after which income decreases. For women the median income of recipients increases through the forty-five to fifty-four age interval and then starts decreasing (Figure 16-2).

Families

Data on the liquid asset holdings of all family units in the United States in 1965 reveals that one in every five families owned no assets and approximately one in every two had less than $500 of liquid assets (*Statistical Abstract of the United States, 1967*, p. 342). The percentage share of aggregated income of families when grouped in income rank reveals that the lowest 20 per cent of the families only received 5 per cent of the income and the top 20 per cent received 41 per cent (Figure 16-3). When the head of the family has had one to three years of college education, the national average is approximately twice as much as when the head of the family has had less than eight years of schooling. The poor (low economic conditions) families have a higher percentage of women (26 per cent) as head of the family than when all families in the

Table 16-1.

MONEY INCOME OF PERSONS FOURTEEN YEARS OLD AND OVER—PERCENTAGE
DISTRIBUTION OF RECIPIENTS: BY INCOME LEVEL, BY SEX, BY TOTAL AND NON-
WHITE POPULATION, AND BY MEDIAN INCOME, 1965.

Item	*Male*		*Female*	
	TOTAL	NONWHITE	TOTAL	NONWHITE
Persons with income vs. no income				
Per cent with income	91.5	87.7	59.5	66.8
Per cent without income	8.5	12.3	40.5	33.2
Total persons	100.0	100.0	100.0	100.0
Money income of persons with income				
$ 1 to $999 or less	13.8	22.8	37.5	44.3
1,000 to 1,999	10.4	15.8	18.9	22.6
2,000 to 2,999	9.3	15.4	12.6	12.2
3,000 to 3,999	8.9	12.6	10.9	8.2
4,000 to 4,999	9.0	10.4	7.9	4.9
5,000 to 5,999	10.3	9.1	5.3	3.3
6,000 to 6,999	9.5	5.5	2.7	2.0
7,000 to 9,9999	17.4	6.5	3.2	1.7
10,000 and over	11.3	1.8	1.0	0.7
Total	100.0	100.0	100.0	100.0
Median income for persons with income.	$4,824	$2,672	$1,564	$1,213

Source: Based upon data from *Statistical Abstract of the United States, 1967,*
88th annual edition, U.S. Department of Commerce, p. 337.

United States are considered (10 per cent). The financial income and
liquid assets of families has such a large range that each family must be
considered separately. The head of the family, years of schooling completed by employed numbers of the family, and the number of employed
persons in the family are all important variables influencing the total
financial income of the family.

Financial Planning

Matching income to outlay both for the present and in the future is
a major undertaking that many, many people never achieve. Short-term
financial planning for items such as clothing, food, shelter, financial
obligations, and other necessities may require information about many

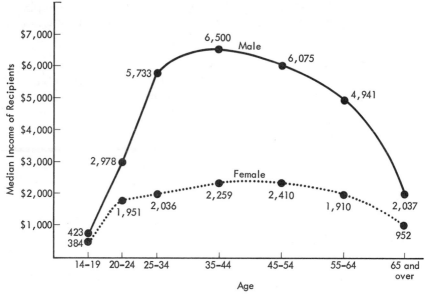

Figure 16-2. MEDIAN INCOME OF RECIPIENTS BY AGE AND SEX, 1964.
Source: Based upon data from Statistical Abstract of the United States, 1966, *87th annual edition, U.S. Department of Commerce, Table No. 484, p. 343.*

things in addition to budgeting. The counselor cannot be all things to all people, but to assist an individual in his total growth and development, in his goals establishment, in self-realization, or in his "becoming" (to use Carl Rogers' word), a counselor may need to have available information on financial planning. The availability may need to be through referral or consultation.

Financial planning never seems to cease. The changing of conditions causes the need for re-evaluation and often the modification of plans. At every age, after one is beyond early childhood, financial plans need to be considered. Courtship, marriage, family rearing, middle age, and retirement, each have different kinds of financial spending, and modification of conditions within each phase also brings new challenges to the individual and those with whom he shares financial responsibilities.

One's future economic conditions as envisioned for himself often have been dreamed without considering means of acquiring the income necessary. One's occupation and other income yield must be realistically considered in developing meaningful avenues for achieving goals. Financial planning without occupational and educational planning may be meaningless. Likewise financial planning without the individual's giving full consideration to his becoming is the performance of an act without recognition of the act as an integral, minute portion of an ongoing process. The counselor can assist the individual by helping make the information processes personal.

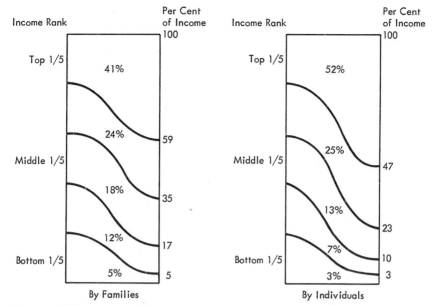

Figure 16-3. FAMILIES AND UNRELATED INDIVIDUALS GROUPED IN FIFTHS BY INCOME RANK AND INDICATED PERCENTAGE OF AGGREGATE INCOME, 1965.
Source: Based upon data from Statistical Abstract of the United States, 1967, *88th annual edition, U.S. Department of Commerce, p. 333.*

Financial Assistance for Obtaining an Education or Training

In recent years financial assistance for obtaining education or vocational training has become big business and now is an accepted procedure and should be considered as a possibility for almost everyone. At the turn of the century only a few could obtain financial assistance for schooling.

Another change has been the extension of education into adult life, including the return of individuals to schools, colleges, or training programs for additional schooling. Each time schooling is considered by a person then financial cost must also be considered. Financial assistance sources include part-time and full-time work, savings, insurance policies, scholarships, assistantships, fellowships, apprenticeships, grants, loans, and special programs, such as military, business and industrial, and governmental programs. Frequently, an individual will use a combination of sources to give him the financial assistance needed. Many educational institutions are helping potential students identify scholarships, loans, savings, and work-study programs for which they are eligible and that may be combined to meet the educational cost. A combination of sources is becoming known as a "package" plan.

The results from a survey sponsored by the Ford Foundation showed that approximately 60 per cent of parents have no financial plan for providing the financial assistance needed when and if their child goes to college. Approximately 11 per cent had college funds in savings accounts and about 6 per cent had savings in Government bonds. Several had life-insurance plans (*Your Child's Future*, 1966, pp. 25–27).

Children in elementary, junior high, and senior high schools often need financial assistance in order to stay in school, as well as youth and adults in vocational schools, training institutions, colleges, and graduate schools. Much of the financial assistance at the elementary and secondary school level will need to come from local sources, including private and community agencies. School counselors in elementary and secondary schools serving districts with low-income families know well the frequency with which they work with children and youth who need clothing, food, and books, and other school necessities, glasses and other medical and dental or psychological services beyond those provided by the school.

Identifying Sources for an Individual

Financial assistance of various kinds is well known but the identification of the specific source or combination of sources to give an individual the package he needs is a personalized process. No one right way seems to exist on how to identify the sources, but some general statements can be made. Even though many national programs exist, often the best ones for many individuals come from local funds, which in many cases can be tailor-made to each individual's needs. A list of steps, which may occur in different sequence for different persons, would include the following:

1. Start with characteristics of the individual that are unique to him and that may assist him in obtaining the outside financial assistance needed.

   Physical and mental impairments.

   Special aptitudes and abilities.

   Place of employment, because many businesses and industries make financial assistance available to employees.

   Military background or eligibility for military service.

   Place of residence, as some financial aids are available only to people in certain geographical locations.

   Economic level of the individual.

   Membership held in different organizations, clubs, societies, and religious affiliations, as some sources are available for certain members and their families.

   Orphan.

2. Next identify characteristics about the individual's family, including parents, that may assist him in obtaining outside aid.

> Military background of parents.
> Place of employment of parents.
> Organizations, clubs, societies, labor unions, and religious affiliation of parents.
> Economic level of parents.

3. Investigate the local situation for financial aids where loans and scholarships are frequently made by local groups.

> Businesses and industries.
> Individuals, wills, estates, and trust funds.
> Local organizations—service clubs, professional associations, churches, philanthropic, civic, and fraternal groups.
> Unions.
> Fraternities and sororities.
> Local educational institutions.
> Banks and savings organizations.

4. Investigate the state financial assistance available to individuals.

> State scholarship plans exist in many states.
> State plans for guaranteed loans.
> State grants for specific purposes.

5. Review the national financial assistance available and identify any that may be applicable to the individual.

6. Identify the educational institutions the individual may attend, and study the financial assistance available. Often the educational institution has a financial aids office that can be used for consulting or referral purposes.

Work-While-Attending

Working while obtaining an education has become an American way of life in all kinds of programs and at various age levels—high school students as well as college students, vocational training enrollees as well as other persons taking courses in recreation or preparation for retirement. In some instances the work is done as employment associated with the school or educational institution, but very frequently the work is done outside the educational setting, where the hourly wage is generally higher. Many educational institutions are recognizing the work-while-attending concept and have established student employment offices to assist enrollees in obtaining jobs either in the school or in a different setting. Educators are beginning to recognize the educational value and frequently the educational motivation produced by coordinating work-job and educational offerings. The program may be structured by the institution, such as the work-study program, also called cooperative education, or through the individual's finding a job that will provide opportunities for the exploration of himself and his educational gains.

The amount of financial assistance obtained by part-time and full-time work varies considerably with the kind of work done, the amount of time spent, the location and setting of the job, and in part the qualifications of the person himself. The proportionate part of schooling paid for by work-while-attending varies from a small percentage to the total amount. Probably for a high percentage of persons the financial assistance from work-while-attending is only an aid rather than the means of meeting total expenses.

As an indication of the number of persons who work while attending school, the eighteen- to twenty-four-year-old civilian noninstitutionalized population of the United States may be studied. In October, 1966, 29.3 per cent of that age group were enrolled in schools, with approximately two in every five students (39.5 per cent) in the labor force with 94 per cent employment. In a comparison of men to women eighteen- to twenty-four-year-old students who work while attending, 41.8 per cent of the men and 35.7 per cent of the women were in the labor force while enrolled (Perrella, 1967, p. A-5).

Savings

The cost of many educational programs, whether for secondary school, vocational school, technical training or college, are so high that individuals and their families frequently have found the financial outlay too extensive unless some long-range planning and money saving have been done. Parents often start savings plans early. Some parents use the systematic payroll-deduction plan, in which the money is invested in Government bonds, bank savings bonds, credit unions, or monthly investment plans where stock is purchased. To assist in saving for an educational program some banks have established college-club savings plans designed on the order of Christmas club plans (Splaver, 1964, p. 39).

Individuals may develop an educational goal and then start saving money to meet the financial obligation associated with achievement of the goal. If the person is older and is employed, he may use one or more of the plans listed for parents. If the person is a child or youth, he may start a savings account in his own name. Counselors may work with parents to facilitate their helping their child establish a savings plan for educational goals. In some elementary and secondary schools weekly deposits are encouraged in savings accounts. Psychologically the savings plans for college education or specific training programs have been effective in motivating the individual to evaluate his goal regularly and to decide whether or not he is still willing to invest now to achieve something in the future.

Insurance Policies

A large number of reliable insurance companies have had educational plans that have been in operation for many years. Life insurance has been used as a method of saving for educational goals. Probably the cheapest type is term insurance, which has no cash surrender value but may be used as a protection to supplement savings plans being developed for another person or to meet loans that have accrued in connection with schooling.

Ordinary life insurance does have a cash surrender value that may serve as a savings or financial assistance (the holder of the policy may borrow on it) for obtaining education or training. The endowment-policy insurance plan is frequently used by parents, who initiate it when the child is young. The insurance policy may be written to mature at the time the person starts his post-high-school training or higher education. The money may be paid in a lump sum or at the beginning of each enrollment period. Many variations have been incorporated into different plans written by different companies.

Scholarships, Assistantships, Fellowships, and Grants-in-Aid

Scholarships were and still are intended primarily as a recognition of talent and ability. However, in recent years a practice has existed whereby need has been recognized as a basis for awarding scholarships. A scholarship is a financial award for furthering one's education that does not have to be repaid. It is an outright grant of money, tuition discount, remission of tuition and fees, or a similar consideration that does not require repayment or a service to be performed on the part of the student (Mattingly, 1962, p. 8). Psychological testing (ability and achievement) and/or a means of assessing need have become bases for selection. The College Scholarship Service (CSS) was organized in 1954 as a subordinate of the College Entrance Examination Board (CEEB) to help colleges and scholarship program sponsors to develop and improve their student-aid program as well as to distribute their financial aid funds both equitably and fairly. CSS has developed a form for evaluating what a family can be expected to contribute toward a child's education; thus CSS has attempted to standardize the determination of need.

Scholarships may be awarded in specified areas, such as music, science, agriculture, and physical education. The sources of scholarships may be classified under educational institutions (school, college, university, or training institution), government (Federal and state), business and industry (local, state, and national), and private organizations and clubs. In a study of how scholarship winners learned about scholarships, Benzing and Hutson (1964, p. 241) found the following categories in rank order: college catalogues, announcements in the guidance office, lists published in the high school, announcements on bulletin boards, other publications, books on scholarships, and announcements in the homeroom.

National scholarships for students going to technical schools have been few in number. A National Technical Scholarship Foundation has been formed. Local and state businesses and industries have been among the best sources.

Assistantships are awarded by educational institutions to students who do work for the financial award. The work generally is associated with the educational program in which the student is majoring; however the kind of work performed has a wide range, from research projects to residence-hall supervision. Assistantships are frequently given to graduate students, but some are becoming available to undergraduates, including first-year post-high-school students. In addition to the financial benefits, assistantships offer valuable experiences to the student. One limitation is the added demand for time and possible distraction from study.

Fellowships are for graduate students and may be comparable to scholarships for undergraduate students. Some graduate fellowships do stipulate a service or work similar to the assistantship. In either case no money has to be repaid upon completing or leaving the program.

A grant-in-aid may be given for a specific project or purpose. The specific project type is usually given at the graduate level. The grant for given purposes may be for financial emergency, financial needs due to physical health limitations, or preparation in specific fields.

Research grants are becoming more plentiful, particularly at the graduate level, but some are being made available to undergraduate students. The sources are government agencies, businesses, and industries, with the funds generally administered through the educational institution.

Contests

Individuals with special talents or aptitudes have earned cash or scholarships by competition in contests. The number and kinds of contests vary considerably. To name but a few of the more commonly known ones would include beauty contests (like Miss America), American Legion Oration contests, science contests, music contests, and the Historical Essay Contest sponsored by the United Daughters of the Confederacy and Sons of Confederate Soldiers.

Loans

Families in the lower-income groups have hesitated to borrow funds for education or training because of the repayment problems and the difficulties they often experience because of their credit standings. More and more individuals are beginning to recognize loans as an economic move. A loan does not incur a debt but merely transfers payment for education from a time when earning capacity is low to a time when it may be higher. In a way, a loan is an "education purchased on an installment plan." A loan to supplement self-help, savings, a scholarship, and other financial aids may be the key to the schooling desired.

Banks have in recent years more readily entered into educational loans. Most of these loans are now protected by insurance on the student and, in the case of a minor, on the parent. Different sponsoring banks have different plans. Some pay tuition and fees as they become due directly to the educational institution. Others make a given amount available during each enrollment period.

According to Cox (1964, p. 119) approximately thirty-five states have established some plan of direct student support. One form of state assistance is the Higher Educational Loan Plan (HELP) established in Massachusetts, where the state guaranteed in part, or in whole, the bank loans to students.

Private agencies also make loans. The United Student Aid Fund, the largest nonprofit organization of this kind, has endorsed low-cost loans to college students through more than seven thousand banks. An undergraduate may borrow up to $1,000 a year. A graduate student may borrow up to $2,000. The total amount in either case is $4,000.

The Federal Government has entered into low-interest, long-term loan plans for students through the National Vocational Student Loan Income Act of 1965, the National Defense Education Act (N.D.E.A.), and the Higher Education Act of 1965. These acts are described in a following section of this chapter, entitled "Federal and State Government Programs."

Many educational institutions have a financial-aid office, which generally has money available to loan. The loans may be of two types— emergency or short-term, and educational expenses or long-term loans. The specific program should be worked out with the financial-aid officer of the institution.

Apprenticeships and Internships

For skilled trades, particularly, and for some other occupations, apprenticeships are the more frequent way to acquire the training to enter the occupation. Apprenticeships are also a financial assistance in that the person generally is paid wages while learning. The unions often control or operate the apprenticeship program.

Internships are also a means of being paid while learning, but internships generally are awarded toward the latter part of an educational program. Usually the term *internship* is used with educational programs designed to prepare persons for professions or semiprofessions.

Federal and State Government Programs

Since World War II, the Federal Government has taken an active role in assisting persons to obtain additional education. The GI Bill was a major undertaking in sending men and women back to school for training and education. The program was considered successful, and other Federal bills have been passed to assist persons.

The National Defense Education Act includes provisions for a student to borrow up to $1,000 a year and a maximum of $5,000 with no interest or repayment while attending school. If an individual enters into the Armed Forces or Peace Corps, no interest will be charged or repayment required for up to three years. The interest is 3 per cent a year. Death or permanent disability cancels all liability. Other special features are also incorporated into the bill. The loan fund is administered through more than 1,500 participating educational institutions, where approximately 90 per cent of the nation's college students are enrolled.

The Higher Education Act of 1965 established a program of educational opportunity grants for students with exceptional financial need who would not, except for the grant, be able to attend college or university. During the first year the grants cannot exceed one half of the student's need and generally range from $200 to $800 a year. After the first year grants may be increased. The grants can be combined with scholarships, loans, or work programs.

The Higher Education Act of 1965 also made provisions for loans to individuals expressing a desire to enter selected professions, including medicine, dentistry, optometry, teaching, and nursing. A forgiveness provision is included in the act for borrowers who subsequently enter the profession for which they trained. Students may borrow up to $2,000 a year to the maximum of $10,000.

In 1965 the National Vocational Student Loan Income Act was passed. The Act provides for loans to students who attend either vocational schools or colleges. For students from a home with a family annual adjusted income under $15,000, the Federal Government will pay interest up to 6 per cent while in school, and 3 per cent during the repayment period, which does not start until after the student leaves school. If the family annual adjusted income is over $15,000, the Government will guarantee the loan but the student must pay the interest.

Federal legislation has also initiated the College Work-Study Program in order to identify, motivate, and recruit prospective students from low-income families. Participants must have an established need for assistance. The work load is generally between fifteen and twenty hours a week, within the educational institution or some approved outside employing agency. Typically, students on the Work-Study Program receive additional assistance through grants, loans, and scholarships.

Under Title II of the Social Security Act are benefits to assist some youth eighteen to twenty-two years old in attending any school, college, or university that is public or accredited. During the school year 1967–1968, an estimated 402,000 students received approximately $355 million in benefit payments. "This resource represents more funds to assist students to further their education than there are in scholarships at all colleges and universities in the United States" (Wieland, 1967, p. 15).

Federal Government programs of financial assistance to veterans, their dependents, and Armed Forces personnel are discussed in Chapter 18.

State governments may have financial assistance through one of their agencies or through the educational institutions within the state.

Disability and rehabilitation programs have financial assistance for individuals who have physical and mental impairment. Counselors in other agencies should use rehabilitation counselors as consultants and for referral in any case where an individual may be eligible.

Financial Assistance in Starting a Private Enterprise

The number of small businesses that start each year is enough to support the belief in need of personalized financial information for thousands of persons. Counselors in most settings do not have nor can they be expected to have the knowledge nor the firsthand information for giving the personalized information needed. Many of them will need to make a referral or obtain consultative help.

Financial assistance is available for assisting individuals in starting a private enterprise. The approach is similar to that for obtaining money to attend school—each case must be considered individually. For those with physical and mental impairments rehabilitation funds are available. For other persons, banks and other lending agencies are the usual sources used to supplement the other funds the individual has. Federal Government small-business loans have been helpful to many persons. Others have formed partnerships or have incorporated and sold stock. Which plan or "package" of sources is best for a given person is an individual case.

Many persons start with a hobby or some self-expressive activity that he then finds has commercial value. To expand his activities necessitates funds for equipment, materials, employees, and facilities. Besides the financial assistance needed, the individual may be in need of many other kinds of general and specific information pertaining to a small business operation.

For youth the Junior Achievement program and other similar programs are beginning to focus attention on private enterprise. Counselors of youth may find more requests in the future for information on financial assistance in starting a private enterprise.

Community Agencies Offering Financial Assistance

From one community to another the agencies available for offering financial assistance vary. Each counselor will need to make a resource and referral directory for those agencies available to serve the clientele with whom he works. The list may also vary from one counselor to another in the same community because of the clientele served. Welfare agencies, rehabilitation counselors, banks and other lending agencies, Travelers' Aid and similar organizations, religious groups, service clubs, professional associations, fraternal and civic groups, fraternities and sororities, labor unions, philanthropic individuals or groups, businesses and industries, governmental agencies, educational institutions, foundations and patriotic organizations are all examples of community agencies that may offer financial assistance at various age levels to meet various needs, such as health services, clothing, and transportation to school.

Relationship Between Economic Conditions and Leisure Time

As the nation becomes more bountifully supplied with material goods, the emphasis in life may shift from work to enjoyment of leisure. The more one satisfies his desires for material things the more he may turn his attention to self-expressive activities. Benson (1966, p. 65) stated, "It is likely that for most of us the skill requirements of leisure will exceed those of work."

Leisure-time Cost

A relationship exists between leisure time and economic conditions. As the economy improves, leisure-time activities increase. When an individual is in need of finances, he tends to work longer hours, including engagement in moonlight jobs. As his work hours increase, his leisure-time hours tend to decrease. As one engages in leisure-time activities, such as hobbies, recreation, reading, and traveling, his financial outlay generally increases. The question is "Can one afford leisure-time activities, both in hours and money?"

Not only does the economic condition of the individual determine in part his leisure-time activities, but also the economic conditions of the society and subgroup of which he is a member. The group's expectations may be sufficient to produce an atmosphere in which he feels he must obtain adequate finances to afford the leisure-time activities approved by his subgroup. One of the drives for working in a financial-return activity is to be able to afford leisure-time activities. Finding self-re-warding, self-fulfilling, self-expressive leisure-time activities may be a major undertaking, but finding ones that are in tune with the subgroups to which one belongs and activities that can be afforded out of the money income remaining after paying for the other necessities of life will require integration of many facts and the personalizing of extensive amounts of information.

Coding, Filing, Storing, and Retrieving Economic Information

Articles on filing economic information for use in counseling and guidance are almost nonexistent. The articles that are available are for filing information for use in secondary schools. Munson wrote an article in 1955 about filing scholarship information, which has been the basis for most authors' suggestions on filing plans (Norris, Zeran, and Hatch, 1966, pp. 398–399, and Isaacson, 1966, p. 323). Munson (1955, pp. 90–92) suggested that three separate but related files be maintained: (1) a scholarship index file that is an alphabetically arranged card file of specific colleges or scholarships and that contains other pertinent facts, such as specific scholarship title, amount, eligibility, application procedures, and where additional information can be obtained; (2) a file of sources of scholarship information that contains alphabetically arranged publications about various scholarships about which specific data has been placed in the scholarship index file card; and (3) a file on scholarships for specific vocations that contains alphabetically ar-ranged folders with publications on scholarships for specific vocations. The third file is formed after the second one has a sufficient volume of material to warrant subdividing.

As indicated earlier financial assistance for education or training has moved from a single source concept to a financial aids package tailor-made for each person planning on attending a given educational or training institution and taking a specific program. As a result most in-stitutions have designated a financial aids counselor, whose job is to assist an individual in developing a financial plan including any and all aids that can be obtained for the program desired at the specific institution. In some secondary schools, counselors are designated the responsibility for contacting post-high-school educational institutions with the specific job of making their financial aids counselors aware of the needs of students who might possibly enroll in the institution. With financial aids counselors now being available as professional per-sons who can join the team for assisting individuals, another type of file needs to be kept—a file on financial aids counselors. The file de-veloped will contain information similar to that obtained in a community resource referral card file, with the person's name, the institution with which he is associated, the kind of services available, how contacts are to be made, the hours and days he is available, and the kind of information that will need to be supplied to him.

The foregoing information is applicable mostly at the secondary school level and to post-secondary-school financial aids. Economic information is much broader and is applicable at elementary and junior high schools, at colleges and universities, at trade and vocational schools, and for adults outside of educational institutions as well as at the secondary school level. The file plans developed will need to be tailor-made for the situation; however, each one should contain financial planning information and general economic information applicable to the clientele served. For counselors working with teen-agers and adults a need will exist for information on budgeting, financial assistance in starting a business or private enterprise, and community agencies offering financial assistance.

Storage and retrieval of information are similar to that provided for educational and occupational information. (See Chapters 7 and 12 respectively)

Subscriptions and Services for Economic Information

Subscriptions and services for economic information useful in counseling and guidance work are almost exclusively directed to educational financial aids information. The materials are applicable primarily at the secondary school level. The following subscriptions and services are available:

Scholarships, Fellowships, and Loans News Service. Bellman Publishing Company; $20.00 a year. Minimum of four issues a year. Binder and index each year. Contains information about new funds and foundations, scholarships, fellowships, loans, work-study opportunities, grants, and research. A service devoted to reporting developments in student aid and aid to education.

Financial Aid News. College Entrance Examination Board; free. Newsletter issued several times a year to report events and offer opinions on matters of concern to persons interested in financial aid affairs. It is intended primarily for college financial aid officers but is useful also to college counselors in schools.

Student Aid Annual and *Student Aid Bulletins.* Chronicle Guidance Publications, Inc.; $10.00. The *Annual* consists of Part I—information on financial aid programs and employment opportunities available to entering freshmen at approximately seventeen hundred higher education institutions. Part II—information on over three hundred financial aid programs available to high school graduates from noncollegiate sources, with national scholarship and loan programs. The *Bulletin* is issued three times during the year to supplement the information provided by the *Annual*.

Financing a College Education: A Guide for Counselors. College Entrance Examination Board; free. Describes sources of financial aid, the work of the College Scholarship Service, and procedures for determining the financial need of the applicant. Routinely sent to guidance directors and financial aid officers.

Reference Books for Economic Information

The economic information reference books for counselor use in counseling and guidance are primarily on financial aids for post-high-school education. The one frequently used by counselors are as follows:

The National Apprenticeship Program. U.S. Dept. of Labor; free. Describes the National Apprenticeship programs. Lists occupations in which training is available, including data on the customary length of apprenticeship and sources for further information.

Need a Lift? American Legion; $0.25. Includes current information on financial assistance.

Manual for Financial Aid Officers. College Entrance Examination Board; $5.00. Loose-leaf binder containing work-study programs of the Economic Opportunity Act of 1964, the National Defense Student Loan Program, commercial and guaranteed loan programs, need analysis, state scholarship programs, and educational opportunity grants program.

Scholarships, Fellowships, and Loans, Vol. IV. Bellman Publishing Company; $10.00. Lists sources of financial assistance—foundations, organizations, industry, unions; qualifications necessary, funds available, and where to apply.

Financial Aids for American Students and Scholars. The College Blue Book, Book Four, Volume III; $75.00 for the three volumes. Lists scholarships, fellowships, loans, research grants, grants to study abroad, training grants, and contests.

Lovejoy's Scholarship Guide. Simon and Schuster, Inc.; $4.95

A National Catalog of Scholarships and other Financial Aids for Students Entering College. W. C. Brown Company, Publishers; $6.00. More than four hundred state and national programs of financial aids to students are listed.

Student Need Analyses Program. Financial Aid Service, American College Testing Programs. Describes the one-page Family Financial Statement and how data-processing machines make the analysis.

National Scholarship Service and Fund for Negro Students. Obtained from association of same name; free. Describes services of organizations that help Negroes choose a college, apply, and obtain financial assistance.

National Register of Scholarship and Fellowships. Vol I: *Scholarships and Loans.* World Trade Academy Press; $15.00.

Grants-in-Aid and Other Financial Assistance Programs. U.S. Government Printing Office; $2.50.

Student Financial Aid in the United States: Administration and Resources. College Entrance Examination Board; $1.50. Contains general information on the principal public and private sources of financial aid for college students.

In addition to the reference material listed, each counselor should obtain directly from training and educational institutions the brochures and booklets on the financial aids available. Catalogues published by the institutions may be helpful; however, specific material prepared on financial aids is generally more comprehensive and provides specific information on procedures.

Sample Material and Sources

Economic information for use in counseling and guidance should be available at every educational level and throughout life. Counselors will need to collect materials from various sources in order that adequate information can be obtained.

In the sample material presented in this section, no attempt has been made to be comprehensive but rather to be illustrative of different kinds of materials, sources, potential uses, and possible coding based upon analysis by the 3-D concept (see Table 7-1 for code). In settings where counselors use extensive economic information, the coding system will probably need additional subdivisions.

The sample materials are arranged according to school levels, plus some illustrations for adults both as parents working with their children in school and as material for the adults' own use. The analysis code could be used in arranging materials in the files.

ELEMENTARY SCHOOL MATERIALS

Our Working World. Books and phonograph records. Science Research Associates, Inc.; $3.10. Economics as it relates to the primary school child's every day experiences. (For teacher to use with pupils. Code: TSk–Pfg–2)

Shoeshine Boy. Book. William Morrow and Company, Inc.; $2.94. Small boy's story in financing his own business. (For pupils. Code: Sk–Pfg–1)

The True Book of Money. Book. Children's Press; $1.88. Concerns use of money and savings. (For pupils. Code: Sk–Pfs–1)

JUNIOR HIGH SCHOOL MATERIALS

Education and Income: Inequalities of Opportunity in Our Public Schools. Book. The Viking Press, Inc.; $5.00. Based on a study of a Midwestern public school system on the limitations on a child's opportunities by the size of his parents' income. (For counselor information. Code: Csi–Pf–2)

Economics in Action Today. Book. Julian Messner, Inc.; $3.95. Broad coverage of life in America—wages, taxes, role of industry and labor, and so on. (For teacher use with students. Code: TSj–Pfg–2)

Money: Make It, Spend It, Save It. Book. Holiday House; $3.95. Information on personal finance: banks, budgets, insurance, investments, and so on. (For students. Code: Sj–Pfg–2)

SENIOR HIGH SCHOOL MATERIALS

How and Where to Get Scholarships and Loans. Book. World Trade Academy Press; $2.95. (For counselor's use with students. Code: CSs–Pff–2)

Why Budget. Film. McGraw-Hill, Inc.; B&W, $60.00. (For students. Code: Ss–Pfp–1)

Extension of Social Security Benefits to Children Attending High School or College After Reaching Age 18 and Up to Age 22 Fact Sheet. American Legion; free. (For counselor and students. Code: CSs–Pff–2)

You Can Win a Scholarship. Barron's Educational Series, Inc.; $3.95. (For students. Code: Ss–Pff–2)

Financing a College Education. Long-playing record, two sides. Guidance Associates; $5.95. (For students. Code: Ss–Pff–1)

Latest Information on Scholarship in the Space Age. Bellman Publishing Company; $0.50. (For students. Code: Ss–Pff–2)

Part-time Jobs for the Handicapped. Book. B'nai B'rith Vocational Service; $0.35. Outlines helpful procedures for obtaining part-time work for the handicapped. (For counselor working with individual. Code: CIh–Pff–2)

Investing for Income and Security. Booklet. Public Affairs Committee; $0.25. (For parents. Code: P–Pfs–2)

How to S-t-r-e-t-c-h Your M-o-n-e-y. Booklet. Public Affairs Committee; $0.25. (For parents. Code: P–Pfp–1)

Money Management for the Young Adults. Booklet. Institute of Life Insurance. (For students. Code: Ss–Pfp–2)

MATERIALS FOR ADULTS

Money Management in Your Family. Book. Children's Press; $3.95. Tips on financial management. (For adults. Code: Ag–Pfp–2)

Utilization

Economic information processes necessitates a developmental approach over an extended period of time. The individual needs broadening and general information, not only in the beginning but throughout life, as changes occur. Broadening can probably take place through the individual's being surrounded with economic information applicable to him and through having time to browse, think, and integrate. Broadening of economic understanding will enable the individual to challenge and perhaps re-evaluate his educational plans, attitudes toward private enterprise and various occupations, leisure-time activities, and economic self-aspiration. To achieve the broadening depth (the first depth in the 3-D concept, utilizing information) various materials, media, and techniques will need to be used, including books, films, trips, brochures, tapes, pictures, and personal contacts.

The second depth, of resource or specific information, can be an important part of the developmental approach and need not be left until a crisis situation when specific information has to be obtained in order that a decision can be made. Such decisions often are formulated under undue pressure. If development of economic information processes is successfully achieved, then second depth personal information will be continually available and utilized by the individual. The specific information materials will need to be available in locations where concentration can be done. Copying specific personal economic information often is necessary. Copying may require some manual duplicating, but whenever possible the material should be located where photocopying machines are available; or, in some cases, duplicate copies of material can be made available free or at nominal cost. Much of the specific and broadening information, which is in a medium that can be, should be available for check-out so that the material can be discussed with others with whom the individual has decided to share life. The discussion of specific information with others may provide a feedback (third depth) for the individual as he integrates other information about himself with the economic information.

Economic information in schools is becoming an important part of the curriculum, starting in lower grades and extending through higher education. Not only are courses offered in economics but units on economic information are included in courses like basic business in junior and senior high schools, home economics courses, and social studies courses. Counselors may work with teachers to develop a portable economic information file for use in the classroom with specific students or by the entire class. The team approach of teacher and counselor may assist individuals in utilizing the information effectively.

In financial planning, financial aids for education, and other economic information, the tendency is to develop the plan, package, or program for the individual instead of assisting the individual in developing one of his own. A developmental long-term approach should provide more opportunity for the individual to be personally involved, thus enabling him to integrate economic aspirations into his overall self-concept and long-term goals. Part of the developmental approach may be personalized counseling with economic considerations part of the counseling process. The feedback from counseling, peer discussions, explorations, and implementations of plans may be essential for reality testing.

In utilizing economic information with different persons, the counselor needs to consider the background of each. Individuals from economically deprived homes often may need economic information for different purposes than persons from upper economic level homes. Individuals from economically deprived homes may need more broadening information, which may serve as a stimulus for increasing economic self-aspiration. The economically deprived background may prevent the person from reading, interpreting, and utilizing economic information as well as persons from upper economic level families. For economically deprived persons, economic information frequently has to have more immediate outcomes, and the time between economic goal establishment and achievement must be of shorter duration than for persons who have lived in families where money was more plentiful.

Summary

Economic conditions do affect the opportunities available and thus the plans that one can form. An understanding of the prevailing economic conditions that are affecting and may affect the individual is an important part of the personalized information processes. Educational opportunities are to a large part dependent upon the financial assistance one can obtain while pursuing an education. Another factor affecting educational decisions is the economic return potential as the individual perceives it.

Financial planning and execution seem to be almost continuous processes, which necessitate personalized information being obtained, integrated, and utilized frequently. The major source of money for the majority of people has been employment for pay; however, the sources are much broader. All present and potential sources of income must be considered in developing financial plans. Not only do the plans need to include the necessities of life, but the trend seems to be toward more of the budget being allocated for leisure and self-expressive time activities. Many leisure-time activities are major expenditures and need to be carefully considered in relation to the total planning.

The available materials for economic information, other than financial assistance for education, seem to have been prepared primarily from theoretical, abstract, and statistical viewpoints. The economic information of a personalized nature most useful in counseling and guidance seems to be lacking except in scholarships, loans, and other financial aids. The amount and sources of economic information applicable for personalized information processes seem to be expanding and are being prepared for use at all age levels.

SELECTED REFERENCES

Adams, James F., ed. *Counseling and Guidance, A Summary View.* New York: The Macmillan Co., 1965. Pp. 316–324.

Arnspiger, V. Clyde. *Personality in Social Process, Values, and Strategies of Individuals in a Free Society.* Chicago: Follett Publishing Company, 1961. Pp. 101–102.

Baer, Max F., and Edward C. Roeber. *Occupational Information: The Dy-*

namics of Its Nature and Use. Chicago: Science Research Associates, Inc., 1964. Pp. 119–127.

Benson, Charles S. *The School and the Economic System*. Chicago: Science Research Associates, Inc., 1966. 117 pages.

Benzing, Cynthia E., and Percival W. Hutson. "Scholarship Guidance Practices," *The School Counselor*, 11 (May 1964), 238–242.

Berdie, Ralph F., and Albert B. Hood. *Decisions for Tomorrow: Plans of High School Seniors for After Graduation*. Minneapolis: University of Minnesota Press, 1965. Pp. 44–46.

Cox, Claire. *How to Beat the High Cost of College*. New York: Bernard Geis Associates, 1964. 298 pages.

"How to Get Financial Assistance for Technical Students," *School Management*, 7 (January 1963), 61.

Humphreys, J. Anthony, Arthur E. Traxler, and Robert D. North. *Guidance Services*, 3rd ed. Chicago: Science Research Associates, Inc., 1967. Pp. 43–44, 57–72, 263, 352–353.

Isaacson, Lee E. *Career Information in Counseling and Teaching*. Boston: Allyn and Bacon, Inc., 1966. Pp. 174–180, 323.

Mattingly, Richard. *Financial Assistance for College Students, Undergraduate*. Washington, D.C.: U.S. Goverment Printing Office, 1962.

Miller, C. Dean, Allen E. Kvey, and Arnold D. Goldstein. "Student Patterns of Financing Education at a Land-Grant University," *The Personnel and Guidance Journal*, 45 (March 1967), 687–691.

Munson, Harold L. "At Your Fingertips, A File Full of Information," *The Vocational Guidance Quarterly*, 3 (Spring 1955), 90–92.

1965 Savings and Loan Fact Book. Chicago: United States Savings and Loan League, 1965. 144 pages.

Norris, Willa, Franklin R. Zeran, and Raymond N. Hatch. *The Information Service In Guidance*, 2nd ed. Chicago: Rand McNally & Company, 1966. Pp. 189–194, 231–238, 398–399.

Perrella, Vera C. "Employment of School Age Youth, October, 1966." *Monthly Labor Review* (August 1967), 20–26. Also see *Special Labor Force Report* No. 87, Reprint No. 2538, pp. 20–26, plus pp. A-1–A-13.

Sherif, Mazafer, and Carolyn W. Sherif, eds. *Problems of Youth: Transition to Adulthood in a Changing World*. Chicago: Aldine Publishing Company, 1965. Pp. 240–260, 315–329.

Splaver, Sarah. *Your College Education—How to Pay for It*. New York: Julian Messner, Inc., 1964. 286 pages.

Wieland, J. Edward, ed. *Need a Lift?* Indianapolis: The American Legion Educational and Scholarship Program, The American Legion, 1967. 128 pages.

Women's Bureau. *1965 Handbook on Women Workers*. Washington, D.C.: U.S. Department of Labor, 1966. Bulletin No. 290. Pp. 124–134.

Your Child's Future. Boston: John Hancock Mutual Life Insurance Company, 1966. Pp. 25–29.

Chapter 17

Information Pertinent to Peer
and Family Relations

The individual is surrounded by a world of information regarding his peers and his family; however, learning how to determine which information is pertinent to him, how to personalize it, and how to get a feedback in terms of his own self-concept may necessitate assistance.

A counselor's decisions concerning what information on peer and family relationships to have available to users will be based on the expected needs of the particular segment of population served. Because peer and family relationships are major influences on an individual's behavior, adjustments, and achievements, need for such information exists over a lifetime in relation to peers and for an extended length of time for the family. The information may be needed as a child, a parent, or another member within a family.

Value and attitude transmittal and formation are centered in family and peer relationships. A counselor works with an individual's peer and family concepts rather than with statistical data and other information about "the American family." Information presented in this chapter for the counselor is to help him facilitate personalizing information and to work with the individual's perceptions, evaluations, and adaptations.

Purposes of Family and Peer Information

Pertinent information pertaining to family and peers, if personalized, serves needs of individuals in promoting their development. The person or persons involved in the information processes may include only an individual or an individual in relationship with peers or the members of his family. The individual may be concerned about his relationship with peers and others who are not members of his family, with any or all members of the family, or between peers and family members. The relationships are pertinent at all ages. A husband may have need for information in order to work more effectively with his wife and vice versa. Parents often have need for additional information so that they can work more effectively with their child and vice versa. An adult needs information to work effectively with a peer associate at work or play. A child needs peer information as he relates to other children. Family and peer information may concern relationships, roles, influences, changes, behavior patterns, interactions, and other knowledge.

The purposes of such information in relation to an individual would include the following:

1. Help understand the effects of family environment and relationships upon behavior, values, and the perceived self.
2. Facilitate communications with and among family members and with peers.
3. Effect assessment (evaluation) of an individual's role in the family and among peers.
4. Stimulate and enhance mobility within or to another family structure and/or peer group(s).
5. Provide pertinent information pertaining to topics on peer and family relationships, including boy-girl relations, dating, sex, and marriage.
6. Help the individual interpret the influences of peer relationships.
7. Provide information on peer relationships pertinent to the individual for evaluation and as a basis for the choice of peers to be influential in his life.
8. Facilitate parents' understanding of their children.
9. Help create a supportive climate where individuals—parents and children—can develop personally, socially, educationally, and vocationally.
10. Promote positive attitudes favorable to being a more active, contributing member as a parent, family member, or peer associate.

Role of Counselor

A counselor's role in personalizing the information process for each individual in relation to family and peers involves many facets. The counselor can facilitate the extension of information necessary for formulating a foundation for decision-making and for implementation by an individual in relation to his family and peers. The counselor must be effective in helping the individual to move from the understanding stage in the information process to the assimilation and utilization stage. Information is meaningful to an individual insofar as he integrates it into his own perceptive structure. Stimulating receptiveness on the part of the individual to consider new or additional information is of major importance.

An individual needs to learn to select from the vast amount of information available that which is of personal value to him. The counselor can enable an individual to become discriminating and to interpret and integrate it into his personal reservoir of information. Peer and family information may help the individual to function successfully and fully within society.

The counselor's role also would involve striving to create a supportive climate of operation for an individual in which to try out and explore certain types of decisions that can be implemented without the full force of risk-taking being involved. If the counselor's setting is a school, this climate could be necessary in the classroom involving peer relationships or at home involving parents and other members of the family. If in youth organizations, it could involve peers, family members, and others not members of the family. If the counselor is working with adults, creating a supportive climate could involve worker to worker relations.

The counselor is concerned not only about cognitive processes or intellectualization, but he is concerned also about the affective processes, particularly in helping the individual keep the two processes attuned to one another.

Parental Expectations

Parents have an expectation of each other and of their children. The expectations may set the stage for what one does.

> If you treat a man as he is, he will stay as he is, but, if you treat him as if he were what he ought to be, and could be, he will become that bigger and better man. (Goethe)

An individual does different things under different circumstances and as a result he is assuming different roles. In fact, different roles are expected of him depending upon the prevailing conditions. Often a child becomes confused because of different role expectations without the child's recognizing or understanding how conditions have changed, and, if they have, how they affect expectations. The child and his parents may need assistance in obtaining the personalized information that may enable each to grow in understanding.

Often parents' expectations are isolated or compartmentalized in regard to what a child should do in a given case. The expectations may or may not be realistic for the child; also, to have the same expectations of two children may be ignoring the differences between them. Parents need to develop a perception that recognizes the relationship among their different expectations and the extent of agreement or inconsistency. If parents would hold a Gestalt view of expectations and would show a willingness toward flexibility as conditions change, children may be able to make more growth than when parents hold compartmentalized expectations with no interrelatedness evident.

During early childhood, parents expect their children to be dependent. In later life, parents expect children to be independent. The transition from dependency to independency presents for many parents a problem of how and when. Parents often want information and assistance on making the transition a process instead of an act, a natural development instead of a major crisis. Cutting the apron string may be hard for both parent and child. Helping parents accept the growing independent behavior of their adolescents may be a major undertaking and equally so may be the job of assisting the adolescent in assuming responsibility for his own behavior.

Parental expectations often are formulated without consultation with their children and in so doing agreements in role expectations often do not occur. Role expectations often are more in agreement when decisions are reached as a family, with the children entering into all decisions to the level of their capabilities. Each child's extent of participation and amount of responsibilities can be increased as he develops in maturity.

A continuous flow of information, with the individual assisted in personalizing the information processes, may help parents and children to have expectations of each other that are realistic. When expectations are attuned to one another, needed modifications can be made with a minimum of difficulty. Parental expectations in such areas as educational achievement, dress, behavior, and performance of the children often are bases for family quarrels. Parental dating expectations often widen the communication gap between youth and their parents. The areas into which parental expectations could be classified would be lengthy and probably not meaningful. Instead, counselors can assist parents in recognizing and understanding the expectations that they have developed for their children. The parents can interrelate the expectations for an examination of consistency. To make an examination may require increased activity in the personalized information processes.

Family Relationships

The family is an important part of the American culture. As Duvall (1962, p. 49) wrote, "Families are the nurturing centers for human personality." They set the emotional climate not only for the children but for the parents as well. The relationships existing among family members have an influence upon each other. The family, though the members may hold divergent views, should be seen as a functioning unit. The interactions among the family members and the way these interactions are perceived are important aspects of the continually shifting, changing family relationships. Assisting an individual in understanding relationships existing between himself and other family members may enable him to be a more effective member and to increase the pace of his own development.

Rosen (1967) from a study of family structure and value transmission found that values are transmitted from parents to children in different ways. In families where children were trained early as compared to later in independent mastery, the value similarity level between mother and son was higher. Love-oriented techniques of discipline were often found present in families where value similarities existed between mother and son. Other factors were parental love and support. He also found that social class did in general make a difference with value similarity scores higher in the middle class than the lower class. The age of the child in comparison to other children seemed also to be a factor, but this varied with social class. Thus, family relationships do make a difference in the value transmissions among the members. Helping parents and children understand potential means for value transmissions may enable them to take a more personal role in those activities, which potentially may facilitate goal achievement.

The relationship existing among family members seems to make a difference in the behavior of individual members. When the husband and wife are involved in the kind of marital relationship that communicate to the children a likelihood of separation, or when the family is fatherless, the children seem to be more vulnerable to influences toward delinquent behavior. When contacts among family members and between the family and community diminish, research data available seem to support that conditions exist that are potential for delinquency. An inconsistent mixture of permissiveness and strictness within the family often is fertile soil for developing delinquency (*The Challenge of Crime*, 1967, p. 63). Parents and children knowing early enough this kind of information about family relationships may be able to obtain other information and help to prevent or reduce the extent of delinquency occurring among their family members. The counselor must guard against generalizing about a specific family based on the general characteristics that have been derived from statistical studies. The general characteristics can be used by the individual to evaluate and study his own conditions as he tries to establish priorities in his plan of action.

The relationship among family members is a complex interrelated network and constantly is undergoing appraisal and frequent modification. The relationship is not simple and cannot be reduced to a single cause and effect. The parents are not independent of one another nor of the child and vice versa. Children affect parents' development as well as parents affecting children's. (Blocher, 1966, p. 189). The family is a unit, but it is not an isolated unit—family members interact with each other as well as with persons outside of the family.

In some communities and among certain families the membership is extended over more than one generation living within the same household at the same time. *The extended* family and relationships existing among the members may be significant in an individual's development. In some households the family has been *expanded* by taking into the home persons other than relatives. The importance of relatives versus nonrelatives does not seem to be the issue, rather the relationship, love, and recognition shown among members. In a research study by Holtzman and Moore (1965, p. 60), no differences in attitudes among high school youth seemed to be found that could be associated with the children being true, step- or half-siblings.

In some cases individuals may lack the kind of relationships among their own family members that may contribute to their development. Some may turn only to peer relationships for the interactions and feedbacks needed. Others may feel the need for a family relationship and try to obtain it through a *quasi* family relationship, where the individual actively engages himself in another family. For that person the family relationships that may be influential in his value formation may be the quasi family as much or more than the blood relation family.

The relationships among siblings is an area of concern for many children. They would like to get along better with brothers and sisters but lack sufficient understanding and know-how to achieve the desired interactions. Older children often are perceived by the younger ones as domineering; the younger children are nuisances as perceived by the older ones. Rivalry may exist for family members' recognition and love. The parents may exhibit too little or too much affection or may show partiality. In lower economic income families conditions may force sharing materials, clothing, toys, and rooms, which may be a breeding ground for friction in sibling relationships. The same conditions may be used for developing attitudes essential for better understandings among people and how each person is somewhat dependent upon but at the same time can contribute to others. The kind of family relationships developed may be somewhat dependent upon an understanding of how to use the information and resources available.

Peer Relationships

One's peers are influential in his behavior, and an understanding of one's peers may assist him in an understanding of himself. Peer relationships start in early childhood and continue throughout life; however, the peer groups change from time to time. One generally selects a few persons from his peers with whom he has influential peer relationships. At times, his needs and those of his peers are at crosswinds to one another. The decision on which shall take precedence or how to reach a compromise may require additional information and perhaps counseling or additional interpersonal relationships with the purpose of feedback. The feedback should help the individual to bring his cognitive and affective processes into focus.

The identification of peers for role models, activity sharing, intellectual exchange, and emotional involvement is often done on a happenstance, situational basis instead of an intellectual or a recognized emotional need basis. Various kinds of peer relationships are essential for feedback so that ideas, decisions, and feelings can be explored at various stages throughout life's developmental stages. Consequently, one's peer group will gain influence as a developing force for the self-concept, educational and occupational aspirations, and behavioral patterns. An individual moves in the direction of his peer group for personal identity and behavior definition. Alexander and Campbell (1967, p. 122) concluded from their research findings that ". . . communication among male high school seniors affects both college plans and attendance." Educational aspirations are associated with one's perceived characteristics of his personal friends.

Counselors need to use caution and not generalize from information about a few people to think that all persons use peer relationships the same way. However, the knowledge of what research studies have found may be beneficial in assisting the counselor in working with individuals. Brittain (1963) in a study of adolescents found that parents are used as competent guides for some things, whereas peers are used for others. Parents tend to be followed on matters of more general importance to adult society, whereas peers are followed on matters of special importance to adolescents (dress, dance, school courses, and so on). Bowerman and Kinch's (1959) research study on children in grades four through ten gave evidence that as children grow older they use their parents less frequently as guides for their actions and use their peers more. Many other studies are available on peer relationships and their influence on the individual.

Peer relationships differ from one group to another and from one subculture to another. The relationships and their influence are often dependent upon the sex of the individual and the sex of the other members in the peer group. The sex role expectations of the peer group also affect the relationship.

The individual's counselor has a major role in helping the individual perceive, understand, and utilize the feedback available from peer relationships. If the family is the nurtured soil for personality origination, then the peer group is the exploration and testing ground. Perceiving the information available from peer relationships is a major task, but even more important are the tasks of personalizing and internalizing the information for maximum utilization in one's growth and development.

Dating Practices

The relationships between boy-girl and man-woman have been bases for hundred of studies and thousands of books. Among teenagers the boy-girl relationship often ranks number one in problems as revealed by various studies. How soon dating practices start or when they end cannot be identified by specific chronological age. Broderick and Fowler (1961) in a study on preadolescents found that almost one half of the boys and over one third of the girls maintained they had begun dating in the fifth grade. Dating practices are common in junior high schools and continue until marriage. Studies often reveal that dating practices continue for some even after marriage. With the high divorce rate existing today, dating practices again become important to a large number of men and women during a period that may be labeled "between marriages."

The reasons for dating vary (Rodman, 1965, pp. 8–13; Williamson, 1966, pp. 170–172). Some individuals use dating as a recreation and go on a date for the pleasure received from the activities in which the two of them engage. In some subcultures or groups a person will not be accepted unless he or she dates. In such groups dating may be done primarily for conformity or status, the gaining and maintaining of prestige. In such cases the group pressure may be determining the dating partner more than the individual's personal evaluation of characteristics sought in a mate. Some persons perceive dating as being an educational process; thus dating becomes an exploration in discovering self and in learning one's own brand of self-expression and emotional attachment to another person of the opposite sex. The dating practices may contribute to the personality growth and maturity development of the individual. For most persons the dating process contributes to selection of a partner for marriage.

The characteristics sought in a dating partner vary from person to person and information about factors contributing to popularity is often desired. Counselors can assist an individual in personalizing information so as to contribute to the person's developmental processes in relationship with the opposite sex. Printed material may be only a partial answer to the kinds of information needed and reading may or may not be an appropriate technique for use with a given person. Information sources, storage, and utilization pertaining to dating may take on a multidimension.

Dating activities are dependent upon many conditions—the reasons for dating, the dating partner, the standards possessed by each of the dating partners, the amount of alcohol and drugs used, and so on. The activities socially accepted in the group or subculture will be major determinants of the dating activities. Dancing, movies, sports participation as a spectator or participating member, TV viewing, car riding, parking, walking, dining out, and others are typical dating activities. Studies conducted in the 1960's provide data to show that intimate forms of premarital sexual behavior are on the increase. Earlier reports and studies by people like Kinsey and Ellis help set the stage for more recent studies. The reasons given for more premarital sexual relationships in this age than in those before seem to vary somewhat. Probably the two more frequent reasons listed are new contraceptive techniques and a change in attitudes regarding premarital sexual relationships. Counselors may find that the next generation will have a new code, one that some counselors may find hard to accept.

The medium for information processes on many topics, including dating practices, has been primarily publications. The trend seems to be toward the individual's taking a more active, rather than passive, role in the information processes. The active role will in many instances require a transition from one code of behavior to another. The value judgment as to whether or not the transition is right or wrong is another issue. However, if the transition is to continue, information will be required on the part of many persons, not only to assist the individual who is taking an active role but also to help others understand the trend and reasons.

Sex Information

Development of body glands as maturity is reached is not always associated with specific chronological age. The changes that do occur in the body may occur prior to or much later than the individual's expectation. Information on physiological changes as the body matures needs to be more than learning of normal expectations; the information needs to be personalized. The physiological developments need to be an integral part of the physical and psychological information (Chapter 14) and should be interwoven with sex information.

Sex roles of men and women vary with the culture and the social class within each culture (Williamson, 1966, pp. 141–163). Each individual has a need for understanding the sex role expectations within his subculture and of other subcultures in which he could potentially become active. Personalizing sex information of the kind needed for understanding, assimilating, and utilizing sex role expectations is not an easy task for an individual; the counselor may facilitate the processes.

An individual's own standards and expectations are what must be considered. Often his standards and expectations, especially in relation to sex roles, are formulated upon insufficient and often inaccurate information. Frequently, the expectations and standards that do exist are incongruent with one another. The individual may be unable to express his standards and expectations verbally and, if he can, he frequently does not have them organized into a meaningful pattern for his own behavior. The ones that can be expressed and intellectually discussed may not be in agreement with the ones emotionally expressed. A given person's standards may even be different from one kind of dating (blind date, double dating, dating after engagement, and so on) to another or from one dating partner to another. Assisting an individual in recognizing and understanding his own standards may be a first step toward helping him develop a sex role within his group or in finding a group in which he can.

Sociologists and psychologists are turning more and more of their studies toward understanding the sexual attitudes, roles, and changes in an increasingly erotic culture. Sexual promiscuity is on the increase. Illegitimate births constituted 5.3 per cent of live births in 1960 in the United States and the number had increased to 6.8 per cent in 1964. Teen-age girls gave birth to 42.5 per cent of the illegitimate children born in 1964, but this was a decrease from 47.9 per cent in 1940. The rate of illegitimate births compared to the total births is increasing with 0.7 per cent in 1940 and 2.3 per cent in 1964. The rate of illegitimate births was 3.4 per cent for whites and 24.5 per cent for nonwhites in 1964 (*Statistical Abstract of the United States*, 1966, pp. 47–48).

Sex information is more than an understanding of physiological knowledge. Sex role expectations, one's standards and own expectations, sociological implications and facts, and one's psychological processes are all interwoven and have major importance in self information. A counselor working in depth with an individual cannot afford to ignore the implications of the sex information processes. Sex information is an integral, not isolated, part of the total personalized information processes that are essential in an individual's growth and development.

Marriage Responsibilities

The median age at time of first marriage is younger for both men and women (22.8 and 20.6 years respectively in 1965) than was the case half a century earlier (24.6 and 21.2 years respectively in 1920). Approximately one out of every four girls is married by age eighteen and approximately one in every two by age twenty-one. Marriages are lasting longer, with the median duration in years of marriages that end in divorces or annulments changing from 5.3 years of marriage in 1950 to 7.3 years in 1962. The divorce rate based on all married females fifteen years old and over has fluctuated from year to year with a high of 1.44 per cent in 1945 but has remained less than one per cent since 1953. The remarriage median age of bride and groom in 1963 was 35.6 and 40.2 years respectively (*Statistical Abstract of the United States,* 1966, pp. 61–64). The average number of years of marriage that is terminated by the death of one partner has increased in recent years not only by marriages occurring at an earlier age but also by the increase in the average life span. Assuming the responsibilities of marriage today means entering into a marriage relationship that has a potential for lasting longer than in any previous period in history. Another interesting point according to Havighurst (1965) is that girls who drop out of school before completing high school more frequently marry than those who are graduated.

Marriage is often thought of in terms of families that include children; however, many marriages result in no children being born or adopted. If children are present in the early years of marriage, the later years may be spent without children present. Almost one half (43.4 per cent in 1965) of all families in the United States had no children under eighteen years old living in the household. Thus, when assuming marriage responsibilities, the man and woman should recognize that they may spend several years together without children in the home, even though children may be present during the early years of marriage.

Marriage counseling prior to and during marriage has become a specialized field, with professional workers concentrating their time and resources in the area. The professional organization to which many of them belong is the American Association of Marriage Counselors. For many counselors who work with clientele regarding topics primarily other than marriage may find that marriage counselors, ministers, priests, and rabbis will be conjoint workers when the major topic for consideration is marriage. The conjoint relationship may be as a resource person, consultant, or a person to whom referrals can be made.

Family and marriage information can assist the man and woman before and after marriage and may be beneficial to all members of their home. Marriage has the potential for bringing many enjoyments, challenges, and problems. Increasing the family members' awareness of different situations and possible problems may reduce friction among family members. The counselor may assist in establishing a framework for communication among family members. Printed material often contains information on family councils that may sound good and are effective where used, but that are found operative only in a small percentage of the families. Other communication means will need to be established in most families. They will probably need assistance in understanding a functional procedure for decision-making on topics of family concern.

Family responsibilities include developing a family socio-economic value structure and a means for modification as the conditions and circumstances change. The associates of the family will have a direct bearing on socio-economic value structure. Thus, the family members may need personalized information that may help them identify persons who will be influential in family activities. The list may need modification as family goals change or new acquaintances are made.

Marriage is more than a legal or religious undertaking. Marriage that results in happiness means the assumption of many responsibilities, including a sharing of oneself with another. The cognitive and affective processes of the family members become intermeshed. The family members often need information in order that they may gain an understanding of how to plan their life for time together, for others to participate in some family activities, and for some independent activities by each member. Personalized family information may assist in developing family patterns that will lead toward family goals and also will aid each member in his development toward his own goals.

Working with Parents

A counselor in an informational role may work with parents to exchange information about the child, to learn how the parents use the child to meet their own needs, to facilitate acquiring pertinent information by the parents, to understand the role of the child in relation to his parents and home environment, and/or to understand the parents' values, prejudices, and expectations. More often work with parents by the counselor will be in a conference, consultative role or facilitator for referrals rather than in a counseling session. For the school counselor the conference will be for the benefit of the student. In order for the counselor to facilitate the development of the student by personalizing the information process he must understand the individual in relation to his parents or parent figures (persons perceived by the child in a parent role—grandmother, aunt, uncle, foster parents, and so on).

In reality not all parents are dedicated to the development of their child for his sake. Some parents use the child to meet their own needs for status and to make themselves appear as successful parents—self-fulfillment through exploitation of the child. The counselor working with parents must understand their expectations for the child as well as understanding the child's expectations. If the expectations of each are not compatible, then pertinent information necessary to help the parents and the child to communicate and to understand each other will be essential.

For communications to be effective for facilitating understanding, parents and child must have or develop respect for each other as individuals. Parents have difficulty viewing their children as individuals. Luckey (1967, p. 207) stated, "One of the greatest contributions a counselor can make to the relationship between parent and child is to demonstrate his own acceptance of and interest in the child and in the parent." For information processes to be effective, openness to receive and understand information must prevail. For a parent or child to accept or integrate additional pertinent information into their value systems, personalization is a must for each as well as receptiveness on the part of the potential user.

Support by parents for considering new information by themselves or by their children can contribute to a positiveness toward information on the part of the children. The reverse may also be true, nonsupport of new information or expanded information on the part of the parents may create a blockage to integrating additional information on the part of children. Parents or the parent figures may be one key to the effectiveness of the information processes.

Coding, Filing, Storing, and Retrieval

The key in relation to information is retrieval and the ease with which it can be done. Material needs to be coded to the subject under which it is most likely to be requested by the potential user. The files need to be *user oriented,* not *information oriented.* What information on peer and family relationships is contained in the files is important only to the extent of its pertinence to the user and the ease with which he can locate and use it.

To establish codes and files, the counselor should analyze the potential users, their expected needs, and other characteristic variables. Materials on peer and family relationships then can be acquired and coded according to users, topics, and depth. The 3-D concept of analyzing materials can facilitate determining the suitability to potential users, the area or topic covered, and the depth of presentation. If established codes and files are not effective or if new files are to be set up and no satisfactory code has been selected, the 3-D concept used in analyzing materials could be used as a code.

Location of files will be comparable to information contained in Chapters 7 and 12.

Material and Sources

Information on peer and family relationships is extensive. The key to effectiveness will be the selectivity of information pertinent to the potential users. For the counselor to keep abreast of the information, regularly consulting the catalogues and brochures from various publishers will prove one effective method for printed materials, films, audio and video tapes, and other audio-visual materials. Much information on family and peers will be produced outside of the guidance and counseling field; therefore, related fields, such as sociology, home economics, family living, or psychology, should be considered for updating materials.

Some illustrative materials and sources available for peer and family relationships information are listed and analyzed for potential use according to the 3-D concept, which could also serve as a code for materials. The materials are listed according to grade levels—preschool, elementary, junior high, and senior high school. The analysis and coding depend upon the segment of population to be served. Some of the following materials although listed under a particular level are also applicable to other levels, including adults. If a counselor is working with more than one level, cross-referencing in the other areas would facilitate use.

PRESCHOOL MATERIALS

Prenatal Care. Booklet. U.S. Government Printing Office; $0.20. Guide for expectant parents. (Code: P–Sf–2)

Laurie's New Brother. Book. Abelard-Schuman Limited; $2.95. A little girl learns to accept and finally to love her new baby brother. (For parents. Code: P–Sf–1)

Enjoy Your Child—Ages 1, 2, and 3. Book. Public Affairs Committee; $0.25. (For parents. Code: P–Sf–1)

ELEMENTARY SCHOOL MATERIALS

Grandfather and I. Book. Lothrop, Lee, & Shepard Company, Inc.; $3.25. (For teacher to use with pupils. Code: TSk–Sf–1)

Grandmother and I. Book. Lothrop, Lee, & Shepard Company, Inc.; $3.25. (For teacher to use with pupils. Code: TSk–Sf–1)

My Sister and I. Book. Lothrop, Lee, & Shepard Company, Inc.; $3.25. (For teacher to use with pupils. Code: TSk–Sp–1)

Theodore's Parents. Book. Lothrop, Lee, & Shepard Company, Inc.; $3.25.

Story of a happy adoption. (For teacher to use with pupils. Code: TSk–Sf–1)

Martha's Secret Wish. Book. Lothrop, Lee, & Shepard Company, Inc.; $3.00. Understanding of the loneliness of a child without a father and whose mother works. (For pupils. Code: Si–Sf–1)

Cousins at Camm Corners. Book. Lothrop, Lee, & Shepard Company, Inc.; $3.00. Orphan goes to live with aunt and family. (For pupils. Code: Si–Sp–1)

Libby's Step-Family. Book. Lothrop, Lee, & Shepard Company, Inc.; $3.50. A thirteen-year-old girl's adjustment to her mother's remarriage. (For pupils. Code: Si–Sf–1)

Meet Miki Takino. Book. Lothrop, Lee, & Shepard Company, Inc.; $3.50. A small boy's search for stand-in grandparents for a school celebration. (For teacher to use with pupils. Code: TSk–Sf–1)

Sibling Relations and Personality. Film. McGraw-Hill, Inc. (For teacher working with pupils. Code: T–Sf–2)

Understand Your Child—From 6 to 12. Book. Public Affairs Committee; $0.25. (For parents. Code: P–Sf–2)

Big Brother. Book. Harper & Row, Publishers; $2.19. (For pupils. Code: Sk–Sf–1)

The Wonderful Story of How You Were Born. Booklet. Doubleday & Company, Inc.; $2.95. (For pupils. Code: Si–Sf–2)

Quiet Street. Book. Abelard-Schuman Limited; $2.73. A quiet street becomes a happy street when Lisa gets a sister of her own at last. A warm story of adoption. (For use in kindergarten through grade three. Code: Sk–Sf–1)

My Family. Book. Abelard-Schuman Limited; $2.89. A youngster explains family relations—how a whole family comes into being, and what keeps them close even when they are separated. (For use in kindergarten through grade three. Code: Sk–Sf–1)

The Daddy Days. Book. Abelard-Schuman Limited; $2.75. Raking leaves, getting a haircut, going to the library, and having supper outdoors are fun on the special days when daddy is home. (For use in kindergarten through grade three. Code: Sk–Sf–1)

Parents and the Counselor. Booklet. National Vocational Guidance Association; $0.50. (For parents. Code: P–Sf–1)

Between Parent and Child: New Solutions to Old Problems. Book. The Macmillan Company; $4.95. (For parents. Code: P–Sf–1)

JUNIOR HIGH SCHOOL MATERIALS

Getting Along with Parents. Booklets. Science Research Associates, Inc.; $0.90. (For students. Code: Sj–Sf–1)

When Children Start Dating. Booklet. Science Research Associates, Inc.; $0.84. (For parents. Code: P–Sb–2)

Helping Boys and Girls Understand Their Sex Roles. Booklet. Science Research Associates, Inc.; $0.84. (For parents. Code: P–Sb–2)

Helping Brothers and Sisters Get Along. Booklet. Science Research Associates, Inc.; $0.84. (For parents. Code: P–Sf–2)

Being Teenagers. Filmstrip. American Guidance Services, Inc.; $3.40. Acceptance by peers and all around development. Human relations skills presented from the eighth grader's viewpoint. (For students. Code: Sj–Ss–2)

Reunion in December. Book, fiction. William Morrow and Company, Inc.; $3.50. Story of girl's adjustment after father's sudden death. (For students. Code: Sj–Sf–1)

Accent on April. Book, fiction. William Morrow and Company, Inc.; $3.50. Sibling relationships in adolescent years. (For students. Code: Sj–Sf–1)

What Should Parents Expect from Children? Booklet. Public Affairs Committee; $0.25. (For parents. Code: P–Sf–2)

Your Child May Be a Gifted Child. Booklet. Public Affairs Committee; $0.25. (For parents. Code: P–Sf–1)

Your Child's Future. Booklet. John Hancock Mutual Life Insurance Co.; free. (For parents. Code: P–Sf–2)

Life with Brothers and Sisters. Booklet. Science Research Associates, Inc.; $0.90. (For students, Code: Sj–Sf–1)

The Boy Next Door. Book, fiction. William Morrow and Company, Inc.; $3.32. Considers a girl's adjustment to school, family, dates, and outside activities. (For students. Code: Sj–Sb–1)

Mrs. Dalling's Daughter. Book. fiction. William Morrow and Company, Inc.; $3.50. Competitive mother-daughter relationship. (For students. Code: Sj–Sf–1)

Classmates by Request. Book, fiction. William Morrow and Company, Inc.; $3.50. Complexities of integration. (For students. Code: Sj–Sp–1)

SENIOR HIGH SCHOOL MATERIALS

Too Bad About the Haines Girl. Book, fiction. William Morrow and Company, Inc.; $3.50. Story of young schoolgirl who becomes pregnant and how she faces her nightmare. (For students. Code: Ss–Sb–2)

Design for Family Living. Book. T. S. Denison & Co., Inc.; $5.95. Written to help parents and their sons and daughters to communicate more easily about personal problems. (For parents and students. Code: PSs–Sf–2)

How to Live with Parents. Booklet. Science Research Associates, Inc.; $0.90. (For students. Code: Ss–Sf–1)

Looking Ahead to Marriage. Booklet. Science Research Associates, Inc.; $0.90. (For students. Code: Ss–Sm–2)

Understanding Sex. Booklet. Science Research Associates, Inc.; $0.50. (For students. Code: Ss–Sb–2)

Guiding Children's Social Growth. Booklet. Science Research Associates, Inc.; $0.84. (For parents. Code: P–Sd–2)

About Marriage and You. Science Research Associates, Inc.; $1.88. Quizzes, charts, and questions to help make a successful marriage. (For students. Code: Ss–Sm–2)

Growing Up Socially. Booklet. Science Research Associates, Inc.; $0.65. (For students. Code: Ss–Sp–1)

Getting Along with Others. Booklet. Science Research Associates, Inc.; $0.65. (For students. Code: Ss–Sp–1)

Catholic Youth's Guide to Life and Love. Book. Random House, Inc.; $3.95. (For students. Code: Ss–Sb–2)

David and Hazel. Film. McGraw-Hill, Inc.; $165.00. Concentrates on how lack of communication in a family is detrimental to the development of a healthy emotional climate in a home. (For students. Code: Ss–Sf–1)

Utilization of Peer and Family Information

The individual probably already has as much or more information pertaining to peer and family relationships as he does to educational and occupational information. Much information that he possesses probably was obtained under conditions that caused him to perceive only part rather than the total and may have caused misconceptions. Much information is obtained by word of mouth and often that is passed in an emotional outburst that is negative. This is not to say that some people never obtain a positive overall viewpoint on peer and family relationships.

Social mores make communications of some peer and family relationships information more difficult than information in many other areas. Thus, the techniques for utilizing peer and family information may require more group interaction and individual conferences between the person and resource people, including the counselor. The person probably will need to take a more active rather than a passive role. Because of social mores the individual is less likely to ask for peer and family information than he is for educational and occupational information. In many subcultures the person is supposed to know these things or learn them on his own; therefore, the initiative for obtaining peer and family information may not be taken by the individual even when he knows he needs it. The utilization of peer and family information by necessity for effectiveness may be somewhat different in that the counselor may have to take more of the initiative.

With the boy-girl relations and sex codes of the past being challenged and possibly modified, the transmittal of much peer and family information becomes a major role for counselors. When does a behavior pattern that has been accepted over an extended period of time no longer have approval? Who has the right to establish behavior patterns? When the new generation establishes a new pattern different from the old generation and the old generation also retains theirs, under what conditions is each pattern used? Probably on the average more value system conflicts will occur in the utilization of peer and family information than in almost any other area. One caution that counselors must consistently remember is to guard against their own value system's being used with individuals who function in value systems foreign to those of the counselor.

For specific techniques on utilization of information, reference should be made to Chapters 8 and 13 particularly, and also to Chapters 14, 15, and 16. For effectiveness the emphasis probably should be more on techniques where the individual can take an active role, including sociodrama, conferences, and other opportunities to interact with resource people, and field trips to various places, such as courts, family counseling centers, mental hygiene clinics, children's homes, child guidance clinics, and family relations classes.

Summary

Peer and family relationship information is extensive. A counselor's role in personalizing such information for the individuals with whom he works necessitates his understanding their needs and the influences of the family and peers. For an individual to understand himself in relation to his family and peers, information concerning parental expectations, family relations, peer relations, dating practices, sex, and marriage responsibilities become necessary.

The counselor's role in working with an individual will be to help the individual and/or his family to be receptive to new information and to be stimulated to integrate it into their present perceived reservoir of information. In order to make available pertinent information a system of coding, filing, storage, and retrieval that is user-oriented rather than information-oriented is essential for effectiveness.

Ease of retrieval and ease of acquiring related information will depend on the counselor's initiative, planning, selection of materials, and his system for making material accessible and personalized for users.

SELECTED REFERENCES

Alexander, C. Norman, Jr., and Ernest Q. Campbell. "Peer Influences on Adolescent Educational Aspirations and Attainments," in *Education: A Book of Readings,* Robert J. Havighurst, Bernice L. Neugarten, and Jacqueline M. Falk, eds. Boston: Allyn and Bacon, Inc., 1967. Pp. 115–122.

Banducci, Raymond. "The Effect of Mother's Employment on the Achievement, Aspirations, and Expectations of the Child," *The Personnel and Guidance Journal,* 46 (November 1967), 263–267.

Bergstein, Harry B. "Individual Parent Conferences in the Junior High School," *The School Counselor,* 13 (December 1965), 88–93.

Blocher, Donald H. *Developmental Counseling.* New York: The Ronald Press Company, 1966. Pp. 188–194.

Bowerman, Charles E., and John W. Kinch. "Changes in Family and Peer Orientation of Children Between the Fourth and Tenth Grades," *Social Forces,* 37 (March 1959), 206–211.

Brittain, Clay V. "Adolescent Choices and Parent-Peer Cross-Pressures," *American Sociological Review,* **28** (June 1963), 385–391.

Broderick, Carlford B. and Stanley E. Fowler. "New Patterns of Relationships Between the Sexes Among Preadolescents," *Marriage and Family Living,* **23** (February 1961), 23–30.

The Challenge of Crime in a Free Society: A Report by the President's Commission on Law Enforcement and Administration of Justice. Washington, D.C.; U.S. Government Printing Office, February, 1967. Pp. 63–66.

Christopher, Samuel A. "Parental Relationship and Value Orientation as Factors in Academic Achievement," *The Personnel and Guidance Journal,* **45** (May 1967), 921–925.

Coser, Rose Laub, ed. *The Family: Its Structure and Functions.* New York: St. Martin's Press, Inc., 1964. 678 pages.

Duvall, Evelyn Millis. *Family Development,* 2nd ed. New York: J. B. Lippincott Company, 1962. 532 pages.

Fullmer, Daniel and Harold Bernard. *Counseling: Content and Process.* Chicago: Science Research Associates, Inc., 1964. Pp. 8–10, 37–41, 207–226.

Garry, Ralph. *Guidance Techniques for Elementary Teachers.* Columbus, Ohio: Charles E. Merrill Books, Inc., 1963. Pp. 115–193.

Goode, William J. *The Family.* Englewood Cliffs, N.J.: Prentice-Hall, Inc., 1964. 120 pages.

Havighurst, Robert J. "Counseling Adolescent Girls in the 1960's," *The Vocational Guidance Quarterly,* **13** (Spring 1965), 153–160.

Holtzman, Wayne H., and Bernice Milburn Moore. "Family Structure and Youth Attitudes," in *Problems of Youth: Transition to Adulthood in a Changing World,* Muzafer Sherif and Carolyn W. Sherif, eds. Chicago: Aldine Publishing Company, 1965. Pp. 46–61.

Humphreys, J. Anthony, Arthur E. Traxler, and Robert D. North. *Guidance Services,* 3rd ed. Chicago: Science Research Associates, Inc., 1967. Pp. 312–313.

Kinnick, Bernard C., and Jack T. Shannon. "The Effect of Counseling on Peer Group Acceptance of Socially Rejected Students," *The School Counselor,* **12** (March 1965), 162–166.

Klemer, Richard H., and Margaret G. Klemer. *Sexual Adjustment in Marriage.* New York: Public Affairs Committee, Inc., 1966. 28 pages.

Landis, Paul H. *Making the Most of Marriage,* 3rd ed. New York: Appleton-Century-Crofts, 1965. 778 pages.

Luckey, Eleanore Braun, "Elementary Guidance. . . . Three Viewpoints: II, The Elementary School Counselor: Counselor for Parents," *The School Counselor,* **14** (March 1967), 204–209.

Mainig, Lawrence R. "Fear of Paternal Competition: A Factor in Vocational Choice," *The Personnel and Guidance Journal,* **46** (November 1967), 235–239.

Mowsesian, Richard, Brian R. G. Heath, and John W. M. Rothney. "Superior Students' Occupational Preferences and their Fathers' Occupations," *The Personnel and Guidance Journal,* **45** (November 1966), 238–242.

Norris, Willa, Franklin R. Zeran, and Raymond N. Hatch. *The Information*

Service in Guidance, 2nd ed. Chicago: Rand McNally & Company, 1966. Pp. 214–224.

Perrone, Philip A. "Stability of Values of Junior High School Pupils and Their Parents over Two Years," *The Personnel and Guidance Journal,* **46** (November 1967), 268–274.

Porterfield, Austin L. *Marriage and Family Living as Self–Other Fulfillment.* Philadelphia: F. A. Davis Company, 1962. 408 pages.

Rodman, Hyman, ed. *Marriage, Family, and Society: A Reader.* New York: Random House, Inc., 1965. 302 pages.

Rosen, Barnard C. "Family Structure and Value Transmission," in *Society and Education: A Book of Readings,* Robert J. Havighurst, Bernice L. Neugarten, and Jacqueline M. Falk, eds. Boston: Allyn and Bacon, Inc., 1967. Pp. 86–96.

Sonstegard, Manford. "A Rationale for Interviewing Parents," *The School Counselor,* **12** (December 1964), 72–76.

Williamson, Robert C. *Marriage and Family Relations.* New York: John Wiley & Sons, Inc., 1966. 618 pages.

Chapter 18

Personalized Military

Information Processes

The counselor should be neither an apologist nor an enthusiast for militarism or pacifism; he should, rather, assist the [individual] in the *discovery* of the nature of the world and of self, in *evaluation* of options, and in *confrontation* of human destiny.
—ALFRED L. BROPHY, 1964, p. 35.

The role of the military today in the lives of individuals may be different than it has been in military crises in America's early history. The Universal Military Training and Service Act touches the lives of more people than any previous military act, not only because of the extent of the compulsory military service, but more so because of the long-range benefits supported as a result of the service and obligations.

Educational and occupational development for individuals in the services has become a major part of military affairs. One reason is that opportunities available for improving oneself educationally while in service or as a result of serving can be entered into by individual choice. The opportunities exist for improvement at all educational levels. Another reason for increased educational emphasis is the Government's efforts to raise the educational level of men and women in the services. Occupationally today, advanced skills and knowledge are necessary to keep pace with the improved technology of machines and equipment used in the armed services. The technical know-how needed for many military jobs requires training that contributes to the individual's occupational development and potentially can be capitalized upon in civilian jobs; thereby an individual may complete while in the service part or all of the training needed in his initial civilian job.

Military information is essential to a wider population than just those individuals actively engaged in the services under the Military Training and Service Act. Parents and relatives of servicemen and -women need military information of various kinds to help in understanding and assisting potential and active duty servicemen and -women. Women may be involved in the military information process as a potential service-woman, or may have friends, husbands, brothers, or sisters affected by it. The extensive benefits for the veteran and his family also involve others in the military information processes.

The need for military information occurs prior to, during, and following the time an individual or associate is in the armed services. Military information may have different connotations to many persons than do other areas of information because of the Universal Military Training and Service Act. An individual may view military information in relation to fulfilling his obligation through understanding laws and opportunities and then planning for avoidance, deferment, regular entry, or early entry.

Military information to be meaningful must be integrated into an individual's long-range plans, whether he will enter military service or not. Physical and mental rejects, other deferees, and conscientious objectors need to consider military information in relation to their long-range plans. The counselor's role is to facilitate information processes with an individual at the time when the information will be most meaningful and in a manner that will assist him in his growth and development.

Purposes of Military Information in Counseling and Guidance

Military information includes all information essential to the individual that will facilitate his understanding of military obligations, opportunities, benefits, and limitations. The information must include training and educational opportunities, career possibilities, and occupational development potential while in service; differences among branches of service; benefits to the individual's family in case of disability or death; benefits available to the individual while in service and upon completion of service; different alternatives open to draft-eligible youth; women's roles in military services; ranks and classifications together with their implications; and an ongoing process whereby the individual can become involved with the information. Military information as used in counseling and guidance is more than material stored on shelves or in boxes and file drawers. With military information being more comprehensive than frequently perceived and with military information being used with and by individuals over an extended period of time, the term *military information* should be expanded to *personalized military information processes.*

Counselor's Role

The laws in regard to military obligation have in the past fifteen to twenty years changed the lives of many people. The Korean and Vietnam conflicts, together with the various kinds of programs offered by different military services, have made youth seek assistance and consultation on military information. The secondary school counselor has many requests for information and for assistance in understanding the implications for the individual.

All young men upon reaching their eighteenth birthday must within five days register for the Selective Service System of the United States. High school youth are aware of the necessity for registration but are often confused and uncertain about the implications. They generally know about the five armed services—U.S. Air Force, U.S. Army, U.S. Coast Guard, U.S. Marine Corps, and U.S. Navy—but frequently are not fully informed about the choices available for fulfilling their military obligation. Selective Service System registration places the young man in a position of making decisions about his choices or the Government will make the choice. In general eight different choices are available:

1. Enlist as a Regular in a branch of the Armed Forces.
2. Enlist in the National Guard.
3. Enlist in an Active Reserve Unit.
4. Enroll as a full-time college student entitled to a deferment dependent upon grades and academic performance.
5. Join a college ROTC program.
6. Obtain an occupational deferment.
7. Volunteer for the draft.
8. Await draft induction.

The military obligation and the uncertainty of it often loom so large on the future horizon that a young person may be blind to career and life planning. The failure to be able to see beyond the years of service often causes youth to see only the present as having meaning. The future is almost void, or when it does become a reality, they try to escape from it. Counselors recognizing causal factors can and should be able to help the individual. Hopefully, military information obtained and utilized over an extended period of time can facilitate a developmental concept and long-range planning; thus the need for therapeutic procedures would be reduced drastically.

Many boys do not serve a period of military service. The reasons vary but could be classified under five major headings: deferment, which includes educational, occupational, and family hardships; health, which includes physical and mental conditions; mental ability because of either insufficient education or ability; conscientious objector; and certain aliens. Some boys think they will be able to serve but will not because of one reason or another (see Figure 18-1). Some other boys think they can avoid the period of military service for what they believe to be an acceptable reason but will not be able to do so. More adequate information about themselves and the Selective Service System operating procedures may facilitate each individual in developing a realistic picture about his role in relation to the military obligation.

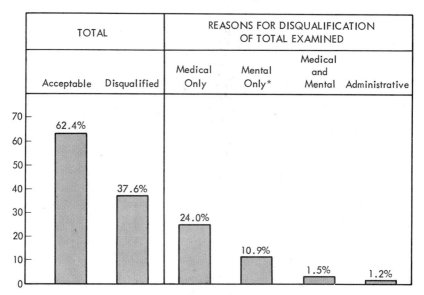

Figure 18-1. SELECTIVE SERVICE DRAFTEES FOUND ACCEPTABLE OR DISQUAL-IFIED, AND REASONS FOR DISQUALIFICATION EXPRESSED IN PERCENTAGE OF TOTAL EXAMINED IN 1966.

Source: Statistical Abstract of the United States, 1967, *88th annual edition,* U.S. *Department of Commerce, p. 269.*

* Failed to meet minimum requirements on mental ability test or the aptitude requirements for trainability.

For those who will serve a period of military service, the counselor's role may be to facilitate career planning that will integrate a period of military service into long-range career plans. The military service may be used to obtain part or all of the education or training necessary and possibly occupational experience. With a long-range plan the individual is better able to select the military service that will provide the greatest benefits for achieving his desired long-range goals.

With Parents

Military service by a boy or girl affects the parents and other family members. If a developmental military information program is formulated, parents will be included. An individual's parents, other family members, and peers need to have some of the same information as the individual in order that they may understand better his attitudes, decisions, and behavior.

Parental attitudes can assist or hinder the individual by creating an environmental climate in which military information is sought or rejected and evaluated objectively or prejudicially. Parental acceptance of the individual and his need for personalized military information can facilitate his making intellectual decisions with full awareness of his emotions and feelings. The counselor's role may be assisting parents to obtain military information of significance to them and their children.

With Girls and Young Women

Women are involved in the Armed Forces and many girls and young women have need for military information in order that they can make decisions about joining. They also have need for military information because a brother, friend, or husband is serving or may serve a period in military service. The projected use will determine the kind of military information supplied. A counselor must be aware of the different purposes for military information and must assume the role that ensures girls and young women that they may obtain personalized military information through a developmental approach.

Women in the Armed Forces

Much of the information for the Armed Forces is applicable to both men and women; however, some information is different. The enlistment requirements for servicewomen are essentially the same in all the armed services. In general the requirements for women are high school education or the equivalent, eighteen years of age or older (if under age twenty-one, parent's or guardian's written permission is required), unmarried, no dependents, good health, and high moral standards. The enlistment period depends upon the branch of service.

Women in all the services are eligible for overseas assignment. Whether assigned overseas or in the United States, every effort is made to assign women to stations where fifty or more are needed. The pay and benefits, including retirement rights and annual leave, are exactly the same for women as men in the same pay grade.

Women enlistees can in some cases be guaranteed a choice of a specific kind of training. Servicewomen are eligible for service school training in most of the career fields to which are assigned. Opportunities for off-duty education are identical to those for servicemen. The same is true about educational opportunities for veterans.

A woman may marry while in the armed services, but in general the rule is that she may not leave the service for this reason until she has completed a stipulated part of her enlistment. The various armed services differ in the exact amount.

Women have an opportunity to become officers in the Armed Forces. College graduates may apply directly from civilian life for a commission as an officer or to attend an officer candidate school or course. Enlisted women, generally those with some college education, can qualify for certain officer candidate programs.

Women who are professionally qualified as physicians, dentists, nurses, dietitians, physical therapists, occupational therapists, and allied scientists may apply for direct commissions.

Educational Opportunities While in Armed Forces

As Clark and Sloan (1964) indicated, the Armed Forces have developed a vast educational complex. By the early 1960's, existing in the United States were some three hundred military schools offering over four thousand technical and semitechnical courses, ranging from elementary subjects to those required for a doctorate. Over one million U.S. military personnel in various parts of the world were taking courses offered by USAFI (United States Armed Forces Institute) and other military agencies. Clark and Sloan indicated that approximately 60 per cent of the subject matter in the various courses was applicable to civilian life.

Military educational programs are constantly under evaluation and are modified as needed. A counselor has the responsibility for assuring that accurate and recent information is communicated to an individual. A review of programs in existence at the time this book was written is supplied on the following pages to provide an idea of the many educational programs available to assist in meeting different objectives while in the military service. Recent and more comprehensive information will be needed before working in depth with individuals.

High School Completion

For those in the Armed Forces who have not completed elementary or secondary education, opportunities are available. Tests of General Educational Development (G.E.D.) are available for those wishing to qualify for high school equivalency certificates. The armed services do not award equivalency certificates, but high schools and state departments of public education can do so on the basis of test results. Many colleges will accept G.E.D. completion as meeting entrance requirements. In some colleges semester hours of college equivalency may be earned through G.E.D. testing.

Specialized courses are available for service personnel. In some cases the courses are offered as part of the regular military training program. The United States Armed Forces Institute (USAFI) offers correspondence courses at the elementary, high school, and college levels. During the fiscal year 1967 over three hundred thousand military personnel enrolled in USAFI courses (Wieland, 1967, p. 108). The cost to the student is so small that it is negligible.

General Academic and Vocational-Technical Schooling

The military services are constantly trying to improve the educational level of their personnel. Many different programs are available to service personnel for general academic improvement.

Vocational and technical schooling has become a major undertaking of the Armed Forces to be able to prepare men and women for the technical work to be performed. The five armed services maintain nearly three hundred technical and specialty training schools. Combined, they offer over one thousand separate courses of instruction. More than three hundred thousand service school students graduate yearly. While in the service, many young men and women learn a trade, skill, or technical occupation that has civilian work application. The programs change frequently to keep pace with the rapid change in equipment and technology.

Officer Candidate School (OCS)

All of the armed services offer officer candidate or training schools. The individual may enter from civilian life or from active duty. The qualifications for admission and length of program vary with the branch of service.

Flight Training Programs

Young men who wish to take training in aviation may find the armed services provide an opportunity for them. Requirements, including school completed, health and physical conditions, and age for entry into the program, vary with the branch of service.

College Programs—Part Time

Servicemen and women may take college credit courses while in the Armed Forces. "During fiscal year 1966 over 380,000 active duty service personnel took off-duty education courses leading to a bachelor's or advanced degrees" (Wieland, 1967, p. 108). Tuition assistance is offered by the Armed Forces for off-duty courses given on military bases or in nearby communities by local colleges or universities. On some military bases college courses are offered by a college or university that has established an educational center on the base. A student may be able to complete a degree or program under the tuition assistance plan. In the fiscal year 1966 over three thousand people earned degrees through off-duty classes. In other cases an individual may take undergraduate or graduate courses that will apply on a program that he hopes to complete upon leaving active military service. After completion of enough courses by working in off-duty time, reassignment may be possible to devote full-time work to completing the degree at the expense of the Armed Forces.

The USAFI offers courses that can be taken for college credit. The courses can then be transferred to a college of the individual's choice to be evaluated for application toward a degree or program.

College Programs—Full Time

Several different full-time college programs are available. These programs may be classified into three groups: (1) ROTC, (2) academies, and (3) college-level specialized programs. Each program is designed to serve a particular need. A brief outline of each of the three groups is presented as first level broad information on educational opportunities available in the armed services for college-level work. For specific and more depth information, resource material should be obtained on the specific program desired.

The Army, Navy, and Air Force have nearly 475 ROTC programs at approximately 300 public and private colleges and universities throughout the United States. ROTC training is comprised of from three to five hours of military instruction a week and some summer training periods. The individual is enrolled in a full-time college program while also taking the ROTC training. ROTC graduates fulfill their military obligation by serving on active duty as reserve officers for stipulated periods of time, ranging from six months to six years. Counselors should help young people know the different colleges offering the ROTC programs associated with the branch of service in which the individual is interested. Because of the role ROTC can have in a young man's life, the counselor may need to help each become aware of the ROTC possibilities in connection with a college education.

The Navy and Marines have had a ROTC scholarship program for several years. When the ROTC Vitalization Act of 1964 was passed, the Army and Air Force were also able to offer a scholarship program. The

ROTC Vitalization Act of 1964 provided increased opportunities and advantages for young men enrolled in, or about to enter, college. It continued the traditional four-year ROTC program and provided a new two-year program for students who were unable to participate in ROTC during their first two years of college or junior college. The Act also authorized financial assistance in the form of ROTC scholarships for carefully selected students in the four-year program. Each branch of service has specific plans, which are modified from time to time. A counselor would need to have general information available on each program and to refer to resource persons for specific information.

The Army, Navy, Air Force, Coast Guard, and Merchant Marine each has an academy offering four years of college education leading to a bachelor of science degree. Cadets and midshipmen receive pay, room and board, books, and tuition free while attending. Upon completion of the program, graduates, with the exception of the Merchant Marine Academy, receive regular commissions and must serve on active duty for at least five years after being commissioned. Merchant Marine Academy graduates are obligated to sail for at least three years in the Merchant Marine. Most appointments to the academies are effective immediately following graduation from high school. The young man, aged seventeen to twenty-two, to be eligible must be single and never have been married, a citizen of the United States, of good moral character, and physically and academically qualified. Appointments to the academies differ. Merchant Marine Academy candidates must receive a Congressional nomination. Coast Guard Academy appointments are made only on the basis of national competition with no Congressional appointments or state quotas. The other three academies have nominations that are grouped into two types: competitive among candidates within each group (such as Presidential nominations, regular and reserve units, sons of deceased veterans, honor military or naval school and ROTC) and noncompetitive, where the nominating authority designates his nominees in order of personal preference.

College-level specialized programs in addition to ROTC and the academies do exist. Each program is designed for a specific function. The following are examples:

Air Force Airman Education and Commissioning Program
Air Force "Operation Bootstrap" Terminal TDY Programs
Army Degree Completion Program
Army Enlisted Schooling
Marine Corps College Degree Program
Navy College Degree Program
Navy Enlisted Scientific Education

Special Military Schools

In addition to the many educational programs previously listed, the Armed Forces have special military schools. Three of these are listed for illustrative purposes.

The National War College is operated as a top-level interservice school for highly selected senior military officers and civilian career officials.

The Industrial College of the Armed Forces is the capstone of the U.S. military educational system. The college offers two extension programs and a ten-month residential course for selected senior officers of the military services and civilian executives of the Government within the national security structure.

The Armed Forces Staff College prepares selected military officers for duty in all echelons of joint and combined commands.

Occupational Development During Military Service

Service in the military is actually time spent in an occupation. Each military man and woman is assigned a job to perform. The jobs performed may vary from time to time and opportunities exist for developing skills and gaining new knowledge that will facilitate occupational mobility. With the average length of time spent in the military service by each individual being only a few years, the turnover in each job classification is high. The number of openings occurring each year in each job classification is generally sufficient to ensure opportunities for occupational mobility to those who want to change and can develop themselves to the extent that they are qualified for advancement.

Jobs in the Armed Forces often are training grounds for civilian occupations. Many of the military occupations have direct relationship with civilian occupations. While in the military service, many young men and women obtain specialized training and education for the military jobs in which they participate. The training and education generally are integrated or closely associated with experience in a particular job. Thus, an individual has during his military service opportunities to learn new occupational skills and to gain the experience that may be essential for his own growth and development.

If military service is perceived as an integral part of an overall life plan, then time spent in the Armed Forces may become a meaningful part of one's occupational development. The Armed Forces of the United States are of such magnitude, with a wide range of occupational potentials, that, if an individual would plan his future, military service may contribute to his occupational development. In some cases qualified enlistees may choose, and be guaranteed, the occupational field of their choice prior to enlistment if an opening is available in the occupational field.

In an examination of the occupations in the different military services, a high percentage (80 to 90 per cent) are in noncombatant roles, including electrical and mechanical equipment operation, maintenance, and repair; administrative and clerical; service and supply; electronic equipment operation, maintenance, and repair; communication and intelligence work; crafts; medical and dental technical specialties; and other technical and allied work. The military service time may be somewhat planned and purposefully integrated into long-range life plans so that military service in relation to occupational development is possibly a forward thrust rather than a segment of time lost. For many, the military becomes the life career for upward to thirty years.

For some individuals, military service may provide the opportunity for a new environment where occupational development may spring forth. Repeatedly in sociological studies data have been gathered to support the concept that environments do affect individual development. The military service may be the environmental change that will enable some persons to perceive themselves differently. The alternatives available in the military service may then become opportunities for occupational development. In some cases, personalized information prior to military service may assist an individual to perceive military service as a time in which occupational development may occur for him. For others the information may have meaning only after entering the service.

Military Service and Implications for the Family

Military information is more than just information on different branches of service and the occupations associated with each. Military information has implications for the individual who may serve and those who associate with him. Each member of the family is affected, not just the one in military service. His family—parents, brothers, sisters, wife or husband, and children—are often deeply affected by the individual's military service—prior to, during, and afterwards.

Development of Family Unit

Thousands of young unmarried men and women enter the service each year. Many of them serve their entire time in the Armed Forces as single persons, whereas many others either enter as married or become married during their military service. The potential for and the effects upon the family unit while one or more of the family members are in the service is of major importance to a large percentage of military personnel. For many persons the length of time they stay in the Armed

Forces, beyond the minimum, may be determined by the opportunities, as they perceive them, for developing the family unit.

Family members or potential family members (bride- or groom-to-be) of military personnel may need information. In some cases the family can stay together, with housing being rented or purchased near the military base or furnished on the military base. In those cases the family unit may be perceived quite differently from those in which the military person is serving in a geographic area other than the one in which the other family members are living.

Opportunities and Privileges

Members of the immediate families of military personnel have various opportunities and privileges. All military installations offer military personnel and their dependents exchange and commissary privileges. At these facilities most necessities can be purchased at prices lower than those paid in civilian-operated stores.

Medical care for dependents of active duty and retired personnel at military facilities is authorized when available. It is also authorized, under certain circumstances, at civilian hospitals for dependents of active duty personnel only. Whereas dental care is authorized for all active duty personnel, routine dental care is provided for dependents at certain remote installations and overseas.

Military personnel of pay grade E-4 or above (Corporal in the Army or Marine Corps, Sergeant in the Air Force, and Petty Officer 3d Class in the Navy or Coast Guard) with at least four years service are eligible for military housing. If government quarters are available, the occupants may choose to relinquish their basic allowance for quarters. Proposed legislation (known as the Hubbell Plan) may change military pay and the allowance for quarters.

Recreation facilities for military personnel and their families are provided at most military bases. The cost to the individual is small in comparison to that in privately operated recreational centers.

Consultation services frequently are available for military personnel and their families. For example, legal assistance officers and supporting agencies under governmental control—local welfare groups and the aid society of each service are available whenever assistance is needed. Help may be obtained in regard to financial and personal affairs through governmental agencies or services offered in the branch of service to which the person is attached.

Sons and daughters of military personnel have opportunities for financial assistance in obtaining education. In obtaining appointments, such as to military academy, a military personnel dependent may have opportunities not available to boys and girls whose parents are not and have not been in military service.

Travel opportunities prevail for families while one or more of the members are in the military services. Travel overseas as well as to different parts of the United States often are afforded families. The entire family may be able to grow and develop as a result of experiencing different cultures, climates, and environments. Travel may be used to broaden the horizons and provide a backdrop of experiences that may help the family achieve goals otherwise difficult or impossible to obtain.

Disability and Death Benefits

A serviceman is assured under Federal legislation that his dependents—wife, children, and financially dependent parents—will be provided financial means if he dies while on active duty or following discharge as a result of disability. The Veterans Administration is responsible for administering most of the programs.

Service personnel are fully covered by the Federal Old Age and Survivors' Insurance (Social Security) program. They pay the same rates for coverage as civilians and receive the same benefits. Thus, Social Security survivors' benefits for a deceased service person's dependents would be additional to those provided through other legislative means.

When a service person suffers physical disability, he may be discharged or, if eligible, retired and given financial compensation. The money generally is paid monthly, either through the branch of service or the Veterans Administration.

Retirement

The retirement plans available to military personnel often affect the family plans and attitudes of family members. The laws under which personnel may meet requirements for retirement are numerous, but in general may be classified under three types of retirement plans: length of service with twenty or more years being the minimum, physical disability, and, in the case of officers only, age.

The amount of retirement pay received is dependent upon various factors. If retiring on the basis of length of service, then the rank or grade held at time of retirement and the length of time in service become the determining factors. If retiring because of physical disability, then the degree of disability governs the amount of compensation. The degree of disability is determined by disability evaluation boards and may range from 10 per cent to total disability.

For many service personnel retirement at twenty to thirty years of active service comes early enough in their lives so that they look forward to a new career in civilian life. Some may work long enough in the civilian job also to build up a regular retirement fund that will begin at age 65 or sooner. The retirement pay may not be as essential in the individual's long-range occupational planning as is the new career in civilian life. Planning for the new career may be very influential in family plans, particularly if children are still in the home.

Transition from Military to Civilian Life

Just as an individual may need information to understand fully the military role and to make the transition from civilian life into military service, he may need information to make the transition back from military to civilian life. After one has spent some two to thirty years in the military service, civilian life and his understanding of how he may fit into it have changed.

Job counseling and job placement for veterans is provided by local state employment offices, in cooperation with the Veterans Employment Service of the United States Department of Labor. Under the law, counseling and priority for training programs or job openings are provided. The law also gives veterans preference in securing civil service jobs.

The job(s) performed in military service may have a direct relationship to civilian jobs. Several publications are available that list military jobs and their relationships to civilian work. Counselors may need such information to help individuals in understanding the relationship between military and civilian occupations.

Returning to civilian life may not be and probably should not be in most cases, a pickup or continuation of civilian life from where it was left prior to military service. Changes have occurred in the individual while in the service. For one thing he or she is older and two to six additional years added when one is eighteen to twenty-four years of age often make major differences in one's life patterns. Also, additional education probably was obtained while in service. The education obtained may enable the person to assume new kinds of responsibilities. Occupational experiences while in service probably also changed the individual. The travel and interpersonal relationships made possible through military service probably also helped to bring about changes in the person.

While in military service many men and women change their family obligations—they marry, are divorced, become parents, or increase the number of children. The assumption of different family responsibilities makes the person a different individual.

Military experiences coupled with time and the processes of living have enabled the individual probably to formulate attitudes and concepts somewhat different from those he held when he entered the service. The same is probably true about the old gang with which the individual did associate. He may find that he is alienated from his own former peers and concepts.

All of the changes may be, but more frequently are not, in the cognitive and affective processes of the individual. An ongoing information process throughout the time one is in the military service may help make the transition, but probably additional information, assistance, and perhaps counseling will be needed to provide a meaningful transition from military to civilian life. The change should be smooth enough to be an integral part of the long-range plans and development of the person rather than a time in which crisis or traumatic experiences are produced.

Veterans' Benefits

Upon having completed a period of military service, an individual has many benefits to which he is entitled under existing laws pertaining to veterans. The Veterans Administration is an active governmental agency that has the responsibility of providing the assistance available under the law for veterans and their families. Each veteran has need for understanding the personal benefits available to him. Awareness of these is only one step in the process. Veterans need to understand the personal implications of available benefits at the times when they are applicable. Because veterans' benefits are dependent upon various factors associated with an individual's period of military service, information pertaining to veterans' benefits may be meaningful prior to and during military service as well as following.

Educational Opportunities

The Veterans' Readjustment Benefits Act of 1966 (Cold War GI Bill) was passed to provide educational assistance for veterans who served on active duty with the Armed Forces after January 31, 1955. A qualified individual can pursue an approved course at a (public or private) college, vocational, business, correspondence, or high school. The bill provides up to thirty-six months of benefit based on length of service. The monthly benefits received are determined by class load in school and number of dependents. Any veteran is eligible who was honorably discharged and meets one of the following: served continuously on active duty for a period of at least 181 days, any part of which was after January 31, 1955; discharged or released from service because of service-connected disability and has less than 181 days; or served on active duty for at least two years and was discharged after the bill was passed.

Loans

To eligible veterans and active duty servicemen the Cold War GI Bill guaranteed loans for homes and farms from private lenders. In certain circumstances direct loans are available from the Veterans Administration. The loans may be for the purchase of homes; to make alterations, repairs, or improvements in homes already owned and occupied; to purchase farms or farm supplies or equipment; to obtain farm working capital; or to refinance delinquent indebtedness on property to be used or occupied by the veteran as a home or for farming purposes.

Many counselors will not be in a position to give all the specifics on loans available to veterans; however, general information about loans available may be needed by individuals as they plan their future. The information may be valuable prior to service as well as during or following.

Medical Care

Veterans are assured under the Cold War GI Bill of medical care including hospitalization, pre- and post-hospital care, outpatient treatment, prosthetic appliances, medical examinations, aid for the blind, and aid for the chronically incapacitated. In addition to the Cold War GI Bill are the Veterans Administration Hospitals to which eligible veterans can go for medical care.

Benefits for Veterans' Children

Several different benefits are available to veterans' children. The Veterans Administration is responsible for administering a bill that provides monthly payments to children of deceased or service-connected disabled (50 per cent or more) veterans of World War I, II, and the Korean War. These benefits are paid to age eighteen but may be extended to age twenty-three if the veteran's child remains unmarried and attends an approved school.

The Junior GI Bill (War Orphans Educational Act) is one of the largest sources of financial aid to children of veterans. Many who are eligible are not taking advantage of the benefits provided. Probably many eligible persons are not aware that the bill applies to them. Eligible persons are students whose parents died or are permanently and totally disabled from disease or injury incurred or aggravated in the Armed Forces after the beginning of the Spanish-American War and prior to the termination of inductions under the Universal Military Training and Service Act. Students generally must be between eighteen and twenty-three years of age and may have one living parent. In exceptional cases, earlier or later use of the benefits may be allowed. The student may receive up to thirty-six months of training and education in an approved (public or private) college, vocational school, business school, or other educational institution. Any student (starting at age fourteen) handicapped by physical or mental functions from normal pursuit of education may obtain special restorative training or retraining to restore or improve his condition. Examples are speech and voice correction, lip reading, and Braille reading and writing. The total number eligible to receive the monthly cash benefits available through the Junior GI Bill is approximately 185,000 (Wieland, 1967, p. 110).

In addition to the programs previously listed, children are often eligible for other benefits. The Veterans Administration should be contacted for the latest information. In some cases assistance can be obtained through programs available for children of each specific branch of service. Army (write The Adjutant General, Department of the Army), Navy and Marine Corps (write the Chief of Naval Personnel), and Air Force (write the Air Force Aid Society).

Keeping Abreast of Changes in Military Information

As in all other educational, occupational, and personal-social information, updating military information requires continuous vigilance on the part of the counselor. Several media are available to facilitate staying abreast of changes in military laws, policies, practices, and educational and vocational opportunities. The media would include subscriptions and services, newspapers and magazine reports, current publications, consultations with local recruiting officers of the various armed services, interviews with members of the draft board, and radio and television broadcasts.

Subscriptions and services received regularly would help the counselor and his counselees to maintain up-to-date information. Also, anticipating the regularity of the arrival of the information could stimulate watchfulness on the part of users. Examples of subscriptions and services are the following:

High School News Service Report, U.S. Department of Defense; free. Published monthly during the school year. Factual information about the Armed Forces. Written for secondary school level. Obtained from High School News Service, Great Lakes, Illinois.

Army Times, Air Force Times, Navy Times: Reports, Army Times Publishing Company; $8.50 a year. Published weekly.

The counselor may obtain military information through *commercial publishers; associations* and *organizations,* such as the American Legion, the Veterans of Foreign Wars, AMVETS, the Disabled American Veterans Auxiliary, and the Central Committee for Conscientious Objectors; and Federal, state, and local *government units.* A counselor, by requesting that his name be included on a mailing list, can receive notifications of publications regularly and may in certain cases receive complimentary copies.

Specific governmental units from which information may be obtained include the following:

Department of the Army
U.S. Air Force Recruiting Service
U.S. Coast Guard
Department of the Navy
Headquarters of the Marine Corps
Defense Advisory Committee on Women in the Services
The National War College
Industrial College of the Armed Forces
Armed Forces Staff College

Consultations with local recruiting officers and members of the local draft board can be excellent sources of information on changes in laws, policies, and procedures. Recruiting officers of the various armed services generally are excellent resource persons; however, they do have a duty to recruit; therefore, certain information obtained may be slanted to this purpose. If both the counselor and the counselee recognize this fact and view such information as only part of the total picture and if other steps can be taken to obtain additional information from various other sources, the information can be meaningful. Policies and procedures of the local draft board members concern the clientele of the counselor under various conditions—as a potential draftee, his parent, a member of potential draftee's family or his friend—as well as help the counselor to keep abreast of the changes.

Radio and television reports frequently are sources for obtaining news items pertaining to changes in military information. The information acquired through these media is usually concise and brief; therefore, additional information probably will be needed before action based on the reports can be implemented.

Coding, Filing, Storage, and Retrieval

Military information by its very nature may have a more compelling need to be known and understood by more individuals than information in any of the other areas. An individual may elect not to investigate educational and occupational information in general, but military information becomes necessary to many people because of the Universal Military Training and Service Act. Boys and young men, their parents, other members of their families, and their friends are forced to be involved with concerns and decisions about the armed services.

The military information needed probably will include at least three major concerns: laws and regulations, educational and training opportunities, and occupational development. Not all military information available can be specifically identified in one of the three major concerns. Some materials requested may be of a general nature. Each of these areas will involve different individuals in various roles, and the information needed by each will vary in depth. Individuals needing information may be students at various school levels; individuals with special needs—handicapped, disadvantaged, academically talented, or potential drop-out; parents, teachers, counselors; or other adults—women veterans, and so on. The depth of information needed may be for gaining broad concepts concerning the armed services, for resource or reference information, or for feedback—to check on the soundness of a decision.

Military information can be analyzed by the 3-D concept (see Table 7-1) to identify the potential users and the depth of the information. If no effective coding system has been established or new files are being set up, the analysis by the 3-D concept could be used effectively as a code. Materials would be coded, filed, stored, and retrieved: first, through identification of the potential users; second, by the area covered by the material; and third, by the depth—broadening, resource, or feedback.

The 3-D concept with its analysis system and symbols provides a coding that could be used for filing military information. The extent of analysis needed for serving the clientele in a given setting may indicate that the symbols used in Table 7-1 are insufficient. If such is the case, then additional symbols could be added and the file code would be expanded accordingly. An example of additional subdivisions could be symbols for each of the five branches of service in order to analyze the extent of information pertinent to each. The counselor in the local setting can determine the number of subdivisions needed and can add the ones most meaningful to his work.

Storage and retrieval for military information are similar to those provided in Chapters 7 and 12 for educational and occupational information.

Sample Materials and Sources

Materials for various age levels concerning the Armed Forces serve different purposes. Individuals may become aware of the armed services and gain certain information from fiction and nonfiction books, films and filmstrips, older brothers and sisters, parents, relatives, friends, and other sources. The military information available to be selected for a particular setting will be determined by the needs of the potential users with whom the counselor works.

Samples of materials and their sources are listed according to elementary, junior high, and senior high schools. Some of these materials are pertinent to individuals in other than school settings and just as well could have been listed for them. The list is not intended to be comprehensive but to be illustrative of various materials available.

In addition to the title of the information and source, each one is analyzed according to the 3-D concept (see Table 7-1 for the analysis code), showing the classification of individuals to whom the information would be suitable, the area and subarea of coverage, and the depth of utilization. This analysis with symbols for classification of material is designated a "code." If a counselor has not developed his own effective filing arrangement, the analysis code could be the arrangement for filing the materials.

ELEMENTARY SCHOOL MATERIALS

They Flew to Glory. Book. Lothrop, Lee & Shepard Company, Inc., $3.50. Account of American fighter pilots during World War I. (For pupils. Code: Si–Pmg–1)

Soldiers and Armies. Book. Lothrop, Lee & Shepard Company, Inc.; $4.95. History of soldiering. (For pupils. Code: Si–Pmg–2)

The Story of Fighting Ships. Book, fiction. Lothrop, Lee & Shepard Company, Inc.; $4.95. Informative survey of ships and weapons. (For pupils. Code: Si–Pmg–1)

The Story of Knights and Armor. Book, fiction and nonfiction. Lothrop, Lee & Shepard Company, Inc.; $4.95. Traces the development of heavy cavalry and is informative on warfare and society. (For pupils. Code: Si–Pmg–1)

Soldiers and Sailors: What They Do. Book. Harper Brothers; $2.19. Beginning reader about military life. (For teacher to use with pupils. Code: Sk–Pmg–1)

The Air Force. Book. The Viking Press, Inc.; $3.00. (For pupils. Code: Si–Pmg–1)

The Army. Book. The Viking Press, Inc.; $3.00. (For pupils. Code: Si–Pmg–1)

The Coast Guard. Book. The Viking Press, Inc.; $3.00. (For pupils. Code: Si–Pmg–1)

The Marine Corps. Book. The Viking Press, Inc.; $3.00. (For pupils. Code: Si–Pmg–1)

The Navy. Book. The Viking Press, Inc.; $3.00. (For pupils. Code: Si–Pmg–1)

JUNIOR HIGH SCHOOL MATERIALS

Annapolis: The Life of a Midshipman, revised edition. Book. Lothrop, Lee & Shepard Company, Inc.; $4.95. Picture-story of midshipman's life. (For students. Code: Sj–Pme–1)

The Coast Guard Academy: The Life of a Cadet. Book. Lothrop, Lee & Shepard Company, Inc.; $4.95. Picture-story of cadet's life. (For students. Code: Sj–Pme–1)

U.S. Air Force Academy: The Life of a Cadet, Revised edition. Book. Lothrop,

Lee & Shepard Company, Inc.; $4.95. Picture-story of cadet's life. (For students. Code: Sj–Pme–1)

West Point: The Life of a Cadet, revised edition. Book. Lothrop, Lee & Shepard Company, Inc.; $4.95. Picture-story of cadet's life. (For students. Code: Sj–Pme–1)

This Is the Air Force Academy. Book. Dodd, Mead, & Company; $1.75. Discussion of life and training of an Air Force cadet through the use of pictures and texts. (Code: Sj–Pme–2)

Air Force Academy: Cadets, Training, and Equipment. Booklet. Coward-McCann, Inc.; $2.86. (Code: Sj–Pme–2)

West Point: Cadets, Training and Equipment. Book. Coward-McCann, Inc.; $2.86. Story of cadet's first days. (For students. Code: Sj–Pme–1)

SENIOR HIGH SCHOOL MATERIALS

One-Third of a Nation—A Report on Young Men Found Unqualified for Military Service. U.S. Government Printing Office. (For counselor's information. Code: Csi–Pmg–2)

Student's Guide to Military Services. Book. Channel Press; $5.95. (For students. Code: Ss–Pmg–2)

Reserve Officers Training Corps—Campus Pathways to Service. Book. Richard Rosen Press, Inc.; $3.78. Different ROTC programs in colleges. (For counselor working with students. Code: CSs–Pme–2)

You and the Armed Services. Book. Pocket Books, Inc.; $1.25. Facts and details of the branches of the armed services. (For counselor working with students. Code: CSs–Pmg–2)

Armed Forces Specialists. Film. A.F. Film Library Center. Description of duties and responsibilities of women officers in Army, Navy, and Air Force who are dieticians, physical therapists, and occupational therapists. (For students. Code: Ss–Pme–2)

Cold War GI Bill: Veterans Readjustment Benefit Act of 1966. Booklet. American Legion; free. (For students. Code: Ss–Pml–2)

Plan Early for Your Future Education: Junior GI Bill. American Legion; free. (For students. Code Ss–Pml–2)

You and the Draft. Book. Richard Rosen Press, Inc.; $3.78. Draft provisions and how they affect young men. (For students. Code: Ss–Pmg–1)

How to Qualify for the Service Academies. Book. Richard Rosen Press, Inc.; $3.78. Steps necessary for entrance into the academies. (For students. Code: Ss–Pme–2)

You and Your Military Obligation. Book. Guidance Associates; $5.95. (For students. Code: Ss–Pml–2)

Classrooms in the Military: An Account of Education in the Armed Forces of the United States. Book. Teachers College Press; $3.95. (For counselor. Code: Csi–Pme–2)

Army Occupations and You. Booklet. Department of the Army; free. (For students. Code: Ss–Pmo–2)

U.S. Military Academy Preparatory School Catalogue. Department of the Army; free. (For students. Code: Ss–Pme–2)

Profile of Entering Class—U.S. Naval Academy. Booklet. Department of the Navy; free. (For counselor working with students. Code: CSs–Pme–2)

Navy Waves (Enlisted Women). Booklet. Department of the Navy; free. (For students. Code: Ss–Pmo–2)

Pocket Guide to Air Force Opportunities. Booklet. U.S. Air Force Recruiting Service; free. (For students. Code: Ss–Pmo–2)

U.S. Air Force Occupational Handbook. Book. U.S. Air Force Recruiting Service; free. (For counselor working with students. Code: CSs–Pmo–2)

A Guide to Occupational Training. Booklet. U.S. Marine Corps; free. (For students. Code: Ss–Pme–2)

What the Marine Corps Offers You. Booklet. U.S. Marine Corps; free. (For students. Code: Ss–Pmg–1)

U.S. Coast Guard—A Career Service. Booklet. U.S. Coast Guard; free. (For students. Code: Ss–Pmo–1)

U.S. Coast Guard Academy. Booklet. U.S. Coast Guard; free. (For students. Code: Ss–Pme–2)

Horizons Unlimited for Women in the Air Force. Booklet. Defense Advisory Committee on Women in the Services; free. (For students. Code: Ss–Pmg–1)

U.S. Service Admission Tests. U.S. Air Force Recruiting Service; free. Air Force material, which consists of colored booklets indicating some of the opportunities in the Air Force. (For counselor working with students. Code: CSs–Pmg–2)

U.S. Service Academy Admission Tests. Book. Arco Publishing Company, Inc.; $4.00. For young men who are interested in one of the five service academies. The book is composed of sample questions, reading comprehension, spatial relations, and many others. (Code: Ss–Pme–2)

Utilization of Military Information

The counselor's role in utilizing military information is similar to that for other areas of information in helping each individual personalize information for his decision-making. Because military information is associated with laws requiring military service, an individual may resist the integration of military information into his own perceived world. Because the individual is anxious about military obligations as they pertain to himself or his friends, he may have emotional anxieties that block him from evaluating military information in the same way he evaluates other educational and occupational information.

An individual must make basic personal decisions concerning his involvement in military services and/or affairs, whether for two years or for a lifetime career, or as one among several alternatives. For the young man considering alternative service, the decision may involve a real identity search. Individual differences are as important in planning for future military service as they are in formulating civilian educational and vocational plans.

Utilizing military information to build a reservoir of accurate, complete, and current information would involve various classifications of media: prestructured and fixed, input controlled by the individual, simulation of situation, and real situation (see Table 8-1). As is true for other areas of information, a combination of these media will need to be used for facilitating personalizing military information for individuals. Individuals of all ages are involved in the need for such information.

The team approach can be effective in assisting the individual to meet his needs in the military information area. The team may be a combination of various people—counselor, teacher, recruitment personnel, religious leaders, and others. For example, the teacher working with students in the classroom can relate the pertinent subject content to military as well as to civilian education, occupation, and benefits. Materials or comments that will pressure or convince any individual to act in one way or another should be avoided. Instead, the individual should have complete and objective information from various sources to use as a foundation in making his decisions and long-range plans. The counselor can work with the teacher by making available pertinent information, participating in classroom activities, and obtaining resource persons in relation to military information.

Many of the media discussed in previous chapters can be used effectively for utilizing military information. Some of the media may need adaptation. One example of adaptation would be an Armed Forces night similar in structure to college or career night. Brophy (1964, p. 34) stated that the counselor's skill is directed toward providing two types of assistance: to help an individual obtain complete and unbiased information and to facilitate reflection and self-analysis by the individual. Military information may be one of the most prejudicially presented materials today. If the counselor and the counselee both understand the biases of the presenter in the information being consulted and will cross-check with additional information, the information even though biased, may meet a need of the individual in affording him the opportunity to consider all angles of military information for himself.

The extent of effectiveness in utilizing military information will depend upon such factors as the availability of information, the attitudinal climate concerning the information both on the part of the provider and the user, the alternatives available, and the impact of the developmental and sequential utilization versus a hit-and-miss approach.

Summary

Military information is interwoven into all areas of an individual's life—personal, social, educational, and vocational. This area of information affects a broader segment of the population than just individuals in active service. It affects families, relatives, and friends as well. Many of the prevailing laws are applicable to families of military personnel; and the benefits, opportunities, and privileges, if fully understood, could be meaningful to individuals and their families. The counselor's role is similar to the personalization required in the other areas of information.

Military information includes educational opportunities made available by the Armed Forces prior to, during, and following military service. The training is varied, with implications for civilian occupations as well as military jobs. Educational courses available range from elementary school subjects through work applicable toward doctorate degrees with all or part of the expenses paid by the Armed Services. The educational programs are of various types including correspondence, off-duty courses, part-time work, and full-time, on-duty, college-level degree programs.

The materials to have available will depend on the needs of the clientele served in the counselor setting—students, parents, and other adults, including servicemen and -women. Such information is available from many sources, including subscriptions and services, commercial publishers, associations and organizations, governmental units, and various people as consultants.

Military information will help the individual who enters the service to obtain the best military assignment for himself, will assist him in gaining maximum benefits for his growth and development during the service, and will enable him to return to civilian life as a contributing member utilizing the experiences and opportunities gained in the service. Counselors in various settings will need to help personalize the military information.

SELECTED REFERENCES

Baer, Max F., and Edward C. Roeber. *Occupational Information: The Dynamics of Its Nature and Use.* Chicago: Science Research Associates, Inc., 1964. Pp. 98–102.

Brophy, Alfred L. "Guidance on Military Alternatives: An Ethical Dilemma," *The Vocational Guidance Quarterly,* 13 (Autumn 1964), 31–36.

Clark, Harold F., and Harold S. Sloan. *Classrooms in the Military: An Account of Education in the Armed Forces of the United States.* New York: Institute for Instructional Improvement, Inc., Teachers College Press, Teachers College, Columbia University, 1964. 154 pages.

Gunderson, E. K. Eric, and Paul D. Nelson. "Personality Differences Among Navy Occupational Groups," *The Personnel and Guidance Journal,* 44 (May 1966), 956–961.

Harwood, Michael. *The Student's Guide to Military Service.* Manhasset, N.Y.: Channel Press, 1963. 313 pages.

Hoppock, Robert. *Occupational Information: Where to Get It and How to*

Use It in Counseling and in Teaching, 3rd ed. New York: McGraw-Hill, Inc., 1967. Pp. 142–144.

Horne, F. W. "Counseling High School Students for Military Services," *National Association of Women Deans and Counselors Journal,* **25,** (April 1962), 117–119.

Isaacson, Lee E. *Career Information in Counseling and Teaching.* Boston: Allyn and Bacon, Inc., 1966. Pp. 255–256.

Norris, Willa, Franklin R. Zeran, and Raymond N. Hatch. *The Information Service in Guidance,* 2nd ed. Chicago: Rand McNally & Company, 1966. Pp. 175–177.

Phi Delta Kappan, **48** (May 1967). Total issue devoted to "The Military and Education."

Wieland, J. Edward, ed. *Need A Lift?* Indianapolis: The American Legion Educational and Scholarship Program, The American Legion, 1967. 128 pages.

APPENDIX

List of Abbreviations

ABE	Adult Basic Education
ACAC	Association of College Admission Counselors
ACE	American Council on Education
ACT	American College Testing Program
BLS	Bureau of Labor Statistics
CAIS	Computer-Assisted Information System
CEEB	College Entrance Examination Board
CIS	Counseling Information Service
CSS	College Scholarship Service
D.O.T.	*Dictionary of Occupational Titles*
EDA	Economic Development Administration
EOA	Economic Opportunity Act
G.E.D.	General Educational Development
HELP	Higher Educational Loan Plan in Massachusetts
HEW	Department of Health, Education, and Welfare
ISVD	Information System for Vocational Decisions
NDEA	National Defense Education Act
NEA	National Education Association
NLRB	National Labor Relations Board
NSF	National Science Foundation
NYC	Neighborhood Youth Corps
OCS	Officer Candidate School
OEK	"Occupational Exploration Kit"
OEO	Office of Economic Opportunity
ROTC	Reserve Officer Training Corps
RVP	Readiness for Vocational Planning
SCOPE	School to College, Opportunities for Postsecondary Education
SICM	*Standard Industrial Classification Manual*
SOS	Specialty-Oriented Student
SRA	Science Research Associates, Inc.
USAFI	United States Armed Forces Institute
USDL	United States Department of Labor
USES	United States Employment Service
USOE	United States Office of Education
VDI	*Vocational Development Inventory*
VIEW	Vocational Information in Education and Work
VISTA	Volunteers in Service to America
VOS	Vocational Orientation System
WORK	"Widening Occupational Roles Kit"

432

Address Index

Commercial publishers, organizations, and companies listed as sources in this book are arranged in alphabetical order with the address for each.

A

Abelard-Schuman Limited, 6 West 57th St., New York, N.Y. 10019

Academic Press, Inc., 111 Fifth Ave., New York, N.Y. 10003

Accrediting Commission for Cosmetology Education, Inc., 1286 West Lane Ave., Columbus, O. 43221

Addison-Wesley Publishing Company, Inc., Reading, Mass. 01867

Adult Education Association, 1225 Nineteenth St., N.W., Washington, D.C. 20036

Air Force Aid Society, National Headquarters, Washington, D.C. 20333

Allis-Chalmers Manufacturing Company, 1126 South 70th St., Milwaukee, Wis. 53201

Allyn and Bacon, Inc., 150 Tremont St., Boston, Mass. 02111

Alp Publications, Inc., 3048 North 34th St., Milwaukee, Wis. 53210

Aluminum Company of America, 1501 Alcoa Bldg., Pittsburgh, Pa. 15219

Alumnae Advisory Center, Inc., 541 Madison Ave., New York, N.Y. 10022

American Association of Advertising Agencies, 200 Park Ave., New York, N.Y. 10017

American Association of Dental Schools, 211 East Chicago Ave., Chicago, Ill. 60611

American Association of Junior Colleges, 1315 Sixteenth St., N.W., Washington, D.C. 20036

American Association of University Women, Educational Foundation, 2401 Virginia Ave., N.W., Washington, D.C. 20037

American Astronomical Society, 211 Fitz Randolph Rd., Princeton, N.J. 08540

American Bakers Association, 20 North Wacker Dr., Chicago, Ill. 60606

American Baptist Education Association, Valley Forge, Pa. 19481

American Chemical Society, 1155 Sixteenth St., N.W., Washington, D.C. 20036

American College Admissions Center, Junto School Bldg., 12th and Walnut Sts., Philadelphia, Pa. 19107

American College Personnel Association, 1607 New Hampshire Ave., N.W., Washington, D.C. 20009

American College Testing Programs, Box 767, Iowa City, Ia. 52240

American Council on Education, 1785 Massachusetts Ave., N.W., Washington, D.C. 20036

American Dental Association, 211 East Chicago Ave., Chicago, Ill. 60611

American Dietetic Association, 620 North Michigan Ave., Chicago, Ill. 60611

American Educational Research Association, 1201 Sixteenth St., N.W., Washington, D.C. 20036

AFL-CIO, 815 Sixteenth St., N.W., Washington, D.C. 20006

American Foot Health Foundation, 3310 Sixteenth St., N.W., Washington, D.C. 20010

American Guidance Service, Inc., Publishers Bldg., Circle Pines, Minn. 55014

American Home Economics Association, 1600 Twentieth St., N.W., Washington, D.C. 20009

American Hospital Association, 840 North Lake Shore Dr., Chicago, Ill. 60611

American Hotel and Motel Association, 221 West 57th St., New York, N.Y. 10019

American Institute of Certified Public Accountants, 666 Fifth Ave., New York, N.Y. 10019

American Iron and Steel Institute, 150 East 42nd St., New York, N.Y. 10017

The American Legion Education and Scholarship Program, Dept. A.P.O. Box 1055, Indianapolis, Ind. 46206

American Library Association, 50 East Huron St., Chicago, Ill. 60611

The American Lutheran Church, 422 South Fifth St., Minneapolis, Minn. 55415.

American Medical Association, 535 North Dearborn St., Chicago, Ill. 60610.

American Nurses' Association, 10 Columbus Circle, New York, N.Y. 10019.

American Personnel and Guidance Association, 1607 New Hampshire Ave., N.W., Washington, D.C. 20009

American Petroleum Institute, 1271 Ave. of the Americas, New York, N.Y. 10020

American Psychological Association, 1200 Seventeenth St., N.W., Washington, D.C. 20036

American School Counselor Association, 1607 New Hampshire Ave., N.W., Washington, D.C. 20009

American Society of Biological Chemists, Inc., 9650 Rockville Pike, Bethesda, Md. 20014

American Society of Traffic and Transportation, 22 West Madison St., Room 404, Chicago, Ill. 60602

American Sociological Association, 1755 Massachusetts Ave. N.W., Washington, D.C. 20036

American Trucking Association, 1616 P St., N.W., Washington, D.C. 20036

American Veterinary Medical Association, 600 South Michigan Ave., Chicago, Ill. 60605

American Vocational Association, Inc., 1025 Fifteenth Street, N.W., Washington, D.C. 20005

Arco Publishers, 219 Park Ave. South, New York, N.Y. 10003

Armed Forces Film Library Center, 8900 South Broadway, St. Louis, Mo. 63125 (for specific films contact local recruiting station)

Armstrong Cork Company, Liberty and Charlotte Sts., Lancaster, Pa. 17604

Army Times Publishing Co., 2201 M St., N.W., Washington, D.C. 20037

Associated Master Barbers and Beauticians of America, 537 South Dearborn St., Chicago, Ill. 60605

Associated Publishers' Guidance Publications Center, 355 State St., Los Altos, Calif. 94022

Association of American Railroads, 815 Seventeenth St., N.W., Washington, D.C. 20006

Association of College Admissions Counselors, 610 Church St., Evanston, Ill. 60201

Association Films, Inc., 347 Madison Ave., New York, N.Y. 10017

Association for Higher Education, 1201 Sixteenth St., N.W., Washington, D.C. 20006

Association Press, 70 Fifth Ave., New York, N.Y. 10011

Audio-Visual Centers, Indiana University, Bloomington, Ind. 47401

B

Barron's Educational Series, Inc., 113 Crossways Park Dr., Woodbury, N.Y. 11797

Bellman Publishing Company, P.O. Box 172, Cambridge, Mass. 02138

Benefic Press, 1900 North Narragansett Ave., Chicago, Ill. 60639

B'nai B'rith Vocational Service, 1640 Rhode Island Ave., N.W., Washington, D.C. 20036

The Bobbs-Merrill Company Inc., 4300 West 62nd St., Indianapolis, Ind. 46206

W. C. Brown Company, Publishers, 135 South Locust St., Dubuque, Ia. 52001

Bruce, Martin M., 340 Oxford Rd., New Rochelle, N.Y. 10804

Bunting & Lyon, Inc., 238 North Main St., Wallingford, Conn. 06492

Bureau of Educational Research and Service (see Iowa, State University of)

Bureau of Publications, Teachers College (see Teachers College Press)

Burgess Publishing Company, 426 South Sixth St., Minneapolis, Minn. 55415

C

California Test Bureau, Del Monte Research Park, Monterey, Calif. 93940

Careers, P.O. Box 135. Largo, Fla. 33540

Cathedral Films, Inc., 2921 West Alameda Ave., Burbank, Calif. 91505

Catholic College Bureau, 25 East Jackson Blvd., Chicago, Ill. 60604

The Center for Applied Research in Education, Inc., 70 Fifth Ave. New York, N.Y. 10011

The Center for Psychological Service, 1835 "Eye" St., N.W., Washington, D.C. 20006

Central Committee for Conscientious Objectors, Room 300, 2006 Walnut St., Philadelphia, Pa. 19103

Chamber of Commerce (contact local office)

Channel Press (see Meredith Press)

Children's Press, Inc., 1224 West Van Buren St., Chicago, Ill. 60607

Chronicle Guidance, Inc., Moravia, N.Y. 13118

The College Blue Book, P.O. Box 311, Yonkers, N.Y. 10702

College Entrance Examination Board, 475 Riverside Drive, New York, N.Y. 10027

College Planning Programs, Ltd., P.O. Box 76327, Sanford Station, Los Angeles, Calif. 90005

Columbia University Press, 2960 Broadway, New York, N.Y. 10027
Consulting Psychologists Press, 577 College Ave., Palo Alto, Calif. 94306
Coronet Films, Coronet Bldg., Chicago, Ill. 60611
Council for Church and Ministry, 287 Park Ave. South, New York, N.Y. 10010
Council on Hotel, Restaurant, and Institutional Education, Statler Hall, Ithaca, N.Y. 14850
Council of Student Personnel Associations in Higher Education, c/o Dr. Thomas A. Emmett, University of Detroit, 4001 West McNichols, Detroit, Mich. 48221
Counseling and Personnel Services Information Center, 309 South State St., Ann Arbor, Mich. 48104
Coward-McCann, Inc., 200 Madison Ave., New York, N.Y. 10016
Croner Publications, 211 Jamaica Ave., Queens Village, N.Y. 11428

D

The John Day Company, Inc., 200 Madison Ave., New York, N.Y. 10016
T. S. Denison & Company, Inc., 321 Fifth Ave., South, Minneapolis, Minn. 55415
Dodd, Mead & Company, 79 Madison Ave., New York, N.Y. 10016
Dorsey Press, 1818 Ridge Rd., Homewood, Ill. 60430
Doubleday & Company, Inc., 277 Park Ave., New York, N.Y. 10017

E

Eastman Kodak Company, 343 State St. Rochester, N.Y. 14650
Edu-Craft Inc., 6475 Dubois, Detroit, Mich. 48211
Educational Directories, Inc., Mount Prospect, Ill. 60056
Educational Research Corporation, 10 Craigie St., Cambridge, Mass. 02138
Educational Testing Service, Princeton, N.J. 08540
Educators Progress Service, Randolph, Wis., 53956
Encyclopedia Britannica Films, Inc., 1150 Wilmette Ave., Wilmette, Ill. 60091
Engineers' Council for Professional Development, 345 East 47th St., New York, N.Y. 10017
Equitable Life Assurance Society of the United States, 1285 Ave. of the Americas, New York, N.Y. 10019
Paul S. Erickson, Inc., 119 West 57th St. New York, N.Y. 10019

F

Family Life Publications, Inc., P.O. Box 6725, Durham, N.C. 27708
J. G. Ferguson Company, 6 North Michigan Ave., Chicago, Ill. 60602
Finney Co., 3350 Gorham Service, Minneapolis, Minn. 55426
Follett Publishing Co., 1010 W. Washington Blvd., Chicago, Ill. 60607
Ford Motor Co., The American Rd., Dearborn, Mich. 48121
Free Press of Glencoe (see Macmillan)
Friendship Press, 475 Riverside Dr., New York, N.Y. 10027
Frith Films, 1816 North Highland Ave., Hollywood, Calif. 90028

Funds for Education, Inc., 319 Lincoln St., Manchester, N.H. 03103

G

General Electric Company, 570 Lexington Ave., New York, N.Y. 10022
General Mills, Minneapolis, Minn. 55440
General Motors, P.O. Box 3097, Detroit, Mich. 48231
Golden Press, Inc., 850 Third Ave. New York, N.Y. 10022
Goodwill Industries, Inc. (contact local office)
Gregg Division (see McGraw-Hill)
Grosset & Dunlap, Inc., Publishers, 51 Madison Ave., New York, N.Y. 10010
Guidance Associates, Harcourt, Brace & World, Inc., Pleasantville, N.Y. 10570
Guidance Exchange, P.O. Box 1464, Grand Central Post Office, New York, N.Y. 10017
Guidance Publication Center (see Associated Publishers' Guidance Publication Center)

H

E. M. Hale and Co., 1201 South Hastings Way, Eau Claire, Wis. 54701
John Hancock Mutual Life Insurance Company, 200 Berkeley St., Boston, Mass, 02117
Harcourt, Brace & World, Inc., 757 Third Ave. New York, N.Y. 10017
Harper & Row Publishers, 49 East 33rd St., New York, N.Y. 10016
Harper Brothers (see Harper & Row)
Hastings House, Publishers, Inc., 151 East 50th St., New York, N.Y. 10022
D. C. Heath and Company, 285 Columbus Ave., Boston, Mass. 02116
High School News Service, Building 1B, Great Lakes, Ill. 60088
Holiday House, 18 East 56th St., New York, N.Y. 10022
Holt, Rinehart, and Winston, Inc., 383 Madison Ave., New York, N.Y. 10017
Houghton Mifflin Company, 2 Park St., Boston, Mass. 02107

I

Illinois Institute of Technology, 3300 South Federal St., Chicago, Ill. 60616
Institute of International Education, 809 United Nations Plaza, New York, N.Y. 10017
Institute of Life Insurance, 277 Park Ave., New York, N.Y. 10017
Institute for Personality and Ability Testing, 1602–04 Coronado Dr., Champaign, Ill. 61822
Interagency Committee on Church Vocations, 222 South Downey Ave., Indianapolis, Ind. 46207
International Film Bureau, 332 Michigan Ave., Chicago, Ill. 60604
The Bureau of Educational Research and Service, East Hall, State University of Iowa, Iowa City, Ia. 52240

J

Jam Handy Organization, 2821 East Grand Blvd., Detroit, Mich. 48211
Jossey-Bass, Inc., Publishers, 615 Montgomery St., San Francisco, Calif. 94111

K

Kansas State Teachers College, Bureau of Educational Measurements, Emporia, Kans. 66802

Kiwanis Club (contact local club)

Alfred A. Knopf, Inc., 501 Madison Ave., New York, N.Y. 10022

L

J. B. Lippincott Company, East Washington Sq., Philadelphia, Pa. 19105

Little, Brown and Company, 34 Beacon St., Boston, Mass. 02106

Lothrop, Lee & Shepard Company, Inc., 419 Park Ave. South, New York, N.Y. 10016

M

The Macmillan Company, 866 Third Ave., New York, N.Y. 10022

Maco Publishing Company, Inc., 757 Third Ave., New York, N.Y. 10017

Macrae Smith Company, 225 S. 15th St., Philadelphia, Pa. 19102

Massachusetts Institute of Technology, Cambridge Mass., 02139

McGraw-Hill, Inc., P.O. Box 402, Hightstown, N.J. 08520

David McKay Company, Inc., 750 Third Ave., New York, N.Y. 10017

McKnight and McKnight Publishing Company, U.S. Route 66 at Towanda Ave., Bloomington, Ill. 61701

Meredith Press, 1716 Locust St., Des Moines, Ia. 50303

Charles E. Merrill Books, Inc., 1300 Alum Creek Dr., Columbus, O. 43216

Julian Messner, Inc., 1 West 39th St., New York, N.Y. 10018

Methods and Materials Press, 6 South Derby Rd., Springfield, N.J. 07081

Metropolitan Life Insurance Company, 1 Madison Ave., New York, N.Y. 10010

William Morrow and Company, Inc., 425 Park Ave. South, New York, N.Y. 10016

N

National Association of Manufacturers, 277 Park Ave., New York, N.Y. 10017

National Association for Practical Nurse Education Services, Inc., 535 Fifth Ave., New York, N.Y. 10017

National Association for Retarded Children, 420 Lexington Ave., New York, N.Y. 10017

National Association of Trade and Technical Schools, 1601 Eighteenth St., N.W., Washington, D.C. 20009

National Broadcasting Company, Inc., 30 Rockefeller Plaza, New York, N.Y. 10020

National Cash Register Company, Main and K Sts. Dayton, O. 45409

National Catholic Welfare Conference (see United States Catholic Conference)

National Commission for Social Work Careers, 345 East 46th St., New York, N.Y. 10017

National Committee for Children and Youth, 1145 Nineteenth St., N.W., Washington, D.C. 20036

National Dairy Council, 111 North Canal St., Chicago, Ill. 60606

National Education Association, 1201 Sixteenth St., N.W. Washington, D.C. 20036

National Home Study Council, 1601 Eighteenth St., N.W., Washington, D.C. 20009

National Industrial Conference Board, 845 Third Ave., New York, N.Y. 10022

National Jewish Welfare Board, 145 East 32nd St., New York, N.Y. 10016

National Merit Scholarship Corporation, 1580 Sherman Ave., Evanston, Ill. 60201

The National Scholarship Service and Fund for Negro Students, 6 East 82nd St., New York, N.Y. 10028

National Society for Crippled Children and Adults, 2023 West Ogden Ave., Chicago, Ill. 60612

National University Extension Association, University of Minnesota, 122 Social Science Bldg., Minneapolis, Minn. 55455

National Vocational Guidance Association, 1607 New Hampshire Ave., N.W., Washington, D.C. 20009

Thomas Nelson & Sons, Copewood and Davis Sts. Camden, N.J. 08103

New American Library, Inc., 1301 Ave. of the Americas, New York, N.Y. 10019

New York Life Insurance Company, 51 Madison Ave. New York, N.Y. 10010

O

Oceana Publications, Inc., 40 Cedar St., Dobbs Ferry, N.Y. 10522

The Odyssey Press, Inc., 55 Fifth Ave., New York, N.Y. 10003

Ohio State University Press, Columbus, O. 43210

P

Park Publishing House, 4141 West Vliet St., Milwaukee, Wis. 53208

Pastoral Psychology Teen-Age Guidance Club, P.O. Box 1079, Westbury, N.Y. 11591

Personnel Press, Inc., 20 Nassau St., Princeton, N.J. 08540

Personnel Research Institute, Western Reserve University, Cleveland, O. 44106

Phi Delta Kappa, Eighth St., and Union Ave., Bloomington, Ind. 47401

Pitman Publishing Corporation, 20 East 46th St., New York, N.Y. 10017

Pocket Books, Inc., 630 Fifth Ave., New York, N.Y. 10020

Prakken Publications, 416 Lonshore Dr., Ann Arbor, Mich. 48107

Prentice-Hall, Inc. Englewood Cliffs, N.J. 07632

Prudential Insurance Company of America, Education Department, Box 36 Prudential Plaza, Newark, N.J. 07101

The Psychological Corporation, 304 East 45th St., New York, N.Y. 10017

Psychometric Affiliates, Box 1625, Chicago, Ill. 60690

Public Affairs Committee, Inc., 381 Park Ave. South, New York, N.Y. 10016

G. P. Putnam's Sons, 200 Madison Ave., New York, N.Y. 10016

R

Rand McNally & Company, P.O. Box 7600, Chicago, Ill. 60680

Random House, Inc., 457 Madison Ave., New York, N.Y. 10022

Research Publishing Company, Box 1474, Madison, Wis. 53701
The Ronald Press Company, 15 East 26th St., New York, N.Y. 10010
Richard Rosen Press, Inc., 15 East 26th St., New York, N.Y. 10010

S

Saint Francis College, Brooklyn, N.Y. 11231
Porter Sargent, Publisher, 11 Beacon St., Boston, Mass. 02108
Scholastic Testing Service, Inc., 480 Meyer Rd., Bensenville, Ill. 60106
Science Research Associates, Inc., 259 East Erie St., Chicago, Ill. 60611
Scott, Foresman and Company, 1900 East Lake Ave., Glenview, Ill. 60025
Sheridan Supply Company, P.O. Box 837, Beverly Hills, Calif. 90213
Simmons College, 300 The Fenway, Boston, Mass. 02115
Simon and Schuster, Inc., 630 Fifth Ave., New York, N.Y. 10020
Society for Visual Education, Inc., 1345 Diversey Pkwy., Chicago, Ill. 60614
Sound Seminars, McGraw-Hill, Inc., P.O. Box 402, Hightstown, N.J. 08520
South-Western Publishing Company, 5101 Madison Rd., Cincinnati, O. 45227
Special Libraries Association, 31 East 10th St., New York, N.Y. 10003
Springer Publishing Company, Inc., 200 Park Ave. South, New York, N.Y. 10003
Stanford University Press, Stanford, Calif. 94305
Sterling Movies U.S.A., Inc., 43 West 61st St., New York, N.Y. 10023
C. H. Stoelting Company, 424 North Homan Ave., Chicago, Ill. 60624
Student Admissions Center, P.O. Box 3601, Grand Central Station, New York, N.Y. 10017
Sun Life Assurance Company of Canada, One North LaSalle St., Chicago, Ill. 60602
Syracuse University Press, Box 87, University Station, Syracuse, N.Y. 13210

T

Teachers College Press, Teachers College, Columbia University, 525 West 120th St., New York, N.Y. 10027
Charles C Thomas, Publisher, 301–327 East Lawrence Ave., Springfield, Ill. 62703
Time Inc., Time and Life Bldg., Rockefeller Center, New York, N.Y. 10020

U

United Business Schools Association, 1101 Seventeenth St., N.W., Washington, D.C. 20036
The United Educators, Inc., Educational Center, 801 Greenbay Rd., Lake Bluff, Ill. 60044
The United Presbyterian Church in the U.S.A., 475 Riverside Dr., New York, N.Y. 10027
United States Catholic Conference, 1312 Massachusetts Ave., N.W., Washington, D.C. 20005
United States Government
Administration on Aging (see Department of Health, Education, and Welfare)

Adult Basic Education Program (see Office of Economic Opportunity)

Adult and Vocational Education, Bureau of (see Office of Education)

Agriculture, Department of, Fourteenth St. and Independence Ave., N.W., Washington, D.C. 20250

Air Force, Department of the, The Pentagon, Washington, D.C. 20330

Apprenticeship and Training, Bureau of (see Department of Labor)

Army, Department of the, The Pentagon, Washington, D.C. 20310

Business Economics, Office of, 1832 M St., N.W., Washington, D.C. 20230

Census, Bureau of the, Washington, D.C. 20233

Children's Bureau (see Department of Health, Education, and Welfare)

Civil Service Commission, 1900 E St., N.W., Washington, D.C. 20415

Coast Guard (see Department of the Treasury)

Commerce, Department of, Fourteenth St. between Constitution Ave. and E St. N.W., Washington, D.C. 20230

Community Action Programs (see Office of Economic Opportunity)

Defense, Department of, The Pentagon, Washington, D.C. 20301

Disadvantaged and Handicapped, Office of (see Office of Education)

Economic Development Administration (write local area or field office)

Economic Opportunity, Office of, 1200 Nineteenth St., N.W., Washington, D.C. 20506

Economic Security, Bureau of (see Department of Labor)

Education, Office of, 400 Maryland Ave., S.W., Washington, D.C. 20202

Educational and Cultural Affairs, Bureau of (see Department of State)

Employment Service (see Department of Labor)

Equal Educational Opportunities, Office of (see Office of Education)

Family Services, Bureau of (see Department of Health, Education, and Welfare)

Government Printing Office, Washington, D.C. 20402

Health, Education, and Welfare, Department of, 330 Independence Ave., S.W., Washington, D.C. 20201

Higher Education, Bureau of (see Office of Education)

Internal Revenue Service, Twelfth St. and Constitution Ave., N.W., Washington, D.C. 20225

Job Corps (see Office of Economic Opportunity)

Juvenile Delinquency and Youth Development, Office of (see Department of Health, Education, and Welfare)

Labor, Department of, Fourteenth St. and Constitution Ave., N.W., Washington, D.C. 20210

Labor Standards, Assistant Secretary for (see Department of Labor)

Labor Standards, Bureau of (see Department of Labor)

Labor Statistics, Bureau of (see Department of Labor)

Labor Statistics, Commissioner of (see Department of Labor)

Manpower Administration (see Department of Labor)

Marine Corps, Navy Department, The Pentagon, Washington, D.C. 20380

National Center for Educational Statistics (see Office of Education)

National Labor Relations Board, 1717 Pennsylvania Ave., N.W., Washington, D. C. 20570

National Science Foundation, 1800 G St., N.W., Washington, D.C. 20550

Navy, Department of the, The Pentagon, Washington, D.C. 20350

Neighborhood Youth Corps (see Department of Labor)

Peace Corps (see Department of State)

Research Bureau of (see Office of Education)

State, Department of, 2201 C St., N.W., Washington, D.C. 20520

Superintendent of Documents, Government Printing Office, Washington, D.C. 20402

United States Coast Guard, Department of the Treasury, 1300 E St., N.W., Washington, D.C. 20226

Veterans Administration, Vermont Ave. between H and I Sts., N.W., Washington, D.C. 20420

Veterans Benefits, Office of (see Veterans Administration)

Vocational Rehabilitation Administration (see Department of Health, Education, and Welfare)

Volunteers in Service to America (VISTA) (see Office of Economic Opportunity)

Welfare Administration (see Department of Health, Education, and Welfare)

Women's Bureau (see Department of Labor)

Work Experience Programs (see Office of Economic Opportunity)

Work Training Programs (see Office of Economic Opportunity)

Youth Conservation Corps (see Office of Economic Opportunity)

United States Savings and Loan League, 221 North LaSalle St., Chicago, Ill. 60601

United World Films, 221 Park Ave. South, New York, N.Y. 10003

University of Chicago Press, 5750 Ellis Ave., Chicago, Ill. 60637

University of Michigan Press, 615 East University, Ann Arbor, Mich. 48106

University of North Carolina Press, Box 510, Chapel Hill, N.C. 27514

W. E. Upjohn Institute for Employment Research, 300 South Westnedge Ave., Kalamazoo, Mich. 49007

V

Vantage Press, Inc., 120 W. 31st St., New York, N.Y. 10001

The Viking Press, Inc., 625 Madison Ave., New York, N.Y. 10022

Vocational Films, 111 Euclid Ave., Park Ridge, Ill. 60068

Vocational Guidance Manuals, 235 East 45th St., New York, N.Y. 10017

Vocational Rehabilitation Office (contact local or state office)

W

Wadsworth Publishing Company, Inc., 10 Davis Drive, Belmont, Calif. 94002

Henry A. Walck, Inc., 19 Union Square West, New York N.Y. 10003

Franklin Watts, Inc., 575 Lexington Ave., New York, N.Y. 10022

Western Psychological Services, 12035 Wilshire Blvd., Los Angeles, Calif. 90025

Westinghouse Electric Corp., 3 Gateway Center, Pittsburgh, Pa. 15230

Westminster Press, Witherspoon Bldg., Philadelphia, Pa. 19107

John Wiley & Sons, Inc., 605 Third Ave., New York, N.Y. 10016
The H. W. Wilson Company, 950 University Ave., Bronx, N.Y. 10452
World Trade Academy Press, 50 East 42nd St., New York, N.Y. 10017

XYZ

YWCA and YMCA (contact local office)

INDEXES

Name Index

A

Abegglen, James C., 175, 183, 196–97

Adams, James F., 76, 126, 191, 227, 253, 383

Albee, George W., 20, 32

Alexander, C. Norman, Jr., 391, 402

Allport, Gordon W., 353, 355

Anderson, Kenneth E., 329

Arbolino, Jack N., 100, 126

Arbuckle, Dugald S., 191, 252, 295, 297, 298, 299

Argyris, Chris, 43, 56

Arnspiger, V. Clyde, 343, 355, 383

Ashby, Jefferson D., 194, 196

Astin, Alexander W., 66, 67–68, 77, 112, 119, 126

Astin, Helen S., 191

Axelrad, S., 174, 175, 180, 193

B

Babbott, Edward F., 329

Bachrach, Paul B., 195

Baer, Max F., 18, 32, 56, 77, 97, 128, 132, 150, 151, 152, 154, 166, 168, 169, 222, 253, 279, 286, 290–91, 294, 295, 296, 297, 298, 299, 329, 383–84, 428

Banducci, Raymond, 402

Bany, Mary A., 157, 168, 169

Barbarosh, Benjamin, 299

Barclay, James R., 355

Barry, Ruth, 191

Baymur, Feriha B., 191

Beck, Carlton E., 77

Beezer, Robert H., 66, 70, 77

Beilen, Harry, 175, 179–80, 182, 191

Belitsky, A. Harvey, 225

Bellamy, William D., 330

Bennett, Margaret E., 158, 169, 286, 289, 300

Bennett, Wilma, 260

Benson, Charles S., 384

Benzing, Cynthia E., 371–72, 384

Berdie, Ralph F., 30, 32–33, 66, 69–70, 72, 77, 160, 169, 361, 384

Berenson, Bernard G., 322, 329

Bergstein, Harry B., 402

Bernard, Harold, 356, 403

Blai, Boris, Jr., 191

Blau, Peter M., 175, 191

Blocher, Donald H., 390, 402

Blum, Lawrence P., 191

Bogan, Forrest A., 205, 206–207, 222

Boocock, Sarene, 49, 189

Bordin, Edward S., 175, 191

Bowerman, Charles E., 391–92, 402

Borow, Henry, 18, 23, 33, 77, 191, 211, 222, 281, 299, 355

Brayfield, Arthur H., 185–86, 192

Brewer, John M., 33

Brickman, William W., 222

Brill, Abraham Arden, 175, 178, 192

Brittain, Clay V., 391, 403

Broderick, Earlfred B., 392, 403

Brophy, Alfred L., 428

Brough, James R., 229

Brown, Roger, 355

Burchill, George W., 253, 300, 322, 329, 339, 355

Burton, Robert L., 329

C

Calia, Vincent, 229, 253, 291, 300

Campbell, Ernest Q., 391, 402

Campbell, Robert E., 50, 56, 185, 190, 192, 200, 210, 223

Caplan, Stanley W., 192

Caplow, Theodore, 175, 181–82, 192, 212, 223

Carkhuff, Robert R., 322, 329

Carp, Frances M., 175, 179, 192

Centers, Richard, 212, 223

Chesler, Mark, 353, 357

Christopher, Samuel A., 403

Clark, Florence E., 253

Clark, Harold F., 82, 90, 97, 175, 177–78, 192, 428

Clarke, R. B., 11, 18, 174, 192

Cogswell, John F., 51, 189

Coleman, James C., 288, 300, 307, 308, 329

Coleman, James S., 49, 189, 355

Combs, Arthur W., 41, 50, 56, 311, 312, 329

Conant, James B., 355

Connors, Ralph P., 195

Cooley, William W., 190

Coser, Rose Laub, 403

Cox, Claire, 373, 384

Crites, John O., 43, 57, 175, 185–87, 192, 195, 275

Crow, Alice, 253, 295, 296, 297, 298, 300

Crow, Lester D., 253, 295, 296, 297, 298, 300, 330, 355

D

Davis, James A., 77

Davis, Russel G., 190

Detjen, Ervin Winfred, 166, 169, 300

Detjen, Mary Ford, 166, 169, 300

Dinitz, Simon, 346, 357

Dolliver, Robert H., 192

Dudley, Gordon, 187, 196, 290, 302

Dunn, Lloyd M., 356

Duvall, Evelyn Millis, 389, 403

E

Eckerson, A. B., 279

Edgar, Thomas, 330

Ehrle, Raymond A., 354

Ellis, Allan B., 190

Erb, Everett D., 312–13, 330

Ervin, Ben, 71, 77

F

Falk, Jacqueline M., 356

Farwell, Gail F., 284, 287, 301

Feingold, S. Norman, 254

Ferguson, Robert H., 254

Field, Frank L., 192

Fine, Sidney A., 175, 192, 279

Flanagan, John C., 190

Ford, Donald H., 8, 18

Form, William H., 175, 194, 208, 212, 213, 224, 356

Forrester, Gertrude, 254, 279

Fowler, Stanley E., 392, 403

Friesen, Delloss, 57

Frost, Joe L., 356

Fullmer, Daniel, 356, 403

G

Gaines, Lynn, 190

Gardner, John W., 93, 97, 330

Garry, Ralph, 330, 356, 403

Gaston, J. Frank, 97

Gelatt, H. B., 11, 18, 174, 192

Gerstein, Martin, 193

Ginsburg, S. W., 174, 175, 180, 193

Ginzberg, Eli, 43, 57, 174, 175, 180–81, 193, 223, 300

Glanz, Edward C., 158, 170, 295, 296, 297, 300

Glick, Peter, Jr., 193, 223

Goldstein, Arnold D., 384

Goldstein, Harold, 89, 97

Gomberg, William, 225

Goode, William J., 403

Goodlad, John I., 57

Gorman, William E., 195

Grant, Claude W., 329

Grant, W. Vance, 75, 77

Gray, Susan W., 284, 300

Gregory, Robert J., 300

Gribbons, Warren D., 43, 57, 175, 186, 193

Grigg, A. E., 185

Gross, Edward, 210, 223

Gunderson, E. K. Eric, 428

Gutsch, Kenneth U., 300, 330

H

Habbe, Stephen, 219, 223

Hagen, D., 185

Hagen, Elizabeth, 175, 183–84, 196

Hall, Donald W., 193

Halpern, Gerald, 190

Hamel, Harvey R., 25, 75, 206–207, 216, 218, 222, 223

Hansen, James C., 19, 33, 194, 301, 357

Harper, William R., 21, 174

Harwood, Michael, 428

Hatch, Raymond N., 19, 57, 98, 126, 132, 155, 166–68, 170, 224, 255, 279, 294, 297, 298, 301, 330–31, 356, 377, 384, 403–404, 429

Hatt, Paul K., 346, 356

Havighurst, Robert J., 356, 395, 403

Hawkes, Glenn R., 356

Heath, Brian R. G., 403

Heinz, Carl A., 192, 279

Henderson, George, 356

Herma, J. L., 174, 175, 180, 193

Herzberg, Frederick, 223

Hewer, Vivian H., 193

Hill, George E., 250, 254, 300

Hilton, Thomas L., 190, 193

Hjelm, Howard F., 66, 70, 77

Hodge, Claire, 215–16, 223

Hoffman, L. R., 224

Holland, John L., 67, 175, 176, 188–89, 193, 308, 310, 330

Holland, Susan S., 205, 218, 223–24

Hollingshead, A. B., 175, 194

Hollis, Joseph W., 16–17, 18, 57, 65, 77, 124, 126, 151, 154, 287, 294, 296, 298, 300, 348, 356

Hollis, Lucile U., 16–17, 18, 57, 65, 77, 124, 126, 151, 154, 287, 294, 296, 298, 300, 348, 356

Holtzman, Wayne H., 390, 403

Hood, Albert B., 30, 32–33, 66, 69–70, 72, 77, 160, 169, 361, 384

Hood, Elizabeth, 330

Hooker, Douglas, 312–13, 330

Hoover, Richard, 176, 189, 193, 194

Hopke, William E., 254

Hoppock, Robert, 18, 57, 132, 154, 166–68, 170, 175, 179, 194, 195, 224, 254, 279, 294, 295, 296, 297, 298, 300, 330, 428–29

Horne, Ferne W., 429

Hoyle, Kathryn D., 216, 224

Hoyt, Kenneth B., 82, 175, 187–88, 194, 293

Hughes, Roland G., Jr., 300

Humphreys, J. Anthony, 330, 356, 384, 403

Hurst, Robert, 57

Hutson, Percival W., 371–72, 384

Hyman, Berman, 300

I

Impellitteri, Joseph T., 50–51, 57, 190, 279

Isaacson, Lee E., 18, 77, 126, 128, 132, 155, 168, 170, 194, 224, 254, 279, 286–87, 294, 295, 296, 297, 298, 300, 330, 356, 377, 384, 429

J

Johnson, Lois V., 157, 168, 169

Johnston, Denis F., 210, 224

Johnstone, John W. C., 83, 90, 97, 355, 356

Jonassohn, Kurt, 355

K

Kaback, Goldie Ruth, 254, 300–301

Katz, Martin, 6, 18, 194

Katzell, Raymond A., 194

Kaufman, Jacob J., 224, 301

Kehas, Chris D., 192

Kell, Bill L., 254

Keller, Franklin J., 22, 23, 33, 175

Kelley, Earl C., 176, 194, 310, 312, 330

Kelly, F. J., 22, 33

Keyserling, Mary Dublin, 69

Kinch, John W., 391–92, 402

Kinnick, Bernard C., 403

Kirk, Barbara A., 262–64, 279

Klemer, Margaret G., 403

Klemer, Richard H., 403

Kohout, Vernon A., 194

Kolb, William L., 332, 356

Krumboltz, John D., 190

Kvey, Allen E., 384

L

Ladato, Francis J., 330

Landis, Paul H., 403

Lane, May Rogers, 248, 254

Learned, Stanley, 203, 224

Lehrer, Stanley, 223

LeMay, Morris L., 258, 279

Lifton, Walter M., 158–60, 168, 170, 287, 301

Lippitt, Ronald, 353, 357

Lipsman, Claire K., 194

Lister, James L., 330

Logan, Richard H. III, 300

Lohnes, Paul R., 43–44, 57, 193

Loughary, John W., 57, 287, 288, 301

Luckey, Eleanore Braun, 397, 403

M

McCreary, Eugene, 337, 356

McCurdy, Harold Grier, 34, 57, 62, 77

McQueen, Mildred, 69, 77

Magoon, Thomas, 190

Mainig, Lawrence R., 403

Mann, Floyd C., 224

Marchese, Theodore J., Jr., 33, 77, 196, 225

Martin, Ann M., 56, 190, 192

Maslow, A. H., 305, 311, 330

Mattingly, Richard, 371, 384

Meadow, Lloyd, 194

Mehrens, William A., 11, 19, 174, 196

Merton, Robert K., 356

Methee, George R., 210, 224

Michels, Marjorie E., 262–64, 279

Miller, C. Dean, 384

Miller, Delbert Charles, 175, 194

Miller, Frank W., 41, 57, 166, 168, 170

Minor, Frank J., 190

Monnens, Lawrence P., 255

Moore, Bernice Milburn, 390, 403

Morrison, Richard L., 194

Moser, Leslie E., 166, 168, 170, 254, 301

Moser, Ruth Small, 166, 168, 170, 254, 301

Mowsesian, Richard Heath, 403

Mueller, Charlotte, 225, 255, 301–302

Mueller, William J., 254

Munger, Daniel I., 301

Munson, Harold L., 377, 384

Murk, Virgil, 301

Murray, Ellen, 346, 357

Murray, Walter I., 355

N

Nachmann, Barbara, 191

Nelson, Paul D., 428

Neugarten, Bernice L., 356

Nichols, R. C., 67

Norris, Willa, 18, 19, 57, 98, 126, 132, 155, 166–68, 170, 194, 224, 255, 279, 294, 295, 296, 297, 298, 301, 330–31, 356, 377, 384, 403–404, 429

North, Robert D., 330, 356, 384, 403

Nosow, Sigmund, 208, 212, 213, 224, 356

O

Odle, S. Gene, 301

O'Hara, Robert P., 175, 190, 194

Ohlsen, Merle M., 166, 170, 279, 295, 296, 297, 298, 301

Olechowski, Nan, 302

Osipow, Samuel H., 194, 196

O'Toole, John F., Jr., 57

Overstreet, Phoebe L., 195, 210, 225, 275, 280, 285, 301

P

Packard, Vance, 221, 224

Parsons, Frank, 20–21, 24, 33, 174

Patterson, Cecil H., 191, 224–25

Patton, Evelyn D., 255

Pearl, Arthur, 345, 357

Pemberton, W. A., 66, 69, 77, 309, 331

Perrella, Vera C., 370, 384

Perrone, Phillip A., 404

Peters, Herman J., 19, 33, 168, 170, 194, 284, 287, 294, 295, 296, 297, 298, 301, 357

Peterson, Peter G., 317, 331

Peterson, Ronald A., 357

Pierson, Glen N., 176, 189, 194

Porterfield, Austin L., 404

Pritchard, David H., 195

R

Reckless, Walter C., 346, 357

Reed, Anna Y., 23, 33

Reiss, Albert J., 225

Rich, Juliet V., 57

Riessman, Frank, 337, 357

Rivera, Ramon J., 83, 90, 97, 356

Robinson, H. Alan, 195

Rodman, Hyman, 392, 404

Roe, Anne, 175, 185, 195, 207, 210, 212, 225

Roeber, Edward C., 18, 32, 56, 77, 97, 128, 132, 150, 151, 152, 154, 166, 168, 169, 222, 253, 260, 279, 286, 290–91, 294, 295, 296, 297, 298, 299, 329, 383–84, 428

Rogers, Carl R., 310–11, 312, 331

Rosen, Bernard C., 389, 404

Rosenfeld, Reba, 357

Rothney, John W. M., 194, 403

Ruble, Ronald A., 192

Rusalem, Herbert, 279

S

Saben, Samuel, 225
Samler, Joseph, 175, 195, 225
Schmuck, Richard, 353, 357
Schwartz, Lester J., 330
Segal, Lenora, 190
Segal, Stanley J., 191
Segel, David, 192
Shannon, Jack T., 403
Shartle, Carroll L., 19, 211, 225, 255, 279–80
Sheppard, Harold L., 225
Sherif, Carolyn W., 361, 384
Sherif, Mazafer, 361, 384
Shertzer, Bruce, 57, 166, 168, 170, 195, 294, 295, 296, 297, 298, 301
Shirts, Garry, 189
Shneidman, Edwin S., 318
Shostak, Arthur B., 225
Siegelman, Marvin, 185, 195, 207, 225
Simon, Kenneth A., 75, 77
Simons, Joseph B., 195
Sinick, Daniel, 195
Skager, Rodney, 357
Slinger, George E., 331
Sloan, Harold S., 82, 90, 97, 428
Smart, Mollie S., 331
Smart, Russell C., 331
Smith, Margaret Ruth, 255
Smythe, Hugh H., 355
Snygg, Donald, 41, 56
Sokoloff, Martin A., 330
Soldahl, Thomas A., 225, 255, 301–302
Sonstegard, Manford, 404
Soper, D. W., 312
Splaver, Sarah, 370, 384
Staton, Thomas F., 357
Stefflre, Buford, 195
Stein, Robert L., 215, 225
Steiner, Dora W., 255
Stewart, Lawrence H., 22, 33, 168, 170
Stiller, Alfred, 357
Stone, Shelley C., 57, 166, 170, 195, 296, 301
Stoodley, Bartlett H., 225, 357
Super, Donald E., 43, 57, 175, 183, 195, 210, 212, 225, 275, 280, 285, 301
Swanstrom, Thomas E., 205, 222

T

Tanner, Daniel, 33
Tennyson, W. Wesley, 225, 255, 301–302
Thomas, Lawrence G., 75, 77, 225
Thomas, R. Murray, 354, 357
Thompson, Albert S., 57, 163–65, 196, 292–93
Thoresen, Carl E., 11, 19, 174, 196
Thorndike, Robert L., 175, 183–84, 196
Tiedeman, David V., 51, 56, 175, 186–87, 190, 192, 194, 196, 290, 302
Tilgher, Adriano, 204, 225
Tillery, Dale, 176, 189, 196
Traxler, Arthur E., 330, 356, 384, 403
Tyler, Leona E., 175, 196, 283, 288, 302
Tyler, Louise L., 57
Tyson, Marion, 190

U

Urban, Hugh B., 8, 18
Useem, Ruth Hill, 343, 357
Utton, A. C., 185

V

Van Hoose, William, 168, 170
Varenhorst, Barbara, 189
Veen, Grant, 26, 33, 74, 77, 89, 91, 93, 98, 196, 225
Viteles, Morris S., 21, 22, 23, 33, 175

W

Walker, Rose Marie, 74, 78
Wall, Harvey W., 194, 196
Walz, Garry, 57, 196
Warnath, Charles F., 22, 33, 168, 170, 258, 279
Warner, William Lloyd, 175, 183, 196–97
Wattenberg, Ben J., 201
Webster, Staten W., 357
Weinberg, Carl, 357
Weitz, Henry, 285, 302, 310, 331
Wellington, John A., 302
Whitfield, Edwin A., 176, 189, 194
Wieland, J. Edward, 384, 412, 429
Wilensky, Harold L., 344, 357–58
Williamson, E. G., 19, 21, 33, 78, 197, 225

Williamson, Robert C., 392, 394, 404
Wilson, Michael J., 190
Witmer, Lightner, 21, 175
Wolf, Beverly, 191
Wolfbein, Seymour L., 24, 33, 78, 226
Wrenn, C. Gilbert, 33
Wurtz, Robert E., 197

Z

Zeran, Franklin R., 19, 57, 98, 126, 132, 155, 166–68, 170, 224, 255, 279, 294, 297, 298, 301, 330–31, 356, 377, 384, 403–404, 429
Zytowski, Donald G., 321, 331

Subject Index

A

Abilities, as variables, 309
Adult Basic Education, 83
Adults; *see also* Community agencies materials
  economic materials, 381
  education, 83, 84 (Fig.), 85
  experiences, 89, 90 (Fig.)
  physical and psychological materials, 327
  social materials, 353
American Personnel and Guidance Association, 26, 32, 121–22
Apprenticeships, 373–74
Aptitudes, as variables, 309
Armed Forces; *see also* Information, military
  educational opportunities, 410–14
  occupational development, 414–15
  privileges in, 416–17
  retirement, 417–18
  women in, 409–10
Assembly programs, 164t, 166, 292t, 295
Assistantships, 371–72
Association for Higher Education, 84–85
Associations and organizations, sources of information, 107, 235–36, 251
Attitudes, 41, 42, 44, 46–47t, 307
Audio-visual materials
  aids, 164t, 166, 292t, 294–95
  evaluation of occupational films, 250–51
  sources, 116–17, 245
Automation, 24–26

B

Bennett Occupations Filing Plan, 260–61
Biography, 242, 292t, 294
Brainstorming, 165t, 168, 292t, 297
Broadening information, depth of, 35, 38, 39, 41, 73, 102, 161
Bulletin board, 164t, 166, 292t, 294

Bureau of the Census, classification, 212
Businesses and industries, sources of information, 111, 239–40

C

California plan, 262–64
Career
  clubs, 293t, 297
  conferences, 292t, 296
  day, 292t, 295
  definition, 210
  development, 173–190
  fiction, 242, 292t, 294
  talks, 292t, 295
Career Exploration Kit, 268, 274
Career Information Kit, 267, 274
Charts, 164t, 166, 243, 292t, 294
Chronicle plan, 266–67
Classification; *see also* Filing plans
  Bureau of the Census, 212
  by occupational group, 200, 201 (Fig.)
  by occupations, 211–13
  origin of, 212
  society as basis of, 212
  Standard Industrial, 212, 262, 269
  theory as basis of, 212
Coding, *see* Filing plans
Cold War GI Bill, 419–20
Collecting information, 53–54, 121–24, 251–52
Collective bargaining, 220–21
College day and night, 164t, 166
College Entrance View-Deck, 146, 164t, 167
College Entrance Examination Board, 371
College Scholarship Service, 371
Colleges and universities
  enrollment, 80, 91, 92 (Fig.), 94–95 (Fig.)
  graduates, 86, 88 (Fig.)
  location, 83–84
  number of, 80
Commercial publishers, 105–106, 233–35

Communication processes, 1–2, 13
Community agencies materials
    educational, 147–48
    occupational, 275
Community survey, 123, 243, 252
Computer-assisted information sys-
    tems (CAIS), 49–51, 54, 164t,
    167, 187, 292t, 296
Conferences, 164t, 167, 292t, 296
Conformity, 342
Conjoint relationships, 284–86, 321–
    22
Contests, 372
Contractual services, 116, 242, 246–
    47, 378–79, 421
Control of educational structure, 81,
    119
Counseling, utilizing information in,
    161–62, 286–89
Counselor
    functions, 161–62
    goals, 5
    implications of educational struc-
        ture, 93–96
    role, 4–7, 13, 63–64, 176, 315–17,
        334–35, 386–87, 396–97, 407–
        409
Criteria
    for educational information, 118–21
    of educational maturation, 148–49
    for filing plans, 133–34
    for housing of information, 129–31,
        258–59
    for occupational information, 244,
        248–51
    of occupational maturity, 275–76
Culturally disadvantaged, 30
Cultures, 335–36
Cybernation, 24–26

D

Dasein-analyse, 7
Dating practices, 392–93
Decision-making processes, 5–7, 10,
    11, 49–50, 93, 174, 176–77,
    181, 187, 189, 203, 208, 314
Demography, definition, 214
Depression, influence of, 23
Depth of information, 7, 35, 37–40,
    73–74, 102, 161
Desk-Top Kit, 266–67, 273, 274

Developmental
    approach, 7, 11, 41, 55–56, 174
        occupation information for, 100,
        227–29
    concept, 34–35
Dictionary of Occupational Titles
    (D.O.T.), 23, 31, 35–36, 46–
    47t, 48, 192, 211, 223, 239,
    246, 253–54, 264–70, 279
Disadvantaged, 336–40
    characteristics of, 336–38
    working with, 338–40
Displays, 164t, 166, 292t, 294
Dramatizations, 165t, 168, 292t, 296
Drop-outs, 29

E

Economic
    information, *see* information, eco-
        nomic
    mobility, 30
    report, 243
    self-aspiration, 361–62
Economic Opportunity Act, 27, 83,
    340
Education
    adult, location of study, 83, 84
        (Fig.)
    college graduates, 88 (Fig.)
    continuing, 27, 28, 61–62, 82
    as determinant of occupational op-
        portunity, 59, 74–76, 182
    financing, 367–75
    high school graduates, 85–86, 87
        (Fig.)
    objectives, 71–72
    role change, 89–93, 94–95 (Fig.)
    unemployment, relation to, 219
Educational
    attainment, 24–26, 25t, 74–75, 75t,
        85, 86 (Fig.), 89–91
    information, *see* Information, edu-
        cational
    institutions, *see* Educational struc-
        ture
    maturity, 72–73, 138
    opportunities
        in Armed Forces, 410–14
        availability, 82–86
        for veterans, 419
        for veterans' children, 420–21

potential
characteristics affecting, 66–70
job determinant, 74–76, 182
research, 66–72
structure
conditions affecting individual, 86–89
control, 81, 119
implications for individual, 79–98
kind of programs, 82, 119
taxonomy, 80–82
and training institutions, sources of information, 111–12, 240
Educational Resources Information Center (ERIC), 103, 153
Elementary school materials
economic, 380
educational, 144–45
military, 424
occupational, 271–72
peer and family, 398
physical and psychological, 325
social, 351
Elementary schools
enrollment, 80
number of, 80
Elementary and Secondary Education Act, 27
Employed persons, definition, 211
Employment
average weekly hours, 31, 318, 319t
high school graduates, 202 (Fig.)
paid holidays, 318–19, 320t
paid vacations, 318–19, 320t
rates, *see* Labor force
trends, 200, 201 (Fig.), 206–210
Enrollments, 80, 91, 92 (Fig.), 94–95 (Fig.), 100
Entry jobs, 293t, 298
Environments, as variables, 308
Evaluative criteria
for educational information, 118–21
for occupational information, 244, 248–51
Exhibits, 123, 124, 164t, 166, 251, 292t, 294
Existentialism, 7–8
Experiences, as variables, 309–10
Exploratory jobs, 293t, 298

F
Family
information, *see* Information, peer and family
military service affect upon, 415–17
relationships, 389–91
Federal Government, role of, 23; *see also* U.S. Government
Federal legislation, 22–23, 26–27, 83
Feedback information, depth of, 7, 35, 38–39, 40, 41, 73–74, 102, 161
Fellowships, 371–72
Feminine roles, 343–44
Field trips, 123, 124, 165t, 168, 293, 297
Filing plans; *see also* housing
alphabetical, 260–61
California, 262–64
chronicle, 266–67
criteria, 133–34, 257–58
Dictionary of Occupational Titles, 264–67
economic information, 377–78
educational information, 132–43
industry, 262
interest, 261
Michigan, 260–61
military information, 422–23
Missouri, 261
occupational information, 260–71
peer and family information, 397–98
physical and psychological information, 323–24
school subject, 261
social information, 349–50
for 3-D concept, 136–43, 137 (Fig.), 140–41t, 144 (Fig.), 268–71, 323–24
values and limitations, 132–36, 260–68
Films, evaluation, 250–51
Financial
income, 362–65
planning, 365–66
Financial assistance
by community agencies, 376
for education, 367–75
apprenticeships, 373–74
assistanceships, 371–72
contests, 372

Financial assistance (*cont.*)
  for education (*cont.*)
    fellowships, 371–72
    government programs, 374–75
    grants-in-aid, 371–72
    insurance policies, 371
    internships, 373–74
    loans, 372–73
    savings, 370
    scholarships, 371–72
    sources identification, 368–69
    work-while-attending, 369–70
  for private enterprise, 375–76
Foster Uncle and Aunt, 165t, 168–69, 293t, 298
Foundations, philosophical, 3–19

G

Game theory activities, 165t, 168, 292t, 297
Government, sources for information, 108–11, 236–39; *see also,* U.S. Government
Graduates
  college, 88 (Fig.)
  high school, 85–86, 87 (Fig.), 202 (Fig.)
Grants-in-aid, 371–72
Group discussions, 164t, 167, 292t, 296
Group work, contribution to individual, 289–90
Guidelines
  communication, 1–2
  information processes, 1–2
  postulates, 8–13

H

Handicapped persons in labor force, 205–206
High schools
  enrollment, 80, 85
  graduates, 85–86, 87 (Fig.)
  number of, 80
Higher Education Act, 27, 373, 374
Horizontal mobility, 344–46
Hours of work, 31, 318, 319t
Housing of information
  criteria, 129–31, 258–59
  physical facilities, 131–32, 259–60

I

Income, 362–65
  by age, 364, 366 (Fig.)
  by educational level, 363–64
  by families, 363 (Fig.), 364–65, 367 (Fig.)
  by individuals, 367 (Fig.)
  by race, 363 (Fig.), 364, 365t
  by sex, 364, 365t, 366 (Fig.)
Individual
  conformity, 342
  differences, 62–70, 305–10
  feminine role, 343–44
  masculine role, 343–44
  social maturity, 342–43
  understanding of others, 340–41
Individuality, 342
Industrial descriptive literature, 243
Information
  in counseling, 161–62
  definition, 3
  depth of, 7, 35, 38–39, 40, 41, 73–74, 102, 161
  economic, 359–84
    financial assistance, 367–76
    financial planning, 365–66
    purposes, 360–61
    sample material, 380–81
  educational, 59–170
    accessibility, 127–28
    within Armed Forces, 410–14
    definition, 14–15
    determinants, 61–78
    developmental approach, 100
    educational attainment, 24–26, 25t, 74–75, 75t, 85, 86 (Fig.), 89–91
    filing plans, 132–43
    objectives of utilizing, 158–59
    research implications, 66–72
    sample materials, 143–48
    sources of, 103–12
    three-dimensional concept, 100–102
    types, 113–17
    types needed, 72–74
    up-dating, 153–54
  explosion, 3–4
  integration, 12
  military, 405–29

counselor's role, 407–409
disability, 417
educational opportunities, 410–14
for family, 415–18
occupational development, 414–15
purposes, 406–407
retirement, 417–18
sample materials, 423–26
transition to civilian life, 418–19
updating, 421–22
veterans' benefits, 419–21
obtaining
 educational, 121–24
 occupational, 251–52
 priority, 53–54
occupational, 171–302
 criteria for, 244, 248–51
 definition, 15
 filing plans, 260–71
 geographical considerations, 208–210
 housing of, 258–59
 literature, definition of, 242–44
 objectives of utilizing, 281–84
 research implications, 176–90
 sample materials, 271–75
 sources, 227–55
 three-dimensional concept, 229–30
 types, 241–48
 updating, 277
peer and family, 385–404
 counselor's role, 386–87, 396–97
 purposes, 385–86
 sample materials, 398–401
personal-social, 332–58, 303–429
 counselor's role, 315–17, 334–35
 definition, 15–16
 economic, 359–84
 military, 405–29
 peer and family, 385–404
 physical and psychological, 305–31
personalizing; see also Media
 experiences, 10
 foundations, 1–2
 need for, 3–7, 9–10, 13
 obtaining, 40 (Fig.)
 philosophy, 7–13

processes, 4, 12–13
purposes, 16–17
role in education, 17–18
selection, 54
physical and psychological, 305–31
 counselor's role, 315–17
 sample materials, 324–27
 self, 310–11
 variables, 305–10
retrieval, 150, 350
social, 332–58
 counselor's role, 334–35
 sample materials, 350–53
sources, *see* Sources
utilization, *see* Utilization
Information Systems for Vocational Decisions (ISVD), 51, 187, 190
Interests
 basic for file plan, 261
 as variables, 308–309
Internships, 373–74
Interviews
 for education information, 164t, 167
 job, 292t, 297

J
Job
 analysis, 243, 292t, 296
 clinics, 292t, 296
 definition, 211
 series, 243
Junior G.I. Bill, 420–21
Junior high school materials,
 economic, 380–81
 educational, 145–46
 military, 424–25
 occupational, 272–73
 peer and family, 399–400
 physical and psychological, 325–26
 social, 351–52

L
Labor force
 boys, 200–201
 change in, 214, 215t
 definition, 211
 employed persons, defined, 211
 girls, 200–201
 growth of, 200, 209–10

Labor force (*cont.*)
   handicapped persons, 205–206
   hours of work, 31, 318, 319t
   marital status, 205, 206 (Fig.)
   men, 216 (Fig.)
   multiple job holders, 206–207
   nonwhites, 200–201, 205, 215, 217t,
      218
   number, 200–201, 209–10, 214–15,
      216 (Fig.), 218
   by occupational group, 200, 201
      (Fig.), 214–15, 216 (Fig.),
      217t
   rising educational level, 74–76
   teenagers, 200–202
   unemployed persons, defined, 211
   unemployment, 215–16, 217t, 219t
   white, 200–201, 215, 217t, 218
   women, 205, 206 (Fig.), 207–208,
      216 (Fig.), 217t
Labor unions, 27, 220–21
Laboratory study, 165t, 168, 293, 297
Leisure time, 318–21, 376–77
Libraries, types, 51–53
Loans, 372–73, 419–20
Location of information, *see* Housing

M
Manpower Development and Training
   Act, 26, 83, 110, 340
Marriage responsibilities, 395–96
Masculine roles, 343–44
Materials, samples
   economic, 380–81
   educational, 143–48
   military, 423–26
   occupational, 271–75
   peer and family, 398–401
   physical and psychological, 324–27
   social, 350–53
Measurement techniques, 64–66
Media
   classifications of, 164–65t, 165–69,
      292t, 294–98
   of educational information, 164–
      65t, 165–69
   information processes, 12
   of occupational information, 292–
      93 (Fig.), 294–98
Methods, *see* Techniques
Michigan file plan, 260–61

Military information, *see* Information,
   military
Missouri file plan, 261
Mobility, 30, 344–46
Monthly Labor Review, 238
Motivation, 307–308

N
National Defense Education Act, 26,
   373, 374
National Education Association, 84
   (Fig.)
National Industrial Conference Board,
   90 (Fig.), 92 (Fig.), 94–95
   (Fig.)
National Vocational Guidance Asso-
   ciation, 23, 242–44, 248–51,
   254–55, 260, 277
   definitions of publications, 242–44
   standards for evaluating materials,
      248–51
National Vocational Student Loan
   Income Act, 374
National Youth Administration, 23
Needs
   determine use, 151, 256–57
   as variables, 306

O
Objectives, *see* Purposes
Occupation
   classification, 211–13
   definition, 210, 211
   demographic factors, 214–18
   education and, 74–76, 182
   geographical consideration, 208–10
   historical events, 20–33
   legislation affecting, 22–23, 26–27,
      221
   prestige, 213, 214 (Fig.)
   ranking of, 213, 214 (Fig.)
   sociological implications, 213
   trends, 28–31, 171, 198–203
Occupational
   abstract, 243, 292t, 294
   biography, 242, 292, 294t
   brief, 242–43, 292t, 294
   courses, 293t, 298
   curriculum, 293t, 298
   description, 243
   development; *see also* Occupational
      maturity definition, 210

group, distribution in labor force, 200, 201 (Fig.), 214–15, 216 (Fig.), 217t
guide, 243, 292t, 294
information, *see* Information, occupational
literature, types defined, 242–44
maturity, 228–29
  criteria, 275–76
  levels, 42–49, 46–47t
mobility, 10–11, 28–29, 216–20
monograph, 242, 292t, 294
research, 173–97
theories, 173–97
units, 293t, 298
Occupational Exploration Kit, 267, 274, 295
Occupational Information and Guidance Service, 23
Occupational Outlook Handbook, 238, 246, 273
Occupational Outlook Quarterly, 238, 247
Occupational Outlook Service, 23
Ohio University checklist, 250
On-the-job training, 293t, 298
Orientation programs, 165t, 168

P

Panels, 164t, 166, 252, 292t, 295
Parent night, 164t, 166
Parental expectations, 387–88
Peer information, *see* Information, peer and family
Peer relationships, 391–92
Perception, 41, 312–13
Periodicals, 116–18, 246–48; *see also* Subscriptions
Personal-social information, *see* Information, personal-social
Personalized information, *see* Information, personalizing, Media
Philosophy, development of, 317–18
Physical information, 305–31
Planning, financial, 365–66
Plant tours, 293, 297
Population, 214, 334
Position, definition, 211
Posters, 243, 292t, 294
Postulates
  basic, 8–13
  guidelines, 1–2

for personalizing information, 8-13
Preschool materials
  peer and family, 398
  physical and psychological, 324-25
  social, 351
Prestige, occupation, 213, 214 (Fig.)
Professional
  journals, 113, 117–18, 242, 247–48
  library, 51
Programs, educational, 82, 119
Psychological information, 305–31
Publications
  media, 164t, 166, 292t, 294
  sources, 105–12, 233–40
Purposes; *see also* Objectives
  of economic information, 360–61
  of military information, 406–407
  of peer and family information, 385–86
  of personalized information, 16–17
  of social information, 334–35
  of utilizing occupational information, 281–84

Q

Quiz contests, 165t, 168, 292t, 296

R

Readiness for Vocational Planning (RVP), 43–44
Recruitment literature, 243
Reference materials, including books, 113–15, 164t, 166, 245–46, 292t, 294, 379–80
Reference library, 51
Research
  contributors, 174–90
  counselor's role, 176
  educational, 66–72
  grants, 372
  implications, 176–90
  recent developments, 173–76
  in vocational development, 176–90
Reserve Officers Training Corps, 412–13
Resources, mobilizing and organizing, 124–125
Retrieval of educational information, 150
Role-playing, 165t, 168, 292t, 296–97

S

Savings, 370

Scholarships, 371–72

School to College: Opportunities for Postsecondary Education (SCOPE), 189

Self, the emerging, 310–11

Self-aspiration, economic, 361–62

Self-concept, 312

Self-expressive time, 318–21

Senior high school materials

economic, 381

educational, 146–47

military, 425–26

occupational, 273–74

peer and family, 400–401

physical and psychological, 326–27

social, 352

Sex information, 393–95

Smith-Hughes Act, 22–23

Social agencies, for referral, 347–49

maturity, 342–43

mobility, 30, 344–46

problems, 346–47

Sources

educational and training institutions, 111–12, 240

for educational information, 103–12

for occupational information, 227–55

people, 104–105, 231–33

places of employment, 241

publications, 105–12, 233–40

associations and organizations, 107, 235–36

businesses and industries, 111, 239–40

commercial, 105–106, 233–35

education and training institutions, 111–12, 240

governments, 108–111, 236–39

tests and test information, 106, 235, 322–23

Specialty Oriented Students (SOS), 82, 187, 268

Specific information, depth of, 35, 38, 39, 41, 73, 102, 161

Standard Industrial Classification, 212, 262, 269

Storage, *see* Housing

Subgroups, 335–36

Subscriptions, 113, 116, 242, 246–47, 378–79, 421

Systems, *see* Computer-assisted information systems

T

Taxonomy, educational structure, 80–82

Teacher, role, 4, 55, 284–86, 321–22

Team approach, 284–86, 321–22

Techniques

in counseling, 161–62

educational information, 121–24, 163–69

needs as a determinant of, 159–60

occupational information, 293–98

selection of, 162–63, 164–65t, 290–93

variation within depth dimension, 160–61

Technological advancement in work, 207–208

Temporary jobs, 293t, 298

Tests, 106, 235, 244, 322–23

Theories

contributors, 174–90

counselor role, 176

implications, 176–90

recent developments, 173–76

in vocational development, 176–90

Three-dimensional concept, 36–40, 48–49, 100–103

area, 37–39

depth, 7, 35, 37–40, 73–74, 102, 161

filing, 136–43, 137 (Fig.), 140–41t, 144 (Fig.), 268–71, 323–24

occupational information for, 229–30

people, 37, 39

Trends, 9–13, 20–33, 29t, 43t, 171, 198–203

implications, 28–31

Try-outs, 165t, 169

Types of information

audio-visual, 116–17, 245

contractual service, 116, 246–47, 378–79, 421

literature, 242–44

professional journals, 113, 117–18, 242, 247–48

reference, 113–15, 164t, 166, 245–46, 292t, 294, 379–80
subscription service, 113, 116, 242, 246–47, 378–79, 421
tests, 106, 235, 244, 322–23

U

Understanding others, 340–41
Unemployed persons, definition, 211
United States Armed Forces Institute, 410–12
U.S. Government
Bureau of the Census, 212
Bureau of Labor Statistics, 25t, 75t, 202 (Fig.)
Department of Agriculture, 108
Department of Commerce, 108, 206 (Fig.), 216 (Fig.), 237, 319t, 320t, 362, 363, (Fig.), 365t, 366 (Fig.), 367 (Fig.), 408 (Fig.)
Department of Defense, 108, 237
Department of Health, Education, and Welfare, 108, 202 (Fig.), 215t, 238
Department of Labor, 23, 25t, 75t, 86 (Fig.), 87 (Fig.), 88 (Fig.), 110, 111, 207, 212, 215, 217t, 238
Employment Service, 23, 110, 265
Office of Economic Opportunity, 108, 237
Office of Education, 23, 108–109, 163, 165t, 293t
Veterans Administration, 110
Women's Bureau, 86 (Fig.), 87 (Fig.), 88 (Fig.), 110, 207
Utilization
concept of, 156–58, 281–84
of economic information, 381–83
of educational information, 150–53, 156–70
improving extensiveness of use, 150–53, 276–77
of military information, 426–27
objectives of educational information, 158–59
of occupational information, 256–302
of peer and family information, 401–402

of physical and psychological information, 310–11, 327–28
point of view, 156–58, 281–84
of social information, 352–54

V

Values, 41, 42, 307
Variables creating individual differences, 305–10
Vertical mobility, 344–46
Veterans' benefits, 419–21
Veterans' Readjustment Benefits Act, 419–20
Vocation, definition, 210
Vocational development
definition, 210
theories and research, 173–90
Vocational Development Inventory (VDI), 43, 185–86, 275
Vocational Education Act, 26–27, 340
Vocational Guidance Quarterly, 248, 260, 277
Vocational Information for Education and Work (VIEW), 153, 164t, 167, 189, 292t, 296
Vocational maturity, 183
Vocational Orientation System (VOS), 190

W

Wagner-Beyser Act, 23
Widening Occupational Roles Kit (WORK), 267, 272
Women
in Armed Forces, 409–10
in labor force, 24–25, 205, 206 (Fig.), 207–208
role in labor force, 205
Work
attitude, 46t, 219–20
changing nature, 198–203
changing role, 203–207
definition, 204, 210–11
governmental influence, 221
psychological implications, 204
sociological implications, 207
technological advancements, 207–208
Work experience programs, 293t, 298
Work-while-attending school, 369–70
World War I, influences, 22–23
World War II, influences, 24